RTC Library

THE ENCYCLOPEDIA OF COOKING

THE ENCYCLOPEDIA OF COOKING

A Complete A-Z of Cooking Terms, Techniques and Recipes

Exeter Books

NEW YORK

© 1964 The National Magazine Company Ltd, England,
Additional material for American edition © 1985 Octopus Books Ltd

First published in USA 1985
Distributed by Bookthrift
Exeter is a trademark of Simon & Schuster, Inc.
New York, New York

ALL RIGHTS RESERVED
ISBN 0-671-07048-7
Printed in Czechoslovakia

CONTENTS

Introduction ii

The Encyclopedia of Cooking 1

Color Plates 440

Menu Glossary 441

Handy Charts

    Cup Measures, Spoon Measures, Metric
    Equivalents, Oven Temperatures 444

    Time-Saving Tips 445

    Money-Saving Tips 445

    Shopping and Catering Guide 447

    Planning a Party 448

    Stocking Your Kitchen Cupboard 449

Recipe Index 451

INTRODUCTION

Every cook occasionally wonders about the origin of a particular food or the reason for using a certain ingredient. At such a time, it is essential to have a reliable guide on hand to provide a concise, informative answer. *The Encyclopedia of Cooking* is just such a book. It is the ultimate reference volume for today's cook – whether a casual Sunday dinner dabbler or a specialist in haute cuisine.

Designed in an easy-to-follow A-Z format, this book is a comprehensive and authoritative guide to every aspect of gastronomy – from culinary terms and techniques to food selection and storage, and from cooking ingredients to information on many favorite American and exotic foreign dishes. Every imaginable type of food is covered, and extensive cross-references and a complete recipe index will enable the busy cook to answer the most obscure question within moments.

Delicious recipes accompany many of the entries (there are over 900), making this book of great practical value in the kitchen. Some recipes are traditional while others will provide new and innovative cooking ideas. Over 100 dishes are shown in stunning, full-color photographs. In addition, 100 easy-to-follow step-by-step illustrations show at a glance how to tackle anything from carving a roast to icing that special occasion cake.

When following a recipe in this book, read through all of the instructions carefully. Assemble the necessary utensils and measure all the ingredients before beginning. Try to avoid substitutions unless they are specifically mentioned in the recipe. Spices and seasonings can be varied according to personal preference.

A menu glossary and a series of handy charts are provided to give information on virtually everything a home cook needs to know, from stocking a kitchen cupboard to planning a large party – including a useful section on time and money-saving tips and a guide to shopping and catering. A variety of charts can be found throughout the book too, giving information on everything from freezing, canning, and cooking to apples and cuts of meat.

Beginners and experienced cooks alike will find *The Encyclopedia of Cooking* to be one of their most valuable kitchen tools.

ABALONE

An edible mollusk also known as the sea ear and ear shell. It is extremely popular as a food in California, but its export in any form is prohibited for reasons of conservation. The flesh is very tough and must be beaten before eating. Cooking time is minimal as overcooking toughens the meat. Abalone is also popular in China, where a dried form is used, and in Japan, where it is the gourmet's delight. The iridescent shell is a source of mother-of-pearl and was prized by the American Indians of the Pacific coast.

ABRICOTINE (APRICOT BRANDY)

A liqueur made from brandy, sugar, and apricots (or apricot kernels).

ABSINTHE

A bitter liqueur distilled from wormwood and flavored with a number of herbs. As it is habit-forming and dangerous to health, it is now banned in many countries.

ACCELERATED FREEZE-DRYING (AFD)

This is a process which was once thought to have great potential as foods treated in this way are superior in quality to conventionally dried ones. However, expense has prevented its development on the scale that was once envisaged.

Frozen food is dehydrated under sufficiently high vacuum to remove the ice directly in the form of water vapor and not as water. Sufficient heat must be applied to the foodstuff to assist this removal without thawing it out and the food gradually dries from its surface inward. Reconstruction consists of soaking in water for a few minutes, or by adding the product to a liquid, e.g. tea or coffee.

Freeze-dried foods are extremely light, as the water content of food accounts for 60 to 90 percent of its weight, depending on the particular type. Foods so treated have a maximum storage life of 2 years; refrigeration is not required.

ACETIC ACID

The essential constituent of vinegar, amounting to not less than 4 percent. A dilute solution of acetic acid (4 to 5 percent) is sometimes used as a cheap substitute for white wine vinegar for pickling purposes. Acetic acid is also used in very small quantities in making some candies. (See Vinegar entry.)

ACETO DOLCE

An Italian pickle, chiefly used as an appetizer.

ACORN SQUASH

A somewhat acorn-shaped winter squash with a ridged dark green skin and orange flesh. (See Squash entry.)

ADDITIVE

Any substance added to foods to perform a special function: this may be to prevent food spoilage or to enhance texture, flavor, or appearance. The purposes legally acceptable are:

Preserving
Coloring and flavoring
Emulsifying and stabilizing
Improving
Processing

The use of additives is very strictly controlled to prevent the careless or criminally-intended inclusion of harmful substances.

ADULTERANT

A substance that is added to another (usually a foodstuff) in order to increase the bulk and reduce the cost, with intent to defraud. The adulterant is usually similar in consistency and color to the food in question and the flavor is either similar or neutral. Common instances of adulterants that were formerly used were starch in spices, curry powder, and cocoa; water in milk, butter, and beer; turmeric in mustard; chicory in coffee.

Since the Pure Food and Drug Act of 1906, control of the adulteration of foods in the United States has improved and there are laws governing the preparation and labeling of food as well as the content. These laws are continually being revised. For many food products, the manufacturer must list on the container the ingredients in order of their respective quantities.

ADVOCAAT

A Dutch liqueur, yellow in color, made with brandy and eggs.

AGAR-AGAR

The gelatin-like product of a red seaweed, which used to be produced chiefly in Japan, China, the Soviet Union, and the United States.

Agar-agar, which is marketed in sheet or strip form, is employed commercially in canning, in the making of gelatins, creams, and emulsions and as a medium for the laboratory culture of bacteria. It has strong setting properties, so a far smaller proportion is required than with gelatin.

AGARIC

A family of fungi, containing many different types of both edible and poisonous mushrooms. (See also Mushroom entry.)

AÏOLI

A garlic sauce popular in the South of France where it is known as the butter of Provence. Aïoli is made like mayonnaise, which it resembles, and is served in fish soups and with vegetables.

AÏOLI

1 thick slice French bread
milk
4 cloves garlic
2 egg yolks
$\frac{1}{8}$ teaspoon salt
1 cup olive oil
1 tablespoon boiling water
lemon juice

Remove the crusts from the bread and soak in milk. Squeeze dry. Place in a large mortar with the garlic and mash with a pestle until a fine paste. Add the yolks and salt and mash in. Drop by drop pound in the olive oil. When the sauce becomes thick, the remaining oil may be beaten in. Thin with water and lemon juice to taste.

AITCHBONE

The rump bone in cattle and the cut of meat containing this bone. The term is not widely used in the United States, although it is in Great Britain.

AJI-NO-MOTO

Japanese trade name for monosodium glutamate (MSG). (See separate entry.)

ALASKA KING CRAB

(See King Crab entry.)

ALBACORE

A large marine fish, a member of the tuna family, sought after by sportsmen and commercial fishers, found in warm waters. It seldom exceeds 50 lb in weight and canned is known as "white" tuna. It is also available fresh as steaks and may be broiled, grilled, roasted, or sautéed. Select steaks 1 to $1\frac{1}{2}$ inches thick and cook 10 minutes per inch, turning once.

ALBUMIN (ALBUMEN)

A soluble protein which forms part of blood, milk, and egg white. When gently heated to 158°, or when mixed with alcohol, it coagulates into a flocculent mass.

ALBUMIN POWDER

This can be used instead of egg whites when making meringues or royal icing. Royal icing made with albumin powder has the advantage of being softer than that made with egg whites.

ALE

An alcoholic drink brewed from malt and hops. The name is generally confined to the lighter-colored malt liquors or beers, though before the introduction of hops it applied to all malt beer. (See Beer entry.)

ALEWIFE

A kind of herring.

ALGERIAN WINES

Various red, white, and rosé wines are made in Algeria, but with one or two exceptions they do not have the quality of the similar French wines and are therefore cheaper.

ALGINATE

(See Seaweed entry.)

ALLIGATOR PEAR

A common name for Avocado. (See Avocado entry.)

ALLSPICE

The pealike berries of an evergreen tree which grows in the West Indies and South America. The berries contain small seeds which are dried to a very dark brown color and are used either whole or finely ground. Their flavor is said to resemble a combination of nutmeg, cloves, and cinnamon and for this reason they are often known as allspice. In the powdered form they are also called pimento and Jamaica pepper (though they lack the hot, pungent taste of true pepper). Allspice is used to flavor pickles, meat dishes, soups, marinades, and broth, and is an ingredient of curry powder; it is also used in sweet dishes – fruit custards, gingerbread, and spicy cakes.

ALLUMETTES

Potatoes cut in "matchsticks" and fried; some-times called straw potatoes. The name is also given to narrow pastry fingers, sweet or savory.

ALMOND

The kernel of the fruit borne by two similar trees – the sweet and the bitter almond. Among sweet almonds the two best types are Jordan and Valencia.

Almonds are used in making cakes, cookies, and desserts, and sometimes in savory dishes. Salted almonds are popular served with drinks. Ground almonds are used in marzipan, macaroons, and other cookies.

Almonds contain a fair amount of protein, fat, and minerals, but no starch.

Bitter almonds contain traces of prussic acid, a poisonous substance. When this has been removed almond oil can be used commercially as a flavoring.

To blanch almonds: Drop the shelled nuts into boiling water and leave for a few minutes. Squeeze each one between thumb and first finger and the brown skin will come away easily. Rinse in cold water and dry on a cloth.

Almond Extract

The flavoring obtained from bitter almonds (after the extraction of almond oil) by fermentation and distillation. It is often added to cakes, cookies, and desserts. Today a synthetic form is generally used. (See Extracts entry.)

Almond Oil

The oil obtained by pressing almonds. It is very expensive and is therefore occasionally adulterated with oil from peach or apricot kernels; the addition is difficult to detect.

Almond Paste (Almond Frosting, Marzipan)

There are many variations of almond paste, but most are made from ground almonds and fine sugar, bound together with egg. It is important to use freshly ground almonds, as they quickly lose their flavor and sometimes become moldy. The paste may be bound with either the yolk or the white of egg, or with both; when the yolk only is used, the paste is richer and more yellow in color, while the white only makes a lighter and more brittle paste. The egg should be added very gradually and the paste kneaded well, to soften it and bring out the natural oil. Almond paste may be colored and flavored as desired for use in cake decorating and candymaking.

Several brands of commercially manufactured

marzipan are on the market. However, instead of the homemade proportions, which are about half ground almonds and half sugar, the commercial type has only 25 percent ground almonds; it is thus sweeter and cheaper than homemade.

ALMOND PASTE

2 cups powdered sugar
1⅓ cups superfine sugar
1 lb ground almonds
1 teaspoon vanilla
2 eggs, lightly beaten
lemon juice

Sift the powdered sugar into a bowl and mix with the superfine sugar and almonds. Add the vanilla, with sufficient egg and lemon juice to mix to a stiff dough. Form into a ball and knead lightly. This makes 2 lb almond paste.

To apply almond paste: Trim the top of the cake. Measure round the cake with a piece of string. Brush the side of the cake generously with sieved apricot jam. Take half the almond paste, form it into a roll, and roll out as long as the string and as wide as the cake is deep. Press the strip firmly onto the side of the cake, smoothing the seam with a knife and keeping the edge square. Brush the top of the cake with jam. Dredge the working surface generously with powdered sugar, then roll out the remaining almond paste into a circle to fit the top of the cake. Turn the cake upside down, center it exactly on the paste and press down firmly. Smooth the seam, loosen the paste from the board and turn the cake right side up. Check that the top edge is level. Leave for 2 to 3 days before coating with royal icing.

ALMOND PASTE DECORATIONS
Simple but attractive decorations for a frosted cake can be made from almond paste and they are particularly suitable for Christmas or birthday cakes. Draw the chosen shape on card and cut it out. (Stars, candles, holly leaves, Christmas trees, houses, or engines make good designs, as they have bold outlines.) Color some almond paste by working food coloring in evenly; roll out very thinly on a board sprinkled with powdered sugar, lay the pattern on it and cut round with a sharp-pointed knife. For holly berries, roll tiny balls of red-tinted paste. Leave the shapes on a plate till quite dry, then stick them onto firm royal icing, using a dab of fresh frosting.

ALPIN (ALPESTRA) CHEESE

A hard, dry, lightly salted cheese, golden in color, made at Briançon and Gap in France.

ALSATIAN WINES

Wines made in the French border province of Alsace. The climate, soil, and grape varieties give the wine its individual characteristics of medium dryness and delicate flavor. The "appellation contrôlée" is imposed by the type of grape rather than the vineyard: principal names are Riesling, Gewürztraminer, Pinot Blanc, and Sylvaner.

ALUMINUM FOIL

Thin, pliable sheets of aluminum can be produced in different gauges, according to the intended purpose. This foil is used to wrap commercially-produced foodstuffs and is sold in rolls for domestic use. It is useful for wrapping food, particularly for bread, sandwiches, and cakes. Meat and poultry can be roasted in it,

TO APPLY ALMOND PASTE
1. Press the strip of almond paste onto the cake by rolling the cake on its side.

2. Invert the cake centering it exactly on the almond paste and press down firmly. Cut away any excess almond paste.

3. Loosen the paste from the board and turn the cake the right way up. Smooth the seam using a spatula.

keeping the oven clean; the foil should be opened for the last 20 minutes to brown the meat. It can be used to line pans, is very malleable, and does not need greasing. Heavy-duty or freezer foil should be used when wrapping food for the freezer.

AMBROSIA

Mythical food of the gods of Olympus. Also a popular dessert in the United States, made of sliced oranges and shredded coconut.

ANADAMA BREAD

A yeast bread of the United States, made with cornmeal and molasses. There are many versions about how this bread was named, but all include the New England farmer yelling at his long-suffering wife, "Anna, damn it."

ANADAMA BREAD

2½–3 cups all-purpose flour
1 teaspoon salt
½ cup yellow cornmeal
1 package active dry yeast
2 tablespoons butter, softened
1 cup hot water (120°–130°)
2½ tablespoons molasses

Combine half of the flour and the salt, cornmeal and yeast in a bowl with the butter. Stir the molasses and hot water together and beat into the flour mixture gradually. Add enough of the remaining flour, about ¼ cup, to make a stiff dough and beat well. Stir in the remaining flour until the dough is no longer sticky. Turn out onto a floured board and knead until smooth and elastic, about 8 minutes.

Place the dough in a greased bowl and cover with greased plastic wrap. Let rise in a warm place until double in bulk. Punch down and form into an oblong ball. Place seam side down in a greased 8 × 4 inch bread pan, cover with plastic wrap and let rise until the center of the bread is above the edge of the pan. Bake in a 375° oven for 45 minutes, or until the loaf sounds hollow when tapped on the bottom.

ANCHOVY

A small fish of the same family as the herring, which it resembles in color and shape, though it is very much smaller. Anchovies are commonly canned in oil or preserved in brine and are used (in small quantities only, as they are very highly salted) for hors d'oeuvres and sauces and as a garnish and flavoring for meat and fish dishes.

To fillet whole anchovies: Salted anchovies should be rinsed under cold water before use. If they are preserved in oil, remove this first by dipping them in water. Wipe on a cloth or scrape to remove the skins and cut off the tails. Split the fish open with the finger and thumb, remove the bone, and cut the flesh into two fillets or smaller pieces, which can be used for hors d'oeuvres, e.g. Anchovy twists.

Anchovy Butter
Mix 1 part of anchovies (boned and pounded to a paste) with 2 parts butter. A little spice or flavoring may be added.

Anchovy Paste
This is commercially made by mixing pounded anchovies, vinegar, spices, and water.

ANGEL FOOD CAKE

An extremely light, feathery cake of the sponge type containing only the whites of the eggs and no shortening. Its success depends on the use of cake flour, the thorough beating of the egg whites with sugar, and the careful folding in of the flour.

ANGEL FOOD CAKE

1½ cups powdered sugar
1 cup cake flour
1½ cups egg whites (about 12)
1½ teaspoons cream of tartar
1 cup granulated sugar
½ teaspoon salt
1½ teaspoons vanilla

Sift the powdered sugar and flour together. Beat the egg whites and cream of tartar on low speed until foamy. Increase speed to high and add the granulated sugar gradually, about 2 tablespoons at a time. Beat until the whites are stiff and glossy; do not underbeat. Beat in the salt and vanilla.

Sift the sugar–flour mixture over the meringue a little at a time, folding in just until the flour disappears. Turn the mixture into an ungreased 10-inch tube pan. Cut through the batter gently with a spatula to remove any air bubbles. Bake on the bottom rack of a 350° oven for 35 to 40 minutes, until the top springs back when touched; cracks in the top of the cake should look and feel dry.

Invert cake on a bottle until cool, about $1\frac{1}{2}$ hours. Remove from pan and serve frosted.

ANGELICA

A tall plant of the parsley family. It is chiefly cultivated in Europe, especially France.

The hollow green stems are candied and used for decorating cakes and desserts. They should be put in hot water for 2 to 3 minutes if necessary, to refresh the color and remove the excess sugar. The seeds are incorporated in certain medicines and a tisane (tea) used to be made from them as a remedy for feverish colds.

ANGOSTURA

A herbal, spiritous compound invented in Venezuela during the last century for medicinal purposes. It is now made in Trinidad with a rum base. It is used in general cuisine and in alcoholic beverages, e.g. Old Fashioned and Pink Gin.

ANISEED

The small seeds of the anise plant, cultivated in Malta, Spain, the Soviet Union, and other places. They contain a volatile oil, with a warm, sweet, aromatic taste and odor. The extract oil of aniseed is used as a flavoring for desserts, pastries, liqueurs, and cordials and has certain medicinal uses.

ANISETTE

An aniseed-flavored sweet liqueur.

ANTIPASTO

A dish served before the main course in Italy. It usually consists of an assortment of fish, cold meats, and vegetables.

APÉRITIF

The French name for a drink taken before meals, differing from a cocktail in that it is lower in alcoholic content and often bitter in flavor. Vermouth and Sherry are popular apéritifs. There are many proprietary brands of apéritif such as Dubonnet, Amer Picon, and St Raphael.

APPETIZERS

This term is applied to finger foods that accompany drinks as well as foods served as a first course. For the latter, see the Hors d'Oeuvre entry.

Appetizers served with drinks or at a cocktail party should stimulate rather than satisfy the appetite, so they should be small and piquant. They should also be easy to eat with the fingers, with nothing that will fall off or smear the hands. Greasy, hot appetizers, such as tiny sausages, should be served on picks.

The following list includes some of the most popular cold and hot cocktail appetizers: olives, radishes, celery, stuffed prunes, salted nuts, potato chips, fried sausages, canapés, barquettes and bouchées, cheese straws, and cheese crackers. (See also Canapé entry.)

Appetizers may be presented in various ways. One of the most usual methods is a spread of some sort (cheese, pâté, fish, etc.) on a base of toast, cracker, crispbread, or pastry. Mushrooms, anchovies, sardines and cheese can all be used in this way, also mixtures such as chopped celery and mayonnaise, chutney and cheese, shrimp and butter, cream cheese garnished with asparagus tips, chopped prunes and mayonnaise, apple and cream cheese, scrambled egg, and watercress.

Another method is to serve bouchées, miniature puffs, tartlets and barquettes made of cheese or other pastry and filled with a meat, poultry, seafood, or cheese mixture; hard-cooked eggs with the yolk removed and the center filled with a tasty mixture (which may include the sieved egg yolk); small tomatoes, celery sticks and Belgian endive with a creamy spread; thick slices of beet or cucumber, hollowed out into a cup shape; soaked prunes with the pits removed and replaced by a spicy cream filling.

APPLE

Apples are grown in most parts of the United States and in temperate climates throughout the world and there are very many varieties, both cooking and dessert.

From the strictly dietetic point of view, apples are not of great value. Although they are rich in minerals, they have a low vitamin content. A crisp apple does have the merit of cleaning the teeth satisfactorily, and apples aid digestion. In addition to their use as dessert, apples can be cooked in a large variety of ways to produce innumerable dishes, and they are sometimes used in combination with meats and cheeses, as in the case of applesauce with pork and certain apple and cheese dishes. They can be baked, stewed, pureed, or combined with pastry, puddings, and many other foods; they can also be preserved in the form of jam, jelly, pickles, chutney, etc., and as dried apple rings and canned fruit or pulp or frozen. Cooking apples are a rich source of pectin and are therefore useful in jammaking to combine with fruits that are poor in pectin. (See Jam entry.)

The following table shows some of the better varieties of apple obtainable in the United States, with the characteristic properties of each.

Name	Description
BALDWIN	Fair for eating, very good for baking and pies
CORTLAND	Very good eating – juicy and aromatic
EMPIRE	Excellent eating – mild, firm, medium sweet. Good for pies and applesauce – fair for baking
GOLDEN DELICIOUS	Sweet, mellow, excellent eating – good for applesauce and baking – excellent for pies
GRANNY SMITH	Excellent for eating, pies, and applesauce
GRAVENSTEIN	Juicy, medium acid – good for eating, cooking, and salad
GREENING	Very sour – excellent for pies, baking, and applesauce
IDA RED	Tangy, firm – good eating – very good for pies, baking, and applesauce
JONATHAN	Excellent eating with crisp flesh and sprightly flavor
LODI	Very tart – good for applesauce and mixing with other apples
MCINTOSH	Crisp, mild, and sweet – excellent for eating and applesauce, good for pies, and fair for baking
MACOUN	Very crisp, aromatic, little acid – excellent eating quality
MILTON	Mild, low acid, aromatic – very good eating
MUTSU	Excellent for eating and baking
NEWTOWN PIPPIN	Medium acid, highly aromatic – very good eating – excellent for dessert and cooking
NORTHERN SPY	Juicy, medium acid, aromatic – very good eating – excellent for dessert and cooking
RED DELICIOUS	Sweet, firm, excellent for eating. Poor for cooking and baking
ROME BEAUTY	Medium acid, fair eating, best for fine cooking and baking qualities
RUSSET	Fair eating – very good for pies, baking, and applesauce
STAYMAN WINESAP	Juicy, sprightly flavor, medium acid – fine for eating and cooking
YORK IMPERIAL	Medium acid, good for eating, and fine for cooking

To stew apples: Wipe 1 lb apples, peel thinly, core and cut into quarters and then into thin slices. Dissolve $\frac{1}{2}$ cup sugar in $\frac{2}{3}$ cup water and boil 5 minutes. Add fruit and simmer very gently until the apples are soft but not broken up.

For stewed dried apples, see Dried Fruit entry.

To bake apples: Wipe even-sized apples and cut through the skin round the center. Remove the cores with an apple corer and stand the apples in an ovenproof dish or baking pan. Pour a few tablespoonfuls of water around and fill up the center of each apple with brown sugar and a lump of butter. Bake in a 400° oven 45 minutes to 1 hour, until tender. Serve hot or cold.

Alternately, the apples may be stuffed with dried fruit or a mixture of chopped dates and nuts, a few shavings of butter being placed on top of the apples before baking. Apples can also be stuffed with a mixture of soft fruits, tossed in sugar and complementary spices.

To preserve apples: In addition to their use in jellies, etc., cooking apples may be quartered, sliced, or pureed, and then jarred and sterilized. (For method see Canning entry.) For directions for dried apple rings, see Drying entry.

Apples can also be frozen in slices or as a puree. Slices should be blanched for 2 to 3 minutes and cooled in ice-cold water before packing; apples stewed for a puree should have very little water added and can be sweetened or unsweetened.

To store apples: Some good keeping varieties of cooking and dessert apples may easily be preserved for winter and spring use.

The apples are best left to mature on the trees until a light twist of the hand will detach them. Pick them carefully, taking care not to bruise them or pull the stems out of their sockets, and place in baskets. Store only unblemished apples, placing them with the stem upward and not touching each other, on slatted wooden shelves in a cool, damp, frost-proof room. They should be looked over once a week and any that show signs of deterioration should be removed and used at once.

Experiments have been carried out to investigate the effect of coating the varieties of apple that do not keep well and the most satisfactory results seem to be given by the use of wax or oil emulsions.

TWO-CRUST APPLE PIE

2 cups all-purpose flour
pinch of salt
5 tablespoons lard or vegetable shortening
5 tablespoons margarine or butter
3–4 tablespoons water
2 lb Golden Delicious apples
$\frac{1}{2}$ cup light brown sugar
2 tablespoons cornstarch
1 piece gingerroot, chopped
milk to glaze
1 tablespoon superfine sugar

Keep hands, utensils, working surface, and ingredients cool. A special pastry blender with wooden handle and wire loops is good for those with warm hands. For a richer pastry increase fats to 6 tablespoons each.

Put flour and salt in a bowl, add firm, not hard, fat cut into small pieces; with fingertips rub in until texture of bread crumbs. Shake bowl from time to time so that any larger crumbs can be seen. The hands should be lifted well up over the bowl so that air is incorporated in the mixture.

Sprinkle liquid over the surface all at once. Gradual addition gives an uneven texture and this tends to cause blisters when the pastry is cooked. Once the liquid is added, use a spatula to distribute liquid as evenly as possible and draw the crumbs together. When large lumps are formed, finish knitting dough together with fingertips into a ball.

With light fingertip handling, knead dough on a lightly floured surface (too much flour makes the pastry tough). When the pastry is smooth and free from cracks, divide in half, round up largest part. Dust rolling pin with flour and roll lightly. Keep edge round. If it begins to break, pinch immediately. Keep pastry circular, turning frequently but not rolling sideways. Roll out to 1 inch larger than the pie plate.

Place a 10-inch inverted pie plate (foil or metal are ideal but ovenproof glass can be used) on pastry; cut round edge with a knife. Knead trimmings with rest of pastry and roll out to fit pie plate 1 inch larger. Fold in half and transfer to plate. Unfold and ease into plate without stretching pastry. Shape into base with fingers and trim off any surplus.

Peel and slice apples to $\frac{1}{4}$ inch thickness. To start cooking and enable more apple slices to be used, plunge slices into boiling water for 2 minutes. Drain at once and cool under running water. Drain again well. In a bowl combine brown sugar and cornstarch, which thickens the juices as they are cooking.

Arrange the apple on the bottom of the pie, scatter the chopped ginger over and sprinkle with half sugar mixture. Repeat with rest of the fruit and sugar, keeping rim of plate clear. Apples should be kept level.

For more tartness add a little lemon juice to filling. Put a baking sheet in oven to preheat. This helps to boost initial sealing of pastry base and prevent a soggy base.

Using a soft pastry brush, moisten pastry rim with milk or beaten egg glaze. Loosely fold pastry round the rolling pin and, with the support of one hand underneath, transfer to pie and guide pastry over filling. This prevents unnecessary stretching of dough. Gently press edges of pastry together with edge of finger to seal. Brush any surplus flour from pastry surface with a dry brush.

Place index finger, knuckle side down, on top of rim. Press lightly. Hold knife horizontally with back of blade toward edge. Beginning near rim of plate and working up toward finger, flake edges by knocking the back of the knife against cut edge.

For a scalloped edge, place thumb on top of pastry and index finger under rim. Press down lightly and, at the same time, move knife, held upright in other hand, up and in to make a small nick. The pressure of thumb against knife makes flute. Slit the center.

Bake unglazed or glaze with milk and dredge with superfine sugar. Place pie on preheated baking sheet and bake in center of 425° oven for 15 minutes. Reduce to 350° for 30 to 35 minutes or until golden brown.

APPLE DUMPLINGS

1 recipe short-crust pastry (see Pastry entry)
4 even-sized cooking apples
$\frac{1}{4}$ cup sugar
milk to glaze
superfine sugar

Divide the pastry into four and roll out each piece into a circle 8 to 10 inches across. Peel and core the apples, place one on each circle and fill the center with some of the sugar. Moisten the edge of the pastry with water, gather to the top, pressing well to seal, and turn the dumpling over. If you wish, decorate with leaves cut from any trimmings of pastry. Brush the tops with milk. Bake on a greased baking sheet in a preheated 425° oven for 10 minutes. Reduce to 325° for 30 minutes, until the apples are soft. Dredge with superfine sugar and serve hot or cold, with custard or cream.

CHICKEN NORMANDE

1/4 cup seedless raisins
1/4 cup butter
4 chicken parts
salt
pepper
1½ lb apples, peeled and sliced
2 tablespoons lemon juice
2 tablespoons cider
½ teaspoon cinnamon
2/3 cup heavy cream

Soak the raisins for 1 hour in warm water. Heat half the butter in a skillet and brown the chicken parts on all sides. Remove to a plate and season well. Add remaining butter and the apple slices. Cook, tossing, so that they become lightly browned only. Place half the apples in the bottom of a casserole and arrange chicken on top. Mix together the lemon juice, cider, salt, pepper, cinnamon, and raisins. Place the remaining apples around the chicken, season, and pour the raisin mixture over the chicken and apples. Cover with a piece of waxed paper and a tight-fitting lid. Cook in a 350° oven for about 1 hour. Stir in the cream and return to the oven to heat through for 5 minutes.

APPLESAUCE

1 lb apples
2 tablespoons butter
sugar or lemon juice if required

Choose good cooking apples; peel and slice them with stainless steel knife and cook gently to a pulp in a covered pan. Beat with a wooden spoon until smooth, then add the butter. Sugar may be added, but to accompany goose, duck, or pork the sauce should be fairly tart; if on the other hand the apples are sweet, a little lemon juice may be added.

TARTE TATIN

The French version of apple pie, made with caramelized apples.

1¼ cup all-purpose flour
pinch of salt
10 tablespoons sugar
½ cup butter, chilled
1 egg yolk
3 teaspoons lemon juice
2 lb cooking apples
½ cup sweet butter

Combine the flour, salt, and 2 tablespoons of the sugar in a bowl and cut in the butter until the mixture resembles fine bread crumbs. Combine the egg yolk and 1 teaspoon lemon juice; stir into the flour to form a ball. Chill 30 minutes.

Peel and slice the apples and place in a bowl of cold water with the remaining lemon juice. Melt the sweet butter and pour 2 tablespoons of it into a 4-cup cake pan, brushing it around the pan. Sprinkle with 2 tablespoons of the sugar. Heat until the butter and sugar mixture sizzles and turns a golden-brown caramel color.

Drain the apple slices and arrange a single, overlapping layer of them in the bottom of the pan. Sprinkle with melted butter and sugar and continue layering, finishing with sugar.

Roll out the dough on a lightly floured surface and cover the apples, tucking the edges inside the rim of the pan. Make a small hole in the center of the pastry and bake in a 375° oven for about 45 minutes, until the apples are tender. Cover the pastry with foil if it becomes too brown.

Let the pie stand for 5 to 10 minutes, then run a knife around the inside edge of the pan. Cover with a warmed serving plate, invert and serve immediately.

APPLE JELLY

5½ lb cooking apples
juice of 2 lemons
water
sugar

Windfalls or cooking apples can be successfully used, but dessert apples should not be used for jellymaking. Wash the apples and remove any bruised or damaged portions, then cut them into thick slices without peeling or coring. Put them in a pan with the lemon juice and sufficient cold water to cover (about 2 quarts). Simmer until the apples are really soft and the liquid is well reduced (by about one-third), then strain the pulp through a jelly bag. Measure the extract and return it to the pan, with 2¼ cups sugar to each 2½ cups of extract. Bring to a boil, stir until the sugar has dissolved, and boil rapidly until a jell is obtained on testing. Skim, jar, and cover the jelly as for jam.

As the color of apple jelly is sometimes unattractive, a few blackberries can be added with the apples; or, if preferred, some raspberries, currants, cranberries, or loganberries may be used instead to give the preserves a better color.

APPLE GINGER PRESERVE

4 lb apples
2½ cups water
1 jar (10 oz) preserved stem ginger
3 tablespoons ginger syrup from jar
grated rind and juice of 3 lemons
6¾ cups sugar

Peel the apples and and slice thinly; tie the cores and peel in cheesecloth; add the water and simmer all in a covered pan until soft. Remove the cheesecloth bag and mash the apples. Cut the ginger into neat pieces and add it to the apples, together with the ginger syrup, the grated lemon rind, the lemon juice, and sugar. Bring to a boil, stirring constantly, test on a cold plate after 10 minutes' boiling and as soon as the preserve sets, jar and cover immediately.

APPLE BRANDY (APPLEJACK, CALVADOS)

A spirit distilled from cider. It is popular in some parts of the United States and in Normandy and the neighboring apple-growing regions of France.

APRICOT

The fruit of a prunus tree, originally a native of China, which is now widely grown in the warmer temperate countries. Apricots are grown in southern California, Spain, South Africa, and Australia. They are marketed in fresh, canned, and dried form.

The apricot somewhat resembles a small peach, being rounded in shape and yellow or orange in color. It has a delicious flavor when ripe and is popular in all its forms, as a dessert fruit, in salads and other fruit dishes and in soufflés and similar confections. Jam is made from both the fresh and the dried fruit. The kernels, which are very like sweet almonds, are crushed to extract the oil for use in the fish-packing industry. The kernels and the fresh or dried fruit are used to flavor abricotine (apricot brandy).

The chief food value of apricots lies in their vitamin A content. Dried apricots are a valuable source of vitamin A, iron, and calcium. They make excellent desserts and fruit compotes.

For preparation and cooking, see Dried Fruit entry.

Apricots can be frozen although they may discolor unless ascorbic acid (vitamin C) is added to the syrup.

The apricots should be plunged into boiling water for 30 seconds to loosen skins and then peeled. They can be sliced, cut in half, or left whole before packing in a syrup made with 1 lb sugar to 5 cups water. For each 1 lb pack add ½ to 1 teaspoon ascorbic acid.

APRICOT JAM
(made from fresh fruit)

4 lb fresh apricots
2 cups water
juice of 1 lemon
4 lb sugar

Wash the fruit, cut in half, and remove the pits. Crack a few pits to remove the kernels and blanch them by dipping in boiling water. Put the apricots into a pan with the water, lemon juice, and blanched kernels, and simmer until they are soft and the contents of the pan well reduced. Add the sugar, stir until dissolved, and boil rapidly for about 15 minutes, or until setting point is reached. Jar and cover in the usual way. *Makes about 6 lb.*

APRICOT JAM
(made from dried fruit)

1 lb dried apricots
7½ cups water
juice of 1 lemon
6¾ cups sugar
¼–¾ cup blanched almonds, optional

Wash the apricots thoroughly, cover with the water, and soak for 24 hours. Put the fruit into a pan with the water in which it was soaked, add the lemon juice and simmer for 30 minutes, or until soft, stirring from time to time. Add the sugar and blanched almonds, stir until dissolved and boil rapidly until setting point is reached; stir frequently as the jam tends to stick. Jar and cover in the usual way. *Makes about 5 lb.*

AQUAVIT

A Scandinavian liqueur, distilled from a variety of substances, including potatoes, grain, and sawdust; it is colorless, unsweetened, and usually flavored with caraway seeds.

ARMAGNAC

A French brandy of excellent quality, named after the district where it is produced.

ARRACK

Also known as Raki or Rakia, it is a spirit made in the Near and Far East. It is made from fermented palm sap (toddy) but other bases such as dates, grapes, and milk are used. Arrack may be flavored, particularly with aniseed.

ARROWROOT

A pure starch powder obtained from the pith of the roots of the maranta plant, which is grown in Bermuda and the West Indies. As purchased in the United States, it is a light, white, odorless powder, which will keep for a considerable time if stored in a dry place.

When mixed with boiling water, arrowroot forms a clear jelly and can be used for thickening fruit juices intended to cover or glaze tarts and similar dishes. Mixed with milk, it may be used instead of flour or cornstarch for puddings and sauces. Arrowroot also makes a popular crisp cookie. It should always be blended with a cold liquid before heating.

ARROWROOT GLAZE

Measure $\frac{2}{3}$ cup of sweetened fruit juice. Blend $1\frac{1}{2}$ teaspoons arrowroot with the juice and pour into a saucepan. Bring to a boil, stirring. When glaze is clear take off heat and leave to cool a little before using to glaze fruit etc.

ARTICHOKE

The name is applied to plants belonging to three different genera: (1) The true or globe artichoke; (2) the Jerusalem artichoke; (3) the Chinese (or Japanese) artichoke or Stachys.

Globe Artichoke

If allowed to reach full maturity the globe artichoke resembles a large thistle. The part eaten is the bud of the flower, which is cut off at the point where it joins the stem. The fond or bottom of the artichoke is particularly highly prized, while the choke, the thistly part, is discarded. Globe artichokes are available year round. They supply a small amount of vitamin C.

To cook globe artichokes: Choose young, compact heads and allow at least one for each person, as they are not easy to divide. Cut off the stalks, level with the leaves; remove the hard bottom leaves and cut about 1 inch off those at the top (using scissors). Wash them in several waters and soak in fresh cold water for at least 1 hour, then place them base downward in a saucepan of fast-boiling water, slightly salted and sharpened with a little vinegar or lemon juice; a small bunch of herbs may be added to give flavor. Let the artichokes boil uncovered until the leaves can be detached quite easily when pulled – 30 to 45 minutes. Drain well and serve piled up on a hot dish, with a sauce served separately.

Melted butter with a dash of vinegar or lemon juice, or hollandaise sauce, are the standard accompaniment for hot artichokes, or they may be served cold with French dressing or vinaigrette sauce. In either case they form a course by themselves, usually the starter to a meal.

The correct way to eat globe artichokes is to pull out the leaves one at a time with the fingers, dip each in the sauce and suck the soft end. When the center is reached, remove the choke or soft flowery part and eat the bottom, which is the chief delicacy, with a knife and fork. The artichoke forms the basis of many main meal dishes as well as appetizers and vegetable dishes.

STUFFED ARTICHOKES

4 artichokes, boiled about 10 to 15 minutes
$\frac{1}{4}$ cup butter
$\frac{1}{4}$ cup finely chopped mushrooms
$\frac{1}{2}$ cup fresh bread crumbs
2 tablespoons chopped parsley
1 teaspoon dried thyme
2 cloves garlic, minced with $\frac{1}{2}$ teaspoon salt
grated rind of 1 lemon
2 tablespoons olive oil
1 cup dry white wine

Remove the chokes from the center of the artichokes. Melt the butter in a small pan and sauté the mushrooms for 2 to 3 minutes. Pour the contents of the pan into a bowl and add all the remaining ingredients except the olive oil and white wine. Toss to mix. Fill the artichokes with the stuffing and place in a casserole that will just hold them. Add the oil and wine and bring to a boil. Cover and bake in a 350° oven for about 40 minutes, or until the artichokes are tender. Serve warm or at room temperature.

ARTICHOKE SALAD

1 head Bibb lettuce, shredded
1 can (16 oz) artichoke hearts, drained
¼ lb mortadella, sliced
black olives
¼ cup olive oil
3 tablespoons lemon juice
1 clove garlic, minced
salt
pepper

Place the lettuce on four salad plates and arrange the artichoke hearts, mortadella, and olives on top of it. Combine the remaining ingredients in a screw-top jar, shake well and pour over the salad.

Jerusalem Artichoke

A member of the sunflower family. The tubers are cooked and eaten as a vegetable during the autumn and winter. The plant is native to the American continent, but is now also grown extensively in Europe.

To cook the tubers, first scrub them, then peel quickly and drop them at once into clean, cold water, using a stainless knife or peeler and keeping them under water as much as possible to prevent discoloration. A little salt and a squeeze of lemon juice added to the water helps keep them a good color. Place in boiling salted water to which a little lemon juice has been added, cook until tender (about 30 to 40 minutes), drain well and serve with butter or a white sauce.

They are easier to peel if cooked first and then allowed to cool.

Artichokes give an excellent flavor to casseroles and are also very good pan-roasted with meat. Cold and sliced, they are a delicious addition to salads.

JERUSALEM ARTICHOKES WITH TOMATOES

2 lb Jerusalem artichokes
juice of 1 lemon
2 tablespoons butter
2 tablespoons olive oil
1 medium onion, thinly sliced
1 clove garlic, minced with ½ teaspoon salt
1 can (8 oz) tomatoes
1 teaspoon dried basil
salt
pepper

Blanch the artichokes in boiling salted water, to which the lemon juice has been added, for about 7 minutes. Drain and cool.

Melt the butter with the oil in a saucepan and sauté the onion and garlic until lightly colored. Stir in the tomatoes, basil, salt, and pepper. Simmer for about 5 minutes, stirring to break up the tomatoes.

Peel the artichokes and slice thickly. Stir into the tomato mixture, cover and simmer for about 30 minutes, or until the artichokes are tender. Stir occasionally to keep from sticking and add water if necessary.

The Chinese or Japanese Artichoke (Stachys)

Rather a rarity in the United States; the tubers, which are the edible portion, resemble Jerusalem artichokes in flavor and may be prepared in the same ways. This vegetable is popular in France, where it is known as Crosne de Japon.

ASCORBIC ACID

The scientific name for vitamin C. (See Vitamins entry.)

ASPARAGUS

This is the cultivated form of a plant of the lily family which originally grew near the seashore. It has been popular for many centuries and there are therefore many varieties, some of them pale green, some almost white, and some with purple tips. The green asparagus grown outdoors in the United States is in season from April until the end of June. Asparagus has very little nutritive value, but is prized as a delicious food. To extend its rather brief season, it may be jarred or frozen and it is also sold canned. It makes a good soup and both canned and packaged soup preparations are available.

To cook asparagus, break off the woody end of the stalks and scrape the white part lightly, removing any coarse spines. Tie in bundles and place upright in a saucepan of boiling water. Boil for 5 minutes, or until just tender when pierced with a knife. Drain very well and untie the bundles before serving with melted butter or hollandaise sauce. Asparagus may also be cooked untied and lying flat in a skillet.

Asparagus may be served cold, with a vinaigrette dressing or with mayonnaise, usually as an appetizer. It may also be served plain as a vegetable accompaniment.

ASPARAGUS AND SHRIMP GRATIN

1 lb asparagus, cooked
2 tablespoons butter
½ cup quartered button mushrooms
⅓ cup chopped shrimp
3 tablespoons half-and-half
salt and pepper
½ cup grated Cheddar cheese
¼ cup grated Parmesan cheese

Place the asparagus in a shallow ovenproof dish. Melt the butter in a small pan and sauté the mushrooms for 5 minutes. Remove from the heat and stir in the shrimp, cream, salt, and pepper. Pour the sauce over the asparagus. Combine the cheeses and sprinkle over the dish. Cook under a moderate broiler until the top is browned and the cheese melted. Serve as a first course.

CREAM OF ASPARAGUS SOUP

1 large bunch of asparagus
½ onion, sliced
2 cups chicken broth
¼ cup butter
4 tablespoons flour
salt
pepper
2 cups milk
¼ cup heavy cream

Wash and trim the asparagus, discarding the woody part of the stem which is tough and inedible, and cut the remainder into short lengths, keeping a few tips for garnishing. Cook the tips for about 5 minutes in boiling salted water. Put the rest of the asparagus, the onion, ½ cup of the broth, and the butter in a saucepan, cover and simmer for about 20 minutes, until the asparagus is soft. Blend the flour and the remaining broth to a smooth cream. Stir in a little of the hot soup and return this mixture to the pan; bring to a boil, stirring until it thickens. Cook for a further 2 to 3 minutes. Season to taste with salt and pepper and puree the soup in an electric blender or food processor. Stir in the remaining milk and the cream, reheat and garnish with asparagus tips.

ASPIC

An amber-colored savory gelatin, deriving its name from a herb called 'spike' which was at one time used to flavor it. Aspic is made from clarified meat stock, fortified if necessary with gelatin and flavored with vegetables, herbs, and sometimes sherry. Prepared aspic may be bought ready-made in cans. As a quick alternative, stock (or water) and gelatin may be used.

Aspic is used to set meat, game, fish, and vegetables, etc., in a mold and as an exterior coating for decorating cold game, hams, tongues, galantines, poultry, fish, and so on. Chopped aspic is used for garnish.

HOMEMADE ASPIC

1 carrot
1 turnip
1 onion
a little celery
grated rind of 1 lemon
2–3 tablespoons lemon juice
2–3 tablespoons tarragon vinegar
2–3 tablespoons sherry
6 peppercorns
½ teaspoon salt
gelatin
4 cups strong stock
shells and whites of 2 eggs

Prepare the vegetables, cutting each into about 4 pieces, and place them in a large saucepan with the lemon rind and juice, the vinegar, sherry, peppercorns, salt, gelatin, and stock. Wash and crush the eggshells and add them, with the egg whites. Put over a low heat, begin to whisk vigorously and bring nearly to the boiling point, whisking meanwhile. Stop whisking and allow the froth to rise to the top of the pan, then allow it to cook without boiling for 20 minutes. Strain the liquid through a sieve lined with 3 layers of wet cheesecloth, passing it a second time through the cloth if not absolutely clear.

ASTI SPUMANTE

The best-known Italian sparkling wine; it is usually a sweet wine best served with dessert but drier types are available.

AU GRATIN

For this and similar phrases, see Menu Glossary.

AVGOLEMONO

A Greek sauce, popular throughout the Balkans, made by whisking a mixture of eggs and lemons into stock. The stock used in the sauce is always the cooking liquid of the food to be sauced. The sauce can be served with chicken, fish, meat, or vegetables, or may be stirred into soup.

AVGOLEMONO SAUCE

2 or 3 eggs
juice of 1 lemon
1 cup hot broth (cooking liquid from the food to be sauced)

Beat the eggs until frothy. Continue beating while adding the lemon juice gradually. Beat in the hot broth drop by drop until the eggs are heated, then beat in in a steady stream. Pour the sauce into a pot containing the food to be served and stir to combine. Serve immediately.

AVOCADO

The fruit of a tree grown in the Americas, Middle East, and parts of Africa. When ripe it is dark purple or green with soft flesh rich in oil, vitamins A, B, C, D, E, and calcium. The flesh has a distinctive bland flavor and buttery texture.

Avocados are usually eaten as hors d'oeuvre. To prepare them, make a lengthwise cut around the center, entirely encircling the fruit and reaching down to the large pit. To separate the two halves, twist them in opposite directions. Discard the pit and sprinkle the flesh with lemon or lime juice to prevent it from turning brown. The center hollows may then be filled with mayonnaise, cream cheese, flaked salmon or tuna, or indeed any desired salad mixture.

AVOCADO AND CRAB GRATIN

2 tablespoons butter
1 onion, finely chopped
2 stalks celery, chopped
1 tablespoon flour
⅔ cup milk
salt and pepper
4 oz crabmeat
2 tablespoons plain yogurt
2 avocados
lemon juice
1 cup soft bread crumbs

Melt the butter and sauté the onion and celery for 5 minutes. Add the flour and cook for 1 minute. Remove from the heat and gradually blend in the milk. Return the sauce to the heat and cook, stirring, until the sauce thickens, then cook for 1 to 2 minutes. Cool slightly. Stir in the salt and pepper, crabmeat, and yogurt and mix well.

Cut the avocados in half and remove the pits. Brush the cut surfaces with lemon juice. Spoon the crab mixture into the center of the avocados and sprinkle with bread crumbs.

Arrange the avocados in a shallow ovenproof dish and cook in a 400° oven for 10 to 15 minutes, or until the crumbs are browned.

AVOCADO APPETIZERS

avocados (allow half per person)
lemon juice
French dressing

Cut the avocados lengthwise, using a stainless steel knife and making a deep cut through the flesh, up to the pit and entirely encircling the fruit. Separate the halves by gently rotating them in opposite directions and discard the pit. Brush the cut surfaces with lemon juice. Serve with a tablespoon of French dressing spooned into the hollow of each avocado half, or fill the hollow with shelled shrimp, flaked crab, or lobster meat, moistened with thin mayonnaise or well-seasoned sour cream. If liked, avocados can be served filled with fresh fruits for a different type of appetizer.

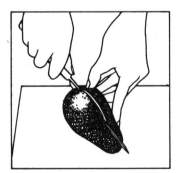 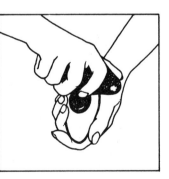 

TO PREPARE AN AVOCADO
1. Using a stainless steel knife cut the avocado lengthwise to entirely encircle the pit.

2. Separate the halves by gently rotating them in opposite directions, and discard the pit.

3. Brush the cut surfaces of the avocado liberally with lemon juice to prevent discoloration.

AVOCADO DIP

2 medium avocados
2 tablespoons milk
8 oz cream cheese
1 teaspoon salt
pinch of cayenne pepper
dash of Worcestershire sauce
1 tablespoon finely grated onion
2 tablespoons lemon juice

Peel and pit the avocados and mash to a smooth puree with the milk. Cream the cheese until soft and beat into the avocado with the remaining ingredients. Serve with crackers and pieces of vegetable as dippers.

AVOCADO AND GRAPEFRUIT SALAD

1 avocado, sliced
1 large grapefruit, peeled and sectioned
Bibb lettuce
watercress
$\frac{1}{4}$ cup grapefruit juice
2 tablespoons honey
1 tablespoon wine vinegar
$\frac{1}{4}$ teaspoon onion salt
$\frac{1}{8}$ teaspoon cardamom

Combine the avocado, grapefruit, lettuce, and watercress in a salad bowl. Combine the remaining ingredients and beat to blend. Pour over the salad and toss gently.

BABA

A rich but light-textured cake, made from a yeast dough and baked in a dariole or individual mold; it is usually soaked in rum syrup after baking and may be served hot or cold as a dessert. When baked in a large ring mold, it is known as a savarin.

BABA AU RHUM

1 oz fresh yeast or 1 tablespoon dry yeast
6 tablespoons tepid milk
2 cups all-purpose flour
½ teaspoon salt
2 tablespoons superfine sugar
4 eggs, beaten
½ cup butter, soft but not melted
whipped cream

FOR THE RUM SYRUP
½ cup honey
½ cup water
rum or rum extract

Lightly grease sixteen 3½-inch ring pans with shortening. Put the yeast, milk, and ½ cup of the flour in a bowl and blend until smooth. Allow to stand in a warm place until frothy – about 20 minutes. Add the remaining flour, the salt, sugar, eggs, and butter, and beat well for 3 to 4 minutes. Half fill the pans with the dough and allow to rise until the molds are two-thirds full.

Bake in a 400° oven for 15 to 20 minutes. Cool for a few minutes, then turn out onto a cake rack.

While the babas are still hot, warm the honey with the water and add rum (or rum extract) to taste. Spoon over each baba enough rum syrup to soak it well. Leave to cool. Serve with whipped cream in the center.

BABKA

A sweet Polish yeast bread, flavored with almonds, raisins, orange peel, and rum.

BACALAO

The Spanish term for dried salt cod. (See Cod entry.)

BACON

The side of a pig, consisting of the skin (rind), fat and a layer of meat, that has been cured in brine or salt and saltpeter and smoked. Sold in one piece or in large hunks for slicing by the butcher or at home, it is known as "slab bacon." Jowl bacon square is the jowl of the pig, shaped, cured, and smoked. Fat is distributed throughout this cut and the outer surface is covered by rind. It can be sliced or cooked in one piece. Because of the presence of sodium nitrite in bacon, used in the preserving process, health food students avoid eating this and many other preserved foods.

PACKAGED SLICED BACON
Before slicing and packaging, the rind or skin of the pig is removed. The greatest amount of fat is on the outside, lean on the inside.

Sliced bacon is available in various sizes of packages. It spoils readily and should be refrigerated in a sealed container or wrapped carefully in foil or plastic wrap.

1. *Regular sliced*: in packages averaging 18 to 22 slices to the lb.

2. *Thin sliced*: in packages ranging from 32 to 40 slices to the lb.

3. *Thick sliced*: in packages averaging 12 to 16 slices to the lb.

4. *Unsliced slab bacon*: available by the piece. It costs less than sliced bacon and lasts longer than sliced bacon when refrigerated unsliced.

5. *Canadian bacon*: available in whole pieces in cans or casings or sliced. It is the eye of the loin of pork and is much meatier with very little fat.

Cooking and serving: Bacon is usually fried or broiled for home service. If fried, add the desired number of slices in one piece to a cold heavy-bottomed skillet, turn the heat to low and cook gently, separating the slices as they warm up. Cook until the fat loses its transparency, turning frequently. Drain on paper towels before serving. Broiled bacon requires greater attention to avoid both burning and fat fires. Microwave ovens give excellent results. Consult the manual accompanying the machine for instructions.

RUMAKI

12 chicken livers
1 can (4 oz) water chestnuts
12 slices lean bacon
24 wooden picks, soaked in water
1 cup soy sauce
1 teaspoon sugar
1 clove garlic, mashed
1 slice gingerroot, minced

Separate the chicken livers into halves, cut the water chestnuts in half and slice the bacon crosswise into halves. Wrap a piece of chicken liver around a piece of water chestnut and enclose with a piece of bacon. Secure with a pick.

Combine the remaining ingredients in a small flat pan and add the rumaki. Allow to marinate 1 hour or longer. Grill over hot charcoal until the bacon is crisp, 5 to 6 minutes. This may also be cooked in the broiler, but the results are not quite as delicious.

SPAGHETTI ALLA CARBONARA

2 tablespoons olive oil
$\frac{1}{2}$ lb bacon, diced
2 cloves garlic, minced
3 eggs
$\frac{1}{4}$ teaspoon pepper
$\frac{1}{4}$ teaspoon dried oregano
8 oz spaghetti, cooked
$\frac{1}{2}$ cup grated Parmesan cheese

Cook the bacon and garlic gently in the olive oil until the bacon is fairly crisp and the garlic golden; do not allow either to burn. Beat the eggs with the pepper and oregano. Pile the hot spaghetti into a bowl and toss with the eggs. Add the bacon sauce and cheese and toss again. Serve immediately, accompanied by more grated cheese.

BAGEL

A ring-shaped roll with a tough, chewy texture. After rising, the roll is dropped briefly in boiling water before baking. Bagels are the foundation of the Jewish snack of lox, bagels and creamcheese.

BAIN-MARIE

A device for keeping foods very hot without actually boiling. A large pan is filled with boiling water and placed over a gentle heat; one or more saucepans or bowls can then be put in it, either to keep their contents hot and ready to serve, or to continue cooking very gently. (A double boiler, though smaller, serves the same purpose.) This is a good way of cooking such things as hollandaise sauce, zabaglione, and any foods or sauces made with eggs, which curdle over high heat.

BAKED ALASKA

A dessert consisting of ice cream mounted on sponge cake and entirely covered with meringue, which is cooked in a hot oven for so short a time that the ice cream remains unmelted. (See Ice Cream entry.)

BAKING

This method of cooking in the oven by dry heat is used for a large variety of foods.

To bake meat: The term generally used for cooking meat in the oven is roasting, with the exception of ham, when the term "baked" is used. (See Roasting entry.)

To bake fish: Baking is a good way of cooking both whole fish and large steaks or fillets; round fish may be stuffed with herbs or breadcrumbs.

To bake vegetables: Generally speaking, baking is not a satisfactory method of cooking vegetables, but potatoes, large zucchini, parsnips, Jerusalem artichokes, carrots, and turnips are excellent when baked in the same pan as a roast; potatoes are also delicious when baked in their skins. (See Potato entry.)

To bake fruit: Fruit contains a high percentage of water, so can be cooked satisfactorily in the oven. Pour in a little water to start the process and to prevent shriveling, add sugar as required and cook slowly in a covered ovenproof dish.

To bake cakes, pastries, cookies, biscuits, muffins, bread: Baking is the method of cooking for almost all these. (See individual entries.)

Times and temperatures for baking are regulated according to the particular food and the necessary details are given in each recipe. (See the Temperatures for Cooking entry.)

BAKING BLIND

A British term applied to pre-baking pastry cases for flans, pies, tarts, etc.

BAKING POWDER

Two types of baking powder are available, single action and double action. Single-action baking powders begin releasing carbon dioxide as soon as they are moistened, which means as soon as they are introduced into the dough. These include the tartrate baking powders and the phosphate baking powders. Double-action baking powders combine soda with sodium aluminum sulfate and calcium acid phosphate. Here too, an immediate reaction occurs when the powder is moistened, but the greatest reaction occurs in the oven when the dough is exposed to heat.

In an emergency, a homemade baking powder can be made. For every cup of flour in the recipe, use 2 teaspoons cream of tartar, 1 teaspoon bicarbonate of soda and $\frac{1}{2}$ teaspoon salt. This is a single-action formula and the dough or batter should be baked or cooked as quickly as possible after the baking powder has been mixed in.

BAKING SODA

(See Bicarbonate of Soda entry.)

BAKLAVA

A sweet Mid Eastern pastry popular in Turkey and Greece. It consists of layers of paper-thin phyllo pastry drenched with melted butter and filled with spices and chopped walnuts and almonds. The pastry is cut into diamonds or triangles and baked. While still partially warm, a honey syrup spiced with cinnamon, cloves and lemons is poured over the pastries to be absorbed by them. (See Phyllo Pastry entry.)

BALM

A fragrant herb, the leaves of which have a flavor and scent resembling those of lemon. Balm is used in punches, fruit drinks, etc., and may also be added to stuffings, soups, sauces, meats, and salads. The leaves may be dried. (See Herbs entry.)

BAMBOO SHOOTS

In many parts of the Orient the ivory-colored shoots of a particular variety of bamboo are eaten. They are cut while they are still young, tender, and crisp – 2 inches in diameter – and before they become large, hollow, and woody. Fresh and canned bamboo shoots are on sale in the United States and are popular with those who enjoy Chinese cookery.

Young shoots may be treated in the same way as asparagus. Larger ones are chopped and may be incorporated with other foods or pickled and candied.

STIR-FRIED BAMBOO SHOOTS

4–5 Chinese dried mushrooms
10 oz bamboo shoots
2 green onions
3 tablespoons peanut oil
1 tablespoon sherry
1 tablespoon soy sauce
2 teaspoons cornstarch
2 slices ham, finely chopped

Soak the mushrooms in warm water for 15 to 20 minutes, squeeze dry and discard the hard stems. Cut each mushroom into 4 or 5 slices. Cut the bamboo shoots into strips. Finely chop the green onions.

Heat the oil in a wok or skillet, add the onions, mushrooms, and bamboo shoots and stir-fry for about 1 minute, then add the sherry and soy sauce. Cook and stir 1 minute. Combine the cornstarch with a little cold water and stir into the wok. Continue stirring and cooking until the sauce thickens. Garnish with chopped ham and serve.

BANANA

The fruit of a tropical tree. The two chief varieties are the Jamaica or Plantain Banana, which is long, fairly large, has flesh of a creamy color and is somewhat insipid in flavor, and the Canary or Dwarf Banana, which is smaller and shorter, with flesh that is more pink in color and has a more aromatic flavor.

The "hands" of bananas are exported to the United States while still green. When buying bananas, avoid those with skins turning black, as the fruit will ripen too quickly and must be eaten immediately. If they are slightly under-ripe and green at the tip, they can be kept in a warm atmosphere until they are yellow all over and even slightly speckled with brown.

Bananas contain a high proportion of starch, which turns to sugar as the fruit ripens. One banana supplies about half the day's requirements of vitamin C and a small amount of other vitamins.

Bananas may be used as a fruit or vegetable, and are delicious served with sugar and cream. As the fruit browns quickly on exposure to the air, it should be prepared just before serving, or sprinkled with lemon juice to prevent discoloration; this also helps to bring out the flavor.

The fruit can be used in a variety of ways in cookery, in shortcakes, pies, cakes, gelatins, salads, etc. Bananas may also be baked or fried as a dessert, or cooked with ham and cheese as an entrée. A cooked banana has a very different flavor to the uncooked fruit. Chartreuse of bananas (see Chartreuse entry) and banana flan are delicious cold desserts.

Dried (Dehydrated) Bananas

These are on sale at health-food stores, etc. Although most unattractive in appearance, they have good flavor and are excellent snacks.

BANANA BOATS

4 medium bananas
¼ cup butter
¼ cup powdered sugar
¼ cup walnuts, chopped
½ teaspoon ground cinnamon
grated rind and juice of ½ lemon

Place the whole bananas, with their peels on, under a preheated broiler for about 15 minutes, turning frequently until the peel turns brown. Cream the butter and sugar, then beat in the remaining ingredients. Split the bananas along the upper surface and press gently at each end to form a hollow in the center. Spoon the walnut butter into each hollow and return to the broiler for 5 minutes, or until the butter is melted. Serve at once.

FLAMBÉ BANANA IN ORANGE SAUCE

8 large firm bananas
2 tablespoons butter
3 tablespoons light brown sugar
2 tablespoons rum
3 medium oranges
2 tablespoons lemon juice
heavy cream to serve

Peel the bananas and cut into four even-sized pieces. Heat the butter in a large skillet. Toss in the bananas and sprinkle with the sugar. Sauté gently, turning the bananas occasionally until golden brown and beginning to soften. Pour in the rum and carefully set on fire with a match. Shake the skillet gently until the flames subside. Coarsely grate in the rind and add the strained juice of 2 oranges with the lemon juice. Cover the skillet and simmer for 5 minutes to thoroughly heat through. Score the third orange at ½-inch intervals with a channel knife, working downward from stem end, not round, to remove narrow strips of rind free of pith. Slice the same orange thinly, discarding any seeds. Serve the bananas very hot with the juices. Decorate with orange slices and serve immediately, accompanied with heavy cream.

BANBURY CAKE

An oval flat cake originating from Banbury, Oxfordshire in England. It is made of flaky pastry filled with dried fruit.

BANNOCK

A large round scone containing oatmeal or barleymeal, baked on a griddle and usually served at breakfast or high tea, particularly in Scotland. There are many variations, including a thin cracker type and a sweet bannock.

BAP

A Scottish type of breakfast roll, eaten hot, which is made from a yeast dough, containing a little fat. Baps are usually made in a flat, oval shape, brushed over with milk and water, then dusted with flour to give them their characteristic floury finish.

BARBECUING

This word – derived from the French barbe-à-queue, literally beard to tail – originally denoted the roasting or broiling of a whole animal, which was fixed to a spit and cooked over a solid bed of glowing coals. Today it is considered an informal way of entertaining. The food at a barbecue party is more likely to be steak, chops, pieces of chicken, sausages, kebabs, hot dogs, previously shaped hamburgers, and so on. Meat is often marinated beforehand (especially if there is any doubt as to its tenderness) and it may be basted during the cooking with a piquant sauce.

The simplest plan is to have a portable barbecue outfit, obtainable from most of the large stores at various prices, and to use ready-made charcoal as fuel (for a meal for 6 to 12 people you would need 2 to 3 lb charcoal). If you prefer to improvise your own fireplace, you will need a few bricks and some iron bars (or the grill shelves from your oven). Arrange 14 to 16 bricks side by side in two rows, to form a rectangular base. Pile more bricks at each side to support the bars, then build the fire on the brick base, using either charcoal or wood – the former takes less time to produce a glowing fire.

Let the fire burn slowly for about 30 minutes; when the coals have burned to a grayish ash, shot with a red glow, the fire is ready for you to start cooking. If you need to add more fuel, place this around the edge of the fire, gradually drawing it into the center as it ignites. Keep a sprinkler bottle handy to quench any flames which might char the food.

The food may be placed directly on the rack (which should be several inches above the fire) or it can be put on aluminum foil or cooked in a thick strong old skillet or saucepan. When cooking such things as a chicken on a spit, you will need some arrangement for collecting the juices and fat which will fall from it.

You will also need a table for food and equipment, tongs, long skewers, and thick oven gloves.

Accompaniments to serve with meats and kebabs can include a variety of salads, vegetable stew such as ratatouille, baked potatoes, crusty bread, rice, or pasta salads. Sauces help to moisten the food so a good tasty one or two should be offered. Serve a variety of salad dressings.

It is a good idea to serve a starter as this can be eaten while food is cooking on the barbecue. If the meal is taken outside it should be something simple such as mugs of soup, slices of melon, dips, or filled patty shells.

Suitable desserts include fresh fruit, individual mousses, shortcakes, or slices of pound or sponge cake followed by coffee. Alternately a cheese board can be served with crackers, crisp celery, and fruit.

To barbecue steak and chops: Prepare the food as for broiling, skewering chops if necessary to keep them a good shape, season and brush with oil. Place on the greased grill and cook over glowing hot coals for about the same time as for broiled meat. (See Broiling entry.)

Alternately, pan broil in a heavy skillet.

BARBECUE SAUCE

$\frac{1}{4}$ cup butter
1 large onion, chopped
1 teaspoon tomato paste
2 tablespoons brown sugar
2 tablespoons cider vinegar
2 teaspoons dry mustard
2 tablespoons Worcestershire sauce
$\frac{2}{3}$ cup water

Melt the butter and sauté the onion for 5 minutes or until soft. Stir in the tomato paste and continue cooking for 3 minutes. Blend the remaining ingredients to a smooth cream and stir in the onion mixture. Return the sauce to the pan and simmer uncovered for 10 minutes.

Serve with chicken, sausages, hamburgers, or chops.

BARBERRY

The fruit of various species of Berberis which grow in different parts of the world. They are used mostly for preserves, tarts, sauces, and flavoring purposes.

BARCELONA NUT

A type of hazelnut from Spain, usually kiln-dried to make it keep well.

BARDING

To cover the breast of a bird with slices of fat before roasting it, to prevent the flesh from drying up.

BARLEY

A cereal grass with a wide climatic range grown

for its seeds. These are used in cooking, for the production of breakfast cereals, and for cattle feed. The grain is also malted and used for the brewing of beer and the distillation of whisky.

Pot Barley, Scotch or Hulled Barley

The most nutritious form, as only the outer husk is removed. It is used in soups and stews and requires 2 to 3 hours' cooking to become tender.

Pearl Barley

For this the grain is steamed, rounded, and polished in the mill, after the removal of the husks. This barley, too, is used for thickening soups and stews (see Scotch Broth under Broth entry), also for making barley water and puddings. It requires rather less cooking time – $1\frac{1}{2}$ to 2 hours.

To blanch pearl barley: This is often done to improve the color of the pearl barley used for barley water or for thickening soups. Wash the barley, put it into a saucepan with sufficient water to cover, bring to a boil, strain, and finally rinse the barley.

Barley Meal

A whole-grain flour made by grinding barley coarsely; it is the crudest ground form and it is still used in some parts of Great Britain for porridge and gruel, also as an addition to a certain kind of bread.

Barley Flour

Is ground and powdered pearl barley. Blended with cold water, it makes a good thickening for soups and sauces made with milk.

BARLEY WATER

2 tablespoons pearl barley
2 cups cold water
$\frac{1}{2}$ lemon
sugar (optional)

Blanch the barley as described above, put it back into the saucepan with the water and the lemon rind (peeled off very thinly) and simmer for $1\frac{1}{2}$ to 2 hours, adding more water if it boils away. Then strain, add the lemon juice and a little sugar if desired and serve hot or cold.

BARLEY SUGAR

A hard toffee flavored with lemon. It was formerly made with a decoction of barley (hence its name), but plain water is now used.

BARM (BREWER'S YEAST)

(See Yeast entry.)

BARON

The two uncut loins and legs of lamb or mutton served as a roast. A baron of beef consists of the two sirloins, left uncut at the bone. It is also served as a roast.

BARQUETTE

A small boat-shaped pastry shell filled with a hot or cold savory mixture. Hot fillings might include a quiche or creamed poultry or seafood mixture. Delicious cold fillings include egg, fish, ham, or seafood salad. Sour cream topped with red or black caviar would also be attractive. These tarts are best made from short-crust pastry.

BASIL

An aromatic annual herb of the mint family with a pungent aroma. There are two varieties, sweet and bush basil. Both are good used with tomato, eggs, and fish, or added to soups, salads, and curries. Basil can be used fresh or dried.

BASMATI RICE

A fragrant and flavorful chewy long-grain rice used in India for curries. It is available in the United States in specialty food stores.

BASS

Any of a variety of widely distributed fresh- and salt-water fish. In North America the freshwater bass are members of the Centrarchidae family, related to sunfish and crappies but larger. They include the small- and large-mouthed, black, and spotted bass.

Saltwater bass include the striped bass and sea bass (see separate entries). The loup and bar of France are Mediterranean species.

BASTING

To ladle hot fat (or liquid) over meat, poultry, etc., at intervals while it is baking or roasting in order to improve the texture, flavor, and appearance. A long-handled spoon or basting tube is usually employed for the purpose.

Basting is not necessary for fatty roasts, especially if the roast can be cooked fat side up.

BATH BUN

A type of yeast bun originally made in the city of Bath in England around AD 1700. A distinguishing feature is the coarse sugar crystals sprinkled on top. The buns contain golden seedless raisins and mixed candied fruit peels.

BATTENBERG CAKE

A two-colored oblong cake, usually covered with almond paste.

BATTER

A thick liquid mixture, consisting essentially of flour, milk, and eggs, but often combined with other ingredients. It forms the foundation for pancakes and popovers and Yorkshire pudding. A thicker coating batter is used for making fritters and for coating fish for frying.

It used to be the custom to make batters at least 1 hour before cooking, the mixture being beaten or whisked to incorporate the air and then allowed to stand in a cool place. Recent experiments show that equally good results are obtained when the batter is beaten just long enough to mix it and does not stand before cooking.

The term is used also for runny unbaked mixtures such as cake "batter."

BASIC RECIPE FOR BATTER

⅔ cup all-purpose flour
pinch of salt
1 egg
1 cup milk

Sift the flour and salt into a bowl. Make a well in the center and add the egg. Add half the liquid, a little at a time, mixing with a wooden spoon from the center outward and gradually drawing in the flour. Mix until smooth and stir in the remainder of the milk.

For batter pudding, melt a little lard in a pan, then pour in the batter and bake in a 425° oven for about 40 minutes.

BASIC COATING BATTER

For fritters containing chopped food.

⅔ cup all-purpose flour
pinch of salt
1 egg
⅔ cup milk or milk and water

Mix together the flour and salt, make a well in the center and break in the egg. Add half the liquid and beat the mixture until smooth. Gradually add the rest of the liquid; beat until well mixed.

THIN BATTER

For fritters where the shape of the food is kept.

⅔ cup all-purpose flour
pinch of salt
1 tablespoon corn oil
⅔ cup water
2 egg whites

Mix together the flour and salt, make a well in the center and add the oil and half the water. Beat until smooth and add the remaining water gradually. Just before using, whisk the egg whites stiffly and fold them into the batter, then use the mixture straight away.

Timbale shells

These require a special iron made in the shape of a basket, which is first heated by being dipped in hot fat, then dipped into pancake batter, plunged into hot deep fat and left for a few minutes, until the batter is golden brown. The batter shell is then slipped off the iron and returned to the fat to finish cooking inside. The shells are filled with a flavorful mixture and served as an entrée or as a hot hors d'oeuvre.

(See Fritter, Pancake, Yorkshire Pudding, and Popover entries.)

BAVARIAN CREAM

A cold dessert consisting of a rich custard combined with whipped cream and set with gelatin. It can be flavored with a fruit puree, chocolate, or extracts.

VANILLA BAVARIAN CREAM

1 recipe Custard Sauce (see Custard entry)
1 teaspoon vanilla
1 envelope unflavored gelatin
2 tablespoons water
1¼ cups heavy cream, whipped

Prepare the custard sauce and flavor with vanilla, adding extra sugar if desired. Soften the gelatin in the water and stand in a pan of hot water to dissolve. When the custard is cool, fold in the gelatin and whipped cream. Turn into a bowl and refrigerate until set. If it is desirable to unmold the dessert, increase the gelatin by 1 teaspoon and use a 4-cup mold.

GINGER BAVARIAN CREAM

Add $\frac{1}{2}$ cup chopped preserved ginger. Soften the gelatin in 2 tablespoons of the syrup and omit the water.

ITALIAN BAVARIAN CREAM

Omit the vanilla and add 1 tablespoon brandy or curaçao.

BAVAROIS

A hot drink, said to have been invented in Bavaria toward the end of the seventeenth century, which used to be served at evening parties. It was made with eggs, sugar, boiling tea, and boiling milk, and flavored with a liqueur or coffee, chocolate, orange, vanilla, etc.

BAY LEAF

The aromatic leaf of the sweet bay tree, a species of laurel originally grown in the Mediterranean zone. (Note: Ordinary laurel leaves cannot be substituted for bay leaves.)

Bay leaves are used fresh or dried for flavoring soups, stews, and sauces and as an essential part of a Bouquet Garni (see separate entry).

BEACH PLUM

The fruit of the beach or shore plum, a low-growing shrub in sandy areas of the east coast of the United States. A wild plum, it is prized for the tangy jelly made from it and used as an accompaniment to meat.

BEANS, DRIED

(See entries for Legumes; Pulses.)

BEANS, GREEN

The edible seeds of leguminous plants grown in various parts of the world. Some varieties are used as green vegetables whereas others are more suitable for drying (pulses).

Green bean (String and French bean)
An annual plant of South American origin. The beans are picked when they are 2 to 4 inches long and topped and tailed before being cooked whole or halved.

Haricot Bean
The name given to a wide range of bean plants, the best known being the Green bean (see above). Haricot beans can be of various sizes and colors. Dried, they can be stored for several months in a cool, dry place and are a useful standby for soups, casseroles, and salads. Flavoring such as onions, herbs, or salt pork can be added while cooking.

Runner bean (Scarlet Runner)
A pole bean, introduced to Europe from Mexico in the mid-seventeenth century.

Snap Wax Bean
Although yellow in color, this bean is similar to green beans in every other way and is prepared in the same fashion.

See separate entries for Fava Bean; Legumes; Lima Bean; Pulses; Soybean.

STIR-FRIED GREEN BEANS WITH PORK

8 oz ground pork
2 tablespoons soy sauce
1 tablespoon cornstarch
8 oz green beans, trimmed
4 tablespoons peanut oil
1 teaspoon salt
1 tablespoon sherry
2 tablespoons chicken broth or water

Mix the pork with the soy sauce and cornstarch. Cut the beans or leave whole, as desired. Heat 2 tablespoons of the oil in a wok or skillet and stir-fry the meat for 1 minute, or until it loses its pinkness. Remove from the pan with a perforated spoon and reserve.

Add the remaining 2 tablespoons oil and stir-fry the beans with the salt for about 1 minute. Return the pork and add the sherry and broth. Blend well and serve.

To salt green beans: This is a simple and excellent way of preserving green beans for winter use. You will need a glass or stoneware jar or crock (glazed earthenware is not suitable, as the salt impairs the glaze and makes the vessel porous).

Choose small, young beans and make sure that they are clean and dry. Break them in two if very long, but do not slice them if very small. Place alternate layers of beans and kosher salt in the jar, allowing about 1 lb salt to 3 lb to 4 lb of beans. Finish with a layer of salt, press down firmly and leave for a few days to settle down. More beans may be added as they become ready, but always finish with a layer of salt and add an extra thick layer when the crock is full. Cover closely with a lid or several layers of paper.

To use the beans, rinse well in cold water or soak for a few minutes only. Cook and serve as for fresh beans, omitting the salt when boiling.

BEAN SPROUTS (MUNG)

A Chinese bean whose young, tender sprouts are famous in Chinese cooking. Fresh sprouts are rich in B vitamins and vitamin C. They can be cooked as a vegetable, added to soups and casseroles just before serving, or eaten raw in salads.

While bean sprouts are widely available, you may wish to make your own. Soak mung beans overnight in cold water. Drain. Place a few layers of blotting paper or absorbent kitchen towels in a shallow dish or plastic tray. Sprinkle enough cold water over to moisten well. Sprinkle beans over the surface, spreading evenly. Slide dish or tray into a large plastic bag to retain moisture and keep in a warm, dark place such as a closet or drawer. Ready to eat when they are about $1\frac{1}{2}$ inches long, about 3 to 4 days after germination.

ORIENTAL SALAD

8 oz cooked shrimp
4 slices cooked ham
1 small green pepper
4–6 green onions
1 cup fresh bean sprouts
3 tablespoons peanut or light sesame oil
1 tablespoon vinegar
2 teaspoons soy sauce
1 teaspoon grated fresh gingerroot
1 small clove garlic, chopped

Shell and devein the shrimp and cut the ham into ribbons. Halve the pepper, remove the ribs and seeds, and shred finely. Cut the green onions into diagonal slices. Rinse the bean sprouts and nip the ends. Combine the shrimp and ham with the vegetables in a bowl and chill until ready to serve.

Combine the remaining ingredients in a bowl and beat with a fork or whisk until the dressing thickens a little.

Just before serving, pour the dressing over the salad and toss thoroughly to coat.

BÉARNAISE SAUCE

A rich sauce in the hollandaise family with a basis of eggs and butter, but flavored with vinegar and tarragon instead of lemon juice. It is served with broiled meat or fish. There are several variations.

SIMPLE BÉARNAISE SAUCE

2 small onions, minced
3 sprigs of tarragon, chopped
3 tablespoons tarragon vinegar
2 tablespoons cider vinegar
1 tablespoon water
2 egg yolks
$\frac{1}{4}$–$\frac{1}{2}$ cup melted butter

Cook the onions and the tarragon leaves in the vinegars until reduced by half, then add the water. Strain into the egg yolks and stir over hot water until the mixture thickens. Remove from the heat, gradually beat in the melted butter and keep warm until ready to serve.

BEATING

To agitate an ingredient or a mixture by vigorously turning it over and over with an upward motion, in order to introduce air; a spoon, fork, whisk, or electric mixer may be used.

To beat raw meat is to hit it briskly all over the surface with a rolling pin or something similar for the purpose of breaking down the fibers and making the meat more tender when cooked.

BÉCHAMEL SAUCE (WHITE SAUCE)

A rich white sauce of coating consistency, used in many recipes for creamed dishes, especially with fish and as the foundation of a number of other sauces. Formerly (especially in restaurant cookery) white stock was sometimes used to replace all or part of the milk, for extra flavor.

BÉCHAMEL SAUCE

1 cup milk
1 shallot, sliced, or a small piece of onion
small piece of carrot, cut up
$\frac{1}{2}$ stalk celery, sliced
$\frac{1}{2}$ bay leaf
3 peppercorns
2 tablespoons butter
3 tablespoons flour
salt
pepper

Put the milk, vegetables, and flavorings in a saucepan and bring slowly to a boil. Remove from the heat, cover, and leave to infuse for about 15 minutes. Strain the liquid and use this with the butter and flour to make a roux sauce. Season to taste before serving.

This sauce is the basis of many other sauces.

BEECH NUTS

The small nuts extracted from beech mast, which may be eaten as they are or salted like almonds. (See Nuts entry.)

BEEF

The meat of the steer or cow, the best (and most expensive) meat being obtained from a steer about 2 years old. (See Veal entry.) The flesh of beef should be deep red – not purple or pale pink – the fat soft and cream-colored. Prime meat is firm, fine-textured, and slightly moist, having no gristle (which is an indication of age).

Beef, like all meat, is a source of protein of good value. It also supplies energy; particularly if there is a lot of fat. The amount of fat in different cuts varies considerably and it is impossible to give exact figures for the nutrients. It is a good source of the B vitamins and a fair source of iron.

Beef is cut in various ways, according to the region or country, but the diagram on page 254 gives a general idea of the method of dividing up the carcass.

How to Cook Cuts of Beef

SIRLOIN STEAK
Broil, pan broil or pan fry

BONELESS SIRLOIN STEAK
Broil, pan broil or pan fry

TOP SIRLOIN BUTT STEAK
Broil, pan broil or pan fry

PORTERHOUSE STEAK
Broil, pan broil or pan fry

T-BONE STEAK
Broil, pan broil or pan fry

CLUB STEAK
Broil, pan broil or pan fry

TENDERLOIN STEAK
Broil, pan broil or pan fry

ROUND STEAK
Braise

TOP ROUND STEAK
Braise or broil (high quality)

BOTTOM ROUND STEAK
Braise

EYE OF ROUND STEAK
Braise

HEEL OF ROUND STEAK
Braise or boil

SIRLOIN TIP
Braise or roast (high quality)

RUMP
Braise or roast (high quality)

FLANK STEAK
Broil or braise

STEWING BEEF
Braise or boil

GROUND BEEF
Broil, pan broil, pan fry, roast or bake (meat loaf) or braise

SHANK AND FORE SHANK
Boil or braise

STANDING RIB OR RIB EYE ROAST
Roast

RIB STEAK OR RIB EYE STEAK
Broil, pan broil or pan fry

BLADE OR ARM POT ROAST
Braise

BLADE OR ARM STEAK
Braise or broil (high quality)

INSIDE CHUCK POT ROAST
Braise

SHOULDER COLD POT ROAST
Braise

ENGLISH CUT
Braise

PLATE AND SHORT RIBS
Braise or boil

BRISKET (BONE IN OR OUT)
Braise or boil

CORNED BEEF BRISKET
Boil

Roast beef

Wipe the meat, note the weight and calculate the

time needed for cooking. For the quick method, it is usual to allow 15 minutes per lb and 15 minutes over for small roasts, 20 minutes per lb and 20 minutes over for thicker roasts, and 25 minutes per lb plus 25 minutes over for larger roasts without bone (since the dense tissues require longer cooking).

For the slow method, the times to allow are 20 minutes per lb plus 20 minutes; 27 minutes per lb plus 27 minutes; and 33 minutes per lb plus 33 minutes, respectively.

Frozen meat can be thawed overnight in the refrigerator and cooked as above. It is also possible to cook roasts from frozen provided care is taken to cook the inside. A meat thermometer should be used to check the internal temperature. For medium cooked meat this should register 160°. First seal the roast in hot fat in a preheated 450° oven for 20 minutes, turning once. Reduce the temperature to 350°, cover the meat carefully and cook for 50 minutes to the lb. (See Roasting entry.)

Serve the meat with Yorkshire pudding, horseradish sauce, and thin gravy.

To boil beef: (See entry under Boiling.) Allow 25 minutes per lb and 25 minutes over.

To cook corned beef: Put the meat in cold water, bring to a boil and discard the water. Then cook but without adding any salt. (See Boiling entry.)

To broil steak: Cook as described in Broiling entry.

BEEF WELLINGTON

3 lb fillet of beef
1 tablespoon oil
salt
pepper
1 lb mushrooms, finely chopped
1 small onion, finely chopped
3 tablespoons butter
4 tablespoons liver pâté
1 lb frozen puff pastry, thawed
beaten egg for glaze

Rub the beef with the oil, salt and pepper and roast in a 450° oven for 40 minutes. Cool.

Sauté the mushrooms and onion in the butter until tender. Drain well and combine with the liver pâté to make a paste.

Roll out the pastry to a rectangle $\frac{1}{4}$ inch thick and large enough to enclose the meat. Dampen the edges. Spread the pâté mixture over the beef and place on the pastry. Wrap the pastry around the beef and seal the edges well. Place the beef, seam side down, on a baking sheet. Roll out the trimmings to make pastry leaves and arrange on the roll. Brush with beaten egg and pierce the pastry in three places. Bake in a 450° oven 40 minutes or until golden brown.

BEEF STEW

$\frac{1}{4}$ cup vegetable oil
2 onions, sliced
1$\frac{1}{2}$ lb stewing beef
$\frac{1}{3}$ cup flour
salt
pepper
bunch of herbs
2–3 carrots, sliced
2 cups beef broth

Heat the oil in a skillet (or casserole), sauté the onions until light brown, then lift out onto a plate. Trim the meat, cut into small pieces, and sauté in the oil until lightly browned on all sides. Add to onions, stir in flour and cook, stirring until it is brown. Add the remaining ingredients and simmer for about 2 hours, or until the meat is tender; taste for seasoning. Take out the herbs and serve the stew garnished with parsley and vegetables – a mixture of small whole carrots and peas may be used.

BOEUF STROGANOFF

1$\frac{1}{2}$ lb thinly sliced sirloin steak
3 tablespoons seasoned flour
4 tablespoons butter
1 onion, thinly sliced
$\frac{1}{2}$ lb mushrooms, sliced
salt
pepper
1 cup sour cream

Pound the steak, trim it, cut it into strips $\frac{1}{4}$ inch by 2 inches and coat with the seasoned flour. Sauté the meat in 2 tablespoons butter until golden brown – about 5 to 7 minutes. Cook the onion and mushrooms in the remaining 2 tablespoons butter for 3 to 4 minutes, season to taste and add to the beef. Warm the sour cream and stir it into the mixture.

CARBONNADE OF BEEF

2 lb stewing beef, cut into $\frac{1}{2}$-inch cubes
salt
pepper
$\frac{1}{4}$ cup vegetable oil
4 strips lean bacon, chopped

4 tablespoons all-purpose flour
1 cup beer
1 cup broth or water
2–3 tablespoons vinegar
3 medium onions, chopped
1 clove garlic, chopped
bouquet garni

Season the meat and sauté in the oil until brown – about 5 minutes. Add the bacon and continue cooking for a few minutes. Remove the meat and bacon from the pan, stir in the flour and brown lightly. Gradually add the beer, broth, and vinegar, stirring continuously or until the mixture thickens. Fill a casserole with layers of meat, bacon, onion, and garlic. Add the sauce and the bouquet garni. Cover and cook for 3½ to 4 hours in a 300° oven. Add a little more beer while cooking, if necessary. Just before serving, remove the bouquet garni. Serve with plain boiled potatoes.

BEEF ROLLS

8 thin slices top round of beef
seasoned flour
2 tablespoons oil
2 cups broth or water
2 onions, sliced

FOR THE STUFFING
3 strips bacon, chopped
1 cup fresh bread crumbs
2 teaspoons chopped parsley
pinch of mixed dried herbs
grated rind of ½ lemon
salt
pepper
beaten egg to mix

Combine the ingredients for the stuffing and bind with the egg. Spread each slice of meat with stuffing, roll, tie with fine string, and toss in seasoned flour. Heat the oil in a skillet and brown the beef rolls lightly, remove and place in casserole. Add 2 tablespoons of the seasoned flour to the skillet, brown well, gradually add the broth and bring it to a boil; season to taste and pour over the rolls. Add the onions, divided into rings, cover and cook in a 350° oven for 1½ hours. Remove the strings to serve.

STEAK AND KIDNEY PIE

¾ lb stewing beef
¼ lb kidney
2 tablespoons seasoned flour
1 onion, sliced

½ package (17¼-oz size) frozen puff pastry, thawed
beaten egg for glaze

Cut the meat into ¾-inch cubes and coat with seasoned flour. Remove the skin and core from the kidney, cut into slices, and roll in seasoned flour. Combine the beef and kidney in a saucepan with the onion and add just enough water to cover. Bring to a boil, reduce heat and simmer, covered, for 1½ to 2 hours, or until the meat is tender. (The meat may also be cooked in a 325° oven in a covered casserole for 2 hours.) Cool.

Place the beef and kidney in a 5-cup ovenproof dish with enough of the cooking sauce to half fill it. Roll out the pastry 1 inch larger than the top of the dish. Cut off a ½-inch strip from around the edge of the pastry and put this strip on the dampened rim of the dish. Dampen the edge of the pastry with water and put on top of the pie. Do not stretch the pastry. Trim if necessary and flute the edge. Decorate, if desired, and brush with beaten egg. Bake in a 425° oven for 20 minutes. Reduce heat to 350° and cook 20 minutes longer.

BEER

An alcoholic beverage produced by the fermentation of malted barley and hops; the barley is wetted, allowed to germinate, and then dried. It is next ground and mixed with water and hops are added; yeast is added to the resulting wort and fermentation takes place. The beer is then filtered and kegged or bottled. Taste, color, and strength vary with type, brewing, and bottling, but it generally contains 3 to 7 percent alcohol. Pale beers are known as ales, though before hops were used the name applied to all malt beers.

Beer is sometimes used in cookery (especially in country districts) and may replace part of the stock or water used in stews, goulashes, meat ragouts, etc. It also helps to mature dried fruitcakes, though owing to its relatively low alcohol content it is not used as much as rum or brandy. Beer is a source of riboflavin and nicotinic acid.

Making beer at home is becoming an increasingly popular pastime. There are many preparations and kits on the market to make it an easy task. It is illegal to sell beer or wine made at home.

BEESTINGS

The first milk drawn from a cow after calving.

BEET (BEETROOT)

Many varieties of this easily grown root vegetable are cultivated in the United States and beets are available year round. They contain a fair amount of sugar – one type is the source of much of the sugar we use in this country.

Small, young beets are best for cooking and are generally boiled or steamed. They may be served hot as a vegetable or cold, usually in a salad. They can also be preserved in vinegar. The leafy tops are sometimes cooked and served as a green vegetable.

To boil beets: Cut the leaves 2 inches above the root but do not cut or damage the root itself, or it will "bleed." If a root is accidentally cut it may be sealed by singeing. Wash the roots in cold water, taking care not to damage the skin. Put into a saucepan of boiling water with a little salt and vinegar and simmer with the lid on the pan until quite tender (30 to 60 minutes for young beets, 1 to 2 hours for old ones), then drain. A well-cooked beet may be easily peeled with the thumb and forefinger. Slice or cube and serve hot with melted butter, or with a horseradish and sour cream sauce; alternately, serve cold, either plain or with vinegar.

To bake beets: Prepare the beet as above, place in a greased ovenproof dish, sprinkle with salt and cook in a 325° oven until tender. Peel and serve.

BORSCH (BEET SOUP)

(See Borsch entry.)

BEIGNET

French word for fritter. See separate entry.

BELGIAN ENDIVE

(See Chicory entry.)

BEL PAESE

An Italian cheese, rather mild in content and creamy in flavor.

BÉNÉDICTINE

One of the most popular of all liqueurs, sweet and aromatic with a base of Cognac. It was devised by the Bénédictine monks at Fécamp in Normandy in the sixteenth century and is still made by them.

BEURRE MANIÉ

A classic thickener of French cuisine. It can be used in place of roux. To make, cream equal volumes of butter and flour together. Swirl into a bubbling sauce bit by bit until thickened to the proper consistency. Beurre manié may be kept in the refrigerator but should be softened before using.

BEURRE NOIR (BLACK BUTTER)

A type of sauce in which butter is browned and combined with vinegar and seasoning. It is served with eggs, fish, and some vegetables.

To make it, melt $\frac{1}{2}$ cup clarified butter in a small saucepan and cook until dark brown. (If literally cooked until black, it would be burned.) Allow to cool slightly, then add 1 tablespoon vinegar, 1 tablespoon chopped parsley, and seasoning. Pour the sauce over the food and serve at once. Served with eggs, vegetables, fish, and brains. Chopped capers are included when served with fish or brains.

BEURRE NOISETTE

Clarified butter browned to a nut-brown color and combined with lemon juice and seasoning.

BEVERAGE

Any liquid, other than water, which is consumed as a drink. (See individual entries.)

BICARBONATE OF SODA (BAKING SODA)

Bicarbonate of soda (also known as baking soda) is used by itself as a leavening agent in recipes where one of the ingredients is an acid and also where a darkening effect is desired, as with gingerbread or chocolate cake. (See Leavening Agent entry and Baking Powder entry.)

At one time bicarbonate of soda was used fairly generally to conserve the color of boiled green vegetables, but this was gradually discontinued when it was found to have a destructive effect on the vitamin C content.

BIGARADE SAUCE

An orange-flavored sauce served with duck. It is made in the pan in which the duck was roasted and piqued with a touch of burned sugar and vinegar. (See Duck entry.)

BILBERRY

The European whortleberry. A small, dark-blue berry which grows wild in Great Britain mostly on moors and hillsides; the fruit ripens in August or September. The berries have a distinctive and delicious sharp flavor and are excellent for tarts, jams, and jellies. They are quite a good source of vitamin C, a serving giving about half a day's requirements. The American blueberry is sometimes known as a bilberry. (See Blueberry entry.)

BILTONG

Strips of meat dried by a method developed in South Africa which enables it to keep for years. The strips can be grated or sliced and eaten raw. It is a form of jerked meat.

BINDING

To add an ingredient, such as flour, eggs, or milk, to a mixture to hold it together.

BIOTIN

One of the B vitamins. (See Vitamins entry.)

BIRD'S NEST SOUP

This Chinese specialty is made from part of the nest of a small species of swallow found on the coasts of Eastern countries. The edible part is a glutinous material that forms the outer supporting wall of the nest; it gives a rich, spicy, aromatic flavor. Birds' nests are available in large cities with a Chinese population.

BISCUIT

A small short quick bread, usually unsweetened. When eaten as a bread, biscuits are served hot from the oven. They may also form the base for creamed mixtures such as chipped beef and may be flavored with herbs or grated cheese. When served as part of a dessert, they are known as "shortcakes." To sweeten the biscuits, add 2 tablespoons sugar to any of the recipes below.

ROLLED BAKING POWDER BISCUITS

$\frac{1}{3}$ cup vegetable shortening
2 cups all-purpose flour
3 teaspoons baking powder
$\frac{1}{2}$ teaspoon salt
$\frac{3}{4}$ cup milk

Cut the shortening into the flour, baking pow-

der, and salt until the mixture resembles dry bread crumbs. Add the milk all at once and stir with a fork just until the dough forms into a ball and the side of the bowl is clean. Knead on a lightly floured surface for about 10 to 15 seconds. Roll or pat out $\frac{1}{2}$ inch thick and cut into 2-inch circles. Place on an ungreased baking sheet; bake in a 450° oven for 10–12 minutes, until golden.

BUTTERMILK BISCUITS

$\frac{1}{3}$ cup vegetable shortening
2 cups all-purpose flour
2 teaspoons baking powder
$\frac{1}{2}$ teaspoon baking soda
$\frac{1}{2}$ teaspoon salt
$\frac{3}{4}$ cup buttermilk

Prepare and bake as for Rolled Baking Powder Biscuits above.

BISCUIT TORTONI

An Italian dessert made of frozen whipped cream flavored with macaroon crumbs.

BISCUIT TORTONI

1 cup heavy cream
$\frac{1}{4}$ cup granulated sugar
2 egg yolks
3 tablespoons powdered sugar
2 teaspoons dark rum
$\frac{3}{4}$ cup dry macaroon crumbs

Beat the cream with the granulated sugar until stiff. Whip egg yolks, powdered sugar, and rum until lemon colored, then fold in $\frac{1}{2}$ cup crumbs. Fold the egg yolks into the whipped cream; spoon into soufflé cups. Freeze. Dip the tops into remaining crumbs before serving.

BISHOP

A favorite drink during the Middle Ages, composed of wine (usually port), sweetened, spiced, and flavored with oranges. It is a popular hot beverage in northern European countries. Bishop can also be prepared with Champagne.

THE BISHOP

2 lemons
12 cloves
5 cups port
2$\frac{1}{2}$ cups water
1 teaspoon ground mixed spices
2 oz lump sugar

Stick 1 lemon with the cloves and roast it in a 350° oven for 30 minutes. Put the port into a saucepan and bring to the simmering point. In another saucepan boil the water with the spices, add to the hot wine with the roasted lemon. Rub the sugar over the rind of the remaining lemon to remove the oil, put the sugar into a bowl, adding the juice of half the lemon, and pour on the hot wine. Serve as hot as possible.

BISMARCK HERRING

A whole herring, pickled and spiced, generally served as an appetizer.

BISQUE

A thick, rich soup, based usually on a white stock made from fish, often shellfish.

BITTERS

An essence or liqueur made from bitter-flavored aromatic herbs, spices, roots, barks, etc. Bitters are used in apéritifs and cocktails and occasionally as a flavoring.

BLACK BEAN

A bean native to the Caribbean and South America, introduced into the United States by the Spanish who brought them to Florida. Although most frequently served as a soup, black beans are delicious served simply as beans.

BLACK BEAN SOUP

1 lb black beans
2 onions, chopped
1 green pepper, chopped
1 clove garlic, chopped
⅓ lb salt pork, diced
2 stalks celery, chopped
1 bay leaf
½ lb ham, cubed
1 cup red wine

Soak beans overnight. Sauté the onions, green pepper, and garlic in a soup pot with the salt pork. When the onions are lightly colored, drain the beans and add to the pot with 3 quarts water, the celery, bay leaf and ham. Simmer for 3 to 4 hours, until the beans are very tender. Remove the bay leaf. Puree the soup and return to the pot. Add the wine and reheat. Serve with lemon slices.

BLACKBERRY (BRAMBLE)

Blackberries, both wild and cultivated, grow extensively in the United States. The cultivated varieties are often larger and more juicy than the wild, but slightly different in flavor. Blackberries are a good source of vitamin C, supplying the day's requirements (20 mg) in an average helping. The name "bramble" applies to any member of the *Rubus* genus, including blackberries and raspberries, but particularly to the common English blackberry.

Ripe blackberries are very good eaten raw and served with sugar and cream; the fruit should be carefully picked over and washed. When cooked, blackberries are often combined with apples. Apples are also added to blackberry jam and jelly to supply the acid and pectin necessary for a good set. As blackberry seeds are very hard, many people use the fruit only in dishes in which it is sieved, as in blackberry fool, blackberry conserve, and blackberry jelly. The fruit and young shoots, make a good wine. (See Wines entry.)

BLACKBERRY JELLY

4 lb blackberries (slightly underripe)
juice of 2 lemons or 1½ teaspoons citric acid
2 cups water
sugar

Wash the blackberries and pick them over. Put them into a pan and crush. Add the lemon juice (or acid) and water, cover and bring to a boil. Reduce heat and simmer for 5 minutes. Strain through a jelly bag, measure the juice and return it to the pan with 3 cups sugar to each 4 cups of juice. Stir until the sugar has dissolved and boil rapidly until the jelly mixture sheets from the spoon. Skim, jar, and cover in the usual way.

BLACKBERRY AND APPLE JAM

4 lb blackberries
2¼ cups water
1 lb sour apples
6 lb sugar

Pick over and wash the blackberries, put them in a pan with ⅔ cup of the water and simmer slowly until soft. Peel, core, and slice the apples and add the remaining water. Simmer slowly until soft and make into a pulp with a spoon or a potato masher. Add the blackberries and sugar, bring to a boil and boil rapidly, stirring frequently, until setting point is reached. Jar and cover in the usual way. *Makes about 10 lb.*

BLACK BUN

A spicy mixture of raisins, currants, candied peel, and chopped nuts enclosed in a flaky pastry. It is eaten in Scotland on Hogmanay (the New Year) and should be prepared several weeks ahead of time and allowed to ripen.

BLACK BUTTER

(See Beurre Noir entry.)

BLACK CURRANT

(See Currant entry.)

BLACK-EYED PEA

The bean of the cowpea, a plant of the South of the United States, grown for forage and incidentally used for food as well. The mottled black and white bean can be eaten fresh or dried. When dried, black-eyed peas improve in flavor if cooked with meat.

BLACK-EYED PEA BALLS

1 lb black-eyed peas
½ lb salt pork, diced
1 onion, chopped
1 green pepper, chopped
salt
pepper
hot pepper sauce
Worcestershire sauce
½ cup cracker crumbs
1–2 eggs

Soak the peas overnight in water to cover. Drain and put in a saucepan with 6 cups fresh water and the salt pork, onion, and green pepper. Simmer for about 2 hours, or until the peas are soft. Drain and put through a food mill. Mix in the seasonings and sauces.

Stir in the cracker crumbs and eggs until thick enough to mold into balls. Shape into small balls, sauté in oil, and serve hot on wooden picks.

BLANCHING

To treat food with boiling water, in order to whiten it, to preserve its natural color, to loosen its skin, to remove a flavor which is too acid, rank, or otherwise too strong, or (in the case of vegetables which are to be canned, frozen, etc.) to kill unwanted enzymes.

The two usual ways of blanching food are:
1. To plunge it into boiling water – use this method for tomatoes and nuts which are to be peeled.
2. To bring it to a boil in the water – used to whiten sweetbreads or veal or to reduce the saltiness of such things as pickled meat or kippers, before cooking them in a fresh lot of water or stock.

BLANCMANGE

A dessert made from milk that is flavored, sweetened, and stiffened either with starch (usually cornstarch) or with gelatin. The hot mixture is poured into a wetted mold to set and is turned out before serving. (See Cornstarch entry for recipe.)

BLANQUETTE

A white stew of chicken, lamb, veal, or sweetbreads, enriched with egg yolk or cream and flavored with a bouquet garni, onion, and lemon juice. It is served hot, with a garnish of croutons of bread or fleurons of pastry, button mushrooms, and onions. (See Blanquette of Veal under Veal entry.)

BLEAK

A small European river fish of the carp family, which may be cooked like the sprat.

BLENDING

To mix flour, cornstarch, rice flour, and similar ground cereals to a smooth paste with a cold liquid (milk, water, or stock), before a boiling liquid is added, in the preparation of soups, stews, puddings, gravies, etc., to prevent the cereal from forming lumps. Use a wooden spoon and add the liquid by degrees, stirring all the time. Experience will soon show the right amount of liquid to use – too little makes hard lumps which are almost impossible to disperse and too much causes smaller, softer lumps which are also difficult to smooth out.

BLENNY

A small European and American sea fish; it may be prepared like whitebait.

BLEWIT

A variety of edible fungus.

BLINIS

Small Russian yeast pancakes, made of buckwheat flour, which are served with smoked salmon, caviar, etc.

BLINTZ

A thin pancake, similar to the French crêpe, that is a mainstay of Jewish cuisine. Depending on its ultimate use, the blintz may be made with milk or water, cooked with butter or oil. Fillings may be of fruit, vegetables, or meat, but the most popular is cheese.

CHEESE BLINTZES

3 eggs
1 cup milk or water
½ teaspoon salt
2 tablespoons salad oil
½ cup all-purpose flour
2 cups drained cottage cheese
1 egg yolk
½ teaspon salt
1 tablespoon melted butter

Combine the eggs, milk, salt, oil, and flour in a blender and mix. Heat a little butter or oil in a 6-inch skillet or crêpe pan and add just enough batter to coat the bottom of the pan, about 2 tablespoons. Cook until the underside is browned. Remove from the pan and place browned side up on a damp towel. Continue until all the blintzes are cooked. Beat the cottage cheese with the remaining ingredients. Place 2 tablespoons of the mixture along one side of the blintz. Fold the sides over and roll like a jelly roll. The uncooked side of the blintz should be outside. The blintzes are now fried in butter or oil, turning once, or baked in a 425° oven, seam side down, until browned. Serve with sour cream.

BLOATER

A herring which has been immersed in brine, smoked and cured by a special process, perfected at Great Yarmouth in England. Unlike kippers, bloaters are not split open and the curing process is not carried so far as with kippers, therefore bloaters do not keep well (except in the form of commercially prepared bloater paste).

BLOOD PUDDING

A kind of sausage, also known as black pudding, popular in the Midlands and North of England. It is made of pig's blood, suet, breadcrumbs, and oatmeal, usually sold ready cooked. It is sautéed and served with mashed potatoes or bacon.

BLOWFISH (SEA SQUAB)

A small saltwater fish, also known as the puffer, capable of inflating itself until it is round. Only the two pieces of flesh along the backbone, marketed as sea squab, are eaten. Sea squab may be sautéed, broiled, or crumbed and deep-fried.

BLUEBERRY

Juicy blue-black fruits commonly found from above the Arctic Circle to Florida. Good blueberries should be plump – whether cultivated or wild. Shriveled or burst blueberries will usually be quite tasteless. One of the most popular berries in the United States, blueberries are excellent raw with cream and sugar or in fritters, pies, cakes, muffins, pancakes, and ice cream.

To make blueberry fritters: Make a fritter batter and add enough blueberries to make it quite thick. Drop spoonfuls into hot shallow fat, fry until golden, drain, and coat with superfine sugar.

BLUEBERRY JAM

2½ lb blueberries
⅔ cup water
¼ cup lemon juice
3 lb sugar
1 (8 fl oz) bottle of commercial pectin

This is rather an expensive jam to make unless you can pick the berries yourself, but it has a delicious flavor.

Pick over the fruit, removing any leaves and stems, wash it lightly and put in a pan with the water and lemon juice. Simmer gently for about 10 to 15 minutes, until the fruit is soft and just beginning to pulp. Add the sugar, stir until dissolved, bring to a boil and boil for 3 minutes. Take off the heat, add the pectin, boil for a further minute and allow to cool slightly before jarring and covering in the usual way. *Makes about 5½ lb.*

BLUE CHEESE

A semisoft cheese made of cow's milk. It is

streaked with a greenish-gray mold and has a flavor similar to Roquefort. Excellent blue cheese is made in the United States, particularly in the state of Wisconsin, and in Denmark.

BLUEFISH

A game and commercial fish of the Atlantic seaboard of North America, with an average range in weight from 2 to 6 lb but growing much larger. They are sold whole or filleted. Somewhat oily and strong-flavored, blues are best cooked by broiling, grilling, or baking.

BOILING

To cook in liquid – usually stock or water – at a temperature of 212°. Vegetables, rice, and pasta, together with syrups, etc. that are to be reduced, are the chief foods that are actually boiled. Although meat, poultry, and fish are put into boiling water, the heat is then lowered and the food is simmered or stewed at a temperature just below boiling point – fast boiling during the whole cooking time causes meat, poultry, etc. to shrink and lose flavor and it also tends to become less digestible.

To boil meat: Wipe the meat thoroughly and remove any superfluous fat.

A large roast such as a round of beef should be tied securely to prevent it from losing shape during the cooking.

Put fresh meat into salted boiling water (1 teaspoon salt to 1 lb of meat). Allow it to simmer gently (i.e. the water should bubble slightly on one side of the pan only) for the required length of time.

In case of corned meat, place it in cold water, bring quickly to the boiling point, throw away this water and commence again with cold. When boiling point has been regained, allow the water round the meat to simmer gently as for fresh meat. Add no extra salt at this stage.

Onions or leeks, carrots, and a little turnip may be added to the pot, also herbs and spices (e.g. clove or mace), according to taste.

The liquor in which meat is cooked contains nourishment and flavor, so some of it can be used to make a sauce or gravy to accompany the meat and any that remains should be used as a basis for soup.

To boil fowl, fish, and vegetables: (See Chicken, Fish, Vegetables, and similar entries.)

BOK CHOY (CHINESE CHARD)

A leafy green vegetable with white stems and tiny yellow flowers. The name is sometimes also used for Chinese cabbage.

BOLETUS

A genus of fungi, including both poisonous and edible varieties, the best-known member of the family being the edible Cèpe de Bordeaux, which is much esteemed in France.

BOLOGNA SAUSAGE

A large Italian smoked sausage of finely chopped pork, veal, and cereal, seasoned and flavored.

BOMBAY DUCK

A fish found in Indian waters, dried and often served with curry. It has a delicate flavor and is very nutritious.

BOMBE

The name given to a mold, usually made of copper with a tightly fitting lid, which is mostly used for shaping different flavors of ice cream and, sometimes, fruits. (See Ice cream entry.)

BONBON

A general name for various kinds of sugar confectionery.

BONDON

A small soft, whole-milk cheese made in Normandy; shaped in the form of a bun.

BONE

Bones contain anything from 20 to 70 percent of mineral elements, 15 to 50 percent gelatin-producing material (cartilage, etc.), 5 to 50 percent of water, and from $\frac{1}{2}$ to 20 percent fat.

In cookery, both raw bones and those taken from cooked meat are used in the preparation of stock which can form the basis of many soups, stews, and sauces. A good flavor and a certain amount of gelatin are obtained from the bones, but stock has practically no nutritional value. (For method of making see Stock entry.)

The fatty substance in the interior of marrow bones is considered by some to be a delicacy and may be served as a garnish in soups and sauces or served as an appetizer with toast.

To prepare marrow: Select large, fresh marrow bones and if possible get the butcher to saw them in half. Scrape and wash the bones and cover the end of each with a paste made of flour and water, in order to prevent the marrow escaping during the cooking. Tie each bone in a small pudding cloth, stand it upright in a pan of boiling salted water and simmer for 1½ to 2 hours, then remove the cloths and paste. Pin a small napkin around each bone and send to table upright on a hot dish, accompanied by dry, crisp toast. Alternately, extract the marrow and serve it already spread on toast. Salt and cayenne pepper are the only flavorings required.

BONITO

A member of the tuna family, caught in the Pacific off the coast of North America.

BONNE-BOUCHE

A small flavorful tidbit, served as an appetizer or, by the British, as a savory at the end of the meal.

BONNE FEMME

This term means cooked in a simple or house-wifely style, with a garnish of fresh vegetables or herbs usually including mushrooms. It is gener-ally applied to cream soups or fish dishes, e.g. Potage à la Bonne Femme – a puree or cream soup garnished with lettuce, tarragon, and chopped chervil; Sole à la Bonne Femme – usually garnished with mushrooms in a sauce flavored with shallots and white wine; Oeufs à la Bonne Femme – hard-cooked eggs, with the yolks pounded with chopped tarragon and butter, then replaced and garnished with beets.

BORAGE

A herb, the young leaves of which are used to flavor claret cup, iced drinks, and occasionally vegetables, and as an addition to salads. They have a cucumber flavor that is particularly refreshing. The blue flowers may be used as a garnish.

BORDEAUX WINES

Bordeaux is the largest fine wine district of France. As a wine region it has the advantages of a stable climate, a position near the sea, and many rivers and forests on the ocean side to protect it from strong salt winds and reduce the rainfall. Although the top soil is often poor, the bed rock is rich in minerals. The wines are made from a mixture of grape varieties, the proportions vary-ing according to each proprietor. The main Bordeaux "rouge" districts are Médoc, St Émilion, Pomerol, and Graves. There are many hundreds of Châteaux making and bottling excellent wines. Most of these will be vintage wines which those bottled overseas are not. The minimum age for a vintage wine is 5 years and some can live for 50 years or more.

Bordeaux white wines are usually medium sweet or sweet. The sweetest are the Barsacs whereas some Graves are quite dry. The best white Bordeaux wines are considered to be the Sauternes. Those of the best vintage will improve for at least 15 years, and even moderate vintages are worth keeping as they gain an added depth of flavor.

BORSCH (BORTSCH)

A Russian or Polish soup made originally from duck, other meat, and beets; nowadays the duck is frequently omitted. The soup may be served hot or cold.

BORSCH

2¼ lb beets, peeled
2 medium-sized onions, chopped
10 cups stock
2 tablespoons lemon juice
seasoning
sour cream
hot peeled boiled potatoes

Grate the beets coarsely and combine them with the onion and stock in a pan. Bring to a boil and simmer, uncovered, for 45 minutes. Strain and add the lemon juice. Adjust seasoning. Serve either well chilled or hot with a whirl of sour cream and a hot peeled boiled potato.

BOTULISM

A form of food poisoning (often fatal) caused by a toxin produced by a bacterium known as *Bacillus botulinus*. It has been known to develop in such low-acid foods as home-canned vegetables, meat, pies, fish and meat pastes, canned and smoked meat, raw and salted fish. Proper pre-paration in a steam-pressure canner in working order destroys the bacteria.

Frequently there is no indication of the presence of toxins and the food may appear, smell, and taste quite normal. For safety, before tasting, all low-acid foods should be boiled for 15 minutes to destroy the toxin and render any contaminated food safe.

BOUCHÉE

A small pastry shell in the shape of a vol-au-vent, filled with a mixture of finely chopped meat, poultry, fish, or game, usually in a thick sauce. Bouchées are served cold or hot as appetizers, with cocktails and at buffet parties.

Typical fillings are: Fish and mayonnaise sauce; chopped cooked mushroom, ham, tongue, shrimp, and chicken moistened with Béchamel sauce, sardine with diced tomato, lemon juice, and a little mayonnaise; cheese preparations.

BOUILLABAISSE

A renowned Southern French fish stew, made of various kinds of fish peculiar to the Mediterranean, cooked with olive oil, spices, and herbs. Saffron is usually included as a flavoring.

BOUILLABAISSE

1 tablespoon oil
1 medium onion, sliced
1 clove garlic, crushed
1 can (14 oz) tomatoes
12 oz fish stock or bottled clam broth
1 tablespoon chopped parsley
salt
pepper
bouquet garni
½ lb monkfish, diced
12 oz red snapper, skinned and filleted
6 oz cod fillet, skinned and diced
6 oz bass fillet, skinned and diced
2 flounder fillets, cut into strips
parsley for garnish

Heat the oil in a large pan and sauté the onion and garlic for 5 minutes. Add the tomatoes with their juice, stock, 1 tablespoon parsley, salt, pepper, and bouquet garni. Bring to a boil, reduce heat, and simmer 10 minutes.

Add the remaining fish, except the flounder, and simmer 5 minutes. Add the flounder and simmer 8 to 10 minutes longer, or until all the fish are cooked. Remove the bouquet garni and taste for seasoning. Pour the soup into a tureen and sprinkle with parsley. Serve with hot French bread.

BOUILLON

Plain unclarified meat or vegetable broth, served as a soup. It is made in a similar way to Pot-au-Feu. (See Pot-au-Feu entry.)

BOULA BOULA

A cream soup made from a puree of green peas combined with turtle soup and cream. It is garnished with diced turtle meat and topped with whipped cream. Served in crocks, it is run under the broiler before being brought to the table.

BOUQUET GARNI

A bunch of herbs, used in soups, stews, and sauces to give flavor. Usually a sprig each of parsley and thyme, a bay leaf and sometimes other herbs or a piece of celery and leek are bound together, or better still tied in a piece of cheesecloth and cooked in the pot with the liquid and other ingredients. The bouquet garni is removed before serving.

There are many variations. In parts of Southern France a strip of dried orange peel is included which gives an excellent flavor to some dishes. Some cooks add marjoram, others, winter savory or lemon thyme.

When fresh herbs are not available, a pinch or so of mixed dried leaf herbs may be used instead. If the dish calls for spices such as cloves, peppercorns and mace, these are usually included in the bag of herbs.

Ready-prepared bouquets garnis are available from gourmet grocery, cookery and gift shops.

BOURBON

A whiskey distilled from mash containing at least 51 percent corn. Bourbon is popular in the South of the United States and is the basis of a mint julep.

BOURGUIGNONNE

A red wine sauce containing onion and sometimes mushrooms. It is also the name for a garnish which incorporates mushrooms, small onions, and broiled bacon in a red wine sauce.

BRAINS

In Europe the brains of calf, sheep, or pig are sold either with the head or separately. In the United States they are sold separately. They are considered a delicacy, calves' brains being generally the most popular. The same recipes can be used for all types of brains.

The brains must be very fresh. Wash them in cold salted water, removing the loose skin and any clots of blood, then let them lie in fresh cold water for at least an hour. When they are thoroughly cleansed, put them into a small saucepan with cold water to cover, a pinch of salt, and a good squeeze of lemon juice. Add a small bunch of herbs (parsley, thyme, and bay leaf), and simmer slowly for 15 minutes, then strain, coat, and fry or sauté or else serve in one of the following ways:

To make calf's brains on toast: Cook the brains as above. Make a good white sauce and add to it the yolk of an egg and a good squeeze of lemon juice. Place the brains on 2 rounds of toast, strain the sauce over and garnish with lemon, a few potato balls or green peas.

To make scalloped calf's brains: Cook as above, then arrange the brains in scallop shells, cover with white sauce and sprinkle bread crumbs and grated cheese on the top. Brown under the broiler.

BRAISING

This combination of stewing, steaming, and roasting is suitable for various meats and vegetables; it gives a delicate flavor and a tender, moist consistency. Meat is first lightly browned in hot fat and then laid on a bed of prepared vegetables, with just enough liquid to cover these. It may be cooked either in a 350° oven or on top of the stove; in this case, bake or roast in the oven for the last 30 minutes of cooking, to give a better flavor to the finished dish.

Preparation
Prepare the meat according to the kind, boning and stuffing if liked. Note the weight to gauge the cooking time and allow 25 to 30 minutes per lb, plus 30 minutes. Then prepare the bed of vegetables, e.g. 1 onion, 1 carrot, 1 small turnip, 2 stalks of celery, and a bouquet garni, with seasoning. Peel and trim the vegetables as usual and cut into pieces.

Cooking
If possible, choose a fireproof casserole or a pan with two handles that may be placed in the oven. Place about 2 tablespoons cooking fat in the pan, together with a few bacon rinds, and brown the meat on all sides in the hot fat. Remove the meat

and add the vegetables, sautéing until lightly browned and soft. Then add the bouquet garni, fresh herbs such as thyme and parsley, and sufficient stock or water to half cover the vegetables. Bring to a boil, then place the meat on top, cover and simmer gently, basting every 15 to 20 minutes with the liquor, for half the cooking time; remove the lid and complete the cooking in a 425° oven, basting frequently. Remove the meat to a hot platter and thicken the pot liquor to make a gravy. Garnish, if liked, with the vegetables, after removing the bacon rinds and the bouquet garni.

Alternate method
Prepare the meat by coating it with seasoned flour. Melt a little dripping and when it is smoking hot sauté the meat, turning it so that it is brown all over, then remove it from the pan. If necessary, add a little more dripping and in this sauté a mixture of vegetables (onions, carrots, celery, etc.) until lightly browned. Put the vegetables into a roasting pan, place the meat on top and add enough stock or water just to cover the vegetables. Add more salt and pepper if necessary and some chopped herbs. Cover and cook in a 325° oven until the meat is tender. Lift it onto a hot dish, arrange the vegetables at each end, and pour the liquor round.

Cooking time
For meat suitable for roasting, allow half as long again as for roasting; for stewing meat (scrag end of neck, etc.) 2 to 3 hours; rabbits, 1 to 2 hours; chicken, 1 hour; fowl, 2 hours.

BRISKET OF BEEF BRAISED IN RED WINE

2 tablespoons vegetable oil
2–2½ lb brisket (thin end), rolled and tied
1 large onion, chopped
1 clove garlic, crushed with ½ teaspoon salt
2 large carrots, sliced
2 leeks, sliced
1 cup red wine
1 cup beef broth
bouquet garni
¼ teaspoon ground cinnamon
¼ teaspoon ground allspice
salt
pepper
1 tablespoon brandy
1 tablespoon softened butter
2 tablespoons flour

Brown the beef in oil in a flameproof casserole. Remove from pot and add the onion and garlic.

Sauté until soft and lightly browned, stirring to prevent burning. Add the carrots and leeks and sauté until softened. Add the wine, broth, bouquet garni, spices, and salt and pepper. Bring to a boil, reduce heat and return the beef to the casserole. Cover and transfer to a 300° oven for 3 hours, or until tender.

Remove the beef and bouquet garni from the pot and cut off any strings. Place the beef on a warmed serving platter. Heat the brandy, ignite it and pour it over the beef. Cream the butter and flour to a paste (beurre manié) and swirl it gradually into the liquid in the casserole over high heat. Bring to a boil and allow to thicken. Taste for seasoning and pour a little of the sauce over the beef. Pass the remaining sauce in a gravy boat with the beef.

BRAISED CELERY

4 small heads celery, trimmed and cleaned
4 tablespoons butter
strong stock, preferably homemade
salt
pepper

Tie each head of celery securely to hold the shape. Sauté lightly in half the butter for 5 minutes, until golden brown. Put in an ovenproof dish, add enough stock to come halfway up the celery, sprinkle with salt and pepper and add the remaining butter. Cover and cook for 25 to 45 minutes in a 350° oven, or until soft. Remove the strings and serve with the cooking liquid poured over; if the stock is homemade reduce it first to a glaze by fast boiling.

BRAMBLE

(See Blackberry entry.)

BRAN

Recent medical research has shown that roughage plays an important part in preventing diseases of the bowel and colon.

About 13 percent of a grain of wheat is bran, which forms the outer layer of cells (pericarp and aleurone). Bran contains cellulose or roughage, which is not digested by the body but has a useful laxative action. The aleurone layer of bran is rich in protein, mineral elements, and niacin, but also contains phytic acid, which tends to prevent the absorption of calcium.

BRANDY

A spirit distilled from wine. Brandy is colorless at first, but darkens in the cask as it matures. The quality of the brandy depends upon the type of wine used, the manner of distillation, and the method and time of storage. The French Cognac and Armagnac brandies are considered the best. V.S.O.P., meaning "very special old pale," denotes a brandy that is 18 to 25 years old, while V.V.S.O.P. applies to one 25 to 40 years old.

Brandy may be flavored with apricots, cherries, or other fruits.

Brandy is frequently found in recipes for fruitcakes and for flambé dishes.

BRANDY SNAP

A crisp rolled cookie served with tea or coffee or as an accompaniment to a dessert such as ice cream; whipped cream or pastry cream is piped into its hollow center; it is sometimes served as a luncheon or dinner dessert.

BRANDY SNAPS

$\frac{1}{4}$ *cup butter or margarine*

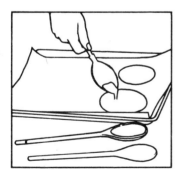

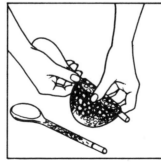

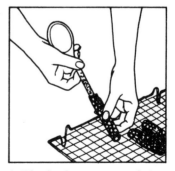

TO MAKE BRANDY SNAPS
1. Drop small spoonfuls of mixture onto a lined baking sheet, allowing plenty of room for spreading.

2. Roll warm brandy snaps around the greased handles of several wooden spoons, leave to cool slightly.

3. When brandy snaps are set and crisp, transfer to a cookie rack.

¼ cup superfine sugar
2 tablespoons corn syrup
½ cup all-purpose flour
½ teaspoon ground ginger
1 teaspoon brandy, optional
grated rind of ½ lemon
whipped cream

Grease the handles of several wooden spoons and line 2 to 3 baking sheets with wax paper.

Melt the butter with the sugar and syrup in a small saucepan over a low heat. Remove from the heat and stir in the sifted flour and ginger, brandy, and lemon rind. Drop small spoonfuls of the mixture about 4 inches apart on the lined baking sheets, to allow plenty of room for spreading. Bake in rotation in a 350° oven for 7 to 10 minutes, until bubbly and golden. Allow to cool for 1 to 2 minutes, then loosen with a spatula and roll them round the spoon handles. If the cookies harden before rolling, return briefly to the oven to soften.

BRAUNSCHWEIGER

(See Liverwurst entry.)

BRAWN

(See Head Cheese entry.)

BRAZIL NUT

The edible seed of a large tree native to Brazil. The fruits are borne in large numbers high on the trees and each contains 12 to 22 nuts, with a distinctive tough, angular shell. The white kernels are eaten plain or used in candies and cakes. Like other nuts, they contain fat and protein.

BREAD

As long ago as 2000 BC bread was an important part of the Egyptian diet. In England there is evidence that it was baked and eaten in the Stone and Iron Ages. Today, bread, with other cereal-based foods, provides more than a quarter of the total energy, protein, carbohydrate, and iron in the average household diet. Bread also provides a good source of calcium, niacin, and thiamin. Although some of these nutrients are lost during the milling of flour, calcium, iron and B vitamins are added to white flour to make good the loss.

There is often controversy as to whether white or whole-wheat bread is better nutritionally. It is now accepted by most nutrition experts that both are a valuable source of nutrients in the diet as white bread is enriched in the United States. Whole-wheat bread is favored by many because of its higher roughage content.

Varieties of Bread

WHITE BREADS
Bread made from wheat flour (see Flour entry) has the light texture which most people like. The nutritive value is high, owing to the additions already mentioned.

Many different varieties and shapes of loaf are made. The most widely sold, because of its convenience, is the wrapped sliced loaf, although connoisseurs prefer crusty, unsliced bread, which should always be served as fresh as possible. Whatever your usual choice, it is a good idea to try some of the scores of varieties now available.

WHITE BREAD MADE FROM UNENRICHED DOUGH
The ingredients of the basic white bread are flour, water, salt, and yeast. A little sugar is usually added to spur the leavening action of the yeast.

Like other breads, this version can be made in a variety of different breads and in different shapes.

Sandwich loaf: Baked in a rectangular pan.

Pullman loaf: May be wrapped or unwrapped. Can be sliced.

Barrel bread: Baked in a cylindrical can.

CRUSTY WHITE BREADS

Coburg: Round, cut on top to form a cross.

Cottage: Made of two rounds, smaller on top of larger.

WHITE BREAD MADE FROM ENRICHED DOUGH
Milk, eggs and/or shortening, sugar, and sometimes other ingredients are added. The addition of milk, butter or shortening, and sugar makes for a lighter loaf, a bit sweeter, and more appealing to American tastes. Eggs and additional oil and sugar will give a softer texture.

SPECIALTY WHITE BREADS
Several of these types of loaf are European in origin.

Poppy seed braid: Crusty braided loaf, with top sprinkled with poppy seeds.

Challa: Jewish bread with added oil, eggs, and sugar, producing a soft texture. Generally braided, sometimes sprinkled with poppy seeds.

Caraway: Contains caraway seeds. Baton-shaped.

Vienna: Enriched with milk, soft and light crumb, but the glazed crust is very crisp. Baked under steam, which keeps crust moist until maximum expansion takes place, giving light, open texture; steam is then withdrawn and crust baked crisp. Various shapes.

French: Made from an enriched dough; very crisp crust. Made like Vienna bread; long shape with a slashed top.

PROTEIN AND GLUTEN BREADS

These have extra protein in the form of added gluten. This gives a lighter texture, but the Caloric value is much the same as for other breads.

WHOLE WHEAT

Made from a mixture of white and whole-wheat flours. (See Flour entry.) Various finishes and shapes.

RYE BREADS

Made from a mixture of rye and wheat flours in varying proportions, so that the color varies from white to black. They have a closer texture than wheat bread and a slightly sour taste. Various shapes.

Pumpernickel is a particularly dark and slightly sour-tasting rye bread.

CRISPBREADS

Flat, crisp wafers, made from rye or wheat flour or a mixture of the two; whole-grain flour, sometimes quite coarsely ground, is generally used. Several commercial varieties are sold here and many more in Scandinavia.

UNLEAVENED BREADS

Made from flour derived from various grains, salt, and water. The dough is kneaded to lighten it somewhat, but when baked it is flat, crisp, and hard. Matzos – the Jewish unleavened bread – is the best known one. Chappatis and many other breads made in different parts of the world are also unleavened.

SODA BREAD

(See Soda Bread entry.)

TYPES OF ROLLS

Dinner: Soft crust, round or long shape.

Vienna: Made from Vienna bread dough; crisp crust, various shapes, with or without poppy seeds.

Croissants: Made from a yeast dough into which butter is folded, as in puff pastry; crescent-shaped. (See Croissant entry.)

Hamburger and Frankfurter: Soft rolls designed to hold respectively a hamburger or frankfurter.

Ingredients Used in Breadmaking

YEAST

Fresh yeast can be bought from health-food stores and some supermarkets and bakers (those who bake their own bread are your best bet), and dry yeast can be found in supermarkets and grocers as well as health-food stores. Which is the best, dry or fresh? Both have their pros and cons. There is nothing to choose between the two as far as taste and texture of the end result is concerned. Fresh yeast is rather like putty in color and texture and should have a faint "winy" smell. There should be no discoloration and it should crumble easily when broken. Although it will store for up to a month in a screw-topped jar or wrapped in plastic or foil in the refrigerator, the best results are obtained when it is absolutely fresh, so buy it in small quantities when required.

Fresh yeast is usually blended with a liquid; it is then ready to be added to the flour all at once. It can also be rubbed directly into the flour or else added as a batter. This batter is known as the sponge batter process where only some of the ingredients are mixed, forming a sponge that is allowed to ferment and is then mixed with the remaining ingredients to form a dough.

Using sugar to cream the yeast before adding the liquid is not advised as concentrations of sugar kill some of the yeast cells and thus delay fermentation. The resulting bread has a strong yeasty taste. Fresh yeast is easiest measured by weight. According to the richness of the mixture, 1 oz fresh yeast is sufficient to raise 3 lb (12 cups) white flour.

Dry yeast is sold in granulated form and is very convenient as it can be stored in an airtight container in a cool place up to the date of expiration. Dry yeast requires sugar and liquid to activate it. The sugar, in the proportion of 1 teaspoon to 1 cup of tepid liquid, is dissolved in the liquid. The yeast granules are then sprinkled over the surface of the liquid and the mixture left to proof, or froth. If a warmer water is used, dry yeast can be added directly to the flour. As it is more concentrated than fresh yeast, generally half of the amount of dry yeast is required to fresh. 1 package of dry yeast is equivalent to $\frac{1}{2}$ oz fresh yeast.

FLOUR

Wheat, before it is made into flour, is either hard or soft. Hard wheat when milled produces a strong flour, rich in protein, which contains a sticky, rubberlike substance called gluten. When combined with the other essential ingredients used in breadmaking, the gluten stretches like elastic and as it is heated, it expands and traps in the dough the carbon dioxide released by the yeast. The gluten then sets and forms the frame of the bread. It is the gluten content in a flour that gives the volume and open texture of baked bread.

Soft wheats when milled produce a flour with different gluten properties, more suited to the making of cakes, pastries, etc. where a smaller rise and closer, finer texture are required.

Although bread flour is now available for consumer use, all-purpose or unbleached flour can make an excellent bread.

It is the flour used that gives each bread its characteristic flavor and texture. Today there are many different flours readily available, from health-food stores if not from your local supermarket or grocer.

Generally bread made with whole-wheat flour has a closer texture and a stronger, more distinctive taste than white bread. As whole-wheat flour does not store as well as white, it should be bought in smaller quantities.

Whole-grain flour contains 100 percent wheat. The entire grain is milled, and bread made with this flour is coarse textured and has a nutty taste.

Whole-wheat flour contains 80 to 90 percent wheat (i.e. some of the bran is removed) and it is more absorbent than white flour, giving a denser textured bread than white but not as coarse as whole-grain. Stone ground refers to the specific process of grinding the flour which heats it and gives it a slightly roasted, nutty flavor. Both whole-wheat and wheat-grain can be stone ground.

Rye flour used on its own produces rather dense, heavy bread as rye lacks sufficient protein for the formation of gluten. Finely milled rye flour gives the densest texture and bread made with coarsely milled rye flour is rougher and more open-textured. The traditional German pumpernickel is made from coarsely ground rye flour. The best results for baking at home are obtained by combining the rye flour with a strong wheat flour.

SALT

Salt is added to improve the flavor. It is essential to measure it accurately, as too little causes the dough to rise too quickly and too much kills the yeast and gives the bread an uneven texture. Salt is used in the proportions of 2 teaspoons to 1 lb flour.

SHORTENING

The addition of shortening to the dough enriches it and gives a moist, close-textured loaf with a soft crust. It also helps keep the bread fresh and soft for a longer time.

LIQUID

Water is most suitable for plain bread, producing a loaf with an even texture and a crisp crust. Milk and water, or milk alone, will give a softer golden crust and the loaf will stay soft and fresh for longer.

The amount of liquid used will vary according to the absorbency of the flour, as too much will give the bread a spongy and open texture. Whole-wheat flours are more absorbent than white.

The liquid is generally added to the yeast at a tepid temperature, i.e. 110°.

GLAZES AND FINISHES

If a crusty finish is desired for bread or rolls, they can be brushed before baking with a glaze made by dissolving 2 teaspoons salt in 2 tablespoons water.

For a soft finish the surface should be brushed with oil and dusted with flour, or alternately brushed with beaten egg or beaten egg and milk.

Some breads and yeast buns are glazed after baking to give them a sticky finish. To achieve this, brush with warmed honey or a syrup made by dissolving 2 tablespoons sugar in 2 tablespoons water; bring to a boil.

There are many ways of adding interest and variety to bread and rolls. After glazing and before baking, lightly sprinkle the surface with one of the following:
1. Poppy, caraway, celery, or fennel seeds.
2. Sesame seeds. Particularly good sprinkled onto the soft rolls eaten with hamburgers.
3. A mixture of crushed rock salt and caraway. This is particularly good on rolls to be eaten with cheese or smoked sausage.

Step-by-Step Processes in Breadmaking

The process used in making yeast mixtures forms the basis of the method followed for nearly all yeast cooking.

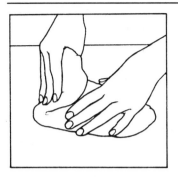

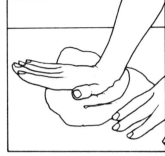

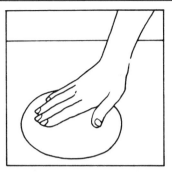

HOW TO KNEAD DOUGH
1. Knead dough by first folding it toward you on a floured surface.

2. Push down and away from you with the palm of the hand. Give the dough a quarter turn and repeat.

3. Continue kneading for about 10 minutes until the dough is firm, elastic and no longer sticky.

1. MIXING THE DOUGH

Measure all the ingredients carefully and sift the dry ingredients (flour, salt, etc.) into a large bowl.

Add the yeast dissolved in the liquid all at once and mix the dry ingredients, using a wooden spoon or fork, until blended. Extra flour (taking care not to upset the balance by adding too much) can be added at this stage if the dough is too soft. Beat the dough by hand until the mixture is completely smooth and leaves the sides of the bowl cleanly.

2. KNEADING THE DOUGH

Kneading is essential to strengthen the gluten in the flour, thus making the dough elastic in texture and enabling it to rise more easily. To do this:

Turn the dough onto a floured working surface, knead the dough by folding it toward you and pushing down and away from you with the palm of the hand. Give the dough a quarter turn and continue kneading for about 10 minutes, until it is firm, elastic and no longer sticky.

If you have a mixer with a dough hook attachment, it can take the hard work out of kneading. Follow manufacturer's instructions; working with small amounts of dough is more successful than attempting a large batch all at once. Place the yeast dissolved in the liquid in the bowl, add the dry ingredients and begin at lowest speed and mix to form dough. Increase the speed for the recommended time.

3. RISING

The kneaded dough is now ready for rising. Unless otherwise stated, place in a greased bowl and cover with a large sheet of plastic, brushed with oil to prevent a skin forming during rising.

Rising times vary with temperature. As only extreme heat kills the yeast and extreme cold retards the growth of yeast, the method of rising can be arranged to suit yourself.

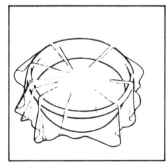

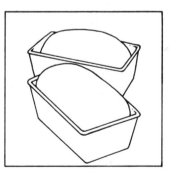

PREPARING BREAD DOUGH FOR BAKING
1. Proof the dough by placing it in a bowl and covering with oiled plastic wrap.

2. Punch down and shape bread dough to fit pan.

3. Allow the shaped dough to rise until it has doubled in size.

The best results are obtained by allowing the covered dough to rise overnight or up to 24 hours in the refrigerator. The refrigerated dough must be allowed to return to room temperature before it is shaped.

Allow about 2 hours for the dough to rise at room temperature (65°). The dough can be made to rise in about 45 minutes to 1 hour if placed in a warm place. The risen dough should spring back when gently pressed with a (floured) finger.

4. PREPARING PANS

While the dough is rising, prepare the pans or baking sheets by greasing and lightly flouring them. Whenever reference is made to a 1-lb loaf pan the approximate size to use is $8 \times 4 \times 2\frac{1}{2}$ inch top measurements. When reference is made to a 2-lb loaf pan, use one with $9 \times 5 \times 3$ inch top measurements.

5. PUNCHING DOWN

The best texture is obtained by kneading the dough for a second time after rising. Put your fist in the center of the dough and punch down to knock out the air. Turn it onto a lightly floured working surface and knead for 2 to 3 minutes to insure an even texture. The dough is shaped as required and placed in pans or on baking sheets at this stage, then covered with plastic wrap.

6. PROOFING

This is the last process before baking. The shaped dough should be allowed to proof, that is, left until it is doubled in size and will spring back when lightly pressed with a (floured) finger. This is done at room temperature. The dough is now ready.

7. BAKING

Basic breads are baked in a 450° oven.

When cooked the bread should be well risen and golden brown and when tapped underneath with the knuckles it should sound hollow. Allow the bread to cool on racks before storing.

8. STORING

Bread should be stored in an airtight container or frozen. Dough must be stored frozen.

9. REFRESHING BREAD

Wrap the bread in aluminum foil and place in a 450° oven for 5 to 10 minutes.

Allow the bread to cool in the foil before unwrapping. For a more crusty loaf omit the foil and bake as above.

To Make Traditional Bread and Roll Shapes

Bread Shapes

PAN LOAF

Roll out dough to an oblong and roll up like a jelly roll. Tuck the ends under and place in the prepared pan. Before baking score the top of the loaf with a knife if wished.

BAGUETTE

Shape into a long roll, with tapering ends, about 8 inches long.

ROUND LOAF

Knead dough into a ball by drawing the sides down and tucking underneath to make a smooth top.

COTTAGE

Divide the dough into two, making one piece twice as large as the other. Knead both pieces well and shape into rounds. Place the smaller round on top of the larger one and place on a baking sheet. Make a hole through the middle of both pieces using the handle of a wooden spoon. Cover and let rise. Glaze with salt water before baking.

BRAID

Divide the dough into three and shape into three long rolls each about 12 inches long. Pinch the ends together and plait loosely crossing each strand alternately. Pinch the ends together. Place on a baking sheet and let rise. Before baking brush with beaten egg and sprinkle with poppy seeds.

Roll Shapes

ROLLS

Can be made in any of the traditional bread shapes by dividing the basic white dough into 2-oz pieces and shaping as for bread. Other variations are:

KNOTS

Shape each piece into a thin roll and tie into a knot.

ROUNDS

Place the pieces on a very lightly floured board and roll each into a ball. To do this, hold the hand flat almost at table level and move it round in a circular motion, gradually lifting the palm to get a good round shape.

CASEROLE
Divide the dough. Knead into small pieces and place together in a greased round layer pan. Pull apart into rolls to serve.

Home Freezing Bread and Dough

FREEZING BAKED BREAD
Baked loaves and rolls, both commercial and home baked, can be home frozen, and it is a successful way of storing bread for up to about a month. There are three points to remember.
1. Only freeze freshly baked bread.
2. Freezer bags are the best containers. Make sure all the air is excluded before sealing the bag tightly.
3. Label to indicate the date of freezing.

STORAGE TIMES
The length of storage depends on the crust, but generally bread stores well for 4 weeks. Bread with any form of crisp crust only stores well for about a week, then the crust begins to flake. Enriched breads and soft rolls store well for up to 6 weeks.

THAWING BREAD
Leave to thaw in the sealed freezer bag (to prevent drying out) at room temperature, or overnight in the refrigerator.

TO MAKE THE CRUST CRISP
Remove the freezer bag and place the thawed loaf or rolls in a 450° oven for 5 to 10 minutes, until the crust is crisp.

Freezing Bread Dough

All bread dough can be home frozen, but the storage time varies with the type of dough – plain or enriched.

Remember these four points:
1. The best results are obtained if the quantity of yeast used in the recipe is increased, for example, increase 1 package dry yeast to 1½.
2. Freeze the unrisen dough in the quantities you are most likely to use.
3. The most successful containers for dough are freezer bags. Oil them lightly and seal tightly. To prevent the dough from forming a skin, the freezer bag should be sealed to exclude air, but if there is a chance of the dough rising slightly before it is frozen leave 1 inch of space above the dough.
4. Label to indicate the date of freezing and type of dough frozen.

STORAGE TIMES – UNRISEN DOUGH
Plain white dough will keep up to 8 weeks; enriched white dough up to 5 weeks. Dough kept longer than these times gives poor results. Loss of resilience and difficulty in punching down the dough begins after about 3 weeks' storage; the dough is also slower to rise.

THAWING DOUGH
Thaw dough at room temperature, 65° to 72°. Dough can be thawed overnight in the refrigerator, but if left overnight at room temperature it will be overrisen. Thaw the dough in the freezer bag to prevent a skin forming, but first unseal the bag and then reseal it loosely at the top, to allow space for the dough to rise.

WHITE BREAD

This is a basic household bread recipe which lends itself to all sorts of variations.

6 cups unbleached flour
2 teaspoons salt
2 tablespoons shortening
1 package active dry yeast
2 cups lukewarm water

Grease a 2-lb loaf pan. Combine the flour and salt in a large bowl and cut in the shortening. Blend the yeast with the water. Make a well in the center of the dry ingredients and add the yeast liquid all at once. Stir in with a wooden spoon or fork. Work the mixture into a firm dough, adding extra flour if needed, until it will leave the sides of the bowl clean. Do not let the dough become too stiff as this produces a heavy close-textured bread.

Turn the dough onto a lightly floured surface and knead thoroughly until the dough feels firm and elastic and no longer sticky – about 10 minutes. Shape it into a ball and place in a large bowl.

Cover the dough with lightly oiled plastic to prevent a skin from forming and let rise until it is doubled in size and will spring back when pressed with a floured finger. Turn the risen dough onto a lightly floured surface, flatten it firmly with the knuckles to punch out the air bubbles, then knead again well. Stretch the dough into an oblong the same width as the pan, fold it into three and turn it over so that the seam is underneath. Smooth over the top, tuck in the ends and place it in the greased 2-lb loaf pan.

Cover the pan with lightly oiled plastic and let rise until the dough comes to the top of the pan and springs back when pressed with a floured finger.

Remove the plastic, glaze and finish as desired. Place the pan on a baking sheet and place in the oven.

Bake in a 450° oven for 30 to 40 minutes, until well risen and golden brown. When the loaf is cooked it will shrink from the sides of the pan and will sound hollow if the bottom is tapped. Turn out and cool on a rack.

TO MAKE ROLLS

After punching down the dough, divide it into about eighteen 2-oz pieces. Place on greased baking sheets about 1 inch apart to allow room for expansion during baking.

QUICK WHOLE-WHEAT BREAD

1 package active dry yeast
1 cup lukewarm water
1 teaspoon sugar
4 cups whole-wheat flour or 2 cups whole-wheat
    and 2 cups unbleached flour
1–2 teaspoons salt
2 tablespoons shortening

Grease two baking sheets. Blend the yeast with the water. Mix the sugar, flour, and salt and cut in the shortening. Add the yeast liquid and remaining water and mix with a wooden spoon to give a fairly soft dough, adding more water if necessary. Turn the dough onto a floured surface and knead well. Divide the dough into two, shape into rounds and place on the greased baking sheets. Cover with lightly oiled plastic and let rise until the two rounds have doubled in size. Bake in a 450° oven for about 15 minutes, reduce to 400° for 20 to 30 minutes longer. Turn out and cool on a rack.

WHOLE-WHEAT BREAD

4 packages active dry yeast
1 quart tepid water
12 cups whole-wheat flour
2 tablespoons sugar
4–5 teaspoons salt
2 tablespoons shortening

Grease two 2-lb or four 1-lb loaf pans. Blend the yeast with 1¼ cups of the water. Mix the flour, sugar, and salt together, cut in the shortening. Stir the yeast liquid into the dry ingredients, adding enough of the remaining water to make a firm dough that leaves the bowl clean. Turn it out onto a lightly floured surface and knead until it feels firm and elastic and no longer sticky. Shape it into a ball, place in a large bowl, and cover with lightly oiled plastic to prevent a skin from forming. Let the dough rise until doubled

in size. Turn it out onto a floured surface and knead again until firm. Divide into two or four pieces and flatten firmly with the knuckles to punch out any air bubbles. Knead well to make it firm and ready for shaping. Shape to fit the pans. Cover with lightly oiled plastic and leave until the dough rises almost to the tops of the pans – about 1 hour at room temperature.

Brush the tops with a salt glaze and bake the loaves in a 450° oven for 30 to 40 minutes. Turn out and cool on a rack.

POPPY SEED BRAID (ENRICHED BREAD DOUGH)

4 cups unbleached flour
1 package active dry yeast
1 cup lukewarm milk
1 teaspoon salt
¼ cup butter or margarine
1 egg, beaten

FOR THE GLAZE AND TOPPING
beaten egg
poppy seeds

Lightly grease a baking sheet. Put 1¼ cups of the flour into a large bowl. Combine the yeast and milk and stir until dissolved. Add to the flour and mix well. Set aside in a warm place until frothy – about 20 minutes. Mix the remaining flour with the salt and rub in the butter. Add the egg and the flour mixture to the yeast batter and mix well to give a fairly soft dough that will leave the sides of the bowl clean. Turn the dough onto a lightly floured surface and knead until smooth and no longer sticky – about 10 minutes (no extra flour should be necessary). Place in a bowl, cover with lightly oiled plastic, and let rise until doubled in size. Knead the dough again lightly on a floured working surface, divide in half, and roll each half into an oblong. Cut each half into three strips lengthwise, pinching the dough together at the top. Braid the strips, dampen the ends, and seal together. Place on the lightly greased baking sheet. Brush with the egg and sprinkle with poppy seeds. Proof again until doubled in size. Bake in a 375° oven for 45 to 50 minutes. Cool on a rack.

CHEESE PULL-APARTS

2 cups unbleached flour
½ teaspoon salt
1 teaspoon dry mustard
½ cup grated Cheddar cheese
2 tablespoons butter or margarine

½ cup finely chopped celery
1 package active dry yeast
⅔ cup milk

FOR THE GLAZE
beaten egg

Grease a 7 × 9¾ × 1¾ inch pan. Mix together the flour, salt, mustard, and cheese. Heat the butter and sauté the celery gently until soft. Add to the dry ingredients. Blend the yeast with the milk, add to the dry ingredients and work to a firm dough. Knead for 10 minutes. Place in a bowl, cover with lightly oiled plastic. Let rise until doubled in size. Turn out and knead again. Cut into eight equal-sized pieces, shape into finger-shaped pieces.

Cut down the length of each with a sharp knife to ¼-inch depth. Place side by side in the pan, not quite touching. Cover with lightly oiled plastic and let rise in a warm place – about 45 minutes. Brush with beaten egg and bake in a 375° oven for about 25 minutes. Cool on a rack. Break apart and serve buttered.

WHOLE-WHEAT FLOWERPOTS

Grease two clean clay flowerpots well and bake them empty in a hot oven before use. This will prevent the loaves sticking.

4 cups whole-wheat flour or 2 cups each whole-wheat and unbleached flours
2 teaspoons each salt and sugar
2 tablespoons lard
1 package active dry yeast
1¼ cups warm water
milk to glaze
cracked wheat

Grease two 4- to 5-inch flowerpots. Mix the flours, salt, and sugar in a bowl, rub in the lard. Blend the yeast with the water and add to the flour, mixing to a soft dough that leaves the bowl clean. Knead the dough thoroughly on a floured surface for about 10 minutes and divide between the two greased flowerpots. Cover with lightly oiled plastic wrap and leave to rise until doubled in size. Brush the tops lightly with milk or water and sprinkle with cracked wheat. Bake in a 450° oven for 30 to 40 minutes. Turn out and cool on a rack.

MALT BREAD

2 packages active dry yeast
13 fl oz tepid water
4 cups all-purpose flour

1 teaspoon salt
3 tablespoons malt extract.
2 tablespoons molasses
2 tablespoons butter or margarine
1½ cups golden seedless raisins

Grease two 1-lb loaf pans. Blend the yeast into the water. Sift the flour and salt together. Warm the malt, molasses, and butter until just melted. Stir the yeast liquid and malt mixture into the dry ingredients and combine well. Stir in the raisins and beat for about 5 minutes. Turn the mixture into the loaf pans. Cover and let rise in a warm place for about 45 minutes, or until the dough almost fills the pans. Bake in a 400° oven for 40 to 45 minutes. When cooked, the loaves may be brushed with sugar glaze, made by dissolving sugar in water and heating gently.

BREAD AND BUTTER PUDDING

3–4 thin slices bread and butter
⅓ cup currants or golden seedless raisins
1 tablespoon sugar
1 cup milk
2 eggs
ground nutmeg

Cut the bread and butter into strips and arrange, buttered side up, in layers in a greased ovenproof dish, sprinkling the layers with the fruit and sugar. Heat the milk, but do not allow it to boil. Beat the eggs lightly and pour the milk onto them, stirring continuously. Strain the mixture over the bread, sprinkle some nutmeg on top and let the pudding stand for 15 minutes. Bake in a 350° oven for 30 to 40 minutes, until set and lightly browned.

BREADCRUMBS

Soft, dry, and browned breadcrumbs are used in cookery. Recipes usually specify which kind. Ready-prepared crumbs may be bought to save time but they are of course more expensive.

Fresh Breadcrumbs

Choose bread that is two to four days old and remove the crusts. The quickest and simplest method is to place the bread in a blender for a few seconds. Otherwise, rub the crumbs through a wire sieve or use a grater (although this will not give such fine or even-sized crumbs). If new bread has to be used, it will be more difficult to handle and will bulk appreciably more than dry bread because of the higher moisture content. For a larger crumb, pull apart with the fingers or a fork.

DRIED BREADCRUMBS

Put unstale pieces of bread on a baking sheet in a 250° oven and let them brown until they are crisp and pale golden brown. Cool, then crush them into fine crumbs with a rolling pin or pass them through a meat grinder. Sieve and store in an airtight container. Alternately use a blender.

BROWNED BREADCRUMBS

Mix 1 cup breadcrumbs and ⅓ cup melted butter and cook over gentle heat until golden brown, stirring constantly to avoid browning unevenly or burning.

BREADFRUIT

A Polynesian fruit that has the texture and taste of bread when roasted. It is a staple food of the South Pacific.

BREADING

To dip food in flour, beaten egg or egg and milk and then toss it in fine breadcrumbs: the crumbs stick to the egg, forming a complete coating around the food. This coating is used for fish, cutlets, rissoles, croquettes, and so on, which may then be either fried or baked. In haute cuisine food prepared in this manner is called "à l'Anglaise."

Put the breadcrumbs on a piece of waxed paper and the beaten egg (or egg and milk) on a plate or dish. Toss the food in a little seasoned flour, then put it in the egg, coating it well, dip it in the breadcrumbs, lift out and pass from one hand to the other until all loose crumbs have fallen off.

Some important points to remember are:
1. Shake off any excess flour. The coating should be complete but light.
2. See that the food is completely coated with the egg before putting it into the crumbs. This is particularly important in deep-fat frying, otherwise the flavor from the food will pass into the fat through the cracks in the coating. The food also becomes hard and spoilt.
3. Dried breadcrumbs are suitable only when the food is cooked and merely requires heating through (e.g. fish cakes). Raw foods, such as fillets of fish, require longer frying and must therefore be coated with light-colored breadcrumbs. Whichever method is used, excess crumbs should be removed to avoid contaminating the oil or fat.

BREAD STICKS

(See Grissini entry.)

BREAKFAST

As the name suggests, breakfast is the breaking of the fast, that is, the first meal of the day. Lack of a satisfactory breakfast can affect dietary intake and nutritional status, particularly in children. Research has shown that to meet the requirements for maintaining alertness throughout the morning and to maintain general physical fitness, breakfast should provide a quarter to a third of the daily protein and energy intake.

The word "breakfast" was first used in the fifteenth century, the meal usually including strong meat and ales. The meal gradually became more important and in the nineteenth century enormous breakfasts were served. These usually included meat dishes, fruit, rolls, and tea. After World War I the traditional "British Breakfast" of cereal, bacon, eggs, and toast became popular in the United States. With changes in life-style this type of breakfast has declined considerably, speed and simplicity now being an important consideration. More popular today are frozen or canned fruit juices, dry cereals or simple egg dishes, toast and coffee; these foods can still provide sufficient nutrients for maximum efficiency.

BREAKFAST CEREALS

There is an enormous choice of breakfast cereals on the market today. These have been developed from dietary research of the nineteenth century. Cornflakes were first made, as a dietetic food, in Michigan. They were so popular that commercial production was started in 1895. At about the same time Dr Bircher-Berner was developing a cereal food mixed with nuts and fruit for patients of his Zürich Clinic. Muesli was the name given to this cereal of which granola is one of the many variations.

Most breakfast cereals are based on corn, rice, wheat, or oats which are modified to make them immediately ready to eat. Some varieties are sugar coated and others have additives for health purposes; these include bran, high-protein and low-calorie cereals.

Although dry cereals contain some nutrients, the milk taken with them is more important in the diet.

BREAM

The European freshwater bream is of rather

coarse texture and flavor but the sea bream (any fish of the Sparidae family) has white, delicate-flavored flesh and is best served baked with a stuffing, but it may also be poached, fried, or broiled.

BRESSE BLEU

A rich, soft, blue-veined cheese, made near Lyons, France, and somewhat resembling Gorgonzola. It is made in small cheeses about 6 inches across and 2 inches high with a thin rind.

BREWER'S YEAST

(See Yeast entry.)

BRICK CHEESE

An American cheese, of medium firm texture, with many small holes. It has a somewhat sweet taste and may be either mild or strong. Brick may be eaten as is or used in cooking.

BRIE

A soft-textured creamy mold-inoculated farm cheese made in the north of France from whole milk. The best variety is that made in the autumn.

BRILL

A European flatfish very similar in flavor and texture to turbot. It may be served boiled whole; filleted and fried like sole; filleted and poached in a white wine sauce; or cut into steaks and baked with a little butter, seasoning, and milk.

BRINING

To immerse food (mainly meat or fish which is to be pickled and vegetables which are to be preserved) in a salt-and-water solution. (See Pickle entry.)

BRIOCHE

A fancy sweet bread or yeast cake, rich in eggs and butter, sometimes containing currants and candied fruit. Round, with fluted sloping side and top knot of dough, brioches come both large and small.

BRIOCHES

1 package active dry yeast
2 tablespoons warm water

2 cups all-purpose flour
pinch of salt
1 tablespoon sugar
2 eggs, beaten
¼ cup butter, melted

FOR THE GLAZE
beaten egg

Oil twelve 3-inch fluted patty pans. Blend the yeast with the water. Mix together the flour, salt, and sugar. Stir the yeast liquid into the flour, with the eggs and butter. Work to a soft dough, turn out onto a lightly floured surface and knead for about 5 minutes. Place the dough in a bowl and cover with oiled pastic wrap. Leave to rise until it is doubled in size and springs back when gently pushed with a floured finger. Knead the risen dough well on a lightly floured surface. Divide the dough into 12 pieces. Shape three-quarters of each piece into a ball and place in the patty pans. Press a hole in the center of each. Shape the remaining 12 pieces of dough into knobs and place in the holes. Press down lightly. Cover the pans with oiled plastic wrap and leave at room temperature until the dough is light and puffy and nearly reaches the top of the tins. Brush lightly with the egg glaze and bake in a preheated 450° oven for about 10 minutes, until golden. Turn out and cool on a rack.

BRISKET

Brisket is the meat covering the breast-bone of any animal eaten for food, but usually the term refers to beef. As it is a rather tough and fat cut of meat, it is usually cheap. Brisket is best boiled, braised, or stewed: it is also good when stuffed, rolled, and roasted. It is often corned and boiled and is then served hot, usually with cabbage and boiled potatoes. It is also enjoyed cold and the leftovers are used for hash.

BRISLING

A small European fish, large quantities of which are canned in Norway for export. Brislings are used like sardines.

BROAD BEAN

(See Fava Bean entry.)

BROCCOLI

There are several varieties, including purple sprouting, available in March and April. Green sprouting is known as calabrese, the spears being cooked like asparagus. Broccoli is a good source of vitamin C, supplying a half-day's needs in an average helping.

BROILER

(See Chicken entry.)

BROILING

The process of cooking food by direct heat, suitable only for cooking thin cuts of meat or fish of good quality. The word "broiling" generally refers to cooking in an appliance, while "grilling" is used for cooking over a charcoal fire. (See Barbecuing entry.)

The broiler should be preheated before use. The heat, turned to high, is adjusted by raising or lowering the broiling pan.

Browning food under the broiler: Many dishes are improved by having the surface browned under a hot broiler. A savory dish is sprinkled with bread crumbs and grated cheese and dotted with butter. A sweet dish may be sprinkled with sugar to give a carameled finish. Put the dish under the hot broiler for a minute or two, until the surface has become a tempting brown.

Broiled Meat and Poultry

Since broiling is a quick method of cooking, it is suitable only for the best cuts of meat — fresh, unhung meat, and poorer cuts will remain tough. The meat may be marinated first and rubbed with flavoring, although a first-class steak or chop requires nothing. Kidney, calf's liver, sausages, bacon, and chicken are other foods suitable for broiling.

For best results, the meat should be at least $\frac{3}{4}$ inch thick and preferably 1 to 2 inches thick, the exception being a ham steak, which may be $\frac{1}{2}$ inch thick. Thinner cuts are suitable for pan broiling (see separate entry) and thicker ones may have to be finished in the oven. Place $\frac{3}{4}$- to 1-inch steaks, chops, and patties 2 to 3 inches from the heat; cuts 1 to 2 inches thick should be 3 to 5 inches from the heat; chicken should be about 6 inches from the source.

Broil until the food is brown. At this point it will be slightly more than half done. Season with salt and pepper and turn. Cook until done (refer to the time chart for approximate timing).

Steak: Trim off excess fat and slash the edges to avoid curling. Marinate, if desired, in a mixture of oil and vinegar. If cooking flank steak, it is customary to score both surfaces and cook a total of no more than 5 minutes. The steak should be taken directly from the refrigerator, unlike most meats which are allowed to come to room temperature before cooking.

Chops: Remove excess fat and slash the edges to avoid curling.

Liver: Wash, wipe, and cut into slices $\frac{1}{2}$ to $\frac{3}{4}$ inch thick.

Kidneys: Wash, skin, and cut them in half, removing the core, then thread them on a skewer so that they can be handled more easily. Veal kidneys are served medium rare, but lamb and pork should be well done. To test for doneness, press with a spoon. Properly done meat will spring back.

Ham steaks: Brush with butter; cook for 2 to 3 minutes — longer for thick steaks. As soon as the fat is transparent on one side, turn them and cook the other side.

Sausages: Prick the sausages and broil them rather slowly until well browned all over, turning them frequently.

Chicken parts: Wipe the parts with a damp cloth, season or rub with flavorings such as garlic, herbs, or lemon. Brush with butter and cook for 20 to 30 minutes.

Whole chicken: Young, $2\frac{1}{2}$ lb or less, birds, are suitable for broiling. Split the bird down the back, flatten it out, and turn the wing tips onto the back side.

Brush the chicken over with olive oil or melted butter, sprinkle with salt and pepper and place under the broiler, skin side down. Broil under a moderate heat for 20 minutes, turn and broil for a further 15 to 20 minutes, basting. Serve with a thin gravy made from the giblets and garnish with watercress.

Times For Broiling

The following table gives approximate times, which vary according to the thickness of the meat:

Steak 1 inch thick:	
Rare	6 to 7 minutes
Medium rare	10 to 12 minutes
Well done	15 minutes
Lamb or mutton chops	10 to 15 minutes
Pork chops	15 to 20 minutes

Veal cutlets	15 to 20 minutes
Liver	5 to 10 minutes
Kidneys	10 minutes
Bacon	2 to 3 minutes
Ham	10 to 15 minutes
Sausages	10 to 15 minutes
(*Allow longer time for pork sausages*)	
Chicken parts	20 to 30 minutes

Mixed Grill

This may consist of a variety of the above meats. Start by cooking those which require the longest time, so that all are ready together. Serve with broiled mushrooms and tomatoes and garnish with watercress and pats of maître d'hôtel butter.

Kebabs

A selection of small pieces of meat and vegetables are threaded onto a skewer, seasoned, and brushed with butter or oil. Turn frequently. The meats can be marinated for extra flavor. (See Shish Kebab entry.)

Fish

Most fish can be broiled, though the drier types are better cooked in other ways. The fish should be seasoned, sprinkled with lemon juice, and (except for oily fish such as herring) brushed with melted butter. Steaks should be tied neatly into shape. Fillets and large fish should be cooked in the broiler pan rather than on the grill.

Steaks and fillets: Broil first on one side, then turn. Brush the second side with oil and broil it. The time varies from 3 to 10 minutes on each side.

Whole fish: Score the fish with a sharp knife in 3 to 4 places on each side, season and brush with melted butter. Place fish on the grill or in the pan and broil slowly, so that the flesh cooks thoroughly without the outside burning. Turn the fish once, handling it carefully to prevent breaking it. To test whether the fish is done, insert the back of a knife next to the bone to see if the flesh comes away easily. Serve with maître d'hôtel butter or melted butter, lemon wedges, and chopped parsley.

Vegetables

Most vegetables contain a large proportion of cellulose, which does not soften under intense, dry heat, and only soft vegetables, such as tomatoes and mushrooms, can be broiled. Brush them well with butter or oil and allow about 5 minutes for halved tomatoes, 10 to 15 minutes for mushrooms.

BROSE

A Scottish dish, somewhat resembling gruel, made by pouring boiling water over oatmeal or barley, stirring well and adding salt. A richer version has additional milk and butter or cream. Fish, meat, or vegetables may be added to make mussel, beef, or kale brose, etc. When made with whisky it is called Athol Brose.

BROTH

Used in a strict sense, this term applies to a stock made from beef, mutton, veal, or chicken, but it has been extended to cover such substantial soups as Scotch broth, which are usually thickened by the addition of a little pearl barley.

SCOTCH BROTH

$1\frac{1}{2}$ lb shin of beef or lamb
5 cups water
salt
pepper
1 carrot and 1 turnip, chopped
1 onion, chopped
2 leeks, thinly sliced and washed
4 tablespoons pearl barley
1 tablespoon finely chopped parsley

Cut up the meat and remove any fat, put it in a pan, cover with the water, add some salt and pepper, bring slowly to boiling point, cover and simmer for $1\frac{1}{2}$ hours. Add the vegetables and the barley. Cover and simmer for about 1 hour until the vegetables and barley are soft. Remove any fat on the surface with a spoon or with paper towels and serve the soup garnished with parsley.

Traditionally, the meat is served with a little of the broth and the remaining broth is served separately.

CHICKEN BROTH

2 lb chicken backs
2 quarts cold water
2 teaspoons salt
pinch of pepper
1 onion, halved
$\frac{1}{2}$ cup each diced carrot and celery
$2\frac{1}{2}$ tablespoons long-grain rice
chopped parsley

Wash the chicken backs, put them into a large pot, cover with water and add the seasoning and vegetables. Bring to a boil, cover and simmer for 3 to $3\frac{1}{2}$ hours, adding more water if necessary. Strain, then remove any grease from the top of the broth with a metal spoon or by drawing a paper towel across the surface of the liquid. Return the broth to the pot, bring to a boil, sprinkle in the rice, and simmer for 15 to 20 minutes, until the rice is soft. Serve sprinkled with chopped parsley. Any meat from the backs can be finely chopped and added to the broth. A fowl may also be used to make the broth, in which case the excess meat can be used in salads or served in a sauce.

The broth can also be made with a chicken or turkey carcass and will need to be simmered for about 2 hours.

BROWNING

To give a dish (usually already cooked) an appetizing golden-brown color by placing it under the broiler or in a hot oven for a short time.

BROWNING, GRAVY

A coloring matter used to darken soups, gravies, etc. There are many proprietary brands on the market, but browning may be made at home in one of the following ways: (1) Heat sugar until it is dark brown and add water (see Caramel entry). (2) Spread some flour on a baking sheet and heat it in the oven until it is brown, stirring it frequently. Keep in a covered jar.

BROWN SAUCE

(See Sauce entry.)

BRUSSELS SPROUT

A member of the cabbage family. Brussels sprouts are best eaten when young and they should be firm, round, and about the size of a walnut. As they are in season during the winter months, when other green vegetables are scarce, and contain a fair amount of vitamin C they are a useful vegetable.

To cook: Wash well, removing any discolored leaves, and cut a little cross in the base of the stalk to enable this part to cook through quickly. Cook in boiling salted water until they are just tender for 5 to 10 minutes, drain thoroughly, return them to the pan and reheat with salt, pepper, and a lump of butter.

To make Brussels sprouts and chestnuts: Prepare the sprouts in the usual way and shell the chestnuts. Put in separate pans and boil them hard for 10 minutes, then drain and remove the thin brown skin from the chestnuts. Melt some butter, allowing $\frac{1}{4}$ cup to about 1 lb of chestnuts and Brussels sprouts, and sauté them in it until both are thoroughly tender – about 15 minutes. Serve very hot. This dish is excellent with roast turkey or goose.

BRUT

A French word applied to the driest type of champagne.

BUBBLE AND SQUEAK

A traditional English dish, originally made from cold boiled beef (thinly sliced, diced, or minced), mixed with cold cooked potatoes and finely chopped cabbage or other greens and then fried; it derived its name from the noises made while it was frying. The cooked dish was sometimes sprinkled with vinegar. In the modern version of bubble and squeak the meat is usually omitted and the dish consists of vegetables only.

BÛCHE DE NOEL

The traditional French Christmas cake made and decorated to resemble a log. A sheet of genoise is rolled into a log shape. It is filled and covered with a chocolate or mocha butter cream that is squiggled with a fork to resemble bark. Further notes of realism may include meringue "mushrooms," chopped pistachio "moss," and a dusting of powdered sugar "snow." It is a delicious but very rich dessert.

BUCK

The male of the roe and fallow deer. (See Venison entry.)

BUCK RAREBIT

A snack served in Great Britain for high tea or supper, consisting of a Welsh rarebit topped with a poached egg.

BUCKWHEAT (SARACEN CORN)

A cereal, a herbaceous plant which will grow on poor soil, used in the Soviet Union, Brittany, and in the United States. Buckwheat is used to make a kind of porridge, also griddle cakes, etc. Commercial preparations of buckwheat can be bought for pancakes.

BUFFET

The word used to describe a method of serving a meal. Buffet parties provide an easier way of entertaining a number of people than a formal dinner party. The buffet may be a fairly grand display of cold dishes or a simpler mixture of hot and cold foods. When no tables are provided, finger or fork foods should be served as these can easily be eaten while standing.

BULLACE

The name given to wild forms of damson plums. They are not suitable for use as dessert fruit, but make good preserves; use any recipe suitable for damsons.

BULL'S EYE

A peppermint-flavored hard round candy, striped black and white.

BUN

Buns should strictly speaking be made from a mixture containing yeast. They are similar in texture to bread, but contain sweetening and usually some shortening, raisins or currants, and spice. Typical examples are Cinnamon, Bath and Hot Cross buns, and Schnecken.

The term is often applied to rolls such as those used to serve hamburgers on.

BURGUNDY

A French province containing several vineyards that produce fine wines. The most important area for red and white wines is the Côte d'Or which includes the Côte de Nuits and the Côte de Beaune. Other areas are Chablis, Beaujolais, and Mâconnais.

Much Burgundy wine is exported as the wine of a district rather than a specific grower. It is bought in barrels from the grower and blended with other wines from the area to achieve certain standards. Most of the "Appellations Contrôlées" in Burgundy refer to the geographical areas, but built into these is also a quality classification. Vintage wines do not improve with very long keeping and many are made for drinking almost immediately. Ten years is usually the maximum time for improvement.

Red Burgundy, which is usually served with roasts or game, should be drunk at room temperature. Well-known types include Vougeot, Chamberton, Pommard, and Beaujolais.

White Burgundy is served slightly chilled. The best-known are Meursault, Montrachet, Corton, and Chablis (the last name is, however, frequently given in error to other white wines).

BUTTER

Butter is made from the fat of milk by churning cream in special conditions of temperature. It may be processed in a plant meeting government requirements. Only butter made in such a plant can carry the USDA (United States Department of Agriculture) shield. These plants are subject to government inspection at regular intervals. The butter is graded by a Department of Agriculture inspector who rates it by color, texture, and body.

There are two types of butter: unsalted (sweet) and salted. USDA grades of butter are AA, A, and B, AA being the best grade.

Whipped butter is made from cream into which air or an inert gas has been whipped. This of course increases the volume and "stretches" the butter, making it easier to spread. May be salted or unsalted.

Storing Butter
Butter should be kept covered in a cool, dark place such as a refrigerator. Butter can be frozen, the unsalted varieties keeping longer than the salted: up to 3 months is recommended for salted butter and 6 months for unsalted. The butter can be left in its retail packaging as long as it is over-wrapped with freezer wrap or foil and freezer tape. Alternately the butter can be removed from the packing and frozen only in freezer wrap. Foil is not recommended as the only packaging as it imparts flavor to the butter.

Clarified Butter
Butter which has been heated and strained to remove salt, water, and solids. This pure butter, which has a higher burning point than unclarified butter, is used in sautéing, omelet making, genoise batter, and pâtés. (See Fats entry.)

Melted (Drawn) Butter
This is a form of dressing served with asparagus, corn on the cob, globe artichokes, and some fish dishes.

Place the required amount of butter in a sauce boat, allowing 1½ to 2 tablespoons per person, and stand the boat in a warm place or in hot water; this avoids waste and prevents the butter becoming brown through overheating.

BUTTER BEAN

(See Pulses entry.)

BUTTER FROSTING

A soft, creamy frosting made with butter and powdered sugar and used for decorating the tops of cakes and as a filling.

VANILLA BUTTER FROSTING

½ cup butter or margarine
1½–2 cups powdered sugar, sifted
vanilla
coloring if required

Cream the butter, add the sugar by degrees, beating until smooth and creamy, then add the vanilla and any coloring.

Chocolate Butter Frosting: Add 1 oz to 2 oz chocolate, melted, to the creamed butter and sugar.

Coffee Butter Frosting: Add 1 to 2 teaspoons extra-strong coffee.

Orange or Lemon Butter Frosting: Add 1 teaspoon of the grated rind and 1 tablespoon of the juice and omit the vanilla.

BUTTERMILK

The liquid left from the cream which has been used for buttermaking. It is composed of water, mineral salts, protein, and milk sugar; its sourness is due to lactic acid.

Buttermilk is also made commercially by adding a culture to skim milk. It can be used in any dish to replace milk if a piquant refreshing taste is required. Buttermilk is often used in biscuits in conjunction with baking soda as a leavening agent. Fruit puree, added to buttermilk, makes a refreshing drink with a slightly acid flavor.

BUTTERSCOTCH

A variety of toffee, made from butter, sugar, and water. The term is also applied to foods flavored with brown sugar.

BUTTERSCOTCH SAUCE

1⅓ cups brown sugar
¾ cup corn syrup
3 tablespoons butter
¼ cup heavy cream

Combine the sugar, corn syrup, and butter in a saucepan and bring to a boil. Boil until thickened, about 1 minute. Cool. Stir in the cream.

CABBAGE

There are many varieties of cabbage, the most important being white and red types, spring greens, Savoy cabbage, turnip tops, and kale. (Brussels sprouts, broccoli and cauliflower belong to the same family). Cabbages are further divided into winter-grown types, available for eating in the spring and early summer, and those planted in the spring to be eaten during the late summer, autumn and winter.

Cabbage contains vitamin A, iron and calcium, and a very variable amount of vitamin C.

To cook: Remove the stumps and any very thick stems or leaf ribs, wash the leaves thoroughly in cold water, and shred them coarsely with a sharp knife just before cooking. Boil them in a small amount of salted water ($\frac{2}{3}$ cup water and 1 teaspoon salt to 1 lb cabbage) for the minimum time – about 5 minutes. Drain thoroughly, press lightly to remove excess water and, if desired, reheat with a lump of butter.

Cabbage is used in various made-up dishes such as Bubble and Squeak and Colcannon; it may be served in the same way as Cauliflower au Gratin (see Cauliflower entry) or pickled (see Pickle entry).

CABERNET SAUVIGNON

A varietal red wine produced in California. This is the same grape grown in Bordeaux for red wines. Cabernet Sauvignon is entering in direct competition for excellence with Bordeaux wines.

CABINET PUDDING

A simple baked or steamed pudding made from bread and butter. A richer version is made with ladyfingers, candied fruits, whipped cream, and gelatin.

CABINET PUDDING

6 tablespoons seeded raisins
4 slices bread
2 eggs
1¼ cups milk
1 tablespoon sugar
vanilla

Grease a bowl and decorate it with some of the raisins by sticking them to the side of the bowl. Cut the bread into ½-inch dice. Beat the eggs, add the milk, sugar, a few drops of vanilla, and the rest of the raisins. Pour the milk over the bread and leave to soak for 30 minutes. Pour into a heatproof bowl, cover with greased waxed paper, and steam for about 1 hour.

CACAO

The cacao tree is native to the tropical countries of South America, but now grows in other parts of the world, notably Africa, the West Indies, and Central America. The fruit is a large pod (ranging in color from purple to yellow, according to variety) containing the seeds or beans. These are allowed to ferment until the pulp drops off. They are then dried and the hard outer skin is removed. Next the beans are roasted and shelled, leaving the kernels or nibs. These nibs are ground and crushed between giant rollers, giving a brown paste. Some of the fat (known as cocoa butter) is then pressed out and the remaining dry cake is reduced to a fine powder, sifted and blended, to become the cocoa powder of commerce.

Nutritionally, cocoa is of no great value, since only 1 teaspoon is used per cup; it does, however, encourage many people to drink milk and the resulting beverage is of good food value. Cocoa is used to give a chocolate flavor to various desserts and cakes. (See Chocolate entry.)

CACCIOCAVALLO

An Italian cheese made from skimmed cow's milk.

CAERPHILLY CHEESE

One of the nine traditional cheeses of the British Isles. It dates from about 1830 and was originally a full cream Welsh cheese made from the milk of Hereford cows. It is now mainly manufactured in the West country. It has a mild flavor and close texture: a whitish cheese which is only matured for about two weeks.

CAESAR SALAD

A salad created in Tia Juana, Mexico by Chef Caesar Cardini, containing romaine lettuce, anchovies, croutons, a raw egg and grated Parmesan cheese. In restaurants it is usually prepared tableside with great ceremony. There are many "original" recipes for this famous salad.

CAESAR SALAD

1 head romaine lettuce
salt
pepper
4 tablespoons olive oil in which 1 clove garlic has
*   been soaked*
1 egg boiled for 1 minute
1 lemon
6 anchovy fillets, cut into pieces
½ cup grated Parmesan cheese
2 cups garlic croutons

Separate the romaine leaves and place in a large salad bowl; season with salt and pepper. Add the oil and gently toss the leaves to coat them. Break the egg over the salad and squeeze the lemon juice over it. Add the anchovies, while continuing to gently mix, and then the cheese. Just before serving, toss with the croutons.

CAFFEINE

A white crystaline substance obtained from coffee, of which it is the active principle. Its main use is as a nonintoxicating stimulant.

CAKE

In the United States cakes may be classed by the manner in which the batter is mixed – by creaming, in one step, or by the sponge or foam method. Whichever method is used, it is important to measure the ingredients carefully. Cakemaking is a highly exacting science. The leavening agents used in the United States are baking powder or air. Recipes for cakes made by all three methods are included here.

Cake Ingredients

FLOUR
Choose a reliable brand of flour and store it in a dry place. Self-rising flour may be used for plain cakes made by the creaming method, but for richer cakes and sponges, which need varying quantities of leavening or none, it is better to use all-purpose flour. The flour should always be sifted before use. Be sure to use the kind of flour called for in a recipe.

SHORTENING
Butter is usually considered most suitable for cakemaking as it gives a good flavor and texture and the cakes made with it keep well. Margarine is the best substitute and can be used alone or mixed with butter. Vegetable shortening is useful, but has little flavor. For certain mixtures (e.g. genoise) butter also needs to be clarified. While butter and margarine are interchangeable in recipes, other shortenings are not.

SUGAR
Granulated sugar is satisfactory for plain cakes, but it is better to use superfine sugar to give a better texture. Brown sugars are good in gingerbreads and spice cakes, giving added flavor.

LEAVENING AGENT
Use a reliable make of baking powder, measure it accurately and sift it with the flour before use.

When sour milk, molasses, or another acidic ingredient is used, the amount of baking powder may be reduced and baking soda (an alkali) added.

EGGS
Eggs improve the flavor of a cake and also help to make it light; like the gluten in flour, they also act

as a structural material, helping to support the cake after it has risen. Sponge cake mixtures contain a high proportion of egg and the beating method incorporates air, so very little, if any, extra leavening is needed. Eggs are also beaten into a butter or shortening cake mixture and again comparatively little additional leavening is required, unless the fat and sugar content is low. In a plain cake, where beaten egg is added together with a liquid, the egg helps to bind and support the mixture, but has little effect as a leavening agent.

Fresh hens' eggs are best, but fresh duck, goose, or turkey eggs may be used.

Use large eggs, unless otherwise stated in the recipe. However, if larger or smaller eggs are used, measure by the cup according to the following formula:

5 large eggs equals 1 cup
8 large egg whites equal 1 cup
12 large egg yolks equal 1 cup.

FRUIT AND NUTS
All fruit must be carefully picked over and cleaned before use and it must be quite dry. (See Dried Fruit entry.) Candied peel, nuts, and large fruit such as dates – and sometimes raisins – are cut up or chopped before use.

Note: Spoon measurements in this book are always level, not rounded. To measure a level spoonful, first heap the spoon with the ingredient, then scrape off the surplus with a knife, making the contents level with the edge of the spoon. The spoons used are the standard measuring spoons.

PREPARING CAKE PANS
An unsalted fat (e.g. sweet butter or shortening) should be used for greasing cake pans and lining papers.

Some recipes, particularly such as for fruitcakes where the baking time is prolonged, require that the cake pan be lined before the cake mixture is put in and waxed paper or baking parchment should be used for this purpose. The lining should be done accurately, so the surface of the baked cake is smooth and unmarked.

When lining pans for rich mixtures which require a long cooking period, use double waxed paper; in addition it is often advisable to put a double strip of thick brown paper round the outside of the pan, fixing it with a pin – this prevents any overcooking of the outside of the cake.

TO LINE A JELLY-ROLL PAN
Cut a piece of paper about 2 inches larger all round than the actual pan. Place the pan on the paper, and make a cut from each corner as far as the corner of the pan remembering to allow for the thickness of the pan. Grease the pan and put the paper in it so that it fits closely, the cut pieces overlapping at the corners. Hold these overlapped pieces firmly in place by greasing each layer. Grease the complete inside of the lining.

TO LINE A ROUND PAN
First draw and cut out a circle of paper to fit the bottom of the pan; allow for the thickness of the sides when cutting out. Now cut a strip long enough to reach around the pan and overlap about 2 inches and high enough to extend about 2 inches above the top edge. Fold up the bottom edge ¾ inch and with scissors make slanting cuts up to the fold at frequent intervals. (The smaller the pan, the closer together the slits should be to obtain a good fit.) Grease the pan and place the strip in position round the inside, overlapping at the seam. Grease the bottom overlapping edge. Put the round paper in position and thoroughly grease all paper surfaces.

LINING A ROUND PAN
1. Draw a circle using base of pan as a guide; cut out a round of waxed paper.

2. Cut a strip of waxed paper and fold up bottom edge ¾ inch. Cut paper along fold at intervals.

3. Line greased pan with paper strip, overlapping at the seam. Press round into base of pan.

TO LINE A SQUARE PAN

This may be done in the same way as for jelly-roll pan. This method is generally used for shallow pans, e.g., for gingerbread. Alternately, if the pan is deeper, line in the same way as for a round pan, making sure that the paper is well greased.

SPONGE AND LAYER PANS

These are used for cakes which do not require a long cooking time and therefore it is not necessary to line them completely. However, a greased circle of paper may be used in the base, to facilitate turning out the cake. Grease all pans well. The quickest way is to use a pastry brush dipped in the melted fat. As an additional precaution, dust the pans with flour.

FOIL AND PAPER BAKING CUPS

These may be used in place of pans for small cakes, etc. They require no preparation. They may be put straight on a baking sheet, but the resulting shape is often better if the cases are placed in muffin pans. Foil may be used to line cake pans and does not require greasing.

SILICONE PAPER

Silicone lining or baking parchment has been found suitable for mixtures containing fat, but not for beaten sponges such as a genoise. It can be used to line a pan in exactly the same way as waxed paper, but is not greased with fat. It is not suitable for lifting a cake out of the pan, as it is rather slippery. When peeled off the cake, silicone paper leaves a smooth, shiny finish, not the characteristic rough surface. Clean for reuse. Silicone paper does not affect cooking time.

Cakes Made by the Creaming Method

1. Have all ingredients at room temperature and measure carefully.
2. Cream the shortening (usually butter) and the sugar together.
3. Add the eggs gradually, while continuing to cream.
4. Add the liquid gradually, usually alternating with the flour.

Cakes made by this method will be lighter if the eggs are separated and the beaten whites folded in at the very end of the process.

CREAMED BUTTER LAYER CAKE

$\frac{1}{2}$ cup butter
$1\frac{1}{2}$ cups sugar
3 eggs
2 cups all-purpose flour

4 teaspoons baking powder
$\frac{1}{2}$ teaspoon salt
$\frac{3}{4}$ cup milk
1 teaspoon vanilla

Cream the butter and sugar until light and fluffy. Beat in the eggs, one at a time. Combine the dry ingredients and add alternately with the milk on low speed. Divide the batter between two greased and floured layer pans and bake in a 350° oven for 30 to 35 minutes, or until a pick inserted in the center comes out clean. Cool in pans for 5 minutes, then turn out on racks to cool.

Cakes Made by the One-Step Method

1. Have all ingredients at room temperature and measure carefully.
2. Place the dry ingredients in the mixer bowl. Add the shortening and liquid ingredients, including eggs.
3. Beat on low speed for about 30 seconds, scraping the bowl down, to moisten the ingredients. Increase speed and beat for the required amount of time.

ONE-STEP SHORTENING CHOCOLATE CAKE

1 cup all-purpose flour
1 cup sugar
$\frac{1}{2}$ teaspoon baking powder
$\frac{1}{4}$ cup shortening
6 tablespoons water
6 tablespoons buttermilk
1 egg
1 teaspoon vanilla
2 oz unsweetened chocolate, melted and cooled

Combine ingredients in a large mixer bowl. Beat on low speed to moisten the ingredients, then on high speed for 3 minutes. Bake in a greased and floured 9-inch square pan in a 350° oven for 30 to 35 minutes, or until a pick inserted in the center of the cake comes out clean. Cool in the pan for 5 minutes, then turn out on a rack to cool.

Cakes Made by the Sponge or Foam Method

These cakes depend for the most part on air for their leavening. They include the Angel Food Cake (see separate entry), sponge cakes, and chiffon cakes. While the European, or true, sponge depends completely on air for its lightness (see Genoise entry), the American sponge contains baking powder. The genoise contains melted butter, but the American cake has no fat other than that in the egg yolks. The chiffon cake, developed in the kitchens of General Mills,

Minneapolis, Minnesota, is a foam cake containing oil that enhances its keeping value.
1. Have all ingredients at room temperature and measure carefully.
2. Heat the eggs and sugar to about 100°. This melts the sugar.
3. Fold in the flour by hand to insure equal distribution.

HOT MILK SPONGE CAKE

1 cup all-purpose flour
1 teaspoon baking powder
3 eggs
1 cup sugar
½ cup hot milk
1 teaspoon vanilla

Combine the flour and baking powder. Beat the warmed eggs and sugar in a large mixer bowl until thick and lemon colored, about 5 minutes. Beat in the milk and vanilla at low speed. Fold in the flour by hand.

Pour the batter into a 9-inch square, greased and floured pan. Bake in a 350° oven for 25 to 30 minutes, or until the top springs back when touched lightly.

JELLY ROLL

A jelly roll contains less flour in proportion to the other ingredients than a regular sponge and is therefore more pliable.

3 eggs
1 cup sugar
⅓ cup water
1 teaspoon vanilla
¾ cup all-purpose flour
1 teaspoon baking powder
¼ teaspoon salt

Beat the warmed eggs and sugar in a large mixer bowl until thick and lemon colored, about 5 minutes. Beat in the water and vanilla on low speed. Combine the dry ingredients and fold in by hand. Pour the batter into a jelly-roll pan lined with greased waxed paper and bake in a 375° oven for 12 to 15 minutes, or until the top springs back when touched lightly. Immediately turn the cake out onto a clean dish towel sprinkled with sugar. Remove the lining paper and cut off the crisp edges. Roll in the towel from the short end and cool on a rack.

When the cake is cool it may be unrolled, filled with jam or butter cream and rerolled. Dredge with sugar or coat with frosting.

TEDDY BEAR CAKE

½ cup sweet butter, softened
2 cups sifted powdered sugar
1 tablespoon orange juice
food coloring
⅓ cup shredded coconut
1 tablespoon apricot jam, warmed and strained
2 jam-filled jelly rolls
assorted sizes of gum drops
½ candied cherry
brightly-colored ribbon

To make the butter frosting, place the butter, sugar, and orange juice in a small mixer bowl and beat on low speed to mix, then beat on high speed until light and fluffy. Tint pale brown with food coloring, following package directions for light brown.

Place the coconut in a bowl and tint with green food coloring. Spread the apricot jam on a serving platter and sprinkle with the coconut.

Cut a 2-inch slice from one of the jelly rolls. Spread the larger piece with butter frosting on all sides. Place upright on the serving platter to form the body of the bear. Cover the 2-inch slice with butter frosting, shaping it into a face by building up the frosting to form a nose and round off the head. Place on top of the body.

Cut the second jelly roll into five pieces. Spread two of these with butter frosting and place at angles to the body to form the legs. Cut a wedge-shaped piece from each of two other pieces, frost and place, wedge side toward the body, against the upper body to form the arms. Build up the shoulders with more frosting. Cut two 1-inch slices from the remaining piece of jelly roll and cover with frosting. Place against the sides of the head for ears.

Place small gum drops at the ends of the arms and legs for paws. Place larger gum drops on the face for eyes and down the body for buttons. Mark the nose with the candied cherry and tie the ribbon into a bow around the neck.

LEMON CHIFFON CAKE

2 cups all-purpose flour
1½ cups sugar
3 teaspoons baking powder
1 teaspoon salt
½ cup salad oil
7 eggs, separated, plus 1 extra egg white
¾ cup water
½ teaspoon cream of tartar
2 teaspoons grated lemon peel
2 teaspoons vanilla

Combine the flour, sugar, baking powder, and salt in a bowl. Make a well in the center and add the oil, egg yolks, water, lemon peel and vanilla. Beat with a spoon until blended.

Combine the egg whites and cream of tartar in a large mixer bowl and beat until stiff peaks form. Fold the egg yolk mixture into the whites. Bake in an ungreased 10-inch tube pan in a 325° oven for 1¼ hours, or until the top springs back when touched lightly. Invert pan on a bottle until the cake is cool, about 1½ hours.

Baking Cakes

MANAGING THE OVEN

Before starting to make a cake, adjust the shelves to the position required. New ovens do not need to be preheated for long, but an older one should be turned on at this stage.

Do not overcrowd the oven. Most cakes bake best in the center of the oven, but foam cakes should be baked on the lowest shelf. Make sure layer cake pans do not touch each other or the sides of the oven.

To maintain a correct temperature, avoid opening the oven door too often or too suddenly while the cake is cooking. Allow the full cooking time given in the recipe.

OVEN TEMPERATURES

It is difficult to generalize about the different oven heats for baking cakes, but obviously the larger and deeper the cake, the longer it will take to cook and the cooler the oven will have to be to avoid overcooking the outside before the cake has completely cooked through. In addition, rich mixtures need to be cooked at lower temperatures than plainer ones.

TO TEST WHEN A CAKE IS COOKED

Small cakes should be well risen, golden-brown in color, and firm to the touch, both on top and underneath. On being taken out of the oven, they should begin to shrink from the sides of the pan.

For larger cakes, the oven heat and time of cooking give a fairly reliable indication, but the following tests are also a guide:
1. Press the center of the top of the cake very lightly with the fingertip. When done, the cake will be spongy, giving only very slightly to the pressure and rising again immediately, leaving no impression.
2. Insert a pick into the center of the cake. It should come out perfectly clean; if any mixture is sticking to it, the cake requires longer cooking.
3. In the case of a fruitcake, lift it gently from the oven and listen to it, putting it fairly close to the ear: a continued sizzling sound indicates that the cake is not cooked through.

COOLING AND STORING

Allow the cake a few minutes to cool before turning it out of the pan; during that time an unlined cake will shrink away from the sides so that it is more easily removed. Turn it out very gently onto a clean towel held in the hand and remove any paper. Invert a cake rake over the cake, then turn it right side up and leave to become quite cold, keeping it in a place away from drafts.

Store cakes in a tightly covered tin. Most cakes are nicest eaten quite fresh, but gingerbread and some rich fruitcakes are improved by keeping.

Rich fruitcakes which are to be kept for any length of time should be wrapped in foil before being put in the tin and left to mature.

Cakemaking Faults

1. IF YOUR CAKE SINKS IN THE MIDDLE

It may be for any of the following reasons:
(a) The cake is not cooked through. Check up on the baking time and temperature and be sure that the cake responds to the test before removing it from the oven.
(b) A sudden drop in the oven temperature at a critical stage of the cooking. Avoid opening the oven door too often or too suddenly and do not alter the position of the cake while it is still soft. See that no draft blows directly onto the oven from the kitchen door or window.
(c) Too much leavening causing the mixture to overwork.
(d) Mixture had too much liquid. Test the consistency of the cake mixture carefully before putting it in the pan.
(e) Too much sugar in proportion to the other ingredients.

2. FRUIT SINKS TO THE BOTTOM OF CAKE

For these reasons:
(a) The mixture is too slack to support the fruit.
(b) The fruit is not properly dried after washing.
(c) The baking temperature is too low.
(d) The fruit is left in too large pieces.

3. A CAKE THAT BOILS OUT THROUGH A CRACK IN THE TOP

Was put into too hot an oven. If the initial temperature is too high, the outside of the cake sets and forms a crust before the cake starts to cook in the center; then instead of rising evenly, the mixture has to force its way out of the top of the cake through a crack.

4. IF YOUR CAKE IS HEAVY AND STICKY INSIDE
It may be due to any of the following:

(a) Baking at too high a temperature and for too short a time, so that the outside cooks too quickly, leaving the center slightly raw. Reduce the heat next time you use the recipe or place the cake lower in the oven. Be sure to allow the full baking time.

(b) Making the mixture too wet, so that the cake does not dry out in the center.

(c) Cooling too suddenly. See that the cake is not put in a drafty place when first taken from the oven.

(d) Putting away while still warm. Make sure the cake is absolutely cold before putting away in the cake tin.

5. A CLOSE OR HEAVY TEXTURE
May be caused by any of the following:

(a) Not enough baking powder. Check up on the recipe and measure baking powder accurately. If the cake is raised by air beaten into the mixture, perhaps you are not beating sufficiently thoroughly.

(b) Heavy handling. Cakes require a very light touch, especially when mixing in the dry ingredients.

(c) Too dry a mixture. If not moistened enough, the cake is likely to be close and dry when baked.

(d) Too wet a mixture. Too much liquid when mixing causes the cake to have a close, heavy texture.

Cake Fillings

Cakes are usually spread with a sweet, well-flavored mixture such as butter frosting and pastry cream. (See individual entries.) Given here are some typical cake fillings.

RICH BUTTER CREAM (CRÈME AU BEURRE)

$\frac{3}{4}$ cup sugar
2 tablespoons water
2 egg yolks
6 tablespoons butter
flavoring

Put the sugar and water in a small saucepan, place over heat and dissolve the sugar. When the syrup is perfectly clear, bring to a boil and boil without stirring until it reaches 238°. While the sugar is

cooking, beat the egg yolks in a bowl, then pour on the syrup in a thin stream, beating all the time. (If the syrup is added too quickly or too hot, the eggs will curdle.) Beat until cool. Cream the butter and beat a little at a time into the egg mixture. Flavor and use very cold.

BANANA FILLING

2 bananas
$\frac{1}{4}$ cup sugar
a little lemon juice
grated rind of $\frac{1}{2}$ lemon
$2\frac{1}{2}$ tablespoons heavy cream

Puree the bananas, add the sugar, lemon juice and rind and finally add the stiffly beaten cream. Beat the whole together for a minute then use as required.

CAKE FROSTINGS

(See Frosting, Piping, and also individual entries, e.g., Almond Paste.)

CAKE MIX

A prepared dry mix to which only water, milk, or egg is added before baking. Various types are available for making a plain sponge, cookies, layer cakes, gingerbread, and other cakes.

The produce generally contains flour, sugar, shortening, leavening, and flavorings. The flour may be a soft cake flour or a high-ratio flour, depending on the type of cake, or even a stronger flour for gingerbread. The shortening has to be of a special quality to resist rancidity. Sometimes dried milk is added and occasionally preservatives of some sort.

A prepared mix is more expensive than a homemade cake, but saves preparation time and is especially handy when unexpected visitors arrive.

CALCIUM

The most abundant mineral in the body and the chief component of bones and teeth. It is of particular importance for children and for expectant and nursing mothers. A deficiency of calcium in the diet of children leads to rickets – badly shaped bones and poor growth. Expectant and nursing mothers pass calcium on to their babies and if there is not enough in their food, will deplete their own stores.

The suggested daily requirement for an adult is 500 mg. Pregnant women and nursing mothers require more. A child needs as much as an adult and an adolescent perhaps more.

Milk and cheese are the best sources of calcium. Vegetables (particularly the pulses) and cereals supply a fair amount. Calcium is added to all flour by law and since flour and bread are eaten each day, generally they are a good source. Fish and eggs supply calcium to some extent. Drinking water in hard-water districts also provides a little.

Acid calcium phosphate is present in some baking powders.

It is essential to have enough vitamin D to permit both the absorption and the use of the calcium in the body. Without it little is absorbed, whereas 20 to 30 percent can be absorbed with adequate vitamin D.

CALF'S FOOT JELLY

A jelly that was at one time often served to invalids. It has little food value but is easily digested. It takes two days to make, as the stock must be made the first day and the jelly finished the second.

To make the stock: Cut 2 calf's feet into pieces and wash and scrape them well. Put the pieces into a saucepan, cover with cold water and bring quickly to a boil, then pour off the water, rinse the pieces and return them to the saucepan. Cover again with $2\frac{1}{2}$ to 3 quarts cold water, cover and simmer slowly for 4 to 5 hours, until the liquid is reduced by half. Strain and leave until cold, when the stock should be a stiff jelly.

TO CLARIFY THE JELLY

To 2 cups calf's foot stock allow the following:

$\frac{1}{2}$ *cup sugar*
$\frac{2}{3}$ *cup sherry*
$1\frac{1}{2}$-*inch stick of cinnamon*
3 cloves
3–4 lemons
2 egg whites and shells
2 tablespoons brandy

Remove all grease from the stock, measure 2 cups of it into a saucepan and add the sugar, sherry, cinnamon stick, and cloves. Wipe the lemons with a damp cloth and peel the rind very thinly off 2 of them. Squeeze and strain the lemon juice, measure $\frac{2}{3}$ pint and add this to the stock, together with the lemon rind, the egg whites, and the well-washed and crushed shells. Bring almost to a boil, then simmer without stirring for 20 minutes; do not allow to boil. Strain through

several layers of washed cheesecloth, repeating the straining process until the jelly runs perfectly clear. The straining should be done in a warm place and out of all drafts; should the jelly stiffen in the cloth before it has all run through, place a small bowl or cup in the center of the jelly and fill it with boiling water. If this fails to melt the jelly, it must be returned to the pan, whisked up again and strained as before. Finally, add the brandy.

Notes: In hot weather, it may be necessary to add a little gelatin to stiffen the stock. On the other hand, if it is too stiff, it must be diluted with a little water.

The amount of sugar used can be altered to suit different tastes and it can be omitted altogether if desired. The amount of wine used can also be altered; if less is included, more lemon juice should be added. A little orange juice may be substituted for some of the lemon juice.

CALF'S HEAD, LIVER, ETC.

(See Head, Liver, and similar entries.)

CALORIE

The term used in dietetics for measuring the heat and energy-producing quality of foods. One Calorie (spelled with a capital letter) is defined as the amount of heat needed to raise the temperature of 1,000 grams of water by 1 degree Centigrade. (Spelled with a lower case "c" a calorie is a term used in physics to denote the amount of heat needed to raise the temperature of 1 gram of water by 1 degree Centigrade.)

Foods vary very much in their caloric content; fats yield about 250 Calories per oz, but vegetables and fresh fruit only 5 to 10. A cup of milk, an average-sized slice of bread, 8 to 12 small lumps of sugar or 2 medium-sized potatoes each yield about 100 Calories.

Calorie requirements vary widely, but it is usual to quote average figures. A moderately active woman or an adolescent girl needs about 2,200 Calories per day; a nursing mother or a boy of 13 to 15 years needs 3,000 and an adolescent youth even more. Men need rather more than women. The exact needs depend of course on the activities and weight and metabolic rate of the individual. For instance, when sitting at rest the average person needs 14 Calories per hour, whereas walking up stairs one uses them at the rate of 900 per hour.

After food has been eaten the body's digestive and metabolic processes are increased, owing to the specific dynamic action of the proteins, fats, and carbohydrates; this results in increased production of heat, proteins producing most and carbohydrates least heat. About a seventh of the Calories consumed by a sedentary person is used up in carrying out physical activities, the remainder being converted into heat, which maintains the bodily temperature.

(See Diet and Joule entries.)

CALVADOS

(See Apple Brandy entry.)

CAMEMBERT CHEESE

A soft French cheese, made from the curd of cow's milk, which is inoculated with a white mold. The best Camembert cheeses are obtained during the summer months, when the milk is at its richest.

This cheese should be eaten soft; it is ready to serve when it will yield to gentle pressure of the fingers; if allowed to become overripe, it develops an unpleasant smell. It should be kept at room temperature, away from drafts.

CAMOMILE

A daisylike plant with an aromatic scent and bitter flavor. The dried flowerheads are used to make a tisane, said to be a mild tonic, popular in the nineteenth century. It is also used as a rinse for hair.

CANADIAN FRUIT PIE

(See Crumble Topping for Pies entry.)

CANAPÉ

Canapés are mouthfuls of flavored food, served on small pieces of bread, toast, or crackers. They are eaten hot or cold, as an hors d'oeuvre, as cocktail snacks or, in Great Britain, as savories at the end of a meal.

The base may be made of buttered bread (close-textured brown or white bread, thinly sliced and cut into circles or fancy-shaped pieces); fingers or shapes of toast or croutons (if the canapés are to be served cold, the bread should be fried in butter, which gives a better flavor); neat fingers of rye bread, assorted crackers, or strips of pastry. The topping may be any kind of meat, poultry, fish, egg, cheese, vegetable, or a mixture, suitably decorated, and is often held in place by aspic.

PÂTÉ WHIRLS

FOR THE BASE
10 slices white bread
6 tablespoons butter, melted

FOR THE TOPPING
8 oz smooth pâté
½ cup butter, softened
½ small clove garlic, crushed
salt
pepper
parsley

Remove the crusts from the bread, squaring up the slices, and cut each into 4 small squares (giving 40 in all). Brush 2 baking sheets with some of the melted butter and put the bread onto them. Brush the bread squares with the remaining melted butter and bake in a 425° oven for 15 minutes until golden brown. Leave to cool on a wire rack.

Cream the pâté with the softened butter and garlic and adjust the seasoning. Using a pastry bag fitted with a large star tube, pipe whirls of the pâté onto the croutes. Garnish each with a minute piece of parsley.

Note: If you wish, use garlic pâté and omit the crushed garlic; use crisp crackers instead of homemade croutes. If using crackers, prepare within 1 hour of serving to prevent them from becoming soggy.

SARDINE PYRAMIDS

1 can sardines, skinless, boneless, drained
lemon juice
salt
pepper
20–24 small crackers
chopped parsley or paprika to garnish

Mash the sardines with a little of the sardine oil, and with lemon juice and seasoning to taste. Mound a little of the mixture onto each cracker and make a cross on the top, using a skewer dipped in the finely chopped parsley or the paprika.

ANCHOVY TOASTS

2 slices bread
1 tablespoon butter
a squeeze of lemon juice
5 anchovy fillets, chopped
a little pepper

a pinch each of ground nutmeg and ground mace
parsley

Toast the bread and cut it into fingers. Melt the butter, add a squeeze of lemon juice, the anchovies, pepper, nutmeg, and mace. Beat well and rub through a sieve. Spread this mixture on the fingers of toast and decorate with sprigs of parsley.

Similar canapés can be made with sardines or herrings.

DEVILED CRAB CANAPÉS

1 tablespoon finely chopped onion
lump of butter
3¼ oz can crabmeat
1 teaspoon Worcestershire sauce or a good dash of
    hot pepper sauce
pinch of dry mustard
2 tablespoons whipping cream
parsley or paprika for garnish

Sauté the onion lightly in the butter for 5 minutes, until golden brown. Drain and add to the crabmeat; stir in the seasonings and cream. Use as a topping for 24 croutes of fried bread. Decorate each with a sprig of parsley or sprinkle with paprika.

CANARY WINES

These wines, made in the Canary Isles, comprise both sherry types (also known as Sack) and port types. The best known is Tenerife or Vidonia, a dry, full-bodied wine produced around Las Palmas. Malvoisie is made from a very sweet grape called Cabosa, which grows in the Canary and Madeira Isles. Canary Sack is a white wine of full flavor, rather similar to a Portuguese Madeira.

CANDIED FRUIT

Fruit that has been preserved by impregnation with a concentrated sugar syrup, giving a fairly firm texture and a shiny, moist and sticky surface. This process is usually carried out commercially, the commonest candied fruit being cherries, although almost any good-quality fruit can be treated in this way. Candied fruits are used in cakes and desserts, and as decorations on these as well.

CANDIED CITRUS PEEL

peel of 2 grapefruits, 3 oranges or 6 lemons

1 cup sugar
¾ cup water
2 tablespoons light corn syrup
sugar for coating

Cover the peels with water and bring to a boil. Cook uncovered for 20 minutes. Drain and repeat. Scrape out any pith remaining on the peel and cut into narrow strips.

Combine the sugar, water and corn syrup and bring to a boil. Add the peels and boil gently, stirring frequently, until most of the sugar is absorbed. Drain and roll in sugar. Spread on waxed paper to dry.

CANDY

The name given to all types of candies including chocolates, fudge, toffees, marzipan, nougats, candied fruit, etc. It is rather difficult to classify candies into exact groups, as there is inevitably a good deal of overlap, but generally speaking the main types made at home are: fondants and creams, both cooked and uncooked; marzipan; fudge; toffee and butterscotch; caramel and nougat; and a miscellaneous group including marshmallows, Turkish delight, and truffles. These can be made very successfully at home in small quantities, but some, such as chocolates are not really suitable for the amateur to tackle.

A selection of recipes is given here for candies in each main group. (For sugar-boiling, see Sugar entry.)

Fondants and Creams
These soft, creamy candies can be given particularly pretty colorings and an unlimited variety of fancy shapes. To make an assortment of different fondants divide the mixture into portions and flavor and color them, using, for instance, lemon, raspberry, violet, orange, coffee, and peppermint flavorings, with appropriate colors.

Roll the fondant out on a slab, dredging this lightly with powdered sugar to prevent sticking. To shape the candies, cut the fondant into triangles, etc., with a knife or tiny cutters or mold it by hand. More elaborate shapes are obtained by melting the fondant over hot water and pouring it into molds. The fondants may be decorated with nuts, candied fruit, crystalized flowers, etc.

(See basic recipes for unboiled and boiled fondant in Fondant entry.)

Marzipan Candies
The quickly made unboiled almond paste or marzipan may be used for the simpler candies, but for those which require molding it is better to

use a boiled paste, as this is less likely to become oily or crack when handled. (For recipes see Almond Paste entry.)

MARZIPAN CANDIES

Make up some unboiled almond paste, adding sufficient egg white to make it bind to a soft but dry paste. Divide into portions, color as desired, roll out, place one layer on another and cut into small squares, triangles, etc. or roll up jelly-roll fashion and then slice.

Marzipan may be used to stuff pitted dessert dates or it may be kneaded with chopped nuts or candied cherries and shaped into balls.

MARZIPAN FRUITS, ETC.

To make fruit and vegetables, take balls of boiled almond paste, plain or colored, and mold them into the desired shapes with the fingers. Using a small paint brush and edible vegetable colorings, tint them all over or touch them up, as necessary. Finish off as follows:

Oranges and other citrus fruit: To obtain a pitted surface, roll the fruit lightly on the finest part of a grater. Use a clove stuck into the "orange" to suggest a calyx.

Strawberries and raspberries: Roll them in fine sugar to give the bumpy surface.

Apples and pears: Use a clove, or part only of its stalk, to suggest the calyx.

Potatoes: Dust with a little chocolate powder.

Flowers: To make flowers, roll out the almond paste thinly and cut it into rounds, using a ½-inch to ¾-inch cutter. Mold these rounds into leaves or petals and fix them together to form flowers. Leave until quite dry, then touch them up with a little coloring, applied with a small brush.

Fudge

VANILLA FUDGE

2¼ cups sugar
4 tablespoons butter
⅔ cup evaporated milk
⅔ cup milk
few drops of vanilla extract

Grease a 6-inch square pan.

Put the sugar, butter, and milk into a 5-pint heavy-bottomed saucepan and heat gently until the sugar has dissolved and the fat melted. Bring to a boil and boil steadily to 240° (soft ball stage), stirring occasionally. Remove the pan from the heat, place on a cool surface, add the vanilla and beat until the mixture becomes thick and creamy and "grains" – i.e. until minute crystals form. Pour it immediately into the greased pan. Leave until nearly cold and mark into squares with a sharp knife, using a sawing motion. When it is firm, cut into squares.

FRUIT AND NUT FUDGE

Add ½ cup chopped nuts and ½ cup seedless raisins; continue as above.

MARSHMALLOW FUDGE

Add ½ lb chopped marshmallows to the mixture before beating; continue as above.

CHOCOLATE FUDGE

2¼ cups sugar
⅔ cup milk
⅔ cup butter
4 oz chocolate
2 tablespoons honey

Grease an 8 × 6 inch pan.

Place all the ingredients in a 6-pint heavy-bottomed saucepan. Stir over a low heat until the sugar has dissolved. Bring to a boil and boil to 240° (soft ball stage). Remove from the heat, stand the saucepan on a cool surface for 5 minutes, then beat the mixture until thick, creamy, and beginning to "grain." Pour into the greased pan, mark into squares when nearly set and cut when firm. *Makes about 1½ lb.*

COFFEE WALNUT FUDGE

3¼ cups sugar
1¼ cup evaporated milk
⅔ cup water
8 tablespoons butter
1½ tablespoons instant coffee
½ cup walnuts, chopped

Grease an 8-inch square pan. Put the sugar, milk, water, and butter into a 7½-pint heavy-bottomed saucepan. Blend the coffee with 1 tablespoon water and add to the saucepan. Stir over a low heat until the sugar has dissolved. Boil gently to 240° (soft ball stage); stir to prevent sticking. Remove from the heat, place the saucepan on a cool surface, add the nuts and beat with a wooden spoon until thick, creamy, and beginning to "grain." Pour into the greased pan and leave until nearly cold; mark into squares. When firm, cut with a sharp knife. *Makes about 2 lb.*

Toffees, Butterscotch, etc.

When making toffee, follow these general rules:
1. Use a large pan and oil the sides, as toffee is inclined to boil over.
2. Do not stir (unless the recipe specially states stirring is necessary).
3. Move the sugar-boiling thermometer from time to time, as toffee may stick to the bulb and give an inaccurate reading. If no thermometer is available, test the temperature by dropping a little syrup into a cup of cold water; it will be at the right temperature when it becomes brittle and snaps easily.
4. Keep the heat very low after the toffee has reached a temperature of 260°.
5. When the required temperature is reached, pour the mixture out quickly.
6. Cool the toffee at an even temperature and when it is lukewarm mark out in squares with an oiled knife.
7. Rub the toffee with absorbent paper, to remove surplus oil, then wrap them individually in waxed papers.

"PULLED TOFFEE"

If toffee and similar boiled sugar mixtures are "pulled" while still warm and pliable, they acquire an attractive satiny, silvery appearance.

A toffee mixture may also be used to make lollipops.

MOLASSES TOFFEE

$2\frac{1}{4}$ cups sugar
$\frac{2}{3}$ cup water
6 tablespoons butter
a pinch of cream of tartar
$\frac{1}{3}$ cup molasses
$\frac{1}{3}$ cup corn syrup

Butter a 12 × 4 inch pan or a 7-inch square pan. Dissolve the sugar and water in a 4-pint heavy-bottomed saucepan over a low heat. Add the remaining ingredients and bring to a boil. Boil to 270° (soft crack stage). Pour into the buttered pan, cool for 5 minutes, then mark into squares and let set. When cold, break into squares and wrap in waxed paper.

NOUGAT

rice paper
$\frac{1}{4}$ cup honey
3 egg whites
$\frac{1}{2}$ cup candied cherries, chopped
$\frac{1}{4}$ cup angelica, chopped
$1\frac{1}{4}$ cups almonds, chopped
$1\frac{3}{4}$ cups sugar
$\frac{2}{3}$ cup water
$3\frac{1}{2}$ tablespoons glucose
vanilla extract

Dampen the inside of a 12 × 4 inch pan or a 7-inch square baking pan and line it with rice paper. Melt the honey in a bowl over hot water, add the stiffly beaten egg whites and continue to beat until the mixture is pale and thick. Add the cherries and angelica to the almonds. Dissolve the sugar in the water in a small heavy-bottomed saucepan. Add the glucose and boil to 245° to 265° (hard ball stage). Pour this syrup onto the honey mixture, add the vanilla extract and continue beating over hot water until a little of the mixture forms a hard ball when tested in cold water. This may take 30 to 40 minutes, but is very important if the nougat is to set firmly. Add the fruit and nuts and put the mixture into the square pan. Cover with rice paper, put some weights on top and leave until cold. Cut into pieces and wrap in waxed paper.

TURKISH DELIGHT

$2\frac{1}{4}$ cups granulated sugar
$3\frac{3}{4}$ cups water
a pinch of tartaric acid
3 oz cornstarch
$1\frac{1}{3}$ cups powdered sugar
2 tablespoons honey
few drops lemon extract
few drops rose water
pink coloring
powdered sugar for dredging

Butter a 12 × 4 inch pan.

Put the sugar and $\frac{2}{3}$ cup of the water into a saucepan. Dissolve the sugar without boiling and bring to a temperature of 240° (soft ball stage). Add the tartaric acid and leave on one side for the short time required to blend the cornstarch. Mix the cornstarch and powdered sugar with a little of the remaining cold water. Boil the rest of the water, then pour onto the blended cornstarch and sugar, stirring hard to prevent lumps forming. Return to the saucepan, boil and beat vigorously until clear and thick. Add the syrup gradually, beating meanwhile over the heat. Continue to boil for 20 to 30 minutes: the time of boiling must not be shortened, as it is essential that the character of the starch be changed by the prolonged boiling with acid. At the end of 30 minutes the mixture should be of a very pale straw color and transparent. Add the honey and flavorings and blend thoroughly.

Pour half the contents of the pan into the buttered pan, color the remainder pale rose pink and pour it on top of the mixture already in the pan. Let stand until quite cold. Dip a sharp knife into powdered sugar, cut the mixture into neat pieces, and toss in powdered sugar.

Cover with parchment paper and let stand in the sugar for at least 24 hours. Pack in boxes in a generous quantity of powdered sugar to prevent the candies from sticking together.

CHOCOLATE TRUFFLES

3 oz chocolate
1 egg yolk
1 tablespoon butter
1 tablespoon whipped cream
1 tablespoon rum
chocolate vermicelli

Melt the chocolate over hot water, without allowing it to become hot. Add the egg yolk, butter, cream, and rum and beat till thick and pasty. Using two teaspoons, form the mixture into balls and roll these in the vermicelli.

COCONUT ICE

2¼ cups sugar
⅔ cup milk
2 cups shredded coconunt
coloring

Oil or butter an 8 × 6 inch pan.

Dissolve the sugar in the milk over a low heat. Bring to a boil and boil gently for about 10 minutes, or until a temperature of 240° (soft ball stage) is reached. Remove from the heat and stir in the coconut. Pour half the mixture quickly into the buttered pan. Color the second half and pour quickly over the first layer. Leave until half set, mark into bars, and cut or break when cold.

CANNED FOOD

The method of preserving foods in special cans serves the double purpose of making seasonal crops available year round and allowing a reserve stock for use in emergencies. Fruits, vegetables, soups, cereals, meats, fish, milk, and many other products are available in this form.

Canning was first used as a form of preservation in the early nineteenth century. It has no practical effect on proteins, carbohydrates, or fats, and, in general, vitamins are well retained.

Buying and Storing Canned Food

Canned foods should be examined for faults and any cans with bulging ends, leaks, etc. should not be bought. Such faults may have been caused by imperfect sterilization, inefficient sealing, or subsequent damage to the cans due to careless handling. If cans develop these faults after purchase, they must be discarded and it is wise to look over your stores from time to time, for a bulging can may burst and scatter its contents. Bulging may be due to the presence of bacteria which form gases or other harmful products, so the contents of such cans should never be eaten. It is also unwise to eat any canned food which has an unusual smell or color, even though the can itself appears sound.

The life of a can of food depends not only on the contents but also on the kind of lacquer, if any, used inside the can and the temperature and humidity of the storage place. Generally speaking, the quality of the food processed under modern scientific conditions is very good and a reputable manufacturer takes care to use good-quality cans and suitable lacquer, so reliable brands, stored in a cool, dry place, should keep well. (Damp conditions cause rusting, which may eventually lead to perforation of the metal.) When a can of food is bought for storage, write the date of purchase on the label.

Research has shown that the nutritive value of canned food is generally satisfactory. Vitamin C and thiamin are less affected by length of storage than by temperature, while for riboflavin and niacin the reverse is the case. Carotene (source of vitamin A) is not severely affected; other nutrients are not affected at all. Water soluble vitamins (B and C) are contained in the liquid in the can; discard the liquid and discard the vitamins.

Canned Fruits: One year is the usual time for storing, provided the cans are kept in a cold, dry place. If they are kept longer, the food value is not impaired, but the fruit may appear less attractive. The natural acidity of the fruit may attack any scratch or otherwise damaged parts of the lacquer; in this case, a metallic flavor develops and a gas (hydrogen) is produced which will eventually cause the can to bulge in which case it should be discarded.

Vegetables will store well for at least 2 years. If kept longer they may become less attractive in appearance, but the food value remains unchanged.

Fish and Meat will keep in good condition for several years. Hams present a special problem in food preservation and the packer's guarantee is usually only for 6 months. If, however, after longer storage the can has not bulged, the contents are sound.

Unsweetened Evaporated Milk should be kept for only 6 months.

Sweetened Condensed Milk remains unchanged for 6 to 9 months.

Dried Milk Powder in cans should be used within a few weeks. It tends to form hard lumps and develop a rancid flavor on long storage.

CANNELLONI

These are numbered among the largest of the stuffed pasta in Italy. They are large squares of pasta cooked in boiling salted water, then stuffed, rolled, and browned in the oven. Sometimes they are baked with butter and sprinkled generously with Parmesan cheese or else, as in Tuscany, they are covered with a sauce and baked until the top is a golden brown. (See Pasta entry.)

CANNING (COMMERCIAL)

The preservation of food in cans is now only carried out on a commercial scale. It is not recommended in the home from a health and hygiene point of view; also the equipment is no longer available to the individual. Today home canning is done in jars.

Traditionally the canning process was carried out by placing the food in the can, sealing it and heating to a high temperature to achieve sterility. In recent years a new method known as aseptic canning has been developed. The food is sterilized by a higher heat treatment for a few seconds before it is placed in a sterilized can and closed with a sterilized lid. The food has a better flavor and a higher nutritional value. The higher, shorter heat treatment also means that the food is sterilized without being overcooked. Many foods are now packed by this method although not all are suitable for the treatment.

CANNING (HOME)

A method of preservation by killing or inhibiting the molds, yeasts, enzymes, and bacteria which are normally present in the tissues of foodstuffs and by maintaining conditions in which new organisms cannot reach the sterilized foodstuffs. Provided it is adequately sterilized and hermeti-

cally sealed, canned produce keeps indefinitely and provides a delicious supply for use in winter time.

Fruits are most suitable for canning as they contain less harmful bacteria than vegetables or meat. The latter are not recommended for canning without a pressure cooker for health reasons. There are only two methods of canning considered safe for all foods – the Boiling Water Bath and the Pressure Canner. The "open kettle," "oven canning," or "steamer canning" methods are dangerous, especially for low-acid foods, although the open kettle is considered safe for jellies. In this process the food is cooked in an uncovered kettle and poured boiling hot directly into hot sterilized jars. Each jar is sealed as soon as it is filled.

Equipment

Elaborate equipment is not essential, but if you intend to do a large amount of canning you will probably like to equip yourself with such apparatus as a sterilizer fitted with a thermometer, a pair of tongs for lifting the hot jars, a long-handled wooden packing spoon and a bottle brush. To can vegetables, a pressure canner is essential, owing to the high temperatures necessary; it may also be used to sterilize canned fruit.

The Fruit Jars

In principle, all jars are the same – that is, they are fitted with a rubber ring and a lid of glass or metal and are provided with some means of holding the lid firmly in position; this may be a metal screw band, a clip, or a metal spring cap.

The jars are made in two shapes, one with rounded shoulders and the other tapered, with a wide neck. It is a good idea to choose at least some jars with wide necks, for they are easier to pack (especially with large fruits such as peaches or pears) and also easier to empty.

If you already have a stock of jars it is well to review them before the preserving season starts. This entails pairing them up with their lids and screws or clips, testing rubber bands, examining lacquered lids, checking jars for nicks on the sealing surfaces, and making any necessary replacements or additional purchases.

As a general rule it is advisable to buy new rubber rings each season, but good quality ones may be used several times if necessary. As soon as they show signs of use or if they become in any way damaged they must be discarded.

Metal lids are lacquered on the inside to protect them from fruit acids, so when using this type of lid it is important to make sure that the lacquer film is intact. Lids should not be used again.

Several types of covers are designed for jelly jars; carefully used these are most satisfactory. The jars must be standard size with rims free from chips or imperfections. Follow the manufacturer's directions.

Preparation of Jars

Wash them thoroughly in warm soapy water and rinse well. Cover with hot water and allow to remain until ready to use.

Soak rubber bands in warm water for 15 minutes, then dip them in boiling water.

The Syrup or Liquid

Fruit may be canned satisfactorily in plain water, but the flavor is much better if syrup is used. A suitable one for most fruits is made with 1 lb sugar to 5 cups water, but as much as 2 lb to 5 cups may be used for very acid fruits. To prepare the syrup, put the sugar and water into a saucepan, cover and bring to a boil; boil for 1 minute, then strain the syrup through cheesecloth. If any syrup is left over after all the jars have been filled, it may be strained, poured into a jar, sealed and sterilized at the same time as the fruit.

For tomatoes, use water with 2 teaspoons salt and 1 teaspoon sugar in each 2 lb jar. Alternatively, use tomato juice (prepared by rubbing stewed tomatoes through a sieve).

The Fruit

Choose firm, dry fruit that is just ripe. When possible, it should be picked on a dry day. Can it as soon as possible after gathering.

Prepare fruit as for stewing, i.e. hull loganberries, blackberries, strawberries, and raspberries, halve and pit plums, if very large; cut rhubarb into convenient-sized lengths. When necessary, wash the fruit gently in plenty of cold water.

Tomatoes may be left whole, if small; large ones are better quartered or sliced. It is best to peel them before canning; to remove the peels easily, first put the tomatoes into boiling water for a few seconds, until the peel starts to split.

Apples, pears, peaches, and some other fruits tend to discolor unless ascorbic acid tablets are added. Dissolve the tablets in the covering liquid and proceed as usual. For each jar use 125 mg.

Apples and pears may, if preferred, be peeled into a bowl of salted water, 2 tablespoons salt to $2\frac{1}{2}$ quarts cold water, to prevent discoloring. The fruit must be well rinsed before it is packed into the fruit jars.

Coloring for Canned Fruit

The addition of a little suitable coloring to the syrup used for rhubarb, strawberries, cherries, etc., gives a better appearance to the fruit.

General Procedure

Whenever possible, grade the fruit according to size and ripeness. Pack it tightly into the jars, without bruising; use a packing spoon or the handle of a wooden spoon if necessary to push the fruit gently into place. Shake the fruit down by striking the bottom of the jar smartly with the palm of the hand. Now follow the detailed instructions for either the boiling-water bath or oven method of sterilization.

Testing for a Seal

When the jars are quite cold, i.e. the next day, remove screw bands or clips. You should be able to lift the jars by the lids, which will show that a vacuum has formed as they cooled and that the jars are now hermetically sealed.

Any jars that are not sealed must be resterilized before storing, or the contents must be used up within a day or so.

Storing

Canned fruit should be stored in a cool, dry place. It is wise to recheck the seal a week or so after putting the jars away and at intervals during the storage period. If, as sometimes happens, sterilization is not complete or if a breakdown in the seal occurs, fermentation or mold growth will set in. If this is noticed at once, while the fruit in the jars is still wholesome, it can be used up at once and need not be wasted.

Slight overcooking, the use of a heavy syrup, or loose packing will cause fruit to rise in the jars during storage, which sometimes worries novices. It is often difficult to avoid overcooking, especially when the oven method of sterilization is used, but it does not affect the keeping quality of the fruit. Provided that sterilization is complete and the jars are hermetically sealed, the fruit should keep.

Boiling-Water Bath

This is, on the whole, the most reliable method of canning fruit. A sterilizer or deep bath fitted with a thermometer is very convenient, but any deep receptacle will do quite well. It should be deep enough to enable the jars to be covered with water by 2 inches and it must be fitted with a rack. Failing this, several thicknesses of cloth or newspaper can be used, but a rack is better as it allows the steam to escape and prevents excessive rattling. Pack a cloth or a pad of crumpled paper between the jars to prevent them touching.

Packing and Processing

Prepare, wash, and grade the fruit and pack it tightly into clean jars. Fill the jars to the top with cold syrup, water, or juice and put on the rubber rings, lids, and clips or screw bands. Loosen the screw bands a very slight amount, by about one half-turn.

Place the bottles in the sterilizer or container with cold water to cover by 2 inches and cover with a lid to prevent evaporation. Heat very gently, so that after 1½ hours the water reaches the appropriate temperature for sterilizing, then adjust the heat and maintain this temperature for the time stated in the chart. If no thermometer is available, heat very gradually to a slow simmering temperature and maintain the water at this heat for 15 to 20 minutes.

Lift the jars out on to a wooden surface or folded newspaper. Tighten the screw bands immediately and again after a few minutes. Leave undisturbed to cool. The next day, test the seals.

Fruit	Temperature	Minutes
Apples sliced	165°	10
Apricots, Peaches	180°	15
Blackberries, Loganberries	165°	10
Blueberries	165°	10
Cherries	180°	15
Currants (black, red, or white)	165°	10
Gooseberries	180°	15
Grapefruit	180°	15
Grapes	180°	15
Mulberries	165°	10
Oranges	180°	15
Pears	190°	30
Pineapple	180°	15
Plums, Greengages, Damsons	180°	15
Quinces	190°	30
Raspberries, Strawberries	165°	10
Rhubarb	165°	10
Tangerines, Lemons	180°	15
Tomatoes	190°	40

Canning Fruit Pulp

Preserving fruit in the form of pulp is quick and easy. It can be stored more compactly in this way and the pulp can either be used for desserts or made into jam at a later date. The pulp can be canned either with or without sugar.

First stew the prepared fruit in the minimum amount of water. When it is thoroughly cooked and mashed and still boiling hot, pour at once into hot sterilized jars and seal at once, as when canning fruit. Deal with one jar at a time and reheat the pulp before filling the next jar. When cold, test the seal in the usual way.

Provided that the fruit is boiling hot when poured into the jar and the filling and sealing are quickly and carefully carried out, the pulp should keep satisfactorily without further sterilization. As an extra precaution, however, the filled and sealed jars may be sterilized. Loosen screw bands by a half-turn, immerse the jars in hot water, standing them on a rack or folded cloth, and bring the water to a boil. Boil for 5 minutes, then remove from the water, cool and test as for canned fruit.

For fruit puree, cook the fruit until tender, puree it in a blender, then bring it back to a boil.

To make tomato puree: Cut up the tomatoes and put into a saucepan with 2½ teaspoons salt to every 2 lb tomatoes. Bring to a boil, stirring frequently, and cook gently until a thick pulp is obtained. Puree and pour into warmed jars. Cover as for canned fruit. To sterilize, put the filled jars into a pan of hot water, bring to a boil and boil for 10 minutes. Test the seal in the usual way.

This pulp is useful for soups and sauces in the winter months.

A quicker method, which dispenses with pureeing, is to peel, cut up, and stew the tomatoes and can them while still boiling hot, as for fruit pulp.

Fruit Juices and Syrups

Sweetened and unsweetened juices make good winter desserts, sauces, and drinks. The best fruits to use are blackberries, raspberries, and strawberries, while rose hips (see recipe) make a syrup rich in vitamin C. The fruit must be really ripe and fresh.

Have ready some small jars and covers suitable for fruit canning or some bottles with screw caps and corks. Heat the jars by bringing them to a boil in water; boil caps or corks for 10 minutes.

Put the fruit in a pan with little or no water (but for blackberries 1¼ cups water per 5 to 6 lb). Bring to a boil, stirring and crushing frequently, and boil for 1 to 2 minutes. Strain the pulp through a jelly bag.

For a very clear liquid, allow the juice to stand for several hours, to let any sediment settle.

For fruit syrup, 1 to 1½ cups sugar per 2½ cups of the strained juice, dissolving it well. Strain through cheesecloth.

Pour the liquid into the bottles to within 2

inches of the cork or stopper and seal tightly, fixing with wire if necessary. Put into a deep pan on a rack and fill with cold water up to the base of the corks. Heat to 170° and maintain this temperature for 30 minutes. (If no thermometer is available, raise to simmering point and maintain for 20 minutes.) Remove the bottles and dip the corks into melted paraffin wax when partly cooled. If no screw caps are used, wire the corks on. Store in a cool, dry place, as for canned fruit.

To make rose hip syrup: The hips should be fresh, fully ripe and deep red. Crush or grate and put at once in boiling water, allowing 2 quarts to 2 lb hips. Bring back to boiling point, then set aside for 10 minutes. Strain through a jelly bag and when it ceases to drip, return the pulp from the bag to the pan, with an additional quart of boiling water. Bring back to boiling point, leave for 10 minutes, then strain as before. Mix the two extracts, and reduce by boiling until the juice measures 1 quart. Add 1 lb sugar and stir until dissolved. Jar, sterilize, and seal.

To make tomato juice: Simmer ripe tomatoes until they are soft, then rub through a sieve. To each 5 cups of pulp add $1\frac{1}{4}$ cups water, 1 tablespoon sugar, 2 teaspoons salt, and a shake of pepper. Put into jars and sterilize as for tomato pulp, above. Use for making tomato juice cocktails; a little lemon juice or Worcestershire sauce may be added to the juice when it is served as an appetizer, etc.

Canning Fruit in a Steam Pressure Canner

This has the advantage of shortening the time and insuring exact control of the temperature. Any pressure canner will take pint canning jars, but for larger jars a pan with a domed lid is required.

METHOD
1. Prepare fruit as for ordinary canning.
2. Pack into clean, warm jars, filling them to the top.
3. Cover with boiling syrup or water to within $\frac{1}{4}$ inch of the top of the jars.
4. Put on the rubber bands and heat-resisting disks and screw bands, screwing these tight, then turn back a quarter turn. As an extra precaution heat the jars by standing them in a bowl of hot water.
5. Place the inverted trivet on the pressure canner and add at least 1 quart water plus 1 tablespoon vinegar or lemon juice to prevent the pan from becoming stained (unless it is nonstick). Bring water to a boil.

6. Pack jars into the canner, making sure they do not touch by placing newspaper between them.
7. Fix the lid in place, put the pan on the heat until steam comes steadily from the vent.
8. Put on the low (5 lb) pressure control and continue heating gently to take about 3 minutes to reach pressure. Reduce the heat and maintain pressure for the time given in the chart below. (Any change in pressure will cause liquid to be lost from the jars and underprocessing may result.)
9. Remove the pan carefully from the heat and reduce the pressure at room temperature for about 10 minutes, before taking off the lid.
10. Lift the jars out one by one, tighten the screw bands and leave to cool.

Fruit	Processing time at Low (5 lb) pressure
Apples (quartered)	1 minute
Apricots (whole)	1 minute
Blackberries	1 minute
Cherries (whole)	1 minute
Currants	1 minute
Damsons	1 minute
Gooseberries	1 minute
Loganberries, Raspberries	1 minute
Pears (eating)	5 minutes
Pears (cooking) (very hard ones can be pressure cooked for 3 to 5 minutes before being packed in jars)	5 minutes
Plums (pricked if whole, pitted if halved)	1 minute
Rhubarb (in 2-inch lengths)	1 minute
Strawberries (not recommended)	—
Soft Fruit (solid pack) Place fruit in a large bowl, cover with boiling syrup ($\frac{3}{4}$ cup sugar to $2\frac{1}{2}$ cups water) and leave overnight. Drain, pack jars and cover with the same syrup. Process as usual.	3 minutes
Fruit Pulp (e.g. apples) Prepare as for stewing. Pressure cook with $\frac{2}{3}$ cup water at high (15 lb) pressure for 2 to 3 minutes; puree in blender. While hot, fill jars and process.	1 minute

Canning Vegetables

This should only be carried out in a pressure cooker. (See Pressure Cooking entry.)

CANTALOUPE

(See Melon entry.)

CAPER

The pickled flower buds of a low-growing deciduous shrub native to the south of Europe. The fresh buds are picked each day during the flowering season, left to dry for 24 hours and put into a cask of pickling brine. They are then canned in good quality vinegar. Capers are used to flavor a sauce which is traditionally served with boiled mutton and are an ingredient of tartar sauce, traditionally served with fish. (See Salad Dressing entry.)

CAPERCAILLIE (CAPERCAILZIE)

A game bird of northern Europe. Similar in size to grouse, it may be cooked in the same way.

CAPON

The term used for a castrated cockerel, specially reared for table purposes and killed at 6 to 9 months old.

CAPSICUM (CHILI)

The family name for a number of varieties of pepper. There are two main types: hot, such as the chili, and sweet, like the ones eaten as a vegetable. Capsicums can be green or red, round or long, and they vary considerably in size. (See Chili and Green Pepper entries.)

CARAMEL (BURNED SUGAR)

A substance prepared by heating sugar very slowly in a thick pan until it is dark brown in color; when water is added it produces a dark brown liquid. Commercially it is used for coloring gravy, fruit cakes, wines, beers, vinegars, soups, sauces, etc.

If the caramel is heated for a shorter time, it will retain its sweet taste, instead of becoming bitter and it then makes an agreeable flavoring for cakes, custards, and sauces.

CARAMEL CUSTARD

$\frac{2}{3}$ cup sugar
$\frac{2}{3}$ cup water
$2\frac{1}{2}$ cups milk
4 eggs

Put $\frac{1}{2}$ cup of the sugar and the water into a small pan and dissolve the sugar slowly; bring to the boil without stirring until it caramelizes, i.e., becomes a rich golden brown color. Pour the caramel into a 6-inch cake pan which has been heated slightly, turning the pan until the bottom is completely covered. Warm the milk, pour onto the lightly whisked eggs and remaining sugar and strain over the cooled caramel. Place the pan in a shallow pan of water and bake in a 325° oven for 1 hour, until set. Leave in the pan until quite cold (preferably until the next day) before turning out.

Note: Individual custards are easier to turn out. Divide the above mixture between 6 caramel coated ramekins. Cook for about 45 minutes.

CARAMEL CANDY

A type of candy made in somewhat the same way as toffee, but not boiled to so high a temperature. Caramels may be either soft or hard in texture, according to the temperature to which they are cooked, and the mixture is usually enriched with butter, cream, condensed milk, etc., which necessitates stirring it occasionally during the cooking.

CARAWAY SEEDS

The caraway plant originated in the Orient and was used as a spice by the Greeks. The seeds have a peculiar pungent, aromatic flavor, similar to cumin. Caraway seeds are used for flavoring cakes, rolls, bread, cheese, pickles, cabbage, sauerkraut, and the liqueur Kümmel. The essential oil distilled from them is used in various medicines, wines, and condiments, while the root is cooked and eaten as a vegetable in some parts of Europe.

CARBOHYDRATE

As the name implies, a carbohydrate consists of carbon, hydrogen, and oxygen (the two latter in the proportions in which they are found in water). Carbohydrates exist as glucose and other simple sugars and also as a number of glucose units combined into one substance. They provide most of the energy of the human diet. Carbohydrates are the cheapest foods, so poor countries and poorer classes in rich countries eat more of them than proteins and fats. They include:

Sugars: Glucose (sometimes called dextrose), fructose, sucrose (better known as the ordinary

domestic sugar), lactose, maltose, and others. These are not of any nutritional value, except as a source of energy.

Starchy Foods: Cereals (grains) and some vegetables store food for the new plant in the form of starch. Cereals include wheat, rice, barley, oats, rye, and corn and their products, flour, cornstarch, pasta, semolina, bread, and many others. Vegetables include pulses, potatoes, and other roots. Most of these foods have other important nutrients such as protein and minerals, besides carbohydrates.

Starch is a more complicated carbohydrate than sugar, being several glucose units linked together.

Cellulose: The cell structure of fruits, vegetables, and grains. Unlike the sugars and starches, cellulose does not provide energy. It is useful to the body as roughage.

Other Carbohydrates: There are many others – for example, glycogen (found in most tissues, particularly of liver and shellfish) and pectin (found in fruit).

The carbohydrates, except cellulose, are broken down in the digestive system and absorbed into the blood stream as glucose. This is stored in the muscles and liver as glycogen, which is converted back into glucose when needed to provide energy.

The energy is the same whether sugar or starch is eaten, but since most starchy foods also provide other materials, they are more valuable. When more carbohydrate is eaten than the body needs, the excess is converted into fat and stored in the tissues, causing obesity.

Some carbohydrate should be eaten at the same time as protein, or some of the protein will be used to produce energy instead of body-building. The habit of eating such combinations as bread and cheese and meat and potatoes is therefore nutritionally sound.

A certain amount of the vitamin thiamin is necessary to make use of the carbohydrate and this is found in most cereals, if they have not been overrefined. It is now added to white flour in the United States to make up for that removed during milling.

CARBONNADE

Originally this was a French culinary term referring to meat grilled over hot coals. Today it generally means a stew or braise of meat, usually incorporating beer. Belgium is famous for its carbonnade of beef. (See Beef entry.)

CARDAMOM

The spicy, bitter seeds of a reedlike plant belonging to the ginger family, grown largely in Malabar; they are dark brown in color and similar in size to mustard seeds. Cardamoms are used in the preparation of sauces, curry powders, cordials, and for spicing cakes and confectionery and are popular in Scandinavian baking. As they lose their flavor quickly once ground, they should be ground just before they are used.

CARDINAL SAUCE

A red sauce served with fish dishes. To make it, prepare some lobster butter (see Lobster entry), using about 1 tablespoon coral and 2 tablespoons butter. Make 1 cup Béchamel sauce (see Béchamel entry), beat it well, and season it with salt, pepper, a little grated nutmeg, and a squeeze of lemon juice. Beat in the lobster butter and last, add 2 tablespoons whipping cream or a little butter. Pass the sauce through a fine strainer and reheat it without boiling.

CARDOON

A plant of the thistle family resembling the globe artichoke; the leaf-stalks and roots can be eaten as a vegetable. The blanched stalks are cooked like celery, while the fleshy main root is boiled and served cold or in salads.

CARMINE

A carnation-red coloring derived from cochineal.

CAROB

The fruit of a Mediterranean shrub, much used in the Middle East; also called locust bean. The whole pod, which is rather sweet and insipid, is used to make a kind of meal and also a syrup. Its taste resembles chocolate, for which it is often substituted by health-food producers.

CAROTENE

The yellow-orange pigment present in yellow and green vegetables and fruit. It is the precursor of vitamin A, being converted into that substance in the body. (See Vitamin A in Vitamins entry.)

CARP

This freshwater fish, found in rivers and ponds, sometimes lives to a great age. It was introduced to the United States in the late nineteenth century and is now abundant in the Midwest. Carp is popular in Jewish and Chinese cooking and in Europe. The French make several delicious dishes with it. If not held alive several days in clear water, it needs washing well in running water or salted water to remove the muddy flavor. It can be broiled or fried and is particularly good when stuffed and baked or cooked in red wine.

CARRAGEEN

(See Irish Moss entry.)

CARROT

Known since Elizabethan times, a useful root vegetable available year round. There are two main types: the long rooted and the shorter or round rooted. Carrots give flavor to stews, casseroles, and soups, or they may be cooked in a variety of ways to serve as a vegetable. They can also be grated and served raw in salads. Carrots are a good source of vitamin A (in the form of carotene) and contain a little of the B vitamins, calcium, and sugar.

To cook: Scrub the carrots and scrape lightly: large old carrots will require peeling thinly and cutting into strips or rounds. Cook in boiling salted water until tender – from 20 minutes for young carrots to 1 hour for coarser ones. Glaze with butter and toss in chopped parsley or coat with a creamy white sauce. Alternatively, mash and reheat with salt, pepper, and some butter.

Carrots may also be baked in a casserole in a very little water; place in a 350° oven for at least twice the usual time. Add a little butter and just before serving sprinkle generously with freshly chopped parsley; serve in the casserole.

CARROT CAKE

$\frac{1}{3}$ cup boiling water
2 cups grated carrots
2 cups all-purpose flour
1 cup sugar
1$\frac{1}{4}$ teaspoons baking soda
1 teaspoon salt
$\frac{3}{4}$ teaspoon ground cinnamon
$\frac{1}{2}$ teaspoon ground allspice
$\frac{1}{2}$ teaspoon ground cloves
$\frac{1}{2}$ cup vegetable oil
3 eggs
1 teaspoon vanilla
1 cup golden raisins
$\frac{1}{2}$ cup chopped walnuts

Combine ingredients in a large mixer bowl and beat on low speed 1 minute, scraping down the side of the bowl constantly. Increase speed to medium and beat 2 minutes; scrape down bowl as needed. Bake in a greased 10-inch tube pan in a 350° oven for 50 to 55 minutes, or until a pick inserted comes out clean. Cool 10 minutes before removing from pan. Frost with Lemon Cream Cheese Frosting (see Cream Cheese entry).

CARVING

Skillful carving makes the most of food, enabling one to obtain the maximum number of neat, appetizing portions and leave the meat looking attractive enough to serve cold. It is advisable to know something about the structure of the different roasts and birds and where the lean and the fat, or the dark and light meat, are to be found. Good carving tools are essential.

KNIVES

For most roasts, a carving knife with a fairly long and broad blade, slightly curved and pointed at the end, is generally satisfactory. Some modern stainless steel carving knives have a hollowed-out grooved blade which does not require sharpening and these knives are perhaps easier for an inexperienced carver to use, though a skillful carver generally prefers a blade with a plain edge.

For carving poultry and game, a knife with a short, straight, stiff blade, pointed at the end and with a comparatively long handle, gives more purchase and makes it easier to sever the joints. When a special game carver is not available use a sharp, pointed kitchen knife in preference to an ordinary carver.

For carving boned hams, the most practical knife is one with a very long, thin, straight and slightly flexible blade; this is usually rounded at the end, for the cuts are invariably made horizontally and a sharp point is unnecessary.

Whatever type of carving knife is used, it should always be very sharp.

FORKS

A carving fork has two sharp prongs, so that it will enter the meat easily, and a guard to prevent the hand from being cut should the knife slip. Forks for carving hams, etc. generally have a square or circular guard, similar to that of a sword.

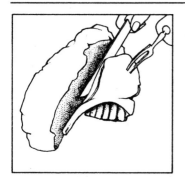
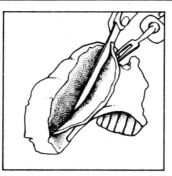
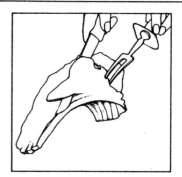

CARVING A ROAST RIB OF BEEF
1. Loosen meat from the narrow ribs. Carve the meat downward.

2. Continue to carve thin slices of the meat, cutting down to the rib bones until you have cut halfway through the roast.

3. Turn the meat and continue carving from the outside to the center of the roast.

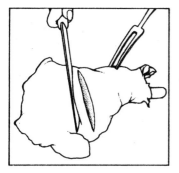
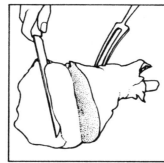
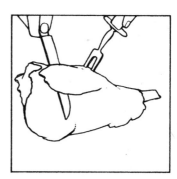

CARVING A LEG OF LAMB
1. Using a sharp carving knife, cut two slices from the center of the leg, cutting down to the bone.

2. Continue carving slices from both sides of the first two cuts and gradually carve longer slices. Carve all the meat from this side.

3. Turn the roast over. Cut away any unwanted fat then carve horizontally along the leg for longer slices. Continue carving down to the bone.

FISH SERVERS

These consist of a blunt-edged knife, with a short, wide, slightly pointed blade, and a wide fork with short, broad prongs. They are generally silver, silver-plated or stainless; ordinary steel should not be used, as it gives the fish an unpleasant taste.

Rules for Carving

1. If necessary, secure the roast before cooking with skewers or string (or both), so that it keeps its shape. This is particularly important when the roast is boned (as in rolled rib of beef or boned sirloin) or stuffed (as with breast of lamb). Take care when trussing birds to give them a good shape.

2. Always use metal skewers, which can be removed with ease when the meat is cooked; wooden skewers swell during cooking, making it very difficult to remove them neatly.

3. Get the butcher to chine roasts such as loin or neck of lamb, mutton, veal, or pork, rather than having them chopped. (See Chine entry.)

4. Bone and stuff a roast such as loin of pork, as it can then be carved much more easily.

5. Score the crackling of pork before cooking – it is difficult to carve if left in thick pieces.

6. Any game birds that require cutting in half should be carved in the kitchen on a board before they are dished up.

7. Choose a large enough dish for the roast and keep the garnishes small; if any gravy or sauce is placed on the dish with the meat, use a small amount only, the rest being served separately in a sauce boat.

8. Arrange for carving to be done at the side table if the carver is inexperienced or if the dining table tends to be crowded. Place a carving cloth or napkin under the dish, to protect the table.

9. Have everything ready and the knife sharpened before beginning to carve and see that the guard of the fork is up.

Carving Meat

Meat is almost invariably carved across the grain, as this makes it more tender to eat. Generally speaking, beef is sliced very thinly (especially when cold); mutton and lamb should be fairly thick, while a medium thickness is best for pork and veal. Slice ham and tongue thinly.

Carving Poultry and Game

CHICKEN
As for Turkey.

TURKEY
Loosen the legs from the body without removing them, then carve thin slices of breast the whole length of the bird. Remove the legs and separate the thigh from the drumstick at the joint. Serve a slice of leg and breast with a portion of stuffing.

DUCK
Cut through the skin with the point of the knife and cut the meat from each side of the breast in long slices, parallel with the breast bone. Cut through the legs and wings at the joint. Serve a piece of leg with a piece of breast.

GOOSE
A goose is carved in the same manner as a duck, but the meat is generally sliced from the legs and wings, these parts being rather large for individual portions.

GAME BIRDS, ETC.
A pheasant or other game bird, if large, is carved in the same manner as a chicken. Partridges, pigeons, and birds of similar size are generally cut in half; if very small, the whole bird may be served as one portion. Special scissors are designed for cutting birds in half, but it can be done with the game carver or with a short, pointed kitchen knife, by inserting the point of the knife in the neck end of the breast and cutting firmly

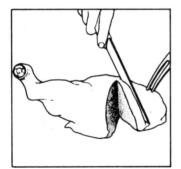

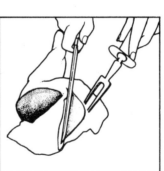

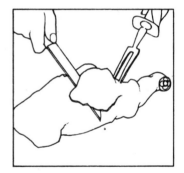

CARVING A SHOULDER OF LAMB
1. Cut a long slice from the center of the roast right down to the bone.

2. Continue to carve thick slices from either side of first slice. Turn the roast and carve from the other side in thin slices.

3. Turn the roast so that the shank end is facing you again and cut horizontal slices from the top.

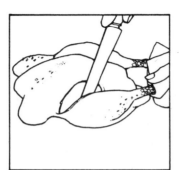

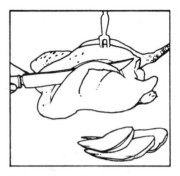

CARVING A CHICKEN
1. Loosen the wings from body then press out and away from body to dislocate. Cut wings through joint.

2. Loosen then cut legs from the body. Separate the thigh from the drumstick at the joint by cutting through ball and socket.

3. Carve slices of the white breast meat in long, thin downward slices from either side of the breast bone.

through the bird in the direction of the breast bone.

Woodcock, snipe, quail, and other small birds are served whole. They can however be cut into two for presentation.

Carving Fish
The aim in carving fish is to serve it in neat portions without breaking up the flakes or mixing them with the bones or skin. The fish is laid flat on the dish, a round fish like cod being placed on its side. For a large fish, run the knife through the middle of the flesh from head to tail and cut slices of flesh from each side of the cut. Remove the backbone and cut the lower half similarly. To serve flat fish, first cut the head off, then cut right through the bone into sections across the fish. In the case of salmon, cut lengthwise through the middle of the flesh and carve the thick part of the fish (the back) in lengthwise slices; include a portion of the thin part (the belly) with each serving, cutting these slices widthwise.

CASEIN

A substance produced from milk by precipitation. It results through the action of rennin on the milk protein caseinogen. This reaction takes place in the stomach as a course of normal digestion; it also occurs in the making of junket when rennet is added to warm milk. The milk sets, but when cut a liquid (whey) separates from the solids (curd); the casein is contained in the curd. The precipitation also takes place when an acid is added to milk although a less firm curd is formed.

The fermentation of casein is the origin of all cheesemaking as the milk is always clotted with rennet and/or acids. The casein clot traps the fat leaving much of the water to be drained off. Cheese is therefore a concentrated form of milk nutrients. (See Cheesemaking under Cheese entry.)

Casein has a high biological value as a protein, making milk and cheese valuable foods in the diet.

CASHEW NUT

A kidney-shaped fruit produced by a tree grown in the East and West Indies and in other tropical regions. The kernel of the fruit has a pleasant taste and is popular roasted and served with cocktails and other drinks. It is used in the making of chocolate and sometimes in Madeira wine.

CASSATA

An Italian frozen dessert consisting of ice cream with chopped nuts, candied fruit, etc., in the center.

CASSATA ALLA SICILIANA

1 cup mixed candied fruits (cherries, angelica,
*   pineapple)*
1½ tablespoons cherry liqueur
1 cup ricotta or cottage cheese
½ cup cream cheese
6 tablespoons granulated sugar
8 individual sponge cake shells
6 oz semisweet chocolate, broken into pieces
¼ cup butter
1 egg, beaten
1⅓ cups sifted powdered sugar

Chop the candied fruits finely and combine with the liqueur. Beat the ricotta in a mixer until no lumps remain and then beat in the cream cheese and granulated sugar. Split the sponge shells and use half of them to line a 5-cup bowl. Stir the fruits and liqueur into the cheese mixture and turn into the cake-lined bowl. Arrange the remaining cake on top and chill overnight.

Put the chocolate and butter in a bowl over a pan of hot water until melted. Mix the egg into the melted chocolate. Remove from the heat and beat in the powdered sugar. Invert the molded cake onto a serving plate and spread with the chocolate mixture. Allow to set.

CASSAVA

A tropical shrub, a native of Central and South America, but now grown in the West Indies, Africa, and some parts of Asia, Cassava is the name used in the West Indies, while the plant is known as manioc in some parts of South America and Africa and as yucca in other regions. The tubers produce a food also known as cassava or manioc.

Cassava is easy to grow, but unfortunately has very little protein and is not as valuable a staple food as wheat; in fact, protein deficiency is a great danger if the cassava is not accompanied by enough foods containing protein.

The large tubers contain hydrocyanic acid, which is removed by washing, exposure to the air, grating, heating, and pressing the tubers; the resultant mass is ground into a coarse meal. This is used to produce a kind of cake, which however, does not rise at all as it contains no gluten. Some variation of this cassava cake is the staple food of millions of people in many tropical countries.

Tapioca and meal, both almost pure starch, are also produced from cassava.

The juice expressed from the tubers and flavored is called cassareep; it is used as a sauce in the West Indies.

CASSEROLE COOKING

The term used to denote the very slow cooking of food placed in the oven in a covered heatproof dish; very often the food is served in the same casserole. It is a simple method, excellent for cooking meat (particularly inferior cuts), fish, and vegetables, as the food becomes very tender and all the nutriment is conserved. The process is economical on fuel; although it takes longer than ordinary methods, only a very low heat is required. Slow cookers, or crock pots, are particularly suitable for this method of cooking. (See Crock Pot entry.)

FLEMISH BEEF IN BEER

2¼ lb chuck
3 tablespoons vegetable oil
7 oz small onions
2 tablespoons flour
finely grated rind and juice of 1 orange
⅔ cup water
1¼ cups pale ale
½ teaspoon dried rosemary
pinch grated nutmeg

Cut the meat into 2-inch cubes. Heat the oil in a skillet or flameproof casserole; sauté meat quickly until browned on all sides. Remove meat and cook whole onions in remaining fat until browned. Stir in flour; return meat to pan. Add orange rind and juice, water, and ale. Stir well, add rosemary and nutmeg. Season. Bring to a boil, stirring. Cover and cook in a 325° oven for 1½ to 2 hours.

CASSEROLE OF CHICKEN

2 medium-sized onions, sliced
2 ribs celery, trimmed and chopped
¼ lb mushrooms, sliced
3 slices bacon, chopped
1 tablespoon vegetable oil
4 chicken parts
¼ cup all-purpose flour
2 cups chicken broth
1 can (16 oz) crushed tomatoes
salt
pepper

Lightly sauté the onions, celery, mushrooms, and bacon in the oil for about 5 minutes, until golden brown. Remove them from the pan with a slotted spoon and use them to line the bottom of the casserole. Sauté chicken parts in the oil for 5 minutes until golden brown. Put the chicken in the casserole on the bed of vegetables. Stir the flour into the remaining fat and cook for 2 to 3 minutes; gradually stir in the broth and bring to a boil. Continue to stir until the mixture thickens then add the tomatoes, with salt and pepper to taste. Pour this sauce over the chicken parts, cover and cook in a 350° oven for 45 minutes to 1 hour, until the chicken is tender.

RICH RABBIT CASSEROLE

1 rabbit, cut into pieces
1¼ cups dry cider
¾ cup pitted prunes
¼ lb unsliced bacon
2 tablespoons butter
½ lb small onions
2 tablespoons flour
⅔ cup chicken broth
salt
freshly ground pepper
1 large tart apple

Place rabbit in a bowl and add the cider. Cover prunes with water. Leave both overnight. Drain and dry rabbit, reserving marinade. Drain prunes. Cut bacon into ¾-inch dice. Melt butter in a skillet and sauté rabbit with bacon and onions until brown. Place in casserole. Stir flour into fat and cook for 1 minute. Blend in broth and cider. Simmer 3 minutes. Season and pour over rabbit, cover and cook in a 300° oven for 1 to 1½ hours. Thirty minutes before end of cooking time, peel, core, and slice apple and add with the prunes. Cover and continue to cook. Garnish with triangles of fried bread.

RAGOUT OF BEEF HEART WITH LEMON

1 lb beef heart
2 tablespoons lard
1 medium onion, sliced
1 tablespoon flour
½ cup beef broth
grated rind of 1 small lemon
1 teaspoon lemon juice
½ teaspoon dried fines herbes
salt
freshly ground pepper
⅔ cup sour cream
1 tablespoon chopped parsley

Trim the heart discarding any little pipes and gristle and cut into strips about ½ inch wide. Melt the lard in a skillet or a flameproof casserole and sauté the sliced onion until golden. Sauté the strips of heart quickly in the fat, to seal on all sides. Stir in the flour and cook for 1 minute, then gradually blend in the broth with the lemon rind, juice, and herbs. Bring to a boil and add salt and pepper to taste. Cover and cook in a 300° oven for about 2 hours. To serve, adjust seasoning, stir in the sour cream and sprinkle with chopped parsley.

CASSIA

The inner bark of a type of cinnamon tree grown in the East, particularly in China. Cassia resembles cinnamon in flavor, color, and aroma and may be used in the same way, but it is coarser and less expensive.

CASSIS

A French liqueur made from blackcurrants, drunk with chilled dry white wine as Kir (5 parts wine to 1 part Cassis).

CASSOLETTE

An individual dish of metal, china, or glass, made to hold one portion of an hors d'oeuvre, entrée, or dessert. The container is sometimes lined with fried duchesse potatoes or puff pastry before the main mixture is put in.

CASSOULET

A haricot bean stew originating in the Languedoc region of France. It is prepared from pork, mutton, and goose (or duck) and is made in an earthenware utensil known as the cassole d'Issel: this name has evolved into the word cassoulet. There are as many recipes for this dish as there are cooks.

CASSOULET

8 oz dried haricot beans
8 oz lean salt pork
8 oz lean shoulder lamb
1 lb onions
2 tablespoons lard
2½ cups water
1 bay leaf
1 clove garlic, crushed
4 oz garlic sausage, sliced
1 teaspoon dried savory

salt
freshly ground pepper

Soak the beans overnight. Drain well. Remove rind from the pork and cut into strips with the lamb. Slice the onions and sauté in the lard in a 3-quart flameproof casserole until soft. Add the meats and cook to seal. Add water, beans, bay leaf, crushed garlic, sliced garlic sausage, savory, and seasonings. Bring to a boil, cover and simmer gently for 1½ to 2 hours, or until the beans and meat are tender.

CATERING

The term usually applied to the business of preparing food for large numbers for special occasions. (See Party entry.)

CATFISH

A name applied to various fish in different parts of the world. In the United States catfish is popular in the South, where it is coated with cornmeal and fried in deep fat.

CATSUP (KETCHUP)

A type of table sauce with one predominating flavour, e.g., tomato, mushroom, cucumber, or walnut, etc. Catsup is made by extracting the juice, boiling it down to a very concentrated form, and seasoning it highly.

TOMATO CATSUP

12 lb ripe tomatoes, sliced
1 lb sugar
2¼ cups spiced vinegar
1 tablespoon tarragon vinegar
pinch cayenne pepper
1–2 teaspoons paprika
2 tablespoons salt

Place the tomatoes in a pan and cook over a very low heat until they become liquid; reduce by boiling until the pulp thickens, then rub it through a sieve. Return the puree to the pan with the remaining ingredients, and boil until the mixture thickens. Pour into warm jars, sterilize for 30 minutes and seal.

MUSHROOM CATSUP

3 lb mushrooms, washed and roughly broken
6 tablespoons salt
1 teaspoon peppercorns

1 teaspoon whole allspice
½ teaspoon ground mace
½ teaspoon ground ginger
pinch of ground cloves
2¼ cups vinegar

Put the mushrooms in a bowl, sprinkle with the salt, cover, and leave overnight. Rinse away the excess salt, drain and mash with a wooden spoon. Place in a pan with the spices and vinegar, cover and simmer for about 30 minutes, or until the vinegar is absorbed. Press the mixture through a sieve and pour into warm jars. Sterilize and seal.

CAUDLE

A hot spiced wine drink, resembling mulled wine, which was popular in earlier centuries as a cure for a cold. It was sometimes made with water in which oatmeal had been soaked, or with gruel.

CAUL

A thin membrane covering the lower portion of an animal's intestines. At one time it was always used commercially for sausagemaking and it is still used for homemade sausages. Pork caul is the best type.

CAULIFLOWER

A member of the cabbage family. It has a compact white head (i.e. flowers), surrounded by green leaves.

The "flower" should be firm and close and protected by young leaves which curl over the flower naturally. Some of the inner green leaves should be kept on the flower when cooked as these add to the appearance of the vegetable. Cauliflower can be served as a vegetable, as part of a main dish (Cauliflower au gratin), or raw as part of a salad. It is also tasty made into soup or pickles. Cauliflower is a good source of vitamin C, an average helping supplying over half a day's requirements.

To cook: Trim off any unwanted leaves, wash the cauliflower, and cut a cross in the stalk to enable this thick part to cook through. Since the stalk takes longer to cook, it is best to place the cauliflower stem downward in the pan. Cook whole in boiling salted water until tender – 20 to 30 minutes. Drain and serve with a white or cheese sauce. Alternatively, the cauliflower can be divided into sprigs or flowerets before cooking, to save time. Many sauces are compatible with cauliflower. These include polonaise and hollandaise sauces and brown butter.

CAULIFLOWER AU GRATIN

1 cauliflower, trimmed
3 tablespoons butter
3 tablespoons flour
1¼ cups milk
1 cup grated Swiss cheese
salt
pepper

Cook the cauliflower in fast-boiling salted water until just tender, drain, and place in an ovenproof dish. Melt the butter, stir in the flour and cook for 2 to 3 minutes. Remove the pan from the heat and gradually stir in the milk; bring to a boil and continue to stir until it thickens. Stir in ¾ cup of the cheese and season to taste. Pour over the hot cauliflower, sprinkle with the remaining cheese and brown under a hot broiler.

CAVIAR

The salted roe of the sturgeon, considered a great delicacy because of its rare flavor, though it is an acquired taste and not appreciated by everyone. Most prized are the Russian varieties: the processed roe of the sterlet from the Caspian Sea consists of a mass of black eggs each about the size of a pinhead. Beluga and sevruga caviar are also highly prized. Once abundant in the United States, caviar is beginning to reappear with the return of sturgeon to the Hudson River.

Caviar should be kept very cold (preferably on ice). It is served either from its jar or from a small barrel placed on a folded napkin and is accompanied by crisp toast or brown bread and butter; or it may be sprinkled with lemon juice if desired. Caviar may also be made into canapés, included in hors d'oeuvre, spread on croutes of fried bread or served in blinis (small Russian pancakes).

CAYENNE

A very hot, pungent variety of pepper, bright red in color, made from the dried seeds and pods of various capsicums. It originated in the district of Cayenne, in South America, from which it takes its name, but it is now grown in other tropical countries. Cayenne is used for flavoring curries and to season cheese and fish dishes.

CELERY

A vegetable of the carrot family widely grown in

temperate regions. It is eaten either raw or cooked and also used as a decoration. (See Garnish entry.) Cream of Celery Soup (made like the tomato soup in the Soup entry) is well flavored and popular, while Celery Consommé makes an excellent first course for a formal dinner.

To prepare raw celery: Wash well to remove any grit and dirt and take off the outside stalks and leaves. (Stalks can be used to flavor stews and soups.) Cut the center part across into halves or quarters, according to the size of the head, the root being scraped and shaped to a point and left on each portion. The celery will keep well if put in a tall glass of water.

The raw stalks can also be chopped or cut up for use in salads.

To boil celery: Wash, cut into even lengths, and tie in bundles. Cook in boiling salted water until tender, 30 to 45 minutes, depending on the coarseness of the stalks. Drain carefully and serve with a brown, white, or cheese sauce.

Braised celery: This has a better flavor than the boiled vegetable. (See Braising entry for recipe.)

To stuff celery: Cut the prepared stalks into convenient pieces, spread thickly with seasoned cream cheese and garnish with paprika. These make good cocktail snacks.

APPLE AND CELERY STUFFING

3 slices bacon, chopped
2 tablespoons butter
2 onions, chopped
2 stalks celery, trimmed and chopped
4 medium-sized apples, peeled, cored, and sliced
3 cups fresh white bread crumbs
2 tablespoons chopped parsley
sugar to taste
salt
pepper

Sauté the bacon in the butter for 2 to 3 minutes until golden brown and remove from the pan with a slotted spoon. Sauté the onions, celery and apples for 2 to 3 minutes, until soft. Mix all the ingredients together.

Use with duck or pork, or make double the quantity and use for goose.

CELERY ROOT (CELERIAC)

A variety of celery, cultivated for its turniplike stem base. The root only is served as a vegetable, made into a cream soup, or grated raw in salads. Cut into julienne strips and dressed with a mustardy mayonnaise, it is delicious as an hors d'oeuvre.

Peel it fairly thickly; the small roots may be cooked whole, but larger ones should be sliced thickly or cut into dice. Cook in boiling salted water or stock until tender, 20 to 60 minutes or even longer. Drain well and serve with melted butter or with a sauce such as Béchamel or hollandaise. It is also delicious pureed and served alone or mixed in equal proportions with mashed potatoes.

CELERY SALT

Salt flavored with dried and powdered celery, used in stews and so on.

CELERY SEEDS

The ground aromatic seeds of a plant related to vegetable celery. It is used as a flavoring in stews, pickling spices, and salads, with fish and meat dishes, etc.

CELLULOSE

(See under Carbohydrate entry.)

CÈPE

A European fungus, *Boletus edulis*, of the mushroom family. They look similar to mushrooms but are a yellowish color. Cèpes can be used in any of the ways appropriate for mushrooms. They are particularly popular in the Bordeaux region of France.

CEREAL

Cereals are grasses cultivated for food. They grow all over the world, even in the Arctic Circle, and generally form the staple food of the population, being a cheap source of energy, protein, some vitamins, and minerals.

The kind of cereal grown depends mainly on climate and soil; wheat and rice are the most widespread.

In general, cereals give economical energy and provide a good accompaniment to protein and stronger flavored foods, e.g., rice with curry, bread with cheese.

Following is a list of the most important cereals. (See individual entries for details.)

WHEAT

In dry, temperate climates. It is ground into flour which is made into bread and cakes.

RICE

In damp, tropical climates. The grain is generally eaten whole (apart from the husk) and it goes with many foods, being served as a side dish or as the basis for entrées or desserts.

RYE

In cold climates, particularly Northern Europe. It is the only cereal besides wheat from which true bread can be made.

CORN

In parts of America, Africa, and India. Ground into cornstarch for puddings and cakes or eaten as the whole kernel or on the cob. Cornmeal is popular as a base for breads in the United States, particularly the South, where grits and hominy are also staples. Tortillas are made with specially treated ground corn.

BARLEY

One of the oldest cereals, but not often used as food now. Pearl barley can be added to soups and stews or sautéed briefly in butter and cooked with mushrooms and broth as a pilaf.

OATS

This cereal also is less used than formerly. It is ground into various grades of oatmeal for porridge, soups, cookies, and scones; rolled oats are also used.

MILLET

In dry, hot climates, mainly in Africa, Asia, and Latin America. It will thrive on poor soil.

PREPARED CEREALS

These are specially treated to make them ready to eat. With milk and sugar, syrup, or fruit, they make a good breakfast. (See Breakfast Cereals entry.)

CHABLIS

A light, dry white Burgundy wine, from the vineyards round Chablis. It is served slightly chilled, with fish or white meat.

CHAFING DISH COOKERY

A chafing dish is a vessel which is used at table for cooking and for keeping food warm. The classic chafing dish consists of two pans, an upper part, which holds the food, and a lower one, which contains hot water. The chafing dish is really the equivalent of a double boiler and is suitable for foods which are normally cooked in that way, for example, Scrambled Eggs or Lobster Newburg. Swiss Fondue can be cooked in the upper pan alone. (See Eggs, Lobster, and Fondue entries for recipes.)

The modern electric skillet, which is becoming increasingly popular, may also be used at table, though the cooking is by dry heat. These skillets are usually sold with a comprehensive book of instructions, giving notes about temperatures and settings, etc., and in some cases, a selection of recipes. Here are some rules to help you make a success of chafing dish cookery:
1. Know your recipe thoroughly, making it up several times.
2. Study the manufacturer's instructions for regulating the heat of your cooker.
3. Have everything ready beforehand – food, seasoning, accompaniments, plates, etc.
4. Plan a first course that will occupy the guests while the second course is being cooked in the chafing dish.

CHALLAH

A rich yeast egg bread, prepared by the Jews for Sabbath, holidays, and other ceremonial occasions. While challah is baked in various symbolic shapes, depending upon the holiday, it usually appears as a braided loaf.

CHALLAH

1 package active dry yeast
2½ cups flour
1 tablespoon sugar
1 teaspoon salt
2½ tablespoons butter or margarine
¾ cup hot water (120°–130°)
1 egg yolk
1 teaspoon cold water

Combine the yeast, 1¼ cups of the flour, and the sugar, salt, and butter in a mixing bowl. Add the water gradually, beating to make a smooth batter. Mix in the remaining flour. Add more flour if the dough is sticky.

Knead the dough on a lightly floured surface until smooth and elastic. Place in a greased bowl, cover with greased plastic wrap and let rise until doubled in bulk, 1½ hours or longer.

Punch the dough down and divide into 3 equal pieces. Roll each out into a strand 12 to 14 inches in length. Lay the strands parallel to each other and braid, starting from the middle of the strands. When one-half is braided, turn and braid the second half. Place on a greased baking sheet and let rise until doubled in bulk, about 50 to 60 minutes. Beat the egg yolk with the water and brush over the top of the loaf. Bake in a 375° oven for 25 to 30 minutes. Cool on wire racks.

CHAMPAGNE

A sparkling wine made from grapes grown within the boundaries of the ancient French province of Champagne. Champagne is always blended, firstly because the wines from different vineyards, although similar in type, are different in style and it is only by judicious blending that the individual wines are improved, the special qualities being merged into a harmonious whole; secondly, because the quantity of wine made each year from individual vineyards is so small that shippers must blend the wine of a number of vineyards in order to have sufficient champagne of uniform style to meet the demands of their customers.

Unlike other wines, champagne is bottled before fermentation is finished, so that the carbonic acid gas remains in solution and escapes when the cork is removed, giving a sparkling effect. A vintage champagne is one bearing the date of an outstanding year. These are not sold until 5 years old but the best will improve for another 5 years.

At formal dinners, champagne is served with the game and desserts. It may also be served as the only wine and this is more usual today. It is the traditional wine for serving at wedding receptions for drinking the health of the bride and bridegroom. It is often served at other celebrations and chilled champagne is sometimes served before a meal. Champagne should be served thoroughly cool, but not icy, or the flavor will be lost.

Fine champagne is a brandy made in the Charentes district of France.

CHAMPAGNE CUP

1 bottle champagne
2 tablespoons sugar
2 oranges, sliced
1 quart chilled carbonated water (optional)

Put the ingredients except the carbonated water into a jug, cover and chill for 2 hours, then decant and add the carbonated water, if used.

CHAMPAGNE COCKTAIL

(See Cocktail entry.)

CHAMPIGNON

French name for the button mushroom found in markets throughout the United States.

CHANTERELLE

A cup-shaped wild mushroom with a frilled edge and a short stem. Widely used in France, it also grows in the United States and can be found in woodlands during the summer months.

CHANUKAH

(See Hanukah entry.)

CHAPATTI (CHUPATTY)

An Indian unleavened bread or pancake, baked on a griddle and served with curry. A paste of flour and water is blended and rolled thinly.

CHAPATTI (CHUPATTY)

2 cups whole-wheat flour
½ teaspoon salt
5–7 oz water

Sift the flour and salt. Add enough water to make a soft dough; blend together with fingertips. Knead well for 10 minutes. Leave covered with a damp cloth for at last 1 hour. Knead well again and then divide into 6 pieces. Roll each out on a generously floured surface to make 4- to 5-inch rounds. Heat up a griddle or a heavy-bottomed skillet, very lightly greased, and cook two chapattis at a time until pale brown on each side. Serve hot, brushed with butter or ghee, to accompany any Indian dish.

CHAR

A freshwater fish, related to the salmon, with a red underside and pink oily flesh, found in lakes and rivers of Scotland, England, Switzerland, and Savoy. It is cooked like trout.

CHARD

(See Swiss Chard entry.)

CHARDONNAY (PINOT CHARDONNAY)

An excellent white wine produced in California from the chardonnay grape. The grape, traditionally called pinot chardonnay, is no longer considered a member of the pinot family. It is from this grape that all white Burgundies, including Chablis, must be made.

CHARLOTTE

A dessert made with stewed fruit and layers (or a casing) of bread or cake crumbs, sponge cake, cookies, etc. In a Charlotte Russe, there is a center of a cream mixture surrounded by cake.

CHARLOTTE RUSSE

2½ cups lemon jello
green grapes, seeded and halved
1¼ cups milk
1 vanilla pod
3 tablespoons water
2 envelopes unflavored gelatin
3 egg yolks
2 tablespoons superfine sugar
10–12 lady fingers
¼ pint carton heavy cream

Pour a little unset lemon jello into a 15-inch/1½-pint sloping-sided russe pan. Allow to set. Arrange a pattern of grapes over, and set carefully with a little more jello. Place remaining jello in a bowl and leave to set.

Heat the milk in a saucepan with the vanilla, do not boil; leave to infuse for 10 minutes, then strain.

Put the water in a small bowl, sprinkle the gelatin over and leave to swell up. Beat the egg yolks and sugar, pour the strained milk over and return it to the pan. Cook gently to a coating consistency. Add the gelatin and stir until dissolved, then cool until beginning to set.

Arrange the ladyfingers (trimmed down each side) side by side around the russe pan. Lightly whip the cream until floppy and fold it into the custard. Turn it at once into the pan. Trim the ladyfingers level with the mixture and arrange the trimmings over the top. Chill until set. Turn out as for molded jello and decorate with the remaining jello, chopped.

RHUBARB BETTY

1½ lb rhubarb, trimmed and wiped
1 cup fresh white bread crumbs
½ cup brown sugar
6 tablespoons butter
grated rind of 1 lemon, or 1 teaspoon ground ginger or cinnamon

Grease a 4- to 5-cup ovenproof dish. Cut the rhubarb into short lengths and place half in the prepared dish. Mix together the crumbs, sugar, butter, and lemon rind, cinnamon or ginger and sprinkle half over the fruit. Add the remaining fruit and top with the remaining crumbs. Bake in a 350° oven for 45 minutes.

CHARTREUSE

One of the most famous French liqueurs, made by Carthusian monks. There are two chief types: yellow and green; a third type is called Elixir.

CHASSEUR SAUCE

A rich, highly-seasoned brown sauce, usually containing white wine, mushrooms, and shallots; it is served with meat, game, or venison, etc. There are a number of different versions, but here is a popular one.

CHASSEUR SAUCE

1 cup chopped mushrooms
butter
salt
1 tablespoon shallot, finely chopped
⅔ cup white wine
⅔ cup Demi-glace sauce (see Demi-glace entry)
⅔ cup tomato sauce
a little chopped parsley, chervil, tarragon

Sauté the mushrooms in butter and season with salt; when they are nearly cooked add the shallot. Stir in the wine, boil in an open pan until reduced by half, then stir in the Demi-glace sauce and the tomato sauce and boil for a minute or two. Just before serving add 2 tablespoons butter and some chopped parsley, chervil, and tarragon.

CHATEAUBRIAND STEAK

A thick steak cut from the middle of the fillet of beef and served with maître d'hôtel butter or Béarnaise Sauce. (See Steak entry.) The traditional accompaniment is château potatoes, turned potatoes cooked in butter.

CHAUD-FROID

A sauce used to coat cooked meat, fish, poultry galantine, etc., which are served as cold entrées.

CHAUD-FROID SAUCE (WHITE)

⅔ cup hot water
2 envelopes unflavored gelatin
1¼ cups Béchamel sauce, warm (see entry)
⅛–¼ pint light cream
salt
pepper

Put the ⅔ cup hot water in a small bowl and stand in a pan of hot water. Sprinkle in the gelatin and stir until it has dissolved, taking care not to overheat the mixture. Stir into the warm Béchamel sauce, beat well and add the cream and extra salt and pepper as necessary. Strain the sauce and leave to cool, stirring frequently so that it remains smooth and glossy. Use when at the consistency of thick cream, for coating chicken, fish, or eggs.

CHAYOTE

A green or white pear-shaped vegetable, with a single seed, related to cucumbers and squashes and native to Mexico and the West Indies. The ridged skin is sometimes covered with small, soft spines; the flesh is pale green. It is now grown successfully in the United States in California, Louisiana, and Florida, and in Algeria, from where it is exported to Europe. It is known under many names – mirliton (New Orleans), vegetable pear (Florida), custard marrow (Great Britain) and brionne (France).

Chayotes may be prepared in a number of ways. After peeling and boiling, they may be sauced as desired or cooled, dressed with a vinaigrette and served as a salad, or they may be parboiled and stuffed and, depending upon the stuffing, served as a main dish or a dessert.

HAM-STUFFED CHAYOTES

2 chayotes
2 tablespoons butter
1 lb ham, finely chopped
¼ cup chopped green onions
2 cloves garlic, minced
1 teaspoon dried thyme
1 cup dry bread cubes
salt
pepper
Tabasco
¼ cup fresh bread crumbs
¼ cup chopped parsley

Cover the chayotes with water and boil until tender, about 45 minutes. Cool and cut into halves. Scoop the flesh out of the chayotes, being careful not to puncture the skin, and combine in a skillet with the butter, ham, green onions, garlic, and thyme. Sauté for 20 minutes then add the bread cubes and seasonings. Pile the mixture into the shells, sprinkle with bread crumbs and parsley and bake in a 350° oven until just browned.

CHEDDAR CHEESE

A traditionally English cheese originally made in the late fifteenth century near Cheddar Gorge in Somerset. It is now made in other parts of England. "Cheddar type" cheeses are also made in other countries including the United States, Ireland, Canada, Australia, and New Zealand.

English Cheddar is a firm, smooth-textured cheese with a clean unbroken rind. It is a straw color and can be mild or strong in flavor. English Farmhouse Cheddar is made from whole milk from a single herd of cows. It is allowed to mature for at least 6 months to produce a rich mellow flavor. Other Cheddar cheese is made from a mixture of ripened and unripened milk; the close texture is obtained by pressing for 3 to 4 days with the pressure increased each day. The cheese can be left to ripen from 3 to 6 months depending on the flavor required. Cheddar is good served alone with bread or in cooked dishes.

CHEESE

Originally a method of preserving milk, cheese became very popular for its own sake at an early stage in man's history and has remained so ever since, for it is a very palatable and versatile food.

It is made by separating the curds from the whey (usually by the action of rennet) and ripening them in some way. The milk can be that of the cow, goat, ewe, camel, mare, llama, or even buffalo, according to the part of the world; in the United States and Europe it is usually cow's, goat's, or ewe's milk.

The process used, the climate and vegetation help to widen the variety of cheeses. Some types cannot be imitated outside their own districts or under factory conditions. Others, such as Cheddar cheese, etc., are made over the world.

Cheese is eaten raw and is also cooked in a large number of dishes, from cocktail snacks to main meals. (See selection of recipes given in this entry.)

Cheesemaking Process
These are the basic principles for cheesemaking, especially the hard Cheddar types. Different

flavors and textures are determined by variations in times and temperatures, in the weight of pressing and the length of maturing.

1. Pasteurized milk is soured or ripened by a "starter" culture or lactic acid bacteria which converts some of the milk lactose into lactic acid. Throughout the cheesemaking process the development of acid is carefully controlled to insure that a good cheese results.

2. Rennet is added to coagulate the milk, and then the coagulum cut to allow the whey to separate from the curd.

3. The curd is scalded or heated to cause shrinkage and release more whey. It is then left to settle which allows further shrinkage and drainage.

4. The curd is broken down and salt added as a preservative and for flavoring.

5. The curd is then pressed in molds for varying times then removed as a whole cheese.

6. The cheese is then left to mature in a special ripening room which is kept at a certain temperature and humidity.

Food Value

Cheese is valuable protein food and plays an important part in the normal diet. The different types vary in composition, but 1 oz gives about one-third of the day's requirement of calcium, also some vitamins A and D and some riboflavin. Bread and cheese are an excellent combination from the nutritional point of view as proteins in the bread enhance those in the cheese.

Cheese Classification

Cheese is classified in several ways. Sometimes it is grouped according to the type of processing — whether the cheese is heated and whether it is hard-pressed and so on. The classification here given is according to the appearance and texture.

Type	Example
Very hard cheese	Parmesan
Hard cheese	
(a) without "eyes"	Cheddar
	Cheshire
	Derby
	Double Gloucester
	Lancashire
	Wensleydale
	Leicester
	Cantal
(b) with "eyes"	Emmenthal
	Gruyère
Semi-hard	Caerphilly
	Edam
	Gouda
	Port-Salut
	Tomme
Blue-veined	Roquefort
	Gorgonzola
	Bresse Bleu
	Stilton
	Danish Blue
	Wisconsin Blue
Semi-soft	Brick
	Munster
	Limburger
	Samsoe
	Mozzarella
Soft	
(a) Ripened	Brie
	Camembert
	Fromage de Monsieur
	Pont l'Evêque
	Bel Paese
(b) Unripened	Coulommier
	Cambridge
	Cottage
	Ricotta
Goat cheese	Chevret
	Saint Maure
	Valençay

SOFT CHEESES (CURD CHEESES)

These are characterized by their small size, high moisture content (50 to 70 percent) and quick ripening properties. They have a mellow, slightly acid flavor and soft spreadable texture. Soft cheeses do not keep as long as the harder varieties, therefore they should be eaten while fresh.

Cream Cheese is made from fresh cream and usually has a fat content of 40 to 73 percent. (See separate entry.)

Cottage Cheese is a skimmed milk soft fat cheese. It is an acid curd cheese made from pasteurized fat-free milk. It is packaged as it is or with the addition of cream. It has a mild flavor which makes it suitable to serve with sweet or savory foods. It is often used as part of reducing or low-fat diets. (See separate entry.)

Packaged and Processed Cheeses, usually sold wrapped in foil, are made by various processes, the ripening being halted at a selected stage. They are generally soft textured and milky and are sometimes flavored with tomato, onion, etc.

European Cheeses

Supplies available vary from time to time, and from one locality to another. Many shops and supermarkets now stock a comprehensive range. Here are some which should be available:

ALPESTRA (ALPIN)
Hard, dry cheese made in the French Alps.

AUSTRIAN SMOKED CHEESE
Cylindrical, with sausage skin covering; close-textured and with distinctive smoky flavor; good with wine.

BEL PAESE
Italian; soft, creamy and rich, very mild in flavor; texture slightly rubbery, but nonetheless agreeable. Good for cooking certain Italian dishes.

BONDON
Small, cylindrical, whole-milk cheese from Normandy. When ripe has a fairly pungent flavor.

BRESSE BLEU
A soft French blue cheese.

BRIE
French; soft, with a crust rather than a rind; when in good condition it is runny in texture, but a poor Brie is dry and chalky; well flavored.

CACCIOCAVALLO
Italian; name due to the fact that the roundish cheeses are strung together in pairs and dried suspended over a pole, as though astride a horse. If eaten fresh, the cheese has a tangy taste and firm, yet soft texture; if kept, it becomes hard and is then grated and used in cooking.

CAMEMBERT
French; soft, and with a distinctive flavor that strengthens as it ripens.

CANTAL
French; a hard strong cheese made in Auvergne.

CHEVRET
French; a Bresse cheese made from goat's milk.

COULOMMIER
French; soft cream cheese, eaten fresh after salting. White crust, creamy to the touch.

DANISH BLUE
Soft and white, with blue veins, sharp and rather salty in taste.

DEMI-SEL
French; a soft, mild, cream cheese.

EDAM
Dutch; bright red outside, yellow inside; mild in flavor, close and fairly soft in texture.

EMMENTHAL
Swiss; hard, pitted with numerous fairly large irregular holes; like Gruyère, which it resembles, it has a distinctive flavor. Used in cooking, especially for cheese fondues.

DANISH EMMENTHAL
A good copy of the Swiss product.

FONTAINEBLEAU
French; creamy cheese, which is sometimes eaten with strawberries.

FROMAGE DE MONSIEUR
French; soft and slightly like Camembert, but milder.

GERVAIS
French; cream cheese, sold packed in boxes of 6 small portions.

GORGONZOLA
Italian; semi-hard, with a creamy texture. It is blue-veined and normally has a strong flavor. However, there are mild varieties of Gorgonzola, the Dolcelatte, made from a sweet milk, being much milder in flavor than the ordinary type; between the two comes the kind known as creamy Gorgonzola.

GOUDA
Dutch; creamier in taste and texture to Edam, and larger and flatter, and with a yellow outside coat. Smaller sizes are available.

GRUYÈRE
Swiss; hard, honeycombed with holes which are smaller and fewer than in Emmenthal; the cheese has a more creamy texture, and a distinctive, slightly acidulous flavor. Used in cooking, particularly for cheese fondues. French Gruyère is also available.

HAVARTI
Danish; foil-wrapped; semi-firm texture, rather open; good full flavor.

KÜMMELKÄSE
German; caraway-flavored; good with cocktails, etc.

LIMBURGER
Belgian or German; strong, ripe flavor and smell.

MARC DE RAISIN
French; semi-hard, with a crust of grape skins and seeds replacing the usual rind. A rather tasteless cheese.

MOZZARELLA
Italian; round, soft cheese, originally made from buffaloes' milk, but now also made from cows' milk. Should be used fresh. Eaten by itself it is somewhat tasteless, and it is more useful in making Italian dishes such as pizza.

MUNSTER
Alsatian; semi-soft cheese, which is good for both cooking and table use; not unlike Pont l'Évêque in flavor.

MYCELLA
Danish; soft textured, creamy with green veins; strong flavor.

MYSÖST (GIETÖST)
Norwegian; whey cheese, principally made from goats' milk. Hard and dark brown, with a sweetish flavor.

NEUFCHÂTEL
French; whole-milk cheese, soft, dark yellow and with a flavor similar to that of Bondon.

PARMESAN
Italian; very hard, ideal for cooking and for grating to serve with pasta, etc. It is also available in packs, ready grated.

PETIT SUISSE
French; soft, creamy and unsalted cheese, made into little cylindrical shapes. Often eaten with strawberries or other fruit, accompanied by sugar.

POMMEL
French; a brand of double-cream cheese, similar to Petit Suisse.

PONT L'ÉVÊQUE
French; semi-hard cheese, sold in small square boxes; delicious mild flavor, somewhere between that of a Brie and a Camembert.

PORT-SALUT
French; semi-hard, with very good mild flavor.

RICOTTA
Italian; a fresh, moist, unsalted variety of cottage cheese.

ROQUEFORT
French; made from ewes' milk; white with blue veins, has a sharp, distinctive flavor; rather salty; creamy and rather crumbly in texture, somewhat like a Stilton.

SAINT MAURE
French; soft, creamy, goats' milk cheese.

SAMSOE
Danish; firm-textured, with regular holes, golden in color; mild and sweet in flavor. Danbo is a small, square-shaped version; Fynbo, Elbo and Tybo are other variants, fairly similar in type; Molbo has a richer, more fruity flavor; Maribo is also more full flavored.

TOMME
French; semi-hard, covered with grape seeds.

VALENÇAY
French; soft, goats' milk cheese.

Cheeses for Cooking
Good cheeses are Cheddar, Cheshire, Parmesan, Gruyère, Emmenthal, Gorgonzola, Bel Paese, Mozzarella, Camembert, Monterey Jack and cream and cottage cheese.

Serving Cheese
When serving cheeses as a separate course, choose varieties which differ in style, flavor, and consistency and arrange them attractively on a board or platter. To accompany them, serve any of the following: plain bread, crackers (plain or very slightly sweetened), hot rolls, toast, rye bread, French bread and so on. Apples, pears, and grapes are popular accompaniments.

Cream cheese may be served plain with crackers; alternatively, paprika, caraway seeds, or chopped chives may be added and some people like chopped pineapple or other fresh fruits or nuts mixed with cream cheese, especially when it is served with salad.

Storing Cheese
Hard cheeses, such as Cheddar, are best kept wrapped in aluminum foil or plastic wrap and placed in a cool storeroom or the least cold part of a refrigerator. The ideal temperature for keeping cheese is 55°. However, the cheese should be brought to room temperature at least one hour before serving. Cheeses bought in vacuum packs are best rewrapped once opened.

Soft cheeses can also be stored in a refrigerator, but ideally they should be eaten as fresh as possible. Some of the soft French cheeses such as

Camembert or Brie may be kept at room temperature for a few days to allow the flavor to develop further. Once ripe they are best eaten the same day.

Hard cheeses can be frozen for up to 4 months if packed in blocks of up to 1 lb. Vacuum-pack cheese can be frozen without repacking, but unwrapped cheese is best frozen in freezer wrap. Cheeses should be thawed in a refrigerator for 24 hours. In some varieties the texture changes and they may deteriorate more quickly than nonfrozen cheese. Curd cheeses can be frozen successfully for up to 3 months. Cream cheese and cottage cheese do not freeze.

Drying and Grating

To make cheese become hard and dry, leave it exposed to the air in a dry but cool place; it is best hung in a cheesecloth bag, as the air can then circulate completely. If the cheese is left on a plate or board to dry, stand it on its rind; a piece that has no rind should be turned occasionally, otherwise the underside will remain soft and will very likely become moldy.

Use a fine grater for a dry cheese; a soft or processed cheese should be shredded rather than grated. Very soft cheese can be sliced and added to sauces etc., without being grated or shredded.

Cooking

The less cooking cheese has, the better. Over-heating tends to make it tough and indigestible, so when making a dish such as Welsh rarebit or cheese sauce, always heat the cheese very gently and do not cook longer than is necessary to melt it. A few recipes are given here. (See Welsh Rarebit entry.)

To toast cheese: Lay a slice of cheese (Cheddar is excellent) on a round of freshly made buttered toast. A dab of mustard may be blended with the butter, if liked. Put under the broiler and leave just long enough for the cheese to melt.

CHEESE SOUFFLÉ

$\frac{1}{4}$ *cup butter*
$\frac{1}{2}$ *cup all-purpose flour*
$\frac{2}{3}$ *cup milk*
1 cup grated Swiss cheese
salt
pepper
$\frac{1}{4}$ *teaspoon dry mustard*
3 eggs, separated

Melt the butter in a heavy pan. Add the flour and cook for 1 minute. Remove from the heat and gradually blend in the milk. Return the sauce to the heat and cook, stirring, until the mixture thickens; cook 1 minute longer. Stir in the cheese, salt and pepper, and mustard.

Add the egg yolks to the mixture and beat well. Beat the egg whites until stiff. Mix 1 tablespoon of the whites into the cheese mixture, then fold in the remainder. Pour the soufflé into a greased 1-quart soufflé dish. Bake in a 375° oven for 35 to 45 minutes, or until brown and firm to the touch. Serve immediately.

STUFFED CHEESE POTATOES

4 large potatoes
2 tablespoons butter or margarine
1 teaspoon chopped onion
1 ripe tomato, peeled and chopped
1 egg, beaten
little milk
$\frac{1}{2}$ *cup bread crumbs*
$\frac{3}{4}$ *cup grated cheese*
seasoning

Cut the potatoes in half lengthwise and scoop out part of the center. Meanwhile, melt half the butter in a pan and add it to the chopped onion and the tomato. Cook gently, shaking the saucepan frequently, for 10 to 15 minutes. Blend thoroughly, add the egg, a little milk, the bread crumbs and the cheese. Season and place a portion of the mixture in each of the potato shells. Finish by baking in a little hot fat in a 350° oven for 30 minutes.

CHEESE STRAWS

1 cup all-purpose flour
pinch of salt
2 tablespoons butter
$\frac{1}{2}$ *cup finely grated Cheddar cheese*
little beaten egg or water

Mix the flour and salt together and rub in the butter, as for short-crust pastry, until the mixture resembles fine crumbs in texture. Mix in the cheese. Add a little egg or water, stirring until the ingredients begin to stick together, then with one hand collect the dough together and knead very lightly to give a smooth dough. Roll out as for short-crust pastry. Cut into $\frac{1}{2} \times 3$-inch strips. Bake until golden (about 7 to 8 minutes) in a 400° oven.

Note: Use a well-flavored cheese with a bite whenever possible; a pinch of dry mustard added to the flour with the salt helps to bring out the cheese flavor.

CHEESECAKE

Traditionally a mixture of soft cheese, eggs, and sugar baked in a pastry case. The term now covers a wide variety of recipes which always include a soft cheese in the filling. It is usual to have a base of pastry, graham cracker crumbs, or sponge cake, and a topping of fruit, nuts, or another layer of the base. Chilled cheesecakes are usually set with gelatin and have a light texture. The European-type cheesecakes have a rich, creamy, smooth texture which is contrasted by the sharpness of a fruit topping. Both varieties are suitable for freezing.

POLISH CHEESECAKE

FOR THE TOPPING
8 oz cream cheese
6 egg yolks
¼ cup butter, melted
¼ cup superfine sugar
¼ teaspoon vanilla extract
icing glaze (see Glaze entry)

FOR THE PASTRY
½ cup butter
2 cups flour
¼ cup granulated sugar
1 egg yolk

Tie the cream cheese in cheesecloth and squeeze out the moisture. When the cheese is dry, grate or crumble it into a mixing bowl. Add the egg yolks, melted butter, sugar, and vanilla extract and beat thoroughly until the mixture is quite smooth. Rub the butter into the flour, add the sugar and work in the egg, with a little water if necessary to give a firm but manageable dough. Roll out and use to cover the base of an 8-inch square pan. Place the cheese mixture on top and bake in a 350° oven for 1 hour. Leave to cool in the pan until the topping is set. Turn out and coat with icing glaze. When set, cut into squares.

LEMON CHEESECAKE

1½ packets of lemon jello
4 tablespoons water
2 eggs, separated
1¼ cups milk
grated rind of 2 lemons
6 tablespoons lemon juice
1 lb cottage cheese
1 tablespoon superfine sugar
¼ pint whipping cream, whipped
candied cherries, and fresh mint sprigs

FOR THE CRUMB BASE
8 graham crackers
¼ cup superfine sugar
¼ cup butter, melted

Put the jello powder and water in a small pan and warm gently over a low heat, stirring until dissolved. Beat together the egg yolks and milk, pour onto the jello, stir and return the mixture to the heat for a few minutes without boiling. Remove from the heat and add the lemon rind and juice. Sieve the cottage cheese and stir it into the jello or put the jello and cottage cheese in an electric blender and puree until smooth; pour the mixture into a bowl. Whisk the egg whites stiffly, add 1 tablespoon sugar and whisk again until stiff; fold into the cool cheese mixture.

Fold in the whipped cream. Put the mixture into an 8-inch spring-form pan fitted with a tubular base.

Crush the graham crackers and stir in the sugar and butter. Use to cover the cheese mixture, pressing it on lightly; chill. Turn the cheesecake out carefully, and decorate with cherries and fresh mint sprigs.

CHENIN BLANC

A varietal white wine produced in California from the grape of that name. This is the same grape used in the Loire valley of France to make the Saumurs and Vouvrays of that region.

CHERIMOYA

(See Custard Apple entry.)

CHERRY

The fruit of the *Prunus cerasus*, some varieties of which are cultivated in most countries.

Eating Cherries
Cherries are delicious eaten raw, either for dessert or in fruit cocktails or salads, but they can also be cooked and may be canned, the red or black varieties being rather more suitable for this purpose, as the white ones turn a somewhat unappetizing fawnish color when canned.

Cherries for Cooking
The Morello and the May-duke are the best-known varieties; they ripen about August. Being very sharp in taste they are not suitable for eating raw, but are delicious when sweetened and cooked. For making preserves, the cooking variety should be chosen (dessert cherries have

insufficient acid and pectin). Red Cherry Soup (see Soups entry) is an unusual way of using this fruit.

Candied Cherries

These are prepared in the same way as other candied fruits and are widely used in cakes, cookies, desserts, etc., both as an ingredient and as a decoration.

Maraschino Cherries

Cherries which have been pitted, cooked in sugar syrup, and flavored with Maraschino liqueur: they are used as a decoration for cocktails, cakes, etc., and occasionally as an ingredient.

CHERRY COMPOTE

Wash the fruit carefully and remove the stems. If a cherry pitter is not available, make a slit down one side of the cherry and remove the pit from the center using a pointed knife.

To each lb of cherries allow $\frac{1}{2}$ cup sugar and the juice of 1 lemon. Put the prepared fruit, sugar, and lemon juice into a nonstick pan, without adding any water, cover and stew slowly until the fruit is tender without being broken. Lift out the cherries, boil the juice a few minutes longer and pour it over them. Cherries cooked in this way are delicious and retain their pretty red color.

DUCK WITH CHERRIES

1 duck
1 onion
1¼ cups broth
finely grated rind of 1 lemon
salt
pepper
1 can (16 oz) black cherries
1 tablespoon cornstarch
watercress sprigs

Place the duck in a casserole with the onion and broth. Cover and cook in a 375° oven for 30 minutes. Drain the liquid from the casserole and reserve. Sprinkle the duck with grated lemon rind and seasoning. Add the cherries, reserving a few for the garnish, and juice. Cover and cook for 1 hour or until the duck is tender. Skim fat from first cooking liquid and thicken with cornstarch. Add to the casserole and cook for 5 minutes longer. The sauce may be served from the casserole or may be strained or pureed as desired. Garnish with watercress and cherries.

CHERRY JAM

2 lb sour cherries
juice of 3 lemons
1¾ lb sugar

Pit the cherries, crack some of the pits and remove the kernels. Put the cherries, kernels, and lemon juice in a pan and simmer very gently until really soft, stirring from time to time to prevent them from sticking. Add the sugar, stir until dissolved and boil rapidly until setting point is reached. Jar and cover in the usual way.

As cherries are lacking in pectin, this jam will give only a light set. *Makes about 2½ lb.*

BLACK FOREST TORTE

1 package (12 oz) chocolate chips
½ cup milk
2 tablespoons sugar
1¾ cups all-purpose flour
1 teaspoon baking soda
1 teaspoon salt
¼ cup butter, softened
⅔ cup sugar
3 eggs
⅔ cup milk
1 teaspoon vanilla
4 tablespoons brandy
2 cups heavy cream, whipped and flavored with 3
    tablespoons brandy and ⅓ cup powdered sugar
1 can (21 oz) cherry pie filling

Combine the chocolate chips, milk, and 2 tablespoons sugar in the top of a double boiler and melt over hot water. Combine the flour, baking soda and salt. In a mixer bowl cream the butter and ⅔ cup sugar until creamy. Beat in the eggs, one at a time. By hand stir the flour mixture in alternately with the milk, beginning and ending with the flour. Stir in the cooled chocolate mixture and the vanilla. Divide the batter between two greased 8- or 9-inch layer pans and bake in a 350° oven for 25 to 30 minutes. Cool for 10 minutes before removing from pans to cool completely.

With a long serrated knife, slice each layer in half horizontally. Sprinkle each of the four resulting layers with brandy. Place one layer on a serving platter and spread with 1 cup whipped cream. Spread about ⅔ cup cherry pie filling over the cream to within ½ inch of the edge. Repeat with the next two layers. Place the final layer on top and cover with the whipped cream. Refrigerate until ready to serve.

CHERRY BRANDY

A liqueur distilled from fermented cherries and their crushed pits.

CHERVIL

Chervil is one of the most common herbs in French cookery, always to be found in the mixture of "fines herbes" for omelets. It is a garden herb of the carrot family with feathery leaves which turn almost purple in the fall; the whole plant has an aroma of aniseed. It is often used for salads (sometimes with tarragon) and in soups and stews.

The bulbous roots of a different plant also called chervil are eaten as a vegetable in France and Italy.

CHESHIRE CHEESE

Probably the oldest English cheese. Like Cheddar, it is a hard type, but rather crumbly in texture. There are two varieties of Cheshire cheese, the red, which is artificially colored with the dye annatto, and the white. Occasionally, more by accident than by design, a red Cheshire cheese will turn blue, that is to say, will develop a system of blue veins which spread all over the cheese and give it a very fine, rich texture and flavor.

CHESTNUT (MARRON)

The edible fruit of the Spanish or sweet chestnut tree. When the fruit ripens the prickly green husks fall to the ground, releasing the reddish-brown nuts. These can be roasted in front of the fire (or in a special chestnut roaster) and eaten with a pinch of salt, or they can be stewed and served as a vegetable. Chestnuts may also be dried and ground into flour, or cooked, pureed, and used to make a variety of garnishes and desserts.

CHESTNUT SOUP

1 lb chestnuts
2 tablespoons butter
1 small onion
1 quart good stock
salt
pepper
1 tablespoon flour
⅔ cup milk
pinch of sugar
2–3 tablespoons cream

Make a slit in the chestnuts at one end with a sharp knife (this facilitates removing the shells), boil them for about 10 minutes in salted water, then remove a few at a time and peel them. Melt the butter in a saucepan and sauté the chestnuts and the sliced onion for a few minutes. Add the stock, salt, and pepper, cover and simmer until the chestnuts are quite tender (about 1 hour), then puree in a blender. Blend the flour with the milk and add to the puree. Bring to a boil, stirring, and cook for 2 to 3 minutes. Taste for seasoning and add the sugar, then stir in the cream.

CHEWING GUM

Sticks and candy-coated pellets usually made of chicle (the coagulated latex of the sapodilla tree), to which syrup, sugar, and flavoring are added.

CHIANTI

The best-known Italian red wine, light and fairly dry. There is also a White Chianti of good quality.

CHICKEN

A young cock or hen for table use, although the term is used more loosely to apply to a fowl of any age. The poultry is classified according to its age and size:

1. SQUAB CHICKEN (POUSSIN)
Very small chicken of 4 to 6 weeks old, 1 lb to 1½ lb in weight. One bird should be allowed for each serving. Broil, grill, or roast.

2. BROILER (POULET NOUVEAU)
Young chicken up to 3 months old weighing 1½ to 2½ lb. It is particularly suitable for broiling or grilling when halved, but may be roasted whole.

3. FRYER (POULET DE GRAIN, POULET REINE)
3 to 5 months old and 2 lb to 3 lb in weight. Fry, sauté, braise, or roast.

4. ROASTER (POULET GRAS, POULARDE)
From 5½ to 9 months old, over 3 lb in weight. Roast, poach, or braise.

5. FOWL (POULE DE L'ANNÉE)
An older bird of 10 to 12 months. It is usually a hen bred to lay eggs then killed once her useful laying life is completed. As the meat is tougher than other birds it should be braised or stewed.

6. CAPON (CHAPON)

A male bird which has beeen neutered. It has been specially fattened for table use to give a lot of flesh and good flavor. 4 lb to over 7 lb in weight. Roast, poach, or braise.

Chicken, like all meat, is a good source of protein and B vitamins. It contains very little fat. For the choice and preparation of a fowl, see Poultry entry.

Frozen Chicken

There has been a rapid increase in the sale of frozen chicken, which are generally of the broiler and fryer type; in fact, the production of thousands of broilers and the freezing of them is a large industry. The freezing does not affect the flavour, texture, or food value in any way, although, because broilers are so young when killed, they have very little natural flavor; they should therefore be well seasoned or dressed in a well-seasoned sauce. Frozen chicken parts are also available.

To roast chicken: This method of cooking is suitable for birds of 9 months or younger.

Prepare the chicken, stuff it if desired and truss neatly. Lay a slice of fat bacon over the breast or put a few dabs of butter over it. A lemon or bunch of fresh tarragon can be placed inside the bird for extra flavor. Place the bird in a roasting pan and cook it in a 425° oven for 15 minutes, then reduce the heat to 350° and continue basting occasionally.

Squab chickens have a total roasting time of 30 to 40 minutes; broilers, 40 to 50 minutes; fryers, 50 to 60 minutes; over 4 lb, allow about 20 minutes per lb. The bird is done when the leg can be easily moved and the juices running from the chicken are yellow.

If the slow method is preferred, cook in a 325° oven for 20 to 22 minutes per lb. Colorless roasting bags are suitable for chicken as they allow the bird to brown without splashing the oven.

Serve with vegetables and potatoes, accompanied by brown gravy and green salad.

An older bird can be steamed or boiled first for about 2 hours to make it tender; do this the previous day, so that it gets cold before it is stuffed. Then roast for 30 to 45 minutes, to make it crisp and brown.

To poach chicken: Poached chicken is the basis for salads or any other recipes calling for cooked chicken – lots of lovely broth, too. Simply wash and dry the chicken, leave whole or cut in serving pieces. Put in a large pot with a tight-fitting lid. Add about 3 cups water, a small sliced onion, cut-up celery top, 2 bay leaves and 1 teaspoon salt. Bring to a boil, reduce heat and simmer for about 1 hour. The heat should be turned down so the liquid barely ripples.

To fry chicken: Young and tender chickens can be fried raw, but older birds are best partly cooked first. Prepare the bird in the usual way. Cut a small bird in halves or quarters and a larger one into neat parts. Season with salt and pepper and coat all over with flour. Then fry in hot fat, turning the pieces so that they brown on all sides, reduce heat and allow 15 minutes on each side. Serve with brown gravy.

Alternatively, season the parts, dip them in egg, coat with soft bread crumbs and fry in deep fat. Serve with fried parsley and accompanied by a cream sauce or gravy. Or, pile the pieces in a napkin-lined basket and garnish as desired.

To broil chicken: Young and tender chickens are suitable for broiling. Split the bird down the back, removing the backbone. Flatten the bird, removing the breast bone and breaking the joints where necessary. Fold the wings back to the body, keeping them flat. Brush with olive oil or melted butter, sprinkle with salt and pepper and place on a greased rack, skin side up. Broil under moderate heat for 20 minutes then turn and broil on the second side for about a further 20 minutes, or longer if necessary, basting. Serve plain with a clear gravy made from the giblets and garnish with watercress.

An alternative method is to sprinkle the chicken with a mixture of finely chopped onion, parsley, and bread crumbs, after brushing it with oil or butter; when it is cooked, garnish it with watercress and serve with brown or tomato sauce.

CHICKEN MARENGO

4 chicken parts
4–5 tablespoons vegetable oil
2 carrots, sliced
1 stalk celery, chopped
1 onion, chopped
3 slices bacon, chopped
4 tablespoons flour
$\frac{2}{3}$ cup chicken broth
1 can (16 oz) tomatoes
2 tablespoons sherry
salt
pepper

bouquet garni
¼ lb mushrooms, sliced
chopped parsley

Sauté the chicken parts in the oil for about 5 minutes, until golden brown; remove them from the pan and put into a casserole. Sauté the vegetables and bacon in the oil for about 5 minutes until golden brown; remove them from the pan. Stir the flour into the remaining fat, cook for 2 to 3 minutes and gradually stir in the broth; bring to a boil and continue to stir until it thickens. Return the vegetables and bacon to the pan and add the tomatoes, sherry, salt, and pepper. Pour this sauce over the chicken parts; add the bouquet garni and sliced mushrooms and cook in a 350° oven for 45 minutes to 1 hour, until the chicken parts are tender. Remove them to a warm serving dish. Strain the sauce from the casserole over them and sprinkle with chopped parsley.

CHICKEN MARYLAND

1 chicken (2–3 lb), cut into parts
4 tablespoons seasoned flour
1 egg, beaten
dry bread crumbs
¼ cup butter
1–2 tablespoons vegetable oil
4 bananas
sweet corn fritters
4 slices bacon

Divide the chicken into fairly small portions, coat each part fairly liberally, with seasoned flour, dip in beaten egg and coat with bread crumbs. Sauté the chicken in the butter and oil in a large skillet until lightly browned. Continue frying gently, turning the pieces once, for about 20 minutes, or until tender. Alternatively, fry in deep fat for 5 to 10 minutes. The fat should be 350° to 375°, hot enough to brown a 1-inch cube of bread in 60 to 70 seconds. Serve the chicken with fried bananas, corn fritters and bacon.

COQ AU VIN

4 slices bacon, chopped
6 oz mushrooms, sliced
16 small onions
lump of butter
1 tablespoon vegetable oil
1 roaster chicken, cut into parts
⅓ cup brandy
3 tablespoons flour
2 cups red wine

⅔ cup chicken broth
1 tablespoon sugar
bouquet garni
pinch of nutmeg
salt
pepper

Sauté the bacon, mushrooms, and onions in the butter and oil for 3 to 4 minutes, until lightly browned; remove from the pan. Sauté the chicken for 8 to 10 minutes, until golden brown and sealed all over. Pour brandy over the chicken, remove the pan from the heat and flame it by igniting the liquid in the saucepan with a match. Remove the chicken when the flames have died down and place it in a casserole. Stir the flour into the fat remaining in the pan and cook for 2 to 3 minutes. Stir in the wine and broth gradually, bring to a boil, and continue to stir until the mixture thickens; add sugar, herbs, and seasonings. Add the browned vegetables to the casserole and pour the sauce over the chicken. Cover and cook in a 350° oven for 45 minutes to 1 hour, until tender. Before serving, remove the bouquet garni.

ARROZ CON POLLO (CHICKEN WITH RICE)

¼ cup vegetable oil
3½ lb chicken parts
salt and pepper
2 onions, sliced
1 clove garlic, minced
1 can (16 oz) tomatoes with juice
¼ teaspoon saffron
2 cups boiling chicken broth
1 cup rice
1 package (10 oz) frozen peas, thawed
2 canned pimientos, slivered

Heat the oil in a skillet, season the chicken parts with salt and pepper and brown. Remove to a casserole. Add the onions and garlic to the skillet and cook until tender; add to the casserole with the tomatoes and saffron. Pour the chicken broth into the casserole and stir in the rice. Cover and bake in a 350° oven for 25 minutes. Add the peas and pimientos, re-cover and bake 10 minutes longer.

CHICKEN LIVER

The livers are usually served as a separate dish, frequently as a luncheon entrée. They are also used to make simple pâtés.

CHICKEN LIVER PILAF

$\frac{1}{2}$ lb chicken livers, cut in strips
4 tablespoons butter
2 onions, finely chopped
2 tablespoons shelled peanuts or almonds
1 cup long-grain rice
salt
pepper
$\frac{1}{4}$ cup currants
2 tomatoes, peeled and chopped
2 cups chicken broth, boiling
little chopped parsley

Sauté the livers lightly in the butter for 2 to 3 minutes and remove them from the fat with a slotted spoon. Sauté the onions for 5 minutes in the same fat until soft but not brown. Add the nuts and rice and sauté for a further 5 minutes, stirring all the time. Add the seasoning, currants, tomatoes, and broth; stir well, cover with a tightly fitting lid and simmer for about 20 minutes until all the liquid has been absorbed. Stir in the livers and parsley, cover again and, before serving, leave for 15 minutes in a warm place.

CHICKEN LIVERS ON TOAST

$\frac{1}{4}$ lb chicken livers
seasoned flour
butter for sautéing
4 rounds of bread about 2 inches in diameter
$\frac{1}{4}$ cup sherry or Madeira
$\frac{2}{3}$ cup sliced mushrooms, optional

Wash and dry the livers, cut them in small pieces and coat with the seasoned flour. Melt some butter in a skillet and sauté the bread rounds for 2 to 3 minutes, until golden; remove them from the pan. Add more butter, put in the prepared livers and stir them over the heat until browned. Add the sherry or Madeira, mix well and cook slowly for 5 minutes. Serve the livers on the rounds of bread. If the mushrooms are used, cook them with the livers.

CHICKPEA (GARBANZO)

A bean of such antiquity that it flourished in the Hanging Gardens of Babylon. Easy to grow, inexpensive, and highly nutritious, the chickpea is a staple in the world's poorer countries. The beans have been popular in the Mediterranean since the time of the early Greeks, were exported by the Romans (Italians know them as *ceci*) and were carried from Spain to Latin America as the garbanzo. They are known in the United States variously as chickpea and garbanzo.

CHICKPEAS WITH SAUSAGES

$\frac{1}{4}$ cup olive oil
1 onion, chopped
2 cloves garlic, minced
4 chorizo sausages, chopped
1 can (16 oz) garbanzos, drained and rinsed
1 bottle (4 oz) pimientos, cut into strips
salt
pepper

Heat the oil in a skillet and sauté the onion, garlic and sausages until the onion is wilted. Add the remaining ingredients and heat through.

CHICORY

Chicory (*Cichorium intybus*) has curly leaves and bright blue flowers. It is quite bitter, so must often be mixed with other salad greens. The large roots of chicory are roasted, ground, and blended with coffee, to which a bitter flavor is imparted.

Witloof chicory (also known as Belgian endive) has fleshy, tender leaves. It may be eaten raw in salads or braised and served with butter.

There is some confusion between the use of the names chicory and endive in the United States, with chicory being miscalled endive and endive sometimes called escarole or chicory.

CHILDREN'S MEALS

The feeding of children has to cover several periods of transition, stretching from infancy to adolescence, but the emphasis throughout must lie on giving an ample supply of protein and the protective foods – that is, milk, meat, fish, eggs, cheese, fruit and vegetables, bread and butter.

Infants

During the first few months a baby has milk only. Breast feeding is now considered the best way to feed the baby during this early and important stage of development. It insures that the baby is receiving the correct quantity of each nutrient and provides the right conditions for the digestive system to give maximum protection against infection. Antibodies from the mother are passed to the baby through the milk. Breast milk is made up of similar constituents to cow's milk but contains less protein and more sugar. Vitamin drops may be given as a supplement from the age of 4 weeks until mixed feeding starts.

If, for any reason, it is not possible to breast feed, or there is a strong reaction against it, modified cows' milk preparations provide an excellent alternative. These are modified to reduce protein content and make them as near to breast milk as possible. They are also fortified with vitamins, making vitamin supplements unnecessary. When bottle feeding it is important to insure that the bottles and nipples are carefully sterilized.

3 to 4 months: Additions may be made to the diet such as cereal, pureed vegetables, or fruits.

5 months: Strained meat, fish, and lightly cooked eggs can be introduced into the diet. Rusks, toast, raw apple, and carrot pieces can be given at this stage to help the baby with teething problems and to teach the process of chewing.

6 to 8 months: Most foods can be given if made to a soft manageable consistency. It is important to give the baby plenty of finger foods to encourage self feeding and chewing.

New foods should be introduced gradually so that by 1 year the baby will be enjoying a mixed diet similar to that of an adult with the exclusion of rich, spicy, or greasy foods.

The Older Child

Children vary enormously in the amount of food they need. There is no need to worry if one child eats less than another as long as he or she is healthy.

Provide three good meals a day and a mid-morning drink. The meals should be based on the protein foods, vegetables, and sometimes fruit. Bread and potatoes should be used as fillers, as they supply protein, vitamins, and minerals as well as energy. Iron to maintain healthy condition of the blood, and calcium for the development of the teeth and bones are two important minerals. Adolescent girls should have food rich in iron to minimize the risk of anemia.

It is a mistake to allow children to eat too many of the less nutritious foods. Obesity in children must be avoided as this can lead to trouble in later life, such as high blood pressure and varicose veins.

CHILI

The small red pod of a type of Capsicum, used widely in Mexico and the southwest of the United States. It may be used raw, dried, or dried and ground into a powder. Chilis are very hot in flavor and are used in pickles, sauces, chutneys, and for flavoring vinegar. Chili powder is ground from chilis.

CHILI CON CARNE

1½ lb ground beef
1 tablespoon vegetable oil
1 large onion, chopped
1 green pepper, seeded and chopped
1 (16 oz) can tomatoes
salt
pepper
1 tablespoon chili powder
1 tablespoon cider vinegar
1 teaspoon sugar
2 tablespoons tomato puree
1 (16 oz) can kidney beans

Sauté the beef in the oil until lightly browned, then add the onion and pepper and sauté for 5 minutes, until soft. Stir in the tomatoes, add the seasoning and chili powder blended with the vinegar, sugar, and tomato puree. Cover and simmer for 2 to 2½ hours. Add the drained kidney beans 10 minutes before the cooking time is completed.

CHINE

The spine or backbone of an animal, or a cut of meat consisting of part of the backbone of an animal and some of the surrounding flesh. It is an uneconomical cut, owing to the quantity of bone, and is difficult to carve. The chine is often severed from the rib bones by sawing through the ribs close to the spine. Cuts such as loin of lamb, mutton, veal, or pork are best chined, instead of merely being chopped through the backbone, as this makes them easier to carve into convenient-sized chops or cutlets.

CHINESE CABBAGE (CELERY CABBAGE)

This type of cabbage looks like a very long cos lettuce. It may be eaten raw or cooked.

CHINESE PARSLEY

(See Coriander entry.)

CHIPOLATA

A very small sausage, made of ordinary sausagemeat filled into a narrow casing. Chipolatas are used to garnish meat dishes and to serve with roast fowl; they are also served on sticks as cocktail food. They may be baked, fried, broiled, or grilled.

CHITTERLINGS

These are the intestines of beef, calf, and pig; the latter being probably the most popular. They are not much eaten today except in country districts, but are used in manufactured meat products. The chitterlings are cleaned and usually boiled before being sold and if fresh will be free of any unpleasant smell. If the chitterlings have not been boiled, wash them very thoroughly and simmer gently for 2 to 3 hours, until tender.

CHIVE

A very small variety of onion; the slender hollow needle-like leaves have a delicate onion flavor. Minced or chopped, chives are excellent for flavoring salads, omelets, sauces, vegetables, and as a garnish for cold entrées and for soups. Use very fresh.

CHOCOLATE

A product of the cocoa bean (see Cacao entry), the three parts of which (nibs, germ, and shells) are separated from each other and treated in various ways to give different products.

Types of Chocolate

COCOA
Cocoa nibs and sugar ground together and mixed with flavorings. Cocoa was manufactured in Great Britain as long ago as 1728, over a century before the introduction of eating chocolate.

EATING CHOCOLATE
This is produced by adding sugar and cocoa butter to slab chocolate. The extra cocoa butter is needed to increase the fat content to approximately 32 percent. Without this, chocolate does not mold satisfactorily. Flavorings such as vanilla, almond, cinnamon, cloves, and cardamom are added in varying proportions.

Semisweet chocolate has some sugar added.

Bitter or unsweetened chocolate is mostly used commercially although a bitter dessert chocolate can be bought. Milk chocolate is sweetened, and powdered or condensed milk is also added.

Chocolate making is a highly skilled process, the quality and price varying according to manufacture.

Chocolate is useful nutritionally as a concentrated form of energy. It is thus of value (e.g., for expeditions) as a compact energy food, easy to carry and to eat.

COUVERTURE CHOCOLATE
A special type of good quality eating chocolate used for coating candies. It is made from selected cocoa beans, mixed with the finest sugar and cocoa butter; the exact proportions depend on the purpose for which the couverture is required and the type of center to be covered. Couverture chocolate retains a high gloss after melting and cooling and is very smooth to eat. A type of couverture can be bought for home use, for cooking and glazing purposes, but it is not of the same high quality as that supplied to candy manufacturers.

Use of Chocolate in Cooking
Many so-called chocolate dishes are actually made with cocoa. However, slab cooking chocolate is used for certain things, especially frostings, cold sweet dishes, and homemade candies; if necessary, it may be replaced by semisweet eating chocolate.

Cocoa, when used in a cake, etc., is usually sifted with the dry ingredients. Cooking chocolate is grated and melted down before being added to other ingredients. Eating chocolate may be grated or flaked and used as a decoration to cold desserts, but is not normally melted down.

CHOCOLATE MOUSSE

6 oz semisweet chocolate
3 eggs, separated
1 tablespoon rum
⅔ cup whipping cream, whipped
grated milk chocolate or finely chopped nuts

Melt the semisweet chocolate in a bowl over a pan of hot water. Beat the yolks into the melted chocolate and add the rum. Beat the whites until stiff and carefully fold into the chocolate mixture. Chill and serve, topped with whipped cream and grated chocolate or chopped nuts.

CHOCOLATE CAKE

¾ cup all-purpose flour
2 tablespoons ground rice
4 oz semisweet chocolate, grated
½ cup butter or margarine
¾ cup sugar
1–2 teaspoons vanilla
2 eggs beaten
chocolate fudge frosting (see following entry)
chocolate glaze (see Glaze entry)

Grease and line a 6-inch cake pan. Mix the flour and ground rice. Put the grated chocolate into a small bowl, place over a saucepan of hot water, and heat gently to melt the chocolate. Cream the fat, sugar, and vanilla until pale and fluffy. Add the melted chocolate (which should be only just warm) to the creamed mixture and mix lightly together. Beat in the egg a little at a time. Fold in the flour. Pour the batter into the pan and bake in a 180° oven for 1 to 1¼ hours. When cold, split in half and fill with chocolate fudge frosting. Glaze the top of the cake, allowing the glaze to run down the sides. Alternatively, fill and decorate with classic butter cream frosting (see Frosting entry) and coarsely grated milk chocolate.

CHOCOLATE FUDGE FROSTING

4 oz semisweet chocolate
¼ cup butter
1 egg, beaten
1⅓ cups powdered sugar, sifted

Break up the chocolate and put in a heatproof bowl with the butter. Place the bowl over a saucepan of hot but not boiling water and melt the chocolate, stirring occasionally. Stir in the egg, then remove from the saucepan. Add the powdered sugar and beat with a wooden spoon until the frosting is smooth.

Use the frosting to fill and cover cakes, swirling the top and sides with a spatula. Set for several hours, then decorate as desired.

For a smooth coating icing, use only 1 cup powdered sugar and pour over the cake.
Sufficient to fill and frost an 8-inch cake.

CHOCOLATE SAUCE

1 tablespoon cornstarch
1 tablespoon cocoa
2 tablespoons sugar
1¼ cups milk
lump of butter

Blend the cornstarch, cocoa, and sugar with enough of the measured milk to give a thin cream. Heat the remaining milk with the butter until boiling and pour onto the blended mixture, stirring all the time to prevent lumps forming. Return the mixture to the pan and bring to a boil, stirring until it thickens; cook for a further 1 to 2 minutes.

RICH CHOCOLATE SAUCE

6 oz semisweet chocolate, chopped
large lump of butter
¼ cup milk

¼ cup corn syrup
1 tablespoon strong coffee

Put the chopped chocolate in a bowl over a pan of hot water. Add the rest of the ingredients and heat gently until melted and warm. Beat well.

BLACK BOTTOM PIE

1 cup sugar
¼ cup cornstarch
2 cups milk, scalded
3 eggs, separated
1 package (6 oz) chocolate chips
2½ teaspoons vanilla
1 9-inch baked pie shell
1 envelope unflavored gelatin
¼ cup cold water
¼ teaspoon cream of tartar
½ cup heavy cream, whipped

Combine ½ cup of the sugar and the cornstarch in a saucepan and gradually stir in the milk. Spoon a couple of tablespoons of the hot milk mixture into the egg yolks, then return to the pan. Cook over moderate heat, stirring, until the mixture thickens. Remove 1 cup of the hot mixture to a small bowl and stir in the chocolate chips until melted. Stir in 1 teaspoon of the vanilla and pour the mixture into the pie shell.

Soften the gelatin in the water. Add the remaining hot milk mixture and stir until the gelatin dissolves. Stir in the remaining 1½ teaspoons vanilla. Cool, then cover the surface with plastic wrap to prevent a skin from forming.

Combine the egg whites and cream of tartar and beat until frothy. Gradually add the remaining ½ cup sugar and beat until stiff peaks form. Fold into the cooled gelatin mixture, then fold in the whipped cream. Pour on top of the chocolate layer in the pie and refrigerate until set, about 2 hours.

CHOCOLATES

For chocolate-dipping, special couverture chocolate is required; even with this it is not possible for the amateur to attain results like those produced by the commercial firms. However, some very delicious candies can be produced at home, using toffee, fudge, marzipan, fondant, nuts, and dried fruit etc., for the centers.

CHOP

A cut of meat 1 to 1½ inches thick, usually lamb, pork, or veal, containing a piece of bone, generally cut from the shoulder, ribs, or loin.

To pan broil chops: When the meat is really tender, this is a very satisfactory method. Cook slowly in a little fat, turning frequently, until they are well cooked (10 to 15 minutes). Alternatively, the chops may be egg-and-bread-crumbed, then cooked. Pork chops should be allowed at least 20 minutes.

To broil chops: Remove the skin and trim off some of the fat from the chops, wipe them with a damp cloth, then brush over with salad oil or butter. Heat the broiling pan and place the chops in position under a preheated broiler. Cook on one side for about 2 to 3 minutes, until the outside is browned, then turn and cook on the other side. Continue to cook, turning frequently, until the meat is just cooked through, 8 to 10 minutes. Use tongs or two spoons for turning, to prevent piercing the meat. Place the chops on a hot dish and garnish lamb chops with broiled tomatoes, mushrooms, or green pepper rings; for pork chops use broiled apple or pineapple rings. Serve with vegetables and accompanied by a well-flavored sauce or gravy.

CHOPPING

To divide food into very small pieces. The ingredient is placed on a chopping board and a very sharp knife is used with a quick up-and-down action.

CHOP SUEY

The name literally means bits and pieces. The dish is the Chinese way of dealing with leftovers in a type of stew; it originated in the United States.

Chop Suey can be made up of thin strips of raw chicken, pork, or beef, cooked with onions in a little oil, with bean sprouts, mushrooms, and other vegetables; chicken broth, soy sauce, sugar, and salt are added to taste and the whole is thickened, if necessary, with cornstarch. It is usually served with rice or noodles.

CHORIZO

A Spanish hot sausage. It is imported into the United States but is also made locally and can be found in Hispanic markets.

CHICKPEA SALAD WITH CHORIZOS

1 can (16 oz) chickpeas, rinsed and drained
¼ lb chorizos, thinly sliced
¼ lb Monterey jack cheese, diced

1 sweet red pepper, chopped
¼ cup chopped parsley
salt and pepper
3 tablespoons olive oil
1 tablespoon wine vinegar

Combine the chickpeas, chorizos, cheese, red pepper, and parsley in a bowl. Toss with salt, pepper, olive oil, and vinegar. Serve at room temperature.

CHOUCROUTE

(See Sauerkraut entry.)

CHOUX PASTRY

A dough prepared by beating eggs into a thick panada of flour, shortening, and liquid. The eggs cause the pastry to swell in cooking. It is used chiefly for éclairs and cream puffs, rich fancy cakes, and entrée or sweet fritters. For basic recipe, see Pastry entry. (See also Cream Puff, Éclair, and Profiterole entries.)

CHOW-CHOW

A Chinese preserve of ginger and orange peel and other fruits in syrup. Also a mixed vegetable pickle, containing mustard and spices.

CHOWDER

A type of dish which originated in France, but is now associated with New England and Newfoundland. It is a thick soup or stew made of shellfish (especially clams) or other fish, with pork or bacon.

FISH CHOWDER

1 onion, sliced
2 slices of bacon, chopped
1 tablespoon butter
3 potatoes, peeled and sliced
1 lb fresh haddock fillet, skinned and cubed
1 (16 oz) can tomatoes
2½ cups fish stock
salt and pepper
1 bay leaf
2 cloves
chopped parsley to garnish

Lightly sauté the onion and bacon in the butter for about 5 minutes, until soft, but not colored. Add the potatoes and the fish. Strain the tomatoes with their juice, add them to the fish stock, combine with the fish mixture and add seasoning and flavorings. Cover and simmer for 30 minutes, until all the fish is soft but still in shape. Remove the bay leaf and cloves and sprinkle with parsley before serving.

CHOW MEIN

A Chinese dish of meat or poultry stir-fried with vegetables (usually bean sprouts, celery, and Chinese cabbage) and served over fried noodles. The dish is so popular in the United States that many mistakenly believe it is of American origin.

CHUB

A freshwater fish resembling carp, rather tasteless in flavor, which when fully grown may weigh 4 to 8 lb. It is seldom used in cookery.

CHUCK

(See Shoulder entry.)

CHUKAR

(See Partridge entry.)

CHUPATTY

(See Chapatti entry.)

CHUTNEY

A pickle or relish of Indian origin. Chutneys vary in type, but are usually composed of fruits (especially mangoes), vegetables, spices, acids, and sugar. Tomatoes, apples, gooseberries, raisins, plums, and zucchini are frequently used for homemade chutneys.

Chutney is served with cold meat, cheese, etc., and with curry and is sometimes mixed with butter to make an accompaniment to fish, etc., or a sandwich filling.

A good chutney should be smooth to the palate, with a mellow flavor. The amount of salt and other seasonings can, of course, be adjusted as required to suit individual tastes. Three points to remember are:
1. Slice or mince the ingredients finely.
2. Allow long, slow cooking. This softens the fruit and blends the flavors. Cooking should be continued until the chutney is of a jamlike consistency.
3. Put into hot jars and use the correct type of covers (see Pickle entry).

APPLE CHUTNEY

3 lb cooking apples, peeled and diced
3 lb onions, chopped
1 lb golden seedless raisins
2 lemons
4½ cups brown sugar
1¼ cups malt vinegar

This is a light chutney, fruity but not spiced, which is good with pork and poultry. Put the apples, onions, and raisins in a pan. Grate the lemon rind, strain the juice and add both to the pan, with the sugar and vinegar. Bring to a boil, reduce the heat and simmer until the mixture is of a thick consistency, with no excess liquid. Jar and cover. *Makes about 4 lb.*

GREEN TOMATO CHUTNEY

1 lb apples, peeled
½ lb onions
3 lb green tomatoes, sliced thinly
8 oz golden seedless raisins
1½ cups brown sugar
2 teaspoons salt
2 cups malt vinegar
4 small pieces dried whole gingerroot
½ teaspoon cayenne pepper
1 teaspoon dry mustard

This is a lightly spiced, smooth-textured chutney. Mince the apples and onions and put in a pan with the rest of the ingredients. Bring to a boil, reduce the heat and simmer until the ingredients are tender and reduced to a thick consistency, with no excess liquid. Remove the ginger, jar and cover. *Makes about 3 lb.*

PEAR CHUTNEY

3 lb pears, peeled and sliced
1 lb onions, chopped
1 lb green tomatoes, sliced
8 oz seedless raisins, chopped
1 cup finely chopped celery
4½ cups brown sugar
pinch of cayenne pepper
pinch of ground ginger
2 teaspoons salt
5 peppercorns, in a cheesecloth bag
1 quart malt vinegar

This is a very dark, smooth, sweet and spicy chutney that is slightly hot. Put all the fruit and vegetable ingredients into a pan, with no added liquid, and simmer gently until tender. Add the remaining ingredients and simmer until of a thick consistency, with no excess liquid. Remove the bag of peppercorns, jar and cover. *Makes about 4 lb.*

ZUCCHINI CHUTNEY

3 lb large zucchini, peeled and seeded
salt
8 oz shallots, sliced
8 oz apples, peeled and sliced
12 peppercorns
$\frac{3}{4}$-inch piece dried whole gingerroot
8 oz golden seedless raisins
1$\frac{1}{2}$ cups brown sugar
1 quart malt vinegar

Cut the zucchini into small pieces, place in a bowl and sprinkle liberally with salt; cover and leave for 12 hours. Rinse and drain, then place in a pan with the shallots and apples. Tie the peppercorns and ginger in cheesecloth and put in the pan with the raisins, sugar, and vinegar. Bring to a boil, reduce the heat and simmer till the consistency is thick, with no excess liquid. Jar and cover. *Makes about 4 lb.*

MAJOR MARSHALL'S CHUTNEY

1$\frac{1}{2}$ lb plums
1$\frac{1}{2}$ tablespoons pickling spice
2 cloves garlic, crushed
2 medium onions, sliced
2 lb tomatoes, peeled and sliced
1 quart malt vinegar
2 lb cooking apples, peeled and chopped
8 oz dried apricots, chopped
1 cup corn syrup
1$\frac{1}{2}$ cups brown sugar
4 teaspoons salt

Wipe the plums, halve, and discard the pits. Tie the pickling spice in a cheesecloth bag. Put the plums and all the other ingredients in a large pan, bring to a boil, reduce the heat and simmer uncovered until the ingredients are soft and well reduced. Remove the cheesecloth bag. Jar and cover. *Makes about 5 lb.*

RHUBARB AND ORANGE CHUTNEY

2 oranges
4–5 cups chopped rhubarb
3 onions, chopped
1 quart malt vinegar
6 cups brown sugar
1 lb seedless raisins

1 tablespoon mustard seed
1 tablespoon peppercorns
1 teaspoon allspice

Squeeze the juice from the oranges and finely shred the peel. Place in a large pot with the rhubarb, onions, vinegar, sugar, and raisins. Tie the spices in a piece of cheesecloth and add to the ingredients in the pan. Bring to a boil and simmer until thick and pulpy, about 1$\frac{1}{2}$ hours. Remove the cheesecloth bag, jar and cover. *Makes about 8 lb.*

CIDER

A bright, honey-colored liquid, the unfermented or fermented juice of the apple. Commercially manufactured cider is made by crushing special cider apples and squeezing out the juice; if not pasteurized, fixed with additives or frozen, the cider will ferment.

APPLE CIDER CUP

2 sweet apples
juice and thinly peeled rind of 1 lemon
8 cloves
4 tablespoons sugar syrup
5 cups dry cider
2 cups soda water

Peel and slice the apples and put into a bowl with the lemon juice and rind and the cloves. Heat the sugar syrup with about 1 cup of the cider; when boiling, pour over the ingredients in the bowl and leave to cool. When cold, add the rest of the cider and the soda water.

HOT SPICED CIDER

1 quart cider
$\frac{1}{2}$ cup sugar
12 whole cloves
4 sticks cinnamon about 2 inches long
8 whole allspice

Put the ingredients in a saucepan and heat until the sugar has dissolved. Strain to serve.

CILANTRO

(See Coriander entry.)

CINNAMON

The bark of a tropical tree of the laurel family, used for flavoring sweet dishes, cakes, fruit, sweet pickles, and mulled wine. The finest quality is a pale yellowish-buff color and has an aromatic flavor; it is sold as stick, broken, and ground cinnamon. It should not be confused with cassia, which although similar, is inferior in flavor.

CIOPPINO

A fish stew that originated in California among Italian fishermen. It is said that the wives of the men awaited their return on the beaches, brewing pots of bubbling sauce. When the fishers returned, part of the catch was tossed into the pot and dinner was ready. Six is the minimum number that this dish should be prepared for.

CIOPPINO

$\frac{1}{2}$ cup olive oil
1 large onion, chopped
2 cloves garlic, chopped
1 green pepper, chopped
4 ripe tomatoes, peeled and chopped
$\frac{1}{2}$ cup tomato puree
2 cups red wine
$\frac{1}{2}$ cup chopped parsley
salt and pepper
1 lb fish fillets
1 lobster
1 lb shrimp
1 quart clams or mussels

Heat the olive oil in a saucepan and add the onion. Cook until soft. Add the garlic and green pepper and cook until the pepper is wilted. Add the tomatoes, tomato puree, wine, parsley, salt and pepper and simmer for 15 minutes.

Meanwhile, cut the fish into 2-inch chunks. Split the lobster and cut into pieces. Scrub the clams, and shell the shrimp. Place the fish and lobster in a casserole. Pour the sauce over them and simmer for 10 minutes. Add the shrimp and clams and simmer until the clams open and the shrimp turn pink. Serve the sauce and seafood together in large soup plates.

CITRIC ACID

An acid obtained from citrus fruits, particularly lemons. The crystals are clear and colorless, with a pleasant, rather sour taste.

Commercially prepared citric acid is used to give a lemon flavor to drinks, fruit dishes, homemade wines, etc.; it is also used to insure a good set in jams and jellies, especially with fruits such as pears and strawberries that have a low acid content.

CITRON

A fruit which resembles the lemon, but is rather longer and larger. The rind is used in crystalized form in cookery, being chopped and added to cakes, puddings, and cookies: a slice of citron peel is the traditional decoration on Madeira cake. The peel is usually bought ready prepared, but it can be made quite successfully at home.

CLAM

A bivalvular shellfish. There are many varieties, varying in size and shape, and nearly all are edible. The commonest forms are those caught on the Atlantic coasts of North America – the hard- and soft-shelled clams. Clams of the Pacific coast include the giant geoduck and the long razor clam. In the United States they are eaten in various ways, especially in chowder and on the half shell.

WHITE CLAM SAUCE

24 hard-shell clams
$\frac{1}{2}$ cup white wine
2 tablespoons olive oil
1 clove garlic, chopped
$\frac{1}{2}$ lb spaghetti, cooked
1 tablespoon butter
2 tablespoons chopped parsley

Put the clams in a pot with the wine and steam just until the clams open. Remove the clams from the shells and chop. Reserve the cooking liquid.

Heat the oil in a skillet and cook the garlic for about 1 minute. Add the clam broth and reduce by about one-half. Add the clams and cook 1 to 2 minutes; do not overcook or the clams will become tough.

Turn the hot spaghetti into a serving bowl and toss with the butter. Add the clams and their cooking liquid and sprinkle with parsley. Toss and serve.

NEW ENGLAND CLAM CHOWDER

2 dozen medium hard-shell clams
$\frac{1}{8}$ lb salt pork, diced
2 potatoes, peeled and diced
1 onion, chopped
2 cups milk, scalded, with $\frac{1}{2}$ cup cream
salt
pepper
$1\frac{1}{2}$ teaspoons butter

Scrub the clams well and shuck, or place in a

heavy-bottomed pan and steam open. Chop finely, reserving the liquor.

Sauté the salt pork in a heavy saucepan until golden. Remove the pieces with a slotted spoon and add the potatoes and onion. Cook for a minute or two, then add the reserved clam liquor and just enough hot water to be seen through the potatoes. Cover and simmer until the potatoes are done. Add the clams and bring to a boil. Remove from the heat and add the scalded milk and cream and season with salt and pepper. Heat just to a boil, add the butter and serve.

Note: 2 cans (8 oz each) clams may be substituted for the fresh clams.

MANHATTAN CLAM CHOWDER

2 dozen medium hard-shell clams
⅛ lb salt pork
2 potatoes, peeled and diced
1 onion, chopped
⅓ cup chopped celery
1 cup water
1 can (16 oz) tomatoes, with the liquid
¼ teaspoon dried thyme leaves
salt
pepper
chopped parsley

Prepare as for New England Clam Chowder (above), adding the celery with the potatoes and onion. Add the clam liquor and the 1 cup water and simmer, covered, until the potatoes are done. Add the clams, tomatoes, thyme, and salt and pepper and bring to a boil. Garnish with chopped parsley and serve.

Note: 2 cans (8 oz each) clams may be substituted for the fresh clams.

CLAM BAKE

New England method for cooking seafood and corn in seaweed, learned by the Pilgrims from the Indians of the region. Today many large coastal New England celebrations during summertime center on a clam bake which, despite its name, would be a sorry affair without the addition of lobsters.

A pit dug in the sand is lined with redhot stones over which is placed rockweed. The pit is then filled with succeeding layers of food and rockweed, the whole covered with a tarpaulin and steamed until done. Besides corn and seafood, traditional foods include chicken and sausages, sweet potatoes, white potatoes, and onions. A clam bake may also be prepared in any

large receptacle, such as a washboiler, with good results. Indispensable to the flavor and outcome, however, is the rockweed.

CLARET

In England the name given to the red wine from the Bordeaux district of France. The term may also be used for other red wines, but in this case the country of origin should be given, e.g., Australian Claret. (See Bordeaux Wines entry.)

CLARET CUP

⅔ cup sugar syrup
juice and thinly peeled rind of 1 lemon and 2 oranges
2 bottles claret (Bordeaux red wine)
2 bottles (10 oz each) tonic water
few thin slices of cucumber
sprigs of borage, if available

Put the syrup and the lemon and orange rind in a saucepan and simmer together for about 10 minutes. Cool and add the strained juice of the lemon and oranges, together with the claret; chill. Just before serving, add the tonic water, cucumber, and borage (if used).

CLARIFYING

To clear or purify. The term is used mainly to denote the freeing of fat from water, meat juices, salt, etc., so that it may be used for sautéing, pastrymaking and so on. The process of clearing consommés is also called clarifying. (See Consommé entry.)

CLEMENTINE

(See Tangerine entry.)

CLOVE

The dried unopened flowerbud of an evergreen shrub that grows in the Moluccas and in other countries with a similar hot, moist climate. When freshly gathered, the flower buds are reddish, but they become dark brown – almost black – when dried. Cloves contain 16 to 20 percent of a volatile oil, which is of medicinal value and has a characteristic hot, spicy, aromatic taste and smell. Whole cloves are used in cookery for flavoring and their flavor blends particularly well with that of apples. Ground cloves are used in some cakes and cookies. For some purposes the flavor of the cloves is obtained by infusion.

COBBLER

A sweetened cooling drink, usually made of a mixture of fruit and wine or liqueur, with ice. The name also applies to fruit dishes which have a topping of biscuit dough.

SHERRY COBBLER

ice
⅔ cup sherry
1 teaspoon sugar
2 teaspoons orange juice
orange sections and a few strawberries

Put a few pieces of ice in a tumbler, add the sherry, sugar, and orange juice and stir well. Put the fruit on top as decoration and serve with a drinking straw.

BLUEBERRY COBBLER

⅓ cup sugar
1 tablespoon cornstarch
1 quart blueberries
1 tablespoon lemon juice
1 cup all-purpose flour
1 tablespoon sugar
1½ teaspoons baking powder
¼ teaspoon salt
3 tablespoons butter
½ cup milk

Combine ⅓ cup sugar and the cornstarch in a saucepan and stir in the blueberries and lemon juice. Bring to a boil, stirring constantly, and boil 1 minute; the mixture should be thickened. Pour into an ungreased baking dish, and keep hot in a 400° oven.

Combine the flour, 1 tablespoon sugar, baking powder and salt and cut in the butter until the mixture resembles bread crumbs. Stir in the milk and drop the dough by tablespoonfuls onto the hot blueberry mixture. Bake for 25 to 30 minutes, until the biscuits are cooked and golden brown. Serve warm, with whipped cream or ice cream if desired.

COBNUT

A type of hazelnut. (See Hazelnut entry.)

COCHINEAL

A red coloring matter obtained from a small beetle, originating in Mexico, which is dried and ground. Cochineal is used to give various shades of pink and red to candies, cakes, buns, cookies, cold desserts, and so on, and also to improve the color of jams and canned fruits.

COCK-A-LEEKIE

A popular Scottish soup made from a fowl boiled with leeks.

COCK-A-LEEKIE SOUP

1 boiling fowl
2 lb lamb neck or knuckle of veal
3½ quarts cold water
salt
pepper
2 cloves
4 leeks
2 tablespoons rice

Wash the fowl well and put it with the meat into a saucepan, then add the water and seasonings. When boiling, add the cut-up leeks and simmer for 1¼ hours. Wash the rice, sprinkle it into the soup, add additional seasoning if necessary and continue to simmer for 45 minutes. The chicken and meat can be served separately, with a parsley sauce made with a little of the broth, or with the soup.

COCKLE

A small bivalvular shellfish found in large numbers around the coasts of the North Atlantic.

Cockles must be washed to free them of sand, then soaked in slightly salted water for an hour or two. To cook, put them in a pan with about 2 tablespoons water at the bottom, cover with a clean cloth and heat gently, shaking the pan to prevent burning. As soon as the shells open (after about 5 minutes) they are done. Serve very hot on a napkin, with bread and butter, or use instead of mussels or oysters in fish sauces and similar recipes.

COCKTAIL

A short alcoholic drink, consisting of a variety of ingredients so well blended together (by stirring or shaking in a cocktail shaker, usually with cracked ice) that no one flavor predominates.

Cocktails, which are offered before lunch or dinner, are served in a small glass and are often decorated with a stuffed olive, a curl of lemon peel, or a Maraschino cherry; they should be served very cold.

Cocktails are rather less popular than formerly, the current fashion being for the simpler

drinks such as dry vermouth, Dubonnet, gin and tonic or whisky and water.

Making Cocktails

Follow the recipe carefully. The total quantities can of course be increased at will, but any variation in the proportions will change the flavor of the drink. It is not normally necessary to follow any particular order in adding ingredients for cocktails, as they are mixed well before being poured into the glasses.

Recipes for a few of the best-known cocktails appear below. In some cases there is more than one accepted recipe and the version you use is a matter of individual taste.

DRY MARTINI

3 parts gin
1 part French vermouth
lemon rind
cracked ice

Stir gently; do not shake.

PINK GIN

Use gin with a dash of Angostura bitters, diluted with iced water. Stir; do not shake.

DAIQUIRI

sugar for glass
2 parts Bacardi rum
1 part fresh lime juice

Dip dampened edge of glass in sugar. Shake rum and lime juice well together and serve in the glass.

BRANDY COCKTAIL

1 glass brandy
2 dashes of Curaçao
crushed ice
lemon rind curl

Shake the brandy and Curaçao with some crushed ice, pour into a glass and serve with a curl of lemon rind.

SIDECAR

2 parts brandy
1 part Cointreau
juice of ¼ lemon for each cocktail

Shake well with cracked ice and strain into cocktail glasses.

HARVEY WALLBANGER

1 part vodka
1 part Galliano
orange juice
orange slice and cherry

Shake vodka and Galliano together, pour into a glass and top up with orange juice. Serve with an orange slice and cherry.

MANHATTAN

2 parts (rye) whisky
1 part French vermouth
dash of Angostura bitters
dash of Curaçao
cracked ice

Decorate with Maraschino cherries

CHAMPAGNE COCKTAIL

4 dashes Angostura bitters
1 small lump sugar
lemon
1 glass champagne

Pour the bitters over the sugar and put into a glass. Add the strained juice of ¼ lemon and fill up with chilled champagne.

COCKTAIL (APPETIZER)

Various kinds of nonalcoholic appetizers served at the beginning of a meal are called cocktails. The best known are made of fish, fruit and fruit juices, and vegetable juices; here are some representative recipes.

FISH COCKTAIL

4–6 oz peeled shrimp or flaked crab or lobster meat
½ head lettuce, washed and shredded
2 tablespoons mayonnaise
2 tablespoons tomato catsup
2 tablespoons light cream
salt and pepper
squeeze of lemon juice or a dash of Worcestershire sauce
cucumber slices, capers, or lemon wedges to garnish

Use either fresh or frozen shrimp; crabmeat may be either fresh or canned – if fresh, use only the white meat; lobster may be either fresh or canned. Line some small glasses with shredded lettuce. Mix the remaining ingredients to make a dressing. Combine the fish and dressing, pile into the glasses and garnish.

TOMATO JUICE COCKTAIL

⅔ cup tomato juice
1 tablespoon lemon juice
¼ teaspoon salt
1 teaspoon sugar
1 small onion, finely sliced
1 bay leaf
1 piece of celery
2 teaspoons chopped parsley
1 teaspoon Worcestershire sauce
2 teaspoons grated horseradish

Combine all the ingredients and chill for several hours. Strain and serve in a glass.

COCOA

(See Cacao entry.)

COCONUT

The fruit of the coconut palm, growing in most tropical climates, though linked mostly with the Pacific Islands. When fully grown, a tree yields upward of 100 coconuts a year. The fresh nut contains a thick jelly and a clear liquid called coconut juice, both of which are delicious. The juice is sometimes fermented to make palm wine.

The flesh is dried (when it is known as copra) and exported to many countries; the coconut oil is expressed from the copra and used in the manufacture of margarine and soap. Shredded coconut is used in cakes, cookies, desserts, and candies.

COCONUT KISSES

2 egg whites
½ cup sugar
1½ cup shredded coconut

Grease a baking sheet and cover with brown paper. Beat the egg whites stiffly and fold in the sugar and coconut, using a metal spoon. Pile in small pyramids on the baking sheet and bake in a 275° oven until pale fawn – about 45 minutes to 1 hour. If desired the mixture can be tinted pink or green.

COCONUT MILK

This is made from the flesh of the coconut and is not to be confused with the coconut juice, the thin liquid found inside a ripe coconut. Coconut milk is very widely used throughout the Orient and in the Pacific islands; it is added to curries, fish and vegetables are cooked in it and it is served (sometimes iced) with fruit salads and so on.

To make rich coconut milk: Grate the white flesh of a ripe coconut, pour a cupful of hot water over, then squeeze through a piece of cheesecloth, producing a thick, creamy liquid. To make a thinner milk, use more water.

Commercially made coconut milk is also available.

COCO YAM

(See Taro entry.)

COD

One of the most important edible saltwater fishes in the world. It belongs to the same family of bony white fish as haddock, whiting, hake, etc. The cod is usually olive-green on the back and sides sprinkled with small dark spots and grows quite long, averaging about 4 feet in length and weighing anything up to 70 to 80 lb. Scrod is the young fish. Cod is caught in North Atlantic waters and is obtainable all year round.

Cod is sold fresh, salted, and in frozen form. As it has only a delicate flavor, it is best baked with stuffing, fried in batter or steamed or poached and coated with a well-flavored sauce; it is often made into fish cakes.

The liver is used to produce cod liver oil. (See separate entry.)

MINT AND CUCUMBER FISH SALAD

2 lb fresh cod fillet (the thick end is the best choice)
juice of ½ lemon
salt
½ cucumber
2 tablespoons chopped mint
2 tablespoons chopped parsley

FOR FRENCH DRESSING
6 tablespoons olive oil
2 tablespoons vinegar
salt
freshly ground black pepper
mustard

FOR GARNISH
1–2 oz peeled shrimp
lemon wedges
sprigs of mint

Wash and skin the fish and cut it into three or four pieces. Sprinkle with lemon juice and salt. Steam or gently poach until just cooked (the flakes should separate easily and look milky white all through). Leave the fish covered until quite cold. Flake the fish very coarsely into a large bowl, removing any stray bones. Wash the cucumber, cut it into small dice and add to the fish with the chopped mint and parsley. Stir the French dressing ingredients together in a bowl and pour over the salad. Using two spoons, lift and turn the salad until all the ingredients are combined and coated with dressing. Take care not to break up the natural flakes of fish. Pile the mixture into individual dishes and garnish each one with shrimp, lemon wedges, and sprigs of mint. Alternatively, serve in a large salad bowl accompanied by mayonnaise, tossed green salad, and French bread.

STUFFED COD STEAKS

4 cod steaks
½ onion finely chopped
6 slices bacon, chopped
1 tablespoon butter
2 tomatoes, peeled and chopped
⅔ cup fresh white bread crumbs
salt
pepper
about ⅔ cup milk

Wash and wipe the fish, trim off the fins and remove the central bone with a sharp-pointed knife; place the fish in a greased ovenproof dish. Sauté the onion and bacon gently in the butter for about 5 minutes, until soft; stir in the tomatoes and crumbs. Season well and add enough milk to bind the mixture. Fill the center of each steak with this stuffing, and skewer the flaps of fish to secure the stuffing. Pour 2 to 3 tablespoons milk around the fish, cover with a lid or foil and bake in a 350° oven for about 20 minutes.

As an alternative filling, use the following mixture.

CHEESE AND TOMATO STUFFING FOR COD

2 large tomatoes, peeled and chopped
¾ cup grated Swiss cheese
⅔ cup fresh white bread crumbs
1 teaspoon dried mixed herbs or sage
salt
pepper
milk to bind

Mix all the ingredients together.

Salt Cod

Salt cod requires soaking to remove the salt and must be very carefully cooked to make it really palatable. Choose thick fillets with firm, close flesh, avoiding stringy or yellow pieces. To prepare it, soak it in cold water for 24 hours, changing the water several times, and place the fish skin side uppermost in the water, to allow the salt to drain out. To cook the cod, put it into a pan with enough cold milk (or milk and water) to cover, bring just to a boil, then draw the pan aside and simmer until tender. Drain thoroughly and use as required. It may be served with maître d'hôtel butter or a well-flavored sauce, or better still dressed with a sauce and served au gratin, creamed, curried, etc.

CODDLING

A method of soft-cooking eggs by steaming in an egg coddler. (See Coddled Eggs recipe in Egg entry.)

COD LIVER OIL

An oil which is extracted from the fresh liver of the cod by heating. It is then cooled and processed. When sold, it is pale yellow in color. The oil can be relatively tasteless if it is prepared from the fish liver when this is absolutely fresh and if it is kept from contact with the air; for this reason the plants for extracting the oil are now sited at or near to ports.

Cod liver oil contains large though varying amounts of vitamins A and D, the approximate figures being vitamin A, 29,000 i.u. per oz; vitamin D, 6,000 i.u. per oz.

The oil used to be given to infants to supply these vitamins, but specially prepared vitamin drops are now available.

COD ROE

(See Roe entry.)

COEUR À LA CRÈME

A French dessert made with Fromage Blanc (see separate entry). The curd is drained, mixed with cream and again drained in heart-shaped molds. It is usually turned out and served with fresh cream and sugar. It can also be served with fresh strawberries or raspberries and sugar.

COFFEE

A shrub, originally African, which produces greenish beans. These are roasted, ground, and used to make a drink. Many varieties are now cultivated in Brazil (which produces about half the world's coffee), Venezuela, Costa Rica, the East and West Indies, India, and various African countries. Colombia, Costa Rica, Kenya, and Jamaica produce particularly good coffees, the Jamaican Blue Mountain having an especially high reputation.

When ripe, the berries are red; they contain 1 or 2 seeds. The berries are usually cleaned and graded before being exported. They must then be roasted and on this depends to some extent the quality of the coffee. They should be roasted evenly, to a light or dark color as desired, and should be cooled rapidly. The aroma and flavor develop during this process.

The beans should preferably not be ground until just before the coffee is needed, or they will lose their flavor and soon become stale. Buy ground coffee in small quantities only. Use it quickly once opened.

The caffeine in coffee generally has a mildly stimulating effect, but people vary in their reactions and some find it relaxing.

INSTANT COFFEE
Coffee which has been ground, dried, and packed as a powder or in granules. It makes quite a good cup of coffee, although not comparable with that produced by the freshly ground product.

DECAFFEINATED COFFEE
A powdered coffee with the caffeine extracted.

To Make Coffee
There are several methods, but the most important point is to use enough coffee – too little produces a tasteless brew. Allow 1 tablespoon at least per person – more for strong, black, after-dinner coffee.

INFUSION
Put 4 tablespoons coffee in a thermos and pour on $2\frac{1}{2}$ cups boiling water, stir, then stand it in a warm place for 10 minutes. Pour the coffee gently through a strainer into a heated coffee pot.

PERCOLATOR COFFEE
The water circulates through the grounds, extracting the flavor and falling through a strainer. Ideally the liquid should be kept at just under boiling point, as boiling spoils coffee.

FILTER COFFEE (CAFÉ FILTRE)
A perforated filter (sometimes used with a filter paper) is filled with finely ground coffee, which is pressed down firmly. Boiling water is poured on and the coffee drips slowly through into the cup.

SUCTION METHOD
A special apparatus must be used, with water in the lower container and a funnel fitted carefully into its neck and filled with coffee grounds. On heating, most of the water is sucked up the funnel, remaining there for about 3 minutes. When the heat is withdrawn, the coffee filters down the lower container, leaving the grounds in the funnel.

ESPRESSO COFFEE
In coffee bar, etc., coffee is prepared under pressure, producing a strong, rather bitter brew.

TURKISH COFFEE
This is said to be the only coffee which should actually be boiled. Finely ground coffee, sugar and cold water are brought to a boil, stirred and allowed to stand away from the heat. The liquid is then reheated and the process repeated two or three times. A few drops of rose water are added and the thick, syrupy brew is served in small quantities.

BLACK COFFEE (CAFÉ NOIR)
Should be strong, clear, and very hot. It is generally served alone, but cream, milk, or sugar may be served with it if desired.

COFFEE WITH MILK (CAFÉ AU LAIT)
This is strong, black coffee to which hot (but not boiling) milk is added, generally in the proportion of 2 to 3 parts milk to 1 part of coffee.

To make Irish coffee: Heat a goblet and put in 2 lumps of sugar. Pour in a jigger of Irish whiskey and fill up two-thirds of the way with hot, strong black coffee. Dissolve the sugar, then carefully add some whipping cream, pouring it in over the back of a spoon, so that it lies on top. Do not mix, but drink the coffee and whiskey through the layer of cream.

To make iced coffee: Make some strong black coffee, using 4 tablespoons ground coffee to 1 quart water. While it is still hot, sweeten to taste. Cool and chill. Pour into glasses, add a cube of ice and top with whipped cream.

COFFEE SAUCE

2 tablespoons butter
4 teaspoons cornstarch
$\frac{2}{3}$ cup black coffee

2 tablespoons sugar
vanilla
1 egg yolk

Melt the butter in a small saucepan and mix in the cornstarch. Add the coffee gradually and stir until boiling. Simmer slowly for 5 minutes, add the sugar and a little vanilla and just before serving stir in the egg yolk. Do not boil again.

COFFEE LAYER CAKE

½ cup butter or margarine
½ cup superfine sugar
2 large eggs, beaten
1 cup all-purpose flour
1½ teaspoons baking powder
½ teaspoon salt

FROSTING
6 tablespoons butter
3 cups powdered sugar, sifted
1 tablespoon extra-strong coffee
1 tablespoon half-and-half

Grease two 7-inch layer pans and line the base of each with a round of greased waxed paper. Cream the butter and sugar until pale and fluffy. Add the eggs a little at a time, beating well after each addition. Fold in half the flour, the baking powder and salt using a metal spoon, then fold in the rest of the flour. Place half the mixture in each pan and level it with a spatula. Bake both cakes on the same shelf of a 375° oven for about 20 minutes, or until they are well risen, golden, firm to the touch, and beginning to shrink away from the sides of the pans. Turn out and cool on a cake rack. For the frosting, cream the butter until soft, but not oily, and gradually beat in the sifted powdered sugar with the coffee and half-and-half. When the cakes are cold, sandwich them together with half the frosting. Top with the rest of the frosting, and mark lines with a fork.

COFFEE CAKE

A sweetened bread, often containing fruits and/or nuts and decorated with frosting, intended to be eaten with coffee.

SWEDISH COFFEE CAKE

½ recipe enriched bread dough, risen (see Bread
  entry)
1 tablespoon butter, melted
¼ cup packed brown sugar
2 teaspoons powdered cinnamon
candied cherries and/or slivered almonds

FOR THE GLAZE
1½ cups powdered sugar, sifted
water
lemon juice

Grease a baking sheet. Roll the dough to an oblong 12 × 9 inches. Brush with the butter, then sprinkle the mixed brown sugar and cinnamon over the dough. Roll up tightly from the long edge and bend around to form a ring. Seal the ends together and place on the baking sheet. Using scissors, cut slashes at an angle 1 inch apart and to within ½ inch of the inside edge. Twist the cut sections to overlap each other. Cover with lightly oiled plastic wrap and put to rise in a warm place for about 30 minutes. Bake in a 375° oven for 30 to 35 minutes. Glaze and decorate (see below) and cool on a cake rack.

To make the glaze, blend the powdered sugar with a good squeeze of lemon juice and just enough water to give a thick coating consistency. While the ring is still warm, dribble the glaze over it with a spoon. Decorate with cherries, angelica leaves, and/or nuts.

COGNAC

Brandy of high quality based on the wines made in the Charente and Charente Maritime *départements* of France, lying around the town of Cognac. The best Cognac brandy is made from Grande Champagne wine. Cognac as sold is generally a blend of Charente brandies – the higher the proportion of best brandy, the finer the Cognac.

One Star Cognac is 3 years old, Two Star 4 years old, and Three Star 5 years old. The initials V.S.O.P., meaning Very Special Old Pale, refer to older brandy.

Cognac is about 72 percent alcohol.

COINTREAU

A French Curaçao, used as an after-dinner liqueur and to flavor punches and cocktails. It has a sweet orange flavor.

COLA

A tropical African tree, the seeds or nuts of which contain a small amount of caffeine and therefore have stimulating properties. It is used in making apéritifs, etc. It is also the name given to certain carbonated soft drinks.

COLCANNON

A mixture of potatoes and cabbage boiled together and mashed, popular in Ireland. It may also be made up with leftover cooked potatoes and cabbage, mixed together and fried in a pan. The dish is very similar to Bubble and squeak (see entry).

COLESLAW

A salad with a base of finely shredded raw white cabbage dressed with cream or mayonnaise. Ingredients that can be added to this type of salad include grated carrot, chopped apple, chopped onion, nuts, dried fruit, cooked corn, chopped celery, and chopped green pepper. The salad may be served in a bowl or in a hollowed-out cabbage. It can be served with any dish but usually accompanies hamburgers, fish dishes, and cold meats.

COLESLAW

½ head white cabbage, finely shredded
1 large carrot, coarsely grated
small piece of onion, finely chopped
1 tablespoon chopped parsley, optional
5 tablespoons salad dressing or mayonnaise
1 teaspoon sugar
salt
pepper
few drops of vinegar or lemon juice

Combine the cabbage, carrot, onion, and parsley (if used) in a large bowl. Mix the salad dressing or mayonnaise with the sugar, salt and pepper and add enough vinegar or lemon juice to sharpen the flavor. Toss with the salad in the bowl until lightly coated, adding a little more salad dressing if necessary.

Note: Coleslaw may be garnished by sprinkling with chopped herbs.

RAINBOW COLESLAW

3 cups shredded red cabbage
3 cups shredded white cabbage
1 large carrot
½ green pepper, seeded
⅔ cup sour cream
2 tablespoons mayonnaise
1 tablespoon lemon juice
½ teaspoon caraway seeds
½ teaspoon celery seeds
salt
freshly ground black pepper

Combine the red and white cabbage in a large bowl. Grate the carrot on a coarse grater straight into the cabbage. Slice the green pepper finely and add it to the cabbage. Mix together the sour cream, mayonnaise, lemon juice, caraway seeds, celery seeds, salt and pepper. Pour this dressing over the coleslaw and mix thoroughly. Chill before serving.

COLLARDS

A green leafy vegetable, member of the cabbage family and closely related to kale. Known to the Greeks and Romans, collards have long been a favorite food in the South of the United States, where they rank high on the list of soul foods. Containing enormous amounts of vitamin A, collards are also a rich source of calcium, phosphorus, and ascorbic acid and may have saved many Southerners with poor means from severe vitamin deficiencies.

To cook collards, sauté a little salt pork or bacon. Add shredded collards, a very small amount of water, and cover and simmer only until tender.

COLLOP

A term derived from the French escalope; it is used (chiefly in Scotland) for a small boneless piece of meat and now often means a dish made of finely ground meat.

COLORINGS

Domestically, colors may be used to tint candies, frostings, cakes, and so on. Commercially, they are used to replace the natural colors lost during the processing of foods.

All prepacked foods must by law include on the label a list of ingredients in descending order by weight; this should include any coloring. It is an offense to mislead the public by the use of food coloring.

A few natural food colors are available, including the well-known cochineal, but in general natural colors are not very strong and are so variable that no two batches are the same; they also tend to fade, being less stable than synthetic colors.

COMPOTE

Fruit stewed with sugar; a compote can be prepared from a single fruit or a mixture and can be served either hot or cold.

To make compote of pears: Make a syrup of sugar and water; 2 lb of stewing pears, $\frac{1}{2}$ to $\frac{3}{4}$ cup sugar, $\frac{2}{3}$ cup water, the juice of $\frac{1}{2}$ lemon, 2 to 3 cloves, and 1-inch cinnamon stick. Put all the ingredients, except the pears, into a heavy saucepan, bring slowly to a boil, and boil for 10 minutes. Peel the pears with a stainless knife, halve and core, taking care not to break the pieces and putting them into cold acidulated water to prevent discoloration. Stew slowly in the prepared syrup until tender, then lift out carefully with a spoon. Reduce the syrup, allow it to cool slightly and then strain. Unless the compote is to be used for children, a little red wine may be added to the syrup when stewing the pears. The pears may also be cooked in a covered dish in a 350° oven for 30 minutes to 2 hours, according to hardness.

Apples may be cooked in the same way.

CONCH

A gastropod sometimes weighing as much as 5 lb, found from Florida south to the West Indies. Its flesh has been savored by settlers since the time of Columbus. Pronounced "conk," it loans its name to the residents of Key West, who refer to themselves as conks. It is delicious in chowders, salads, and fritters.

CONDE, À LA

Culinary term for soups and desserts in which rice plays an important part.

CONFIT

Meat or poultry cooked and preserved in its own fat. Confit of goose is often an ingredient of cassoulet.

CONGER EEL

A scaleless marine fish, grayish or dusky brown on top and silver underneath, up to 8 feet long, which is often found in European waters. Conger eels are cooked like freshwater eels when small; when large they are somewhat coarse. They make good soup and are included in bouillabaisse.

CONSERVE

A preparation of two or more fruits in sugar, very similar to jam, the chief difference being that a conserve often contains raisins and nuts.

STRAWBERRY AND RHUBARB CONSERVE

1 quart of strawberries
4 cups cut-up rhubarb
7 cups sugar
$\frac{1}{3}$ cup lemon juice

Select strawberries which are just ripe, red and firm. Prepare and wash them in the usual way and drain them well. Then place in a large kettle with the rhubarb. Add the sugar and lemon juice and bring slowly to a boil; boil until thick, stirring frequently. Pour into hot jars and seal.

CONSOMMÉ

A clear soup, made with the stock from fresh meat, chicken, or even fish. Consommé can be served hot or cold and is usually garnished. Various commercial consommés are available.

BROWN STOCK FOR CONSOMMÉ

1 lb marrow bone or knuckle of veal, chopped
1 lb shin of beef, cut into pieces
2 quarts water
bouquet garni
1 carrot, sliced
1 medium onion, sliced
1 stalk celery, sliced
$\frac{1}{2}$ teaspoon salt

To give a good flavor and color, brown the bones and meat in the oven (exact temperature not important) before using them. Put in a pan with the water, herbs, vegetables, and salt, bring to a boil, skim and simmer covered for 5 to 6 hours. *Makes about 1$\frac{1}{2}$ quarts.*

Note: For a more economical brown stock, use 2 lb bones, omit the shin of beef and sauté the onion until well browned.

CLASSIC CONSOMMÉ

1$\frac{1}{2}$ quarts brown stock (cold)
4 oz lean ground beef
1 carrot, chopped
1 small onion, chopped
bouquet garni
1 egg white
salt
2 teaspoons dry sherry, optional

A completely clear, well-flavored broth, made from good brown stock. Both the stock and the utensils must be quite free from any trace of grease to prevent droplets of fat forming on the surface of the soup.

Remove any fat from the stock. Put the meat, vegetables, stock, and bouquet garni into a deep saucepan; lastly add the egg white. Heat gently and beat continuously until a thick froth starts to form. Stop beating and bring to a boil. Reduce the heat immediately, cover and simmer for 20 minutes. If the liquid boils, the froth will break and cloud the consommé.

Scald a clean cheesecloth, wring it out and line a strainer with it. Pour the soup through into a large bowl, keeping the froth back at first with a spoon, then let it slide out onto the cloth. Again pour the soup through the cloth and through the filter of egg white.

The consommé should now be clear and sparkling. Reheat it, add salt if necessary and a little sherry to improve the flavor, but add nothing that would make the liquid cloudy.

COOKIE

Any of a variety of sweet filled or unfilled little cakes. The word is probably derived from the Dutch "koekje." Some, like brownies, are soft and chewy, while others are crisp to the bite. Cookies in one form or another are popular in almost every country and each country has its own specialty. They are usually easy to make and most cookies freeze well.

Cookies are classified by the way they are formed – drop (dropped from a spoon onto the baking sheet), bar (cut into squares or bars after baking), molded (shaped by the fingers), rolled (rolled out like pie crust and cut into desired shapes), pressed (made with a cookie press or pastry bag into fancy shapes), or refrigerated (chilled and cut before baking).

To mix: Follow the recipe carefully. Heat the oven before you begin.

To bake: Use shiny baking sheets at least 1 inch smaller on all sides than the oven. Bake only one sheet at a time in the center of the oven. Remove cookies from the sheet as soon as they are baked unless the recipe has other instructions. And always put unbaked cookies onto cold baking sheets.

To store: Cookies must be cold before they are put away. Crisp cookies should be stored in a container with a loose lid. Soft cookies should be stored in an airtight tin and never in the same container as a cake. Cookies may be recrisped in a 300° oven for a few minutes.

Drop Cookies

These cookies are dropped from a spoon onto the baking sheet and should be uniform in shape and slightly mounded. If they spread too much, it means that something was too warm – the dough, the baking sheet, or the oven. One of the most popular drop cookies is the chocolate chip cookie.

CHOCOLATE CHIP COOKIES

Developed in 1930 by Mrs Wakefield, owner of the Toll House Inn in Massachusetts, these cookies vie with brownies for the number one place in the hearts of American cookie lovers.

$2\frac{1}{4}$ cups all-purpose flour
1 teaspoon salt
1 teaspoon baking soda
1 cup butter, softened
$\frac{3}{4}$ cup granulated sugar
$\frac{3}{4}$ cup packed brown sugar
1 teaspoon vanilla
2 eggs
1 package (12 oz) chocolate chips
1 cup chopped nuts

Combine the flour, salt, and baking soda. In a mixer bowl beat the butter, sugars, and vanilla until creamy. Beat in the eggs, one at a time. Stir in the flour gradually by hand, then the chocolate chips and nuts. Drop by rounded teaspoonfuls onto ungreased cookie sheets and bake in a 375° oven for 8 to 10 minutes.

Bar Cookies

These are rich, moist cakelike cookies. They should be cool before you cut them.

RICH BROWNIES

$\frac{3}{4}$ cup all-purpose flour
$\frac{1}{4}$ teaspoon baking soda
$\frac{1}{4}$ teaspoon salt
$\frac{1}{3}$ cup butter
$\frac{3}{4}$ cup sugar
2 tablespoons water
1 package (12 oz) chocolate chips
1 teaspoon vanilla
2 eggs
$\frac{1}{2}$ cup chopped nuts

Combine the flour, baking soda, and salt. Melt the butter with the sugar and water and bring just to a boil. Remove from heat immediately and stir in 1 cup of the chocolate chips. Stir until melted, then stir in the vanilla. Pour the mixture into a mixing bowl and add the eggs, one at a time, beating well. Gradually stir in the flour, then the remaining chocolate chips and the nuts. Spread the mixture in a greased 9-inch square baking pan and bake in a 325° oven for 30 to 35 minutes. Cool completely before cutting into squares.

Molded Cookies

It is important that the cookies all be shaped uniformly so that they will bake evenly. If a recipe tells you to flatten the cookie, do it with a fork, your thumb or a glass dipped in sugar. A very buttery dough may need refrigeration before shaping.

OATMEAL COOKIES

$\frac{3}{4}$ cup all-purpose flour
$\frac{1}{2}$ teaspoon baking soda
6 tablespoons sugar
$\frac{3}{4}$ cup rolled oats
6 tablespoons butter or margarine
1 tablespoon milk
1 tablespoon corn syrup

Grease 2 baking sheets. Sift the flour and soda and stir in the sugar and oats. Heat the butter, milk, and corn syrup together until melted, pour onto the first mixture and mix well. Roll into small balls and place 4 inches apart on the baking sheets. Flatten slightly and bake in a 300° oven for about 25 to 30 minutes. Cool on the sheets for 2 to 3 minutes then transfer the cookies to a rack to cool completely.

Rolled Cookies

These versatile cookies can be crisp and thin or thick and soft. It is easier to roll chilled dough using a stockinette-covered roller and a pastry cloth. Roll the dough out evenly, so that the cookies will be of the same thickness and brown evenly. Flour the cutter and stamp out the cookies working from the edge of the dough toward the middle and using the dough as economically as possible. Any remaining dough may be lightly kneaded and rolled out again, but the cookies from this second rolling are never as good as the first ones.

MORAVIAN GINGER COOKIES

These cookies should be rolled as thinly as possible and outlined with a piping of frosting made with powdered sugar.

$1\frac{1}{4}$ cups all-purpose flour
$\frac{1}{4}$ teaspoon salt

$\frac{1}{4}$ teaspoon nutmeg
$\frac{1}{4}$ teaspoon cinnamon
$\frac{1}{4}$ teaspoon allspice
$\frac{1}{2}$ teaspoon ground ginger
3 tablespoons butter
2 tablespoons brown sugar
$\frac{1}{3}$ cup molasses

Sift the flour and spices together. In a small mixer bowl cream the butter and sugar. Add the molasses. By hand, stir in the flour only until incorporated. Cover and refrigerate for 4 to 6 hours.

Work with $\frac{1}{4}$ or $\frac{1}{3}$ of the dough at a time, keeping the rest chilled. Roll out on a cloth-covered board with a cloth-covered pin, working quickly as the dough can become sticky. Roll as thinly as possible, $\frac{1}{8}$ inch being the thickest allowable, $\frac{1}{16}$ inch being preferable. Bake on an ungreased baking sheet in a 350° oven, about 8 minutes for thicker cookies, 5 minutes for thin ones. When cool, decorate with a frosting made from 1 cup powdered sugar mixed with 2 to 3 tablespoons cream.

Pressed Cookies

Decorative fancy cookies may be made with a press. This consists of a tube which holds the mixture and a plunger to force it out through one or other of several perforated disks (which can be easily fitted and changed). The mixture must be fairly rich, sufficiently soft to come easily through the tube when pushed by the plunger and yet stiff enough to retain its shape on the pan during the cooking. You will need a little practice in manipulating the cookie press.

If preferred, the cookie mixture may be piped with an ordinary pastry bag and a fluted tip.

ORANGE GLAZED MELTAWAYS

1 cup butter
$\frac{1}{2}$ cup powdered sugar
grated rind of 1 orange
2 cups all-purpose flour
2 tablespoons apricot jam, strained
3 tablespoons powdered sugar
1 tablespoon orange juice

Cream the butter until soft. Sift in the sugar and beat until light and fluffy. Stir in the orange rind and flour until well blended. Put the mixture into a cookie press and fit the disk of your choice on the end. Hold the press over the greased cookie pan and press the plunger downward, making each cookie a neat, even shape. Chill for 30 minutes. Bake in a 325° oven for 20 minutes.

Remove from the oven, brush each cookie with a little apricot jam. Combine the sifted sugar with orange juice and brush over the jam. Return the cookies to the oven for 5 minutes longer, or until the sugar glaze begins to go slightly crystaline. Cool on a rack.

STAR COOKIES

2 cups all-purpose flour
¼ cup semolina
¾ cup butter
⅔ cup sugar
1 egg, separated
2 tablespoons water
jam or jelly

Combine the flour and semolina in a bowl. Cut in the butter, then stir in the sugar. Mix the egg yolk with the water and use to bind the dry ingredients into a stiff dough. Divide the dough in half and shape each into a roll about 2 inches in diameter. Refrigerate for 3 hours.

Cut off as many thin slices from a roll as you wish to make cookies, returning any unused dough to the refrigerator for future use. Using a solid star, heart, moon, or other shape press an indentation into each cookie. Place on a greased baking sheet and brush with egg white. Bake in a 400° oven for 8 to 10 minutes, or until golden. Cool on a rack. Fill the indentations with jelly or jam.

Refrigerated Cookies

These rich cookies are always ready when you need them. The dough can be frozen, if desired. Wrap well in aluminum foil or freezer wrap. When ready to use, thaw just enough to slice. Refrigerator cookies must be evenly sliced to insure even cooking.

NUT REFRIGERATOR COOKIES

½ cup butter or margarine
½ cup sugar
1 egg, beaten
1½ cups all-purpose flour
½ teaspoon salt
¼ cup finely chopped walnuts or almonds

Cream the butter with the sugar and beat in the egg gradually. Stir in the flour, salt, and chopped nuts to give a fairly firm dough. Shape into a long roll, wrap in waxed paper or aluminum foil and refrigerate for several hours to chill thoroughly.

To finish, grease 2 baking sheets, cut the roll into ¼-inch slices, place the cookies about 1 inch apart on the sheets and bake in a 400° oven for 10 to 12 minutes. Cool on a rack.

CORDIAL

A spirit sweetened and infused with fruit or other agent to add flavor and scent. It was supposed to have some stimulating effect on the heart hence the name, meaning of or belonging to the heart. This product is now more often called a liqueur.

CORIANDER (CHINESE PARSLEY)

An Eastern spice, which was introduced into Europe by the Romans. The strongly scented plant has leaves similar to those of parsley and the flowers grow around the stem in tassels. The fragrant dried seeds are used as a flavoring for gin and in dishes such as curry, pickles, and gingerbread; they are also used to flavor medicine. The flavor resembles a mixture of sage and lemon peel and therefore may be added to stuffing. Coriander is favored in Chinese and Hispanic cooking.

CORING

To remove the central membranes, seeds, etc., from apples, pears, and so on, either by quartering the fruit and cutting out the core or by using a special corer on the whole fruit. Also to remove the tough central membrane from kidneys.

CORN

A general term applied to all kinds of grain, such as wheat, rye, oats, barley, maize, etc. As a cooking term it usually means sweet corn or maize. Special varieties of corn are grown for use in this way, and they include ears with white, yellow, and white and yellow kernels, each having its advocates. Corn of good quality has a fresh-looking green husk, with a brown silk tassel. The ear should be filled with plump, milky kernels, firm but not hard. Corn with yellow or dried-out husks or an ear full of very small, immature seeds should be rejected.

Choose the ears when they are plump, well formed and of a pale golden yellow color and cook them as soon as possible. Remove the outside leaves and silky threads, put the cobs into boiling unsalted water (salt toughens corn) and cook for 5 to 10 minutes, depending on their size – overcooking also makes them tough. Drain well and serve with plenty of butter, salt, and freshly ground pepper. *Allow 1 to 2 ears per portion.*

Corn Fritters: Make up a batter from 1 cup all-purpose flour, a pinch of salt, 1 egg and $\frac{2}{3}$ cup milk. Fold in 1 cup corn. Fry in spoonfuls in a little hot fat until crisp and golden, turning them once. Drain well on crumpled paper towels.

CORNED BEEF

A preparation of pickled beef cooked slowly in simmering water and generally served with boiled potatoes and cabbage. Ways of using leftover corned beef are very numerous, the simplest being to slice it and serve it cold with salads, but many people prefer it in cooked dishes, such as ragouts, stews, curries, fritters, etc.

Corned beef has approximately the same protein and fat content as fresh meat, but contains less of some of the B vitamins.

CORNED BEEF HASH

2 cups chopped corned beef
2 cups cooked and chopped potatoes
1 onion, chopped
$\frac{1}{4}$ cup oil
pepper
salt
Worcestershire sauce
parsley

Combine the corned beef, potatoes and onion. Heat the oil in a skillet and add the meat, potatoes, and onion and season with pepper, salt, and sauce. Combine well, then smooth out the mixture and cook very slowly until piping hot and nicely browned underneath – about 30 minutes. Turn onto a hot dish, brown side uppermost, garnish with parsley and serve immediately.

When cooked chopped beets are added to the mixture, the resulting dish is known as Red Flannel Hash.

CORNET

A hollow conical pastry in the shape of a horn, filled with pastry cream. The term is also used for thin slices of meat similarly rolled.

CORNICHON

(See Gherkin entry.)

CORNISH PASTY

A small meat pie originating in Cornwall, England, where it was carried by the tin miners for their lunch in the bowels of the earth. It is usually baked in a pastry shaped like a turnover. It is delicious hot or cold.

CORNISH PASTIES

12 oz chuck steak
1 potato, peeled and diced
1 small onion, chopped
salt
pepper
1 recipe short-crust pastry (see Pastry entry)

Cut the steak into small pieces, add the potato and onion and season well. Divide the pastry in four and roll each piece into a round 8 inches in diameter. Divide the meat mixture between the pastry rounds, dampen the edges, draw the edges of the pastry together to form a seam across the top and flute the edges with the fingers. Place on a baking sheet and bake in a 425° oven for 15 minutes to brown the pastry, then reduce the oven to 325° and cook 60 minutes longer. Serve hot or cold.

CORNMEAL

A meal made from ground corn. It is a staple in areas in which corn grows and is the basis of Italy's polenta and Mexico's tortilla. (See separate entries.) In the United States it is a staple of the South and the Southwest. In New England it is used to make Johnny cakes and Indian pudding. It is universally popular in the United States as a quick bread served either as muffins, corn sticks, or cut into squares.

CORN BREAD

$1\frac{1}{2}$ cups cornmeal
$\frac{1}{2}$ cup all-purpose flour
2 teaspoons baking powder
1 teaspoon sugar (optional)
1 teaspoon salt
$\frac{1}{2}$ teaspoon baking soda
$\frac{1}{4}$ cup vegetable shortening
$1\frac{1}{2}$ cups buttermilk
2 eggs

Combine and beat all ingredients for 30 seconds. Pour into a greased 8-inch square pan and bake in a 450° oven for 25 to 30 minutes. Serve hot. If baking as muffins, bake 20 minutes only; corn sticks, 12 to 15 minutes.

Note: Depending upon the part of the country you live in and your personal taste, crisp cooked bacon, canned whole kernel corn, chilis, and/or grated cheese can be stirred into the batter.

SPOON BREAD

White stone ground meal is considered the best for spoon bread, but yellow or white regular cornmeal will do. This bread is more like a pudding than a bread and is served in place of potatoes as the starch.

1½ cups boiling water
1 cup cornmeal
1 tablespoon butter
3 eggs
1 cup buttermilk
1 teaspoon salt
1 teaspoon sugar (optional)
1 teaspoon baking powder
¼ teaspoon baking soda

Stir the water into the cornmeal, then the butter. When tepid, stir in the remaining ingredients. Pour into a greased 2-quart baking dish and bake in a 375° oven for 45 to 50 minutes, or until a knife inserted in the center comes out clean. Serve with plenty of butter.

INDIAN PUDDING

4 cups milk, scalded
½ cup yellow cornmeal
2 tablespoons melted butter
½ cup molasses
1 teaspoon salt
1 teaspoon cinnamon
¼ teaspoon ginger
2 eggs, beaten

In the top of a double boiler pour the milk slowly over the cornmeal, stirring constantly. Cook over hot water 20 minutes, stirring occasionally. Combine the remaining ingredients and stir into the cornmeal. Pour into a 6-cup greased baking dish. Place in a larger pan and add about 1 inch boiling water. Bake in a 350° oven for 60 minutes.

CORN OIL

The germ of the corn kernel contains an oil, which is expressed and then refined. It is used for frying, in salad oils, and in the manufacture of some cakes and biscuits. It has a high percentage of unsaturated fats.

CORNSTARCH

Cornstarch is the inner part of the kernel of corn, very finely ground. It consists mainly of starch and is used for making puddings and dessert sauces and for thickening soups, sauces, and stews; it is also used in a few cakes, cookies, etc.

CORN SYRUP

This product, which varies in color from clear white to amber, is manufactured from cornstarch by treatment with an acid. It may be used as a table syrup or as a sweetening agent, but is not as sweet as ordinary cane sugar. It is also possible to use corn syrup in preserving, brewing, and cakemaking, but some additional sugar is needed for certain of these purposes and less liquid should be used, as the syrup contains 20 percent water.

COTTAGE CHEESE

A low-fat soft cheese with a mild flavor and granular texture. It can be used in entrées or desserts, or it may be served with salad. Cottage cheese is also available with flavoring additions such as chives and pineapple.

COTTAGE PIE

A homely dish usually made with leftover cooked meat, often thought to be identical with Shepherd's Pie (see separate entry). Some people, however, assert that while Cottage Pie may be made with any meat, only lamb or mutton should be used for Shepherd's Pie.

COTTONSEED OIL

(See Oil entry.)

COULIS

Originally this meant the juices that ran out of meat in the natural way while it was cooking. It then came to mean various sauces, but especially a rich gravy or concentrate made from meat and/or poultry, used in making sauces, soups, and stews, etc. Veal stock is also called by this name.

The French term coulis is also used for a thickened type of soup made with a puree of game, poultry, fish, or shellfish (though some authorities say that the last named should be called a bisque).

COUPE

A combination of fruit and ice cream served in a glass goblet.

Coupe Jacques: Half fill some glass goblets with fruit salad, flavored with Kirsch, cover this with a layer of vanilla ice cream and then add a layer of strawberry ice. Decorate with a candied cherry.

COURGETTE

(See Zucchini entry.)

COURT-BOUILLON

A stock used instead of plain water to cook fish which is inclined to be flavorless. There are various types of court-bouillon, some containing white or red wine, vinegar, or milk.

To each 2 cups water (or water and white wine mixed), allow:

1 onion
1 clove garlic
1 carrot
small stalk celery
bunch of herbs
small clove
1 tablespoon vinegar
1 teaspoon salt
freshly ground black pepper

Put all the ingredients together in a pan, cover and simmer for 20 minutes or longer. Strain this liquor and use for cooking the fish.

COUSCOUS

A North African culinary specialty made with millet flour, or fine semolina made from wheat germ, cooked in water until fluffy and served with mutton stew.

COW HEEL

The foot of a cow cleaned and with the hoof removed. It is very gelatinous, and is usually used to make head cheese.

COWSLIP

These sweet-scented flowers can be used to decorate salads and also to make syrup, vinegar, or wine.

CRAB

The United States has many wonderful and varied species of crab. The West coast brings Alaska king crab and Dungeness crab from California and Washington. On the East coast, from Maine to Florida, the blue crab and the stone crab (Florida) are available. Blue crab is sold as "soft shell crab" when it sheds its shell in the summer.

Crabs should be alive when purchased. Place in cold water and very gradually raise the temperature to the boiling point, then cook for 10 to 20 minutes, according to size; if overcooked, crabs become hard and thready.

To shell a crab: Lay the cooked crab on its back, hold the shell firmly with one hand and the body (to which the claws are attached) in the other hand, then pull apart.

The edible portion of the crab consists of two main parts: the white flesh of the claws and body,

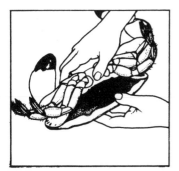
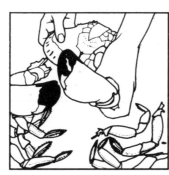

PREPARING A CRAB
1. Hold the shell firmly in one hand and the body in the other hand, pull the shell and body apart.

2. Remove the stomach bag, found just below the head and discard. Remove and discard the "dead men's fingers."

3. Crack the claws, except the very tiny ones. Take out all the flesh from the legs using a skewer.

and the liver, or soft yellow substance, which almost fills the shell.

Take the shell apart; using a spoon remove the stomach bag (which lies just below the head) and discard it. Then carefully scrape all the brown meat from the shell into a bowl and reserve it. Wash and dry the shell, then knock away the edge as far as the dark line.

Take the body and remove the legs and the grayish-white, frondlike pieces, the so-called "dead men's fingers" which are inedible. Remove the white flesh. Crack the claws (except the very tiny ones) with a nut cracker or a hammer and take out all the flesh. Use a skewer to get into the crevices and take great care not to get splinters of shell amongst the meat.

Crabmeat simply dressed: Add 1 tablespoon fresh bread crumbs to the brown meat, season with salt, pepper, lemon juice, and a little chopped parsley and pack it into the sides of the prepared shell, leaving a space in the middle. Season the white flesh with salt, pepper, cayenne, and lemon juice and pile it into the center of the shell.

Decorate with parsley. Dip the back of a knife into cayenne pepper and mark diagonal lines across the dark meat. Alternatively, decorate with sifted egg yolk and chopped egg white. Lay the crab on a dish and garnish with the small claws.

SCRAMBLED CURRIED CRAB

hot buttered toast
¼ cup butter
1–2 teaspoons curry powder
1 can (6½ oz) crabmeat, flaked
4 eggs
¼ cup cream or milk
celery salt or salt
little black pepper

Have ready some hot buttered toast. Melt the butter and stir in the curry powder and the flaked crab. When it is thoroughly hot, pour in the beaten eggs mixed with the cream or milk; season and cook quickly, scrambling in the usual way. Serve piled onto the buttered toast.

CRAB APPLE

A variety of apple native to North America, Europe, and Asia and cultivated for its fruit and for ornamental purposes. The small, sour apples of the European and North American varieties make excellent jelly and pickles. The Siberian crab apple is grown for ornamentation.

CRAB APPLE JELLY

6 lb crab apples
6 cups water
cloves or bruised gingerroot, optional
sugar

Wash the crab apples and cut into quarters, without peeling or coring. Put into a pan and add the water. Bring to a boil and simmer for about 30 to 35 minutes or until the fruit is soft, adding a little more water if necessary. A few cloves or some bruised gingerroot may be added while the apples are cooking, to give extra flavor. Strain through a jelly cloth, measure the extract and return it to the pan with 1 cup sugar to each cup of juice. Stir until the sugar has dissolved and boil rapidly until the jelly sheets from the spoon. Skim, pour into hot jars and cover in the usual way.

CRACKER

Various thin, crisp wafers, or biscuits made from unleavened dough, that are suitable for eating with cheese, serving with soup, or eating with milk or a soft drink as a snack. The name is derived from the "cracking" sound made when the wafers are broken. Crackers may be plain, salted, or sweet and are made from a large variety of flours.

CRACKLING

The crisp brown rind on a fresh ham after baking; the rind is usually scored before cooking, to prevent it pulling the roast out of shape, and is rubbed with salt, then brushed with oil to make it crisp.

CRACKNEL

A type of hard, plain cracker made of paste which is boiled before being baked; this causes it to puff up.

CRANBERRY

The red berry fruit of a small low-growing evergreen shrub, which occurs wild on peaty soil in North America and northern Europe. It is cultivated extensively in the United States.

Cranberries, which are very sour, are usually used in conjunction with another fruit, such as apple, for making fruit pies and tarts. They can also be canned whole and made into jams and jellies; a good jam is made with equal quantities of cranberries and apples. Cranberry sauce and jelly are traditional accompaniments to roast turkey; the fruit can also be used in relishes.

Cranberry Sauce: Pick and wash 1 lb cranberries and put them into a saucepan with $1\frac{1}{4}$ cups water. Cook until reduced to a pulp, bruising them well with the back of a wooden spoon, then add 1 to $1\frac{1}{2}$ cups sugar, stirring until dissolved, and a little port wine (if desired). Serve as an accompaniment to roast game or turkey.

CRAYFISH (CRAWFISH)

These variants of the same word are used almost indiscriminately to denote the two different shellfish described below, although, strictly speaking, only the first of them is entitled to the name. Crawfish is the name used in the southern United States.

1. The freshwater crayfish (French *écrevisse*) is like a miniature lobster and inhabits rivers and lakes; slightly different varieties are found in many parts of the world. When caught, they are a dull green or brown, but they turn a brilliant red on being boiled. Crayfish have a very delicate flavor and are used extensively in New Orleans cookery, France, and Scandinavia. Small ones are used for soup and garnishes, while the larger ones can be boiled and served hot in a good cream sauce, or cold with brown bread and butter.

To prepare crayfish, wash them well and with a pointed knife remove the intestinal tube under the tail, as it has a bitter flavor. Place them in salted water or court-bouillon and cook for about 10 minutes after the liquid has reached the boiling point.

CREAM

Cream is produced from whole milk by separation and can be described as the fat of the milk with a varying proportion of other milk constituents and water. These differ according to the type of cream.

As fat is lighter than the rest of milk it can be separated by gravity. However, in modern manufacture, the cream is separated by centrifugal force in a mechanical separator, the action being similar to that of a spin dryer.

All cream sold as fresh cream is pasteurized; this kills harmful bacteria and improves the keeping quality without affecting the flavor. The cream is heated to 175° for 15 seconds then cooled to 40° before packing.

Government regulations require the butterfat content of the different creams to be uniform throughout the nation. For longer shelf life, most cream is now ultra-pasteurized as well as homogenized.

Half-and-half: 11.7 percent butterfat, for coffee, pouring cream for cereals and cooking.

Light cream: 20.6 percent butterfat, also for coffee and food which call for a richer cream. This cream will not whip.

Whipping cream: 31.3 percent butterfat. Lighter than heavy cream, but it does whip and costs less than heavy cream.

Heavy cream: 37.6 percent butterfat. Will whip to at least twice its volume. Suitable for cake decorating or enriching sauces and soups.

Sour cream: 18 percent butterfat. Sour cream is not soured cream. It is sweet cream blended with a culture and allowed to ripen to a tart flavor.

Freezing Cream

Only heavy and whipping creams can successfully be frozen. Whipping cream can be frozen for up to 2 months, but heavy cream gives better results if only frozen for up to 1 month. Both creams benefit by being semi-whipped to the desired consistency after thawing. (See Freezing entry.)

CREAM CHEESE

This cheese originated in the United States. It is an unripened cheese made from a coagulated mixture of milk and cream. The butterfat content ranges from 40 percent to as high as 73 percent. Cream cheese is used in sandwiches and as a base spread for canapés and is indispensable in the service of lox and bagels. Sweetened, it is used in cheesecakes and desserts and as the basis of cake frostings.

LEMON CREAM CHEESE FROSTING

1 package (8 oz) cream cheese, softened
1 tablespoon milk
1 teaspoon vanilla
5 cups sifted powdered sugar
1 tablespoon grated lemon peel
about 3 tablespoons lemon juice

Beat ingredients until the frosting is fluffy and of spreading consistency. Add more lemon juice if necessary.

CREAM HORN

A favorite pastry confection, which may be made large or small and may be filled with any suitable sweet or savory mixture.

CREAM HORNS

8 oz puff pastry – ready-made weight
1 egg, beaten
raspberry jam
1 cup whipping cream
powdered sugar

Roll out the pastry to a strip 26 inches by 4 to 4½ inches. Brush with beaten egg. Cut eight ½-inch strips from the pastry with a sharp knife. Wind each round a cream horn tin, glazed side uppermost; start at the tip, overlapping fractionally, and finish neatly on the underside. The pastry should not overlap the metal rim. Place on a damp baking sheet seam-side down. Bake near the top of a 425° oven for 8 to 10 minutes. Cool for a few minutes. Carefully twist each tin, holding the pastry lightly in the other hand, to ease it off the horn. A clean towel helps if the tin is too warm to hold. When cold, fill the tip of each horn with a little jam. Beat the cream and fill horns. Dust with powdered sugar.

CREAMING

The beating together of fat and sugar to resemble whipped cream in color and texture. This method of mixing is used for cakes with a high proportion of shortening.

Put the shortening and sugar into a bowl and mix them with a wooden spoon. (The bowl may be slightly warmed to make the process easier.) Now beat the fat and sugar hard until the mixture is light and creamy. An electric mixer can be used to make the task easier and quicker.

CREAM OF TARTAR

(see Tartaric Acid entry.)

CREAM PUFF

A popular pastry made of choux pastry (see Pastry entry) with a filling of whipped cream or pastry cream. It also may be filled with a mixture of cheese, meat, seafood, or poultry and served as an hors d'oeuvre. When prepared in this fashion, the puffs are usually no larger than a walnut.

FILLING
Cream together a 3 oz package cream cheese and 3 tablespoons softened butter; add 1 teaspoon of lemon juice and salt and pepper to taste.

CREAM PUFFS

choux paste, made with ½ cup flour
1 cup whipping cream, whipped
melted chocolate or powdered sugar

The characteristic light, crisp texture and crazed tops of cream puffs are achieved by the swelling of the eggs during baking.

Pipe or spoon the paste into rounds 1½ to 2 inches in diameter 3 inches apart on 2 baking sheets. Bake in a 400° oven for 35 to 40 minutes. Pierce the side of each puff with a sharp-pointed knife and allow the puffs to cool in the oven with the door ajar. When they are cold, fill with whipped cream and dip the tops in melted chocolate or dust with powdered sugar.

CRÈME ANGLAISE

The French term for Custard Sauce. See Custard entry.

CRÈME CHANTILLY

Cream, whipped as the French do just until it forms soft peaks. Unlike cream more heavily beaten, it increases in volume by only one-half. To each cup of cream, fold in 1 tablespoon powdered sugar and ½ teaspoon vanilla after whipping.

CRÈME DE CACAO

A very sweet French liqueur, chocolate in color, with the flavor of cocoa.

CRÈME DE MENTHE

A pale-green liqueur, made of wine or grain spirit, flavored with peppermint and sweetened.

CRÈME FRAÎCHE

Heavy cream that has had the natural lactic acids and ferments destroyed by pasteurization returned to it after the pasteurization process. It is thick, with a nutlike flavor and slight tang. Available in France, it is imported into the United States in small quantities and can be found at specialty food stores. It keeps well and can be used on top of fruit, to enrich sauces, and in any ways that heavy or sour cream is used. Unlike the latter, it can be whipped and does not curdle if boiled. A similar cream can be made at home.

CRÈME PÂTISSIÈRE

The French term for Pastry Cream. (See separate entry.)

CRÊPE

The French word for a very thin pancake. It may be made without sugar and used to enclose vegetable, meat, poultry, seafood, or cheese fillings and served as an appetizer or entrée, or it may be made with sugar, sauced or filled with fruit, and served as a dessert.

CRÊPES

1 cup all-purpose flour
pinch of salt
2 eggs, separated
1 cup milk
2 tablespoons sugar (for dessert crêpes)

Sift the flour and salt, add the egg yolks and beat in about half the milk. Beat thoroughly, then add the remaining milk. Beat the egg whites until stiff, beat in the sugar (if using) and fold this mixture into the batter.

Heat a 7-inch skillet until hot. Grease lightly. Raise the handle side of the pan slightly, pour a little batter in from the raised side, so that a very thin skin of batter flows over the pan; move it back and forth until the base is covered. Place over a moderate heat and leave until the crêpe is golden brown. Turn with a spatula or by tossing and cook the second side until golden. Turn out onto waxed paper. Repeat, greasing the pan each time.

If you are cooking a large number of crêpes, keep them warm by putting them as they are made between two plates in a warm oven. Cooked crêpes will keep for up to 1 week if wrapped in waxed paper and stored in a refrigerator. Reheat them in a hot skillet, without any fat, turing them over once.

Crêpe Fillings

APPETIZER OR ENTRÉE
Diced meat or poultry in sauce
Fried mushrooms or tomatoes
Chopped fried sausage
Asparagus tips
Green peas and diced fried potato

Canned salmon and cooked mushrooms, heated in white sauce
Grated cheese, seasoning and chopped parsley

SWEET
Sugar and lemon juice
Sugar and ground cinnamon
Jam (with whipped cream if desired)
Fruit puree
Cleaned raisins, or chopped dates
Raspberry jelly and apple puree
Banana and sugar
Hard sauce

Freezing Crêpes
Crêpes freeze successfully. They should be wrapped with waxed paper between each crêpe, then wrapped in foil and a freezer bag. Use within 2 to 3 months.

CRÊPES SUZETTE

crêpes (from recipe above)
¼ cup sugar
¼ cup butter
juice of 2 oranges
grated rind of 1 lemon
3 tablespoons Cointreau
2 tablespoons brandy

Put the sugar in a skillet and heat gently, shaking the pan occasionally until the sugar has melted and turned golden brown. Remove the pan from the heat and add the butter, the lemon rind and the orange juice. Fold each crêpe in half and then in half again to form a quarter circle. Add the Cointreau to the sauce, place the crêpes in the pan and simmer for a few minutes until heated, spooning the sauce over them. Warm the brandy, pour it over the crêpes, and ignite it. Serve at once.

CRÉPINETTE

Crépinettes are little flat sausages, wrapped in caul, or very thin slices of salt pork. They are usually broiled, but may be baked or sautéed. They are generally served on a bed of mashed potatoes.

CRESS

Any of several plants native to Europe and North America; cultivated or wild, it grows very quickly and easily on any damp patch of ground and is a popular salad ingredient. Cress appears to be a fairly rich source of vitamins A and C, but the amount consumed at a serving is too small to contribute much of value to the diet.

Cress should be washed very carefully, as grit and soil cling firmly to its stalks. It can be used as a garnish for roast game and poultry, hot and cold entrées, meat, cheese, fish, etc. It may be cooked in the same way as watercress.

CRISPBREAD

Bread made from crushed whole grains, such as rye and wheat, and prepared in large, thin, brittle crackers.

Crispbread can be served at breakfast instead of toast, offered with the cheese course and used as a base for cocktail canapés. Crispbreads are of course very popular in Scandinavia, where they originated, and always appear on the Smörgåsbord; they may also form the base of Smørrebrød (see separate entry).

CROCK POT

An electric casserole or crock which can be left on the low setting all day without worry of the food spoiling. Food simmers at a temperature low enough that the liquid will not boil. Also, water condensing inside the lid runs down to form a liquid seal around the lid rim so there is no loss from evaporation.

The pots are particularly suitable for foods that require long, slow cooking such as stews, pot roasts, boiled ham, etc., as the meat becomes tender and holds its shape well with virtually no shrinkage. However, it is necessary to sauté meat and vegetables on the stove before putting into a slow cooker. The pots can also be used for cooking soups, vegetables, and fruit. As it is a very different method of cooking certain adjustments have to be made. Instructions and recipe booklets are supplied by the manufacturer with each pot.

The main advantage of the crock pot is the large fuel savings which can be as much as 40 percent. However, this has to be offset by the initial cost of the crock pot so it should be used regularly to make it a worthwhile buy.

CROISSANT

Croissants are crisp, crescent-shaped, flaky yeast rolls served for a French breakfast, and are best eaten hot. They reheat well if lightly wrapped in foil. The secret of success in making them lies in layering the butter well, chilling the pastry while it is standing to keep it firm and working quickly so that the dough does not become too warm and soft through overhandling. The dough is only allowed to rise at a warmer temperature after shaping.

CROISSANTS

2 packages dry active yeast
1 cup milk
1 tablespoon sugar
4 cups bread flour
2 teaspoons salt
1½ cups butter

FOR THE GLAZE
1 egg
2 teaspoons water
½ teaspoon sugar

Blend the yeast with the milk and sugar. Sift together 3½ cups flour and the salt and rub in 2 tablespoons of the butter. Add the yeast liquid and mix well together. Knead on a lightly floured surface only until the dough is smooth. Let rest in the refrigerator 10 to 15 minutes. Roll the dough into a strip about 20 × 8 × ¼ inches, taking care to keep the edges straight and the corners square.

While the dough is resting, mix the remaining ½ cup flour with the remaining butter. Dot the butter over two-thirds of the dough. Cover the center with the unbuttered third, then fold over the remaining buttered third. Leave a ½-inch margin all round. Turn the dough so that the fold is on the right-hand side. Seal the edges with a rolling pin.

Reshape to a long strip by gently pressing the dough at intervals with a rolling pin. Refold into thirds. Cover the dough with plastic wrap to prevent it forming a skin or cracking. Allow to rest in the refrigerator for 30 minutes. Roll out as before, and repeat the folding and rolling two more times. Place in the refrigerator for at least 1 hour.

Roll out the dough to an oblong about 22 × 13 inches. Cover with plastic wrap; leave for 10 minutes. Trim with a sharp knife to 21 × 12 inches and divide in half lengthwise. Cut each strip into six triangles 6 inches high and with a 6-inch base. To make the glaze beat the egg, water, and sugar together. Brush glaze over the triangles then roll each one loosely from the base, finishing with the tip underneath. Curve into a crescent shape.

Put the shaped croissants onto ungreased baking sheets. Brush the tops with egg glaze, cover with a clean towel and leave at room temperature for about 30 minutes, until light and puffy. Brush again with egg glaze before baking in a 425° oven for about 20 minutes.

CROQUEMBOUCHE

A crackling French pastry dessert, usually served at Christmas time. It consists of small profiteroles, filled with pastry cream or whipped cream, piled into the shape of an inverted cone. The "glue" of this construction is caramelized sugar cooked to the cracking point.

CROQUE-MONSIEUR

The French version of a ham and cheese sandwich. Butter one slice of bread and place on it a slice of Swiss cheese. Cover with ham and a second slice, unbuttered, of bread. Fry in butter until golden brown and the cheese melted, turning once.

CROQUETTE

A light entrée or garnish made from cooked and finely ground meat, fish, eggs, mushrooms, etc., mixed with a panada, or thick binding sauce, formed into cylinders or balls, bread coated and fried.

SAVORY CROQUETTES

1 cup milk
piece of onion
1 bay leaf
3 tablespoons butter
6 tablespoons flour
1 cup ground ham
¾ cup grated Cheddar cheese
salt
freshly ground white pepper
2 eggs
bread crumbs

The thickness of the panada (basic sauce) is critical. Its proportions are carefully balanced to insure that the finished filling will set firmly enough for shaping and yet not be heavy and stodgy to eat. Place the milk in a saucepan with the onion and bay leaf. Bring slowly to just below the boiling point, then remove from the heat and cover with a lid. Infuse for 10 minutes. In a separate pan, melt the butter and stir in the flour. Cook gently, stirring, until the mixture bubbles. Take off the heat and stir in the milk. Bring to a boil, stirring continuously for smoothness. Cook for about 2 minutes over a gentle heat – it is important to cook the sauce well or the filling will taste raw. Take pan from the heat and cover with a lid or place buttered waxed paper on the sauce to stop a skin forming.

Add the ham and cheese to the sauce, beating well to combine evenly. Season generously with salt and freshly ground white pepper, tasting as you go. Beat one egg lightly with a fork and beat into the filling. (For added richness, use 2 egg yolks in place of the whole egg.) Leave in the pan, covered, for the flavors to mingle.

When cool, but not cold, turn out the ham mixture onto a buttered plate or dish. Spread it evenly with a spatula to give a thickish layer – about ½ inch. Brush the surface with a little melted butter and cover with a second plate or cover with buttered waxed paper to prevent a skin forming. Allow to cool completely in the refrigerator before shaping. When quite cold divide the mixture into 8 to 10 equal parts. On a lightly floured surface neatly mold each piece into a cork shape ready for coating, making sure that the ends are kept square. For this stage use a small spatula and lightly floured fingertips.

Break the second egg into a shallow dish or plate and beat lightly with a pinch of salt and a teaspoonful of oil for a really crisp coat. Put the bread crumbs on a sheet of waxed paper. Lightly flour croquettes first, then place in the beaten egg. With the help of a small spatula and fork, gently turn to coat thoroughly. Lift out carefully, one at a time, allowing the surplus egg to drain off. Transfer the croquettes to the crumbs and with the aid of the paper gently roll croquettes to and fro until well and evenly coated, pressing crumbs in with spatula. Coat all the croquettes before starting to fry. If time permits, put the coated croquettes in the refrigerator for an hour to set. Alternate coatings to bread crumbs are finely chopped nuts, crushed cornflakes, crackers, or rolled oats.

In a deep, heavy-bottomed pan heat enough oil to give a depth of 3 inches. If a fat thermometer is available heat the oil to 375°. Otherwise test the temperature by dropping in a small cube of white bread – it should turn golden in about 20 seconds. The number of croquettes fried at one time should not be more than will cover the base of the pan. Either place the croquettes in a frying basket if you have one and lower into the pan, or slide in one at a time with the aid of a pancake turner or tongs. Fry until crisp and golden: this will take 3 to 4 minutes. Lift croquettes out in the basket or use a slotted spoon. Transfer to absorbent paper toweling. While frying the next batch, keep hot on a baking sheet in a cool oven.

CROUSTADE

A container (usually small) made of fried bread, pastry, duchesse potatoes, etc. for serving entrée foods.

FRIED BREAD CROUSTADES

Use bread which is at least 2 days old. Cut it into fingers or rounds about $\frac{3}{4}$ inch thick and scoop out the center part; then fry the cases in deep fat until they are golden brown.

Fill with a hot mixture such as chopped ham or chicken and mushroom in sauce.

CROUTONS

Small, crisp pieces of fried or toasted bread, often seasoned with a variety of herbs and spices. Croutons can be used to enhance soups, salads, and stuffings.

CROUTONS

Cut slices of bread $\frac{1}{4}$ to $\frac{1}{2}$ inch thick, remove the crust and cut into $\frac{1}{4}$-inch dice. Sauté these in butter and drain, or bake or toast until golden brown and crisp.

CROWN ROAST OF LAMB OR PORK

A handsome roast dish for a party, consisting of (1) 6 to 7 lamb rib chops or (2) half a dozen ribs from each side of a loin of pork. The chop bones are partially separated and neatly trimmed and scraped, then the meat is bent round and secured in a circular shape, the center being filled with stuffing. Protect the tips of the bones with greased paper caps to prevent burning. After roasting, the crown is decorated with small white onions, balls of potato or paper frills stuck on the end of the chop bones. Instead of stuffing, the crown may be filled with vegetables after roasting.

CRULLER

A breakfast bun made from a baking powder dough and fried in fat; crullers are very similar to doughnuts, but are rolled into strips and twisted before cooking.

CRUMB

To cover an ingredient with crumbs, either bread or cracker. The food to be coated is usually dipped in flour and eggs before being rolled in crumbs.

CRUMBLE TOPPING FOR PIES

A rubbed-in plain cake mixture, used instead of pastry as a topping over fruit. A savory mixture can be made to top meat by omitting the sugar and adding cheese and seasoning.

FRUIT CRUMBLE

1½ lb raw fruit, e.g. apples, plums, blueberries, rhubarb
granulated sugar
6 tablespoons margarine or butter
¾ cup all-purpose flour

Prepare the fruit as for stewing and layer it in a 4- to 5-cup ovenproof dish with $\frac{1}{4}$ cup or more sugar, depending on the sharpness of the fruit. Rub the butter into the flour until the mixture is the texture of fine crumbs; stir in $\frac{1}{4}$ cup sugar. Sprinkle the mixture on top of the prepared fruit and bake in a 400° oven.

CRUMPET

A small English cake made of a yeast mixture, which is baked on a griddle in special metal rings. Underneath, the cake is smooth and brown; the top is full of small holes. They are served toasted and hot, thickly buttered, for tea.

CRUMPETS

3 cups bread flour
1 package active dry yeast
1½ cups warm water
scant cup milk
½ teaspoon baking soda
1 teaspoon salt
oil or butter for greasing

Place half the flour in a bowl with the yeast and warm water. Blend until smooth, cover and leave until frothy, about 20 minutes. Stir in the remaining ingredients gradually, beating until smooth. Add more milk if necessary to make a pouring batter. Grease a griddle or heavy skillet and about six crumpet rings or metal cutters, 3 inches in diameter. Heat thoroughly. Pour about 2 tablespoons of the batter into the rings on the hot griddle. Cook until set and holes are formed before removing rings. Turn crumpets over to brown lightly on the other side. Cool on a wire rack. Toast lightly on both sides and serve hot and buttered with jelly.

CRUST

The commonest meaning of this term is the crisp or outer part of a loaf, pie, or other baked dish. As applied to wine, crust means the deposit of organic salts which wines throw off as they age.

CUBEB

A kind of pepper, native to the East Indies. The gray beans when dried somewhat resemble peppercorns. They have a pungent, spicy flavor like camphor and are used in Eastern cookery and also in some medicines.

CUCUMBER

The fleshy fruit of the gourd family originally from northern India. Cucumbers are eaten raw, sliced thinly and served as a salad vegetable or as an accompaniment to cold entrées, fish dishes, etc.; they also make an attractive decoration. (See Garnish entry.) They can also be cooked in a variety of ways and have a distinctive but delicate flavor. Braised, stuffed, or made into soups, are popular ways of serving cucumbers. Small varieties of cucumber, known as gherkins (Kirbys) are often pickled. When buying cucumbers, choose those with a firm smooth skin. Commercial cucumbers must be peeled before using as the skin is waxed.

Cucumbers have little food value.

BUTTERED CUCUMBER

1 large cucumber
water
salt
1 tablespoon butter
freshly ground black pepper

Thinly peel the skin from the cucumber using a vegetable peeler. Halve the cucumber lengthwise and remove the seeds. Cut lengthwise again and into 2-inch strips. Place the sticks in a saucepan with just enough water to barely cover, add salt and cook for about 7 minutes, making sure they remain crisp. Drain off the liquid and, just before serving, add the butter and some freshly ground pepper.

MINTED CUCUMBER AND CELERY

½ medium cucmber, finely diced
3 to 4 stalks celery, finely sliced
⅔ cup plain yogurt
large pinch celery salt
pinch of dried mint or 1 teaspoon fresh chopped
    mint
grated rind of ½ lemon
freshly ground black pepper

Put the cucumber and celery into a bowl. Add the yogurt, celery salt, mint, lemon rind, and pepper. Mix them well together and chill before serving.

RAITA

A cool fresh-tasting accompaniment to Indian dishes that is made from a variety of fresh raw vegetables.

½ cucumber
1 onion, finely chopped
1 clove garlic, crushed
1¼ cups plain yogurt
½ teaspoon salt
pinch of black pepper

Dice the cucumber finely. Combine with the other ingredients and chill thoroughly for 1 hour before serving.

CUMBERLAND SAUCE

A delicious, somewhat sweet sauce used to enhance the flavor of duck, ham, lamb, and venison.

CUMBERLAND SAUCE

1 orange
1 lemon
5 tablespoons currant jelly
5 tablespoons port
2 teaspoons arrowroot
2 teaspoons water

Peel the rind thinly from the orange and lemon, free of all the white pith, using either a very sharp, small vegetable knife or a vegetable parer. Cut it in fine strips, cover with water and simmer for 5 minutes. Squeeze the juice from both fruits. Put the currant jelly, orange juice, and lemon juice in a pan, stir until the jelly dissolves, simmer for 5 minutes and add the port. Blend the arrowroot and water to a smooth cream and stir into the jelly mixture. Heat, stirring, until it thickens and clears. Drain the strips of rind and add to the sauce.

CUMIN

A plant of the carrot family native to Egypt, Asia, and the Mediterranean. Its strong spicy seeds are used to flavor liqueurs, cordials, cheese, breads, sauces, curries, and pilafs.

CUMQUAT

(See Kumquat entry.)

CUP

A type of warm weather drink usually made from red or light white wine diluted with ice or soda water, and with sprigs of herbs, fruit and flavorings added.

CURAÇAO

A sweet liqueur made of wine or grain spirit, sugar, and orange pulp and peel. It is usually white but there are also some red, orange, green, and blue types. Cointreau and Grand Marnier are both Curaçao liqueurs.

CURDS

Curds are formed by milk when it coagulates – either naturally or because acid or rennet have been added. They consist of the proteins plus other constituents trapped with them. They may be eaten as they are or pressed to form cheese.

To make curds: Put 2 cups milk into a saucepan with a squeeze of lemon juice and heat very slowly until a curd has formed; the milk must not be allowed to boil. Turn into a sieve lined with cheesecloth and leave until the whey has drained away and the curd is dry. Serve with cream and sugar.

CURING

The process of salting and smoking fish or meat to preserve it.

CURLY ENDIVE

(See Endive entry.)

CURRANT

This term is used both for the dried fruit and for a group of fresh fruits known as black, red, and white currants.

Dried currants are very small seedless grapes deriving their name from Corinth, the Greek region from which they originally came. They are used in fruitcakes, cookies, mincemeat, puddings, and breads. The fresh currant is a small translucent berry that is seldom seen in markets in the United States. Although native to North America as well as Europe, its growth is discouraged in the United States because it is host to a parasitic fungus causing blister rust to valuable white pines. There are three varieties of currants – white (the sweetest), red (eaten raw or turned into preserves and tarts), and black (the least sweet and usually used for cooking). In France black currants are used to make cassis.

CURRANT JELLY

3 lb currants
2¼ cups water
sugar

Wash the fruit, but do not remove the stalks; put it into a pan with the water and simmer gently until the currants are soft and pulped. Strain through a jelly cloth, measure the juice and return it to the pan with 1 lb sugar for each pint of extract. Stir until the sugar has dissolved and boil rapidly until a "jell" is obtained on testing. Skim, jar, and cover in the usual way.

CURRANT FOOL

1 lb currants with stalks removed
2 tablespoons water
½ cup sugar
⅔ cup heavy cream
⅔ cup custard
red food coloring

Cook the currants with the water and sugar until the fruit is soft and well reduced, then sieve it. Whip the cream. Fold the custard and then the cream into the puree. Add a few drops of coloring and chill. Divide the fool between four sundae glasses.

CURRY

A dish of Oriental and particularly Indian origin, highly seasoned with a mixture of condiments and spices, many of which are grown in India and similar regions. The main characteristics are that it is spicy, often hot, and both sweet and acid in taste.

Lamb, chicken, fish, and vegetables are the foods most usually served in the form of a curry. The cooking time naturally varies with the ingredients used: uncooked fish needs 15 to 20 minutes; uncooked meat or chicken 1 to 2 hours and vegetables about 30 minutes to 1 hour, according to type. All curries and curry sauces should be thoroughly cooked, to develop the flavor and blend the ingredients.

The seasonings may be varied to suit individual tastes and they should be so skillfully blended that no individual flavor predominates. Great variety may be achieved by adding, for example, ½ teaspoon of powdered mixed spice, mace, cinnamon, or allspice, or a very little garlic vinegar (vinegar in which a few chopped cloves of garlic have been steeped) or 1 tablespoon of preserved tamarinds instead of the lemon juice. Small quantities of freshly shredded coconut and a little coconut milk, or grated almonds, walnuts, or Brazil nuts, give soft, mellow flavor.

The coconut milk mentioned in many recipes means an infusion of the coconut flesh, not the liquid found in the fresh nut. (See Coconut entry.)

Curry Powder and Paste

Curry powder is a commercially prepared mixture of finely ground spices and different makers have their own recipes. Curry paste sometimes contains spices that are now included in the powder form. Both can be bought in prepared form and if you get a reliable brand and use it while it is still fresh, you can make very palatable but not true Indian curries.

Connoisseurs of Oriental cooking usually prefer, however, to use fresh spices of which these preparations are composed; they are chiefly cayenne, coriander, turmeric, cumin seed, ginger, mace, cloves, cardamom, fenugreek, and pepper. Spices should be freshly ground if possible, so the best plan is to buy them in seed or whole form and pound them in a mortar or electric grinder. To prevent deterioration, keep them in a dry place in airtight containers. If you prefer, you can grind sufficient to make up a small supply of curry powder.

Making and Serving Curries

The cooking of many curries starts with the sautéing of the spices. Generally, begin with the mustard seed (which has a disconcerting habit of jumping, so don't be startled); add fenugreek last, as it burns rather easily. Sauté the spices gently, turning them frequently, and avoid overcooking, which makes a dish taste pungent and bitter. If you are using curry powder, this too is often cooked to get rid of the raw taste.

The amount of either curry powder or individual spices and condiments can, of course, be varied to suit your own taste when you make a particular curry.

Here are some other notes about the art of currymaking:
1. Always cook curries slowly to extract the richness which is so characteristic of the dish.
2. Curries are rarely thickened with flour – the long cooking should give the sauce the required consistency.
3. In many Oriental recipes a sealed casserole is recommended. A thick flour-and-water paste is put around the rim of the casserole to reduce the amount of moisture escaping as steam and the cooking is done in a very little liquid.
4. If onions and garlic are sautéed as a preliminary step, do not allow them to brown unless this is specifically mentioned – to prevent browning, cover the pan with a lid and cook very slowly.
5. Although apples (as a substitute for mangoes), raisins, almonds, etc. are sometimes included, these are not used in a true Indian curry, though they may appear in the accompanying rice or in pilafs and similar dishes.
6. Another habit that is not known in India is that of serving curry on rice – the two are always served separately.
7. The main ingredients of a curry should be cut up small enough so that the curry can be eaten with a spoon.

Accompaniments for Curries

Dry boiled rice (see Rice entry for method of cooking) is the almost invariable main accompaniment. Unpolished rice is more nutritious than polished.

Many types of side dishes are served with curry in different Oriental countries and these accompaniments are known by such names as *sambals*, *santals*, *agram-bagrams*, and *toulimoulis*. They may include tomato, sweet peppers, chutneys, cucumbers, mangoes, sliced hard-cooked eggs, grated fresh coconut topped with a sprinkling of red chili, young green beans sautéed in oil and garnished with sautéed onion and many other attractive and colorful garnishes. Serve each separately. Chapattis and pappadams are types of Indian breads often eaten with curries. (See separate entries.)

A suitable drink to serve with the curry would be an iced lager beer.

VINDALOO

From Western India a dish traditionally based on pork. The marinade imparts a characteristic hot and sharp flavor. You can use other meats, duck, or here we introduce shrimp.

1 teaspoon coriander seeds
1 teaspoon cumin seeds
1 teaspoon mustard seeds
1-inch piece of fresh gingerroot, peeled and chopped
1 teaspoon ground cloves
½ teaspoon ground turmeric
⅔ cup white vinegar
3 cloves garlic, crushed
2 onions, chopped
1 lb cleaned shrimp

4 tablespoons vegetable oil
2 tomatoes, peeled and chopped
1 teaspoon salt
½ teaspoon black pepper

Grind the seeds, ginger, and spices in an electric mill or mortar. Blend this to a paste with the vinegar adding the garlic and half the onion. Add to the shelled shrimp and leave for an hour to marinate. Heat the oil and gently sauté the remaining onion. Gradually add the marinated shrimp mixture. Continue to cook for 2 to 3 minutes, stir in the tomatoes. Season with salt and pepper. Simmer gently for 5 to 10 minutes.

ROGAN JOSH

A popular richly spiced Northern Indian curry that tends to be drier than some. Mutton is the traditional choice for the meat, but lamb is perfectly acceptable.

4 tablespoons vegetable oil
1 onion, sliced
3 cloves garlic, crushed
2 teaspoons ground ginger
2 teaspoons paprika
1 tablespoon ground coriander
1 teaspoon ground cumin
1 teaspoon ground turmeric
½ teaspoon cayenne pepper
large pinch of the following: ground clove, nutmeg,
    mace, and cardamom
1½ lb boned lean mutton or lamb, cubed
1 cup plain yogurt
1 teaspoon salt
4 tomatoes, peeled and chopped
chopped parsley for garnish

Heat the oil in a large pan and brown the onion. Add the garlic and all the other spices with the meat and gently sauté for 5 minutes. Stir in the yogurt, salt, and tomatoes. Bring to a boil, simmer, reduce heat and stir occasionally, until the meat is tender and the sauce thick, about 1½ hours. If the sauce thickens too much before the meat is cooked, add some extra water or tomato juice. Serve hot, garnished with chopped parsley and accompanied by plain rice.

SAMOSAS

These are deep-fried pastries containing a spicy filling that can be meat or vegetables. The little extra effort required in their making is worthwhile; they are delicious as an appetizer or snack.

PASTRY
1 cup all-purpose flour
½ teaspoon salt
2 tablespoons butter
4–6 tablespoons water

FILLING
1 onion, finely chopped
2 cloves garlic, crushed
1 green chili, seeded and finely chopped
1-inch piece of gingerroot, peeled and chopped
2 tablespoons butter
½ teaspoon ground turmeric
½ teaspoon chili powder
1 teaspoon salt
2 teaspoons garam masala
12 oz raw ground lean meat

Make pastry as for short-crust, then knead for about 5 minutes, until smooth and elastic. Leave covered with a damp cloth while making the filling. Gently sauté the onion, garlic, fresh chili, and ginger in the butter for 5 minutes. Stir in the seasonings and the meat, mix well and cook for 15 minutes. Remove from the heat and allow to cool while shaping the pastry. Divide the dough into 15 equal pieces. Roll out each to form a 4-inch round. Cut each round in half and lightly dampen the edges of these semicircles. Shape each up to form a cone and fill each with some of the mixture. Seal the edges well and set aside in a cool place for 30 minutes. Deep-fry in hot oil, a few at a time, for 2 to 3 minutes, until a golden brown. Drain and serve hot.

AVIAL (AVIYAL)

A mild vegetable curry with coconut and yogurt. The choice of vegetables is wide open, a variety is best. Indians always include okra (ladies' fingers) to this or any other vegetable dish whenever they get the chance.

1 teaspoon mustard seeds
1 onion, finely chopped
1 green chili, seeded and finely chopped
1 teaspoon ground turmeric
1 tablespoon ground coriander
5 tablespoons oil
1 lb mixed vegetables, prepared and sliced (choose
    from eggplant, carrots, beans, cauliflower, green
    pepper, okra, potatoes, tomatoes)
1 teaspoon salt
fresh grated coconut
⅔ cup plain yogurt
2 tablespoons butter, melted

Gently sauté the mustard seeds, onion, chili, and spices in the hot oil. Add the prepared vegetables, season with the salt, and simmer with sufficient water to just keep the vegetables moist. Cook until the vegetables are virtually done though still crunchy (the time will depend on the choice of vegetables used; those needing a little longer cooking can be started first). Stir in the coconut and simmer for a further 5 minutes. Remove from the heat, stir in the yogurt and melted butter and serve.

TANDOORI CHICKEN

A hot, but not fiery, spiced chicken which is marinated overnight and then baked in a Tandoor oven. Here it is adapted for roasting and basting in a gas or electric oven.

3 lb chicken
1 teaspoon salt
2 teaspoons chili powder
½ teaspoon ground black pepper
2 tablespoons lemon juice

MARINADE
¼ cup plain yogurt
4 cloves garlic, chopped
2-inch piece of fresh gingerroot, peeled and chopped
1 teaspoon cumin seeds
1 tablespoon coriander seeds
1 teaspoon paprika
½ teaspoon ground turmeric
½ teaspoon ground cinnamon
¼ cup butter

Pierce the chicken flesh all over with a sharp, thin skewer or needle. Sprinkle salt inside the bird. Stir together the chili powder, seasonings, and lemon juice. Rub this well into the chicken flesh and leave for 20 minutes. Prepare the marinade by blending all the ingredients to form a smooth paste. (Grind the spices first in an electric mill or mortar.) Place the chicken on a wide shallow plate or dish and cover with the marinade, again rubbing well into the flesh. Cover and refrigerate for 24 hours. Place the chicken on a rack and the whole over a roasting pan containing 1 inch cold water. Spoon any remaining marinade from the bowl over the chicken and cover it with small dabs of softened butter. Roast the chicken in a 400° oven for about 1 hour, until tender, basting frequently with the liquid in the pan.

BIRYANI

A dish from the Moglai area in which rice is layered with spicy meat and onions. Originally made with lamb but adapts well to chicken pieces. May also be served as a vegetable dish.

1½ cups long-grain rice
1 teaspoon saffron threads
5 tablespoons oil
2 cloves garlic, crushed
1-inch piece fresh gingerroot, peeled and chopped
1½ lb boned lean lamb, cubed
pinch of cayenne pepper
1 teaspoon ground cumin
1 teaspoon ground coriander
1 teaspoon black pepper
1 teaspoon salt
1 teaspoon ground cloves
1 teaspoon ground cinnamon
1¼ cups plain yogurt
2 onions, sliced
¼ cup shredded almonds
¼ cup golden seedless raisins
2 tablespoons butter

Soak rice in cold water to cover. Put saffron to soak in 5 tablespoons hot water. Leave both for about 30 minutes. Heat the oil and lightly sauté the garlic and the ginger. Add the meat and sauté for 5 minutes. Stir in the spices and yogurt, blend well together and simmer for about 35 minutes. Meanwhile bring to the boil 1 quart lightly salted water. Drain the rice and plunge into the boiling water, bring back to a boil and boil for 2 minutes. Drain well and then divide into three portions. Place one-third of the rice in a 6-cup casserole dish. Soak another third of the rice in the saffron water to color it yellow. Place half of the lamb on top of the rice in the casserole and top with half the onion. Next add the drained saffron rice and repeat with the rest of the lamb and onion, using the remaining rice as the top layer. Cover the casserole with aluminum foil and then the lid of the casserole and bake in a 350° oven for 30 minutes. Sauté the almonds and raisins in the butter and sprinkle on top of the biryani to garnish.

CURRY SAUCE

2 medium-sized onions
2 tablespoons butter
1 tablespoon curry powder
1 teaspoon curry paste
1 tablespoon flour
1 clove garlic, crushed
1 cup broth or coconut milk
salt
little cayenne pepper
2 tablespoons chutney
1 tablespoon half-and-half, optional

Slice the onions and chop them finely. Melt the butter and sauté the onions until golden brown.

Add the curry powder, paste, and flour. Cook for 5 minutes, then add the garlic, pour in the broth or coconut milk and bring to a boil. Add the seasonings and chutney, cover and simmer for 30 to 40 minutes. This sauce is improved by the addition of the cream immediately before use. Less curry powder may be used for those who prefer a mild dish.

Note: The flour can be omitted, since a curry is thickened by reduction of the liquid through long, slow simmering.

CUSTARD

A mixture of eggs and milk, with a characteristic somewhat soft consistency due to the way in which eggs coagulate when heated. Special care is needed when making egg custards to heat the mixture only sufficiently to cook the eggs, as overheating results in curdling. The use of a double boiler, or waterbath when baking, helps to control the temperature.

Custards can be served alone or as an accompaniment to other dishes and often form part of cold desserts such as trifles. Custards are also the bases of quiches.

BAKED CUSTARD

1½ cups milk
3 eggs
3 tablespoons sugar
ground nutmeg

Scald the milk in a saucepan. Beat the eggs and sugar lightly in a bowl; pour in the hot milk, stirring constantly. Strain the mixture into a greased ovenproof dish, sprinkle with nutmeg and bake in a 325° oven for about 45 minutes, or until set and firm to the touch.

Note: The dish containing custard can be stood in a shallow pan containing water – this helps to insure that the custard does not curdle or separate through overheating. Bake in individual custard cups if preferred.

CUSTARD SAUCE (CRÈME ANGLAISE)

1½ eggs or 3 yolks
1 tablespoon sugar
1¼ cups milk
few strips of thinly pared lemon rind or vanilla pod, split

Beat the eggs and sugar lightly. Warm the milk and lemon rind and leave to infuse for 10 minutes. Pour the milk onto the eggs and strain the mixture into the top of a double boiler or into a heavy-bottomed saucepan. Stir over a very gentle heat until the sauce thickens and lightly coats the back of the spoon. Do not boil.

Serve hot or cold with fruit desserts, or as a base for Bavarian Cream (see entry).

CUSTARD PIE

FOR AN 8-INCH PIE SHELL
3 eggs
3 tablespoons sugar
1¾ cups milk
little grated or ground nutmeg

Roll out the pastry and line an 8-inch pie plate; flute the edge. Place on a baking sheet. Beat the eggs lightly with the sugar, warm the milk and pour it over the egg mixture. Strain the custard into the pastry shell and sprinkle the top with nutmeg. Bake in a 425° oven for about 10 minutes, until the pastry begins to brown. Reduce the oven temperature to 350° and continue cooking for a further 20 minutes, or until the custard is just set. Serve cold.

Note: If you have trouble with the crust bubbling when making a custard tart, this is probably due to a small break in the pastry. Avoid stretching the pastry when lining the pie plate; brush the lined pie plate with raw egg white before adding the custard mixture to seal the pastry.

CUSTARD APPLE (CHERIMOYA)

The fruit of a tree grown in the West Indies and South America. The large sweet fruit resembles a small pineapple; the flesh is yellow and pulpy.

CUSTARD MARROW

(See Chayote entry.)

CUTLET

A thin cut of meat cut out from the ribs or leg of lamb, veal, or pork. Cutlets are usually broiled or sautéed. The term is also applied to a flat croquette of meat, fish, eggs, or vegetables shaped like cutlets.

VEAL CUTLETS IN LEMON SAUCE

4 veal cutlets, about $\frac{1}{4}$ inch thick
seasoned flour
4 tablespoons butter
2 tablespoons olive oil
$\frac{1}{4}$ cup chicken broth
2 tablespoons lemon juice

Coat the cutlets in seasoned flour, shaking off any excess. Melt 2 tablespoons of the butter with the oil. Add the cutlets and sauté until golden brown, turning once. Remove the cutlets to a warm serving platter and drain off any fat in the pan. Add the chicken broth and cook over high heat, scraping the pan. Cook until the broth becomes syrupy. Swirl in the butter until melted, then add the lemon juice and remove from the heat. Serve the cutlets with the sauce poured over them.

CUTTING-IN

To combine one ingredient (usually shortening) with others, by means of a pastry blender knife used with a repeated downward cutting motion.

DAB

A small flatfish related to flounders. It is light brown in color, with small dark spots and white underside and has close-set scales. Generally 4 oz to 6 oz in weight. Dabs are considered to be the sweetest-flavored fish of the flounder family. They are found on North Atlantic coasts.

DAIKON

A Japanese large white radish, varying in length from 6 or 7 inches to several feet. It is a frequent ingredient of Japanese salads.

SWEET-SOUR DAIKON

5 daikons (the size of cucumbers), peeled
$\frac{1}{2}$ cup sugar
$\frac{1}{4}$ cup rice or cider vinegar
1 cup water
$\frac{1}{4}$ cup salt

Slice the radishes thinly. Combine the remaining ingredients in a saucepan and bring to a boil. Remove from heat immediately and cool. Pour the sweet-sour mixture over the radish slices and marinate in the refrigerator for 3 days. Serve as a side salad.

DAIQUIRI

A Cuban rum, also a drink made with the rum, fresh lime juice, and sugar.

DAMSON

A very small variety of plum, dark blue in color and slightly pointed at one end, originating in Eurasia. If absolutely ripe, damsons can be eaten raw, but they are much better cooked in pies or preserves.

DANDELION

The flowers of this wild plant may be used for making wine, while the leaves may be eaten raw in salads or boiled and served as a vegetable. If they are to be cooked, wash them well and cook them like spinach; when they are quite tender, puree them, season well and add a lump of butter.

DANDELION SALAD WITH BACON

12 oz dandelion greens
3 tablespoons wine vinegar
4 oz slab bacon

Clean the dandelion greens well and dry between paper towels. Sprinkle with the vinegar. Cut the bacon into cubes, discarding the rind, and sauté until golden brown. Pour the bacon and fat in the pan over the greens and toss well. Serve immediately.

DANISH BLUE CHEESE

A soft white cheese made from full-cream cow's milk and veined with blue mold. It is produced in Denmark and has a sharp, strong flavor.

DANISH OPEN-FACE SANDWICHES

(See Smørrebrød entry.)

DANISH PASTRY

A rich yeast dough into which butter is rolled, used to make sweet breakfast rolls or coffee cakes with a cheese, jam, or other sweet filling.

DANISH PASTRY

2 packages dry yeast
1 cup milk (110°–115°)
½ cup sugar
5 cups flour
1½ teaspoons salt
¼ cup melted butter
3 eggs
1 cup butter

Dissolve the yeast in the milk with 2 tablespoons of the sugar. Combine the remaining sugar with 4 cups of the flour and the salt. Beat in the milk mixture, melted butter, and eggs. Knead in the remaining flour to make a medium soft dough. Refrigerate for 15 minutes. Roll the dough out into a rectangle ½ to ¾ inch thick, three times as long as it is wide. Dab the 1 cup butter over two-thirds of the rectangle. Fold the third without butter over the center third. Cover with the remaining third, making three layers of dough with two layers of butter. Refrigerate for 20 to 30 minutes.

Place the dough on a lightly floured board, narrow end toward you. Roll out into a rectangle as before. Again fold into thirds and refrigerate. Repeat twice more, always refrigerating between rollings and rolling from the narrow side. Refrigerate for 4 to 5 hours before shaping.

CREAM CHEESE FILLING
1 cup cream cheese, softened
¼ cup sugar
1 tablespoon flour
1 egg yolk
1 teaspoon melted butter
1 tablespoon sour cream
½ teaspoon vanilla

Cream the cream cheese with the sugar and flour. Stir in the remaining ingredients.

PRUNE FILLING
1 cup pitted cooked prunes, chopped
2 teaspoons grated lemon rind
3 tablespoons melted butter
¼ cup chopped nuts
2 tablespoons sugar

Combine ingredients and stir well.

To prepare: Roll out dough ¼ inch thick and cut into 4-inch squares. Place a spoonful of filling in the center of each square. Fold two opposite corners of the pastry to the center and pinch to hold together. Place on a lightly greased baking sheet and let rise until puffy:

To bake: Bake in a 450° oven for 10 minutes. Reduce heat to 375° and cook for 15 minutes or until golden.

DARIOLE

Originally the name of a small cake, the word now means a small, narrow mold with sloping sides.

DATE

The fruit of the date palm which is cultivated in southern California, North Africa, and western Asia. The best quality dates, which come from Tunis, are large, tender, and very sweet, with unwrinkled skins of a golden brown color. Dessert dates are usually dried before they become very ripe and are loosely packed (often on the stem) in long boxes. Other less expensive varieties, quite suitable for cooking are pitted when they are quite ripe, pressed into a block and sold in bulk. Fresh dates are becoming more readily available.

Dietetically, dates are primarily of value for their sugar content (about 50 percent), which means that they are useful as a concentrated source of energy.

DATE-BRAN MUFFINS

1¼ cups all-purpose flour
1 teaspoon salt
1 tablespoon baking powder
1½ cups bran
¾ cup milk
½ cup vegetable oil
3 tablespoons sugar
1 egg, beaten
½ cup pitted chopped dates

Grease twelve 2½-inch-deep muffin cups. Sift the flour, salt, and baking powder. Soak the bran in the milk for 5 minutes. Stir in the oil. Add the flour mixture and remaining ingredients, stirring only until just mixed. Fill the muffin cups two-thirds full and bake in a 400° oven for 20 to 25 minutes, until golden and well risen. Cool on a rack.

DATE BARS

1 cup all-purpose flour
½ teaspoon baking soda
1 teaspoon cream of tartar
pinch of salt
¼ cup butter or margarine
2 tablespoons sugar
¾ cup pitted dates
¼ pint milk

Preheat a baking sheet. Sift together the dry ingredients. Rub in the butter until the mixture resembles fine bread crumbs; add the sugar. Using kitchen shears, snip the dates into small pieces and add to the mixture. Mix to a light dough with the milk. Roll out the dough into an oblong 12 by 14 inches. Brush with milk and place on the baking sheet. Mark into eight bars, using the back of a knife. Bake in a 450° oven for about 15 minutes. Break apart and cool on a rack. Eat on the same day.

PICKLED DATES

3 lb dates
1½ quarts white vinegar
1 generous cup brown sugar
⅓ cup pickling spices

Pit and halve the dates. Boil the vinegar, sugar, and spices together until a syrup is formed. Place the dates in a jar, pour the hot syrup over them, and allow to cool. Cover tightly and keep for 3 months before use.

STUFFED DATES

Fill pitted dates with marzipan or cream cheese.

DATE-MARKING

This applies to two methods of coding food to indicate its shelf life.

(a) Most packaged, canned, and prepared foods are coded by the manufacturer to indicate the date of delivery. The retailer has a key to the code and can therefore place food on the shelves in rotation.

(b) Sell-by dates are stamped on certain short-life foods (yogurts, cream, milk, etc.) for the benefit of the customer. The food should still keep for 2 to 3 days after this date.

DECANTING

Pouring wine carefully from a bottle into a glass decanter, leaving any sediment in the bottle. It is only necessary with fine wines which have been long aged in the bottle, such as old clarets and ports. However, younger wines can also benefit from being exposed to the air before serving. Decanting is also done for aesthetic reasons, the color of the wine showing more clearly in the glass container.

DEEP FRYING

(See Frying entry.)

DEGLAZE

To swirl liquid in a skillet or roasting pan to dissolve the bits of meat sticking to the pan. The liquid then becomes part of the sauce. Any cooking fat in the pan is first poured off, stock or wine is added to the pan and brought to a boil, stirring to dislodge browned bits of food clinging to the pan.

DEHYDRATED FOODS

Foods commercially dried to preserve them as bacteria cannot thrive without moisture. They keep well if stored in an air-tight container and have the advantage of taking up less storage space than most other preserved foods.

Due to entirely new methods of processing, foods can now be reconstituted to resemble the fresh product quite closely, unlike those treated by previous drying methods. The food value is also well preserved; the only nutrients affected are vitamins B and C, the small losses of these being no more than in fresh vegetables and fruit when cooked and eaten a day or two after picking.

The process can be applied to vegetables, fruit, meat, soups, salad dressings, and other foods. Quite frequently, dehydrated foods are included as ingredients in mixes, e.g. dehydrated onion in onion sauce mix, packaged stuffings or soups.

The reconstitution rarely takes more than 30 minutes' soaking depending on the size of the particles, but exact instructions are given on the packet.

(See Accelerated Freeze-Drying entry.)

DELICATESSEN

The name given to ready-to-eat foods such as cold meats, smoked sausages, poultry, pickled and smoked fish, potato salad, coleslaw, olives, etc. The name also means the store where this type of food is sold.

DEMERARA SUGAR

Originally the cane sugar produced in British Guiana, but the phrase now refers to all crystalized cane sugars from the West Indies and nearby countries. It is a raw sugar, in which a little of the color from the cane juices remains in the sugar along with traces of minerals and other impurities; this gives it a honey color.

DEMI-GLACE (DEMI-GLAZE)

Espagnole sauce to which has been added meat glaze, meat extract or, if preferred, brown or white stock or clear soup. The sauce must then be well reduced; finally, sherry or Madeira may also be added, if desired. Demi-glace is served with high-class meat dishes.

To make it, put about 2 cups Espagnole sauce in a pan and add $\frac{1}{4}$ cup liquid meat glaze. Boil for 20 minutes, skimming frequently to remove all the fat, then strain.

DEMI-SEC

Term for sweet champagne.

DEMI-SEL

A soft, whole-milk French cheese.

DERBY CHEESE

A British cheese originally made in the North of England where it is still more widely available than in the South. It is a mild, moist cheese with a honey color. As it darkens in color and sharpens in taste with age, there is a tendency to sell Derby when it is young. A sage Derby is made by flavoring and coloring the cheese with chopped sage leaves. The cheese is traditionally associated with Christmas in England.

DESSERT

Originating from the French "le dessert." The last course of a formal dinner, usually consisting of fresh, dried, and crystalized fruit of various kinds and sometimes in addition ices, petits fours, or fancy cookies. The fruit may be placed on the table in dishes, as part of the decoration scheme, or it may be handed separately (after the table has been cleared of all unwanted dishes, glasses and cutlery and a dessert knife, spoon, and plate have been set in front of each guest). The fresh fruits offered are usually tangerines, oranges, apples, pears, peaches, pineapple, bananas, or black and white grapes. In addition, dates, raisins, figs, almonds, crystalized fruits, and preserved ginger may be served. If ices and similar sweet dishes are to be included, they should be served before the fruit. Today the term is used with reference to any sweet course which may include tarts, mousses, pies, trifles, cheesecakes, fruit compote, meringues, pancakes, and profiteroles.

DEVILING

The process of applying a highly flavored paste, or a mixture of dry condiments, to legs of poultry, game, fish roes, etc., and then broiling them, or coating them with bread crumbs and frying them. Various mixtures of condiments are used, but they usually include some very hot ingredients and something piquant; prepared mustard is often used. Turkey legs and similar foods are slashed in several places so that the mixture may be inserted or rubbed in.

DEVILED BUTTER

$\frac{1}{4}$ *cup butter*
squeeze of lemon juice
little cayenne pepper
pinch of white or black pepper
1 teaspoon curry powder

Blend all the ingredients thoroughly with a wooden spoon and use as required.

DEVILED HAM

Make some deviled butter as above, adding a pinch of ginger and substituting Worcestershire sauce for the lemon juice. Spread ham steaks fairly generously with the mixture, place them under a broiler and cook slowly, turning once. Serve immediately.

DEVILED CHICKEN

2 broiling chickens
little cayenne pepper
$\frac{1}{4}$ teaspoon black pepper
2–3 teaspoons Worcestershire sauce
2–3 teaspoons prepared mustard
2–3 teaspoons vinegar
3–4 tablespoons vegetable oil

Split the birds down the back and open them out. Blend all the remaining ingredients and when smooth spread the mixture on the chickens. Place them under a medium heat and broil, turning them once or twice, for about 30 minutes, until tender.

DEVILED TURKEY DRUMSTICKS

Cut the drumsticks from a cooked turkey. (Other fair-sized portions can be used in the same way.) Score with a sharp knife, then brush with melted butter. To prepare the deviled mixture, mix on a plate 1 teaspoon each of French and English mustard, 2 teaspoons finely chopped chutney, a pinch of ground ginger and a little pepper, salt, and cayenne. Spread this mixture over and into the cuts and leave the turkey legs for 1 hour or longer. Broil them on a greased pan under a medium heat until crisp and brown, turning them regularly to insure even cooking. Serve garnished with watercress.

DEVIL'S FOOD CAKE

A moist chocolate cake that is a great favorite in the United States. It is usually iced with White Mountain Frosting, but die-hards hold out for an all-chocolate cake and chocolate frosting.

DEVIL'S FOOD CAKE

1 cup cake flour
$\frac{3}{4}$ teaspoon salt
$\frac{3}{4}$ teaspoon soda
$1\frac{1}{4}$ cups sugar
$\frac{1}{2}$ cup vegetable shortening
$\frac{2}{3}$ cup water
2 oz unsweetened chocolate
2 eggs
1 teaspoon vanilla

Place the shortening in a large mixer bowl and sift in the dry ingredients. Beat on low speed to moisten the ingredients, then beat on medium speed for 2 minutes. Add the melted chocolate, eggs, and vanilla, and beat 1 minute longer.

Pour the batter into two greased and lined 9-inch layer pans. Bake in a 350° oven for 25 to 30 minutes. Let cake rest in pans 10 minutes before removing to cool completely on racks. Frost as desired.

DEVONSHIRE CREAM

Name sometimes given to clotted cream with a minimum butterfat content of 55 percent. The cream is scalded in hot water after being separated from the milk. It is made chiefly in Devon, Cornwall, and Somerset, England, and is considered a gourmet treat.

DEXTROSE

Another name for Glucose. (See Glucose entry.)

DHAL

A lentil grown in India. It is used to make a dish similar to kedgeree or stew; or it can be pureed to serve with curry.

LENTIL PUREE (DHAL)

$\frac{1}{2}$ cup lentils
$\frac{2}{3}$ cup cold water
pepper
salt
1 medium onion
vegetable oil for sautéing
2 tablespoons butter

There is no need to soak the lentils. Wash them, put them into cold water, add pepper and salt and let them cook steadily for about 1 to $1\frac{1}{2}$ hours, adding more water if they get too dry. Meanwhile, chop the onion finely and sauté it. When the lentils are tender, remove them from the heat and stir vigorously. Add the butter and the sautéed onion and stir over the heat to blend well. Serve with curry.

DIABETIC FOODS

Specially prepared foods containing reduced amounts of carbohydrate. Diabetic jams and marmalades, chocolates, and candies may be bought. Saccharin is also available to replace sugar. On the whole, however, it is considered better for the diabetic to get accustomed to doing without sweet foods and to build his diet on the foods he is allowed, rather than perpetuate his sweet tooth by buying expensive substitutes. These foods may, however, be useful in certain circumstances—sugarless drinks, for example, for children during illness. (See Saccharin entry.)

DIET

The food eaten regularly, or the pattern of eating. A diet also means, in a narrower sense, a special regime, generally followed for medical reasons.

The normal diet should provide sufficient protein, carbohydrates, fats, vitamins, minerals, and water. Actual requirements of these nutrients are difficult to assess and can at best only be a rough estimate, for individual requirements vary enormously.

People on special diets need the same nutrients, so it is important to check the diet and, if certain foods have to be omitted, to make sure the missing nutrients are made up in some other way.

Overweight Diet

Overweight (obesity) is becoming an increasing problem as today's lifestyle encourages over-eating and less exercise. There are many ways of cutting down on intake of food, but it is important that a diet suits the individual.

Snacks and between-meal nibbles of carbohydrates are a cause of obesity and should be rigorously avoided. If in any doubt about diets, medical advice should be obtained before starting one.

Diabetic Diet

A correct diet is of great importance in keeping the diabetic healthy. It resembles a diet for overweight in that carbohydrate foods are cut down, but the essential point is that the carbohydrate content should be kept at the same level every day, depending on the doctor's orders.

Light Diet

Frequently ordered for a patient in bed. It may occasionally be a fluid or soft diet, if the patient has difficulty with swallowing. Otherwise, it simply means avoiding rich, highly spiced, or fried foods.

Ulcer Diet

The many specialized ulcer diets have largely disappeared, leaving in use a fairly simple diet, rather like the light diet. Foods with seeds and skins should be avoided and so should spiced and fried items. As this means no fruit or vegetables (unless strained), fruit juice or vitamin C tablets should be taken instead. But more important than the diet are the following principles:

Do not worry
Eat slowly and rest after meals
Eat small meals at regular intervals.

Other Diets

The doctor may in certain cases prescribe a low-fat, low-salt, or low-protein diet. There are also other diets that control disorders in metabolism. None of these should be attempted except on specific medical orders.

Vegetarian Diet

(See Vegetarian Diet entry.)

DIGESTION

With one or two exceptions, foods cannot be absorbed straight into the blood stream as they are. They have to be broken down, first physically into a soft mass and then chemically by the digestive juices into soluble products which can pass through the wall of the intestine into the blood stream. The cellulose in fruit and vegetables, together with the skins and seeds, the coarse fiber and other indigestible material, are passed on and evacuated.

In the mouth, the food is ground to small pieces and mixed with saliva, which starts the process. Very little digestion takes place in the stomach, the gastric juice being mainly hydrochloric acid; the stomach acts as a food reservoir, makes the food more fluid and allows it to pass gradually into the small intestine. There the digestive juices break down proteins to amino acids, fats to fatty acids, and starches to sugars. They are then absorbed into the blood stream, along with the mineral salts, vitamins, and water. The indigestible material is moved onto the large intestine.

The word "indigestible" in this context merely applies to the coarse residue that the body cannot absorb but which is useful roughage. The popular idea of indigestible food means food that causes pain or discomfort. There are very few foods indeed which are in themselves indigestible, apart from poisonous fruits and fungi. The indigestion is caused by other circumstances, such as eating too quickly, too much, or while very worried, or it may be caused by an individual idiosyncrasy or by swallowing air. Psychological considerations of stress and overwork have far more effect on digestion than the food itself. In fact, over 95 percent of the digestible parts of foods (i.e., excluding fiber and skins) is normally digested. Contrary to popular belief, foods that are disliked are apparently digested as thoroughly as those that are liked.

Foods vary in the time they take to pass from the stomach into the intestines, but this does not appear to have any special importance, apart from the fact that the quick passage of food leaves you feeling hungry sooner, so for dieters it may be advisable to eat foods that are not digested quickly.

DILL

An aromatic plant similar to fennel; it originated in Spain. The seeds are used for flavoring soups, sauces, and pickles. Oil of dill, used in the manufacture of dill water for infants, is distilled from the seeds. The leaves have a strong flavor and can be used sparingly fresh or dried, in soups, salads, and fish dishes. Dill seeds make an unusual but interesting addition to a salad. They can be mixed into a coleslaw, sprinkled over a cucumber and yogurt salad, or even mixed with yogurt or a vinaigrette dressing to add an interesting flavor variation. It is an extremely popular flavoring in Scandinavia.

DINNER

The name usually given to the main meal of the day when served in the evening. (If it is eaten at midday, it is more often called lunch or luncheon.) The accepted plan for a formal dinner is soup or hor d'oeuvre (melon, grapefruit, shrimp cocktail, pâté, etc.), a main dish plus vegetable accompaniments, salad, and a dessert (which can be hot or cold). For simple family dinners, two courses only may be served.

Sample Family Dinner Menus

Veal Goulash
Boiled Rice   Green Beans
Apple Pie à la Mode

London Broil
Mashed Potatoes   Brussels Sprouts
Caramel Custard

Meat Loaf
Scalloped Potatoes
Stewed Tomatoes   Peas
Chocolate Cake

Pork Chops
Baked Potatoes
Broiled Tomatoes   Salad
Sliced Oranges

Tomato Soup
Hamburgers
Fried Potatoes   Fried Onions
Fruit Crumble

Sample Formal Dinner Menus

Jellied Consommé
Broiled Salmon   Sauté Potatoes
Peas   Cucumber Salad
Baked Alaska

Hors d'oeuvre
Sole Véronique
Rice
Creamed Spinach
Tossed Green Salad
Charlotte Russe

Grapefruit
Roast Loin of Pork
Roast Potatoes   Broccoli Spears
Belgian Endive Salad
Orange and Lemon Sherbet

Shrimp Cocktail
Boiled Lamb Chops   Duchesse Potatoes
Asparagus with Melted Butter   Watercress Salad
Lemon Meringue Pie

Dinner Party
(See Party entry.)

DIP

A dip is a fairly soft, well-flavored mixture, often served at a cocktail or wine and cheese party or similar occasion; guests help themselves by dipping or dunking small crackers, potato chips, short sticks of celery, or something of the kind into a bowl of the mixture. Cheese, soft cheese, whipped cream and yogurt form ideal bases for the mixtures.

BLUE CHEESE DIP

4 oz Danish Blue or Roquefort cheese, softened
1 package (3 oz) cream cheese, softened
1 tablespoon lemon juice
pinch of salt

Blend all the ingredients to a smooth cream and serve with chunks of French bread or vegetable dunks.

This dip can form the basis of an interesting relish to serve at barbecues with grilled meats and hamburgers.

HOT MUSTARD DIP

1 tablespoon Dijon mustard
2 teaspoons prepared English mustard
2 tablespoons vinegar
2 tablespoons butter
3 tablespoons flour
1¼ cups broth
1 tablespoon cream, optional

Blend the mustards and vinegar together. Melt the butter in a pan and stir in the flour. Cook for 2 to 3 minutes, stir in the broth, bring to a boil and stir until the mixture thickens. Remove from the heat and add the prepared mustard. Serve hot. If a milder flavor is preferred, stir in the cream just before serving with chipolatas, meatballs, or potato chips.

DOBOS TORTE

The famous seven-layer cake of Hungary, made with a genoise sponge, filled with a rich chocolate frosting and topped with crunchy caramel. This extravagant version has eight layers.

DOBOS TORTE

1 recipe Genoise (see Genoise entry.)
1 recipe Butter Cream (see Frosting entry)
3 oz unsweetened chocolate
¾ cup sugar

Divide the cake batter between two greased and lined jelly-roll pans. Bake at 350° for 10 to 12 minutes, until the cakes are golden brown. Remove from oven and invert pans. Strip off the paper. Return cakes to pan; cut each cake cross-wise into four strips. Remove to racks to cool.

Flavor the butter cream with the chocolate. Reserve the eighth layer and stack the other seven with frosting between each layer and on top of the top layer. Melt the sugar slowly in a heavy skillet, stirring continuously until the sugar is melted and brown. Place the reserved layer on waxed paper and pour the caramelized sugar over it, spreading evenly. Cut through the caramel with a warmed knife at 1-inch intervals so that the torte can be sliced. Place on top of the stacked layers and frost the sides of the torte with the remaining frosting. Rosettes of butter cream can be piped along the top of the torte if desired.

DOGFISH

A name given to various fishes of the shark family found in different parts of the world; some types can be eaten.

DOLMAS

A Turkish dish prepared by stuffing grape, fig, cabbage, or other edible leaves with a mixture such as ground lamb and cooked rice, then braising the rolled-up leaves. The term is some-times applied in the Middle East to stuffed eggplant, zucchini, etc.

Dolmades is the name given to stuffed grape leaves in Greece. (See Grape Leaves entry.)

DOLPHIN

A game fish of southern waters, iridescent in color, reaching 50 to 60 lb. It is unrelated to the mammal of the same name. Dolphin may be cooked like swordfish, and is prized for its flavor.

DOUBLE GLOUCESTER CHEESE

A traditional British cheese with a smooth mature flavor and open buttery texture. Its light orange color is achieved with the addition of the dye annatto.

Until the end of World War II there was a Single and Double Gloucestershire cheese. Both were made by similar methods but the Single Gloucester was smaller in size and less acid: this cheese is still made in small quantities on a few farms.

DOUGH

A thick mixture of uncooked flour and liquid, often combined with other ingredients. The term is not confined to the typical yeast dough, but is also applied to mixtures such as pastry, cakes, biscuits, and cookies. In pastry making the dough is termed "stiff" when only sufficient liquid is added to bind the ingredients together (e.g. short-crust pastry), whereas in cakemaking a stiff dough contains sufficient liquid to make it too sticky to handle, though it is still stiff enough to hold its shape when dropped from a spoon (e.g. fruitcake dough). A "firm" dough is slightly softer, though still fairly stiff – for example, the mixtures for biscuits; a "soft" dough contains an amount of liquid that makes it only just firm enough to handle, e.g. bread dough and other yeast mixtures. (See Bread entry.)

Refrigerated fresh dough is a live dough product in pressure-packed cylinders found on the refrigerator shelves of supermarkets. Once purchased, store in the coolest part of the refrigerator and use by the date stamped on the can. Do not freeze refrigerated fresh dough. For use follow manufacturer's instructions on the pack.

DOUGHNUT

A cake made of slightly sweetened dough cooked in hot fat and dredged with sugar. Doughnuts can be made with either yeast or baking powder as a leavening agent. They can be filled with jam, jelly, or cream, or dipped in sugar.

JELLY DOUGHNUTS

1 package dry active yeast
5 tablespoons tepid milk
2 cups all-purpose flour
½ teaspoon salt
1 tablespoon butter or margarine
1 egg, beaten

jelly
deep fat for frying
sugar and ground cinnamon to coat

Blend the yeast with the milk. Mix the flour and salt and rub in the butter. Add the yeast liquid and egg and mix to a soft dough, adding a little more milk if necessary. Beat well until smooth, cover with a cloth and leave to rise until doubled in size. Knead lightly on a floured surface and divide into 10 to 12 pieces. Shape each into a round, put 1 teaspoon jelly in the center and draw up the edges to form a ball, pressing firmly to seal them together. Heat the fat to 350°, or until it will brown a 1-inch cube of bread in 1 minute. Fry the doughnuts fairly quickly until golden brown (for 5 to 10 minutes, according to size). Drain on crumpled paper towels and toss in sugar mixed with a little cinnamon. Serve the same day.

CAKE DOUGHNUTS

2 cups plus 2 tablespoons all-purpose flour
2 teaspoons baking powder
pinch of ground cinnamon
2 tablespoons butter
¼ cup sugar
1 egg, beaten
milk
deep fat for frying

Sift the flour, baking powder, and cinnamon and rub in the butter until the mixture resembles fine bread crumbs. Stir in the sugar. Make a well in the center, pour in the egg and gradually work in the dry ingredients. Turn the dough out onto a floured board and lightly knead until free from cracks; then roll out until ½ inch thick and cut into rings with a doughnut cutter. Heat the oil to 375° and slide the doughnuts into the oil. Fry until they are golden brown on each side, turning once. Drain on paper towels and sprinkle with sugar.

DOVE

(See Pigeon entry.)

DRAGÉE

A French candy made of fruit, nuts, etc., coated with a hard sugar frosting; sugar almonds are the best-known example. In Greece, it is traditional to serve sugar almonds at weddings, festive occasions, and parties.

DRAINING

The two main methods of removing surplus liquid or fat from foods are by means of a sieve or colander or by placing them on crumpled absorbent paper towels.

DRAMBUIE

A Scotch liqueur, golden in color, made of whisky and heather honey.

DRAWN BUTTER

Melted butter, used as a dressing for cooked vegetables, etc.

DREDGING

The action of sprinkling food lightly and evenly with flour, sugar, etc. Fish and meat are often dredged with flour before frying, while cakes, cookies, pancakes, etc., may be sprinkled with fine sugar to improve their appearance. A pierced container of metal or plastic (known as a dredger) is usually used.

DRESS, TO

To prepare for cooking or serving in such a way that the food looks as attractive as possible. The term sometimes denotes a special method of preparation, as in dressed crab.

DRIED FRUIT

This term includes both small and large fruits, such as currants, raisins, dates, prunes (plums), apricots, peaches, figs, pears, and apples, which are used in cakes, breads, desserts, and other dishes.

Their chief food value lies in their sugar content. Apricots and prunes have a useful amount of vitamin A, but no dried fruit retains its original vitamin C.

Cake Fruit (Currants, Raisins, and Dates)

Most dried fruit is available ready prepared, but fruit not prepacked must be carefully cleaned before being used. A small quantity of currants, etc., which is required in a hurry may be cleaned by mixing the fruit with a little dry flour and rubbing on a sieve to remove the stems, etc. If the fruit is really dirty, however, it must be washed. Place it in a colander resting in a bowl and pour cold water over, shaking the fruit in the colander meanwhile. Drain the fruit well, spread it out on a cloth and leave to dry overnight; if necessary finish the drying in a very cool oven. Finally, pick the fruit over and pack it into clean, dry jars. It is most important that the fruit should be quite dry before it is stored or it will not keep, while if it is wet when used in a cake, it will sink to the bottom.

Raisins (unless seedless) need to be pitted before use: do this by hand, dipping the fingers into hot water after dealing with every 2 to 3 raisins. Dry the fruit and if necessary cut it up before use.

Dates should also be cut up before use.

Prunes, Apricots, Peaches, Figs, Pears, and Apples

These need to be washed and then soaked in cold water overnight; they should be cooked in the same water. They swell considerably and 8 oz will provide average-sized portions for 4 to 6 people, except in the case of apples, which will give about 12 servings per 8 oz. The cooking time ranges from 20 to 30 minutes for figs and pears to 30 to 40 for apricots and apples and 40 to 60 for peaches and prunes. About 2 tablespoons sugar to $\frac{1}{4}$ cup fruit (unsoaked weight) is required: figs and prunes usually need less sweetening, apricots and apples more.

Stewed Dried Fruit

Apricots, prunes, and figs should be washed, then soaked for some hours (or overnight) in fresh water. Cook them in this water, adding $\frac{1}{3}$ to $\frac{1}{2}$ cup sugar and a piece of lemon rind per pint. Stew gently till soft and serve cold.

DRIED VEGETABLES

(See Dehydrated Foods, Drying, Pulses entries.)

DRINKS

(See individual entries – Tea, Coffee, Lemonade, Spirits, Wine, Cocktail, etc.)

DROPPING CONSISTENCY

The term used to describe the texture of a cake or pudding mixture before cooking. To test it, well fill a spoon with the mixture, hold the spoon on its side above a bowl and count slowly – the mixture should drop in about 5 seconds without your having to jerk the spoon.

DRYING

One of the most natural ways of preserving fruits and vegetables. If the sun is hot enough the process can be done in the open air over several days. As the climate is not always suitable it is best to alternate sessions between sun and artificial heat (low oven, airing cupboard, top of boiler, or warming tray). The temperature should be between 120° and 150°.

Prepared fruit or vegetables should be spread out so that air can circulate freely. Slatted frames or large sieves are ideal, although some method can usually be improvised. It is also important to protect the food from dust and insects by covering with cheesecloth. When drying is complete, the fruit or vegetables should be left for 48 hours to cool completely. They can then be stored in a cool, dry, well-ventilated place within jars, tins, or boxes. Unlike most foods they do not need to be in airtight containers. Food stored in this way should keep for about a year as long as the containers are moisture free.

Fruits Suitable for Drying

APPLES

Prepare the fruit by peeling, coring, and slicing in rings about $\frac{1}{4}$ inch thick, using a stainless steel knife or peeler. Put the sliced fruit in a solution of $\frac{1}{4}$ cup salt to 5 quarts water, leave for 5 minutes, then dry on a cloth. Spread the rings on trays or thread on thin sticks and dry in a very cool oven (lowest setting) until leathery in texture – about 6 to 8 hours.

PEARS

These should be nearly ripe. Peel, core, and cut into halves or quarters, dip into salted water, spread on trays and dry.

FRUIT WITH PITS

Dry these whole; large fruits, such as plums or greengages, can be cut in half and pitted. Dry them until no juice comes out when the fruit is squeezed.

GRAPES

Spread out, and continue drying until the grapes are no longer juicy.

Vegetables Suitable for Drying

ONIONS

Drying is an excellent way of treating onions which are unsuitable for ordinary harvesting. Peel them, slice into rings, then steam for 1 to 2 minutes or blanch in boiling water for $\frac{1}{2}$ minute. Plunge the rings into cold water, drain, and spread out to dry until crisp.

MUSHROOMS

Choose young, tender mushrooms, peel them and cut or slice if very big. Spread out or string (with knots between) and dry until leathery.

GREEN BEANS

Slice the beans, then blanch them in boiling slightly salted water for 3 to 5 minutes. Plunge them into cold water, drain, and spread out to dry until crisp.

LIMA BEANS

Shell them and blanch in boiling water for 3 to 5 minutes. Plunge into cold water, drain, and spread out to dry.

PEAS

These are best left upon the plants until the pods become yellow. Gather the pods, shuck them, and spread the seeds out to dry before storing. Late crops should be pulled up bodily and hung in a dry, airy place to ripen before shelling.

To cook home-dried vegetables: Soak them for at least 12 hours before use and then cook in the same water; season, bring to a boil and simmer until tender.

Herbs are also suitable for drying. (See separate entries.)

DUBLIN BAY PRAWN (LANGOUSTINE)

The largest and best of the prawn family, obtainable fresh during the summer months. To prepare prawns, break off and discard the head, take the flesh intact from the shell and remove the black filament in the back. Serve the prawns on a bed of lettuce, garnished with cucumber or with their own claws, with mayonnaise as an accompaniment.

DUBONNET

A well-known and popular quinine-flavoured French apéritif. A fortified wine which may be drunk neat, with ice and lemon, or made into a cocktail with vodka or gin.

DUCHESSE POTATOES

(See Potato entry.)

DUCK

A web-footed bird, of which there are various wild and domestic varieties. The flesh is dark, and though ducklings have more fat than chicken, there is little flesh on the bones, so it is necessary to allow about 12 oz dressed duck per person. Wild duck is classed as game and is only in season for a short time (see Wild Duck entry). It is served roasted and undercooked. Domestic duckling bred for the table is classed as poultry and is readily available frozen. It can be roasted and served with stuffing, applesauce, or orange sauce. When choosing fresh duckling for the table, select a young bird, as the flesh is more tender.

Preparation and roasting: A young duckling does not require stuffing, but it is usual to stuff an older one. Truss for roasting (the wings are not drawn across the back) and sprinkle the breast with pepper and salt. Prick skin all over. Cook in a 400° oven, allowing 15 minutes per lb. To cook by the slow method, put it in a 325° oven and allow 20 minutes per lb. Remove the trussing strings and skewers and serve the bird on a hot dish, garnished with watercress and accompanied by potatoes or other vegetables, applesauce, and thin brown gravy. Orange salad is also popular.

DUCK WITH BIGARADE SAUCE

1 roasting duck
1 tablespoon butter
salt
pepper
⅔ cup white wine
4 oranges
1 lemon
1 tablespoon sugar
1 tablespoon vinegar
2 tablespoons brandy
1 tablespoon cornstarch
1 bunch watercress

Rub the breast of the duck with the butter and sprinkle with salt. Put the duck in the roasting pan with the wine and cook in a 375° oven for 30 minutes per lb basting occasionally with the wine. Squeeze the juice from 3 of the oranges and the lemon and grate the rind from 1 orange. Melt the sugar in a pan with the vinegar and heat until it is a dark brown caramel. Add the brandy and the juice of the oranges and lemon to the caramel and simmer for 5 minutes. Cut the remaining orange into segments.

When the duck is cooked, remove it from the roasting pan, carve it and place the pieces on a serving dish. Drain the excess fat from the roasting pan and add the grated rind and the orange sauce to the sediment. Blend the cornstarch with a little water, stir it into the pan juices, return the pan to the heat, bring to a boil and cook for 2 to 3 minutes, stirring. Season and pour the sauce over the duck. Garnish with orange wedges and watercress.

DUCK AND ORANGE CASSEROLE

1 duck, quartered
seasoned flour
2 tablespoons butter
4 oz mushrooms, sliced
2 onions, chopped
¼–½ cup flour
1 quart broth
⅔ cup orange juice
1 orange

Coat the duck with the seasoned flour. Sauté the duck in the butter for 8 to 10 minutes, until well browned, and transfer to a casserole. Sauté the mushrooms and onions lightly in the hot butter for about 3 minutes, remove from the pan, and add to the casserole. Stir the flour into the remaining fat and brown it over a very low heat, stirring all the time. Remove from the heat, gradually stir in the broth and orange juice and bring to a boil, continue to stir until it thickens. Pour over the duck, cover and cook in a 350° oven for 1 hour, until the duck is tender.

Serve garnished with orange slices.

Duck Eggs
(See Egg entry.)

DULSE

(See Seaweed entry.)

DUMPLING

A small ball of dough cooked by steaming or boiling with a stew or soup. It may be plain or flavored with herbs or cheese. The term also refers to a piece of fruit enclosed and baked in pastry.

DUMPLINGS FOR STEW

3 tablespoons vegetable shortening
1½ cups all-purpose flour
2 teaspoons baking powder
½ teaspoon salt
¾ cup milk

Combine the dry ingredients and cut the shortening into them until the mixture resembles small bread crumbs. Stir in the milk. Drop the dough onto the stew (the dough should rest on top of the stew and not be immersed in the liquid). Cook 10 minutes. Cover and cook about 10 minutes longer.

MATZO BALLS

4 eggs, separated
1 teaspoon salt
dash of cayenne pepper
2 teaspoons grated onion
2 tablespoons melted chicken fat
¾ cup matzo meal

Combine the yolks, seasonings, onion, and chicken fat and beat until fluffy. Beat the egg whites until stiff and fold into the yolk mixture. Fold in the matzo meal and chill for 30 to 60 minutes.

Wet the hands with cold water and shape the dough into ½-inch balls. Cover and cook in boiling stock until the balls rise to the surface of the liquid, about 15 minutes.

PEACH DUMPLINGS

1 recipe short-crust pastry (see Pastry entry)
6 peaches, peeled, halved and pitted
lemon juice
½ cup brown sugar, packed
3 tablespoons raisins
3 tablespoons chopped nuts
¼ cup butter, softened

Roll the pastry out and cut into six 7-inch squares. Sprinkle the peaches with lemon juice. Combine the brown sugar with the raisins, nuts and butter and stuff the peaches. Re-form the peaches and place each peach on a pastry square. Draw the corners up and pinch to seal. Place in a baking dish and bake in a 425° oven for 40 minutes. If desired when the pastry begins to brown, heat ½ cup brown sugar with 1 cup water to a boil. Pour over the dumplings and continue to cook until done. The liquid will form a sauce. Otherwise, serve warm or cold with Hard sauce.

DUNDEE CAKE

A fairly rich fruitcake, decorated with halved blanched almonds.

DUNDEE CAKE

2 cups all-purpose flour
pinch of salt

1 cup butter
1 cup sugar
4 eggs, beaten
2¼ cups yellow raisins
2¼ cups currants
1 cup chopped mixed peel
¾ cup candied cherries
grated rind of ½ lemon
1 cup whole blanched almonds

Grease and line an 8-inch round cake pan, 3 inches deep. Sift together the flour and salt. Cream the butter, add the sugar and beat together until light and fluffy. Gradually add the beaten eggs one at a time. Fold in the flour, fruit, peel, cherries, lemon rind, and ⅓ cup of the almonds, chopped. Turn the mixture into the prepared pan and level the surface. Split the remainder of the almonds in half and arrange neatly over the cake, rounded side up. Bake in a 300° oven for about 2½ hours. When quite firm to the touch, remove from the pan and cool on a rack.

DUTCH CHEESE

There are several varieties of Dutch cheese, the best known being Edam and Gouda. (See individual cheese entries.) There are also some spiced Dutch cheeses.

DUXELLES

French name for finely chopped mushrooms sautéed with shallots or onion in butter and used for stuffings and in sauces.

EASTER

A number of traditional dishes are associated with the religious festival of Easter, particularly special breads, eggs, and cakes. Simnel Cake is usually eaten on Easter Sunday or on Mother's Day, while Hot Cross Buns are by tradition eaten on Good Friday. (See separate entries for recipes.)

Pashka is a traditional Russian dish eaten at this time. It is a rich sweet mixture containing soft cheese, cream, candied peel, and fruit.

Decorated Eggs

Boiled eggs can be painted or decorated. This is particularly popular with children.

Chocolate Easter Eggs

Tin molds may be bought in various sizes. Use good quality couverture chocolate and break it up small. Melt the chocolate over gently simmering water in a double boiler then remove half of it and stir until almost set. Return this chocolate to pan and mix well. Polish inside the molds with cotton wool, half fill with chocolate and tilt so as to run the couverture to the edge of the mold quite evenly all round. Do this two or three times, then pour the surplus back into the chocolate pan. Run the finger round the edge of the mold, then turn it upside down on a cool, flat surface. As the shells cool, they will contract slightly and may be removed from the tins by pressing gently at one end. The outer glazed surface given by the contact with the bright metal must not be handled more than can be helped. The shells can be joined by lightly touching the two halves onto a warm, flat pan, so that just sufficient chocolate melts to enable them

to set firmly together.

Wrap the eggs in foil, or decorate them with ribbon, frosting, chocolate piping, and so on.

ECCLES CAKES

A pastry with a filling of dried fruit moistened with melted butter and sugar, famous throughout England but originating in the Lancashire town of Eccles.

ECCLES CAKES

1 sheet frozen puff pastry

FOR THE FILLING
2 tablespoons butter, softened
2 tablespoons brown sugar
2 tablespoons finely chopped mixed candied peel
$\frac{1}{4}$ cup currants

FOR THE GLAZE
egg white
superfine sugar

Cut the pastry into $3\frac{1}{2}$-inch rounds. Bind the ingredients for the filling and place a small spoonful of mixture in the center of each pastry round. Draw the edges together and reshape into a round. Turn it over and roll lightly until the currants just show through. Score with a knife in a lattice pattern. Allow the cakes to rest on a baking sheet for about 10 minutes in a cool place. Brush them with egg white and dredge with sugar. Bake in 450° oven for about 15 minutes, until golden. Cool on a rack.

ÉCLAIR

A small finger-shaped cake prepared from choux pastry (see Pastry entry) and filled with whipped cream or pastry cream; the top is iced with chocolate or coffee glaze.

Small éclairs made in the same way, but with a cheese or other tasty filling, make a delicious hors d'oeuvre for cocktail parties.

ÉCLAIRS

choux pastry (see Pastry entry) made with ½ cup flour
⅓ cup whipping cream or pastry cream
chocolate or coffee glaze, (see icing glaze under Glaze)

Put the choux pastry into a pastry bag fitted with a plain round tip ½ inch in diameter and pipe in fingers 3½ inches long onto the baking sheet, keeping the lengths even and cutting the dough off with a wet knife against the edge of the tube. Bake in a 400° oven for about 35 minutes until well risen, crisp, and golden brown. Remove from the pan, slit down the sides with a sharp-pointed knife to allow the steam to escape and leave on a cake rack to cool. When the éclairs are cold, and shortly before serving, fill with whipped pastry cream, then ice the tops with chocolate glaze or dip in melted chocolate.

FILLINGS
1. Cream together a 3 oz package cream cheese and 3 tablespoons softened butter; add 1 teaspoon of lemon juice and salt and pepper to taste.
2. Cream together a 3 oz package cream cheese, 3 tablespoons softened butter and 2 teaspoons tomato paste, add a few drops of Worcestershire sauce and seasoning to taste.
3. Cream ¾ to 1 cup butter with 2 teaspoons anchovy paste and pepper to taste.

EDAM CHEESE

A rounded dark yellow Dutch cheese with a bright red rind made in Holland, Germany, Belgium, Yugoslavia, and the United States. It is a pleasant cheese to eat with bread, crackers, and fruit and is often served by the Dutch for breakfast.

EEL

A long, snakelike fish found in fresh and salt waters.

Eels can be jellied, fried, or stewed. Smoked eels are considered delicious by many people and are often a highlight of a Japanese meal.

To prepare eels: First skin the fish: cut off the head, turn back the skin at the top and peel it off. Clean the fish thoroughly, wash it in salted water and cut into 2- to 3-inch pieces.

STEWED EELS

2 lb eels, cleaned
salt
pepper
squeeze of lemon juice
few sprigs of parsley
3 tablespoons butter
5 tablespoons flour
1¼ cups milk
2 tablespoons chopped parsley

Split open the body and remove the backbone. Clean well and wash the eels in salted water. Cut the eels into 2-inch pieces, cover with water and add the seasoning, lemon juice, and sprigs of parsley.

Simmer for about 45 minutes, until tender. Drain, and reserve 1¼ cups of the cooking liquid; keep the fish warm. Melt the butter, stir in the flour, and cook for 2 to 3 minutes. Remove the pan from the heat and gradually stir in the reserved cooking liquid with the milk. Bring to a boil, stirring until the sauce thickens. Remove from the heat, stir in the parsley, add seasoning to taste, and serve the eels coated with this sauce.

FRIED EELS

Prepare the eels as above, dry the pieces, dip them in seasoned flour, coat with egg and bread crumbs or batter and fry until crisp and brown.

EGG

Usually refers to the hen's egg although those from other birds can be used.

A plentiful supply of eggs is one of the greatest aids when planning meals and cooking.

From the dietetic point of view, eggs provide protein and fat; one egg has a similar protein value to that of 1 oz of beef and rather more fat; it supplies calcium, iron, and vitamins A, D, B_1 and B_2 in useful amounts.

Apart from their use as a main dish at almost any meal of the day, as an ingredient in entrée dishes and salads and as a garnish, eggs are employed in cookery for three purposes:

1. *Emulsifying*: the yolk only is used, as in mayonnaise.

2. *Thickening and binding*: these properties are important in the making of sauces, custards, fish cakes, meat loaves, and as a coating for foods, which may disintegrate in cooking, e.g. croquettes, fritters.

3. *Leavening or "foaming"*: eggs are widely used as a leavening agent in cakes and batters. Additional lightness is given by whisking the whites separately and folding into the mixture. Beaten egg whites are also used for meringues, soufflés, and light foamy desserts.

The egg yolks alone are often added to pastry, almond paste, etc., to give extra richness and color and sometimes to bind the mixture.

Egg Grading
The United States Department of Agriculture sets the standards for egg grading – both for size and quality. There is no difference between white and brown eggs except in the color of the shell.

SIZE CLASSES	MINIMUM WEIGHT PER DOZEN
Jumbo	30 oz
Extra large	27 oz
Large	24 oz
Medium	21 oz
Small	18 oz
Peewee (bantam)	15 oz

QUALITY GRADES
The USDA quality grades are AA, A, B, and C. The grading is based on the area covered by a freshly broken egg, the thickness of the white, how high it stands and the firmness and height of the yolk. AA graded eggs, for example, will cover the smallest area when broken. The white will be thickest, stand the highest and the yolk will be the most firm and also stand the highest.

Accelerated Freeze-Dried Eggs
Eggs can be preserved by AFD (see Accelerated Freeze-drying entry).

Powdered Eggs
These are made by spraying pulped fresh eggs in hot air. The resulting powder (1 oz of which is equivalent to 2 fresh eggs) is similar in use to fresh eggs, though it does not aerate as well. Powdered eggs can be of great help during times of food shortage, but are generally used only in commercial baking. They are not generally available.

Liquid Frozen Eggs
These also are used mainly for commercial purposes. The eggs are shelled, placed in containers, frozen, and kept in cold storage.

Freezing Eggs
Eggs can be frozen if the whites are separated from the yolks, each being stored in an airtight container. Whole eggs do not freeze as they will crack and hard-cooked eggs become rubbery if stored in a freezer. However, beaten whole eggs can be frozen, providing they are mixed lightly together with a little salt or sugar.

Eggs From Other Birds

DUCK EGGS
These are similar in food value and cooking properties to hens' eggs, though they are larger and somewhat richer. As they are sometimes contaminated with bacteria which give rise to gastroenteritis, they should be cooked very thoroughly (14 minutes being allowed for boiling) and they should not be preserved or stored in any way, nor should they be used for making meringues as they will not give satisfactory results.

GOOSE EGGS
Any of the ordinary cooking methods may be used for goose eggs, which may also be used in cakes and custards. As they are larger than hens' eggs, more time should be allowed for cooking – to soft cook, allow 7 minutes. They should not be preserved unless they are known to have been laid under strictly controlled hygienic conditions.

TURKEY EGGS
Although larger than hens' eggs, turkey eggs are just as delicate in flavor. They may be cooked in all the same ways and can be used in all cakes and custards. Allow longer time for boiling – e.g. about 7 minutes to soft cook.

GUINEA FOWLS' EGGS
When they are available, they make a good hors d'oeuvre; cook the eggs for 10 to 15 minutes, shell, and serve on a bed of watercress.

QUAIL EGGS
These are available preserved, canned, or fresh.

To test eggs for freshness: These homely ways of testing freshness are based on the fact that there is always a small amount of air inside the shell of an egg, which increases as the egg ages, so the fresher the egg the fuller it is.
1. Place the egg in a pan of water. If fresh, it will remain resting at the bottom of the pan. If not quite fresh, it will rest with the large end higher than the small end; in this case it is probably not

suitable for boiling or poaching, but will fry or scramble satisfactorily. The higher the large end is raised, the older the egg. If the egg floats, it is very likely bad; as an additional test, shake it – the contents will shift about if the egg is bad, because the shell is not full.

2. Make a brine solution, using $\frac{1}{4}$ cup salt to $2\frac{1}{4}$ cups water, and place the egg in it. If good it will sink; if bad it will float.

3. Hold the egg to the light. If transparent in the center, it is good; if transparent at the ends, it is bad. It is also bad if it does not look clear, but appears watery or has dark spots or patches.

To separate eggs: Crack the egg sharply with a knife or on a sharp edge and open the crack only just enough to let the white slip out into a cup. Tip the yolk carefully from one half of the shell to the other to release all the white. There is also a special gadget available for separating eggs.

To store eggs: Eggs deteriorate unless special measures are taken to preserve them. They should be kept in a cool, airy place, although not necessarily in the refrigerator.

If eggs are kept in a refrigerator they should be taken out at least 30 minutes before they are to be used. Store eggs with the pointed end down as the air cell is at the rounded end.

To pickle in spiced vinegar: This is a way of preserving hard-cooked eggs, which can be used as a snack or buffet dish or with salad.

PICKLED EGGS

For every 6 hard-cooked eggs allow:

$2\frac{1}{4}$ *cups white wine or cider vinegar*
6 cloves garlic
pickling spice
small piece of orange peel
piece of mace

Boil all the ingredients (except the eggs) for 10 minutes in a heavy pan with a well-fitting lid. When the mixture is cool, strain it into a wide-mouthed glass jar with a screw-lid or a tight cork. Put in the eggs (shelled but whole) and leave for at least 6 weeks before eating.

More hard-cooked eggs can be added as convenient, but they must always be covered by the liquid.

SOFT-COOKED EGGS

Eggs should be simmered rather than actually boiled, or the shells may break and the whites

become tough. Put them into boiling water, lower the heat, and cook for 3 to $4\frac{1}{2}$ minutes, or put in cold water and bring slowly to a boil, when they will be lightly set.

Whatever method is used, fresh eggs tend to take a little longer to cook than those which are a few days old. The water in each case should be just sufficient to cover the eggs.

HARD-COOKED EGGS

Put in boiling water, bring back to a boil, and cook for 10 to 12 minutes.

Hard-cooked eggs should be placed at once under running cold water until they are cold; this prevents the yolk discoloring on the outside and enables the shell to be easily removed – tap all round the egg with the back of a knife and draw off the shell.

CODDLED EGGS

These are very soft eggs, cooked by steaming in an egg coddler. Break the egg into a coddler, screw or clamp on the lid. Place the coddler in simmering water coming three-quarters of the way up the side; simmer for 6–8 minutes.

POACHED EGGS

Eggs for poaching are at their best when about 2 days old; very fresh eggs and staler ones are both difficult to keep whole.

The eggs may be cooked in a special poaching pan or in a skillet. To use an egg poacher, half fill the lower container with water and place a small piece of butter in each cup. When the water boils, break the eggs into the cups, season lightly, and cover the pan with the lid. Simmer gently until the eggs are lightly set and loosen them with a knife before turning out.

To use a skillet, half fill it with water, adding a pinch of salt (to lower the temperature at which the eggs coagulate). Bring the water to a boil and break the required number of eggs into the water. Cook gently until lightly set, then lift out with a slotted spoon. Drain the eggs and then serve them as desired – on hot buttered toast, or on spinach, etc. garnished with small sprigs of parsley.

Milk may be used instead of water and it is usually served with the eggs.

Note: Eggs may be poached in water to which a little vinegar has been added, held in cold water until ready to use, and reheated briefly in boiling water. The vinegar helps to keep the white from disintegrating.

FRIED EGGS

If the eggs are to be served with bacon, cook this first, then remove the slices and keep them hot. Break each egg separately into a cup, drop it carefully into the hot fat and cook gently, basting with the fat so that it cooks evenly on top and underneath. When the eggs are just set, remove them from the pan with a broad spatula and serve with the hot bacon. Some people prefer the egg to be turned just before being served.

SCRAMBLED EGGS

Beat the eggs and add salt and pepper. A little milk can also be added. Pour into the saucepan and stir over a gentle heat until the mixture begins to thicken, then remove from the heat and stir until creamy. Mound it on hot buttered toast and serve immediately.

Scrambled eggs can be flavored by adding finely chopped fresh or dried herbs, small pieces of cooked bacon or ham, mushrooms, flaked cooked fish, tomatoes, etc.

BAKED EGGS

Use individual ovenproof dishes (ramekins). Place the dishes on a baking sheet, drop a teaspoon of butter in each and put in a 400° oven for a minute or two. When the butter has melted, break a fresh egg into each dish, season with pepper and salt and return the dishes to the oven, leaving them until the eggs are just set, 4 to 5 minutes. Serve at once.

SHIRRED EGGS

Break the eggs into a dish, add some bread crumbs and a little cream and cook in a 400° oven for a few minutes, until the eggs are set and the crumbs are brown.

FRAMED EGGS

4 slices white bread
butter
4 eggs

With a biscuit cutter, cut a hole in the center of each slice of bread, leaving a "frame." Cook the frames in the hot butter until brown, turn them over and brown the second side. Break an egg into the center of each frame and fry until the eggs are set. Lift out with a broad spatula, draining off any butter, and serve on a hot plate.

EGG CROQUETTES

3 tablespoons butter
⅔ cup water
¼ cup all-purpose flour
1 egg, beaten
½ teaspoon mild curry powder
salt
pepper
2 hard-cooked eggs
¼ cup toasted chopped almonds
1 small egg, for coating
1 cup fresh white bread crumbs
oil for frying

Melt the butter in the water and bring to a boil. Remove from the heat and quickly add the flour. Beat well until smooth and the dough forms a ball. Allow to cool for a few minutes and then beat in the egg. Season well with curry powder, salt, and pepper. Chop the hard-cooked eggs and add with the almonds to the pan. By heaping spoonfuls, roll the mixture to a sausage shape on a floured surface. Pat the ends flat. Coat with beaten egg and bread crumbs. Chill, then deep fry in oil at 300° for about 5 minutes, until puffed and golden brown. Drain on paper towels. Serve immediately with tomato sauce.

HUEVOS RANCHEROS

1 tablespoon chopped onion
2 tablespoons vegetable oil
1 clove garlic, chopped
¼ teaspoon oregano
2 green chilis, mashed and strained
1 cup tomato sauce
4 eggs
4 tostados

Cook the onion in the oil until soft. Add the garlic, oregano, chilis, and tomato sauce. Simmer for 5 minutes. Add the eggs and poach until done. Serve on tostados.

DEVILED EGGS

6 eggs
3 tablespoons mayonnaise
2 teaspoons French mustard
salt
pinch cayenne pepper
strips of red pimiento

Lower the eggs into a saucepan of gently boiling water to which a good pinch of salt has been added. Cook gently for 10 to 12 minutes. Stir the eggs for the first 8 minutes so that the yolks will be centered. Remove from the heat and plunge immediately into cold water.

When the eggs are completely cold shell them and cut in half lengthwise, using a stainless steel knife (other metals will discolor the eggs). Remove the yolks carefully and push through a sieve.

Mix in the remaining ingredients. If the mixture is too thick for piping add a little more mayonnaise. Using a $\frac{1}{2}$-inch plain rosette tube, pipe the mixture into the egg whites and decorate with strips of red pimiento.

VARIATIONS

Small jars of chopped ham, chicken or smoked ham can be worked into the yolks, or use any of the suggested variations:

Chicken and ham: Boil 6 eggs, shell, and cut in half lengthwise. Remove yolks carefully and push through a sieve. Add $\frac{1}{4}$ cup finely chopped chicken, $\frac{1}{4}$ cup finely chopped ham, $\frac{1}{4}$ cup butter, and salt and pepper to taste to the yolks. Pipe or spoon into the whites and garnish each half with a tiny sprig of parsley.

Anchovy: Chop 4 anchovy fillets very finely. Stir into the sieved yolks of 6 eggs with $\frac{1}{4}$ cup butter, and pipe or spoon into the egg whites. Garnish with anchovy fillets to serve. (A little cayenne pepper may be added to the yolk mixture if desired.)

Caviar: Mash the yolks of 6 eggs with $\frac{1}{4}$ cup butter or 3 tablespoons mayonnaise, 1 teaspoon lemon juice and 2 tablespoons caviar. Fill into the egg whites and garnish with red or black caviar or lumpfish roe.

Smoked salmon: Mash 3 slices of smoked salmon with a fork and stir into the mashed yolks of 6 eggs with 3 tablespoons mayonnaise. Pipe or spoon into the whites and garnish with a small strip of smoked salmon.

Shrimp: Finely chop $\frac{1}{4}$ cup cooked shrimp. Stir into the mashed yolks of 6 eggs with 3 tablespoons mayonnaise, a pinch of cayenne pepper and a pinch of nutmeg. Pipe or spoon into the whites and garnish each half with a small whole shrimp.

SCOTCH EGGS

4 hard-cooked eggs
2 teaspoons seasoned flour
Worcestershire sauce
8 oz sausage meat
1 egg, beaten
dry bread crumbs
deep fat
parsley

Dust the eggs with the seasoned flour. Add a few drops of Worcestershire sauce to the sausage meat and divide it into 4 equal portions. Form each quarter into a flat cake and work it round an egg, making it as even as possible and making sure there are no cracks in the sausage meat. Brush with beaten egg and toss in bread crumbs. Heat the fat to 375°. (As the sausage meat is raw, it is essential that the frying should not be hurried unduly, so the fat must not be too hot.) Fry the eggs for about 7 to 8 minutes. When they are golden brown on the outside, remove them from the fat and drain.

Cut the eggs in half lengthwise, garnish each half with a small piece of parsley and serve either hot with tomato sauce or cold with a green salad.

HOT STUFFED EGGS

4 hard-cooked eggs
$\frac{1}{2}$ cup chopped mushrooms
1 onion, chopped
3 tablespoons butter
$1\frac{1}{4}$ cups tomato juice
1 teaspoon sugar
salt
pepper
2 teaspoons cornstarch

Cut the eggs in half lengthwise and remove the yolks. Lightly sauté the mushrooms and onion in the butter for 5 minutes, until golden brown. Put half the mixture in a bowl. Add the tomato juice, sugar, and seasoning to the remaining mixture in the pan and cook for 5 minutes. Blend the cornstarch to a smooth cream with a little water. Stir in a little of the hot tomato juice and return it to the pan; bring to a boil, stirring until it thickens, and continue cooking for 1 to 2 minutes. Keep this tomato sauce hot. Meanwhile mix the egg yolks with the remaining onion and mushroom mixture in the bowl and use to stuff the eggs. Place on a dish and pour the tomato sauce around the eggs.

PIPÉRADE

$\frac{3}{4}$ lb green peppers
1 lb tomatoes
$\frac{1}{2}$ cup butter
1 large onion, finely chopped
3 cloves garlic, crushed
salt and freshly ground pepper
8 eggs
$\frac{1}{4}$ cup milk
fried croutons

Shred the peppers finely. Peel the tomatoes, cut into halves, discard the seeds, and roughly chop the flesh. In a medium-sized pan, melt the butter; when it is frothy, add the onion and garlic and cook for 1 to 2 minutes, then add the peppers and simmer for 4 minutes. Add the tomatoes. Season well and leave to simmer while you beat the eggs, milk, and seasoning with a fork. When the vegetables in the pan are well reduced, pour in the beaten eggs. Cook for 3 to 4 minutes, stirring continuously. When a soft scrambled egg is obtained, turn onto a hot serving plate.

EGG FLIP

1 egg
1 tablespoon sugar
$\frac{1}{4}$ cup sherry or brandy
$1\frac{1}{4}$ cups milk

Beat the egg and sugar together and add the sherry or brandy. Heat the milk without boiling and pour it over the egg mixture; stir well and serve hot in a stemmed tumbler of heavy glass.

FRUIT FLIP

1 egg
2 teaspoons superfine sugar
juice of 1 orange
juice of 1 lemon

Beat the egg and sugar together for a few moments. Add the strained orange and lemon juice, strain and served chilled.

CURRIED EGGS

(See Curry entry; see also Omelet, Soufflé, etc. entries.)

EGGPLANT (AUBERGINE)

This plant is a member of the nightshade family, a native of SE Asia. Its fruit, usually egg-shaped, is somewhat akin to the tomato; it varies in color from a yellowish-white to deep purple.

Eggplants can be sliced and then fried, broiled, or sautéed; baked with a savory stuffing; made into fritters; used in soups and casseroles.

To prepare them cut off the stem and peel or wipe the skin carefully. Slice or cut in half, according to the dish being made, and sprinkle with salt. Leave them for 20 to 30 minutes to get rid of excess water before rinsing and wiping. This helps to remove any bitterness and bring out the flavor. While exposed to the air the eggplant will discolor slightly.

BAKED STUFFED EGGPLANT

2 eggplants, about $\frac{3}{4}$ lb each
salt
6 tablespoons vegetable oil
1 small onion, chopped
2 tablespoons tomato paste
freshly ground black pepper
4 eggs
chopped parsley to garnish

Wipe the eggplants and trim off the stems. Halve lengthwise and score the cut surface well. Sprinkle with salt and leave to stand for about 20 minutes to draw out the indigestible bitter juices. Pat the eggplants dry using kitchen toweling and sauté the eggplant halves gently in the hot oil (adding more oil if necessary), turning once, until just tender. Remove from the pan. Add the onion and sauté to a golden brown in the remaining oil. Meanwhile scoop out the eggplant flesh leaving a good edge on the skin. Chop the flesh roughly and stir into the pan with the tomato paste and seasoning. Simmer gently until well combined. Pack the eggplants into a shallow ovenproof dish. Break the eggs, individually, into a cup and pour carefully into the eggplant shells. Spoon the cooked mixture along each end of the eggplants. Bake in a 350° oven for about 20 minutes or until the eggs are just set. Sprinkle with chopped parsley for serving.

EGGPLANT FIESTA

1 eggplant, about 1 lb
boiling water
1 can (16 oz) tomatoes, drained
2 tablespoons butter
1 clove garlic, crushed
salt and freshly ground pepper
1 can (12 oz) whole kernel corn
$\frac{1}{2}$ cup grated Parmesan cheese
chopped parsley for garnish

Peel the eggplants, cut into 1-inch slices and cut each slice into 4 triangular chunks. Put in a saucepan, cover with boiling water, and boil gently for 5 minutes; drain well. Roughly chop the tomatoes. Butter the inside of an ovenproof dish and put in the eggplants, tomatoes, garlic, seasoning, and corn. Sprinkle evenly with the cheese. Bake uncovered in a 450° oven for about 20 minutes, until the sauce is bubbly and the cheese has melted. Garnish with chopped parsley.

EGG ROLL

A small Chinese fried pastry served as an hors d'oeuvre. It is usually filled with shredded pork, chicken, or shrimp (or a mixture of these), and shredded vegetables.

EGG ROLLS

2 tablespoons peanut oil
½ lb boneless pork, shredded
1 scallion, white part only, shredded
10 water chestnuts, shredded
½ cup shredded bamboo shoot
½ cup shredded celery
½ cup pea beans
½ teaspoon salt
2 teaspoons soy sauce
2 teaspoons cornstarch
8 egg-roll skins
oil for deep-frying

Heat the 2 tablespoons peanut oil in a wok or skillet and add the pork. Stir-fry until the pork loses color, about 3 minutes. Remove the pork and add the vegetables. Cook, stirring, for 2 minutes, then return the pork and cook 1 minute longer. Add the seasonings and cook to blend. Pour into a strainer to drain; cool.

When filling is thoroughly cool, place ¼ cup filling on lower third of each egg-roll skin. Fold bottom of roll over the filling, turn in the sides and roll up. Seal with a paste made of flour and water. Heat oil in a deep-fryer to 380° and fry the egg rolls, two at a time, until golden brown. Drain and keep warm while cooking the remainder. Serve with a sharp mustard.

ELDERBERRY

The fruit of a tree common in North America and Europe. It was formerly used for medicinal purposes, but today is only used in the home for making elderberry jelly, jam, and wine.

ELDERBERRY JELLY

2 lb elderberries
2 lb cooking apples
1¼ cups water
sugar

Wash the elderberries. Wash the apples and chop roughly without peeling or coring. Cook the fruits separately with just enough water to cover, until they are soft and pulped. Strain the combined fruits through a jelly bag, measure the juice, and return it to the pan with ½ cup sugar to each cup of juice. Stir until the sugar has dissolved and boil rapidly until the jelly sheets on testing. Skim, jar, and cover in the usual way.

ELDERFLOWER

The flowers of the elder tree are sometimes used to make wine. When infused they have a delicate flavor. They can also be used to flavor preserves, e.g. rhubarb jam, to which they impart a taste resembling that of muscat grapes.

ELECTRIC MIXERS AND THEIR USE

For anyone who does a fair amount of cooking, an automatic electric food mixer is likely to save both time and energy. The small portable ones (some held in the hand, some used with a stand) will carry out creaming, beating, and whipping operations. The large mixers are normally used on a stand, but a few can also be hand-held for such jobs as beating eggs and sugar for a sponge. These models will of course deal with bigger quantities of food and they have a wide range of optional attachments for carrying out such operations as grinding coffee, slicing and shredding, sharpening knives and so on. The machines known as blenders are primarily intended for pureeing cooked foods and vegetables (especially for soupmaking), for extracting juice from fruit, and so on, but can also be used for mixing and in some cases for cakemaking; the manufacturer's instructions must be closely followed.

Most of the attachments for a mixer have names that are self-explanatory and if you study the maker's leaflet or booklet you will be in no doubt as to when and how to use them.

An electric mixer can be used (with correct attachments) for cutting in (the fat must be at room temperature), for creaming fat and sugar, for making frosting, for kneading dough, and for whipping cream.

The lighter kind of mixing known as "folding in" (for example when the flour is added to the beaten sugar and eggs in making a sponge) should only be done on a very low speed to avoid overbeating.

BLENDERS

Blenders chop and blend and are generally versatile in terms of simplifying and speeding up the preparation of food.

Blenders may be an independent unit or an attachment to a food mixer. All blenders perform the same functions, the difference lying in the power of the motor and the size of the blending container. A freestanding blender is useful for people who do not have a mixer or who have a small hand-held one with no blender attachment.

Blenders can be used for making bread crumbs, mixing instant foods and drinks, making salad dressing, chopping raw vegetables, pureeing fruit and vegetables, making soups and batters, and mixing pie fillings. Sauces such as mayonnaise and hollandaise can also be made in a blender.

EMINCÉ

The French culinary name for a dish of meat cut into thin slices, put into an earthenware dish, and covered with some suitable sauce, which can be sauce bordelaise, chasseur, italienne, poivrade, tomato, or mushroom.

It is essential that the meat is simmered and not cooked quickly so that it remains tender.

EMPANADA

A turnover usually filled with meat, poultry, or seafood and fried. Originating in Spain, it is popular throughout Latin America. Large empanadas are good for lunch, while small ones, called empanaditas, are excellent served hot as an appetizer with drinks. Empanadas may also contain sweet fillings, e.g. jam.

EMPANADAS

2 cups all-purpose flour
½ teaspoon salt
1 teaspoon baking powder
½ cup vegetable shortening
⅓ cup ice water
oil for deep-frying

Combine the flour, salt, and baking powder in a bowl and cut in the vegetable shortening until the mixture resembles fine bread crumbs. Stir in the

water and gather the pastry into a ball. Roll out on a lightly floured board until very thin. For luncheon empanadas, cut into 4-inch circles; for appetizers, 2-inch circles. Fill with leftover meats finely chopped and combined with sautéed chopped onion and moistened with tomato sauce. Wet edges of pastry and pinch together to seal. Deep fry until golden brown. Drain and serve hot.

ENCHILADA

A tortilla that is fried briefly in lard to soften it and is then stuffed and sauced and served hot. Shredded lettuce, radishes and olives are a usual accompaniment.

ENDIVE

There are many forms of this plant, but in the United States the name usually refers to one of the curly-leaved varieties, rather like lettuce, but with stronger and tougher leaves. The flavor is more bitter than lettuce. Curly endive has narrow spiky leaves and is frequently miscalled chicory. Another variety with flat broad leaves is called escarole. Belgian endive is a form of chicory.

ENRICHMENT

The addition of nutrients to food. This may be done to replace nutrients removed during processing (as when calcium, iron, thiamin, and niacin are added to flour, which loses these nutrients during milling), or it may be to improve a substitute (as when vitamins A and D are added to margarine to make its food value comparable with that of butter). Occasionally the enrichment is to insure a constant level of a particular nutrient in an otherwise variable food (as when vitamin C is added to fruit juice).

ENTERTAINING

(See Party entry.)

ENTRECÔTE

A steak cut from the middle part of the sirloin of beef; in France it means a steak taken between two ribs. (See Steak entry.)

ENTRÉE

A main dish, consisting of meat, poultry, game, fish, eggs, or vegetables, etc. (e.g., cutlets, fillets, croquettes, quenelles), served either hot or cold, complete with sauce and garnish.

It was originally a dish forming a complete course in itself and in the days of long dinner menus the entrée followed the fish course and preceded the roast.

ENTREMETS

Formerly a light dish served between the roast and the dessert at formal dinners. Today the word means dessert, either hot or cold.

ENZYME

A catalyst (that is, a substance which induces a change in other substances without being affected itself) found in various foodstuffs and in the digestive juices. Enzymes are soluble proteins that are destroyed by heat, strong acid, or alkalis; their effect is retarded by low temperatures. Examples are B vitamins (thiamin, riboflavin, and nicotinic acid) which act as enzymes on carbohydrates, oxidizing them into sugars, etc., for absorption; oxidase in vegetables which destroys vitamin C; and the digestive enzymes in the alimentary tract which break down carbohydrates, fats, and proteins into substances that can be absorbed into the body.

ESCALOPE

(See Scallop entry.)

ESCAROLE

The name sometimes given to the broad-leaved endive. Escarole may be cooked like spinach and served hot, as a vegetable accompaniment or in soup.

ESPAGNOLE SAUCE

A rich brown sauce, used in the preparation of many entrées.

ESPAGNOLE SAUCE

1 slice bacon, chopped
2 tablespoons butter
1 shallot, chopped, or a small piece of onion, chopped
$\frac{1}{4}$ cup mushroom stems, chopped
1 small carrot, chopped
2–3 tablespoons flour
$1\frac{1}{4}$ cups beef broth
bouquet garni
2 tablespoons tomato paste
salt
pepper

This classic brown sauce is used as a basis for many other classic sauces.

Sauté the bacon in the butter for 2 to 3 minutes, add the vegetables and sauté for a further 3 to 5 minutes, or until lightly browned. Stir in the flour, mix well and continue cooking until the vegetables brown. Remove from the heat and gradually add the broth, stirring after each addition. Return the pan to the heat and stir until the sauce thickens; add the bouquet garni, tomato paste, and salt and pepper. Reduce the heat and allow to simmer very gently for 1 hour stirring from time to time to prevent sticking; alternately, cook in a 325° oven for $1\frac{1}{2}$ to 2 hours. Strain the sauce, reheat and skim off any fat, using a metal spoon. Taste for seasoning. A tablespoon of sherry may be added just before the sauce is served.

EVAPORATED MILK

(See Milk entry.)

EWE'S MILK

This contains a higher proportion of protein, fat, and sugar than cow's milk; it is used in making a number of European cheeses, e.g., Roquefort, Brousses, Cachat.

EXTRACT

Originally, an extract was a solution of essential oils or other flavoring ingredients in alcohol, the best-known examples being almond, anise, orange, lemon, citron, peppermint, vanilla, ginger, cinnamon, and caraway, but today many synthetic extracts are prepared from esters (compounds of alcohol and an organic acid). They often resemble the natural flavoring closely, but tend to lack the delicacy and richness of the natural substances; they have, however, the advantage of being decidedly cheaper. For family cooking, they make a suitable alternative to their more expensive counterparts. Synthetic products are labeled as imitation flavors.

Both natural and synthetic extracts help to make food more palatable and varied. They should be used sparingly and when possible they should be added during the final stages of cooking, to prevent loss through volatilization.

The following are the most frequently used extracts:

VANILLA

The genuine extract is a dilute alcoholic extract of the vanilla bean; the synthetic type is produced by oxidation of a compound obtained from clove oil and has a somewhat crude flavor.

MEAT AND FISH

A preparation obtained from various foodstuffs such as lean meat, by means of mincing, boiling, and evaporation or some other process. Extracts are usually commercially manufactured and sold in concentrated form as proprietary brands.

Meat extracts consist of natural juices and mineral salts and are used to flavor soups and gravies. Yeast extracts, which are similar in flavor to the meat products, are often used to dilute them and also to flavor soups, etc. They are a useful source of B vitamins.

ALMOND

The essential oil obtained from pressed almonds after the almond oil has been extracted. An imitation almond flavoring almost identical with the natural product is produced synthetically from benzaldehyde.

FRUIT

Genuine extracts are obtained from rind and pulp of various fruits, but they are difficult to make sufficiently concentrated and are often replaced by artificial flavorings made from esters.

FARCE

The French term for stuffing. (See Forcemeat and Stuffing entries.)

FARINA

The term used generally to denote the fine meal produced from cereal grain or starchy root (e.g., cassava). Farina is also the name of a cereal product made from wheat other than the durum type.

FARINACEOUS FOODS

Foodstuffs which consist very largely of starch – for example, bread (which contains 50 percent), oatmeal, flour, pasta and semolina (which contain 70 to 75 percent).

FATS

Fats are compounds of fatty acids and glycerol. Like many organic compounds, they contain carbon, hydrogen, and oxygen. They are valuable "fuel" foods, supplying more than twice as many Calories (kilojoules) for heat and energy than either protein or carbohydrates. If more fat is taken than is needed for these purposes, it is stored in the body. Some fats (though not vegetable fats nor mineral oils such as paraffin) also supply vitamins A and D.

The chief sources of fats are animal foods (meat, dairy produce, and oily fish) and vegetable foods such as nuts, from which oil is extracted. The normal diet must contain a proportion of natural fats: an average of 3 oz daily for adults.

Oils

These are fats that are liquid at ordinary room temperature. (See separate entry.)

Fatty Acids

The three fatty acids which, when combined with glycerol, make up a fat, can be of different kinds. In saturated fatty acids each link in the molecular chain of acids is single, but in the unsaturated fatty acids one or more is double.

In general, fats containing saturated fatty acids are more solid than those containing unsaturated fatty acids; animal fats contain mostly saturated fatty acids, while corn, olive, and sunflower oils are mostly unsaturated. When fats such as peanut, coconut, palm, and whale oils are hardened to make margarine and cooking fats, hydrogen is added to take up the extra links, thus converting unsaturated to saturated fatty acids. The resulting solid fat seems for some reason to be composed of even more saturated fatty acids than naturally solid fats.

There are three fatty acids which cannot be made within the body yet are required in small quantities for normal health. These are known as "essential fatty acids." However, a normal diet will contain enough of these fatty acids.

People who have a high blood cholesterol level should reduce the amount of fat in the diet, limiting it to unsaturated fatty acids. It is believed by many medical experts, although not proved, that a high proportion of saturated fatty acids is a contributory factor to heart disease. It should, however, be emphasized that this is not a sole cause.

Fat in Cooking

Fats used in cooking are butter, lard, drippings, suet, and various vegetable fats and oils, including margarine and vegetable shortenings which are a mixture of fats. Oils (chiefly olive, nut, and vegetable) are mainly used for frying and for salad dressings, but may also be used for cakes and pastry.

PASTRY

Flavor and shortening power are the most important factors in pastrymaking. Butter or margarine provide flavor whereas lard has more shortening properties, hence for some pastries a mixture of the two fats is used. Solid margarine is more suitable for pastry than soft margarine. Whipped vegetable fats and oil can also be used for pastry, but these are usually added to the flour with the water and mixed with a fork, rather than by the usual cutting in method.

CAKES

Butter is considered to give the best flavor, although margarine is usually easier to cream. Vegetable shortenings are often preferred for cakemaking and certainly give a better result in the one-stage method. Oils can also be used in cakemaking.

FRYING

A good frying fat should be free from moisture, which makes it splutter when heated, and it should have a high smoking temperature, that is, it should be capable of being heated to high temperatures (not less than 360°) before it smokes and burns. Butter is not suitable for general frying purposes, although good for cooking omelets and certain vegetables; a mixture of butter and oil is sometimes used to give flavor and enable the use of a higher temperature. The best fats are olive oil, vegetable oil, clarified dripping, and lard.

Rendering

To render means to extract the fat from pieces of meat or poultry. There are two methods of doing this:
1. Cut the fat in small pieces, place them in a pan and place in a 300° oven until the fat has melted, leaving only crisp, brown pieces of tissue. Strain the fat into a clean bowl.
2. Cut the fat into small pieces, place them in a pan with very little water and boil without a lid until the water has evaporated. Continue to heat very gently until the fat has melted and left only crisp brown pieces of tissue. Strain as before.

Note: with both methods care must be taken not to have too high a heat, or the fat will burn and be spoiled.

Clarifying

Fats which are to be used for cakemaking, frying, and so on sometimes need to be freed of water, meat juices, salt, and other ingredients that may be present.

To clarify butter or margarine: Heat the fat gently until it melts, then continue to heat slowly without browning until all bubbling ceases – this shows that the water has evaporated. Remove it from the heat and let it stand a few minutes for any salt and sediment to settle, then gently pour off the fat. If there is much sediment, the clarified fat may be strained through cheesecloth, but this is seldom necessary.

Rancidity

This is due mainly to slight oxidization changes, whereby a fat acquires an unpleasant acrid taste and smell, though the condition is not necessarily harmful. Hot weather, exposure to air and light, and prolonged storage are the usual causes of rancidity, which occurs more quickly if there is much water present in the fat. To guard against fats turning rancid, they should be kept in a refrigerator.

The addition of a little baking soda helps to neutralize slight rancidity and make butter or other fat more palatable. Put the fat in a saucepan, pour boiling water over it, melt it gently, and allow it to cool. Strain off the liquid. Again melt the fat slowly in a pan with a very little hot water containing $\frac{1}{2}$ teaspoon baking soda to $2\frac{1}{4}$ cups of water. Skim, allow to cool, and strain off the liquid. Warm the fat up again with plain water, skim if necessary, allow to cool, and finally strain off all liquid from the fat before using it.

FAVA BEAN (BROAD OR WINDSOR BEAN)

It is considered to be the original bean and was first grown in North Africa. The beans are encased in a thick, tough pod with a furry lining. When very young and tender, the pods can be cooked whole, but usually they are shelled. As the plant matures the beans develop a gray outer skin which gradually becomes tougher. This can be removed before cooking by blanching for a few minutes in boiling water. The beans can be served tossed in melted butter and garnished with chopped parsley or other herbs. In season, early June to end July.

FAVA BEANS WITH GARLIC SAUSAGE

*2 packages (10 oz each) frozen shelled fava beans
  or lima beans, thawed*
2 tablespoons butter
2 shallots or green onions, finely chopped
4 oz garlic sausage, chopped
salt
pepper
⅔ cup half-and-half

Cook the beans according to package directions. Meanwhile, melt the butter and sauté the onion until soft and lightly colored. Add the sausage and cook, stirring, for 2 to 3 minutes. Drain the beans and add. Season to taste with salt and pepper. Stir in the cream and heat gently to warm through; do not boil.

FEIJOADA

The national dish of Brazil, made with black beans, various meats and spices and served with yellow rice. The last word in boiled dinners, it is not unusual for a feijoada to contain four different kinds of meat plus sausages. The cooking liquid is flavored with orange juice and wine.

FENNEL

The name given to a variety of aromatic plants native to Europe but now grown in North America as well. One variety is a hardy perennial, growing 4 to 5 ft high, with hollow, deep-green stalks and finely cut leaves of a rich green. The flower stems appear soon after mid summer and bear heads of bright yellow flowers, but as seed formation shortens the lives of the plants, gardeners generally remove the stems to prevent flowering. The stalks, leaves, and seeds give a delicate licorice flavoring. The feathery foliage is used like parsley for garnishing and for flavoring sauces to serve with salmon and mackerel. Fennel seeds can also be used for flavoring and in making liqueurs.

Another variety has solid white stems with a swollen base, rather resembling celery roots; they can be eaten raw as an hors d'oeuvre or with cheese or may be cooked in the same way as celery and served hot. This vegetable is popular in Italy as *finocchio* and in France as *fenouil tabereux*.

FENUGREEK

An aromatic, bittersweet spice, the flavor resembling celery. It is an essential ingredient in many Indian dishes and is also used in Mediterranean cooking. It is a leguminous plant looking rather like a tall clover and is native to Eurasia.

FERMENTATION

This term is used to denote chemical changes (deliberate or accidental) brought about by ferments – for example, the decomposition of carbohydrates, with the production of alcohol and carbon dioxide caused by the action of yeast. This process is utilized in the making of breads, wines, etc. (See Yeast entry.)

Malt and wine vinegars are produced by a ferment action which converts alcohol into acetic acid. The souring of milk, with the formation of lactic acid, is another well-known example and there are many more. Jams sometimes show signs of fermentation when they are stored, if they have not been carefully made and covered: for preventive measures, see Jam entry. Fresh fruit, for example cherries, sometimes ferment when kept and develop a slight alcoholic flavor. The change is entirely harmless and the fruit can be eaten with perfect safety. If, however, fermentation occurs in jarred or canned fruit, it denotes incomplete sterilization and it is unwise to eat the fruit, since other undesirable changes may also have occurred.

FETA

A soft, crumbly white cheese made of goat's milk. Occasionally sheep's milk is added, in which case the cheese is less salty. It is extremely popular in Greece where it is eaten as a table cheese and used in cooking.

FETTUCCINE

An Italian noodle, about ¼ inch wide; with tagliatelle it is the best known of the Italian noodles. Although it can be purchased dried, it is better when fresh. It is delicious tossed with butter and grated Parmesan cheese, but is most famous served tossed with butter, cream, and cheese. This dish is generally served tableside in restaurants.

FETTUCCINE ALFREDO

1 lb cooked fettuccine
1 cup sweet butter, softened
2 cups grated Parmesan cheese
¾ cups heavy cream
freshly ground pepper

Drain the fettuccine and place in a chafing dish over heat. Add the butter, cheese, and cream gradually, tossing. Grate fresh pepper over each serving.

FIDDLEHEAD FERN

The young frond of various species of ferns of Canada and the United States. It is good eating only before it unfurls. Fiddleheads are usually cooked briefly in boiling water and served with butter or hollandaise sauce.

FIG

Numerous species of fig are grown in hot climates, including southern Europe, the Near East, and extensive areas of the United States, where they were introduced into California by the Spanish in 1769. The fruits have a fleshy exterior enclosing small, hard seeds. They can be purchased canned in syrup or fresh in season.

Most figs, however, are sold dried, the chief varieties used for this purpose being the Smyrna (the best-known kind) and the Adriatic fig. They may be dried in the sun or by artificial heat; after drying they are pressed flat and packed between laurel leaves.

Fresh figs make a delicious dessert fruit, while dried figs are used as a stewed fruit (either by themselves or in fruit salads), in various cakes and puddings, and in some candies. (See Dried Fruit entry for the method of cooking them.)

FILBERT

A species of hazelnut grown in California, England, Turkey, Italy, and Spain. The nuts may be recognized by their long, fringed husks and elongated form.

Like all nuts, filberts have a fairly high proportion of fat. They also contain a little protein, minerals, and thiamin.

FILET MIGNON

A very tender cut of beef.

FILLET

A boneless cut from the loin of beef, pork, etc.; also the boned breast of a bird or the boned side of a fish.

FILTER

To strain a liquid through a special fine filter, as when making coffee, or through a cloth, as when making jelly.

FINES HERBES

Fresh herbs (usually parsley, tarragon, and chives) which are finely chopped and used to flavor omelets etc. It is quite common to only include parsley and chives.

FINNAN HADDIE

(See Haddock entry.)

FISH

There are many varieties of fish and the United States is particularly fortunate in the quality and quantity of its supply. The value of fish as a food has now been realized, hence the increase in fish farming.

Fish is an important source of protein, although it contains slightly less than meat. Fish oils – for example cod and halibut liver oil – contain vitamins A and D in large quantities. Some of the small fish, such as sardines, may supply a useful amount of calcium when the bones are eaten.

Fish may be classified in more than one way. Sometimes they are grouped according to type of flesh, thus:

> *White fish*: cod, sole, turbot
> *Fat fish*: herring, salmon, sardine
> *Shellfish*: crab, shrimp, lobsters, etc.

Another grouping is according to shape, thus:
> *Round fish*: cod, haddock, herring
> *Flat fish*: flounder, sole, skate
> *Shellfish*: as above

Fresh fish is cheapest and best when it is in season and has the finest flavor just before spawning; during the spawning season it is poor in flavor and flesh of white fish is inclined to be of a bluish tinge, watery, and lacking in firmness. Some fish, such as cod, are available throughout the year, but for most there is a closed season. (See individual fish entries.)

Fresh fish rapidly becomes stale and should be cooked as soon as possible after it is caught. When really fresh, it should have no unpleasant odor, the flesh should be firm and the body stiff, the gills red, the eyes bright and not sunken and the scales plentiful and sparkling. Fish of a medium size are superior in flavor and finer than over-large ones; a thick steak from a smaller fish is preferable to a thin steak from a large one.

A large percentage of fish in the United States

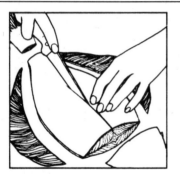 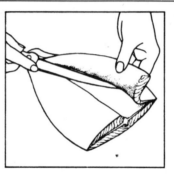 

FILETING FLAT FISH
1. Place fish on a wooden board. Cut straight down the back, following the line of the bone.

2. Insert the knife under one side of the flesh and carefully cut it away from the bone, working from head to tail.

3. Turn fish over and fillet the other side of the fish in the same way so that you are left with four fillets of fish.

is sold frozen. Contrary to belief this does not mean that it is inferior in any way. As only the best quality fish are frozen it may be superior to fresh fish. Furthermore, as it is frozen as soon as it is caught (on the boat or on reaching land) all the nutrients are preserved. Other advantages of frozen fish are that they are usually gutted and boned, and sometimes coated ready for frying. Also it has less odor than fresh fish which makes storage in a refrigerator more acceptable. Ready-prepared "fish in sauce dishes," breaded or battered fish, and smoked fish are all available frozen; these make serving quick and simple.

Also available frozen are scallops, shrimp, and lobster tails. The range of frozen fish is always increasing, and it is likely that more and more fish will be sold frozen in years to come.

Canned fish is a good standby as the preservation is permanent and there are no inedible parts of the fish included; it is also ready to serve hot or cold. The oily fish are particularly suitable for canning, such as sardines, pilchards, herring, roes, mackerel, sprats, brisling, anchovies, tuna, and salmon. Also sold in cans are mussels, shrimp, kipper and herring fillets, lobster, crab, fish balls, quenelles, fish soups, and chowders.

Preparation of Fish

Whole fish: Scrape off any scales on both sides of the fish using a knife and scraping from tail to head, with frequent rinsing to loosen the scales. To remove the entrails from round fish, make a slit along the abdomen from the gills halfway to the tail, draw out the insides and clean away any blood. Rub with a little salt to remove black skin.

With flat fish, such as sole and flounder, open the cavity which lies in the upper part of the body under the gills and clean out the entrails as above.

Cut off the fins and gills and remove the head and tail if desired. If the head is left on, the eyes must be removed. Finally rinse the flesh thoroughly in cold water.

Cut fish, fillets, and steaks: Wipe with a damp cloth. Do not wash or leave lying in water, as this draws out the juices and impairs the flavor.

Skinning round fish (Haddock, Whiting, etc.): Round fish are skinned from head to tail. Cut across the skin just below the head and loosen the skin under the head with the point of a sharp knife, then dip the fingers in coarse salt and gently pull the skin down toward the tail, working very carefully. Skin the other side in the same way, dipping your fingers in coarse salt to prevent slipping.

Filleting round fish: Cut down the center back to the bone with a sharp knife and cut along the abdomen. Remove the flesh cleanly from the bones, working from the head down, pressing the knife against the bones and working with short, sharp strokes. Remove the fillet from the other side in the same way. The fillets may be cut slantwise into two or three pieces if desired.

Skinning whole flat fish (Sole, Flounder, etc.): The black skin is usually removed, whatever the mode of treatment. A sole skins easily, so do this before filleting; a flounder is more difficult, so fillet it first and then skin the fillets. First wash the fish and cut off the fins, then make an incision across the tail, slip the thumb between the skin and the flesh and loosen the skin round the sides of the fish. Now hold down the fish firmly with one hand and with the other take hold of the skin

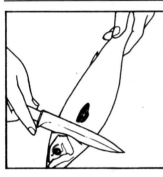

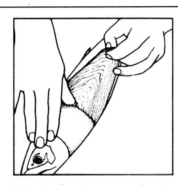

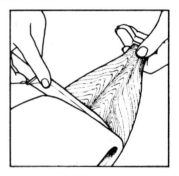

SKINNING ROUND FISH
1. *Lay fish on a board and cut across the skin just below the head to loosen the skin under the head.*

2. *Dip the fingertips in coarse salt and grip the skin. Gently pull the skin toward the tail, working carefully.*

3. *Skinning flat fish: Hold tail of fish and separate the flesh from the skin with a sharp knife.*

and draw it off quickly, upward toward the head. The white skin can be removed in the same way.

Filleting flat fish: With a sharp, flexible knife, cut straight down the back of the fish, following the line of the bone. Then insert the knife under the flesh and carefully remove it with long, clean strokes.

Take the first fillet from the lefthand side of the fish, working from head to tail, then turn the fish round and cut off the second fillet from tail to head. Fillet the other side of the fish, in the same way. When the operation is finished, no flesh should be left adhering to the bone.

Skinning fillets of flat fish: Lay the fillet on a board, skin side down, salt the fingers and hold the tail end of the skin firmly. Then separate the flesh from the skin by sawing with a sharp knife from side to side, pressing the flat of the blade against the flesh. Keep the edge of the blade close to the skin while cutting, but do not press heavily or the skin will be severed.

(See individual entries for preparation of shellfish.)

Methods of Cooking

Fish can be boiled, poached, steamed, stewed, baked, fried, or broiled. Most fish requires a good sauce or accompaniment to bring out the flavor.

We give below notes on the most usual methods of cooking, followed by a small selection of recipes; other recipes will be found under the names of the individual fish, e.g., Sole.

Boiling: This is only to be recommended for a few fish such as salmon and large cuts of cod, etc. (Fish which is called "boiled" is in fact often poached.)

Rub the cut surface of the fish with lemon juice to keep it firm and of a good color, then put it in sufficient hot salted water or court-bouillon (see Court-bouillon entry) to cover it. (A common fault is to put insufficient salt in the water.) If possible use a fish poacher, to enable the fish to be lifted out of the container without breaking; failing this, tie in cheesecloth and place on a plate in the bottom of a roasting pan. A small bunch of herbs and a little cut-up carrot, onion, and celery can be added to the water if the fish is of a tasteless kind. Bring the water to a boil and then simmer very slowly (removing any scum as it rises) until the fish is cooked, i.e., when the flesh comes away easily from the bone. The time depends on the shape and thickness of the fish, the average being 10 minutes per inch thickness of fish. Drain well, place on a hot plate, garnish with parsley and lemon, and serve with a suitable sauce.

(See Salmon entry.)

Poaching: Suitable for cuts of fish, particularly for small pieces and for small whole fish. Roll or fold the fish fillets to a convenient size. Heat sufficient milk and water in a saucepan or casserole to half cover the fish. When this is simmering, lay the fish in the pan, season, cover, and simmer very gently until tender allowing 10 minutes for each inch of thickness. Lift out the fish, drain, place on a hot dish, and serve coated with sauce made with the liquor in the pan.

Steaming: Prepare the fish as for boiling. Place large pieces or whole fish directly in the steamer; small fillets or thin steaks will cook satisfactorily if laid on a greased deep plate with 1 tablespoon milk and some seasoning, placed over a saucepan of boiling water and covered with the lid or a second plate. For a large fish allow 15 minutes per lb and 15 minutes over. Cook fillets for about 20 minutes. Serve with a sauce.

Frying: Almost any kind of fish is suitable for this method of cooking. Shallow frying is best for thick pieces such as cod steaks and for whole fish such as soles, which require a fairly long time to cook through. Deep frying is better for fillets and small fish. Small fish can be fried whole, while the large ones should be filleted and cut into convenient-sized pieces. The fish must be made quite dry and the outside coated so as to prevent the fat soaking into the fish itself. There are several methods of coating fish for frying.

Coating for shallow frying: The simplest method is to coat the fish with seasoned flour. Fine oatmeal may also be used, particularly for herring and mackerel.

A slightly more elaborate method is to dip the fish into seasoned flour, then into milk, and into flour again. Do not prepare the fish until just before frying it.

Coating for deep frying: Small pieces of fish may be dipped in batter. Season them with pepper, salt, and a little lemon juice, then drop them into the batter and lift them out with a skewer, draining off any surplus batter before putting the fish into the frying fat. Do not coat the fish until just before frying it.

The fish may also be breaded, which gives it a very attractive appearance when cooked. It should be breaded well before cooking as the coating becomes drier on standing and the food fries all the better.

To serve fried fish: Garnish with lemon and parsley or maître d'hôtel butter and if desired with French fried potatoes. Any sauce should be served separately.

Broiling: Herrings, mullet, mackerel, flounder, and sole are suitable fish to broil, as well as steaks and fillets of thick fish, such as halibut, cod, salmon, etc. (See Broiling entry.)

Baking: Weigh and wipe the fish, place it in a greased pan lined with a double fold of greased aluminum foil, sprinkle with salt and pepper and, if desired, a little lemon juice, then add a few dots of butter. Bake in a 400° oven until the flesh is white and firm, with a creamy curd between the flakes, and will come away easily from the bone.

Allow 6 to 10 minutes per lb and 6 to 10 minutes over, according to the thickness. Thin fillets of fish will take about 15 minutes.

Fish baked in foil: Steaks of fish just need wiping over, but if the fish is to be cooked whole, clean it, leaving on the head, tail, and skin. Place in the foil, dot with butter, sprinkle with salt, pepper and a little lemon juice and then completely enclose the fish in the foil. Place on a baking sheet or shallow dish and bake in a 350° oven allowing 15 minutes per lb, plus 15 minutes over. When the fish is cooked, remove it from the foil, skin carefully and serve hot or cold, garnished as desired.

Any fish can be cooked in this way, but it is particularly suitable for salmon.

Baking whole fish: A large sole or flounder or a small cod, hake, or fresh haddock, served on a long platter and attractively garnished, makes a decorative dish. Wash the fish, remove any scales, clean it carefully, but leave the head on, removing the eyes. Stuff with fresh bread crumbs, salt and pepper, a little chopped fat bacon, some chopped parsley and a pinch of mixed herbs, moistened with beaten egg and a little milk.

With a round fish, such as cod, place the stuffing in the cavity from which the entrails have been removed. Roll any remaining stuffing into small balls and dust them with flour. Place the fish on a greased baking sheet with some firm tomatoes (if desired) and the balls of stuffing.

In the case of a flat fish, such as flounder or sole, lay the fish on a board and cut through the flesh right down to the backbone; then, using the point of a sharp knife, loosen the flesh from the bone on each side as far as the fins, but not right through the skin. Fill the stuffing into the cavity thus formed, lay some small tomatoes along the center of the fish and place it on a greased baking sheet.

Dot the stuffed fish with butter and bake in a 400° oven for 45 minutes to 1 hour (according to size and thickness). Lift carefully onto a hot dish, using broad spatulas.

Garnish with lemon wedges and fresh parsley or fennel and serve with melted butter.

CURRIED FISH

1½ lb filleted cod, haddock, or similar white fish, skinned
1 large onion, chopped
2 tablespoons butter
1 teaspoon curry powder
5 tablespoons flour
1¼ cups chicken broth
1¼ cups milk
1 small apple, peeled and chopped
2 tomatoes, peeled and chopped

$\frac{1}{4}$–$\frac{1}{2}$ cup golden seedless raisins
salt and pepper
boiled rice

Cut the fish into 1-inch cubes. Sauté the onion gently in the butter for 5 minutes without browning. Stir in the curry powder and cook for 2 to 3 minutes, add the flour and cook for a further 2 to 3 minutes. Remove the pan from the heat, stir in the broth and milk gradually and bring to a boil, stirring until the sauce thickens. Add the apple, tomatoes, raisins, salt and pepper, cover and simmer for 15 minutes.

Add the fish, stir and simmer for a further 10 minutes, or until the fish is tender. Add more salt and pepper if necessary and serve with boiled rice.

FISH CAKES

8 oz fish, e.g. cod or haddock
1 lb potatoes, peeled and cut up
2 tablespoons butter
1 tablespoon chopped parsley
salt
pepper
milk or beaten egg, to bind
1 egg, beaten, to coat
dry bread crumbs
fat for frying

Cook and flake the fish. Boil and drain the potatoes and mash with the butter, or use 1 cup leftover mashed potatoes or instant potato. Mix the fish with the potatoes, parsley, and salt and pepper to taste, binding if necessary with a little milk or egg. Form the mixture into a roll on a floured board, cut it into 8 slices and shape into cakes. Coat them with egg and crumbs, fry in hot fat (deep or shallow) until crisp and golden; drain well. Vary the flavor of the cakes by using canned tuna or salmon instead of white fish.

As fish cakes tend to be dry, serve with a sauce such as tomato.

BAKED FISH

$\frac{1}{4}$ cup olive oil
1 clove garlic, crushed
2 sprigs parsley, finely chopped
$\frac{1}{4}$ teaspoon oregano
4 cod steaks
salt
pepper
1 cup dry bread crumbs
$\frac{1}{2}$ cup grated Parmesan cheese

Combine the olive oil, garlic, parsley and oreg-

ano in a shallow dish. Season the fish with salt and pepper and place in the marinade, turning to coat. Cover and refrigerate for 3 to 4 hours, turning once. Drain, reserving the marinade.

Mix together the bread crumbs and cheese and use to coat the fish. Strain the marinade into an ovenproof dish and add the fish. Moisten the coating with a spoonful or two of marinade. Bake in a 375° oven 20 to 25 minutes. Serve garnished with lemon.

FISH PROVENÇALE

1 onion, chopped
1 small green pepper, seeded and chopped
3–4 slices bacon, chopped
2 tablespoons butter
1 lb fillet of cod or haddock, skinned
seasoned flour
1 can (16 oz) tomatoes, drained
1 bay leaf
2 teaspoons sugar
salt and pepper

Sauté the onion, pepper, and bacon gently in the butter for 5 to 10 minutes, until soft but not browned. Wash and dry the fish and cut it into 1-inch cubes. Toss the fish in seasoned flour and cook with the vegetables for a further 2 to 3 minutes. Stir in the tomatoes, bay leaf, sugar, and seasoning, bring to a boil, stirring gently, cover with a lid and simmer for 10 to 15 minutes, until the fish and vegetables are cooked. Serve with boiled rice.

FRIED FISH

4 flounder fillets
seasoned flour
1 egg
$\frac{1}{4}$ cup milk
corn meal
oil for frying

Cut the fillets into strips and dust with flour. Beat the egg with the milk and dip the fish in the mixture. Roll in the cornmeal. Heat the oil in a skillet and fry the fish until golden, turning once. Serve garnished with lemon wedges.

FLAGEOLET

A type of kidney bean with pale green, tender skin and a delicate flavor.

FLAMBE

French term meaning to flame foods with

warmed alcoholic spirits, such as brandy or rum, which have been ignited.

FLAN

A round tart with a filling of cheese, fruit, or custard. The shell is free-standing and made of pastry. The shells are made on baking sheets inside special flan rings which are removed after baking.

COOKIE CRUST

1½ cups cookie crumbs
3 oz melted butter

Grease a shallow 8-inch pie plate or layer cake pan. Crush the cookies with a rolling pin and bind together with the melted butter. Spoon the crumbs into the pie plate, pressing them firmly into shape to make a shell. Chill until set.

VARIATIONS
1. Replace ¼ cup of the crumbs by ¼ cup shredded coconut or chopped nuts.
1. Add the grated rind of 1 lemon.
3. Add 1 to 2 teaspoons ground ginger or mixed spice.
4. Blend the crumbs with 3 to 4 oz chocolate and a walnut-sized knob of butter, melted together.
5. Use ginger snaps and bind with melted semisweet chocolate.
6. Add finely grated orange rind from one orange.

FRESH FRUIT FLAN FILLING

8 oz fresh fruit, e.g., strawberries, raspberries
currant jelly

Pick over the fruit and arrange in the flan shell. Make a glaze by melting 2 to 3 tablespoons currant jelly with about 1 tablespoon water; pour the glaze over the fruit when it begins to thicken.

Note: Adapt the quantity to suit the size of flan.

CANNED FRUIT FLAN FILLING

1 can (15 oz) fruit
1 tablespoon cornstarch
⅔ cup fruit juice

Arrange the drained fruit in the flan shell, filling it well. Blend the cornstarch with a little of the fruit juice to a smooth cream. Boil the rest and stir into the blended cornstarch. Return this mixture to the pan and bring to a boil, stirring until a clear thickened glaze is obtained. Spoon over the fruit to coat it evenly.

Note: Adapt the quantity to suit the size of flan.

FLAPJACK

A pancake.

FLAVORING

Almost as old as the art of cookery itself is the practice of adding or enhancing taste, or disguising a poor flavor, by the use of extra ingredients. Herbs and spices (see separate entries) are added to innumerable dishes during the cooking to give flavor. Flavoring extracts are also very widely used, especially in candies and in the making of wines, liqueurs, and cordials. (See Extract entry for fuller details.)

Wines and liqueurs, such as Madeira, port, sherry, Kirsch, Cointreau, etc., are much used in high-class cookery, as are the different types of brandy – Cognac, Calvados and so on.

FLEURON

A small fancy-shaped piece of pastry (usually puff pastry) used for garnishing entrées, ragouts, etc.

Roll the pastry thinly, then stamp it into crescents with a small round cutter, place the cutter about ½ inch onto the edge of the pastry for the first cut, then move the cutter a further ½ inch inward and cut again, thus forming a crescent; continue the length of the pastry, moving the cutter ½ inch each time. Alternatively, cut the pastry into rounds, squares, triangles, diamonds, etc. Place on a baking sheet, brush the tops lightly with beaten egg, and bake in a 450° oven until well risen, golden brown and firm underneath – 7 to 10 minutes. Use at once, while crisp.

FLIP

A drink made with beaten egg and milk, wine, spirit or beer, and sugar.

FLORENTINE

A crisp lacy cookie, made with cream and containing chopped nuts and candied orange peel. The cookies are dipped into chocolate after baking.

FLORENTINES

½ cup heavy cream

½ *cup sugar*
5 *tablespoons butter*
1¼ *cups chopped almonds*
¾ *cup finely chopped candied orange peel*
⅓ *cup all-purpose flour*
1 *oz unsweetened chocolate*
1 *oz semisweet chocolate*
1 *tablespoon honey*

Combine the cream, sugar, and 3 tablespoons of the butter in a saucepan and bring to a boil. Remove from the heat and stir in the nuts, orange peel, and flour.

Drop the batter by the tablespoon onto a greased and floured baking sheet. Bake in a 350° oven for about 10 minutes. Remove from the oven and let stand on the sheet for about 5 minutes. Remove to a wire rack to cool.

When the cookies are completely cool, melt the chocolate. Add the remaining 2 tablespoons butter and the honey and stir until the butter is melted. Spread on the bottom of each cookie. Chill.

FLOUNDER

A small marine flatfish resembling sole, but of poorer texture and flavor. Flounders are found in the North Sea, the Baltic, the Mediterranean, and off the Atlantic coast of the United States.

Flounders are good broiled or fried, but may be cooked in any way suitable for sole.

FLOUR

Any fine, soft, white powder prepared from a grain, e.g. cornstarch, rice flour, and wheat flour. Unless otherwise indicated, however, the word usually implies wheat flour, obtained by milling the wheat grain. This is the staple food in most temperate climates and can be made into a wide range of products – breads, biscuits, cookies, cakes, pastry, pasta, puddings. It is important as a thickening agent.

Types of Wheat Flour
The flour varies according to the type of wheat used. Hard spring wheats, like those grown in the United States and Canada, produce strong flours. These contain a large amount (10 to 15 percent) of a protein-forming substance, gluten. Soft wheats, grown in milder climates, produce a soft or weak flour, containing 7 to 10 percent gluten. It is the gluten which gives wheat flour its elasticity, allowing it to rise and trap the bubbles of gas produced by a leavening agent and then be set by baking. A strong flour is necessary to bake yeast goods and puff pastry. A weak flour is better for biscuits, cakes, and short-crust pastry, where the rising power is not so important as the ability to carry fat.

Millers select different wheats and blend them to produce different grades of flour. Most flours on the market, sold as "all-purpose," are milled from a mixture of hard and soft wheats and are therefore of medium strength. Self-rising flour is generally a softer flour to which baking powder and salt have been added.

High-Ratio Cake Flour is a special type of flour used in the United States. It is made from a soft variety of flour from winter wheats containing about 7 percent protein and is Patent Grade (i.e., a purer flour obtained early in the milling process). This flour is generally employed in cake mixes and commercial cakemaking; a higher ratio of sugar, fat, and liquid to flour is possible where it is used – hence the name.

Extraction Rates
When wheat is milled, it is crushed between rollers to split the husk and release the contents (including the wheat germ). The amount of bran and germ that remains determines the kind of flour. Whole meal contains the whole of the cleaned wheat grain, nothing must be added to it or taken from it; white flour is produced from the inner endosperm and contains no bran or germ. The extraction rate of flour means the percentage of the whole grain that remains in the flour after milling, thus: whole meal and whole wheat flour is 100 percent extraction of the cleaned wheat grain; wheat meal usually contains 80 to 90 percent of the cleaned wheat grain; white flour usually contains 70 to 72 percent of the cleaned wheat grain.

On the whole, millers prefer to make white flour, as it keeps better than whole meal; the fat in the wheat germ goes rancid so whole meal flour is best kept no longer than 2 months.

Bleaching and Improving Agents
Storage of flour in the quantities required today is a difficult matter, so the bleaching and improving which used to take place naturally, as the flour aged, are now carried out chemically.

Self-rising Flour and Leavening Agents
To make self-rising flour, a leavening agent is added during manufacture and mixed in thoroughly. The agents used are sodium bicarbonate and calcium acid phosphate or sodium pyrophosphate.

Self-rising flour is considered by some to be

more convenient. It gives perfectly good results for most recipes, though it is not necessary for very rich creamed mixtures and beaten sponges, where eggs are a sufficient leavening agent; for crackers and plain pastries, which are not meant to rise; for bread, where yeast is the leavening agent; and for batters, which are raised by steam.

Food Value of Wheat Flour

Flour is a cheap and valuable food. It supplies energy, protein, calcium, iron, and vitamins of the B group. White flour has only about half the minerals and B vitamins contained in whole meal flour, although it has much the same amount of protein and energy value. With the policy of enrichment of flour nutritionally, there is little difference in value between brown and white flour.

The higher extraction flours contain a substance called phytic acid which is thought to decrease the absorption of calcium to some extent, so probably enriched white flour supplies considerably more available calcium. In fact, odd though it seems, whole meal flour is probably a poorer source of calcium than other flours.

To sum up, the advantages of white flour are that it has better baking qualities and produces a whiter loaf; it has less fat and therefore stores better; it has less phytic acid interfering with the absorption of calcium. On the debit side, as milled it contains less calcium, iron and vitamins of the B group, but since these nutrients are now added, this does not matter. It does not contain roughage as the bran has been removed. For this reason many people prefer to use whole meal flour in bread and cooking.

Whatever kind of flour and bread is chosen, all types are easily digested, very nutritious and comparatively economical.

Flours from Other Cereals

RYE FLOUR
This ranks next to wheat flour as a breadmaker. It is extensively employed in black bread, such as pumpernickel, and in rye bread. The flour is deficient in proteins as compared with wheat.

RICE FLOUR
By itself this is unsuitable for bread- or cakemaking, as it contains no gluten. Rice flour can, however, be combined with wheat flour to make bread and cakes.

CORNSTARCH
A corn preparation which consists almost entirely of starch, since the proteins and fats are

removed. It is used for thickening sauces, gravies, and soups; it may also be used for cakemaking in conjunction with wheat flour.

Flouring: To dredge flour over the surface of a food in order to dry it or coat it for frying, or to sprinkle flour over a pastry board before use.

FLUMMERY

An old English cold dessert made of a cereal (originally oatmeal), set in a mold and turned out. Other types were Dutch Flummery, made with gelatin or isinglass, egg yolks, and flavorings, and Spanish Flummery, made of cream, rice flour, cinnamon, and sugar.

FOIE GRAS

The liver of a goose which has been specially fed and fattened. These very large goose livers are esteemed a great delicacy in Europe and are cooked in various more or less elaborate ways. They may be served hot or cold as an hors d'oeuvre.

Goose livers are also combined with pork, truffles, and other ingredients to make the smooth rich paste known as pâté de foie gras, which is imported from France in terrines (small earthenware pots). This pâté is often eaten as an hors d'oeuvre and may be served in the terrine or cut into thin slices and garnished with chopped parsley and sliced lemon. Pureed foie gras may be served as an hors d'oeuvre and the pâté may also be used in making sandwiches and canapés.

FOLDING

A method of combining a beaten mixture with other ingredients so that it retains its lightness; it is used for mixing meringues, soufflés, and certain cake mixtures. A typical example is folding dry flour into a beaten sponge cake mixture. First sift the flour on top of the beaten mixture. Using a large metal spoon, take up a spoonful of the sponge mixture from the bottom of the bowl, drawing the spoon across the base, then fold it over the top, enclosing the dry flour in between. Repeat until all the flour is incorporated, occasionally cutting through the mixture with the spoon held at right angles to the direction of the folding.

Important points to remember are that the mixture must be folded very lightly and that it must not be agitated more than is absolutely necessary, because with every movement some of the air bubbles are broken down.

FONDANT

This forms the basis of a large number of candies and is also used for chocolate centers and for frosting cakes, etc. True fondant is made by boiling sugar syrup to a temperature of 240° to 245° but an unboiled version may be used for making simple candies.

BOILED FONDANT

1 cup water
3 cups sugar
good pinch cream of tartar

Put the water into a pan, add the sugar and let it dissolve slowly. Bring the syrup to a boil, add the cream of tartar and boil to 240°. Sprinkle a little water on a marble slab or other suitable surface, pour on the syrup and leave for a few minutes to cool. When a skin forms around the edge, take a spatula and collect the mixture together, then work it backward and forward, using a figure-of-eight movement. Continue to work the syrup, collecting it into a small area until it changes its character and grains, becoming opaque and firm. Scrape it off the marble and knead it in the hands until of an even texture throughout.

Fondant Icing

Make the fondant as described above and prepare it for use as follows:

Put the required amount in a bowl; stand the bowl over hot water and melt over a very gentle heat. Take care not to overheat the fondant, as this makes the texture rough and destroys the gloss. Dilute the melted fondant with sugar syrup or with plain water to the consistency of heavy cream – or until the mixture will just coat the back of a wooden spoon. To make sugar syrup, dissolve 1 cup sugar in 1 cup water, then boil without stirring to 225°; cool before using. Cakes which are to be coated with fondant should be glazed first with apricot glaze and then coated with almond paste in order to appear professional. To cover small cakes or pastries, spear them on a fork or skewer and dip them in the fondant.

To cover a large cake, put it on a wire rack with a plate below and pour the fondant quickly over the cake. Don't touch the fondant with a knife or the gloss will be spoiled. Add any desired decoration and leave the cake to set.

UNBOILED FONDANT

1 box (16 oz) powdered sugar
pinch cream of tartar
1 teaspoon lemon juice
1 egg white
coloring

Sift the powdered sugar with the cream of tartar. Add the lemon juice and sufficient egg white to make a pliable paste, add a few drops of coloring as required. Knead thoroughly for 5 minutes, then set aside to mellow for 1 hour before using.

Fondant Fruits: These make attractive petits four. Prepare neat and fairly small pieces of crystalized ginger, candied pineapple, clusters of raisins, etc., and dip them in liquid fondant (which may be colored or plain, as desired).

Lift them out onto waxed paper and allow to dry. If the fruit is fresh and juicy, serve it within 2 to 3 hours, or the juice will spoil the fondant.

FONDUE

A specialty of Savoy and Switzerland, made basically of melted cheese, with wine and flavorings. There are many variations of cheese fondues which provide a popular way to entertain informally. Recipes for sweet fondues are also available. A French dish, Fondue Bourguignonne, consists of small cubes of tender steak impaled on a long fork and cooked in hot oil and served with a selection of sauces. Pieces of chicken, shrimp, and scampi may also be used.

FONDUE

1 clove garlic, crushed
⅔ cup dry white wine and a squeeze of lemon juice
8 oz cheese, cut in thin strips (half Gruyère and half Emmenthal)
2 teaspoons cornstarch
1 tablespoon Kirsch
pepper
grated nutmeg

Rub the inside of a flameproof dish with the garlic, place the dish over a gentle heat and warm the wine and lemon juice in it. Add the cheese and continue to heat gently, stirring well until the cheese has melted and begun to cook. Add the cornstarch and seasonings, blended to a smooth cream with the Kirsch, and continue cooking for a further 2 to 3 minutes; when the mixture is of a thick creamy consistency, it is ready to serve.

Traditionally, fondue is served at the table in the dish in which it was cooked, kept warm over a small spirit lamp or hot tray. To eat it, provide cubes of crusty bread which are speared on a fork and dipped in the fondue.

An anglicized version of fondue can be made using a strong-flavored Cheddar cheese, cider instead of white wine, and brandy instead of Kirsch.

HOT CHEESE DIP

$\frac{2}{3}$ cup medium dry white wine
1 teaspoon lemon juice
14 oz Gouda cheese, grated
1 tablespoon cornstarch
1 teaspoon prepared English mustard
pepper

Put the wine and lemon juice into a heavy saucepan and heat until nearly boiling. Add the cheese and beat well with a wooden spoon.

Blend the cornstarch with a little water and add to the cheese mixture, beating well. Stir in the mustard and season with pepper.

Serve at once with chunks of French bread.

Note: Serve as a traditional fondue for leisurely eating. Supply each guest with a fork for spearing the bread and then dipping into hot cheese mixture. Accompany with a well-tossed salad.

FONDUE DU RAISIN

A mild French cheese, covered with grape seeds, which comes from the Province of Savoy. This cheese tends to be rather mild in flavor but it adds color to a cheese board.

FONDUTA

A famous dish from Piedmont in Italy made with Fontina cheese and truffles.

FONTAINEBLEAU CHEESE

A French cheese of the cream type, soft and fresh, made in the country round Fontainebleau, mostly during the summer.

FONTINA D'AOSTA

One of Italy's great cheeses which comes only from the valley of Savoy.

FOOD

Food is essential for life. Plants can make their own from minerals, water, and the gases in the air, but animals have to obtain their food ready-made. Basically, all animals get their food from plants, although many of them obtain it indirectly by eating other animals. The water, minerals, and gases thus used are eventually returned to their original state through breathing, excretion, and decay after death, and are then once more available to build new plants. This cycle is continuous and the total amount of food available to life on the earth remains constant. The human race is able to direct and improve the cycle, but it is not able to alter the basic principles or increase the amount of the basic ingredients.

All plant and animal life should theoretically be available as food for animals, but most species are restricted in their choice of foods. Sheep eat mainly grass and can get the necessary nourishment from it, whereas humans are so adapted that they could not be well fed on grass. However, human beings are able to eat a very much wider variety of foods than most animals.

No single food eaten by humans supplies all that is necessary, although milk comes near to doing so. Each food supplies nutrients of some kind in varying amounts and it is difficult to say that this food is more valuable than that one. What we can say is that the wider the choice of food, the more likely it is that all the necessary food factors will be obtained.

FOOD POISONING

Any poison transmitted by food and drink is covered by this term, but it is generally used only for certain infections.

The number of cases due to natural poisons, such as deadly nightshade and certain fungi, and to artificial ones (such as insecticides, etc.) accidentally added to food, or lead derived from lead pipes, is not nearly so great as that due to bacterial infections.

A steady increase in these cases has led to food poisoning being made a reportable disease, though many cases are still not reported, since a mild attack is easily overlooked and the doctor is not necessarily called in. Attacks are more frequent during the summer than in winter and they may set in within 6 to 24 hours after the infected food has been eaten. The symptoms are generally vomiting and/or diarrhea. Such disorders, frequently dismissed as "only a germ going around," are in fact due to a lack of hygiene somewhere.

The increase in food poisoning is probably due in part to changing food and eating habits. Much more use is made of communal feeding centers – restaurants, cafés, snack bars and school and industrial cafeterias. Practices that cause no harm in the home may be dangerous in the large-scale kitchen. Some of the possible causes are:
1. Lack of hygiene – poor personal hygiene, lack

of washing facilities, unnecessary handling of food.

2. Lack of trained staff to instruct the workers, point out the dangers and supervise the preparation and storage of the food.

3. Lack of good cold storage facilities.

4. Cooked food not being reheated sufficiently. The actual poisoning can be caused either by bacteria or by toxins produced by bacteria. Bacteria thrive in warm, moist conditions, where there is a supply of food. Some of them produce poisons which cannot be destroyed except by thorough cooking, even though the bacteria themselves are killed.

Types of Food Poisoning

SALMONELLA GROUP
Many varieties, producing mild or severe illness. Amongst them are the bacteria that cause gastro-enteritis, typhoid fever, and enteric fever.

Some of the foods that can be infected are meat, egg, and milk dishes.

STAPHYLOCOCCAL GROUP
These produce harmful toxins.

BOTULISM
Caused by a powerful poison from *Bacillus botulinus*, but fortunately very rare.

HEPATITIS
Caused by infectious or toxic agents found in raw clams and oysters taken from polluted waters.

DYSENTERY
Particularly prevalent in tropical climates.

CHOLERA
Very rare in Western countries.

FOOD PROCESSOR

A compact table-top machine with a heavy motor. Depending upon the blade inserted in it, this machine is capable of pureeing, grinding, slicing, making dough, etc.

FOOD STORAGE

Different kinds of food have different storage requirements.

Perishable Foods

Meat, fish, milk, fats, cheese, eggs, fruit, and vegetables come into this group, since they all deteriorate fairly quickly owing to the action of bacteria and enzymes. Low temperatures slow down this action, so perishable foods should ideally be stored at a temperature low enough to delay such activity – that is, at about 40° or just under. The domestic refrigerator, which is normally kept at 35° to 45° is thus suitable for storing fresh foods, milk, fats, etc. (See Refrigeration entry for further details.) In general, however, no attempt should be made to store these foods for a long period, even when a refrigerator is available, and most of them should be bought and used within a few days. Cream, yogurt, and soft cheeses are usually marked with a date indicating the last day on which they can be sold. They will keep for a few days after this in a refrigerator. Failing a refrigerator, perishable foods should be kept covered in a cold, well-ventilated place.

MEAT AND FISH
Raw meat and fish should be stored in the refrigerator covered lightly with foil, etc.

Cooked meat or fish should be wrapped in waxed paper or plastic wrap or placed in a covered container.

MILK
Keep this in its container in the refrigerator. Pitchers of cream should be covered.

BREAD
Air circulation is necessary, so keep bread in a ventilated metal or plastic bread box or in a loosely wrapped plastic bag.

FATS AND OILS
Should be kept cool and if possible in the dark, since the light has a destructive effect on their vitamin content and tends to hasten rancidity.

CHEESE
For table use should be stored in conditions that prevent both mold growth and excessive drying. A cheese dish with a ventilated cover is good, provided it is placed in a cool, dry, airy place. Alternatively, wrap the cheese in plastic wrap or aluminum foil, or place it in a plastic container large enough to allow air circulation. Hard cheeses can be kept in a refrigerator, but soft ones should be kept in the special cheese compartment of the refrigerator. Cheese for cooking should be allowed to harden, especially if it is soft or immature when bought. (See Cheese entry.)

EGGS
Should be kept in the refrigerator or in a cool, airy place.

FRUIT, VEGETABLES

Most of these foods contain some vitamin C and since the vitamin content diminishes rapidly during storage, they should be used fresh and stored for as short a time as possible in a cool and well-ventilated place. Root vegetables should be placed on a vegetable rack with slatted shelves. Green vegetables should be washed and put in the salad crisper or a plastic container in the refrigerator.

FROZEN FOODS

(See separate entry.)

LEFTOVERS

Cool these rapidly by putting them in a cold place. Do not leave them on the stove or in a warm part of the kitchen. They are then best covered and stored in the refrigerator. Failing this, use them up as soon as possible, preferably the next day.

Storage Times for Perishables
(not Frozen Foods)

	IN REFRIGERATOR
MEAT	
Raw: roasts, chops	3 to 5 days
Variety meats, ground meat	1 to 2 days
Cooked	2 to 5 days
FISH	
Raw	1 to 2 days
Cooked	2 days
DAIRY PRODUCTS	
Milk	3 to 4 days
Butter and Cheese	2 to 4 weeks

Dry Stores

Under this heading are included cereals, sugars, syrups, dried fruits, herbs, extracts, flavorings, condiments, and spices, etc. Deterioration during storage is not as a rule a serious problem, but most cereals are subject to attacks by weevils and mites and will mold if allowed to become damp. Oatmeal, since it contains an appreciable amount of fat, will become rancid if kept too long or in a warm place. In certain cases, notably with dried fruit, fermentation may set in after prolonged storage.

Cupboards should be cool and dry, well-ventilated but dustproof and the stores must be examined from time to time. A small cupboard or shelf near the range should be used for the stores which are constantly required, such as sugar, salt, pepper, tea, and coffee.

Ideally the shelving in cupboards should be so arranged that the jars can be kept in single rows, and in any case not more than two deep, so that they can be easily seen. The shelves should be removable and adjustable so that they can be adapted for jars and cans of different heights. Stepped shelves for small bottles, also shelves that slope backward, economize on space.

Plastic or glass jars are excellent for cereals and dried fruits, etc., for quick identification and also to see immediately how much is in stock. Smaller plastic or glass jars with well-fitting lids are suitable for herbs and spices. Airtight containers are needed for cakes, biscuits, baking powder, and coffee. A container with slight ventilation is needed for bread; a plastic bag is also suitable, if not wrapped too tightly round the loaf. Flour is best left in the package and stored in a bin. Make sure the bin is kept clean by regular washing. Make sure to dry the bin thoroughly, as a damp atmosphere should be avoided at all costs.

Storage Times for Dry Goods

Cereals, flour (*except whole meal*) and pulses	Several months
Whole meal flour	1 to 2 months
Sugar	Indefinitely
Preserves, pickles, jarred fruit and vegetables	1 to 2 years
Dried fruit	2 to 3 months
CANNED FOODS	
Fruit	1 year
Vegetables	2 years
Fish and meat (*except large hams*)	5 years
Evaporated milk	2 years
Soups	2 years
Mixes, e.g. cake	6 months

Refrigerator Storage

Allow hot foods to cool before putting them in the refrigerator.

Plastic wrap, plastic containers, or foil prevent food drying out.

All foods should be covered.

Wipe up spilled foods at once.

Cover any foods that are highly flavored or strong smelling to avoid flavors transferring from one food to another, for example, the strong smell of onion to milk.

Defrost according to the manufacturer's instructions and wipe the inside of the refrigerator with a clean, damp cloth. Do not use scouring powder.

(See Refrigeration and Freezing entries.)

FOOL

A puree of fresh, or sometimes canned, fruit with cream and/or custard. (See recipe in Fruit entry.)

FOO YUNG

Chinese for hibiscus; a thin patty of egg mixed with green onions, water chestnuts, bean sprouts, dried mushrooms, and shredded meat, poultry, or seafood. It is the Chinese answer to the omelet.

PORK EGGS FOO YUNG

$\frac{1}{4}$ cup dried mushrooms, soaked 15 minutes
6 eggs
$\frac{3}{4}$ cup shredded cooked pork
3 green onions, sliced $\frac{1}{4}$ inch thick
6 water chestnuts, diced
$\frac{3}{4}$ cup bean sprouts
1 teaspoon salt
5 tablespoons oil

Shred the mushrooms finely. Break the eggs into a bowl and stir to blend; do not beat. Add the remaining ingredients except the oil. Heat 3 tablespoons of the oil in an 8-inch skillet and add half the egg mixture. Cook until golden brown on one side, then turn and cook on the second side. Put on a warm plate, add the remaining oil to the skillet and cook the rest of the mixture. Serve with soy sauce.

FORCEMEAT

Finely ground meat or poultry used for stuffing. The mixture can also be rolled into small balls, fried or baked and used as a garnish. There are several types of forcemeat and the basic recipe can be altered according to the dish which it accompanies.

HAM FORCEMEAT

$\frac{1}{4}$ onion, chopped
1 tablespoon butter
2 mushrooms, chopped
$\frac{1}{4}$–$\frac{1}{3}$ cup cooked ham, chopped
$\frac{1}{2}$ cup fresh white bread crumbs
salt and pepper
little dry mustard
few drops of Worcestershire sauce
beaten egg or milk to bind

Lightly sauté the onion in the butter for 1 to 2 minutes; add the mushrooms and ham and sauté until the onion is soft but not browned. Remove from the heat and add the crumbs, seasonings, and Worcestershire, and bind with beaten egg or milk. Use as a stuffing for vegetables, tomatoes, small zucchini, peppers, etc. *Makes enough for a $3\frac{1}{4}$ lb chicken.*

VEAL FORCEMEAT

4 oz lean veal
4–5 slices lean bacon
1 small onion, finely chopped
2 tablespoons butter
1 cup fresh white bread crumbs
1 large mushroom, wiped and chopped
1 teaspoon finely chopped parsley
salt and pepper
cayenne
ground mace
1 egg, beaten

Pass the mixed veal and bacon twice through a grinder, then beat them well in a bowl. Lightly sauté the onion in a little of the butter, until soft but not browned – 2 to 3 minutes; add to the meat. Add the bread crumbs, mushroom, and remaining butter, parsley, and seasonings, and lastly the beaten egg. Mix well; if the mixture is too stiff, add a little milk.

Use for veal or lamb; double the quantities for a 13 lb turkey.

FOWL

An edible bird especially the domestic cock or hen. As a general term, the word can apply to a bird of any age, but it is often applied more particularly to an older tougher bird, suitable for boiling, steaming, or fricasseeing.

For general directions regarding drawing, trussing, etc., see Poultry entry. (For methods of cooking and recipes, see Chicken entry.)

FRANGIPANE (FRANGIPANI)

Originally frangipane was a jasmine perfume, which gave its name to an almond cream flavored with the perfume. The term is now usually applied to a small tart filled with an almond-flavored mixture. It also applies to a type of choux pastry.

FRANKFURTER (HOT DOG)

A long, reddish smoked sausage made from ground pork or beef and pork or poultry, and served with mustard and/or sauerkraut on a long, soft bread roll. The frankfurters are usually boiled for a few minutes before being used, but are sometimes fried or grilled. The name originated in the city of Frankfurt, Germany, but frankfurters have become a national dish in the United States, traditional at baseball games and for Fourth of July picnics.

FREEZER

Freezers are increasingly popular and valuable pieces of equipment in the home. They are also invaluable in any establishment that has to cater for large numbers. The main advantages are:

1. To make good use of abundant supplies of fruit, vegetables, and other food.
2. To enable foods to be eaten when out of season.
3. To take advantage of bulk buying, thus reducing costs and shopping time.
4. To cook food in bulk, saving on cooking time and fuel.
5. To be able to store meals and foods which can be used when shopping and cooking are not possible for various reasons.

Apart from the advantages, the cost of running the freezer must be taken into account. On top of the cost of the freezer, the cost of electricity, packing materials, and insurance must be considered. Most people feel that the convenience of having a freezer outweighs these costs even if they do not save a great deal on the contents.

Types of Freezer

Freezers are of two main types – the upright kind (with a door) and the chest models (with a lift-up lid). There is also the combination refrigerator-freezer which is useful for processing small quantities of food and where space is limited.

The type to choose depends on your requirements. It is reckoned that each cubic foot of space will store about 20 lb of frozen food, depending on kind. A useful guide is to allow a minimum of 3 cubic feet space per person. Sizes range from 1.75 cubic feet up to 25 cubic feet.

UPRIGHT TYPE

This model takes up less floor space and the food is easier to get at. On the other hand, the cold air inside tends to spill out when the door is opened and warm, moist air enters. This kind of freezer frosts up more quickly for this reason, but the frost is easily scraped out. Sizes range from 1.75 cubic feet to 20 cubic feet.

CHEST TYPE

This type retains the cold better and is slightly cheaper to run. It is not so easy to see the contents nor to reach foods at the bottom. Most models are supplied with plastic covered wire baskets to hold the most often needed or delicate items, making them easier to find. Defrosting is required less frequently, but takes more effort to carry out. 4 cubic feet to 25 cubic feet include range of sizes.

COMBINATION REFRIGERATOR-FREEZER

This has two separate units, the freezer section being insulated from the refrigerator. The thermostat controls the refrigerator temperature without altering that of the freezer and the refrigerator can be defrosted without affecting the freezer.

It is important to distinguish between the refrigerator with a true freezer compartment and the one with a frozen food compartment. Although the latter (and ice cube section) is often incorrectly called a freezer, it does not provide a sufficiently low temperature for freezing foods, but will store frozen food for a certain length of time, depending on its rating. In many freezers a dial or switch can be set to give a lower temperature or fast-freezing setting. This should be lowered before use so that the freezing process is speeded up, quick freezing being important. Once the foods have been frozen the setting should be returned to normal, maintaining an internal temperature of 0°.

A freezer is capable of freezing food without any change in the temperature of the food already being stored. It has the ability to freeze in 24 hours a specified quantity of fresh or cooked foods and to store them for periods of up to one year or more depending on the product.

It is an advantage to have a warning device (a light is the usual arrangement) which comes on when the temperature starts to rise above 0°. Alternatively, a warning buzzer or light may be fitted to the plug which will come on when the current is cut off.

Maintaining a Freezer

Most freezers are supplied with full instructions from the maker. Defrosting should be carried out every 9 to 11 months, or when the ice coating is $\frac{1}{2}$ inch thick on the sides of the wall plates. Defrost at a time when the freezer contains as little as possible. Remaining food can be placed in a refrigerator or wrapped in newspaper and blankets until the freezer is ready for use again. Pans of hot water may be used to hasten the defrosting process but they must not touch the freezer walls.

Power Failure

If the power fails, do not open the freezer unless it is really necessary. The contents of the freezer will keep cold for at least 12 to 24 hours. When you do open the freezer, inspect the packages; provided there are still ice crystals present in them it is safe to keep them in the freezer. If, however, the food has thawed it should be used as soon as possible, certainly within three days, and not refrozen. It is possible to have the contents of the freezer insured for a small premium per annum. Several companies will handle such claims and some stores offer cover if the freezer is purchased from them. Always check exactly what the policy covers.

FREEZING

Although it has been known for thousands of years that cold retards the decay of food, only in the past few decades has the freezing and long-term cold storage of a variety of foods been widely developed.

It is the easiest and safest way of preserving food. It is a simple process of reducing food to a temperature at which bacteria become inactive. Home freezing is carried out at a temperature of $-5°$.

Foods for Freezing

Most foods will freeze successfully, but it is important that they are of good quality: freezing does not improve the quality of food. Particularly suitable for freezing are meat, fish, vegetables, fruit, and dairy products. Any of these foods can be frozen raw or made into dishes and frozen: bread, cookies, cake, pancakes, puddings, pastries, and sauces can all be frozen and make useful standbys. If more convenient bread dough can be frozen uncooked. This also applies to pastry dough and cake mixtures.

The few foods which do not take kindly to freezing are whole eggs, hard-cooked eggs, potato in cooked dishes, custards, mayonnaise, dishes containing a high proportion of gelatin and light cream. However, with correct treatment some of these can be frozen for short periods. Eggs can be separated and frozen in individual containers; they should be lightly whipped and a small amount of sugar or salt added to the yolks; potato is more satisfactory if mashed and custards can be frozen before being cooked.

Salad ingredients such as lettuce, watercress, celery, and cucumber cannot be frozen successfully at all. The same applies to some fruits, such as melon, bananas, and pears (discolor badly).

Some frozen foods can be cooked from frozen such as meat for broiling or roasting, vegetables and fruits, but most need to be thawed first.

Cooked dishes, such as stews and quiches, can be cooked from frozen but extra cooking time must be allowed. Slow thawing can be done in the refrigerator, which is most suitable for dairy products and dishes including them, or at room temperature for a shorter time. It is very important to allow frozen poultry to thaw thoroughly before cooking. It is possible to refreeze foods as long as there has been no risk of contamination: the quality will, however, be impaired slightly, so it is not advisable as a general rule.

General Notes on Freezing

All food stored in a freezer must be carefully wrapped and sealed. There are many packaging materials available in supermarkets. These include heavy-duty polyethylene and aluminum foil, rigid plastic boxes, wax cartons, foil containers, and freezer tape. It is also possible to use yogurt and cottage cheese cartons provided they are carefully cleaned and sealed with freezer tape before being placed in the freezer. Food should be packed in portions to suit the family needs to save time and waste. When packing food, as much air as possible should be excluded, except with liquids when a space of $\frac{1}{2}$ inch should be left at the top to allow for expansion. All foods should be labeled with the contents, date of packing, and weight or number of servings. It is also advisable to keep an inventory of the contents of the freezer so that food can be used in rotation.

Freezing Fruits

PREPARATION

Clean, stem, and sort the fruit, handling it carefully and working with small amounts to avoid bruising. Discard overripe parts, blemishes and green sections.

WASHING AND DRAINING

Use clean utensils and wash your hands before handling the fruit. Cold (or better still ice) water should be used for washing fruits, to firm them and prevent waterlogging and seepage of juice. Drain in a colander. Fruit to be frozen in a dry pack should be dried on absorbent paper towels.

PACKING

The flavor, color, and texture of most fruit will be better retained if it is frozen with sugar or syrup. The amount used depends upon personal taste, the tartness of the fruit, and the way it is to be served. Fruits contain chemical substances called enzymes that hasten chemical changes. Instead of being blanched (as are vegetables) to stop enzymatic action, they are packed in sugar or syrup that protects them in two ways: the sugar retards the action of enzymes during frozen storage; and the syrup (either prepared and poured over, or formed by the sugar and juice drawn from the fruit) keeps the air out and retards oxidation (browning).

Soft fruits may be packed without sugar or syrup but are usually preferred with one or the other. As already mentioned, some fruits, particularly pears, discolor badly when frozen, so they should either be blanched or packed in an ascorbic acid solution or lemon juice; on the whole, they are perhaps better not frozen.

Method I – Dry pack: This method is used chiefly for fruits that are to be made into pies, jellies, or preserves. It is satisfactory for cranberries, blueberries, currants, and other small fruits that can be washed and prepared without breaking the skin and that do not darken easily upon exposure to the air. Carefully wash and sort the fruit, drain on absorbent towels, fill the containers full and freeze.

Method II – Free flow dry pack: This method is suitable for small fruits (or pieces of fruit), e.g. raspberries, cherries, grapefruit segments. Pick the fruit over, prepare as necessary; spread out on a baking tray and freeze until firm, then pack for storage.

Method III – Sugar pack: Use this method for juicy fruits that are sliced, crushed, or pureed. The sugar draws the juice from the fruit, forming a natural syrup that covers and protects it. Allow $\frac{1}{2}$ to $\frac{3}{4}$ cup sugar to each 1 lb fruit. The fruit must be mixed with the sugar until each piece is coated, so use a sifter to distribute the sugar and add alternate layers of fruit and sugar, shaking the contents after each addition to distribute the sugar and coat the fruit with natural syrup.

Method IV – Syrup pack: Syrup is used for packing fruits that have little free juice, e.g. peaches, apricots, greengages, and plums. A syrup consisting of $1\frac{3}{4}$ cups sugar to 1 pint water is sufficient for 1 lb fruit. Pit and peel the fruit, place in the containers, and cover with syrup. Leave $\frac{1}{2}$ to $\frac{3}{4}$ inch head space for expansion during freezing. Keep syrup-packed fruits submerged by placing a piece of crumpled waxed paper under the cover of the container or in the top of the bag.

Method V – Fruit purees: Fruit that is not of prime quality can be made into a puree before freezing. This takes up less space and is useful for making mousses and sauces to accompany ice cream and other desserts. Some fruits such as rhubarb, apples, apricots, blackberries, raspberries, currants, gooseberries, and plums will need to be stewed before pureeing. Softer fruits such as strawberries can be pureed without cooking. Purees should be placed in rigid containers allowing $\frac{1}{2}$ inch head space to allow for expansion.

THAWING AND COOKING FRUIT

If the fruit is to be served raw, thaw it slowly in the unopened container and eat while still slightly chilled. Fruits which tend to discolor, like peaches, should be thawed rapidly. Allow 6 to 8 hours per 1 lb of fruit to thaw in a refrigerator, and 2 to 4 hours at room temperature. For quick thawing, place container in warm water for 30 minutes to 1 hour.

If the fruit is to be cooked, thaw until the pieces are just loosened. Cook as fresh fruit, adding sugar to taste (remember that it will be fairly sweet if packed in dry sugar or syrup).

Freezing Vegetables

Most vegetables are suitable for freezing, except cucumber, radishes, lettuce, watercress, and other green vegetables that are eaten raw. New potatoes and onions do not freeze well; celery loses its crispness. Tomatoes are best frozen pureed. Asparagus, corn, peas, spinach, green beans, and cauliflower are very successful frozen.

PREPARATION

Speed is important here, for deterioration after harvesting is rapid at warm temperatures and vegetables lose some of their food value and garden freshness if allowed to stand for even a few hours in a warm place. They must be frozen immediately after harvesting or refrigerated and frozen within 12 hours.

Carefully trim and wash the vegetables, i.e. prepare them as for cooking: large vegetables such as cauliflower and broccoli should be divided into pieces of the right size for serving. Small pieces of uniform size can be scalded and packaged more easily than large ones.

BLANCHING (SCALDING)

Fresh vegetables contain chemical substances called enzymes which help in the growing and ripening, but which after harvesting cause serious destruction of vitamins, texture, and color – even during storage at 0°. Therefore, all vegetables must be blanched to destroy these enzymes. Take a pan large enough to hold the colander, wire basket, or net bag in which the vegetables are to be placed and put in about 6 to 10 pints of water for each 1 lb of vegetables. The food should be weighed into suitable quantities according to the number of portions needed at one time. Place in the colander or other container and immerse in fast-boiling water for the appropriate time, counting from the moment when the water returns to a boil. Put the colander into ice-cold water to cool, drain the vegetables, pack into containers, seal, and label. It is best to blanch 1 lb amounts to insure bringing the water quickly back to a boil each time.

Scalding Times

Brussels sprouts	3 to 4 minutes
Lima beans	3 minutes
Green beans	2 to 3 minutes *according to size*
Peas	1 to 2 minutes
Asparagus: young thin stalks	2 minutes
thick stalks	up to 4 minutes
Cauliflower	3 minutes
Carrots	5 minutes
Broccoli	3 minutes

Freezing Fish

Freeze fish the same day as they are caught. Prepare as for cooking – scale, gut, wash thoroughly, cut off head and fins. Freeze small fish whole, but cut large ones into steaks or fillets.

PACKING

Pack in moisture-and-vapor-proof paper or sheeting, or put into shallow rectangular waxed cartons or aluminum foil. Seal carefully and label.

THAWING

Thaw slowly unopened in a cool place long enough to separate the pieces of fish (45 minutes at room temperature, 3 to 4 hours in refrigerator). Small fish may be cooked frozen; cook for a few minutes longer than usual.

FREEZING SHELLFISH

Freeze within 12 hours of being caught. *Oysters and Scallops:* wash outside of shell thoroughly, open carefully and drain, retaining the liquor. Wash in a brine solution (1 tablespoon salt to 1 pint water). Drain and pack in small containers with reserved liquor. *Shrimp:* freeze raw, removing heads but not shells. Wash in brine solution, drain and pack. *Crab and Lobster:* cook before freezing; remove the meat from the shells and pack in small containers. The brown and white meat of crab should be packed separately.

Freezing Meat

If good-quality meat is available from a farm or wholesaler, freezing it is practical if the meat is selected carefully. Ready-frozen meat is available in whole carcasses, halves and quarters. Beef and mutton should be hung 5 to 7 days before freezing, veal, lamb, and pork for at least 24 to 48 hours. Always buy meat from reliable suppliers.

PREPARATION

Cut the meat into convenient pieces or roasts; trim off excess fat and bone. Trim steaks and chops as usual and separate with waxed paper. Many butchers will prepare meat as ordered.

PACKAGING

Polyethylene bags or sheeting or aluminum foil; seal and label.

THAWING

Allow 6 hours per lb in the refrigerator or 3 hours at room temperature.

COOKING ROASTS FROM FROZEN

Place in cold oven set to required temperature and time from when this is reached. Always use a meat thermometer. (See Beef, Lamb, Pork entries for details.)

Freezing Poultry and Game

KILLING AND PLUCKING

Kill the bird and pluck; leave overnight in either refrigerator or cool larder. Game must be hung before freezing as for immediate use.

PREPARATION

Remove the head and feet (and the oil sac from ducks, geese, and turkeys). Singe and trim the bird. Draw carefully, making sure that the lungs are completely removed. Wash well in cold running water, drain and discard the gall bladder. Clean and wash the gizzard, liver, and heart.

PACKAGING WHOLE BIRDS

Truss the bird as for the table. Wrap the giblets in polyethylene and place by the side of the bird.

Package the bird in a moisture-and-vapor-proof container (a bag is the most suitable for quick handling) or in aluminum foil. If the bones of the legs are sharp and pointed, wrap small pieces of foil round them so that they do not pierce the bag. Label, marking the weight of the bird and the date when frozen.

The bag should then be sealed either by heat-sealing or with a bag fastener. With a large bird it is advisable to overwrap the bag with brown paper to prevent its being torn.

PACKAGING CUT-UP BIRDS

Prepare as above but do not draw. Cut up the bird and remove the giblets. Clean the heart and gizzard. Wrap each piece of bird separately in polyethylene and package either in a waxed carton or moisture-and-vapor-proof bag, wrapping up the giblets separately. Label and freeze.

THAWING

Thaw the bird completely in its wrapping either under cold running water 30 minutes per lb or at room temperature 8 to 10 hours for a 3 lb bird or 15 hours in a refrigerator.

Freezing Dairy Products

With the exception of milk, cottage cheese, and cream with a fat content of less than 35 percent, dairy products can successfully be frozen.

CREAM

Heavy cream can be frozen for up to 1 month and whipping cream for up to 2 months. It can be stored in retail cartons if sealed with freezer tape. However, better results are obtained if the cream is partially whipped then stored in rigid containers. 10 percent sugar by weight can be added to the cream to act as a stabilizer, but this limits its use to sweet dishes.

CHEESE

Cottage cheese does not freeze because of its high water and low fat content. Cream cheese can be frozen for up to 3 months, the best results being achieved when it is left in the retail carton. The higher fat content cream cheeses are not so successful as they produce a buttery granular texture on thawing.

Hard cheeses freeze for a considerable length of time; most for 4 months and Cheddar for up to 6 months. The texture may be more crumbly on thawing but still acceptable. Vacuum packs of cheese can be frozen without repacking, but unwrapped cheese should be packed in freezer polyethylene or cling wrap. (Aluminum foil tends to impart flavor to the cheese.) Grated cheese can be frozen in rigid containers or polyethylene bags with all air excluded.

YOGURT

Fruit yogurts can be stored for up to 3 months with little or no deterioration. Some may separate slightly but this disappears on stirring. Nut yogurts can also be frozen for up to 3 months, but after this the nuts become soft.

The freezing of natural yogurt depends on the way it has been manufactured; those that have been heavily homogenized or have had stabilizers added are more successful than set type yogurts. There is a slight loss of flavor after 2 months.

The addition of sugar aids freezing but limits the use of the yogurt. Homemade yogurt does not freeze well.

Ideally yogurt is best frozen in the retail carton with freezer tape to secure the lid. Yogurt should be thawed in a refrigerator for 24 hours.

Freezing Cooked or Prepared Foods

Foods should be prepared and cooked in the normal way, taking care not to overcook them. It is also important not to season heavily as flavors tend to develop in the freezer. Some of the liquid may be reduced while the food is in the freezer but this can be corrected on thawing and reheating.

Cooked food should be carefully packed, the container depending on the nature of the food. Many dishes and casseroles available are suitable for oven and freezer use, which means that food can be taken straight from the freezer and placed in an oven (not preheated). If it is not possible or desirable to freeze the dish, it can be lined with aluminum foil, allowing enough to cover the top. When the food is frozen, it can be removed from the dish and overwrapped with polyethylene. When it is required, the food will then fit back into the dish for reheating.

Details of freezing prepared foods are given in the chart.

Approximate Storage Times in Freezer

Vegetables	10 to 12 months
Fruits	9 to 12 months
Beef	8 months
Lamb	6 months
Pork	6 months
Veal	6 months
Variety meats	3 months
Ground meat	3 months
Sausages	3 months
Chicken	12 months
Giblets	2 to 3 months
Turkey	6 months
Duck	4 to 5 months
Goose	4 to 5 months
Game birds	6 to 8 months
Fish	2 to 3 months

FOOD	TYPES TESTED AND RECOMMENDED	PREPARATION AND FREEZING	PACKAGING	PREPARATION BEFORE SERVING
CAKES Storage time in freezer 6 months. Fruitcakes improve with keeping so may be stored longer; frosted cakes 2 months. Uncooked mixture 2 months.	Fatless sponge cakes. Layer cakes. Cup cakes, frosted fancy cakes. Fruitcakes.	Loaf and square cakes are easier to wrap and store than round ones. Make and bake as usual. Cool to room temperature. Cakes may be frozen frosted or plain, filled or unfilled, though they keep longer if not frosted. Frosted cakes are easier to pack placed in the freezer for 1 hour to harden the frosting; butter frosting freezes.	Polyethylene bags, aluminum foil, waxed cardboard boxes, or plastic boxes. Seal. Wrap plain cake layers separately or together with waxed paper between layers.	Thaw buns, cakes, unfrosted layer cakes, 1 to 2 hours. Frosted layer cakes 4 hours.
COOKIES Storage time in freezer 6 months for baked and unbaked.	Almost any type (preferably unfilled).	Make and bake as usual. If fragile keep a day before packaging. Alternatively, freeze cookie dough.	Waxed cardboard boxes; separate each layer with waxed paper. Seal. Cookie dough may be molded into a bar or roll and wrapped in polyethylene.	Baked cookies: thaw for 15 to 30 minutes. To crisp up place them in a fairly hot oven for 3 to 5 minutes. Dough: thaw until it can be easily handled, about 30 minutes.
ICE CREAM Storage time in freezer: Commercial 3 months; Homemade 1 month.	All types	Make as usual.	$\frac{1}{2}$-pint or 1-pint containers. Seal.	Thaw in freezing compartment of refrigerator for 6 to 8 hours. Some may be used straight from freezer.
MEAT DISHES Storage time in freezer – 2 months.	Stews and casseroles. Meatballs made with fresh meat. Meat croquettes, made with cooked meat.	Make as usual but cook for slightly shorter time. Cool. Make and cook as usual, freeze in gravy. Freeze, uncooked (if soft, freeze before packing).	1-quart cardboard containers. Seal. Plastic boxes. Aluminum foil dishes covered with foil; polyethylene bags. Seal. Waxed cardboard boxes. Seal.	Reheat foods from cartons or bags in a pan for 30 minutes. Place in casserole, heat in 350° oven for 1 hour. If in foil dishes, remove top; reheat in 350° oven for 50 minutes.

FOOD	TYPES TESTED AND RECOMMENDED	PREPARATION AND FREEZING	PACKAGING	PREPARATION BEFORE SERVING
MOLDS, MOUSSES, CREAMS, Storage time in freezer 2 to 3 months.	Orange, lemon mousse. Chocolate, coffee, vanilla cream. Dairy cream.	Make as usual.	Aluminum foil dishes covered with foil. Seal. Waxed carton.	Thaw slowly in refrigerator for 6 hours or at room temperature for 2 hours.
PASTRIES Storage time in freezer. Baked: 3 to 6 months. Unbaked: 3 months.	Short crust: pie crusts, jam tarts, pie shells, etc. Puff: Vol-au-vent cases, cream horn cases, pie crusts. Choux: éclairs (unfilled) and cream puffs.	Make and bake as usual. If they are to be reheated, bake for shorter time. Fruit pies, to be served hot, should be frozen unbaked, as this saves double cooking time. Puff and choux pastry shells should be frozen baked but not filled. Éclairs can be frozen filled for short periods only.	Pies: aluminum foil plates. Freeze before wrapping if they seem tender to handle. Seal. Bouchée shells and tartlets: waxed cardboard boxes. Seal.	Pies, filled and baked: thaw for 1 to 1½ hours. Heat in 375° oven for 30 to 50 minutes. Filled and unbaked: do not thaw, bake in hot oven for 40 to 60 minutes. Flan or vol-au-vent shells. Baked: do not thaw, heat in fairly hot oven for 15 minutes. Unbaked: do not thaw, bake in hot oven for 20 minutes.
STOCKS AND SOUPS Storage time in freezer 2 to 3 months. Sauces – entrée and dessert. Storage time as above. If highly seasoned – 2 weeks.	Almost any type (e.g. tomato, chicken, etc.) but excluding onion and celery. Curry, barbecue, tomato, lobster. Butter-scotch, chocolate. Highly spiced sauces should not be stored too long as some spices develop a musty flavor.	Make as usual, but blend the fat and flour in sauces particularly well to prevent separation during storage. Cool quickly to room temperature.	1-pint or ½-pint containers. Seal.	Thaw in container for 2 hours. Pour into double boiler. Heat slowly, stirring all the time until hot.
SANDWICHES Storage time in freezer 1 to 2 months.	Most types may be frozen but those filled with hard-cooked egg, tomato, cucumber, or bananas tend to become tasteless and soggy.	Use freshly sliced bread; warm the butter so that it spreads easily. Do not use mayonnaise. Cut off the crusts.	Polyethylene bags or plastic boxes. Package in small amounts; do not pack too many layers. Seal.	Thaw in unopened package, 3 to 4 hours.

FOOD	TYPES TESTED AND RECOMMENDED	PREPARATION AND FREEZING	PACKAGING	PREPARATION BEFORE SERVING
YEAST MIXTURES Storage time in freezer 4 weeks.	White and brown bread rolls. Chelsea buns.		Polyethylene bags or foil.	Leave to thaw in sealed bag or wrapper 3 to 6
Storage time up to 1 week in wrapper.	Bought bread.		Original wrapper or polyethylene bag or foil.	hours at room temperature or overnight in the refrigerator; or leave foil-wrapped and crisp in 400° oven for about 45 minutes.
Storage time up to 4 months.	Bought part-baked bread.	Freeze immediately.	Leave loaf in bag, rolls in polyethylene bag.	Follow package instructions.

Notes:
1. Pies, tarts, tartlets: fillings thickened with cornstarch freeze very well, but should be packaged separately from the pastry shell. Custards may curdle. Jam, fruit, and mince pie fillings all freeze satisfactorily in the pastry shell.
2. All pastries are improved by reheating.
3. Cakes and pastries: if you use waxed cardboard boxes, and wish to keep the foods for the maximum period, enclose the boxes in polyethylene bags.
4. Particular care should be taken with the sealing of all meat dishes.

FRENCH BREAD

(See Bread entry.)

FRENCH DRESSING

(See Salad Dressing entry.)

FRENCH FRY

To fry in hot deep fat. The food may be fried plain, e.g. potatoes, or first dipped in batter, e.g. onion rings.

FRENCH TOAST

Bread soaked in a mixture of eggs and milk and sautéed in butter until golden brown. It is usually served for breakfast, with jelly or maple syrup. Bacon or sausages often accompany the toast.

FRENCH TOAST

2 eggs
½ cup milk
1½ teaspoons sugar
pinch of salt
6 slices white bread
1 tablespoon butter

Beat the eggs, milk, sugar, and salt together in a flat dish. Soak the bread on both sides in the egg mixture, until the liquid is absorbed. Melt the butter in a skillet and cook the bread over low heat until golden brown, turning once.

FRICASSEE

A stew of poultry or meat served in a creamy sauce.

CHICKEN FRICASSEE

1 fowl, cut into serving pieces
1 carrot, chopped
1 stalk celery, chopped
1 onion, chopped
seasoned flour
bacon fat
2 tablespoons butter
2 tablespoons flour
½ cup heavy cream

salt
pepper

Combine the fowl, carrot, celery, and onion in a soup pot and cover with water. Bring to a boil, reduce heat and simmer for 3 to 4 hours, until the chicken is tender. Remove the chicken and strain the broth reserving 1½ cups for use in this recipe.

Coat the chicken pieces with flour and brown in a skillet in bacon fat. Remove to a hot platter and drain the skillet. Melt the butter in the skillet and stir in the flour. Remove from the heat and stir in the chicken broth. Add the cream and return to the heat. Bring to the boiling point, then pour the sauce over the chicken and serve.

FRITTATA

An Italian omelet, cooked slowly in a heavy pan and then turned or finished under the broiler. The filling of leftover vegetables, cheese, meat, poultry or seafood is stirred in before cooking. Although anything goes, vegetables are the most popular filling for a frittata.

FRITTATA

4 tablespoons butter
1 onion, chopped
1 clove garlic, minced
8 eggs
2 cups chopped cooked zucchini
1 tablespoon chopped parsley
salt
pepper

Melt 2 tablespoons of the butter in a heavy skillet and sauté the onion and garlic until limp. Beat the eggs in a bowl and add the onion, garlic, and remaining ingredients. Melt the remaining butter in a skillet, swirling it to coat the side, and pour in the egg mixture. Cover and cook over low heat until the egg begins to pull away from the side of the pan, about 10 minutes. Finish under the broiler.

FRITTER

A small dumpling of fried batter, often containing small pieces or purees of fruit, vegetables, meats, or fish. One of the mixtures given under Batter may be used for the coating. Note that different batters are used for chopped foods and sliced foods where a shape is to be preserved. If desired, ground cinnamon may be added to the plain batter used to coat a fruit filling such as apple or pineapple.

To cook fritters: Prepare the filling and cut it into slices or small pieces. Apple should be peeled and sliced about ¼ inch thick (keep the slices in the batter or under water to prevent discoloration). Bananas should be cut in half lengthwise, then halved crosswise. Oranges are divided into sections, the pith being removed. Fruit pieces should be dusted with flour.

Prepare the batter and heat a pan of clean oil until a faint haze appears (approx 350° to 375°). Lift the fruit or other filling on a skewer one piece at a time and dip it into the batter, coating it well; allow it to drain and place it in the hot oil. Chopped ingredients are stirred into the batter. When the fritters are brown on both sides, drain them on crumpled paper towels. Sprinkle sweet fritters with sugar. Serve immediately.

CORN FRITTERS

1 cup all-purpose flour
1 teaspoon baking powder
1 teaspoon salt
½ cup milk
2 eggs
1 teaspoon vegetable oil
1 cup corn kernels
oil for frying

Mix together the flour, baking powder, and salt. Beat in the milk, eggs, and oil. Stir in the corn. Drop the batter by tablespoonfuls into the hot oil and fry about 5 minutes, until golden brown. Serve at once. Maple syrup is a traditional accompaniment.

FRITTO MISTO

An Italian dish consisting of a variety of small mouthfuls of meat, fish, poultry, and vegetables, which are coated with either bread crumbs or batter and deep-fried.

FROG

Although it has never won general acceptance in the United States, the edible frog (*grenouille* in France) is of real gastronomic merit. Only the hind legs are used, sautéed in butter. The meat is delicate in flavor, resembling the flesh of a chicken.

FROMAGE BLANC

A soft French summer cheese, consisting of a thick curd drained of the whey and usually eaten with salt and pepper and herbs. (See Coeur à la Crème entry.)

FROSTED FRUIT

Soft, juicy fruit such as grapes and fresh currants may be given a crisp, sparkling coating of superfine sugar and served as a dessert or used as garnishes.

Wash the fruit if necessary, dry it carefully and divide into small clusters. Tie a short length of strong thread to each bunch. Either whip an egg white lightly, or make a syrup with $\frac{1}{4}$ cup sugar and 2 tablespoons water and boil it for 2 to 3 minutes. Dip the bunches one at a time in the egg white or the cooled syrup, toss them in superfine sugar and dry on a rack. Remove the threads before serving.

FROSTING

A sweet coating or covering for cakes, cookies, pastries, etc., which improves their flavor and appearance and forms a good background for other decoration; frosting also helps to keep a cake moist. The art of making and applying simple frosting is easily learned, and full directions for the following types are given under the individual entries or below.

Almond paste	for coating and molding into flowers, etc.
Butter cream	for coating and piping
Classic butter cream	for coating and piping
Fondant	for coating and simple decoration
Icing glaze	for coating and simple decoration
Royal icing	for coating and elaborate decoration
Seven-minute frosting	for coating
Transparent icing	for finished coating

CLASSIC BUTTER CREAM FROSTING

$\frac{2}{3}$ cup sugar
$\frac{1}{3}$ cup water
pinch of cream of tartar
6 eggs, beaten
$\frac{3}{4}$ cup butter, softened

Combine the sugar, water, and cream of tartar in a saucepan and cook over low heat, stirring until the sugar is dissolved. Raise heat and boil to 238° on a candy thermometer. Pour the boiling syrup into the eggs, beating continuously. Beat until the mixture is cooled, then beat in the butter. Flavor as desired.

FROZEN FOODS

The first experiments in freezing foods were carried out by Lord Bacon who tried freezing foods in snow.

A very wide range of frozen foods is now available and the present high degree of technical skill results in the supply of excellent products. They include fruit, vegetables, fish, meat, and poultry in bags and cartons; pies and complete meals in foil containers; prepared dishes such as hamburgers, fish cakes, and fish sticks; pastry dishes, raw and cooked; cakes, desserts, ice cream, sorbets; boil-in-the-bag; fruit juices.

The three great assets of frozen foods are that they retain a high proportion of their vitamins and other nutrients, as well as their flavor, color, and good general appearance; they require very little preparation and entail no waste; they enable the consumer to enjoy out-of-season delicacies. They are thus particularly useful in menu planning.

(See Freezer and Freezing entries.)

Storage

The foods should be kept frozen and in their original packages until actually required; failing a refrigerator, keep them in a cool place, wrapped in a few layers of newspaper, for not more than 24 hours. The length of time they can be kept in the frozen storage compartment of a refrigerator depends on the temperature maintained:

Max. Temperature of Frozen Food Compartment	Max. Storage time for:	
	Frozen Foods	Ice Cream
0°	2 to 3 months	1 month
+10°	4 weeks	1 to 2 weeks
+21°	1 week	1 day

Thawing and Cooking

Follow meticulously any special directions on the packet.

FRUIT

Botanically speaking, a fruit is the ovary or seed-bearing part of any growing plant. In cookery it refers to those edible parts of a plant which are usually served at the dessert course of a meal. There are three main types of fruit used in cookery:
1. Fruits such as the apricot, plum, peach, and cherry, containing a single pit.

2. Berries and other soft fruits, such as the raspberry, strawberry, currant, grape, and blackberry.

3. Citrus fruits (orange, lemon, grapefruit, etc.) and other large fruit, such as apple, pear, banana, and melon.

In addition there is rhubarb, which since it comes from the stems of a plant, is not a fruit, but is served as such.

The supply of fruit in the United States is excellent, most of the usual varieties being available year round, either nationally-grown or imported from various parts of the world.

Food Value of Fresh Fruit

Fruit is particularly valuable for its pleasant flavor and wide variety and it does much to relieve the monotony of diets which might otherwise be dull. Fruits also supply some vitamins and minerals. They contain varying amounts of carbohydrates in the form of sugar, cellulose, and occasionally starch. Their protein and fat content is negligible. Pectin is present in most fruits.

Practically all fruits have a high proportion of water or juice (75 to 93 percent), which contains the characteristic flavor and also much of the vitamins, mineral salts, and acids.

The fruit acids (which the body converts into alkalis) and also the cellulose or fibrous framework of fruit, have a laxative effect. However, some unripe fruits containing a higher proportion of acids are irritating to the digestive tract.

VITAMINS IN FRUITS

Although vitamin A, thiamin, riboflavin and vitamin C are represented in some fruits, vitamin C is the most important and the most widely represented in fresh fruit. Of the winter fruits, the grapefruit, orange, and lemon are richest in vitamin C; of the summer fruits, strawberries, cantaloup, tomatoes and watermelon are best.

Cantaloupe, watermelon, tomatoes, and peaches are good sources of vitamin A.

Any of the following contains the day's quota of vitamin C for one person.

1 small orange
1 grapefruit
$\frac{1}{4}$ cup orange juice
1 cup tomato juice
$\frac{3}{4}$ cup strawberries
$\frac{1}{4}$ cup cantaloup
2 small raw tomatoes

Serving Fruit

Fruit may be eaten at any meal. It should be carefully looked over and wiped or washed as necessary before it is served. Some fruits, such as berries, are usually accompanied by sugar and sometimes by cream. Others, such as apples and pears, may be served as they are.

Raw fruit also makes an effective garnish for all kinds of dishes.

Cooked fruit may form a dish by itself or the basis of various more elaborate desserts and is also used as a decoration. Fruit soups are popular in some European countries, particularly in Scandinavia.

Fruit may be preserved at home by canning, freezing, and drying, and in jams, jellies, and similar preserves; it may also be candied and crystalized. (More information will be found under the respective headings.)

The most usual way of cooking fruit is by stewing it, but it may also be baked or steamed and it is included in many baked desserts and pies. (See recipes under individual fruits.)

STEWED FRUIT

Peel, core, or pit the fruit and if necessary cut up into neat pieces. If you wish to keep individual pieces of fruit whole and well shaped (e.g. to serve as stewed fruit), stew gently in a syrup made from sugar and water. The proportions will vary with the juiciness and sweetness of the fruit, but 1 cup water and $\frac{2}{3}$ cup sugar to 1 lb fruit is the average. Lift out the fruit, simmer the juice until it is slightly syrupy and pour it over the fruit. Serve warm or chilled with cream.

If the fruit is to be pureed, it is better to cook it without sugar and in a minimum of water until tender and then to sweeten it, since the addition of sugar to the raw fruit toughens it and prevents it from being mashed properly.

Some fruits are improved by additional flavoring. Apples may be flavored with lemon juice, grated lemon rind, cloves, stick cinnamon or marmalade (remove cloves or cinnamon before serving); pears are improved by cloves or stick cinnamon. Plums may be flavored with their kernels or a few sweet almonds; rhubarb with gingerroot, stick cinnamon, or a strip of lemon or orange rind; remove before serving as all the flavor will have gone.

(See Dried Fruit entry.)

FRUIT SALAD

$\frac{1}{2}$ cup sugar
$\frac{2}{3}$ cup water
juice of $\frac{1}{2}$ lemon
selection of fruit, e.g. 2 red apples, 2 oranges, 2
 bananas, 4 oz black or green grapes

To make a syrup, dissolve the sugar in the water over a gentle heat and boil for 5 minutes; cool and add the lemon juice. Prepare the fruits as required and put them into the syrup as they are ready. Mix them all together and if possible leave to stand for 2 to 3 hours before serving, to blend the flavors. Any other combinations of fresh fruits can be used, such as pears, strawberries, raspberries, cherries, and melon.

To give additional flavor, add to the syrup:
1. a pinch of ground cinnamon or nutmeg or infuse a piece of stick cinnamon when preparing the syrup; this will avoid clouding the syrup.
2. 1 to 2 tablespoons fruit liqueur, brandy, or rum.

Fruit salad can be served in a hollowed-out melon or pineapple; in either case the flesh which has been removed should be cut into chunks and used in the salad. Melon shells look particularly attractive especially when filled with melon balls of various colors, e.g. honeydew, watermelon, and cantaloup.

Canned fruit such as apricot halves, sliced peaches, and pineapple chunks can also be used in fruit salads or the more exotic canned guavas and lychees. If you use canned fruit, use some of the syrup from the can, sharpened with lemon juice, to replace sugar syrup. Liqueurs can also be added to complement the individual fruits.

WINTER FRUIT SALAD

½ cup sugar
1¼ cups water
peeled rind and juice of 1 lemon
½ cup pitted prunes, stewed and drained
¾ cup dried apricots, stewed and drained
1 banana, sliced
2 oranges, segmented
1 grapefruit, segmented

Make a syrup by dissolving the sugar in the water over a gentle heat; add the lemon rind, heat and boil for 5 minutes. Add the lemon juice. Strain the syrup over the prepared fruits and leave to cool.

Alternatively, use mixed dried fruit as a basis, cooking it in the usual way and adding any fresh fruit that may be available.

FRUIT FOOL

1 lb rhubarb
½ cup sugar
2 cups whipped cream or 1 cup whipped cream and
   1 cup boiled custard
chopped nuts

Stew the fruit in 2 tablespoons water, with the sugar. Puree the fruit in a blender. Cool. Fold the puree, custard, and whipped cream together. Pour into glasses and decorate with chopped nuts. Serve with ladyfingers or a plain sweet cookie. This dessert can also be made with apples, blackberries, apricots, or raspberries (the last should not be cooked, just puree, strain and sweeten).

FRUIT BUTTER

A preserve which has the spreading consistency of butter.

QUINCE BUTTER

4 lb quinces, peeled and roughly chopped
water
1 teaspoon citric or tartaric acid
sugar

Put the quinces in a pan, almost cover with water and add the acid. Bring to a boil and simmer gently until the fruit is soft and broken down, then press it through a fine sieve and measure the pulp. Return this to the pan, add 1 generous cup sugar to 2 cups pulp. Dissolve, bring to a boil again and boil for 45 minutes to 1 hour, stirring continuously to prevent burning. The doneness is determined by the consistency rather than by set or temperature: the butter should be thick but semisoft, so that it can be spread. Jar and cover immediately.

FRUITCAKE

A spiced cake containing dried or preserved fruit. It may be simple, containing only raisins and/or currants, and baked for a family dessert or as an after-school snack, or it may be quite rich and contain a variety of raisins, nuts, and candied fruits. In this form it is usually baked for Christmas entertaining and often forms the base of the traditional wedding cake.

CHRISTMAS FRUITCAKE

This is the famous Christmas cake of England.

1½ cups currants
1½ cups golden seedless raisins
1½ cups dark seedless raisins, chopped
¾ cup mixed chopped peel
¾ cup diced candied cherries
½ cup chopped almonds
1½ cups all-purpose flour

pinch of salt
½ teaspoon ground mace
½ teaspoon ground cinnamon
1 cup butter
1 cup, tightly packed, light brown sugar
grated rind of 1 lemon
4 large eggs, beaten
2 tablespoons brandy

Line an 8-inch cake pan, 3 inches deep, using two thicknesses of waxed paper. Tie a double band of brown paper around the outside. Mix the currants, dark and golden raisins, peel, cherries, and nuts. Sift the flour, salt, and spices. Cream the butter, sugar, and lemon rind, until pale and fluffy. Add the eggs a little at a time, beating well after each addition. Fold in half the flour, using a rubber scraper, then fold in the rest and add the brandy. Lastly fold in the fruit. Put into the pan. Spread the mixture evenly, making sure there are no air pockets, and make a depression in the center. Stand the pan on a baking sheet in the oven and bake at 300° for about 3¾ hours. To avoid overbrowning the top, cover with several thicknesses of waxed paper or aluminum foil after 1½ hours. When the cake is cooked, leave it to cool in the pan and then turn it out onto a cake rack.

To store, wrap it in several layers of waxed paper and put it in an airtight container. If a large enough container is not available, cover the wrapped cake entirely with aluminum foil. If desired, prick the cake top with a fine skewer and slowly pour 2 to 3 tablespoons brandy over it before storing.

FAMILY FRUITCAKE

2 cups all-purpose flour
3 teaspoons baking powder
1 teaspoon salt
1 teaspoon ground cloves
1 teaspoon ground ginger
½ cup vegetable shortening
½ cup brown sugar
2 eggs
2 tablespoons milk
2 cups dried fruit

Grease a 7-inch round cake pan and line the base with greased waxed paper. Sift the flour, baking powder and spices into a large bowl, add the rest of the ingredients, except the fruit, and beat until thoroughly combined. Fold the fruit into the mixture. Put into the pan and bake at 325° for about 1¾ hours. Turn out to cool on a wire rack.

FRUIT CUP OR COCKTAIL

Cut-up fruit served as an appetizer or as a dessert. When served as a dessert, the fruit is usually first steeped in a liqueur such as Kirsch.

FRESH FRUIT COCKTAIL

2 navel oranges, peeled, sectioned and diced
1 grapefruit, peeled, sectioned and diced
2 slices fresh pineapple, cubed
1 cup seedless green grapes, halved
sugar
½ cup boiling water
1 cup sliced strawberries

Combine the fruits, except the strawberries, in a bowl and sprinkle with sugar to taste. Add the boiling water; refrigerate for 24 hours. Before serving, drain, and fold in the strawberries.

FRUMENTY

A traditional British dish, which used to be made from the new wheat. The grains were steeped in water and left in a warm place for hours, then husked and boiled with milk to make a kind of porridge, which was spiced, sweetened, and sometimes enriched with cream or egg yolks.

FRYING

The process of cooking food in hot oil or fat to seal in and give extra flavor (see Fats and Oils entries). There are two main methods of frying:

Sautéing and Shallow Frying
Only a small quantity of fat is used, in a sautéing pan. This method is used for steak, chops, sausages, fish steaks or white fish such as sole, and pancakes, which need only sufficient fat to prevent them from sticking to the pan. Dishes such as fish cakes or rissoles require enough fat to half cover the food and are shallow-fried. The fat should be heated until a faint haze rises before the food is added; take care not to overheat it. Sometimes the food is breaded. Cook it fairly quickly for a few minutes, until the surface is browned on each side, reduce the heat and finish cooking slowly. Turn the food carefully, to avoid destroying the coating, if used. When it is cooked, lift it from the pan, drain on paper towels to remove any surplus fat and serve at once.

Deep Frying
This method is suitable for dishes such as croquettes and fritters, fish coated with batter, and

for French fried potatoes, doughnuts, etc.

The food is cooked in sufficient oil to cover it completely. A deep pan and a wire basket are required, with enough oil to come about three-quarters up the pan; corn oil, peanut oil, and clarified beef fat are suitable. The fat should be pure and free from moisture to avoid spurting or boiling over. It must be heated to the correct temperature (see below); if not hot enough, the food will be sodden with grease, if too hot, the food will burn without cooking through.

Most deep-fried food (except potatoes, pastry, doughnuts, etc.) should be breaded or coated with a batter. Place the food in the wire basket and lower the basket slowly into the oil. When a large quantity of food is to be fried, cook it a little at a time to avoid lowering the temperature of the oil. As soon as the food is golden brown, lift it out. Drain, using paper towels, and serve.

After use, strain the frying oil into a clean bowl and keep it for further use; with care it can be used many times and will keep for months.

See Fritter, Fried Potatoes (under Potato entries.)

TEMPERATURES FOR DEEP FAT FRYING
Most foods should be deep-fried at temperatures of 350° to 375°. See recipes for exceptions.

If you have no thermometer, temperature may be tested as follows: put one or two 1-inch cubes of bread into the hot fat. If they take: 60 seconds to brown, the fat is 350° to 370°; 40 seconds, it is 370° to 380°; 20 seconds, it is 380° to 390°.

FUDGE

A candy made from sugar, butter, milk, and cream, in varying proportions. By using different flavorings and such additions as chopped nuts, candied or dried fruit, many varieties of fudge can be made – chocolate, vanilla, honey, etc. The mixture is heated to a temperature of about 240° and then it is grained, that is, stirred until minute crystals are formed. The mixture is also stirred during the cooking to prevent burning. While it is still liquid, the fudge is poured into a greased pan and cut as soon as it is firm.
(See Candy for recipes.)

FUMET

French name given to a liquid used to give flavor and body to soups and sauces. It is prepared by cooking fish, meat, game, or vegetables in stock or wine. It may be used as a cooking stock or, considerably reduced, as a flavoring agent.

FUNGUS

A mushroom, toadstool, or similar plant. A large number of fungi are edible, but since some types are poisonous, it is essential to be able to distinguish between them or to buy only from a reliable source. A number of well-illustrated books on the subject have been published and will help you to recognize the main edible fungi, but it must be emphasized that if there is any doubt about a particular type, it should be rejected. All fungi should look fresh, not dried up or slimy, when picked or bought.

Mushrooms, blewits, morels, and some species of boletus (cèpes) are the chief edible fungi. The field mushroom is the most widely known. This grows wild, at its name suggests, but is also cultivated; most mushrooms for sale are in fact cultivated field mushrooms. (See Mushroom entry for recipes.)

The food value of fungi is negligible, apart from a little thiamin, and they are eaten for their excellent flavor. They may be used in many ways, either as the main ingredient of a dish or as a flavoring, accompaniment, or garnish, particularly with fried and broiled foods.

FUNNEL CAKE

A deep-fried cake prepared in Pennsylvania in the United States by those descendants of Germans known as the Pennsylvania Dutch. The thin batter is poured through a funnel into hot fat. The skillful manipulator of the funnel can form the cakes into fanciful shapes by tilting and moving the funnel and by controlling the flow of dough with the fingertip.

FUNNEL CAKES

2 eggs, beaten
2 cups milk
2 or more cups all-purpose flour
1 teaspoon baking powder
½ teaspoon salt
oil for deep-frying

Mix the eggs and milk. Combine the flour, baking powder, and salt and stir into the flour. If necessary, add additional flour so that the batter is just thin enough to pour. Heat the oil to 375° and swirl the batter through a large funnel into the oil. Cook until golden brown. Funnel cakes are usually served with powdered sugar but may also be accompanied by sausages or bacon for a light lunch or supper.

GALANTINE

A cold dish made of poultry or white meat, which is boned, stuffed, shaped and cooked with herbs, vegetables, etc. The galantine is then chilled before being glazed and garnished with its own clarified jellied stock.

CHICKEN GALANTINE

$3\frac{1}{4}$–4 lb chicken
1 onion
1 carrot
3 parsley stalks
1 bay leaf
6 peppercorns
8 oz pork sausagemeat
8 oz lean ground pork
2 shallots, chopped
salt
pepper
$\frac{1}{4}$ cup Madeira
3 slices cooked ham
6 slices cooked tongue
3 slices bacon
2 tablespoons pistachio nuts, blanched
6 black olives, pitted

FOR FINISHING
2 cups chicken stock
1 envelope gelatin
$\frac{1}{4}$ cup Madeira
cucumber, radishes, and black olives for garnish

Lay the bird on a board, breast side up. Using a sharp boning knife, cut off the wings at the second joint and the legs at the first. Turn the bird over and make an incision down the center of the back. Keeping the knife close to the carcass and slightly flattened, to avoid damaging the flesh, carefully work the flesh off the rib cage, scraping just enough to expose both of the wing joints.

Take hold of the severed end of one wing joint. Scrape the knife over the bone backward and forward, working the flesh away from the bone. Continue until both wing and socket are exposed. Sever all the ligaments and draw out the bone. Repeat for second wing.

Continue working the flesh off the carcass until the leg and socket are reached. Sever the ligaments attaching the bone to the body flesh and break the leg joint by twisting it firmly in a cloth. Hold the exposed joint firmly down in one hand and scrape away all the flesh down to the broken leg joint. Working from the opposite end of the leg, ease out the bone, scraping off the flesh until the bone is completely exposed. Pull the leg bone free; repeat for the other leg. Continue working the flesh cleanly off the body and breast, being careful not to break the skin.

Lay the boned chicken, skin side down, on the board and turn the legs and wings inside out. Make a stock using the chicken bones, giblets, onion, carrot, parsley, bay leaf, peppercorns, and enough water just to cover.

Work together the sausagemeat, pork, shallots, salt, and pepper in a bowl. Moisten with the Madeira wine. Slice the ham, tongue, and bacon into long strips about $\frac{1}{4}$ inch wide.

Spread half the stuffing over the boned chicken. Lay along the bird, in alternate lines, strips of ham, tongue, and bacon, pistachio nuts and the olives. Cover with the remaining stuffing. Draw the sides of the chicken together and sew up, using a trussing needle and fine string.

Wrap the galantine in a double thickness of cheesecloth and tie the ends to make a neat shape. Strain the stock, pour it into a large pan and immerse the galantine in it. Cover well and simmer for about $2\frac{1}{4}$ hours. Drain, reserving the stock.

Place the galantine, still wrapped in cheesecloth, on a plate; cover with another plate and top with a weight. When nearly cold, remove the cheesecloth, and when thoroughly cold, carefully remove the trussing string.

Heat 2 cups clear chicken stock, soften the gelatin in $\frac{1}{4}$ cup Madeira and dissolve in the hot stock for the aspic.

Place the chicken on a wire rack with platter or baking pan underneath. When the aspic is on the point of setting, pour it over the chicken to coat it thoroughly reserving a small amount.

When the aspic is set, decorate the galantine with slices of cucumber, radish, and olive, dipped in aspic. Cover with a thin coat of the reserved aspic jelly. Refrigerate to set. Any leftover aspic may be allowed to set in a shallow pan and then chopped and used to garnish the serving platter.

GALETTE

A cake made in France to be served on Twelfth Night, the Feast of the Three Kings. In the north of France it is made from a flaky pastry, while south of Paris it is made from a yeast dough. However the cake is made and wherever baked, it contains a bean or small porcelain figure. Whoever finds this treasure is king or queen for the day.

GALLIMAUFRY

A hash or ragout of poultry or meat.

GAMAY AND GAMAY BEAUJOLAIS

Varietal red wines made in California from the Gamay and Gamay Beaujolais grapes. The Gamay grape, also cultivated in the Beaujolais region of France, makes fruity and appealing wines. The Gamay Beaujolais, which makes a less fruity wine than the French Beaujolais wine, is now recognized as an offshoot of Pinot Noir and can legally be sold under either name. Lighter red wines are usually marketed as Gamay Beaujolais, while heavier wines are sold as Pinot Noir.

GAME

Wild animals and birds hunted for food. (See individual entries for game animals.)

Choosing and Cooking Game Birds

1. Look for birds which have firm, plump flesh and weigh heavy for their size. Spurs should be short and round, flight feathers pointed and the feathers under the wing downy. As the bird gets older, the flight feathers become rounded and the spurs pointed. The feet should be supple and the vent firm.
2. Game birds are hung before they are plucked and cooked, the time varying with the bird, with individual taste and with the season; in hot weather they are drawn in the field and hung for a shorter time than in winter, when the birds may be hung for as long as 2 to 3 weeks. For the average taste they are considered sufficiently mature after 3 to 5 days. A green or bluish discoloration of the flesh shows that the bird has hung too long. Wild duck and other water fowl should be hung for a few days only, as the flesh tends to turn rank if kept too long.
3. Roasting is the best method of cooking game, as the full flavor is then retained, but if birds are old and likely to be tough, they are best braised or fricasseed.
4. Game birds lack fat, so it is usual to cover the breast with pieces of fat bacon before roasting (i.e. to bard them) and to baste them frequently during the cooking. When they are half cooked, the bacon can be removed and the breast dredged with flour and basted. Game birds are generally roasted in a 425° oven. They can also be broiled, grilled, braised or fricasseed. Carcasses can be used to make soup.

GAME SOUP

game carcass
1 onion
1 small carrot
1 small piece of turnip
butter for sautéing
1 tablespoon flour
2 cups broth (approx.)
bouquet garni
1–2 slices bacon
salt
pepper
little red wine (optional)

Cut or break up the carcass. Prepare and cut up the vegetables. Melt a little butter in a saucepan and sauté the game and vegetables lightly, then stir in the flour and cook this also. Cover with broth and add the bouquet garni and bacon. Season, cover, and simmer gently for 1 to 2 hours, then strain the soup and return it to the pan with any meat from the bones, cut in neat dice.

Taste for seasoning. A little red wine may be added just before serving.

GAMMON

The British term for the hind-quarter of a hog which has been cured in a brine solution before being cut off. Gammon is either cooked whole and served as ham, or cut into large slices, which have a high proportion of lean to fat and are usually cut thicker than bacon slices. Gammon steaks are also available, usually in vacuum packs.

GAR (GARFISH, GARPIKE)

A slender fish, found off most European coasts; it has green bones. Garfish is usually skinned and may then be cooked in any way desired.

It is also the name of a freshwater fish found in the east and south of the United States. It is not a food fish, and preys on other valuable fish.

GARBANZO

(See Chickpea entry.)

GARBURE

A thick cabbage soup, almost a stew, from the southwest of France. Made in season with fresh fava and haricot beans, in winter it substitutes dried beans. The soup, thick enough to support a spoon, is usually enriched with a piece of preserved goose or duck. If you have a duck or goose carcass handy, add that instead.

GARBURE

1 cup dried navy beans
½ lb salt pork
2 carrots, diced
2 potatoes, peeled and diced
2 leeks, white part only, sliced
1 white turnip, diced
2 cloves garlic
¼ teaspoon dried thyme
¼ teaspoon dried marjoram
1 small head cabbage

Soak the beans overnight. Drain and place in a heavy pot. Add the remaining ingredients, except the cabbage and water to cover. Cook until the vegetables are almost done. Shred the cabbage and add to the pot. When the cabbage is done, taste for seasoning and serve.

GARLIC

A plant of the onion family, with long flat leaves and a bunch of small white flowers at the top of each flower stalk. Each garlic head is really a collection of several small bulbs, called "cloves," which are bound together by the outer skin. The heads will keep for months in a dry place and are not impaired when some of the cloves are removed.

Garlic has a powerful acrid taste, due to the oil it contains. It gives a good flavor to soups, stews, reheated dishes, curries, gravies, and sauces, while a mere suggestion of garlic in salad dressings is excellent.

Owing to its strong flavor, garlic should be chopped very finely before use and the addition of one or two cloves to a dish is usually enough for conservative tastes. For a salad, it is often sufficient to rub the bowl with a cut garlic clove before using.

A garlic press is useful in that it extracts all the juice and flavor from a clove without leaving its taste on kitchen equipment in general use.

GARLIC BREAD

Cut a loaf of French bread into 1-inch slices almost through to the bottom crust. Mix some softened butter with a generous amount of chopped parsley and a very finely chopped clove of garlic (use a garlic press if available). Spread this butter mixture between the slices, brushing the top of the loaf with any left over. Wrap the whole loaf in aluminum foil, and place in a 400° oven for 15 to 20 minutes. Serve in the aluminum foil to keep it hot. This is very good with salads and stews.

GARLIC SOUP WITH EGGS

5 tablespoons olive oil
2 cloves garlic
4 thin slices bread
1 teaspoon paprika
4 cups chicken broth
4 eggs
salt
pepper

Heat the oil in a skillet and sauté the garlic cloves until brown; discard. Add the bread and cook until browned. Add the paprika and broth and stir until the bread is broken up. Cover and simmer 15 to 20 minutes. Add the eggs and poach until done. An egg accompanies each serving.

GARNISH AND DECORATION

Decorative touches are added to a dish to improve its appearance and to some extent its flavor and texture. All garnishes should be edible and must, of course, be chosen to suit the particular dish. Here are some general rules:

1. The garnish of any dish should be decided on beforehand, since the more elaborate ones take time to prepare.

2. As a rule, hot garnishes should be served with hot dishes and cold with cold dishes, though there are one or two exceptions. For hot food the decoration needs to be simple and quickly prepared, or the food may become lukewarm before it reaches the table.

3. The garnish should be comparatively small and must not obscure the main dish. It is often better to put the decoration round the edges of the dish rather than in the center.

4. For soft food such as ground meat, a crisp garnish like toast provides a pleasant contrast in texture.

5. Colors should be chosen to agree with both the food and the serving dish. Two or at most three colors are sufficient.

Types of Garnish and Decoration

GREENS

Probably the most commonly used. Parsley (in small sprigs, chopped or fried), watercress (small bunches, or groups of three leaves arranged to resemble clover), green peas, spring onions, finely chopped chives, sliced gherkin, olives (whole or stuffed and sliced), young celery leaves or celery "curls" (made by fringing a small length at each end and leaving in water till it curls), radishes (used whole or made into radish roses or lilies), tomatoes (sliced, quartered, or made into flowers), cucumber cones or slices (for decorative edges, slices, remove lengthwise strips of peel about $\frac{1}{8}$ inch wide and $\frac{1}{8}$ inch apart, then slice the cucumber very thinly).

ROOT VEGETABLES

Carrots, rutabagas, and turnips may be grated and used raw; cut into julienne strips (matchlike sticks) about $1\frac{1}{4}$ inches long, cooked and arranged in small piles; or cut into balls, which must be cooked carefully to keep them whole; fancy shapes may be stamped out of sliced root vegetables with small cutters.

POTATOES

Use fried as slices, strips, lattice-work (a special cutter is required for these), or rounds. Roasted potatoes may be turned into small shapes before cooking. Mashed or Duchesse potatoes may be piped into fancy shapes or borders.

MUSHROOMS AND TRUFFLES

Cooked and used whole, sliced or chopped.

ONIONS

Usually cut into rings and fried.

HARD-COOKED EGGS

Sliced or quartered and used to decorate salads, cold dishes, or entrées. The white may be cut into fancy shapes or rounds and the yolk can be sifted, or the two combined to make daisies.

BREAD, PASTRY, ETC.

Toasted or fried bread croutons are used with entrées and with soups; pastry fleurons are also used with entrées and so are noodles and fancy forms of pasta.

FRUITS

Strawberries, raspberries, cherries, grapes, sliced bananas, etc., may all be used to decorate desserts. Melon, pears, and apples can be used in small, thin slices or cut into balls with a scoop. (These fruits turn brown if exposed too long to the air, but a coating of apricot jam or marmalade will prevent discoloration or they may be soaked in lemon juice.)

Oranges and lemons look well if peeled, quartered and peeled or thinly sliced. Lemons (and sometimes oranges) are used to garnish some hors d'oeuvres and entrées. To make lemon fans for use with fish, etc., cut slices $\frac{1}{8}$ inch thick and cut each in half. Cut the rind in half again, leaving the center membrane whole, and spread out the lemon into a fan shape.

ALMONDS, WALNUTS, PISTACHIO, HAZEL, BRAZIL AND PINE NUTS

After shelling and blanching, are used whole, or halved, chopped, sliced, shredded or grated. Almonds are sometimes lightly toasted. Chopped nuts are often used to decorate the side of a cake.

HEAVY CREAM

Can be whipped until stiff, sweetened and flavored, then piped onto desserts with a pastry bag and decorative tips.

MINIATURE MERINGUES

May be stuck around the side of a dessert or a meringue mixture piped through a decorative tip.

CANDIES AND COOKIES

Chocolate drops, gumdrops, chocolate sprinkles, grated chocolate, marshmallows (whole or cut up), and colored sugar, all make attractive garnishes for desserts.

CANDIED AND CRYSTALIZED FRUIT AND CRYSTALIZED FLOWERS

Often used for desserts.

Soup Garnishes: (See Soup entry.)

GÂTEAU

The French term for cake. Most French gâteaux are made from a number of basic doughs (puff pastry, short and sweet short pastry, brioche and savarin doughs, genoise and choux pastry), alone or in combination with each other and with the addition of various pastry creams, etc.

GÂTEAU ST HONORÉ

short pastry, made with 1 cup flour, see Pastry entry
choux pastry, made with ½ cup flour, see Pastry entry
1 egg, beaten, to glaze
2 egg yolks
¼ cup sugar
2 teaspoons flour
5 teaspoons cornstarch
1¼ cups milk
1 teaspoon vanilla
3 egg whites, stiffly beaten
⅔ cup heavy cream, whipped
¼ cup sugar
¼ cup water
angelica and candied cherries

Roll the pastry into a 7-inch round, prick well and put on a lightly greased baking sheet. Brush a ½-inch band round the edge with beaten egg. Using a ½-inch plain tip, pipe a circle of choux paste round the edge of the pastry and brush it with beaten egg. With the remaining choux paste, pipe about 20 walnut-sized rounds onto the baking sheet and brush with beaten egg. Place the baking sheet in a 375° oven and bake for about 35 minutes, or until the pastry is well risen and golden brown. Cool on a rack.

Meanwhile prepare the pastry cream filling. Cream the egg yolks with the ¼ cup sugar until pale, add the flour and cornstarch with a little of the milk and mix well. Heat the remaining milk almost to the boiling point; pour onto the egg mixture, return this to the pan and bring to a boil, stirring continuously. Boil for 2 to 3 minutes, then turn the mixture into a bowl to cool. Stir in the vanilla. Beat with a rotary beater till smooth, then fold in the egg whites. Pipe some of the whipped cream into the cold choux puffs, reserving a little for the top of the gâteau.

Dissolve the ¼ cup sugar in the water and boil until the edge just begins to turn straw-colored. Dip the tops of the choux paste puffs in this syrup, using a skewer or tongs to hold them. Use the remaining syrup to stick the puffs onto the choux pastry border. Fill the center of the gâteau with the pastry cream mixture and cover this with the remaining cream. Decorate with angelica and candied cherries.

GAZPACHO

A famous Spanish soup which is served cold. It is a mixture of raw salad ingredients made into a puree. There are as many recipes as there are cooks for this dish.

GAZPACHO

1 medium cucumber
3 ripe tomatoes
1 green pepper, seeded
1 onion
1 clove garlic
¼ cup olive oil
¼ cup wine vinegar
2 cups tomato juice
2 tablespoons tomato paste
pinch salt

Wash and roughly chop the cucumber, tomatoes, pepper, onion, and garlic. Mix all the ingredients together in a bowl. Puree them in a blender in small batches. Return the puree to the bowl and add a few ice cubes. Serve the soup with very finely diced green pepper and croutons.

GEFILTE FISH

Small fish dumplings, made with freshwater fish, seasoned with onion and bound with matzo meal and eggs. Gefilte fish is part of traditional Jewish holiday feasts and the Friday night Sabbath dinner.

GEFILTE FISH

2 lb assorted whitefish, pike and carp fillets, trimmings reserved
2 onions
salt
pepper
1 egg

$\frac{1}{4}$ cup ice water
$\frac{1}{4}$ teaspoon sugar
1 tablespoon matzo meal
1 carrot, sliced

Combine the fish trimmings with $1\frac{1}{2}$ of the onions in a saucepan with 2 cups water and salt and pepper. Cook over high heat while preparing the fish.

Grind the fillets and remaining half onion. Place in a chopping bowl with the rest of the ingredients except the carrot. Chop until very fine. Moisten the hands and form into balls. Add to the stock with the carrot, cover loosely and simmer for $1\frac{1}{2}$ hours; remove the cover for the last 30 minutes. Cool the fish in the stock. Serve in the jellied stock garnished with the sliced carrots. Accompany with beet horseradish.

GELATIN

A protein substance made chiefly from calves' heads, cartilages, tendons, etc., which are boiled with acid and then submitted to various refining and purifying processes. Gelatin is equally satisfactory in granulated or sheet form, though it is most commonly sold as granules. Two envelopes ($\frac{1}{4}$ oz each) are the equivalent of three $4\frac{1}{2} \times 6$ sheets. Gelatin should be colorless and have no offensive smell. As the setting power of gelatin differs according to the make, it is essential to follow the manufacturer's instructions closely. Sweetened fruit-flavored gelatin is a popular and easy-to-make dessert. When using commercial gelatin, always use according to the manufacturer's instructions.

GELATIN

A mixture, savory or sweet, to which gelatin is added, so that it will set firm when it cools and can be turned out, keeping the shape of the mold in which it is made.

Method of Making Gelatin

1. Allow 1 envelope unflavored gelatin for each 2 cups liquid. Do not use fresh or frozen pineapple juice. Decrease liquid by $\frac{1}{4}$ cup if gelatin is to be molded.
2. Soak the gelatin in a little of the cold liquid for 5 minutes. (This is not essential but does help to make thorough mixing easier.) Dissolve the soaked gelatin, preferably by placing the bowl over a pan of hot water; the mixture must not be allowed to become hot.
3. Measure the correct amount of fruit juice, other liquid or puree, add flavoring, coloring, and sugar if necessary. Add the lukewarm dissolved gelatin, pouring it through a strainer and stirring if necessary with a spoon or whisk.

When adding gelatin to the very cold mixtures, make sure it is stirred in very quickly, to avoid partial setting.
4. Clarify the gelatin if necessary (see below).
5. Pour the gelatin into a damp mold or other container or into small individual molds and when nearly cold place in the refrigerator. Alternatively, stand the molds in a dish and surround with ice.
6. When solid ingredients (such as fruit and nuts) are included, they should be stirred in when the gelatin is just beginning to set. Alternatively, proceed as directed in the recipe Molded Fruit Gelatin.
7. When making a gelatin from fresh pineapple juice, boil the juice for 2 to 3 minutes first. This kills an enzyme contained in the juice which would otherwise break down the gelatin and destroy the setting properties.

To Clarify Gelatin

Use 1 egg shell and 1 egg white to 2 cups of liquid gelatin. Wash the eggshell well before breaking it, separate the egg very carefully and add the white and the crushed shell to the liquid. The pan should not be more than half full, as the mixture is apt to boil over. Bring it nearly to the boiling point, whisking all the time, then stop whisking and allow the froth to rise to the top of the pan. Draw the pan away from the heat, but leave it in a warm place for five minutes. Strain the gelatin through a scalded jelly bag while it is still hot and repeat the process if it is not clear, using a fresh bowl. Do not touch the bag during the straining.

To Unmold and Serve Gelatin

1. Half fill a bowl with very hot water.
2. If a metal mold is used, hold it in the water for a few seconds, wipe with a clean cloth, dabbing the top of the gelatin to dry it. Place a plate over the top of the mold, then invert the two, and give a good shake. When the gelatin slips out, lift off the mold.
3. If a china mold is used, stand or hold it in the hot water (which should come just to the top of the mold) for 1 to 2 minutes, according to the thickness of the mold. Then loosen round the edge with the fingers and turn out as above.
4. Decorate with chopped gelatin, whipped cream or fruit etc. (To chop gelatin, cut it up on wet waxed paper.)

To Line a Mold with Gelatin

1. Fill a large bowl with ice; nest the mold in it.

2. Pour 2 to 3 tablespoons cold but liquid gelatin into the damp mold and rotate this slowly until the inside is evenly coated. Continue pouring in and setting cold liquid gelatin until the entire surface is lined with a thin coat of the gelatin.
3. Dip the decoration (slices of pistachio nuts, cherries, etc.) in liquid gelatin with the aid of skewers or a pointed knife, then place in position in the mold, allowing each piece to set firmly.
4. Finally, pour a thin coating of gelatin over the whole and allow it to set before pouring in the remainder of the gelatin.

JAMBON PERSILLÉ (HAM AND PARSLEY IN ASPIC)

An excellent dish for a buffet.
2 envelopes unflavored gelatin
½ cup water
1½ cups white wine
2 tablespoons butter
2 green onions, finely chopped
1 clove garlic, minced
½ cup chopped parsley
½ cup chopped chives
pepper
1 lb cooked ham, diced

Soften the gelatin in the water and then set in hot water to dissolve. Stir into the wine. Melt the butter in a skillet and sauté the onions and garlic. Remove from the heat and stir in the herbs and pepper. Add to the wine mixture. Rinse out an 8 × 4 inch loaf pan with cold water and add enough of the aspic mixture to cover the bottom of the pan; refrigerate for about 30 minutes, or until just beginning to set. Place one-quarter of the ham in the bottom of the pan, pressing it down lightly. Return to the refrigerator until completely set.

Pour another layer of aspic over the ham and continue making and refrigerating layers, finishing with a layer of jelly. Refrigerate overnight, then run a knife around the inside edge of the pan and unmold on an inverted serving plate. Serve accompanied with mayonnaise or aïoli.

BASIC DESSERT GELATIN

1 envelope unflavored gelatin
¼ cup cold water
4 tablespoons sugar
1¾ cups fruit juice

In a saucepan, sprinkle the gelatin over the water, add the sugar and dissolve over a low heat; do not boil. Add the juice to the mixture. Leave to set.

CLEAR LEMON GELATIN

4 lemons
whites and shells of 2 eggs
3 envelopes unflavored gelatin
¾ cup sugar
4 cups cold water
3 cloves
¾ inch stick cinnamon

Wash the lemons and the eggs. Pare the rind in thin strips from 3 of the lemons and squeeze the juice of 4, adding water if necessary to make up to 1 cup. Combine the lemon rind, lemon juice, gelatin, sugar, and water, with the cloves and cinnamon, in a large saucepan. Add the egg whites and the crushed eggshells, place over a gentle heat and start to whisk at once. Continue to whisk the mixture until nearly boiling, by which time there should be a thick froth on the surface. Stop whisking and allow the froth to rise and crack, then reduce the heat and simmer gently for 5 minutes. Strain through several layers of dampened cheesecloth. Pour into individual glasses or a mold and refrigerate until set.

MOLDED FRUIT GELATIN

Make some lemon gelatin as above or with a flavored gelatin and prepare some fresh fruit such as grapes, cherries, raspberries, sections of oranges, or sliced bananas (dip banana slices in lemon juice first to prevent discoloration), or well-drained canned fruit such as peaches, apricots, mandarin oranges, and pineapple. Pour about 1 inch of gelatin into the mold and arrange a few fruits in this; allow the gelatin to set. Add more gelatin and fruit and again allow to set. Continue until the mold is completely filled. It is essential that each layer of gelatin poured into the mold be allowed to set before more is added, otherwise the fruit will move and the finished appearance will be spoiled.

ORANGE SNOW

Follow the recipe for Basic Dessert Gelatin using orange juice. When the gelatin is just beginning to set, whip it until it is light and frothy, then fold in the stiffly beaten whites of 1 to 3 eggs. Set as usual.

GENOISE

A light, rich European sponge cake that, unlike sponges made in the United States, contains butter and depends solely on well-beaten eggs for its leavening. It is used as the basis for fancy cakes or petits fours which are to be coated with fondant or glaze; it can also be served as an undecorated sponge cake.

GENOISE

6 tablespoons unsalted butter
1 cup all-purpose flour
6 eggs
¾ cup sugar

Grease and flour two 8-inch layer pans. Heat the butter gently until it is melted, remove it from the heat and let it stand for a few minutes to allow any sediment to settle. Sift the flour. Put the eggs and sugar in a mixer bowl; stand this over a saucepan of boiling water to warm slightly, about 30 seconds. Beat with the mixer attachment until light and creamy, about 10 minutes. The mixture should be stiff enough to retain the impression of the beater for a few seconds. Sift the flour over the mixture while carefully folding it in. Pour the butter around the edge of the mixture and fold it in. Pour the mixture into the pans and bake in a 350° oven until golden brown and firm to the touch, about 25 minutes. Let stand 5 minutes then turn out and cool on a cake rack. Use as required.

GERVAIS

A small, soft, delicately flavored cream cheese made in France.

GHEE

A type of fat or liquid butter made from cow or buffalo milk and used extensively in Oriental countries. It is allowed to go rancid and all the water is extracted. Salt is then added and when the ghee is bottled or canned it will keep for several years.

GHERKIN (CORNICHON)

The pickled fruit of a small variety of cucumber. The best gherkins are small and dark green and have a rough skin; large quantities are exported from France and Holland and are sold jarred in brine.

Gherkins are used as one of the ingredients in mixed pickles, as an accompaniment to cold meats and in sauces, etc. They also make an attractive garnish for cocktail hors d'oeuvres and cold appetizers.

GIBLETS

The edible parts of the entrails of birds, consisting of the gizzard, liver, heart, and also the neck. With the exception of the liver, they are largely used in making gravy or soup. The liver is cooked separately, but may be chopped and included in the gravy.

To make giblet stock for gravy, cover the giblets with stock or water and simmer for 1 hour or longer.

Giblet soup is made in a similar way to Game Soup. (See Game entry.)

GIN

A colorless alcoholic beverage made from rye and barley or corn and flavored with juniper berries. Gin is the purest of all alcoholic beverages, being distilled at high strength. It does not improve with keeping in the same way as brandy.

Gin is used as the basis of many cocktails, such as the Martini. It is also used for various other long and short drinks, being diluted to the required strength with water, fruit juice, ginger ale, or soda water. Holland gin, from the Netherlands, is too strongly flavored to be used in mixed drinks.

GINGER

The underground stem of a reedlike plant which grows in Asia, the West Indies, South America, Western Africa, and Australia. Both the knotty, fibrous roots and the stems have the characteristic hot flavor and are used in various forms in cookery and also in medicine.

The young green stems are used fresh in the Orient. They are also preserved in syrup and often crystalized and served as a dessert; so are the roots, though these are fibrous and not so good. The dried roots are ground to produce powdered ginger for use as a spice in cakes, cookies, desserts, and curries, or may be used whole for pickling and jammaking. Jamaican ginger, which is generally considered the best variety, is buff-colored and has a pleasant odor and pungent taste.

GINGERSNAPS

1 cup all-purpose flour
½ teaspoon baking soda
1–2 teaspoons ground ginger
1 teaspoon ground cinnamon, optional
2 teaspoons sugar

$\frac{1}{4}$ *cup butter or margarine*
$\frac{1}{4}$ *cup molasses*

Grease two baking sheets. Sift together the flour, soda, ginger, cinnamon, and sugar. Melt the butter and stir in the molasses. Stir these into the dry ingredients and mix well. Roll the dough into small balls, place well apart on the greased baking sheets and flatten slightly. Bake in a 375° oven for about 15 minutes. The gingersnaps will have the traditional cracked tops. Cool for a few minutes before lifting carefully from the baking sheet.

Finish cooling on a rack and then store in an airtight can.

If desired, these biscuits may be covered with lemon-flavored glaze.

GINGER ALE

Colored water aerated with carbon dioxide and flavored with ginger. It is used as a soft drink, in punches and in place of soda to dilute alcoholic beverages such as whisky and brandy.

GINGER BEER

A non-alcoholic effervescent beverage with a flavor of ginger. Ginger, cream of tartar, and sugar are fermented with yeast, water is added and the liquid bottled before fermentation is complete.

GINGERBREAD

This is a moist brown cake flavored with ginger and containing molasses; it is usually served cut into squares. There are many different forms of gingerbread, varying in color from light brown to a very dark shade, according to the amount of baking soda and the type of molasses used.

GINGERBREAD

$2\frac{1}{3}$ *cups all-purpose flour*
1 teaspoon salt
2 teaspoons ground ginger
1 tablespoon baking powder
1 teaspoon baking soda
$\frac{1}{3}$ *cup sugar*
$\frac{1}{2}$ *cup shortening*
1 cup molasses
$\frac{3}{4}$ *cup hot water*
1 egg

Grease and flour a 9-inch square cake pan. Sift the flour, salt, ginger, baking powder, and soda.

Place all the ingredients in a mixer bowl and beat until combined, about 3 minutes. Pour the mixture into the pan and bake in a 325° oven for about 50 minutes or until firm to the touch. Turn out to cool on a rack.

GINGERBREAD CHILDREN

$1\frac{2}{3}$ *cups all-purpose flour*
$\frac{1}{2}$ *teaspoon salt*
2 teaspoons ground ginger
$\frac{1}{2}$ *cup butter*
$\frac{1}{2}$ *cup granulated sugar*
$\frac{1}{2}$ *cup molasses*
$\frac{1}{2}$ *teaspoon baking soda*
$\frac{1}{4}$ *cup hot water*
raisins
cinnamon candies
$\frac{2}{3}$ *cup powdered sugar*
$\frac{1}{2}$ *teaspoon vanilla*
1–2 tablespoons heavy cream

Combine the flour, salt, and ginger. Melt the butter in a large saucepan. Remove from the heat and stir in the sugar and molasses. Dissolve the baking soda in the hot water. Beginning and ending with the flour, stir it alternately with the hot water solution into the molasses mixture. Cover the dough with plastic wrap and chill for 2 to 3 hours.

Using only as much dough as you can handle at one time, roll it out $\frac{1}{8}$ inch thick. Cut with girl and boy cookie cutters dipped in flour and transfer to a baking sheet with a wide spatula. Decorate with raisins for eyes and red candies for buttons. Bake in a 350° oven for 10 to 12 minutes, until the cookies are lightly browned. Cool for 2 to 3 minutes on the baking sheet before transferring to racks to cool.

Sift the powdered sugar into a bowl and add the vanilla. Stir in the heavy cream bit by bit until the icing is of the proper consistency for piping. Using a fine plain tip, outline the cookies and decorate as desired.

GLASSWORT

(See Samphire entry.)

GLAZE

A substance used to give a glossy surface to certain candies, nuts, and desserts, and savory dishes as well. Different materials are used for different dishes. A glaze improves both appearance and flavor and many dishes (such as fruit tarts) are incomplete without it.

Some glazes, e.g. beaten egg or milk for pastry, are put on before cooking, while others are poured or brushed on after cooking.

MEAT GLAZE
(For galantines, cutlets, head cheese, etc.)

Place 5 quarts of good stock (made from meat and bones) in a heavy saucepan, first skimming off any fat. Bring to a boil and continue to boil for several hours, until the stock is reduced and is of the consistency of glaze. It can then be brushed over hot or cold roasts, galantines, and so on. This quantity of stock should give approximately 2 cups of glaze.

QUICK MEAT GLAZE

1 envelope gelatin
2 bouillon cubes
2 cups hot water

Soften the gelatin, then dissolve with the bouillon. Use within 2 to 3 days, as this glaze will not keep.

ASPIC JELLY

(See Aspic entry for method of preparing.)
This is used for glazing meat and fish molds, cocktail hors d'oeuvres, and open-face sandwiches.

ICING GLAZE
(For cakes)

Sift 1 to $1\frac{1}{2}$ cups powdered sugar and gradually add 2 to 4 tablespoons warm water. The glaze should be thick enough to coat the back of a spoon. If necessary, add more water or sugar to adjust the consistency. Add a few drops of coloring, if required, and flavoring, and use at once.

For glaze of a finer texture, put the sugar, water, and flavoring into a small pan and heat, stirring until the mixture is warm – don't make it too hot. The glaze should coat the back of a wooden spoon and look smooth and glossy.

ORANGE GLAZE
Substitute 2 to 4 tablespoons strained orange juice for the water in the above recipe.

LEMON GLAZE
Substitute $1\frac{1}{2}$ tablespoons strained lemon juice for the same amount of water.

CHOCOLATE GLAZE
Dissolve 3 tablespoons cocoa in a little hot water and use to replace the same amount of plain water.

COFFEE GLAZE
Flavor with 1 tablespoon instant coffee, dissolved in a little of the water.

MOCHA GLAZE
Flavor with 1 teaspoon cocoa and 3 teaspoons instant coffee, dissolved in a little of the measured water.

LIQUEUR GLAZE
Replace 3 to 4 teaspoons of water with liqueur as desired.

When using flavorings of your own, do so carefully so as not to upset the basic consistency of the glaze. Always add flavorings a little at a time rather than all at once.

To use glaze: Allow the cake to cool, see that any decorations are prepared and insert the filling if any. Cut small cakes to the required shape before glazing them and make a large cake level on top by cutting off any peak; brush the surface free of crumbs. For a really smooth finish the cakes can then be given a thin coating of strained apricot jam, which is brushed on and left to dry for a few hours. Place the cake or cakes on a wire rack over a piece of waxed paper.

When the glaze is of the correct consistency, pour it onto the center of the cake and allow it to run down the sides; if it runs too much to one side, use a spatula knife to divert the flow. Fill any gaps with glaze from the tray, but try to avoid doing this as it often gives an untidy finish. If only the top surface is to be glazed, pin a double band of paper around the cake to protect the sides, removing it with the help of a hot knife.

Small cakes can be coated in the same way or may be dipped into a bowl of glaze, the cake being held in tongs or between the thumb and forefinger; this method is excellent for éclairs, when only a strip of glaze is required on top. Any decorations should be put on immediately, for the glaze may wrinkle or crack if they are added when it is at the point of setting.

CORNSTARCH GLAZE
(For fruit tarts, etc.)

1 teaspoon cornstarch
$\frac{1}{3}$ cup strained fruit juice or water

1 tablespoon sugar
lemon juice (optional)
2½ teaspoons currant jelly or apricot jam (optional)
coloring, if required

Blend the cornstarch with a little of the fruit juice. Put the rest of the juice and the sugar into a saucepan to warm gently. Add the blended cornstarch and bring to a boil. Reduce heat and simmer until the syrup is quite clear and of a coating consistency. Add a squeeze of lemon juice, the jelly or jam, and the coloring (if used). The syrup should be well flavored and of a thick glazing consistency – if too thin, it will soak into the pastry and make it soggy. It must be used while still warm, as it sets quite quickly.

Other Types of Glaze

GELATIN GLAZE (FOR MOLDS, TARTS, ETC.)
Any type of gelatin can be used. For coating molds, a thin lining of gelatin is set in the mold. For tarts, etc. it is spooned over the food when it is about to set – it must not be poured on when liquid, as it is then absorbed by the material which it should coat.

SYRUP GLAZE (FOR TARTS, TARTLETS, GÂTEAUX)
A concentrated syrup made from sugar and water or fruit juice, suitably flavored. It should be boiled until it coats the back of the spoon.

GLAZE FOR YEAST BUNS
Brush the buns as soon as they come out of the oven with ¼ cup sugar boiled in 3 to 4 tablespoons water.

SIEVED APRICOT JAM GLAZE (FOR SAVARINS, FRUIT TARTS, CAKES, ETC.)
Warm the jam in a pan of hot water before using.

GLAZES FOR PASTRY
Brush before baking with beaten egg or milk or, for sweet dishes, with beaten egg white and sugar.

GLAZE FOR VEGETABLES
Toss the cooked vegetables in melted seasoned butter.

SAUCES
These can be regarded as glazes when they are used to coat a dish. A sauce intended for the purpose should have a good sheen, which it acquires through thorough cooking and beating.

GLOBE ARTICHOKE
(See Artichoke entry.)

GLOUCESTER CHEESE
(See Double Gloucester Cheese entry.)

GLUCOSE (DEXTROSE)
A simple sugar. It is a white, crystaline substance with a faintly sweet taste. Glucose is a constituent of ordinary cane sugar and of starch and when carbohydrates are digested, they are broken down to glucose, which is then absorbed by the blood stream. The level of glucose in the blood goes up after a meal, then returns to normal about an hour or so later, depending on the individual and on the kind of meal.

Commercially prepared glucose which is made by heating a starchy food (often corn) with an acid, is used in candymaking, because it does not crystalize to the same extent as other sugars, and also in the less expensive jams.

Glucose has no food value and is only taken for its energy value. It has no advantages over other sugars except that it is absorbed into the blood stream a little quicker. Medically, it is sometimes used for a patient who is too ill to eat properly, since it can be taken in greater quantities than other sugars as it does not taste so sweet.

GLUTEN
An insoluble protein which forms the major part of the protein content of wheat flour. Gluten gives flour its elasticity and enables it to hold air or carbon dioxide, thus producing light, well-risen breads and cakes.

The strength and elasticity of gluten depends in the first place on the part of the world in which the wheat is grown, some wheats being hard and others soft. Most millers blend flours to produce the strength they require. Bread needs a hard flour, rich cakes and cookies a soft type. The flour sold on the retail market is usually all-purpose, made by mixing hard and soft flours.

The "strength" or toughness of gluten is modified by water, by handling and mixing and by very acid or alkaline conditions. Thus pastry becomes tough if the fat is not cut in sufficiently to prevent the water having access to the particles of flour; overmixing a cake or pastry makes it tough because it causes the gluten to develop too much; again, a cake mixture containing an excess of lemon juice or acid may be tough.

GLYCEROL OR GLYCERINE

A sweet, colorless, oily liquid. It is a compound of carbon, hydrogen, and oxygen, formed by the breaking down of fats and produced chiefly as a by-product of the manufacture of soap. Glycerol is occasionally added to royal icing to keep it moist.

GNOCCHI

An Italian dish, consisting of squares, rounds, or other shapes made from semolina or potatoes. The dumplings are served boiled or boiled and fried or baked accompanied by a variety of sauces.

SEMOLINA GNOCCHI ALLA ROMANA

3 cups milk
¾ cup semolina
salt
pepper
pinch of grated nutmeg
2 eggs, beaten
¾ cup grated Parmesan cheese
¼ cup butter, melted
extra cheese for topping

Bring the milk to a boil, sprinkle in the semolina and seasonings and stir over a gentle heat until the mixture is thick enough for the spoon to stand up in it. Beat well until smooth and stir in the eggs and cheese. Return the pan to a low heat and stir for 1 minute. Spread this mixture, about ¼ to ½ inch thick, on a shallow buttered dish and allow to cool. Cut into 1-inch rounds or squares and arrange in a shallow greased ovenproof dish. Pour the melted butter over them and sprinkle with a little extra cheese. Brown under the broiler or toward the top of a 400° oven. Serve with more cheese and tomato.

POTATO GNOCCHI

3 boiling potatoes
1½ cups all-purpose flour
2 tablespoons vegetable oil
2 eggs, beaten
½ cup grated Parmesan cheese
salt
pepper

Boil the potatoes, peel and mash while still warm. Place in a mixer bowl and add the remaining ingredients, beating until well mixed. The dough must be stiff enough to roll into ¾-inch thick ropes. If not, add additional flour.

Roll the dough with the hands, a little at a time, on a floured surface into ropes. Cut into 1-inch lengths. As the dough is cut, place it on a floured board. Bring 6 quarts water to a boil and cook the dumplings until they rise to the surface of the water. Drain and serve with butter and grated Parmesan cheese.

GOAT

(See Kid entry.)

GOATS' MILK

Goats' milk has a higher percentage of fat and protein than some varieties of cows' milk and it has a somewhat stronger flavor. It is widely used for making cheeses (for example, Saint Maure); in Scandinavia it is used for such cheeses as Gjetøst. Goats' milk can also be used for ordinary household purposes. It is useful for feeding babies who are allergic to cows' milk, although it must be adjusted to their needs.

GOLDEN SYRUP

A light colored syrup produced by the evaporation of cane sugar juice. Golden syrup is used in Great Britain to sweeten and flavor cakes and puddings, to make sauces, as a filling for tarts, and in gingerbreads.

GOOSE

A goose for the table should be under 6 months. The birds may be purchased fresh from late November through early March and are available frozen year-round. Frozen birds should be defrosted in the refrigerator or under cold running water.

Goose fat is highly prized as a cooking fat and once rendered keeps well in the refrigerator. (See Fats entry for rendering.)

Geese generally weigh between 8 and 12 lb, with a range of 9 to 11 lb being most satisfactory. A 9 lb bird will serve 6 to 8 and an 11 lb bird 10 or 11. Larger birds should be braised rather than roasted as they are probably older and tougher. Prunes, apples, and chestnuts are traditional stuffings for goose, and when combined with sausagemeat make the bird go further. Allow 1 cup stuffing per lb of bird, and increase the cooking time by 20 to 40 minutes. An unstuffed 9 lb bird will cook in about 2 hours, an 11 lb bird will take only 20 to 25 minutes longer. See also Wild Goose entry.

ROAST GOOSE

Bring the bird to room temperature. Salt the cavity lightly and stuff if desired, sewing or skewering the vent. Secure the legs and wings to the body with string. Salt and pepper the bird and prick all over with a kitchen fork. Place breast up on a rack in a roasting pan and put in a 425° oven. After 15 minutes, reduce the heat to 350°. Fat accumulating in the pan must be removed about every 15 minutes, a bulb baster being the handiest utensil for this operation. Cook the goose until the juices run yellow or a meat thermometer inserted in the inside of the thigh reads 180°.

Serve with giblet gravy (made in the pan after the fat has been poured off), and red cabbage.

Confit d'Oie is goose preserved in its own fat, a specialty of southwestern France. The large geese raised in the area of Toulouse for foie gras are preserved in this fashion.

Goose Livers

Have an excellent flavor and are converted into pâté de foie gras. (See Foie Gras entry.)

Goose Eggs

(See Egg entry.)

GOOSEBERRY

The fruit of a prickly bush native to North Europe and Asia. The berries, which hang down from the underside of the stem, are green when first formed. There are many different varieties of gooseberries.

Gooseberries have a good vitamin C content. The young fruit has a high percentage of acid and pectin and is useful in jammaking, but the riper fruit contains less.

Preparation and cooking: The stalk and the flowering end should be either pinched or cut off (called "topping and tailing") and the fruit should be thoroughly washed. They are stewed in the ordinary way (see Fruit entry), but being acid they require at least ½ cup sugar per 1 lb of fruit. Some of the acid can be counteracted by adding a pinch of bicarbonate of soda. If the fruit is soft, less water is required and sometimes less sugar.

GOOSEBERRY SAUCE

Puree in a blender slightly sweetened stewed gooseberries and reheat with a lump of butter. Serve with goose or duck.

GOOSEBERRY JAM

3 lb gooseberries (slightly underripe)
2½ cups water
7 cups sugar

Top, tail, and wash the gooseberries and put them into a pan with the water and sugar. Bring slowly to a boil and cook for about 30 minutes until setting point is reached. Stir frequently, to avoid sticking. Jar and cover in the usual way. *Makes about 5 lb.*

GOOSEFISH

(See Monkfish entry.)

GORGONZOLA

A popular, semihard, blue-veined cheese of sharp flavor, made from cows' milk; it is named after the Italian town where it is produced. Gorgonzola is aged for 3 to 4 months in moist, drafty caves to encourage the formation of the blue veins. The cheese is made up in a small drum shape, weighing about 15 lb and wrapped in foil. The white variety of Gorgonzola has a slightly bitter flavor appreciated by cheese connoisseurs.

GOUDA CHEESE

A wheel-shaped Dutch cheese, not unlike Edam in taste and texture, but flatter in shape, with a yellow rind and very much larger, approximately 9 lb in weight. It is an excellent cheese for cooking. There are also small Goudas, about 1 lb in weight. Gouda has a smooth, mellow flavor.

GOUGÈRE

A French pastry that is a specialty of Burgundy. It is made with choux pastry, flavored with cheese and baked in a ring. Gougère may be served hot as an hors d'oeuvre or cold. It may also be prepared with eggs or other fillings in the center of the ring.

HAM GOUGÈRE

1 recipe choux pastry (see Pastry entry)
½ cup grated Cheddar cheese
2 tablespoons butter
2 onions, sliced
½ cup sliced mushrooms
2 teaspoons flour
¼ cup ham broth
3 tomatoes, peeled and quartered
½ cup chopped cooked ham

salt and pepper
1 tablespoon grated Parmesan cheese

Make the choux pastry according to directions. Stir in the cheese. Spoon the mixture around the edge of a shallow 9-inch ovenproof dish, leaving a space in the center.

Melt the butter in a skillet and sauté the onions for 5 minutes. Add the mushrooms and sauté for 1 minute. Blend in the flour and broth. Bring to a boil and simmer 5 minutes or until thick.

Add the tomatoes and ham and season to taste. Pour the filling into the middle of the choux ring. Sprinkle the Parmesan cheese over the top. Bake in a 400° oven for 30 to 40 minutes, or until well risen and golden brown. Serve hot.

GOULASH

A rich meat stew flavored with paprika, Hungarian in origin, but found in several European countries. Sour cream can be stirred in or served separately.

GOULASH

1½ lb stewing beef, cut into ½-inch cubes
¼ cup seasoned flour
2 medium-sized onions, chopped
1 green pepper, seeded and chopped
3 tablespoons vegetable oil
2½ teaspoons paprika
¼ cup tomato paste
little grated nutmeg
salt and pepper
½ cup flour
1¼ cups broth
2 large tomatoes, peeled and quartered
bouquet garni
⅔ cup beer

Coat the meat with seasoned flour. Sauté the onions and pepper lightly in the oil for about 3 to 4 minutes. Add the meat and sauté lightly on all sides until golden brown, about 5 minutes. Add the paprika and sauté for about 1 minute longer. Stir in the tomato paste, nutmeg, seasoning, and flour and cook for a further 2 to 3 minutes. Add the broth, tomatoes, and bouquet garni, put into a casserole and cook in a 325° oven for 1½ to 2 hours. Add the beer, cook for a few minutes longer and remove the bouquet garni.

GOURD

In the United States this is the name given to several vines of the Cucurbitacenae family, related to pumpkins, cucumbers, and squashes. Their shells are dried for use as utensils or as decoration. In Europe the name is applied to the edible members of the family as well as the inedible.

GRAHAM FLOUR

Graham flour is ground from whole wheat grain and is similar to whole wheat flour. It was named for Sylvester Graham, a nineteenth-century minister who advocated its use in the diet.

Graham crackers are crisp wholemeal biscuits, often flavored with honey.

GRAHAM CRACKER PIE CRUST

1½ cups graham cracker crumbs (about 20 crackers)
3 tablespoons sugar
½ cup butter, melted

Grease a shallow 8- to 9-inch pie plate or pan. Combine the crumbs, sugar, and melted butter. Line the pie plate with the mixture, pressing it firmly into place. The crust may be baked in a 350° oven for 10 minutes or refrigerated until chilled and set. This pie crust makes a popular alternative to a pastry crust, particularly for recipes such as cheesecakes and pies made with fruit.

GRANADILLA (PASSION FRUIT)

The fruit of the passion flower, of which there are numerous varieties bearing different-sized and colored fruits. The type commonly grown in the United States is large and has seedy pulp similar to a pomegranate. Other types are grown in tropical climates, the smaller, darker ones often being more juicy. Although their appearance is unattractive, granadillas have a delicious and refreshing flavor. They are served as a dessert fruit, or made into ices and other desserts. They are available fresh or canned in syrup.

GRAND MARNIER

A French liqueur based on Cognac, light brown in color and orange flavored.

GRANITA

An Italian ice. The name, meaning "granite," somewhat describes the pleasing hard and granular texture of this confection.

GRANITA DI CAFFÈ (COFFEE ICE)

$\frac{3}{4}$ cup sugar
2 cups water
2 cups strong espresso coffee

Melt the sugar in the water and add to the coffee. Place in ice-cube trays and freeze, stirring frequently. It is not desirable to obtain a smooth-textured product; a true granita is full of ice crystals. Granita is delicious alone or served with whipped cream.

GRAPE

The fruit of the vine, of which there are many varieties in Europe and elsewhere.

GRAPEFRUIT

A large, yellow-skinned citrus fruit which originated in China and the East Indies. It is now grown in many hot countries. The fruit resembles an orange, but the flesh is yellow or pink in color. The grapefruit is larger than an orange, varying from the size of a large orange to types weighing several pounds. The thickness of the skin varies and most grapefruit contain a number of seeds.

The juice of the grapefruit is more acid than that of the orange and it has a sharp flavor, which makes it a suitable appetizer for a meal. It is particularly popular served for breakfast. It is usually eaten uncooked, either alone or in fruit salads, though it may be lightly broiled to serve as an appetizer or dessert. For more unusual dishes it can be mixed with vegetables and salad ingredients. Grapefruit cans well. Like all citrus fruits, it is a good source of vitamin C.

Grapefruit marmalade can be made either thick or clear; grapefruit can also be mixed with other citrus fruits. It can be frozen in segments.

To serve grapefruit: 1. Peel the fruit, cutting off the inner as well as the outer skin. Cut down the skin dividing the segments and remove the section of pulp. Remove the seeds and place the sections of pulp in fruit glasses. Sprinkle freely with sugar and add 2 teaspoons of sherry to each glass. Place a Maraschino or candied cherry in the center and serve iced.
2. Cut the grapefruit in half across the sections. Using a grapefruit or other sharp knife, cut round the skin to loosen the pulp from the pith. Remove the center pith and core and loosen each section from the surrounding skin. Put sugar in the center, place a cherry on top and serve cold. The edges of the grapefruit may be pinked with scissors if desired.

GRAPEFRUIT COCKTAIL

2 grapefruits
2 oranges
sugar
$\frac{1}{4}$ cup lemon juice
Maraschino cherries

Prepare the fruit in segments as described above. Add sugar and lemon juice to taste. Serve well-chilled in individual glasses, each garnished with a cherry.

CHICKEN WITH GRAPEFRUIT

2 tablespoons butter
4 chicken parts
salt
pepper
2 teaspoons brandy
$1\frac{1}{4}$ cups chicken broth
2 tablespoons sherry
1 teaspoon dried herbs
1 grapefruit
1 tablespoon cornstarch
2 tablespoons sugar
watercress

Melt the butter in a skillet and brown the chicken on all sides. Remove to a casserole and season well. Heat the brandy in a ladle and flame. Remove the chicken from the heat and add the brandy. Add the broth, sherry, and herbs. Cover and cook in a 325° oven for 1 hour. Meanwhile remove thin strips of grapefruit peel with a sharp knife. Cut the grapefruit across the top and cut round skin, removing all the white pith. Cut into segments. Squeeze remaining grapefruit with the hand into the casserole juice. Taste for seasoning. Thicken the broth if necessary with the cornstarch, adding the sugar and strips of grapefruit peel. Garnish the chicken with watercress and grapefruit segments.

GRAPEFRUIT SALAD

Place halved sections of grapefruit (prepared as in method 1 above) on a bed of lettuce leaves or watercress and serve with French dressing. Equal parts of avocado may be added for variation.

GRAPEFRUIT AND SHRIMP SALAD

lettuce
1 grapefruit
½ cucumber
8 shrimp, cooked and shelled
French dressing

Prepare the lettuce and arrange a neat bed of the leaves in a shallow salad bowl. Peel the grapefruit, remove the pith, and divide it into sections; cut each section into three and put the juice and grapefruit into a bowl. Peel the cucumber, cut it into small dice and add it and the shrimp to the grapefruit. Pour on French dressing and mix lightly with a spoon and fork. Pile the mixture on the lettuce leaves and serve cold.

GRAPE LEAVES

Young grape leaves are much used in Greek and Turkish cooking. They are usually wrapped round a stuffing which may include meat and rice, then cooked in a sauce.

The Greek dish is known as Dolmades and the Turkish as Dolmas. (See Dolmas entry.)

DOLMADES

1 jar (16 oz) grape leaves
3 tablespoons lard or cooking oil
1 lb ground lamb or beef, cooked
1–2 onions, chopped
2 tablespoons cooked long-grain rice
chopped parsley
tomato sauce (to moisten)
salt
pepper
juice of 1 lemon

Dip the grape leaves in boiling water for 1 to 2 minutes and allow to drain while the stuffing is prepared. Put 2 tablespoons of the lard in a skillet with the meat, onions, rice, parsley, tomato sauce, and seasoning; mix well and sauté. Add the lemon juice. Place a small portion of the stuffing in the center of each grape leaf; roll up and fold envelope fashion. Secure if necessary with fine string. Put in a saucepan with the remaining lard, a little more tomato sauce, and a little water. Cook over a low heat until the sauce is well reduced.

GRAPPA

A strong Italian brandy. Like its French counterpart, marc, it is distilled from the residue of grapes.

GRATE

To rub foods such as cheese and vegetables against a coarse surface to produce small particles of food.

Foodstuffs to be grated must be firm and cheese should be first allowed to harden.

As foods deteriorate in quality when they are grated and thus exposed to the air, they should be grated only just before serving.

GRAVES

The name given to the Bordeaux wines produced from the vineyards of the Graves district, west and south of Bordeaux, in France. Both red and white wines are made, the red being the better of the two. The parishes which produce the best wines are Léognan, Martillac, Villenave d'Ornon and Mérignac. There are many famous château names for Graves: Château Haut-Brion is considered the best, followed by La Mission Haut-Brion, Pape Clément, etc. White Graves wines are usually sold under the name Graves and are often blended. The wine is medium-dry and is served with fish, poultry, veal, etc.

GRAVLAX

A Scandinavian dish of raw salmon marinated in salt, pepper, sugar, and dill for at least 24 hours. It is served sliced paper thin, cut on the bias as smoked salmon is.

SCANDINAVIAN GRAVLAX

⅓ cup kosher salt
¼ cup sugar
1 tablespoon crushed black pepper
1 salmon, dressed and split but unskinned
fresh dill

Combine the salt, sugar, and pepper. Rub the skin sides of the salmon with about half of the mixture. Line a glass baking pan with dill. Rub the remaining mixture into the flesh of each half. Place one half, skin side down, in the dish and cover with dill. Place the second half on top, skin side up, and cover with aluminum foil. Place a board on top and weight it down with a couple of cans, or whatever can be found. Refrigerate 24 to 36 hours.

GRAVY

A type of sauce made from the juices which run out from meat during cooking. These juices are sometimes served as they are, but they can be thickened, diluted, or concentrated; a little extra flavoring may be added, but too much tends to mask the true meat flavor.

Natural Gravy

Pour the fat very slowly from the pan, draining it off carefully from one corner and leaving the sediment behind. Season well with salt and pepper and add 1 cup hot vegetable water or broth. Stir thoroughly with a wooden spoon until all the sediment is scraped from the pan and the gravy is a rich brown; return the pan to the heat and boil for 2 to 3 minutes. Serve very hot.

This is the "correct" way of making thin gravy, but some people prefer to make a version of the thick gravy given below, using half the amount of flour.

Thickened Gravy

Leave 2 tablespoons of the fat in the pan, add 1 tablespoon flour, blend well and cook over the heat until it turns brown, stirring continuously. Slowly stir 1 cup hot vegetable water or broth and boil for 2 to 3 minutes. Season well, strain, and serve very hot.

NOTES
1. If the gravy is greasy (due to not draining off enough fat) or thin (due to adding too much liquid) it can be corrected by adding more flour, or by cooking down.
2. If the gravy is pale, a little gravy browning may be added. (See Browning entry.)
3. Meat extracts are sometimes added to give extra taste; however, they do tend to overpower the characteristic meat flavor. A sliced carrot and onion cooked with the meat in the gravy will give extra body to the taste without impairing it. A dash of wine added at the last moment does wonders for the gravy.

GRAYLING

A freshwater game fish of the northern hemisphere, resembling trout but with a large dorsal fin. It is cooked in the same ways as trout and is noted for its delicious flesh.

GRAY MULLET

(See Mullet entry.)

GREEN BUTTER

(See Ravigote Butter entry.)
A green butter for sandwiches and canapés

can also be made by creaming 4 tablespoons butter with $\frac{1}{2}$ cup chopped watercress that has been pureed in the blender. Season with salt and cayenne pepper.

GREENGAGE

A variety of plum, considered by many to be the finest flavored of all. The fruit is round and green in color, becoming yellowish when fully ripe.

Greengages are chiefly used as a dessert fruit, but may also be stewed and they make excellent tarts. They can well and make good jam.

Preparation and cooking: Remove the stalks and wash the fruit. If it is required for salads, etc., remove the skin, cut the fruit in half and remove the pit.

Greengages may be stewed like other fruit and require about 6 tablespoons to $\frac{1}{2}$ cup sugar and $\frac{2}{3}$ cup water for every 1 lb of fruit.

GREENGAGE JAM

3 lb greengages
1¼ cups water
7 cups sugar

Wash the fruit, cut in half and pit. Crack some of the pits to obtain the kernels and blanch. Combine the plums, water, blanched kernels, and sugar in a pan. Bring slowly to a boil and boil about 30 minutes, until setting point is reached. Jar and cover in the usual way. *Makes about 5 lb.*

GREEN GODDESS DRESSING

An herby mayonnaise with a tang of anchovies. It was created at the Palace Hotel in San Francisco, California, in honor of the English actor George Arliss who was opening in the play *Green Goddess*. There are many variations of the recipe, but to be savored fully, the herbs must be fresh. It is excellent with cold seafood.

GREEN GODDESS DRESSING

1 cup mayonnaise (preferably homemade)
2 tablespoons anchovy paste
¼ cup chopped parsley
2 tablespoons minced chives or green onion tops
1 tablespoon chopped tarragon or 3 tablespoons tarragon vinegar
1 tablespoon lemon juice
½ cup heavy cream
salt
pepper

Combine the ingredients in a small mixer bowl and beat to combine. Chill before using.

GREEN ONION

Also called scallions, these are onions that have no bulb. They have hollow green tops and about 2 to 3 inches of white above the roots.

Wash the onions, remove the outer skin, and serve them whole in salads, or chopped and sprinkled over green salad, tomato salad, etc. They can also be used for flavoring a wide variety of dishes.

GREEN PEA

(See Pea entry.)

GREEN PEPPER

The fluted, pear-shaped fruit of the capsicum plant. The shiny skin is green, yellow, or red, according to the degree of ripeness and the variety. Red peppers are often known by the Spanish name pimiento.

Fresh peppers have many uses in the kitchen: their sweet piquancy will enhance a salad if they are finely chopped, or cut in rings they make an attractive garnish. They give flavor to stews and casseroles or they may be stuffed and baked to serve as a main dish or vegetable. Suggested fillings are a mixture of some of the following: cheese, cold meats, bacon, cooked rice, bread crumbs, chopped nuts, onions, mushrooms, herbs, canned fish. They may be served with a sauce.

STUFFED PEPPERS

4 green peppers, halved lengthwise and seeds removed
1 onion, chopped
¼ lb bacon, chopped
3 tablespoons butter
4 tomatoes, peeled and sliced
⅔ cup long-grain rice, boiled
salt
pepper
¼ cup grated Cheddar cheese
⅔ cup fresh bread crumbs
⅔ cup broth

Put the halved peppers in an ovenproof dish. Lightly sauté the onion and bacon in 2 tablespoons of the butter until golden brown. Add the tomatoes, cooked rice, seasoning, and half the cheese. Mix the rest of the cheese with the bread crumbs. Put the bacon stuffing into the peppers and sprinkle with the bread crumb mixture. Pour the broth round the peppers, top each with a lump of butter and cook in a 375° oven for 15 to 20 minutes, or until the peppers are cooked. Carefully lift the stuffed peppers out of the dish and serve.

SWEET PEPPERS WITH TOMATOES

2 tablespoons oil
½ onion, chopped
1 clove garlic, crushed
4 tomatoes, peeled and sliced
2 tablespoons tomato paste
⅔ cup dry white wine
4 peppers, seeds removed and thinly sliced, about 1 lb
salt
pepper

Heat the oil in a large skillet or saucepan and lightly sauté the onion and garlic for 5 minutes without coloring. Add the tomatoes, tomato paste, and wine and simmer for 5 minutes. Add the peppers, cover and simmer gently for 15 to 20 minutes. Season if necessary. Serve as an accompaniment to broiled meats and fish.

ITALIAN PEPPER SALAD

2 green peppers
2 red peppers
2 tablespoons red wine vinegar
2 tablespoons olive oil
1 teaspoon Worcestershire sauce
1 teaspoon tomato paste
½ teaspoon paprika
salt
pinch of sugar
4 black olives, pitted and quartered

Slice the peppers, remove the core and seeds. Put the slices in a pan of cold water, bring to a boil, then drain and cool. Meanwhile, make the dressing. Put all the remaining ingredients (except the olives) into a bowl and beat well together. Arrange the cold peppers in a serving dish. Pour the dressing over and let stand for 30 minutes. Scatter the olives over the top. Serve as a side salad.

GREEN TEA

(See Tea entry.)

GRENADIN

A French term used for a small slice of fillet of veal. A grenadin is usually larded and braised, then served with a vegetable garnish, e.g., braised celery, chicory, or lettuce, or buttered carrots.

GRENADINE

A French syrup made from pomegranate juice. Bright red in color, it is used as a sweetening and coloring agent in a variety of cocktails, fruit drinks, etc.

GRIBICHE SAUCE

A French cold sauce made with oil beaten into the yolks of hard-cooked eggs and flavored with mustard, gherkins, capers, and herbs. It is served with fish and cold meats.

GRIDDLE CAKE

(See Pancake entry.)

GRILLING

(See Barbecuing and Broiling entries.)

GRILSE

A young salmon.

GRINDING

The process of reducing hard foodstuffs such as nuts and coffee beans to small particles by means of a food mill, coffee grinder, food processor or electric blender.

GRISSINI

Crisp bread sticks, baked at a high temperature in finger widths. Grissini are easily digested and very dry.

GRISTLE

Gristle or tendon is part of the connective tissue of an animal's body, forming the soft skeleton which supports the other tissues and organs. The principal constituent of gristle is collagen, which is converted into gelatin by prolonged cooking. It is usually inedible.

GRITS OR GROATS

The hulled and coarsely crushed grain of corn or oats (or occasionally other cereals such as buckwheat.) (See Hominy entry.)

GROG

An alcoholic drink, usually of rum, made with water and sweetened with sugar.

GROUND MEAT

(See Hamburger entry.)

GROUNDNUT

(See Peanut entry.)

GROUPER

Any of a variety of fish belonging to the sea bass family, found in warm waters around the world. They range in length from 2 to 12 feet. The average market weight is 5 to 15 lb and they are sold whole, filleted and cut into steaks. They can be cooked in any way that striped bass is.

GROUSE

Any of a variety of game birds native to the cooler climates of the northern hemisphere, related to the pheasant. Best known in the United States is the ruffed grouse (sometimes called partridge) and the prairie chicken, and sage grouse of the West. Ptarmigan, which turns white in winter, inhabits arctic and subarctic regions. The red or Scotch grouse, in fact a ptarmigan, is prized in Great Britain for its fine-flavored meat.

Grouse are cooked by roasting, broiling, grilling, or braising. As it is a small bird allow one bird per person.

ROAST GROUSE

After hanging, pluck, draw, and truss the bird, season inside and out and lay some fat bacon over the breast. Put a lump of butter inside the bird and roast in a 450° oven for 25 minutes, basting frequently.

Remove the trussing strings before serving the bird on toast.

GRUEL

A thin porridge, made with fine oatmeal or barley.

GRUNION

A small fish found off the coasts of California and Mexico. It comes ashore to spawn during spring tides that coincide with the full moon, at which time it is gathered from the beaches. Grunions are served whole and are delicious when coated with cornmeal and deep-fried.

GRUYÈRE CHEESE

A large, flat, whole-milk cheese, originally made in the Swiss town of Gruyère, but now also made in France and elsewhere. It is easily distinguished by its large holes caused by the gas produced by the bacteria with which it is inoculated. Gruyère is firm and rather rough in texture, but it has a pleasant taste. Its flavor and its firm texture make it second only to Parmesan cheese in popularity for cooking. Unlike Parmesan, however, it also makes a good table cheese.

When buying Gruyère cheese, avoid ones that have a very large number of irregularly shaped or unduly small holes, as they are likely to be of poor quality.

A considerable amount of Gruyère is pasteurized, compressed, shaped in small wedges, wrapped in foil, and sold in boxes; these processed cheeses have the same flavor as the ordinary cheese, but are unsuitable for cooking.

GUACAMOLE

A Mexican appetizer made from mashed avocados, popular in all parts of the United States. It may be incendiary – with Tabasco and chili – or mild and varies in texture from traditional chunkiness to a smooth paste. It is usually served as a dip in the United States. When chilling guacamole, cover the surface carefully with plastic wrap, pressing it down, to avoid discoloration of the dip.

GUACAMOLE WITH GREEN CHILI PEPPERS

2 avocados, mashed or pureed
¼ cup finely chopped canned green chili peppers
2 tablespoons grated onion
salt
2 tablespoons lemon juice

Combine the ingredients in a mixing bowl. Cover with plastic wrap and chill.

GUACAMOLE WITH BACON

2 avocados, mashed or pureed
2 tablespoons lemon juice
Tabasco sauce to taste
1 clove garlic
6 strips bacon, cooked until crisp and crumbled

Combine the avocados, lemon juice, Tabasco, and garlic in a mixing bowl. Cover with plastic wrap and chill. When ready to serve, stir in the bacon.

GUAVA

The fruit of a tropical tree. It has pink flesh and numerous seeds. A delicately flavored, stiff-textured jelly, and a paste are made from guavas.

GUDGEON

A freshwater fish similar to carp, found in European rivers. It grows to about 8 inches in length and has barbels at each corner of its mouth and black spots along the side of its body. Like all freshwater fish, gudgeon needs soaking in salted water before cooking. It is best fried or broiled.

GUINEA FOWL

A breed of domestic poultry developed from a wild species native to Africa. Related to the pheasant, the Guinea fowl is raised in a semiwild state in many parts of the world. Because its flesh is similar to that of game birds, it is in demand by restaurants that serve its roasted breasts under glass.

ROAST GUINEA FOWL

Allow one bird for each person and truss it for roasting, tying a piece of fat bacon over the breast. Roast in a 400° oven for 30 minutes or longer, according to size, basting frequently with butter. Garnish with watercress and serve with a mixed green salad.

GUINEA FOWLS' EGGS

(See Egg entry.)

GUM

A sticky substance, which hardens somewhat on exposure to the air, obtained from various trees and plants. The two chief types used in cookery are gum arabic and gum tragacanth. The former, which is derived from Arabian and Indian species of acacia, is used in the manufacture of jujubes, pastilles, and gumdrops, as well as in medicine; gum tragacanth, which is obtained from a spiny shrub grown in western Asia, is used for thickening creams, gelatins, and pastes, particularly the special stiff royal icing formerly employed to make ornaments for wedding cakes, etc.

GUMBO

A regional United States dish that was originated in New Orleans by Créole cooks. A souplike stew or stewlike soup, depending upon who is describing it, gumbo is New Orleans' most characteristic dish. Containing shellfish, poultry, meat, or a combination thereof, gumbo is thickened with okra in most of the South. The exception to this is the gumbo filé of New Orleans, thickened with filé powder ground from the leaves of young sassafras plants. Gumbo is served in soup plates on rice.

CRAB GUMBO

$\frac{1}{4}$ cup diced ham
$\frac{1}{2}$ clove garlic, crushed
2 cups sliced okra
2 tablespoons lard
6 tomatoes, peeled and diced
1 cup hot water
$\frac{1}{8}$ teaspoon thyme
salt and pepper
1 lb crabmeat
cooked rice

Sauté the ham, garlic, and okra in lard, until the onion is softened. Add the tomatoes, water, and seasonings. Cook 30 minutes. Add the crabmeat and cook to heat through. Serve on rice.

GUMBO FILÉ

1 (4 lb) fowl
2 quarts water
2 tablespoons lard
$\frac{1}{2}$ lb ham, diced
2 onions, chopped
2 tablespoons flour
salt
pepper
cayenne pepper
1 pint oysters, opened (reserve liquor)
2 tablespoons filé
cooked rice

Cook the chicken in the water until tender. Skin and bone it and cut the meat into dice. Melt the lard in a large heavy pot and brown the ham and onion. Sprinkle with flour and stir in. Flavor with the salt, pepper, and cayenne. Add the chicken and oyster liquor and pour in the boiling chicken stock; simmer for 2 hours. Add the oysters and cook until plump and the edges curled. Moisten the filé with stock, remove the gumbo from the heat and stir in. Do not heat after the filé is added nor attempt to reheat, for the gumbo will become stringy. Serve on a bed of rice.

GURNET OR GURNARD

A small European marine fish. It has a large, angular, bony head and firm, white flesh of good flavor. Gurnets are best baked but can be cooked by any recipe suitable for haddock.

GUTTING

To clean out the inside of a fish, removing all the entrails.

HADDOCK

A fish somewhat similar in appearance and color to the cod, but with a more pronounced flavor, it may be identified by a black streak down the back and two black spots, one at each side, above the gills. It can weigh from 1¾ lb to 3¼ lb. Haddock may be cooked by any method suitable for white fish; small or medium-sized fish can be cooked whole, but larger ones should be filleted or cut into steaks. The flesh tends to be dry, so the fish should be accompanied by a sauce.

SMOKED HADDOCK

When smoked, haddock is known as finnan haddie, named for the Scottish village of Findon near Aberdeen, where it originated. In Great Britain smoked haddock is served for breakfast, lunch, or high tea, is a frequent ingredient of kedgeree (see entry), and is served in soufflés and scalloped.

BAKED STUFFED FRESH HADDOCK

3 lb haddock
stuffing (see recipe)
bacon

Slit the haddock, leaving the head and tail on, and fill with the stuffing. Sew up and cover with a slice or two of bacon. Place in a well-greased pan and bake in a 425° oven. Cook 10 minutes per inch, measured at the thickest point of the fish. Garnish with parsley and serve with lemon butter.

STUFFING FOR BAKED HADDOCK

¼ cup butter
½ cup chopped onion
2 cups dry bread crumbs
½ cup chopped parsley
¼ cup chopped mixed herbs
salt
pepper
1 egg, well beaten

Melt the butter and sauté the onions until soft but not brown. Combine with the remaining ingredients, tossing well.

HADDOCK JULIENNE

1½ lb haddock or cod fillet
2 tablespoons butter
salt
pepper
ground coriander
juice of ½ lemon
1 small onion
2 tomatoes, peeled and seeded
¼ cup grated Cheddar cheese
1 teaspoon cornstarch
chopped parsley

Remove the skin from the fillet. Cut the fish into 4 portions. Use half the butter to grease a shallow ovenproof serving dish. Arrange the fish in a single layer, with salt, pepper, and a little coriander. Sprinkle with lemon juice. Cut the onion thinly into rings. Cut the tomato into strips. In a small skillet, melt the remaining butter and cook the onion until soft and beginning to color. Combine with the tomato and cheese.

Spoon the onion mixture evenly over each fillet. Cover and cook in 425° oven for 20 minutes.

In a small pan, blend the cornstarch with 1 tablespoon water, add the drained-off fish liquor and bring to the boil, stirring. Pour it over the fish and serve garnished with chopped parsley.

POACHED FINNAN HADDIE

Cut the fins from the fish and, if the fish is large, cut it into serving pieces. Place in a skillet or large saucepan, barely cover with milk, or milk and water, sprinkle with pepper, and simmer gently for 10 to 15 minutes, or until tender. The Finnan haddie can be served topped with a poached egg.

HAGGIS

A Scottish dish made from oatmeal, suet, and the internal organs of a sheep, the stomach of the sheep being cleaned and used as a casing for the pudding or sausage. A simpler type is made with liver and cooked in a saucepan.

HAKE

A white fish, long and slender, with a pointed snout and large mouth, related to the cod. It has flesh of a close texture and a delicate flavor. Hake is available year-round and is found in the Atlantic and Pacific waters of both the northern and southern hemispheres. It is cooked in any way suitable for cod.

HALIBUT

A very large flat fish found in the North Pacific and the North Atlantic. The young fish, which weighs about 3 lb, is in season year-round and has the best flavor. Larger ones, which can weigh up to 200 lb, are sold in steaks and sometimes as fillets.

Halibut can be broiled, steamed, baked, or served with a piquant sauce, and can replace turbot or cod in many recipes.

BAKED HALIBUT IN WINE

4 small halibut steaks, about 1½ lb
½ small onion, chopped
3 slices bacon, chopped
2 tablespoons butter
1 tablespoon flour
2 large tomatoes, peeled and chopped or 1 (16 oz)
    can tomatoes, drained
¼ cup dry white wine
salt
pepper
pinch of sugar
½ bay leaf
3–4 peppercorns

Rinse and dry the fish and place it in a greased ovenproof dish. Sauté the onion and bacon in the butter until soft but not brown, about 5 minutes, and stir in the flour. Add the tomatoes, wine, seasonings, and flavorings and pour over the fish. Cover with foil and bake in a 425° oven for about 20 minutes, or until the fish is tender. Remove the bay leaf and peppercorns before serving.

Halibut Liver Oil

This is a very good source of vitamins A and D (containing a higher proportion than cod liver oil); it is generally taken in a capsule.

HAM

The thigh of the hog, specially prepared and cured in a mixture of salt and saltpeter. The shoulder prepared in the same fashion is often referred to as ham.

The food value of ham is similar to that of all meat. It is a good source of protein, fat, and thiamin.

There are many variations in the curing of hams, some are smoked and some are not. Here are a few of the many varieties.

VIRGINIA
Special spicing and smoking with apple and hickory wood give these hams their individual flavor.

SMITHFIELD
A very popular type of Virginia ham, fed on acorns and beech and hickory nuts, later on peanuts and corn and, after curing, smoked with apple, hickory and oak wood.

KENTUCKY
Fed on acorns, beans, and clover, later on grain and, after curing, smoked with apple and hickory wood.

BAYONNE
An uncooked smoked ham, usually served as an hors d'oeuvre, best known of the French hams.

WESTPHALIA
An uncooked ham, served as an hors d'oeuvre, best known of the German hams.

DANISH

These hams are generally smaller in circumference but longer than the other types. They are exported to the United States boned and canned.

PARMA

An uncooked, smoked ham served very thinly sliced, usually eaten as an hors d'oeuvre with melon or figs; best known of the Italian hams.

YORK

Pale-dried ham, with a mild, delicate flavor and a pale lean meat; the fat is a very faint pink color. It is expensive because it is prepared by a special process which takes several months; when well matured, York ham should have a greenish mold on the outer surface. It keeps well and is the most famous of the British hams.

BRADENHAM

A British ham. It is sweet-cured, almost black in appearance, processed in molasses instead of brine, and needs long soaking and cooking.

TENDERIZED OR READY TO EAT

Cured but unsmoked ham that has been treated with heat. Always check the cooking directions, but usually this ham needs no more cooking than that to heat it through. These hams are mild and lack the flavor of smoked hams.

Cooking Ham

Whole hams are generally baked before serving. Aged hams, such as Smithfield, Virginia, and Kentucky, must be boiled before baking. And before boiling, they must be scrubbed with soap and water and a stiff brush to remove mold and dirt. They are then soaked for 24 to 48 hours before boiling. Country hams are usually accompanied by directions for cooking and generally do not have to be boiled before baking. If in doubt, however, and the ham is dry, hard, and smoky in odor, boil it first. Tenderized and ready-to-eat hams should not be boiled.

BOILING A HAM

Cover the ham with water and bring to a boil, removing any scum. Reduce heat and simmer for 20 minutes per lb. The ham is done when the shank bone removes easily. Remove from the water at once and cool.

BAKING A HAM

When the boiled ham has cooled, skin it. Loosen the fat at the butt end using a long sharp knife and slipping your fingers between the fat and the skin, peel it back. If the layer of fat is very thick, it may be trimmed. The ham is then studded with cloves and covered with brown sugar or brushed with a mixture of pineapple juice and sugar. The ham is then put in a 350° oven until glazed. It is served tepid or cold, sliced thinly. Follow package directions for baking country and tenderized or ready-to-eat hams, decorating them first as above.

BROILED HAM STEAK

Select a ham steak about 1 inch thick and slash the fat at intervals to prevent the steak from curling. Place in a broiling pan, turn the broiler to 550° or broil and cook 3 inches from the heat until lightly browned. Turn and continue cooking for about 6 minutes. Just before the steak is done, brush with jelly, marmalade, or apricot jam and allow to glaze.

HAM STEAK AND RED-EYE GRAVY

Select a slice of country ham $\frac{1}{4}$ to $\frac{3}{8}$ inch thick and cook it slowly in a skillet until browned on both sides and cooked through. Remove from the pan and pour off any excess fat. Add a little water and about 2 tablespoons strong coffee to the pan and bring to a boil, stirring and scraping the pan. Serve the steak with the gravy and grits.

HAM AND SCALLOPED POTATOES

4 cups sliced potatoes
4 tablespoons butter
3 tablespoons flour
$\frac{1}{2}$ teaspoon salt
$\frac{1}{4}$ teaspoon pepper
$2\frac{1}{2}$ cups milk
1 onion, finely chopped
$\frac{1}{2}$ pound cooked ham, diced

Put the potatoes in cold water to soak. Melt 3 tablespoons of the butter and stir in the flour, salt, and pepper. Cook, stirring, about 1 minute. Remove from the heat and add the milk all at once, stirring until smooth. Return to the boil, stirring.

Drain the potatoes and arrange $\frac{1}{3}$ of them in the bottom of a greased casserole. Sprinkle with $\frac{1}{2}$ of the onion and $\frac{1}{2}$ of the ham and cover with $\frac{1}{3}$ of the sauce. Make a second layer with $\frac{1}{2}$ of the remaining potatoes and sprinkle with the remaining ham and onions. Cover with $\frac{1}{2}$ of the remaining sauce. Add the remaining potatoes, cover with sauce and dot with 1 tablespoon butter. Cover and bake in a 325° oven 40 minutes. Uncover and cook for a further 70 minutes.

HAMBURGER

A patty of freshly ground beef cooked by pan broiling, broiling, grilling, or baking, usually served on a soft round roll. Catsup, relishes, and slices of raw tomato or onion are favorite accompaniments. It may be topped with a slice of American or Swiss cheese and returned to the broiler to melt and brown the cheese, and served as a Cheeseburger, or the cheese may be sealed between two thin patties, which are then cooked as one patty. Considered a national dish of the United States, it is becoming popular in Great Britain and in Europe.

HAMBURGERS

1 lb lean ground chuck, round or sirloin
½ onion, grated, optional
salt
pepper

Mix the meat well with the onion (if used) and a generous amount of salt and pepper. Shape lightly into 4 round patties. To cook, broil for 4 to 6 minutes on each side for rare, or fry in a pan, turning once and allowing the same amount of time; hamburgers can also be baked in a 350° oven for 20 minutes.

VARIATIONS
Traditionally, hamburgers contain no other ingredients but they can be varied as follows: To 1 lb hamburger add any of the following when mixing the hamburgers:

½ to 1 cup grated cheese
1 tablespoon sweet pickle
1–2 teaspoons prepared mustard
1 teaspoon dried mixed herbs
1 tablespoon chopped parsley
2 teaspoons prepared horseradish

HANGING

The practice of allowing meat, poultry and game to hang in a cool well-ventilated area to tenderize the meat and allow it to gain flavor. Beef and lamb, with enough fat covering to protect them from bacteria and drying, can be aged. Veal cannot, and pork requires no aging. Because storage is expensive, meat is increasingly being cut into smaller portions and wrapped in air- and moisture-proof plastic bags. This is called "Cryovac aging." Kosher meat is not allowed to hang or be aged and is consequently relatively tough and tasteless.

HANUKAH (FESTIVAL OF LIGHTS)

The Jewish eight-day feast that commemorates the victory of the Maccabees over the Syrians in 165 B.C. and the rededication of the Temple. It is one of the most joyous of the Jewish holidays, celebrated with gift-giving and top-spinning. Foods particularly associated with Hanukah are Kreplach and Potato latkes (see entries).

HARD SAUCE

A sauce served with Christmas and other rich puddings, which is made with butter and superfine or brown sugar. It is usually flavored with brandy or rum; as the name suggests, it becomes firm when cold. Ground almonds or stiffly beaten egg white are sometimes added and the sauce is usually sprinkled with grated nutmeg before serving.

HARD SAUCE

6 tablespoons butter
½ cup superfine sugar
2–3 tablespoons brandy

Cream the butter until pale and soft. Beat in the sugar gradually and add the brandy a few drops at a time, taking care not to allow the mixture to curdle. The finished sauce should be pale and frothy. Mound it in a small dish and leave to harden before serving.

Traditionally served with hot plum pudding and mince pies, but excellent with fruit pies and desserts such as Brown Betty.

Note: If you prefer a less granular texture, use sifted sugar or half powdered and half superfine sugar.

To make with rum: Make this as above, but use brown sugar, replace the brandy with 5 tablespoons rum and include the grated rind of half a lemon and a squeeze of lemon juice.

HARE

A wild animal resembling the rabbit, but somewhat larger and with flesh that is darker in color and richer in flavor. Although plentiful in many parts of the country, hare has never been as popular in the United States as it has in Britain and Europe.

Hare may be jugged, roasted, fricasseed, braised or made into terrines. Perhaps the most satisfactory portion is the saddle, or thigh section, of the hare. This can be roasted or sautéed in butter for about 25 minutes. Cream is then added to the pan and the hare simmered an additional 10 minutes. Fried grits are a good accompaniment to this dish.

JUGGED HARE

A very famous British recipe.

1 hare
3 slices bacon, chopped
2 tablespoons lard
1 onion, stuck with 2 cloves
1 carrot, sliced
1 stalk celery, sliced
4 cups broth
bouquet garni
juice of ½ lemon
¼ cup flour
1 tablespoon currant jelly
⅔ cup port or red wine, optional
salt
pepper

Prepare the hare, retaining the blood; wipe and cut into pieces. Sauté the pieces with the bacon in the lard until they are lightly browned (about 15 minutes). Transfer to a deep casserole and add the vegetables, enough broth to cover the parts, the bouquet garni, and lemon juice. Cover and cook in a 325° oven for 3 to 4 hours, or until tender.

A few minutes before serving, blend the flour with a little cold water to a smooth cream, stir in the blood of the hare and add to the casserole, with the jelly and wine (if used). Adjust seasoning. Reheat without boiling and serve with currant jelly.

HARICOT BEAN

(See Beans, Green entry.)

HARICOT OF MUTTON

A thick stew, which originated in France, of mutton, turnips, and potatoes. It contains no haricot beans and the French claim the name derives from "halicoter," to chop finely.

HASH

A dish of diced cooked meat reheated in a lightly flavored sauce. Hash provides a good way of serving the last of a roast (the bones can be used to make stock as a basis for the sauce). It can be served with a border of creamed potatoes or savory rice.

CORNED BEEF HASH

(See Corned Beef entry.)

HASTY PUDDING

Cornmeal mush. In Great Britain it is a very simple pudding, made by boiling milk with tapioca, sago, semolina, or even flour. Sugar is added to taste and the pudding is served hot.

HAZEL HEN

A game bird of northern Europe and Asia. The birds have white tender flesh tasting slightly of pine. About the size of a partridge, they may be prepared in the same ways.

HAZELNUT

The hazel tree is found all over Europe, but the best nuts come from southern Europe, particularly Spain. Cultivated varieties include the filbert. Hazelnuts are used in cooking for flavoring and decorating cakes, cookies, and desserts, etc.

HEAD

Heads contain a large amount of well-flavored meat, the tongues and brains being especially good. The other meat can be removed and made into head cheese. Calf's head is popular in France. One head will serve about 6.

CALF'S HEAD (TÊTE DE VEAU)

1 calf's head
1 gallon water
½ cup all-purpose flour blended with enough water
*   to make a paste*
2 carrots
2 stalks celery
1 leek, white part only
1 bay leaf
salt
12 peppercorns
1 teaspoon thyme
¼ cup lemon juice

Remove the brains and blanch, reserve. Wash the head thoroughly, paying particular attention to nostrils and ears and cut into 8 pieces. Soak in cold water for 24 hours, then cover with fresh water and blanch for 4 minutes. Rub with cut lemon to whiten it. Combine remaining ingredients and add the tongue from the head and the pieces of head, reserving the brain. Bring to a boil, reduce heat and simmer for 2 hours.

Meanwhile prepare the brains (see separate entry).

To serve, cut off all the meat, arrange it on a hot dish, and garnish with the sliced skinned tongue and the brains. Accompany with boiled potatoes and vinaigrette sauce.

HEAD CHEESE

Head cheese is a preparation of boned meat made from pig's head and is eaten cold. Sheep's head, veal, and other meats may be used to make this delicious cold cut which is also known as brawn.

The meat is stewed with spices and seasoning until very soft, then picked from the bone and finely chopped. It is then set in molds with some of the stock which is reduced sufficiently for the mixture to set to a jelly. Head cheese is served cold and thinly sliced.

HEAD CHEESE

$\frac{1}{2}$ pickled or fresh calf's head
bouquet garni
6 peppercorns
1 large onion
pieces of carrot and turnip
salt
freshly ground black pepper
ground nutmeg
1 hard-cooked egg, sliced

Wash the head thoroughly, making sure the ear and nostril are clean; soak it in salted water for about 6 hours. Cut off the ear and remove the brains. Scald the ear, scrape it free of hair, and wash well. Place the head in a large pan with the ear, bouquet garni, peppercorns, vegetables, and 1 teaspoon salt if the head is pickled, 2 teaspoons if it is fresh. Cover with water, bring to a boil, skim, cover, and allow to cook very slowly until the meat is tender – about 2 to 3 hours. Strain off the liquid, reserving it; remove the meat from the bones and cut it into small pieces. Peel the tongue and slice it thinly. Cut the ear into strips. Skim off the fat from the remaining liquid, add the brains tied up in cheesecloth, then boil uncovered until the liquid is reduced to half. Chop the brains and add to the meat. Season the mixed meats well with salt, pepper, and nutmeg.

Garnish the bottom of a mold or cake pan with sliced hard-cooked egg, pack the meat in tightly and pour some of the liquid over. Put a plate and a weight on it and leave till cold and set. When the head cheese is required for use, dip the mold into hot water and turn the head cheese out onto a dish.

HEART

Though somewhat neglected, hearts can be used to make a variety of economical and tasty dishes.

Beef heart is the largest and tends to be rather tough unless cooked long and slowly. It can be parboiled whole and then roasted, or cut up and braised or used in stews, but in any case it needs strong seasonings. When cooked whole, beef heart is often stuffed. A beef heart may weigh about 4 to 5 lb and is enough for 6 people.

Veal heart is small and more tender, but still needs slow cooking to make it enjoyable. It may be roasted, braised, or stewed. One veal heart will serve 2 people.

Lamb heart is the smallest kind, one of which serves only 1 person. More tender than veal or beef heart, it has a finer flavor and is usually stuffed and either roasted or braised.

BAKED STUFFED HEARTS

4 small lambs' hearts
1 cup fresh white bread crumbs
1 medium-sized onion, finely chopped
$\frac{1}{4}$ cup melted butter
$2\frac{1}{2}$ teaspoons dried mixed herbs
salt
pepper
2 tablespoons seasoned flour
2 tablespoons vegetable oil
$1\frac{1}{4}$ cups broth
1 onion
4 stalks celery, sliced
4 carrots, sliced

Wash the hearts, slit open, remove any tubes or gristle and wash again under cold, running water. Fill with a stuffing made from the bread crumbs, onion, melted butter, mixed herbs, and seasonings. Tie the hearts firmly into the original shape with string, coat with seasoned flour and brown quickly in the hot oil. Place in a casserole with the broth, cover and bake in a 325° oven for $2\frac{1}{2}$ hours, turning them frequently. Add the onion, celery, and carrots for the last 45 minutes of the cooking time.

BRAISED SLICED HEART

1 beef heart, $2\frac{1}{4}$ to 3 lb
$\frac{1}{4}$ cup vegetable oil
2 onions, sliced

¼ cup flour
⅔ cup broth
salt
pepper
8 oz carrots, grated
½ small rutabaga, grated
rind of 1 orange
6 walnuts, chopped

Cut the heart into ½-inch slices, removing the tubes, and wash it well. Sauté the sliced heart in the oil until slightly browned and put into a casserole. Sauté the onions and add to the casserole. Add the flour to the remaining oil and brown slightly. Add the broth, season to taste with salt and pepper, bring to a boil and simmer for 2 to 3 minutes, then strain into the casserole; cover and cook for 3½ to 4 hours in a 300° oven, adding the carrots and rutabaga after 2½ to 3 hours. Pare the rind from the orange, shred it finely, cook in boiling water for 10 to 15 minutes, then drain. Add the walnuts and orange rind to the casserole 15 minutes before the cooking is completed.

Note: 1 can (8 oz) tomatoes, chopped, can be substituted for the orange rind and walnuts.

HERBS

The addition of suitable herbs so greatly improves the flavor of soups, stews, and other slow-cooking dishes that a supply should be available in every kitchen. If it is not possible to have a small herb garden, flowerpots and window boxes can often be used to grow herbs.

Fresh herbs are superior to dried in cooking, although dried herbs have a stronger flavor. It is therefore important to be more generous with fresh herbs. Fresh herbs can be frozen successfully.

Herbs can be dried for the winter months; a wide variety can be bought ready dried. It is advisable to store each kind separately, and it is useful to have also a jar of mixed herbs. The following are the most commonly used. (See individual entries.)

Balm	Fennel	Oregano
Basil	Garlic	Parsley
Bay	Horseradish	Rosemary
Borage	Lemon Thyme	Sage
Celery seeds	Lovage	Savory
Chervil	Marjoram	Sorrel
Chives	Mint	Tarragon
Dill	Nasturtium	Thyme

MIXED HERBS
Usually a mixture of equal quantities of parsley, chives, tarragon or chervil and thyme.

BUNCH OF HERBS OR BOUQUET GARNI
A bunch of herbs, including a sprig of parsley, thyme and marjoram and a bay leaf, is used for flavoring stews, etc. Fresh herbs should be tied together, dried ones tied in a cheesecloth bag, so that they can be easily removed when serving.

TO DRY HERBS
Pick the herbs on a dry day shortly before they flower. Wash them and pick off any damaged leaves. Dry the herbs by hanging in the sun or by placing in a cool oven. When the herbs are ready the leaves will crumble easily. Parsley and mint will keep green if dipped in boiling water for a minute and then dried fairly quickly. Crumble the leaves, put in jars and store in a cool, dry, dark place. Alternatively, tie them in bunches with a paper bag fastened over the leaves. Approximately 1 teaspoon dried equals 3 teaspoons fresh.

HERB VINEGAR
Using young, fresh, dry herbs (e.g. mint, tarragon), fill a jar three-quarters full, fill up with warm vinegar, put on the lid and leave for 3 weeks, shaking at intervals. Strain and bottle the vinegar. Store in a cool dark place.

HERB BUTTER
Fresh herbs such as chopped parsley, thyme, tarragon, and chives can be added to creamed butter and used as a sandwich spread, or, with the addition of lemon juice, as a sauce for fish or meat (see Maître d'Hôtel).

HERO

A sandwich of "heroic" size. It is made on a split loaf of Italian bread and contains a variety of fillings, including meat, sausages, cheese, and pickled vegetables.

HERRING

A small, oily fish, caught in large quantities in the Atlantic. While herrings are obtainable year-round, it is the fresh young herring of spring that is considered the greatest delicacy, particularly in Holland, where they are sold on every street corner. Many young herrings are canned under the name of sardines.

The herring is economical and a good source of first-class protein; it also contains niacin, vitamin A and some D, calcium, and phosphorus.

Fluorine, iodine, riboflavin, and vitamin B_1 are present in small amounts.

Herring can be served at any meal of the day and pickled herring make appetizing hors d'oeuvres. The full flavor of the fish is best obtained when it is sautéed or broiled. Herring roes have a delicate flavor and are excellent poached or sautéed.

The fish may be preserved in brine. After soaking in cold water for 24 hours, changing the water several times, the fillets may be prepared as rollmops or Bismarck herring (see separate entries) or marinated or pickled or served in a salad of cold boiled potatoes and beets and tart apples dressed with oil and vinegar. The fish may also be preserved by smoking, the bloaters and kippers (see separate entries) of Great Britain being famous examples. Smoked fillets should be soaked for 2 hours in water or milk and can then be marinated in oil with onions, carrots and bay leaf for 2 or 3 days before serving.

To prepare fresh herrings: remove the head and entrails which usually come away with it – if not they should be removed separately. Remove any black skin by rubbing with salt and wash the fish well. Scrape off the scales and trim off fins and tail with scissors. Score on each side, if the fish are to be broiled or sautéed.

SAUTÉED HERRING IN CRUMBS

Prepare and bone the herrings, then sprinkle them with pepper and salt; dip into milk and then fine crumbs. Sauté on both sides in hot butter until a light golden color, drain well and serve garnished with lemon wedges and parsley.

BROILED HERRINGS

Score the skin diagonally two or three times on each side, season with pepper and salt and let the fish lie for a short time before cooking. Broil in the usual way, lowering the heat if the fish are large and thick, and cook for 7 to 10 minutes.

Alternatively, split and bone the herrings and arrange flesh side upward on the broiling pan. Dab with butter and cook until it melts. Sprinkle with bread crumbs and cook until the fish are brown and done. Garnish with parsley or watercress and lemon.

SOUSED HERRING

4 large or 6–8 small herrings, cleaned and boned
salt and pepper

1 small onion, sliced into rings
6 peppercorns
1–2 bay leaves
few parsley stalks
$\frac{2}{3}$ cup cider vinegar
$\frac{2}{3}$ cup water

Sprinkle the fish with salt and pepper. Roll up from the head end and secure with wooden picks. Pack them into a fairly shallow ovenproof dish and add the onion, peppercorns, and herbs. Add the vinegar and enough water to almost cover the fish. Cover with foil and bake in a 350° oven for about 45 minutes or until tender. Leave the herrings to cool in the cooking liquid before serving as an appetizer or with salad. To serve as an appetizer, cut each herring into bite-sized pieces and secure on cocktail picks. Alternatively, serve them whole or halved on slices of rye bread with a garnish of onion and green pepper rings.

HICKORY

Any of several deciduous trees of the genus *Carya*, native to North America and bearing edible nuts. The pecan (see separate entry) is the most famous of these.

HIPPOCRAS

A medieval drink, heavily sweetened with honey and flavored with herbs and spices. It is likely that soured wine was used up in this way.

HIPS, ROSE

(See Rose Hip entry.)

HOCK

The name given by the British to white wines from the Rhine Palatinate and other parts of Germany. The original name, Hochheimer, was given to the wine made in the vineyards close to the town of Hochheim and this region still produces the best Hock, which is sold under a number of well-known names, e.g. Johannisberger, Steinberger, Liebfraumilch, Marcobrunner, Hochheimer.

The term also applies to meat taken from just above the forefoot of a hog.

HOECAKE

A primitive cornbread baked on a hoe by early settlers in the United States and slaves. The batter is made of cornmeal, salt, lard, and boiling water.

HOI SIN OR HOISIN SAUCE

A thick Chinese condiment sauce with a sweet-spicy flavor. Red in color, it is served with duck, used as a dip, cooked with chicken and shrimp, and combined with soy to make a delicious barbecue sauce. It is available in cans and after opening keeps well tightly covered in the refrigerator.

HOLLANDAISE SAUCE

A rich sauce made of egg yolks, butter, and lemon juice and served with fish, asparagus, artichokes, or eggs. Mousseline and Béarnaise are variations of hollandaise (see separate entries).

HOLLANDAISE SAUCE

3 egg yolks
4 tablespoons lemon juice
½–¾ cup butter
salt
cayenne pepper

Put the egg yolks in a bowl and stir in the lemon juice. Put over a pan of hot water and heat gently, stirring all the time, until the egg mixture thickens (never let the water go above simmering point). Divide the butter into small pieces and gradually whisk into the sauce; add seasoning to taste. If the sauce is too sharp add a little more butter – it should be slightly piquant, almost thick enough to hold its shape and warm rather than hot when served.

BLENDER HOLLANDAISE

While not as thick as regular hollandaise, this sauce takes only about 30 seconds in the blender.

3 egg yolks
2 tablespoons lemon juice
pinch of salt
pinch of cayenne
½ cup hot melted butter

Combine the egg yolks, lemon juice, and seasonings in a blender container, cover and blend on high for 2 to 3 seconds. Remove cover and slowly pour in the hot butter.

MOCK HOLLANDAISE SAUCE

2 egg yolks
2 tablespoons cream

1 cup Béchamel sauce (see entry)
lemon juice or vinegar

Beat together the egg yolks and cream and add to the Béchamel sauce. Heat carefully in a double boiler until thickened, but do not allow to boil. Add a very little lemon juice or vinegar drop by drop, to give a slightly sharp taste to the sauce.

HOLLAND GIN

A type of gin distilled in Holland and highly prized by the Dutch. It is made from barley, malt, rye, and juniper berries.

HOMINY

The whole kernel of dried corn treated with lye to remove the hulls. Grits, coarser than cornmeal and resembling broken rice, are the ground particles of hominy. Extremely popular in southern United States, grits are served boiled, with butter or gravy, as a breakfast cereal or a side dish and are particularly popular with game. Leftovers can be baked or molded and sliced and fried in bacon fat or lard. In the Southwest, hominy is baked in various combinations with cheese and chili.

HONEY

This natural liquid sugar is prepared by bees from the flower nectar which they collect; the honey acquires the flavor of the flower predominantly used in its production, so that clover honey, for instance, has a different taste from that of garden flower honey.

Bees make from 20 to 50 lb of honey per year per hive, according to the size of the hive and the food available. They secrete an enzyme by which they convert the nectar sucrose they collect into invert sugar (dextrose and levulose), which represents 70 to 80 percent of the total weight of the honey; water accounts for about 15 to 25 percent and there is up to 8 percent of unchanged sucrose. Honey is a good source of energy but has no other food value.

Natural honey is sold in various states:

In the honeycomb: The comb from a virgin hive (a hive from which the bees have not swarmed) is the whitest and best. It should be served by cutting or scooping horizontally, not vertically, as this keeps the honey from running out of the comb. Store in a warm, dry place and handle by the wooden casing.

Clear honey, which is extracted by hanging up the combs (after damaging the cells) and allowing the honey to drip out; it is then strained and jarred. Clear honey varies in viscosity, flavor, and color. The viscosity depends on the manner in which the honey is collected and extracted and the flavor of the flowers the bees have visited; these also affect the color and it is generally considered that the light-colored honey is better than the dark. Heather honey is light golden in color and rather thick, with a bitter taste; clover honey is a clear greenish yellow and thin; mountain honey is the best type and has a exquisite flavor; it varies in color though it is usually whitish.

Clear honey should be stored in a warm, dry place, otherwise it crystalizes out and this spoils the flavor. If it does crystalize gentle warming will liquefy it.

Solid (thick) honey: This is merely clear honey which has solidified. The flavor is not generally considered so good as that of clear honey, but the texture is often preferred.

Use of Honey

Though honey is principally served as a preserve, which enables its full flavor to be appreciated, it has many other uses, especially in the preparation of candies such as nougat. It can be substituted for sugar in the making of desserts and cakes, but a larger quantity of honey than sugar and less liquid will be required; thus 1 cup of honey will replace $\frac{3}{4}$ cup of sugar and $\frac{1}{4}$ cup of liquid. The texture of some mixtures (e.g. cakes made by the creaming method) is adversely affected if honey alone is used instead of sugar, but even in these a proportion of about 25 percent can be used successfully. Clear honey is better for these mixtures. Honey also give a delicious flavor to stewed fruit and hot drinks.

HONEYDEW MELON

(See Melon entry.)

HOPPING JOHN

A dish originally served in the Carolinas for good luck on New Year's Day and now prepared throughout the South of the United States to fend off bad luck in the New Year. In South Carolina it is made with red cowpeas, elsewhere black-eyed peas can be used.

HOPPING JOHN

1 lb red cowpeas or black-eyed peas
$\frac{3}{4}$ lb salt pork, cubed
1 cup rice
salt
pepper

Soak the peas overnight. Drain and cook with the salt pork in 1 quart water until almost tender, 30 to 40 minutes. Add the rice and 2 cups water. Bring to a boil and cook 20 minutes. The liquid should be almost all absorbed and the rice and peas done.

HOPS

The ripened flowers of a climbing vine, the hop plant, which are used to impart a bitter flavor to beer. The tender shoots are eaten as a vegetable in France and Belgium.

HORS D'OEUVRE

Small cold or hot snacks served as an appetizer at the beginning of a meal. They may be served with drinks before dinner or at table as a first course. If served with drinks, they usually take the form of canapés, pâtés, or spreads that can be eaten from a cracker, shrimp, or cut herring served with picks, or any food that can be eaten with the fingers.

When served at the table, an hors d'oeuvre is eaten with knife and fork, but the portion should still be small and appetizing and provide contrast to the meal to come. An hors d'oeuvre can be made of seafood, meat, cheese, vegetables, or fruits. Oysters and clams on the half shell, shrimp and crabmeat cocktails, herring in sour cream, smoked salmon or gravlax and caviar might precede a roast. Pâtés, foie gras, sausages, and thinly sliced hams are among the meats available. Fried mozzarella with anchovy sauce and baked goat's cheese are popular hors d'oeuvre. Asparagus, artichokes, peppers green and red, caponata, and salads of cucumber, tomatoes or beets are among the vegetable appetizers, while grapefruit, fruit cocktail, and melon are among the fruit.

Hors d'Oeuvres Variés (Mixed Hors d'Oeuvre)

While this term is the French one, many countries have this custom. There are the Antipasto of Italy, the Smörgåsbord of Scandinavia and the Zakuski of the Soviet Union. (See separate entries.) In summer they may be served as a complete meal. They are presented in special dishes divided into sections. Small separate dishes can also be arranged on a tray, or the hors d'oeuvre may be set on a large platter, with the items separated by a garnish of watercress or parsley. The individual dishes (there should be at least four) can be chosen from meat, poultry, game, fish, eggs, cheese, nuts, vegetables, fruits. Starches should be used with caution, as they are substantial. Serve hors d'oeuvres very cold, accompanied by crisp rolls and butter.

The following is a list of suitable ingredients for mixed hors d'oeuvre; unless otherwise stated, salad vegetables, etc., should be tossed in French or other dressing before being served.

Salad and Other Vegetables

LETTUCE
Crisp hearts or shredded leaves.

CURLY ENDIVE OR ESCAROLE
Shredded, or torn into small pieces.

BELGIAN ENDIVE
Sliced.

RADISHES
Left whole or cut into fancy shapes, or sliced, tossed in French dressing and sprinkled with chopped parsley.

CUCUMBER
Peeled, thinly sliced and laid in vinegar; or cut into small dice.

TOMATOES
Peeled, sliced, dressed and garnished with chopped parsley or onion or mixed with fine green beans and vinaigrette.

MUSHROOM CAPS
Sautéed and stuffed with a mixture of the chopped stalks, onion and ham sautéed and mixed with bread crumbs.

SPRING ONIONS
Left whole, cut into a uniform length, or sliced and tossed in dressing.

BEETS
Sliced or diced, sprinkled with finely chopped onion or chives.

CELERY
Sliced, tossed in dressing and garnished with chopped parsley; cut into short lengths and stuffed with cream cheese or other filling; braised, sliced and dressed as above.

RED OR GREEN PEPPERS
Shredded or chopped and mixed with dressing.

POTATO
Cooked and sliced or diced, coated with mayonnaise and garnished with chopped parsley or chopped chives.

PEAS, GREEN BEANS
Cooked and tossed in dressing, or included in mixed vegetable mayonnaise.

ASPARAGUS TIPS
Cooked and dressed with vinaigrette dressing, or wrapped in smoked salmon or ham.

CARROTS, TURNIPS, AND ARTICHOKES
Cooked and diced, these are included in Russian salad or may be used alone in mixed hors d'oeuvre. They are usually tossed in mayonnaise, but a simple dressing may be used if preferred.

CABBAGE
Shredded raw cabbage (possibly with caraway seeds) tossed in dressing, or pickled red cabbage served in its own liquor.

OLIVES
Whole or stuffed. Chopped olives are sometimes mixed with other hors d'oeuvres such as Russian salad, to give piquancy.

PICKLES
Pickled gherkins, mixed pickles, piccalilli, etc., served in their own liquor.

WATERCRESS AND PARSLEY
Used as garnishes.

HERBS
Chopped chives, tarragon, parsley or mint, etc., may be used to mix with, or sprinkle over, the hors d'oeuvre.

Fish

SALTED AND PICKLED FISH, SUCH AS SARDINES, ANCHOVY FILLETS, ROLLMOPS, SOUSED HERRINGS AND SO ON
Usually served in their own liquor or with a simple dressing.

SHELLFISH
Shrimp, mussels, lobster, crab or crayfish — usually served dressed with mayonnaise dressing.

Other fish include: cold salmon, dressed with mayonnaise; tuna; herring.

Meats

Salami, garlic sausage, and various other types; usually served sliced and do not require dressing.

Cold cooked meats, such as roast beef, ham or tongue, chicken, game, etc.; usually cut up neatly and sometimes soaked in a marinade of oil and vinegar, with chopped parsley and perhaps chopped onion or chives.

Eggs

Hard-cooked eggs, sliced neatly, coated with mayonnaise and garnished with paprika or capers.

Starches

WHOLE BEANS
Cooked, mixed with tomato sauce and garnished with chopped parsley or chopped chives.

RICE
Dry boiled rice, mixed with chopped raisins with curry-flavored dressing.

PASTA
Cooked, cut into short lengths, mixed with chopped ham and moistened with salad cream.

HORSE MEAT

In many parts of Europe horsemeat is extensively eaten. In the United States and Great Britain horseflesh serves as a valuable feeding stuff for domestic animals.

HORSERADISH

A plant with a pungent, acrid root, used as a condiment. The root is grated and made into a cream or sauce for serving with roast beef and some other meat entrées, and for adding to sandwiches.

HORSERADISH SAUCE

2 tablespoons grated fresh horseradish
2 teaspoons lemon juice
2 teaspoons sugar
pinch of dry mustard, optional
$\frac{2}{3}$ cup whipping cream

Mix the horseradish, lemon juice, sugar, and mustard. Whip the cream until it just leaves a trail, then fold in the horseradish mixture.

Serve with beef, trout, or mackerel. Horseradish sauce may also be added to sandwich fillings to add a piquant flavor.

HORSE'S NECK

A long drink. Put 2 to 3 pieces of broken ice in a tall glass, fill with ginger ale and hang a long curl of lemon peel over the side of the glass. A "stiff Horse's Neck" is made by adding a dash of Angostura bitters and $\frac{1}{8}$ pint spirits.

HOTCHPOTCH

A thick soup made of meat and vegetables, popular in Scotland.

HOT CROSS BUN

A yeast bun traditionally eaten in the United States during Lent. The buns are flavored with nutmeg and, as the name implies, have a cross on top, made by cutting the buns with scissors before setting them to rise. A cross is frosted on the buns after baking.

HOT CROSS BUNS

4 cups bread flour
2 packages active dry yeast
$\frac{2}{3}$ cup tepid milk
$\frac{1}{3}$ cup tepid water
pinch of salt
$\frac{1}{2}$ teaspoon grated nutmeg
$\frac{1}{4}$ cup superfine sugar
$\frac{1}{4}$ cup butter, melted and cooled, but not firm
1 egg, beaten
1 cup raisins
$\frac{1}{4}$ cup chopped citron
1 egg white, slightly beaten

FOR THE FROSTING
2 teaspoons milk or water
$\frac{3}{4}$ cup powdered sugar

Flour a baking sheet. Put 1 cup of the flour in a large mixing bowl. Dissolve the yeast in the liquids and add to the flour; mix well. Set aside in a warm place until frothy, about 15 to 20 minutes. Sift together the remaining flour, salt, nutmeg, and sugar. Stir the butter and egg into the frothy yeast mixture, add the flour and the fruit, and mix together. The dough should be fairly soft. Turn it out onto a lightly floured surface and knead until smooth. Place in a bowl and cover with greased polyethylene. Allow to rise until doubled in size.

Punch down the dough and turn out onto a floured working surface. Divide the dough into twelve pieces and shape into buns. Arrange them well apart on the floured baking sheet, cover and let rise until doubled in size. Brush the tops of the buns with egg white. Bake in a 375° oven for 15 to 20 minutes, until golden brown and firm to the touch. Meanwhile, heat the milk and water and sugar gently together. Cool the buns on a rack. Mix the milk and sugar to spreading consistency and frost a cross on each bun.

HOT DOG

(See Frankfurter entry.)

HOTEL RACK

(See Rib entry.)

HOT POT

A layered stew of meat or fish baked with very little liquid in a pot with a tight-fitting lid. The lid is removed for the last 30 minutes of baking to brown the top layer of potatoes. Popular in Great Britain, the dish has many regional variations. Perhaps the best known is the Lancashire hot pot, consisting of lamb, onions, kidneys, and potatoes. In its original form, it also contained oysters.

HOT WATER CRUST

The traditional pastry used in Great Britain for raised pies. Stiff enough to stand by itself, it is made with hot water, melted lard and flour. While still warm, the pastry is molded into the desired shape and filled with a veal, ham or pork filling.

HUBBARD SQUASH

A large dark-green hard-shelled squash, nearly round in shape and with a warty rind and orange flesh. (See Squash entry.)

HUCKLEBERRY

The black or blue fruit of a shrub native to North America and related to the blueberry, with which it is often confused. Huckleberries are used for pies, preserves, and sauces, and are prepared in the same ways as are blueberries.

HUMMUS

A puree of chickpeas flavored with a paste of sesame seeds, garlic, and lemon juice. It is a popular Middle Eastern dish.

HUMMUS DIP

1 can (1 lb) chickpeas
1–2 cloves garlic
salt
4–6 tablespoons lemon juice
6 tablespoons tahini (sesame seed paste)

Puree the chickpeas. Pulverize the garlic with the salt and add to the puree. Add the lemon juice with the tahini. The consistency should be that of thick mayonnaise; no one taste should predominate.

Note: Tahini is available in some supermarkets and most health food stores.

HYDROMEL

A drink of honey and water, flavored with herbs and spices; when fermented, it becomes mead.

HYSSOP

A plant of the mint family with dark green leaves and deep blue flowers. Its pungent, aromatic leaves may be used in salads and soups. Honey made from hyssop flowers is said to be particularly good. The oil distilled from the leaves is used in liqueurs.

ICE CREAM

A frozen dessert made of cream (Philadelphia ice cream) or cream and a custard base (French custard ice cream), to which flavorings or fruit are added before freezing. Hand-churning produces the best ice cream with the smoothest texture, but battery- and electric-operated machines produce excellent results. Failing a machine, ice cream can be made in the ice-cube trays of a freezing compartment, but special steps or recipes must be used in their preparation.

Hand-Churned Freezer
Pour the ice cream mixture into the canister, insert the dasher and set the top firmly in place. Fit the canister into the wood tub and fill one-third full of ice. Layer with rock salt and ice (6 parts ice to 1 part salt) until filled. Turn the crank until it becomes difficult to turn. Drain water from wood tub, remove the top of the canister and take out the dasher. Pack the ice cream down, cover the canister with waxed paper and then its top. Repack the tub with ice and salt, using 4 parts ice to 1 part salt. Cover with burlap or newspapers and leave to ripen for about 2 hours.

Electric- or Battery-Operated Machine
Follow the manufacturer's directions. Some of these machines use plain table salt and some are operated from inside the freezer and need neither ice nor salt.

In the Refrigerator
If not using a special recipe intended for unchurned ice cream, use a French custard as the base. Prepare the custard as directed. Pour the custard into ice-cube trays and freeze for 30 to 60 minutes, until partially frozen. Turn the mixture into a bowl and beat until smooth. Whip the cream lightly, until the beater just leaves traces, and fold it into the custard with any fruit puree. Return to the freezer trays, cover with foil and freeze until firm, about 4 hours. Stirring from time to time will improve the texture.

FRENCH CUSTARD VANILLA ICE CREAM

1 cup milk
½ cup sugar
3 egg yolks, beaten
1 tablespoon vanilla
2 cups heavy cream

Combine the milk and sugar in a saucepan and heat, stirring to dissolve the sugar. Pour the hot mixture over the egg yolks, stirring constantly. Return the mixture to the saucepan and cook it over gentle heat, stirring until the custard thickens. Cool and stir in the vanilla.

If freezing in hand-churned or electric- or battery-operated freezer, add the cream and proceed as directed above. Otherwise follow the directions for freezing in the refrigerator above.

CHOCOLATE ICE CREAM
Melt 2 oz semisweet chocolate with the milk.

COFFEE ICE CREAM
Add ¼ cup instant coffee, dissolved in 2 tablespoons hot water.

BANANA ICE CREAM
Add 3 mashed or pureed bananas with the cream.

GINGER ICE CREAM

Add 1 jar (10 oz) preserved stem ginger, pureed in its syrup, with the cream.

CHOCOLATE CHIP ICE CREAM

Add 6 oz chocolate chips or grated semisweet chocolate with up to 1 tablespoon orange juice or liqueur.

PHILADELPHIA ICE CREAM

1 quart whipping cream
1 cup sugar
2 teaspoons vanilla

Heat the cream until lukewarm. Stir in the sugar until dissolved. Cool and add the vanilla. Freeze in a hand-churned or electric- or battery-operated machine.

To serve ice cream: Use an ice cream scoop to dish the ices (or, failing that, a soup spoon), dipping it in tepid water before scooping up the ice cream. Serve in any of the following ways:
1. Plain or topped with whipped cream, accompanied by cookies.
2. In individual glasses, decorated with fresh or preserved fruits (cherries, angelica, etc.).
3. Place a spoonful of ice cream between two meringue shells, pipe with whipped cream and decorate with fruit or chocolate sauce.

Sundaes, etc.
These have a basis of ice cream of any flavor, combined with a fruit or other sweet sauce, fresh or canned fruit, grated chocolate, chopped nuts, or whipped cream. (See Parfait, Sundae, and Peach Melba entries.)

Neapolitan Ice Cream
Use three or four kinds of ice cream, usually white (vanilla), green (pistachio or almond), brown (chocolate), and pink (raspberry). Use a square or oblong mold and pack in the half-frozen mixtures in layers; cover and freeze as a bombe (below).

Bombes
These are made by freezing ice cream mixtures in a decorated bombe mold. Numerous variations can be made by altering the flavoring and adding fruit or nuts.
   Plain mixtures should be half frozen, i.e. frozen to a mushy consistency, before being molded. Mousse and parfait mixtures, being fluffy in texture, can be molded when cold and then frozen. The preliminary freezing may be

carried out by any method, but if the mixture is too hard, it will not mold satisfactorily. Pack it into the chilled mold, filling it to the brim and taking care to leave no air spaces, press on the lid and freeze in one of the following ways:
1. By freezing in a refrigerator. Place the filled and covered mold in the coldest part of the freezing unit and leave undisturbed, with the temperature control set to "coldest" for about 2 hours or longer.
2. By burying the mold in ice and salt. Either wind a piece of adhesive tape round the edge of the lid or wrap the whole mold tightly in foil to prevent the salt seeping through to the mixture and spoiling the flavor. Bury the mold in a bowl or bucket of 4 parts crushed ice and 1 part rock salt. Cover with a sack or blanket and stand it in a cool place for at least 2 hours, draining off the melted ice from time to time and adding more ice and salt if necessary.

To unmold the bombe: Brush a piece of sponge cake the same size and shape as the bottom of the mold with apricot jam and roll the side in chopped nuts. Have ready some whipped cream in a pastry bag and any decorations, e.g., angelica or candied cherries, etc. If the mold has been buried in ice and salt, rinse it in cold water. Dip in tepid water for a few seconds, then remove any adhesive tape and the lid and invert the ice cream onto the cake base. Pipe a border of whipped cream round the base, decorate, and serve at once.

MAKING BOMBES WITH TWO MIXTURES
Bombes may be made with two mixtures, one as the lining and the other as the filling. Chill the mold, then line it to a thickness of 1 inch with one of the frozen mixtures, put the other frozen mixture in the center and fill up with the first mixture. Cover and freeze as for a plain bombe. Good combinations are vanilla and raspberry ice cream, coffee and vanilla ice cream, chocolate and orange ice cream. Three flavors may be used if desired.

PRALINE BOMBE

$\frac{1}{2}$ *cup sugar*
$\frac{2}{3}$ *cup hot water*
4 egg yolks, beaten
4 oz almond toffee, crushed
1 teaspoon vanilla
pinch of salt
1$\frac{1}{4}$ cups heavy cream, whipped
1 pint vanilla ice cream

Put the sugar into a heavy skillet and heat very

gently until coffee-colored: add the hot water, redissolve the caramel and cool. Put the egg yolks in the top of a double boiler over hot water and add the caramel. Stir until the mixture is thick. Cool, add the crushed toffee, vanilla, and salt and fold in the cream. Pour the mixture into a freezing container and freeze until half-set. Line a bombe mold with vanilla ice cream and fill it with the half-frozen praline mixture. (See making bombes above.) Freeze, and turn out just before serving.

BAKED ALASKA

This delicious dessert is sometimes served at a dinner party as a surprise item.

7-inch round sponge cake
1 package (10 oz) frozen raspberries, thawed with liquid reserved
1 pint ice cream
3 egg whites
¾ cup sugar

Preheat the oven to 450°. Place the sponge cake on a flat ovenproof dish and just moisten with the reserved raspberry juice. Put the ice cream in the center of the cake and pile the fruit on top. Beat the egg whites stiffly, beat in half the sugar, then fold in the remaining sugar. Pile the meringue mixture over the cake, covering the cake, ice cream, and fruit completely and taking the meringue down to the dish. Place in the oven immediately and cook for 2 to 3 minutes, or until the outside of the meringue just begins to brown. Serve at once.

VARIATIONS
1. Use fresh crushed fruit, e.g. strawberries, when in season.
2. Sprinkle 1 to 2 tablespoons sherry or rum over the cake before the ice cream is added.
   (See Ices, Mousse, Parfait, Sherbet, Sorbet, and Sundae entries.)

ICELAND MOSS

A lichen closely resembling Irish moss, but darker in color, which grows on barren mountains in Iceland and other northern regions; it is sometimes used in cooking in the same way as Irish moss (see entry).

ICES

Refreshing frozen desserts, made from a sugar syrup flavored with fruit juice or puree. Ices are best made in an ice cream maker, but they can be made in a refrigerator if the mixture is stirred frequently during the freezing, although there will be a certain amount of crystalization. Two especially delicious types of ice are made by adding stiffly beaten egg white or by flavoring with a liqueur. (See Granita, Sherbet, and Sorbet entries.)

LEMON ICE

1 cup sugar
1¼ cups water
rind and juice of 3 lemons
1 egg white, beaten

Dissolve the sugar in the water over a low heat, add the thinly pared lemon rind and boil gently for 10 minutes; leave to cool. Add the lemon juice and strain the mixture into ice-cube trays. Freeze to a mushy consistency. Turn the mixture into a bowl, fold in the egg white, mixing thoroughly, replace in the tray, and refreeze.

ORANGE ICE

½ cup sugar
⅔ cup water
1 tablespoon lemon juice
grated rind of 1 orange
grated rind of 1 lemon
juice of 3 oranges and 1 lemon, mixed (about 1¼ cups)
1 egg white, beaten

Dissolve the sugar in the water over a low heat, bring to a boil and boil gently for 10 minutes. Add 1 tablespoon lemon juice. Put the grated fruit rinds in a bowl, add the boiling syrup and leave until cold. Add the mixed fruit juices and strain into an ice-cube tray. Freeze to a mushy consistency. Turn the mixture into a bowl; fold in the egg white, mixing thoroughly, replace in the tray and freeze.

Other flavors of ices (e.g. raspberry, strawberry) can be made by adding 1¼ cups fruit puree and the juice of ½ lemon to 1¼ cups of the syrup; continue as above.

PINEAPPLE ICE

2¼ cups sugar
2 cups water
2 cups unsweetened pineapple juice
4 envelopes gelatin

Dissolve the sugar in the water over a low heat. Bring to a boil and boil for 5 minutes. Strain and add pineapple juice, reserving $\frac{1}{2}$ cup. Soak gelatin in reserved juice, then dissolve over a gentle heat and stir into liquid. Allow to cool.

Pour into a well-chilled tray, put into freezer, and leave for 30 minutes. Turn into a bowl and beat. Return to tray and freeze for 40 to 50 minutes, or until frozen.

ICING

(See Frosting, Glaze, Royal Icing entries.)

INDIAN CORN

(See Corn entry.)

INFUSING

To extract the flavor from such things as spices by steeping them in a liquid, as when preparing milk to make Béchamel sauce. Tea and coffee are also infusions. The usual method of making an infusion is to add boiling liquid, to cover and leave in a warm place, without further cooking or heating.

IODINE

An element found in salt beds and some seaweeds and stored in the thyroid. A minute amount of iodine is necessary in the diet for the prevention of goiter. Usually there is enough present in drinking water, in fish and some vegetables (watercress and onions). In inland areas, however, such as Switzerland and the Great Lakes region of the United States, there is a deficiency. Under these conditions, it is usually considered advisable to use iodized salt in cooking.

IRISH COFFEE

A beverage that doubles as dessert, served in a stemmed glass. For each serving you will need: 3 small lumps of sugar, $\frac{3}{4}$ cup hot coffee, 1 oz Irish whiskey and whipped cream to float on top.

IRISH (CARRAGEEN) MOSS

A dark purple or green seaweed, *Chondrus crispus*, found on many coasts of northern Europe. When dried and bleached it can be used as a substitute for gelatin. Commercially, it is used as a thickening agent.

IRON

Nutritionally, iron is essential as a component part of hemoglobin – the substance which gives the red color to blood. The amount contained in the body at birth is sufficient to last for the first six months of life; the level is gradually raised by the iron contained in the diet.

The daily requirement of iron varies from about 6 mg for babies under one year to about 15 mg for expectant or nursing mothers and during adolescence. Iron is lost from the body when any bleeding occurs and possibly as a result of the daily wear and tear of the tissues. Insufficient iron in the blood stream will eventually lead to anemia. General symptoms include tiredness, lassitude, irritability, and loss of appetite.

Not all the iron contained in food is available to the body, but eggs, liver and other meat, green vegetables, and dried fruits are useful sources. Iron is now added to flour which makes this a good source.

ISINGLASS

This is a pure and practically tasteless form of gelatin prepared from the air bladders of fish, especially sturgeons. It is used commercially to clarify beer and wine. It is also used to preserve eggs.

JAGGERY

A brown sugar made from palm juice; also brown cane sugar.

JAM

Jammaking is a useful method of preserving fruit and it always tastes superior to commercial varieties. Even if fruit is not available from the garden, it can be bought when in season and at its cheapest. However, it is important that it is of good quality.

To obtain consistently good results – a jam that looks clear, has an attractive color, is set but not stiff and will keep well – demands care, not guesswork, but the process is not difficult.

Jam sets because of a substance called pectin which is released when the fruit is boiled with sugar. The acid in the fruit and the added sugar are both important in the setting process. The correct amount of sugar will also prevent fermentation or crystalization. During the boiling, some of the water evaporates until the correct sugar concentration is obtained.

The Fruit

This should be of good quality, freshly picked, dry and underripe rather than overripe. Some fruits, such as cooking apples and currants are rich in pectin and acid and easily set as jam. Apricots, rhubarb, and strawberries need added pectin; sweet apples, figs and peaches (also beets, carrots, and turnips, which are sometimes mixed with fruit in jammaking) need added acid. Ripe blackberries and strawberries, sweet cherries and pears need both acid and pectin.

The following fruits are sufficiently rich in both pectin and acid for jammaking:

Apples (sour)	Greengages
Blackberries	Lemons
(underripe)	Limes
Crab apples	Oranges (Seville)
Cranberries	Plums (some
Currants	varieties)
Damsons	Quinces
Gooseberries	Raspberries (slightly
Grapefruit	underripe)

PECTIN

If there is any doubt as to whether a given fruit has sufficient pectin, test as follows: after simmering a small sample of the fruit in a little water until the skins are soft (and without adding any sugar), take 1 teaspoon juice, cool it and add 3 teaspoons methylated spirit; shake gently and leave for 1 minute. If there is plenty of pectin in the fruit, a transparent, jellylike lump will form; but if there is very little pectin, the clot will be broken up into small scattered pieces. In this case, it will be necessary to do one of the following: use less water in making the jam and cook it longer; mix the fruit with some that is rich in pectin; add the juice of a fruit rich in pectin (see recipe); or add a pectin extract in liquid or powder form.

According to the type of fruit, $\frac{2}{3}$ cup homemade pectin extract may be needed with 2 to 5 lb of fruit. (If a manufacturer's extract is used, follow the instructions as to quantities.) Boil the fruit for a short time, add the sugar and continue to boil for a little while, then remove the pan from the heat and add the pectin extract. Stir well, test for a set and jar and cover at once. The short boiling time conserves the fresh fruit flavor and shortens the whole operation, so some people prefer to use pectin extract even when making jam with fruit of good pectin content.

GOOSEBERRY, RED CURRANT, OR APPLE JUICE (PECTIN EXTRACT)

Wash 6 lb fruit (slice apples if used), and simmer it in a pan with 5 cups water until tender, then mash well and strain through a jelly bag. Remove the pulp left in the bag, add enough water to make a mash and simmer again for 1 to $1\frac{1}{2}$ hours, then strain again. Mix the two extracts, which should give a fairly thick liquid; if it is slightly watery, reduce it by boiling. When a good pectin clot is obtained on testing with methylated spirit, the juice may be jarred and sterilized for future use. Bring it to a boil and pour immediately into hot, clean preserving jars, filling them to the brim. Seal at once with hot lids, place the jars on a rack in a pan of hot water, just deep enough to cover them, bring the water to a boil and boil for 5 minutes.

ACID IN JAMMAKING

A certain amount of acid is required to enable the pectin present to set the jam and convert some of the cane or beet sugar into invert sugar, which prevents the jam from crystalizing. Some fruits (and vegetables) are lacking in acid and extra must be added in the form of a more acid fruit juice or some tartaric acid. (To tell whether acid is required see list page 222.) To every 4 lb acid-deficient fruit add one of the following:

$\frac{2}{3}$ cup currant or gooseberry juice
2 tablespoons lemon juice
$\frac{1}{4}$ teaspoon tartaric or citric acid

Jammaking Processes

PREPARATION OF THE JARS
Wash them thoroughly, rinse in clear water and invert to drain. Dry in a warm oven.

PREPARATION OF THE FRUIT
Remove stalks, leaves, and any damaged parts, then wash and drain the fruit. Remove pits from large fruits with a knife and use a cherry pitter for cherries (tie the pits in a cheesecloth bag to boil with the jam). Apricot and plum pits can be cracked and the kernels mixed with the fruit.

'BREAKING-DOWN' PROCESS
Water and/or acid are added, according to the particular recipe, and the fruit is simmered gently until it is completely cooked. With fruits rich in pectin, the yield of jam is increased by adding a fairly large quantity of water. Fruits lacking in pectin, such as strawberries, are simmered with acid alone. This cooking is best done in a preserving pan, but a large saucepan may be used. Aluminum, enamel, brass, and copper pans are suitable; in the case of both brass and copper it is essential to see that the inside surface is immaculately clean and free from discoloration.

BOILING WITH SUGAR
The quantity depends on the pectin strength of the fruit; if too little sugar is used, the preserve is apt to go moldy on keeping; if too much is used, it may tend to crystalize. The sugar should form about 60 percent by weight of the finished preserve, the amount varying according to the amount of water added, which in turn depends on the pectin content of the fruit. The following table shows the average proportions:

$2\frac{3}{4}$ cups sugar to 1 lb fruit rich in pectin
$2\frac{1}{4}$ cups to 1 lb fruit fairly rich in pectin
$1\frac{1}{2}$ cups sugar to 1 lb fruit weak in pectin

Warm the sugar before adding it, so that it dissolves more rapidly. Once it has dissolved, boil the jam quickly until setting point is reached. Too little boiling will not convert a sufficient proportion of the sugar into invert sugar and the jam will therefore crystalize, while overboiling makes too much invert sugar, producing a syrupy consistency.

TESTING FOR SETTING POINT
There are several methods, number 1 being the simplest.
1. Place 1 tablespoon jam on a saucer and leave it to cool. If a skin can be seen on the surface when the little finger is pulled lightly across, setting point has been reached.
2. Drop some of the jam from the side of a clean spoon that has been dipped in cold water; if it is at setting point it will not run off easily, but the drops will fall very slowly and run together.
3. Use a jelly thermometer: setting point is reached at a temperature of 220°, provided the fruit has been cooked sufficiently, before the sugar is added.

FILLING THE JARS
Remove the scum from the surface. Strawberry jam, shred marmalade, etc., in which fruit or peel

is likely to rise, should be allowed to cool until the jam thickens enough to hold the fruit throughout before it is jarred. (Do not leave for too long, however, or mold spores may be introduced.) Other types, such as plum, can be put at once into the prepared jars. Pour the jam into a jug and fill the jars nearly to the top. Cover the jam immediately with a round of waxed paper, making sure the disk touches the whole surface of the jam. Put on a round of cellophane, wiping it with a damp cloth to make it stretch and insure a good seal; when the jars are cold, label them with the name of the jam and the date.

(See various fruit entries, such as Currant, Raspberry, etc., for individual recipes.)

MAKING JAM FROM CANNED FRUIT

Drain the fruit in order to weigh it and calculate the sugar needed, but save the liquid, which should be used instead of water in making the jam. Otherwise, make in the usual way.

MAKING JAM FROM FRUIT PULP

Fruit which has been preserved as pulp can be made into jam at any time convenient. To ascertain the amount of sugar required, use the pectin test; weigh the pulp and add sugar. (See boiling with sugar.) Add the sugar as soon as the excess water has been boiled off and finish the jam in the usual way.

JAM SAUCE

5 tablespoons jam, sieved
$\frac{2}{3}$ cup water or fruit juice
$2\frac{1}{2}$ teaspoons arrowroot

$2\frac{1}{2}$ tablespoons cold water
squeeze of lemon juice, optional

Warm the jam and water and simmer for five minutes. Blend the arrowroot and cold water to a smooth cream and stir in the jam mixture. Return the sauce to the pan and heat, stirring, until it thickens and clears. Add the lemon juice before serving. Serve hot or cold.

Note: A thicker sauce is made by just melting the jam on its own over a gentle heat and adding a little lemon juice.

JAMAICA PEPPER

(See Allspice entry.)

JAMBALAYA

A stew of meat, poultry, and/or seafood with rice that originated in the United States as a Cajun country dish in the Louisiana bayous; with refinements, it is now claimed by New Orleans Créoles as well. Jambalaya was probably a ham dish originally. The rice, simmering in stock with the other ingredients, absorbs the various flavors of the cooking foods.

HAM AND SHRIMP JAMBALAYA

$1\frac{1}{2}$ cups diced ham
$\frac{3}{4}$ lb shrimp, shelled
2 tablespoons olive oil
1 tablespoon butter
2 onions, finely chopped
1 clove garlic, minced
1 cup rice

TESTING FOR THE SETTING POINT
1. Place jam on a saucer; leave it to cool. It is ready if a skin can be seen on the surface when a finger is pulled lightly across it.

2. Dip a spoon into cold water then dip into the jam; if setting point has been reached the jam will drip slowly from the spoon.

3. Setting point is reached when the sugar boiling thermometer reaches a temperature of 220°.

3 cups chicken broth
½ green pepper, finely chopped
1 can (8 oz) tomatoes
1 bay leaf
salt
pepper
cayenne pepper

Sauté the ham and shrimp in the oil and butter until the shrimp are partly done. Remove the shrimp with a slotted spoon and add the onion and garlic and sauté until the onion is soft. Add the rice and cook, stirring, until it is golden brown. Pour in the broth, green pepper, tomatoes, and bay leaf. Cover and simmer 15 minutes. Add the shrimp and cook 5 minutes longer, until the rice is done. Season with salt, pepper, and cayenne.

JAPONICA FRUIT

The fruits of the ornamental Japonica tree, sometimes used to make jam or jelly.

JELLY

The principle of jellymaking is similar to that of jammaking, but it is even more important that the fruit should have a good pectin and acid content, since a runny jelly is very difficult to manipulate. Most fruits can be made into jelly, except a few that are poor in acid or pectin, such as strawberries and cherries.

There are two processes in jellymaking: first to extract the juice; and second to set it by boiling it with sugar. For the first, the fruit is put into a pan with water (the amount varying according to the pectin content) and is then cooked gently to a mash, so that the tissues are broken down and juice extracted; it is next strained through a scalded jelly bag, plenty of time being allowed for the juice to drip – it should not be squeezed through or the jelly will be cloudy. Fruits rich in pectin may be given a second boiling; the pulp in the bag is boiled again with more water, then strained and the two extracts are mixed together.

For the second stage the extract is weighed and an equal weight of sugar is added; or the juice can be measured and 2¾ cups sugar allowed for each 2½ cups. (Some authorities consider that 1 lb sugar to 2½ cups of juice gives a better set, less sugar being used if the pectin content is low and more if it is high.) Boil briskly until the preserve jells when tested on a cold saucer, taking off any frothy scum that is thrown up during the boiling process; if this is difficult to remove, strain the jelly through a cheesecloth into the jars. Cover in the same way as jam, and store in a cool, dry place.

(See individual fruits for individual recipes.)

JERKED BEEF (JERKY)

Beef cut into wafer-thin strips and dried or cured in the sun. The name is a corruption of the Spanish *charqui* used in South America.

JEROBOAM

A large bottle of wine. In champagne, it is equivalent to a double magnum, or four bottles.

JERUSALEM ARTICHOKE

(See Artichoke entry.)

FILLING THE JARS
1. Place the warmed jam jars on a wooden board to prevent them from slipping and, using a jug, pour jam into warmed jars.

2. Make sure that the jam reaches top of each jar before placing a waxed disk on top of the jam to completely cover the surface.

3. Place a round of dampened plastic wrap over top of each jar, secure with elastic band. When cold label, giving the date and contents of jar.

JICAMA

A root tuber of the tropical Americas. It resembles the rutabaga in appearance and the water chestnut in taste. In Mexico they are used as potatoes are in the United States, but may also be eaten raw, sprinkled with lime juice and a dusting of cayenne pepper or sugar, according to taste. These juicy vegetables are found in the United States in West Coast Chinese markets.

JOHANNISBERG RIESLING OR WHITE RIESLING

A United States varietal white wine produced in California from the grape of the same name. Besides medium-dry to sweet Johannisberg rieslings, California also produces Late Harvest wines similar to the German Auslese, Beerenauslese and Trockenbeerenauslese wines. This late-maturing grape is the same one that produces Germany's finest Mosel and Rhine wines.

JOHN DORY (ST PIERRE)

A European marine fish, rather ugly, with a curiously shaped mouth and compressed body; called John Dory in Great Britain and St Pierre in France. The skin is an attractive golden color and the white flesh has a delicious flavor.

John Dory may be cooked whole by baking or by sautéing in butter but it is usually filleted and cooked in any way suitable for sole. Porgy is a good substitute in any recipe.

JOHNNYCAKE

A primitive cornmeal bread that was originally an American Indian food. No two experts agree on the origin of the name, recipe, or color of the cornmeal used. Some say the name is a corruption of Shawnee, the tribe that passed the recipe onto the settlers, while others claim the original was a Journey Cake, made by circuit riders and others going on long trips. Rhode Islanders hold that johnnycakes are made with white cornmeal.

RHODE ISLAND JOHNNYCAKE

1 cup white cornmeal
1 teaspoon salt
1¼ cups boiling water

Combine the dry ingredients and stir in the boiling water to make a thick batter. Drop by tablespoons onto a well-greased skillet and cook about 10 minutes, turning once.

JOULE

A unit of energy or work; 4,186 joules of heat energy are required to raise the temperature of 1 kg of water through 1° celsius.

1 kilocalorie (k cal), equal to 1,000 Calories, will supply the same heat. As joules are so small they are often expressed as kilojoules (kj) or megajoules (MJ).

Food tables and labels in Europe may quote Calories and/or joules.

JUGGED HARE

(See Hare entry.)

JUICE

The liquid part of fruits and vegetables; the word is also sometimes applied to the liquid from meat.

The juices of fruits and vegetables can be extracted to use as a drink or in cooking, some of them are especially valuable for their vitamin C content. They are most easily extracted by using an electric squeezer, which obtains the liquid very rapidly, leaving the fibers behind. Many whole fruits or vegetables can be pulped in a blender. The pulp can then be strained to remove the fibers if desired, but for most purposes the pulp is sufficiently pureed to make straining unnecessary. Tomato, carrot, mixed vegetable, orange, and many other juices obtained in this way make delicious drinks. Fruit juice can be extracted manually in a hand press or (with suitable types) on a squeezer. Tomato juice can be obtained by putting tomatoes through a sieve.

The commercial canned products are very good and save time and trouble. Many of these consist of the natural juice and sometimes they are sweetened; certain permitted additives can be included but the label must state what they are.

JUJUBE

Originally the name of a shrub of the buckthorn family growing in the East, the fruit of which is eaten candied or made into jelly. The name is also applied to a cherry candy. Jujubes are sometimes medicated or scented.

JULEP

A drink popular in the southern United States, made traditionally with bourbon and mint.

MINT JULEP

1 teaspoon sugar
6 sprigs of mint, crushed
bourbon
lemon

Half fill a julep glass or silver goblet with shaved ice and add the sugar and crushed mint. Cover with the bourbon and mix well. Pack the glass with shaved ice and let stand until frosted. Garnish with lemon and mint and serve with a straw.

JULIENNE

The name of a clear vegetable soup first made by a noted eighteenth-century French chef named Jean Julien.

The term is also used for julienne strips – thin pieces of vegetables, meat, or poultry, shaped like matchsticks, which are used to garnish soups, stews, etc. Cut the peeled vegetable into oblong-shaped blocks of equal size, cut these into very thin slices, place one on top of the other and slice down in the opposite direction, to give matchstick pieces. Blanch in boiling salted water, put under running cold water, then drain and add to the dish just before serving.

JUNIPER BERRY

The fruit of the juniper tree, which grows throughout the northern hemisphere. The small, dark, purple-blue, aromatic berries (which take two years to ripen) are used to flavor sauces, stuffings, gin, and medicines.

JUNKET

A dessert made of curds, produced by treating milk with rennet. The action of the rennet on the milk protein makes it easily digested, so junket is very suitable for children and invalids.

KAFFIR OR KAFIR CORN

(See Millet entry.)

KALE (KAIL)

A green, curly-leaved vegetable of the cabbage family; unlike the cabbage, however, it does not form a head.

Kale has a good flavor when picked young and is a rich source of vitamins A and C. Prepare and cook it like cabbage, discarding the tough midribs.

KASHA

Buckwheat groats, much used in Russian and Jewish cooking. Kasha is often part of the cholent, the bean stew started before sundown Friday so it can be eaten hot on the Sabbath. Kasha is also served as the starch of a meal.

KASHA VARNITCHKES

1 cup finely chopped onions
2½ tablespoons chicken fat
1 cup cooked kasha
1½ cups cooked broad noodles, drained
salt
pepper

Sauté the onions in the chicken fat until browned. Toss with the kasha and noodles and season with salt and pepper.

KEBAB

(See Shish Kebab entry.)

KEDGEREE

A dish of Anglo-Indian origin, consisting of rice, cooked white or smoked fish and usually hard-cooked eggs. It is traditionally eaten for breakfast, but can be served for supper or a light lunch, accompanied by a fresh salad.

KEDGEREE

1 lb smoked haddock
¾ cup long-grain rice
2 hard-cooked eggs
6 tablespoons butter or margarine
salt
cayenne pepper
chopped parsley

Cook and flake the fish. Cook the rice in the usual way and drain if necessary. Shell the eggs, chop one and slice the other into rings. Melt the butter in a saucepan, add the fish, rice, chopped egg, salt, and cayenne and stir over a moderate heat for about 5 minutes, until hot. Pile the mixture into a warmed dish and garnish with chopped parsley and the sliced egg.

KEFIR

A cultured milk product which originated in Russia and Poland. It is made from whole or skimmed cows' milk to which Kefir grain is added. It differs from yogurt in that additional cultures are introduced which produce alcohol. Kefir is a milky white, slightly greasy, homogenous product resembling liquid cream. It has a lactic flavor and usually no additional flavor is introduced. (See Koumiss entry.)

KETCHUP

(See Catsup entry.)

KID

A young goat. Kid is seldom eaten in the United States, but is popular in some Mediterranean regions. The flesh is sweet and tender if properly prepared but inclined to be dry and a little lacking in flavor. Marination and seasoning are recommended.

Kid is usually roasted whole, like suckling pig. Prepare and cook as for young lamb.

KIDNEY BEAN

A New World bean, a member of the haricot family. It was brought by sixteenth-century sailors to Italy, where both the red and white (the latter known as cannellini) varieties of the kidney-shaped bean still flourish. The red kidney bean is widely distributed in the United States and is popular in Mexico as the *frijol rojo*, or red bean. A well-known Mexican dish is refried beans.

FRIJOLES REFRITOS CON QUESO (REFRIED BEANS WITH CHEESE)

¼ cup (or more) lard
1 can (16 oz) kidney beans
½ cup cubed Monterey jack cheese

Heat 1 tablespoon of the fat in a skillet and add the beans. Mash and cook slowly, gradually stirring in the remaining lard. Add more lard if necessary; the beans should be dry but creamy. Just before serving, stir in the cheese. The beans are ready as soon as the cheese is melted.

KIDNEYS

The kidneys of many different animals are eaten, from the small ones of rabbits and hares to the large beef kidneys. Like other forms of meat, they supply protein; they are rich in iron and contain a certain amount of other minerals and vitamin A and niacin.

Kidneys give a rich, distinctive flavor to steak pie; they also make good casserole dishes, stews, and curries, as well as a filling for omelets. Broiled or fried sheep's, pig's and calf's kidneys may be served for breakfast or as part of a mixed grill (see Broiling entry). Beef kidneys require long, slow, moist cooking.

Preparation: Remove excess fat (suet) surrounding the kidney, then remove the skin. Cut it through at the thickest part to the center fatty "core," peel off the outer skin and cut out the core, using kitchen scissors. Wash and dry.

KIDNEYS WITH SHERRY

2 tablespoons butter
1 onion, chopped
2 cloves garlic, crushed
2 tablespoons flour
⅔ cup stock
2 tablespoons chopped parsley
1 bay leaf
2 tablespoons oil
8 lamb's kidneys, prepared
6 tablespoons dry sherry
salt
pepper

Heat the butter and sauté the onion until transparent. Add the garlic, sprinkle in the flour and stir to blend. Gradually add the stock, stirring until thick and smooth. Add the parsley and bay leaf and leave over a low heat. Heat the oil, add the kidneys and brown evenly; transfer them to the sauce, draining carefully. Add the sherry to the pan drippings, and bring to a boil, add to the kidneys and mix all together. Simmer for 5 minutes, remove the bay leaf and adjust the seasoning.

KIELBASY (POLISH SAUSAGE)

A reddish brown sausage that is most familiar when sold in a ring. Fresh varieties must be cooked longer than cured ones.

KILOJOULE

A unit of energy 100 times greater than a joule.

KING CRAB

One of the largest edible crabs, with a leg span of 4 to 5 feet, found in northern Pacific waters and the Bering Sea, off the coast of Alaska. A similar variety is found in cold southern Pacific waters off the coasts of Chile and southern Australia. The easily extracted leg meat is sold in chunks canned or frozen while the body meat is packaged shredded in cans.

KIPPER

A herring split, salted and dried in smoke. Kippers can be broiled, baked, fried, or poached. If very salty, trim them, place in a bowl and pour boiling water over them. Leave for 3 minutes, then finish as directed below, cooking the skin side first. Frozen kippers should be cooked as directed on the package.

To broil: Cook slowly for 4 to 5 minutes on each side.

To bake: Cover with greased paper and cook for 15 minutes in a 400° oven.

To fry: Cook in a very little fat for about 4 minutes on each side.

To poach: Place in a bowl, pour boiling water over and leave for 10 to 12 minutes. Alternatively, the kippers can be cooked in a skillet of hot water: this method does away with the disagreeable odor accompanying the other methods.

KIR

(See Cassis entry.)

KIRSCH OR KIRSCHWASSER

A colorless liqueur made from black cherries, produced in Germany and Switzerland. The special flavor comes from the crushed pits of the fruit; glucose is added for sweetening. Kirsch is excellent for adding to fruit salads and desserts.

KIWI FRUIT (CHINESE GOOSEBERRY)

An oval fruit, $2\frac{1}{2}$ to $3\frac{1}{2}$ inches in length, with a brown furry skin and a delicate green interior. It is native to China and has been grown in New Zealand since 1906. Its name, given it by New Zealand merchandizers, identifies it with that country and with the bird of the same name whose body it resembles. The beautiful coloring of the kiwi flesh and its concentric pattern of tiny seeds makes it a favorite for fresh fruit tarts.

KNAIDLACH

A small dumpling made with matzo meal instead of flour for the Jewish festival of Passover. It may be served in soup (see separate Dumpling entry) or as a dessert.

CHEESE KNAIDLACH

2 cups pot cheese
2 eggs, separated
$\frac{1}{2}$ teaspoon salt
$\frac{1}{4}$ cup matzo meal
3 tablespoons butter, melted
2 tablespoons sugar

Puree the cheese with the egg yolks in a blender. Stir in the salt, matzo meal, butter, and sugar. Beat the whites until stiff and fold in. Refrigerate for 30 minutes to 1 hour. Moisten your hands and form the mixture into balls, about 2 tablespoonfuls in each. Cook in boiling water until the balls rise to the surface. Drain and serve with cinnamon, sugar and sour cream if desired.

KNEADING

Working dough with the hands to blend and to obtain a required consistency. This is done by stretching and folding on a floured surface. It is a particularly important process in breadmaking. It can be done in an electric mixer if there is a dough hook attachment. (See Bread for kneading diagrams.)

KNISH

A baked Jewish pastry with a filling of potatoes, cheese, meat, or chicken. It may be served as an entrée or, in a smaller version, as a cocktail appetizer. Knishes may be filled like turnovers or prepared like a jelly roll and sliced before baking.

KOHLRABI

A stem vegetable, with a turniplike globe (the enlarged stem), topped with curly green foliage, which grows above ground. It is a member of the cabbage family and leaves of the young vegetables can be eaten.

To prepare and cook: Choose young, small globes. Wash, peel, and cut into cubes or slices (very young ones can be scrubbed and left whole) and boil in a small quantity of salted water until tender – 30 to 50 minutes. Drain and toss in butter and chopped parsley or serve with a white sauce, garnished with chopped chives. Alternatively, steam for 30 to 50 minutes until tender. Kohlrabi can also be served cold with vinaigrette sauce.

KOLA NUT

The nut of the Kola tree, which grows in Africa and is chewed by natives for the caffeine that it

contains. Kola nuts are used in pharmaceuticals and in "cola" beverages.

KOSHER FOOD

Food prepared especially for the Jewish community in accordance with their religious rules.

Certain foods are forbidden and restrictions govern the consumption of others.

Only fish which have fins and scales (not shellfish) may be eaten; game birds and all pig products are forbidden. Milk and meat may not be cooked or eaten together. Separate and easily distinguishable sets of cooking utensils, china, cutlery, table linen, bowls, and working surfaces are required for meat and milk. All manufactured products must be known to be free from non-kosher ingredients.

KOSHER SALT

A coarse salt used in kosher cooking. Unlike table salt, it contains no fillers to prevent it from caking and is therefore ideal for use in canning and pickling as it will not cloud the liquid contents of the jars.

KOUMISS

A weak alcoholic sour beverage similar to kefir (see Kefir entry). Koumiss is made from mares' milk which has a fat content of 1.7 percent. A culture and yeast are added to give the sour taste. It is a milky white mixture with a gray tinge; the texture is similar to that of cream except that it is permeated by small gas bubbles. A characteristic odor reflects the alcoholic content and sour taste.

In the Soviet Union, where koumiss originated, there were numerous sanitoria where koumiss therapy was available for the treatment of tuberculosis. As this is no longer such a common illness, many of these institutions have now closed. Many cultured milk products were thought to have therapeutic value but there is no modern evidence of this.

KREPLACH

Small triangles of noodle dough encasing a filling of kasha or potatoes, meat or liver, cheese or chicken. A prominent feature of Jewish cuisine, kreplach are usually served boiled in soup, but may be fried after a preliminary boiling of the noodle and its filling.

KROMESKI

A Russian and Polish dish, consisting of a mixture of ground poultry, game, or meat, bound to a stiff paste with sauce and wrapped in bacon, then coated with batter and fried.

KUGEL

A Jewish pudding-soufflé that is served as a main dish, side dish or dessert depending upon its contents.

POTATO KUGEL

2 eggs
2 cups grated potatoes
$\frac{1}{4}$ cup potato flour
$\frac{1}{2}$ teaspoon baking powder
salt
pepper
2 tablespoons grated onion
$2\frac{1}{2}$ tablespoons melted butter

Beat the eggs until thick and light-colored. Stir in the remaining ingredients. Pour into a greased 4-cup soufflé dish and bake in a 350° oven for about 50 minutes, or until browned.

NOODLE KUGEL

$\frac{1}{2}$ lb medium noodles, cooked and drained
$\frac{1}{4}$ cup melted chicken fat or butter
2 eggs
$\frac{1}{3}$ cup sugar
2 teaspoons ground cinnamon
$\frac{1}{2}$ cup raisins, soaked in hot water

Toss the noodles with the melted fat. Beat the eggs with the sugar and cinnamon. Add to the noodles with the raisins and toss to mix well. Place in a greased 5- to 6-cup soufflé dish and bake in a 350° oven for 30 minutes.

KUGELHOPF

A French Alsatian yeast cake, similar in texture to the savarin, containing currants and almonds and baked in a fluted tube pan.

KULICH

A Russian yeast cake, baked in a cylindrical mold and served at Easter with Pashka (see separate entry).

KULICH

1 cup milk
2 packages active dry yeast
⅓ cup warm water
4½–5 cups all-purpose flour
½ cup sugar
1 teaspoon salt
3 eggs, beaten
¾ cup butter, melted
¼ cup blanched shredded almonds
¼ cup candied citron
¼ cup candied orange peel
½ cup raisins
1½ teaspoons ground cardamom
½ teaspoon vanilla

FONDANT ICING

½ cup powdered sugar
2 teaspoons warm water

Scald the milk and cool to 105° to 115°. Dissolve the yeast in the warm water and stir in the milk, ½ cup of the flour and the sugar and salt. Let stand in a warm place until doubled in bulk.

Stir the eggs into the risen batter and then alternately stir in the butter and remaining flour. Knead on a lightly floured board until smooth and elastic; this may take much longer than ordinary doughs. Place in a greased bowl, cover and let rise in a warmed place until doubled in bulk.

Punch down the dough and knead in the remaining ingredients. Divide in half and form into two balls. Place in two well-greased 1-lb coffee cans and let rise until the dough begins to puff over the top of the cans. Bake in a 375° oven, on a low rack, for 40 to 45 minutes, or until browned. Remove from the cans and cool on a wire rack.

Combine the powdered sugar with the water to make an icing. Spoon it over the tops of the cakes.

KÜMMEL

A sweet, colorless liqueur, originally made in the Baltic countries, which is flavored with caraway seeds, cumin, and fennel. It is now also distilled in England, France, and Holland.

KÜMMELKÄSE

A German cheese, flavored with caraway. Good with cocktails.

KUMQUAT (CUMQUAT)

A small subtropical fruit of a bright yellow color, with an edible rind, juicy pulp and a sweet though slightly bitter flavor. Kumquats are eaten raw as dessert and they can also be cooked or used in preserves. The Chinese make a delicious sweetmeat by preserving them in sugar. Kumquats may be baked as follows: cover the fruit with sugar syrup and bake in a 350° oven for about 50 minutes, or until tender. Serve with whipped cream or ice cream.

KVASS

A home-brewed drink made from rye, malt, and yeast and often flavored with mint. It is made in the Soviet Union.

LACTOSE

A type of sugar (disaccharide) found in milk. As it is very much less sweet in taste than cane sugar, it is sometimes used for invalids to make drinks with a high energy content without being sickly sweet. It is also used in milk formulas for babies.

Lactose aids the absorption of calcium in the intestine.

LADYFINGER

A small sponge cake, about the size and shape of a finger. They are served as cookies or used to line molds for elaborate Charlotte desserts.

LADYFINGERS

3 eggs, separated
pinch of salt
½ cup sugar
½ teaspoon vanilla
⅔ cup all-purpose flour
powdered sugar

Beat the egg whites with the salt until stiff. Gradually beat in the sugar. Fold in the vanilla and the broken egg yolks. Sift the flour over the mixture and fold in.

Using a pastry bag, pipe the batter onto 2 greased and floured baking sheets. The fingers should be about 1 inch wide and about the length of the middle finger. Lines drawn in the flour will help keep the cakes a consistent length. Sprinkle with powdered sugar and let stand 5 minutes. Knock off the excess sugar and bake in a 325° oven for 12 to 15 minutes, or until beige in color. Allow to cool on the pans.

LAGER

A type of beer which can be dark or pale. For centuries it was made in Bohemia and for a long time in Germany and elsewhere. In many countries it is now produced on a massive scale in a lighter form. Although based on hops, the process is slightly different from beer. Lager is a carbonated drink which is best served chilled.

LAKE TROUT

Any of several species of game trout found in North American lakes as far south as the Great Lakes. There are several European species as well. Small specimens are prepared in the same way as other trout, while large ones can be cooked in any of the variety of ways that salmon is cooked.

LAMB

The meat from a sheep under one year old. (For Mutton, see separate entry.) Lamb should be light in color and firm in texture; the fat should be firm and white and there should be a fair proportion of it in the cuts of meat.

Cuts of Lamb and Methods of Cooking

Leg	Roast, boil
Loin	Roast; fry or broil chops
Rib chops	Roast, braise; fry or broil cutlets
Middle neck or scrag	Stew, braise, make into soups
Breast	Roast slowly, stew
Shoulder	Roast

Roast Lamb

Cut	Time when cooked at 300°–325°
Leg – plain	30 to 35 minutes per lb
boned and stuffed	40 to 45 minutes per lb
Shoulder – plain	30 to 35 minutes per lb
boned and rolled	40 to 45 minutes per lb
boned and stuffed	40 to 45 minutes per lb
Rib	35 to 45 minutes per lb
Crown roast	25 to 30 minutes per lb
stuffed	30 minutes per lb
Loin – plain	1 hour 45 minutes to 2 hours
boned and rolled	40 to 45 minutes per lb
boned and stuffed	40 to 45 minutes per lb
Breast – boned and rolled	1 hour 30 minutes

Note: Always calculate the cooking time of stuffed roasts by weighing them when stuffed.

Frozen lamb can be thawed overnight in a refrigerator and cooked as above. It can also be cooked in the frozen state provided time is allowed for the meat to cook through. A meat thermometer is essential to check this: the temperature should reach 175°–180° when the meat is cooked through. Sear the roast in hot fat in a preheated 450° oven uncovered for 20 minutes, turning once. Reduce the temperature to 350°, cover the meat and cook for 60 minutes per lb, basting frequently.

(See Mutton and Carving entries.)

COUNTRY LAMB POTAGE

1½ lb stewing lamb
2 quarts of water
bouquet garni
8 oz carrots
2 bouillon cubes
¼ cup vegetable oil
1 large onion, sliced
8 oz leeks, sliced and washed
1 large turnip, diced
1 cup cooked macaroni
salt and pepper
chopped parsley

Place the lamb in a saucepan, cover with cold water, bring to a boil, drain and refresh under cold running water. Replace drained meat in pan; cover with the water. Add bouquet garni tied in cheesecloth, carrots and bouillon cubes. Bring to a boil, reduce heat and simmer, covered, for about 1 hour. Cool sufficiently to skim off fat.

Heat the oil in a large saucepan. Add the onion, leeks and turnip; cook over gentle heat, covered, for about 10 minutes. Strain the lamb stock over the vegetables. Strip the meat off the bones, slice the cooked carrots and add to the pan with the pasta. Adjust seasoning. Simmer for about 45 minutes. Add chopped parsley to serve.

LAMB AND POTATO PASTIES

1 tablespoon oil
8 oz potatoes, peeled and diced
1 small onion, diced
12 oz boned lean shoulder of lamb, coarsely ground
1 beef bouillon cube
salt
freshly ground pepper
1 package (17¼ oz) frozen puff pastry, thawed
milk to glaze

Heat the oil in a skillet and gently sauté the potato and onion for 3 to 4 minutes. Remove with a slotted spoon. Sauté meat quickly to seal, then mix with the potato, onion, crumbled bouillon cube, salt and pepper. Cool. Roll out pastry thinly and cut out four 7-inch rounds. Divide the filling between the rounds, brush the edges with milk, then bring the pastry up and seal on top by pressing together with fingertips. Place the pasties on a baking sheet, brush with milk and bake in a 425° oven for 15 minutes; reduce the heat to 350° for a further 20 to 25 minutes.

SPICED LAMB WITH EGGPLANT

2¼ lb lean breast of lamb, boned
2 tablespoons lard
2 medium-sized onions, chopped
1 teaspoon turmeric
1 teaspoon chili powder
1 teaspoon ground cumin
1 teaspoon salt
2½ tablespoons curry paste
¼ cup mango chutney
¾ cup golden seedless raisins
2½ tablespoons peanut butter
1 tablespoon Worcestershire sauce
⅔ cup beef broth
1 lb eggplant, sliced

Grind the lamb coarsely and sauté in the melted lard until brown. Add the onions, spices, salt and curry paste and cook for 5 minutes, stirring. Stir in the chutney, raisins, peanut butter, Worcestershire sauce and broth. Bring to a boil, reduce heat and simmer for 1 hour.

Sprinkle the sliced eggplant and leave for 5 minutes. Rinse and dry thoroughly, add to the pan. Simmer gently for 30 minutes and serve with boiled rice.

LAMB'S FRY

Lamb's liver, sweetbread, heart and some of the inside fat.

LAMB'S WOOL

An old English drink, mentioned by Pepys, made by pouring hot ale over pureed roasted apples and adding sugar and spices.

LAMPREY

An eellike fish of the Atlantic and Mediterranean, which can reach a considerable size.

Formerly considered a great delicacy, lampreys may be prepared like eels, but require longer cooking.

LANCASHIRE CHEESE

A white crumbly English cheese with a clean mild flavor after maturing for four to eight weeks. It has excellent toasting properties so is frequently used for cheese on toast and similar dishes. Traditionally it was sprinkled over Lancashire Hot Pot. Lancashire cheese was originally made in farm kitchens until the factory production of the cheese became well established. A small amount of Farmhouse Lancashire is still available, this being made in the traditional cylindrical shape. Most of the cheese is consumed locally.

LANCASHIRE HOT POT

(See Hot Pot entry.)

LANGOUSTE

The spiny lobster, sometimes called the "sea crayfish," resembles a lobster, but without the big claws.

It is found off the shores of Europe, America, Africa, etc. Langouste is prepared and cooked like lobster. It is sold frozen in supermarkets as "lobster tails."

LANGOUSTINE

(See Dublin Bay Prawn entry.)

LANGUE DE CHAT

A sweet cookie, flat and finger-shaped; also a piece of chocolate shaped in the same way.

LAPWING

(See Plover entry.)

LARD

The inside fat of a hog, which is melted down, freed from fibrous materials and stored in airtight containers for future use. The best-quality lard (sometimes called "leaf" lard) comes from the abdomen and around the kidneys. Ordinary commercial lard comes from fat from all parts of the pig.

Lard is suitable for pastry making, but is inclined to make cakes heavy, so it is better mixed with butter or margarine for this purpose. It is suitable for both deep and shallow frying. As pure lard is 99 percent fat, it does not splutter when heated and it has high "smoking" temperature (i.e., it can be heated to a high temperature – not less than 360° – before it smokes and burns).

LARDING

To insert small strips of pork fat or bacon into the flesh of game birds or meat before cooking, to prevent it from drying out when roasted. A special larding needle is used for the purpose. It is long and has a large eye into which the fat is inserted.

LARDY CAKE

A type of cake made with bread dough, lard, sugar, and dried fruit. It is mostly found in the English counties of Sussex, Wiltshire, and Oxfordshire.

LARK

A small wild bird of northern Europe. Larks may be roasted, broiled, or set in aspic. They are caught by nets and considered a great table delicacy in France, where they are also prized for pâté.

LASAGNE

Wide strips of pasta which can be plain or flavored with spinach (lasagne verdi). They are cooked in salted boiling water until soft, then layered with cooked ground meat in a dish, covered with cheese and tomato sauce and browned in the oven. There are slight variations to this popular Italian dish. Green or mixed salad makes an excellent accompaniment.

LASAGNE AL FORNO

8 oz ground beef
2 cans (16 oz) tomatoes
¼ cup tomato paste
½–1 teaspoon dried marjoram
salt
pepper
1 teaspoon sugar
4 oz lasagne
¾ cup ricotta or cottage cheese
¼ cup grated Parmesan cheese
8 oz Mozzarella cheese

Brown the meat in a skillet. Add the tomatoes, tomato paste, marjoram, seasonings, and sugar; simmer gently for about 30 minutes. Cook the lasagne in boiling salted water according to the package directions; drain well.

Cover the bottom of a fairly deep ovenproof dish with a layer of the tomato and meat sauce. Add half the lasagne, put in another layer of the sauce, then cover with the cheese, using half of each kind.

Repeat these layers with the remaining ingredients, finishing with a layer of cheese. Bake in a 375° oven for 30 minutes, until golden and bubbling on top. Serve at once. The tomato and meat sauce can be replaced by a Bolognese sauce (see Pasta entry).

LAVER

(See Seaweed entry.)

LAYER CAKE

A butter cake baked in two, three, or more separate pans; the layers are put together when cold. Each layer can be spread with jam, cream, butter cream frosting, or other filling and the top or the complete cake may be frosted.

LEAVEN

A substance such as yeast, baking powder, or baking soda used to raise batters, doughs, and pastries. Also a piece of sour dough, kept to ferment the next batch of bread; used in the days before yeast was generally obtainable.

LEAVENING AGENT

Any means whereby air or gas is introduced into bread, cake, pastry or pudding mixtures to make them rise during the cooking process. For example, in the making of sponge cakes, air is introduced by the beating of egg and sugar over hot water, and this air acts as the leavening agent. Batters, such as Yorkshire pudding, depend principally on the conversion of water into steam to make them rise, for the steam has 1,600 times the volume of the original water. The most usual leavening agent, however, is carbon dioxide, produced either by the action of yeast or by chemicals.

For domestic use, the chemical agents most commonly employed to produce the carbon dioxide are baking powder or, when sour milk or some other acidic factor such as chocolate, molasses, or spices are present, baking soda.

The amount of baking powder used varies considerably according to the richness of the mixture and whether any other leavening agent is also being used, e.g., eggs, which introduce air in creamed mixtures.

(See Yeast and Baking Powder entries.)

LEBKUCHEN

A spiced cookie containing honey, nuts, and candied citron peel. Glazed or covered with chocolate, Lebkuchen are made in Germany for Christmas and are a specialty of Nuremberg.

NÜRNBERGER LEBKUCHEN

1 cup honey
1 cup sugar
4 eggs
2 tablespoons cocoa
1 cup milk
2 cups all-purpose flour
½ teaspoon baking soda
¼ teaspoon ground cloves
¼ teaspoon ground cardamom
¼ teaspoon ground ginger
¼ teaspoon ground allspice
½ teaspoon ground cinnamon
½ cup finely chopped citron

FOR GARNISHING
fondant icing
blanched almonds
citron

Beat the honey, sugar, and eggs until thick; beat in the cocoa and milk. Combine the flour, baking soda and spices in a strainer and sift over the honey mixture, stirring it in with the citron. Refrigerate for at least 8 hours.

Roll out the dough ¼ inch thick on a lightly floured surface. Use only a small amount at a time, keeping the rest refrigerated. Cut into small rectangles or triangles and place on a greased baking sheet. Bake in a 400° oven for 10 to 12 minutes or until no imprint remains when touched lightly with the finger. Remove from the sheets and cool on wire racks.

When cool, coat with fondant icing made with ½ cup powdered sugar mixed with ½ teaspoon vanilla and 1 tablespoon warm water. Decorate with almonds and citron.

LEEK

A vegetable belonging to the same family as the onion and garlic, although it does not form a bulb. The flavor is mild but distinctive. The lower part of the stem is covered with earth and therefore remains white. Leeks are excellent in soups and stews and as a vegetable. They supply a small amount of vitamin C.

Preparation and cooking: Remove the coarse outer leaves and cut off the tops and roots. Wash the leeks very thoroughly, splitting them down to within an inch or so from the bottom, to insure that all the grit is removed; if necessary cut them through completely. Leave leeks whole or slice and cook them in boiling salted water until they are tender, 15 to 25 minutes. Drain very thoroughly. Serve coated with butter or a cheese sauce.

CREAM OF LEEK AND POTATO SOUP

4 medium-sized leeks, sliced and thoroughly washed
1 small onion, sliced
3 medium-sized potatoes, peeled and sliced
¼ cup butter
5 cups chicken broth
salt and pepper
¼ cup cream

Lightly sauté the vegetables in the butter for 5 minutes, until soft but not colored. Add the broth, cover and simmer for about 45 minutes until the vegetables are cooked. Puree the soup in an electric blender and return to the pan.

Reheat, season to taste and stir in the cream just before serving.

LEEK AND POTATO BAKE

Choose a dish for baking that is suitable for the table. Serve golden and bubbling; this recipe is especially good with baked pork chops.

1 lb potatoes, peeled and thinly sliced
1 lb leeks, sliced and thoroughly washed
¼ cup grated Cheddar cheese
salt
pepper
1¼ cups milk
1 egg

In a buttered ovenproof dish, layer the potatoes and leeks, sprinkling each layer with half the Cheddar and salt and pepper to taste. Mix together the milk and egg and pour over the dish. Sprinkle the remaining cheese on top. Bake, uncovered, in a 350° oven for 1¼ hours, or until the potatoes are tender.

LEFTOVERS

The food remaining after a meal. Leftovers should be kept to the minimum by buying and cooking only as much food as required, but inevitably there will be some remaining and it is an important part of housekeeping to use these to best advantage.

Leftovers should be stored with care and used as quickly as possible, before they deteriorate. Meat, fish, and milk products, in particular, can become harmful if not treated correctly. Cooked meats and fish should be cooled rapidly and placed in a refrigerator. If they are to be reheated, they should be brought rapidly to the boiling point and allowed to simmer for at least 15 minutes or cooked thoroughly in some other way, and never just warmed through.

(For ways of using leftovers, see Réchauffé entry.)

LEG OF MUTTON

(See Mutton entry.)

LEGUMES

These are the vegetables which consist of seed-bearing pods including peas, beans, lentils, soybeans, peanuts, chickpeas, and kidney beans.

Unlike most vegetables, legumes are a good source of protein and when fresh, they also supply vitamins A and C. Dried legumes, also called pulses, are important in various parts of the world where animal protein foods are scarce. They are also important in vegetarian diet. (See separate entries on individual legumes.)

LEICESTER CHEESE

A mild mellow English cheese (pronounced less-ter) that has much in common with Cheddar. The texture is slightly flaky and the color is a rich orange red due to the addition of annatto. The cheese is famous for its use in Welsh Rarebit; it is also a good dessert cheese.

LEMON

The fruit of the lemon tree, *Citrus limonum*, which is now cultivated in most warm countries; the chief source of United States supply is southern California, producing 80 percent of the U.S. crop. Italy, Sicily, Spain, and Australia are also chief growers. The lemons are usually gathered when green and are ripened in special storehouses. Although those which ripen on the tree have the finest flavor, they decay sooner than those ripened after being picked.

Lemons are an excellent source of vitamin C. Their acid and pectin content make them useful in jammaking and they are often included in marmalade. The rind and juice of lemons are used in small quantities to flavor many sweet and savory dishes and in larger quantities to make desserts, fillings, and beverages such as lemon meringue pie, lemon curd and lemonade and also ice cream and sorbets. Lemon juice can be used instead of vinegar in salad dressings. The essential oil contained in the skin is used to make a flavoring extract; it may be obtained from a fresh lemon by rubbing a sugar cube over the well-washed surface. Lemons are available year-round and a ripe, unbruised lemon stored at about 40° will keep for 8 to 12 weeks.

Slices of lemon can be frozen and used in drinks, for decoration and garnishes.

LEMON CURD

grated rind and juice of 4 lemons
4 eggs, beaten
½ cup butter
2¼ cups sugar

Put all the ingredients into the top of a double boiler or in a bowl over simmering water. Stir

until the sugar has dissolved and continue heating, stirring occasionally, until the curd thickens. Strain into small ramekins and cover. *Makes about 1½ lb.*

LEMON MERINGUE PIE

½ recipe short-crust pastry (see pastry entry)
3 tablespoons cornstarch
⅔ cup water
juice and grated rind of 2 lemons
½ cup sugar
2 eggs, separated
⅓ cup superfine sugar

Roll out the pastry and use it to line a 7-inch flan ring or pie pan. Trim the edges, line with foil, fill with pie weights and bake in a 425° oven for 15 minutes. Remove the foil and pie weights and return the shell to the oven for 5 minutes more. Reduce the oven to 350°. Mix the cornstarch with the water in a saucepan, add the lemon juice and grated rind and bring slowly to a boil, stirring until the mixture thickens, then add the sugar. Remove from the heat, cool the mixture slightly and add the egg yolks. Pour into the pastry shell. Beat the egg whites stiffly, beat in half the sugar and fold in the rest. Pile the meringue on top of the lemon filling and bake in the oven for about 10 minutes, or until the meringue is lightly browned.

LEMON ICE CREAM

grated rind of 1 lemon
juice of 1½ lemons
¾ cup superfine sugar
⅔ cup heavy cream
⅔ cup milk
angelica leaves, to decorate

Place the lemon rind, juice, and sugar in a mixing bowl. Stir well. Add the cream and beat until thickened enough to show the trail of the beater. Slowly beat in the milk. Transfer to an ice tray and freeze until slushy.

Place the ice cream in a large bowl. Beat until smooth and return to the freezer, either in individual ramekins or one large container. Decorate with angelica leaves and, if desired, serve with fresh raspberries.

LEMONADE

A refreshing drink made from the juice of lemons, the rind (or zest), sugar, and water. The name is also applied to many drinks tasting of lemon. In some commercial products the water is replaced by carbonated water, the sugar by a cheap form of glucose and artificial sweeteners and the lemon by citric acid and yellow coloring.

LEMONADE

1 lemon
¼ cup sugar
1 cup boiling water

Wash the lemon and peel the rind very thinly; put it with the sugar into a jug, pour on the boiling water, cover and allow to stand until cool, stirring occasionally. Add the lemon juice and strain the lemonade.

LEMON BALM

A herb of the mint family, used for flavoring stuffing, etc., also in drinks. It has a pronounced lemon aroma and flavor.

LEMON SOLE

This fish, which actually belongs to the flounder, not the sole family, inhabits the sea from the north of Scotland to the Mediterranean, but it is most abundant in the cold waters of the North Atlantic and the English Channel; it is in season year-round. Lemon soles are smaller than ordinary soles (the largest on record being 14 inches long).

Lemon soles may be cooked by any of the usual methods used for fish, particularly frying and broiling. Fillets are delicious when steamed, baked, or poached and served with a rich cream, white wine, or mushroom sauce.

LEMON THYME

A herb used for flavoring stuffings, soups, fish, etc.; its strongly flavored leaves are sometimes used as a substitute for lemon.

LENTIL

A pulse vegetable, the seeds of a leguminous plant. Lentils are about half the size of a pea and have a characteristic flavor. In the Orient, especially Egypt, they have been a staple item of diet for many centuries; they are now grown in the United States and all over the south of Europe. Three main varieties are marketed: Egyptian or red lentils, grown in Arabia and Palestine as well as in Egypt; European or yellow lentils, grown chiefly in France and Germany; German lentils, a variety of European lentils which are dark green

and supposed to be more palatable than the yellowish-red variety.

Lentils are a cheap and useful source of protein, which they contain in a form known as legumin. They also supply carbohydrates, thiamin, iron, and calcium.

Lentils are generally used in soups and stews. Bacon, sausage or ham should be added to the cooking liquid to give extra flavor.

To cook lentils: Wash them thoroughly, cover with boiling water and soak for 6 hours (or overnight, if convenient). Cook the lentils in the water in which they were soaked, as this contains some of the mineral matter and other nutrients that have been extracted. Bring to a boil and simmer very gently until they are tender and the liquid is absorbed, adding more liquid if necessary; the time needed is about 30 minutes. If desired, the lentils may then be rubbed through a sieve or pureed; this makes them more digestible by removing their outer shell.

LENTIL AND BACON SOUP

¾ cup lentils
6 cups beef broth
1 clove garlic, crushed
1 clove
salt
pepper
7 oz lean slab bacon, rinded and diced
1 can (8 oz) tomatoes
1 cup chopped onions
1 lb potatoes, peeled and diced
2 tablespoons lemon juice
crisply fried bacon strips, chopped parsley, grated cheese, or croutons for garnish

Wash the lentils and put them in a saucepan with the broth. Add the garlic, clove, salt, pepper, bacon, tomatoes, and onion. Bring to a boil, cover and simmer for about 1 hour, until the lentils and bacon are soft. Add the potatoes and cook for 20 minutes more. Remove the clove, pour the soup into a blender and puree until smooth. Add the lemon juice and reheat to serving temperature. Garnish as desired.

LETTUCE

A green plant, which is used chiefly as a salad though it can also be cooked and served as a vegetable or made into soup. There are several species and about a hundred varieties, grouped into five classes: Crisphead, with a firm head and brittle texture; cos or romaine, with a long-shaped head and narrow leaves, either self-closing or loose-closing; butterhead, with soft leaves and a buttery taste; leaf lettuce, which does not form a head; and stem lettuce, the only variety of which sold in the United States is celtuce. Of the crispheads, which are the most important commercial lettuces in the United States, iceberg is best known. Of the butterheads, Boston and Bibb lead the field.

Lettuce is rich in vitamins A, B, C, and E, as well as calcium, iron, and magnesium.

Preparation: Remove any old or badly damaged leaves. Wash the lettuce quickly but thoroughly in cold running water and drain it well, then place the leaves in a wire salad basket or clean towel and shake with a smooth, swinging movement to remove the remaining moisture. Toss in vinaigrette or serve as desired.

LEVERET

A young hare (see Hare entry).

LIAISON

A thickening – for example, blended cornstarch and milk – used to thicken puree soups and sauces. Other liaisons include flour and eggs. (See Thickening entry.)

LICORICE

The black juice prepared from the roots of this plant is used to make candy, as well as a flavoring agent and in medicine.

LIEDERKRANZ

The adaptation in the United States of Belgian Limburger cheese, this is a semisoft cow's milk cheese with a similar but slightly milder flavor and aroma than its Belgian cousin.

LIGHTS

The lungs of sheep, calves, beef, or pigs, used for feeding pets and in stews in various parts of Europe. In the United States lights are considered unfit for human consumption and their sale is prohibited.

LIMA BEAN (BUTTERBEAN)

A bean originally grown in South America. The seeds are short, flat, slightly kidney shaped and used fresh or dried as a vegetable.

LIMBURGER CHEESE

A semisoft Belgian cheese, of extremely strong flavor and smell. Named for the Belgian town of Limbourg, it is now also produced elsewhere, including the United States, Austria, and Germany.

LIME

The fruit of the citrus lime tree, which requires the same subtropical climatic conditions as the orange tree, grows in Florida, Mexico, the West Indies, the last two being chief producers. There is also a small amount of production in California. The lime, which is oval and of a pale yellowish-green color, is very acid. The rind and juice of limes are used in the same ways as lemon rind and juice. Limes contain about half the amount of vitamin C found in lemons. Two popular Florida varieties are the Key Lime and the Tahiti Lime.

KEY LIME PIE

The use of canned milk in many recipes from the Florida Keys is a reminder of early days without refrigeration.

3 eggs, separated
1 can (14½ oz) sweetened condensed milk
⅓ cup lime juice (preferably from Key limes)
1 baked pie shell
1 cup heavy cream
sugar

Beat the egg yolks and add the milk and lime juice. Beat the egg whites until stiff and fold into the yolk mixture. Pour into the pie shell and bake in a 250° oven for 10 minutes. Cool. Just before serving, beat the heavy cream and sweeten to taste. Mound it on top of the pie and serve.

LIME BLOSSOM

The dried flowers of the lime (linden) tree can be infused to make a pleasant, delicately flavored tea or tisane, which used to be regarded as a medicinal drink for debility, indigestion, and sleeplessness.

LIMPET

This small, single-shelled mollusk which clings to rocks like abalone is found on the Atlantic and Pacific coasts of North America. It can be prepared, cooked, and served in ways suitable for clams, oysters, and mussels.

LING

A large fish of the cod family, which grows to about 7 feet in length and weighs about 120 lb. It is found in Eastern Atlantic waters. Ling is generally sold salted and sometimes passed off as cod. Salted ling should first be soaked to remove the salt and then requires careful cooking to make it palatable.

LINGUINE

This pasta looks like a narrow thick noodle but is actually a spaghetti. One of its more famous associations is with clam sauce.

LINGUINE WITH RED CLAM SAUCE

2 tablespoons oil
1 clove garlic, minced
¼ cup chopped parsley
1 can (16 oz) tomatoes, drained and crushed
12 little neck clams, scrubbed
1 can (7½ oz) minced clams
8 oz linguine, cooked

Heat the oil in a skillet and sauté the garlic for 1 minute. Add the parsley, tomatoes, and little neck clams. Cover and cook over high heat until the clams open. Remove the clams from the skillet and add the minced clams. Simmer, uncovered, for 30 minutes. Return the little necks to the skillet to heat through. Toss the linguine with the sauce and serve garnished with the clams in their shells.

LINZER TORTE

A lattice-top cake, buttery and crumbly and tasting of nuts and spices. It is filled with jam. The cake originated in Linz, Austria, and is now world famous.

LIQUEUR (CORDIAL)

This name is applied to a variety of alcoholic beverages sweetened with sugar, flavored with extracts, and sometimes scented and colored. In the preparation of liqueurs the fruits or herbs are first bruised and are then steeped in diluted grain alcohol or rectified alcohol; after sufficient steeping the volatile constituents extracted by the alcohol are separated by distillation and the distillate is sweetened. The product is stored in wooden casks to mature and is finally bottled. Liqueurs are principally served as after-dinner drinks; they are also used to flavor desserts.

Some of the best-known liqueurs are: Advocaat, Bénédictine, Brandy (also Apricot Brandy and Cherry Brandy), Chartreuse, Crème de Cacao, Crème de Menthe, Curaçao, Drambuie, Grand Marnier, Kirsch (or Kirschwasser), Kümmel, Maraschino, Sloe Gin and Anisette. (For details, see individual entries.)

LIQUORICE

(See Licorice entry.)

LITCHI

(See Lychee entry.)

LIVER

The livers of calves, beef, pigs, and sheep, also those of poultry and game, are all used in cooking.

Calf's liver, which is regarded as the best, is popular when sautéed and served with bacon or mushrooms. Sheep's and lamb's liver can also be sautéed. Beef liver is coarse in texture (and therefore much cheaper) and it needs to be braised or cooked in some similar way to prevent its becoming hard and granular. Pig's liver is normally used in sausages of various kinds and in liver pâté. (See Pâté entry.)

Pâté de foie gras, made from the livers of specially fattened geese, is regarded as a great delicacy. Chicken livers have a good flavor and are used in pâté and appetizers.

The food value of liver is high. It contains protein, vitamin A, the vitamin B complex and iron in appreciable amounts. Liver eaten once a week supplies a good portion of the iron required.

LIVER AND ONIONS

1 lb onions, chopped
2 tablespoons bacon drippings or oil
salt
pepper
½ teaspoon dried sage or mixed herbs, optional
1 lb calf's liver

Sauté the onions lightly in the hot drippings or oil until they begin to color, then add the seasoning (and the herbs, if used). Cover the skillet and simmer very gently for about 10 minutes until the onions are soft. Meanwhile wash and trim the liver and cut it into thin strips. Add to the onions, increase the heat slightly and continue cooking for about 3 to 7 minutes, stirring continually, until the liver is just cooked. Remove it from the pan, drain and serve with boiled rice and salad.

LIVER MARSALA

1 lb calf's liver
lemon juice
seasoned flour
4 tablespoons butter
¼ cup Marsala
⅔ cup beef broth
whole broiled tomatoes, matchstick potatoes, and
parsley to garnish

Wash and slice the liver. Sprinkle it with the lemon juice and coat with seasoned flour. Melt the butter in a skillet and sauté the liver quickly on both sides until lightly browned. Stir in the Marsala and broth and simmer until the meat is just cooked and the sauce syrupy. Arrange the liver on a serving dish and garnish with the tomatoes, potatoes, and parsley.

CHOPPED CHICKEN LIVERS

¼ cup butter
½ cup rendered chicken fat
1 Spanish onion, chopped
½ lb chicken livers
2 hard-cooked eggs, chopped
salt
¼ cup chopped parsley

Combine the butter and 2 tablespoons of the chicken fat in a skillet and add the onion. Sauté until golden, allowing a tablespoon or two to become deep brown. Remove from the pan with a slotted spoon and add the livers over high heat. Cook, shaking the pan, until just done; they should still be faintly pink on the inside.

Turn out the livers, fat and all, onto a chopping board with the onions and hard-cooked eggs. Season with salt and chop until the livers are fine, then mix in the chopped parsley. Add as much of the remaining chicken fat as the mixture will absorb. Refrigerate until ready to serve.

LIVERWURST (BRAUNSCHWEIGER)

A smoked liver sausage, originally made in Germany, popular in the United States.

LOACH

A small freshwater fish of the carp family found in Europe and Asia; it is prepared like smelt.

LOAF

A neatly shaped mass of a foodstuff, such as bread, cooked meat, sugar, etc.

LOBSCOUSE

A sailor's stew of meat, vegetables, and hardtack.

LOBSTER

A saltwater crustacean found in waters all over the world and prized for its sweet tender meat. The American lobster (*Homarus americanus*) is larger than the European species. The best ones are in the colder northern water of the Atlantic off the coasts of Maine and Nova Scotia. Its natural color is a mottled greenish black which turns bright red-orange after cooking.

Other crustacea often named lobster, including spiny lobster and Norway lobster, are not of the same family. Preferred cooking methods are boiling and steaming, but lobsters may also be broiled or baked.

CHOICE, BOILING, AND PREPARATION
When purchasing a live lobster, look for one that is lively and heavy for its size. When buying a pre-boiled lobster look for plenty of "spring" in the tail, a good indicator of freshness. For eating purposes, the male or cock lobster is superior to the hen and is more delicate in flavor; it does not grow to so large a size and is generally narrower in the back part of the tail. On the other hand, the hen lobster is prized for its red coral (or roe), which is useful for garnishing and for making cardinal sauce.

If the lobster is bought alive, tie up the claws securely and wash it in clean water. Then place it in salted cold water, bring slowly to the boiling point, and let it boil fairly quickly and without stopping for 10 to 20 minutes, according to size; lift the lobster out of the water with tongs and let cool until it can be handled. If a lobster is boiled too long, the flesh becomes hard and thready. Remove any scum from the shell before lifting out the lobster flesh and if the shell is to be used, rub it with a little oil to give it a gloss.

To serve, first twist the claws off the lobster and crack them without injuring the flesh. Then split the lobster right down the middle of the back from head to tail, using a strong, pointed knife. Remove the intestine (which looks like a small vein running through the center of the tail), the stomach, which lies near the head, and the spongy-looking gills. Arrange the halves of the body on a dish with the cracked claws around it and garnish with parsley or salad. Serve any sauce or condiments separately; boiled lobster tastes best when served simply with melted butter.

LOBSTER SALAD

Cut the lobster meat into small, neat pieces and slice a hard-cooked egg. Line a salad bowl with lettuce and watercress, mix the lobster with mayonnaise and pile in the center. Decorate with lettuce heart, sliced egg, and lobster coral (if available) or the lobster claws and head.

LOBSTER NEWBURG

1 small cooked lobster
2 tablespoons butter
white, cayenne, and paprika pepper
salt
⅓ cup Madeira or sherry
2 egg yolks
⅔ cup light cream
buttered toast or boiled rice
chopped parsley to garnish

Cut the lobsters in half, carefully detach the tail meat in one piece and cut it into fairly thin slices. Crack the claws and remove the meat as unbroken as possible. Melt the butter in a skillet, lay the lobster in it, season well and heat very gently for about 3 minutes, without coloring. Pour the Madeira or sherry over and continue to cook a little more quickly until the liquid is reduced by half. Beat the egg yolks with a little seasoning and add the cream. Take the lobster off the heat, pour the cream mixture over and mix gently over a slow heat till the sauce reaches the consistency of heavy cream. Adjust the seasoning, pour at once onto hot buttered toast or boiled rice and sprinkle with parsley.

LOBSTER THERMIDOR

2 small cooked lobsters, 1 lb each
4 tablespoons butter
1 tablespoon chopped shallot
2 teaspoons chopped parsley
1–2 teaspoons chopped tarragon
⅓ cup dry white wine
1 cup white sauce
¼ cup grated Parmesan cheese
mustard
salt
paprika

Remove the lobster meat from the shells, reserving the shells. Chop the claw and head meat coarsely and cut the tail meat into thick slices. Melt half the butter in a saucepan and add the shallot, parsley, and tarragon. After a few minutes add the wine and simmer for 5 minutes. Add the white sauce and simmer until it is reduced to a creamy consistency. Add the lobster meat to the sauce, with 2 tablespoons of the cheese, the remaining butter (in small pieces), and mustard, salt, and paprika to taste. Arrange the mixture in the shells, sprinkle with the remaining cheese and put under the broiler to brown the top quickly. Serve at once.

LOBSTER BUTTER

Remove the coral from a cooked lobster, wash it and dry it in a cool oven, without allowing it to change color. Pound it in a mortar or process in a food processor with double its weight in butter, season to taste and rub it through a fine sieve. Use to make lobster bisque, sauces or spread on toast.

LOCUST BEAN

(See Carob entry.)

LOGANBERRY

A succulent aggregate fruit, larger and more acid than raspberries, with a hardish hull and when fully ripe of a dark purplish red. It was discovered in California a century ago growing in the garden of Judge J. H. Logan. Really ripe loganberries are suitable for dessert and they also make good tarts, pies, wine and preserves; loganberry jam, which is made in the same way as raspberry jam, is particularly delicious.

LOIN (SHORT LOIN)

The name given to the lower back of beef, veal, pork, and lamb as well as other meat animals. The cut extends from the last rib to the hip bone and, with the exception of the beef club steak which may contain a piece of the 13th rib, contains only the back bone. This consists of three parts – the spine bone, chine bone and finger bone (the center bone of a T-bone or porterhouse steak and of veal, pork, and lamb loin chops). The loin is considered one of the choicest cuts of any animal.

The muscles of the loin are the top loin and the tenderloin or fillet. When the flank muscle is included, it is the tail of a steak or chop. The tenderloin muscle extends into the sirloin and only its thin end is contained in the short loin.

Beef cuts from the loin include the club steak, the T-bone and porterhouse steaks (each containing part of the top loin and tenderloin); the top loin steak (New York cut and Kansas City steak); and tenderloin (filet mignon) steak.

Veal cuts include the kidney chop, with the flank enclosing a piece of the kidney, and the loin chop.

Pork cuts include the butterfly, top loin and loin chops and the tenderloin, a long narrow strip.

Lamb cuts include the English and loin chops and the loin roast. The saddle of lamb, the double loin, is rarely served because of its cost.

LOLLIPOP

A hard candy stuck on a small wooden stick and called a sucker. (See Candy entry.)

LOQUAT

A Japanese species of medlar, with yellow fruit the size of a large grape with a tart/sweet taste. It is used for jams and jellies. Though developed in Japan, it's now grown in the United States.

LOTE

(See Monkfish entry.)

LOVAGE

A perennial herb similar to angelica in appearance and a member of the parsley family. Every part is aromatic and can be used for culinary purposes. The seeds, leaves, and stems all have a slightly celery flavor and fragrance which is retained when dried. The stems are thick and hollow and are often candied and used in candymaking. Lovage was known to the Greeks and Romans as a medicinal herb. The fresh leaves can be used in salads and broths, but should be used sparingly as the taste is somewhat strong.

LOVE APPLE

An old name for the tomato.

LOX

Jewish smoked salmon, a little oilier and saltier than top grade smoked salmon. Lox are usually served with cream cheese and bagels and make a fine breakfast, lunch, or snack.

LUNCHEON (LUNCH)

The midday meal. It varies so much in character according to taste and circumstance that no hard-and-fast description is possible, for the word may cover anything from the sandwich lunch taken by some office and factory workers to the fairly elaborate formal meal given when guests are entertained at a public function or private party.

LUTING

A British term for the strip of pastry placed around a dish to seal the lid or pastry cover; used when preparing potted game, etc., in covered dishes.

LYCHEE (LITCHI)

The fruit of a tree of Chinese origin that grows in many parts of the Orient as well as in the Southern United States, Hawaii, the West Indies, South Africa, and Australia. Lychees have a scaly, reddish-brown outer covering, white, pulpy flesh and a hard brown pit; their flavor is very attractive, acid yet sweet. The fruit is available in the United States fresh and in cans.

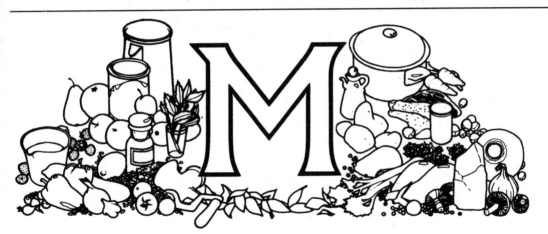

MACADAMIA

The edible nut of a species of macadamia trees, native to Australia, a specialty of Hawaii and now grown in California as well. The shell is almost unbreakable and the nut is marketed shelled and usually roasted.

MACARONI

One of the most widely known types of pasta, this long hollow tube shape is made from durum wheat flour and water. It is also made into shapes such as the letters of the alphabet, shells, rings and stars as well as in various colors. It is a staple food of Italy and it is said that the name derives from the Greek meaning of the word which is "blessed bread." This is an allusion to the ancient custom of eating it at feasts for the dead.

Macaroni can be served in innumerable ways, the simplest being with plenty of butter, pepper, salt, and grated Parmesan cheese. It can be served as an accompaniment or added to soups and stews and is occasionally made into desserts and salads.

To cook macaroni: Macaroni is cooked in boiling salted water or stock. Allow plenty of liquid (2 pints to 4 oz) as the macaroni absorbs a great deal of fluid – for example 4 oz weight about 14 to 16 oz when cooked. Bring the liquid to a boil and add salt with flavoring such as a small onion if desired. If not already in small pieces break the macaroni into 2-inch lengths and boil, stirring occasionally, until the macaroni feels soft but not mushy; cooking times vary considerably, but the time suggested on the box is almost always too long. Then drain off the liquid. Toss in a little melted butter.

MACARONI AND CHEESE

6 oz elbow macaroni
3 tablespoons butter
4 tablespoons flour
2 cups milk
pinch grated nutmeg or ½ teaspoon prepared mustard
1½ cups mature cheese, grated
2 tablespoons fresh white breadcrumbs (optional)

Cook the macaroni in rapidly boiling salted water for 10 minutes only and drain it well. Meanwhile melt the butter, stir in the flour and cook for 2 to 3 minutes. Remove the pan from the heat and gradually stir in the milk. Bring to a boil and continue to stir until the sauce thickens; remove from the heat and stir in the seasonings, 1 cup of the cheese, and the macaroni. Pour into an ovenproof dish and sprinkle with the breadcrumbs (if used) and the remaining cheese. Place dish on a baking sheet and bake in a 400° oven for about 20 minutes or until golden and bubbling.

VARIATIONS
Add to the sauce any of the following:

1 small onion, chopped and boiled
¼ lb bacon or ham, rinded, chopped and lightly fried
½–1 green pepper, chopped and blanched
½–1 canned pimiento, chopped
1 medium can of salmon or tuna, drained and flaked
2 oz mushrooms, sliced and lightly sautéed
1 medium can of sardines, drained and flaked
1 small can tomatoes

MACAROON

A chewy cookie made of sugar, egg whites, and either shredded coconut, almond paste, or ground almonds, and baked on rice paper. Small macaroons can be served as petits fours and the mixture may also be used as a filling for tarts. In Italy almond macaroons, called amaretti, are very popular.

MACAROONS

1 egg white
½ cup ground almonds
7 tablespoons superfine sugar
½ teaspoon almond extract
egg white to glaze

Line 1 or 2 baking sheets with parchment paper. Beat the egg white until stiff and fold in the ground almonds, sugar, and almond extract. Place spoonfuls of the mixture on the baking sheets, leaving plenty of room for spreading. (Alternatively pipe the mixture onto the paper, using a pastry bag and ½-inch tube.) Brush each cookie with egg white. Bake in a 350° oven for 20 to 25 minutes, until just beginning to color. Cool on a wire rack.

MACE

The second covering of the nutmeg, which is used in both "blade" and powder form. Its flavor is similar to that of nutmeg and cinnamon and it is usually one of the ingredients of curry powder. It is occasionally added to the other herbs forming a bouquet garni, and is used in sauces, stews, and soups as well as in meat and fish dishes and puddings.

MACÉDOINE

This French term is used to denote a mixture of vegetables or fruit, diced or cut into various shapes and served as a cocktail, a salad or a garnish.

Macédoine of vegetables

Dice such vegetables as carrots, turnips, and celery, add some peas and boil in salted water until tender. Serve plain, tossed in butter or in a white sauce. For Russian salad, mix with mayonnaise.
Macédoine of fruit: See Fruit salad, in Fruit entry.

MACKEREL

A round fish found in the Pacific and on both sides of the Atlantic, which is in season from April to October, but at its best during April, May, and June. Mackerel has distinctive blue-black markings on the back and silvery underside; when fully grown it may be 18 inches in length. The flesh is oily and the strong flavor is best when the fish is eaten fresh from the sea. Chub or Pacific mackerel is most common on the west coast. The much larger King mackerel is found south of the Chesapeake Bay. When buying mackerel make sure that it is perfectly fresh; choose a fish that has clear eyes, bright coloring, and bright-red open gills. It should also be stiff although this is not an infallible guide, as stiffness may be due to ice storage. Frozen and canned mackerel are also available.

Mackerel is a good source of protein and vitamins A and D; it also contains small amounts of minerals.

Cooking

Mackerel may be steamed, broiled, fried, or baked. Suitable accompaniments to serve with them include parsley, fennel, apple, caper and mustard sauce and maître d'hôtel butter. The British and French serve it with a tart/sweet gooseberry sauce. They are also delicious split in half, dipped in oatmeal and fried. Soused mackerel is prepared like soused herring (see Herring entry).

If desired the prepared and scored mackerel may be soaked in a marinade for 1 hour before broiling, then served hot or cold, garnished with lemon or parsley.

Smoked mackerel: serve broiled or fried.

Canned mackerel: serve cold in hors d'oeuvres and salads or hot with sauce.

BAKED MACKEREL

Score the mackerel 2 to 3 times on each side. Sprinkle lightly with salt and pepper and a squeeze of lemon juice and place on a greased baking dish with a few pieces of butter on top, then cover lightly with a piece of waxed paper. Bake in a 350° oven for 20 to 30 minutes, basting twice during the cooking. Serve with mustard sauce and garnish with parsley.

MACKEREL IN CREAM SAUCE

4 mackerel
bunch of parsley
little butter
2 tablespoons flour
oil for frying
salt
⅔ cup water
⅔ cup sour cream

Wash the fish, then fillet them and sprinkle with chopped parsley and a few flakes of butter. Roll up and tie with fine string. Toss in flour and fry in a skillet until brown. Add salt to taste, the water and sour cream. Cover and simmer for 10 minutes. Remove strings and serve with sauce.

MADEIRA

A fortified wine from the island of Madeira; the grapes are grown on the rich volcanic soil which gives an individual flavor. Before being fortified the wine is subjected to heat in the maturing casks. There are several types of Madeira with different flavors and characteristics. Malmsey is rich, sweet and dark and can be very old: there is some known to be over 100 years old. It is good served after dinner. Boal is a less expensive form of Malmsey and essentially a dessert wine; Sercial is a light dry Madeira and Verdelho is medium sweet. These are more suitable to serve as an apéritif.

MADEIRA OR MARSALA SAUCE

Add up to ⅔ cup Madeira or Marsala to 1 cup espagnole sauce (coating consistency) and reheat but do not reboil. The juice and extracts from the pan in which meat was roasted can also be reduced and added to give extra flavor.

Serve with any meat or game.

MADEIRA CAKE

A rich classic Portuguese cake that does not contain madeira but is often saturated or served with it. The characteristic decoration consists of candied lemon peel which is placed on top during baking.

MADEIRA CAKE

2 cups all-purpose flour
1 teaspoon baking powder
½ teaspoon salt
¾ cup butter
¾ cup superfine sugar
1 teaspoon vanilla
3 eggs, beaten
1–2 tablespoons milk
2–3 thin slices lemon peel

Grease and flour a 7-inch cake pan. Sift the flour, baking powder and salt together. Cream the butter, sugar, and vanilla until pale and fluffy. Beat in the egg a little at a time. Fold in the flour, adding a little milk if necessary to give a dropping consistency. Put into the pan and bake in a 350° oven. After 20 minutes put the lemon peel on top of the cake and continue to cook for a further 40 minutes. Cool on a wire rack.

MADELEINE

A small French tea cake made of a genoise-type sponge batter baked in a scallop-shaped mold.

MADELEINES

2 eggs
¾ cup sugar
1 teaspoon grated lemon rind
½ teaspoon vanilla
1 cup all-purpose flour
¾ cup melted clarified butter

Combine the eggs and sugar in a large mixer bowl and heat over hot water until the eggs are warm. Beat at high speed for about 10 minutes, or until light and very fluffy. Add the vanilla and the lemon rind, then fold in the flour. Fold in the melted butter, making sure it does not settle in the bottom of the bowl. Fill greased madeleine molds ⅔ full and bake in a 450° oven for 10 minutes, or until the cakes are golden. Remove from the molds immediately and cool on wire racks.

MADRILÈNE (À LA)

A name given to many foods flavored with tomato, particularly a consommé that is usually served jellied.

MAGNUM

A large wine bottle, containing ⅓ gallon.

MAID OF HONOR

Small British tarts filled with flavored milk curds that originated in Henry VIII's palace where they were popular with the queen's maids of honor.

MAISON

Such a description of a dish, e.g. Pâté Maison, should indicate that it is a specialty of a restaurant.

MAÎTRE D'HÔTEL

Literally, head waiter's style; the name given to simply prepared dishes garnished with maître d'hôtel butter – for example Filet de Sole Maître d'Hotel. The name is also given to a sauce.

MAÎTRE D'HÔTEL BUTTER

2 tablespoons butter
2 teaspoons finely chopped parsley
1 teaspoon lemon juice
salt
cayenne pepper

Soften and cream the butter with parsley, lemon juice, and seasonings. Shape into a sausage roll, wrap in waxed paper and chill until firm. Unwrap and cut into ½ inch thick slices.

When served with hot food a pat of maître d'hôtel butter should be added only just before the dish is put on the table, or it will melt and lose its decorative appearance.

MAKO

An edible species of shark. With a texture and taste akin to swordfish, mako can be cooked in the same ways.

MALAGA

A sweet fortified Spanish wine. It is made from local wine to which Pedro Ximenez sherry and grape brandy are added.

MALLARD

(See Wild Duck entry.)

MALT

The substance produced by allowing barley to germinate to a certain stage under controlled conditions, the starch being converted into dextrin and malt sugar; when the correct stage of germination is reached the grains are dried by heating and become malt: which is largely used by brewers of beer and ale of which it is a major ingredient. Malt extract, a dark sticky syrup made by evaporating malted barley at a low temperature or in a vacuum, is used in cakes, bread, and puddings to which it imparts a distinctive flavor and a rather moist texture. Used in medicines etc., its flavor helps to mask unpleasant-tasting ingredients such as cod and halibut liver oils. Malt bread is a sweet dark bread made by the British with malt extract and molasses.

MALT BREAD

1 teaspoon superfine sugar
⅔ cup lukewarm water
1 package active dry yeast
4 cups plain flour
1 teaspoon salt
4 tablespoons malt
1 tablespoon molasses
2 tablespoons butter or margarine
sugar and water glaze, optional

Dissolve the sugar in the water, sprinkle the yeast over it and leave until frothy. Mix the flour and salt. Warm the malt, molasses, and butter until just melted. Stir the yeast and malt mixtures into

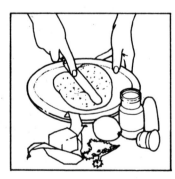

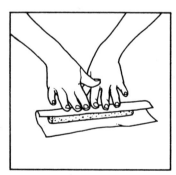

MAKING MAÎTRE D'HÔTEL BUTTER
1. Cream the butter, chopped parsley, lemon juice and seasoning together on a small plate.

2. Roll the butter into a sausage shape in a piece of waxed paper, wrap and refrigerate until firm.

3. Unwrap butter roll and cut into thin slices approximately ½ inch thick.

the dry ingredients and mix to a fairly soft, sticky dough, adding a little more water if necessary. Turn onto a floured board, knead well until the dough is firm and elastic. Divide into two pieces. Shape both into an oblong, and roll up like a jelly roll and put into two prepared 2-cup loaf pans. Leave to rise in a warm place (about 75°) until the dough fills the pans; this may take about 1½ hours as malt bread dough usually takes quite a long time to rise. Bake in a 400° oven for 30 to 40 minutes. When cooked the loaves can be brushed with a sugar glaze of 1 tablespoon water and 2 tablespoons sugar.

Serve cut into slices and buttered liberally.

MALTOSE (MALT SUGAR)

This form of sugar is one of the intermediate "break-down" products occurring when starch-splitting (diastatic) enzymes work on starches such as wheat (during the making of bread). This disaccharide is also significant in converting starch to sugar in the fermentation of alcohol.

MANDARIN ORANGE

(See Tangerine entry.)

MANGEL-WURZEL (MANGOLD)

A coarse beet, related to the garden beet, and usually grown for cattle feed; it can be cooked like a turnip. Mangel-wurzel beer is made from this beet.

MANGE TOUT

(See Snow Pea entry.)

MANGO

A tropical fruit combining a distinctive, sweet and spicy flavor with slight acidity and a smooth texture. The fruit varies considerably in size, ranging from the size of a plum to about 5 lb in weight; its color also varies from green to yellow and red. Some varieties are delicious, others are most unpleasant in taste.

Chief sources of the United States supply are Mexico, Southern California, and Hawaii.

MANGOSTEEN

A tropical fruit with a refreshing, pleasant flavor. It is the size and shape of a tangerine but is dark brown with white spots and has rose-colored pulp, with a wonderfully soft texture.

MANHATTAN COCKTAIL

(See Cocktail entry.)

MANICOTTI

Large squares of fresh pasta wrapped around a filling such as cheese or ground meat and baked in a sauce. Dried manicotti is sold commercially in the form of a large tube, usually grooved, about 1 inch in diameter.

MANIOC

(See Cassava entry.)

MAPLE SUGAR

This sugar is derived from boiling down maple syrup. It has a characteristic flavor and may be used to replace part or all of the ordinary sugar in cakes, puddings, etc. It is also used in candy-making (often mixed with brown sugar) and in sauces for ice cream, waffles, etc. It is a staple sweetener in the Northeastern States, particularly Vermont, and in Canada.

MAPLE SYRUP

A very sweet syrup, made from the sap of various species of maple tree. It has a distinctive but delicate flavor, and is used in sweet dishes and as an accompaniment to ices, waffles, etc., as well as in the manufacture of candy.

MARASCHINO

A liqueur made from a type of small, sour, black cherry grown in Dalmatia, known as Marasca. The kernels are distilled together with the leaves and this distillate gives a bitter tang to an otherwise sweet drink. Maraschino is often used to flavor desserts, punches, cocktails, etc.

MARC

The name generally used for marc eau-de-vie, a French brandy made from the residue of grapes after winemaking.

MARC DE RAISIN

A French semi-hard cheese with a "crust" of grape skins and seeds replacing the ordinary rind.

MARENGO

A chicken dish named after the Italian village of Marengo. Here the dish is said to have been invented by Napoleon's chef and cooked after the battle in 1800 with ingredients foraged from the countryside. Traditionally the chicken is sautéed in oil and flavored with tomato, garlic, and brandy and garnished with eggs and crayfish. There are variations to this original recipe and it is also made with veal.

MARGARINE

This manufactured fat was first produced as a substitute for butter. It was invented by a Frenchman, Megès Mouriés, in 1869 and was originally made from a mixture of animal fats.

Present-day margarine includes vegetable and/or animal fats and cultured or sweet fat-free milk, all blended together as an emulsion. A wide range of oils are used; these include palm oil, peanut, coconut, sunflower, cottonseed and soybean oils. The blend varies according to the supply and cost of the ingredients at any given time.

Almost all margarine is enriched with vitamins. Like butter, it is required by law to contain 80 percent fat and may be substituted for butter by weight or volume.

Margarine in the diet

It is principally a source of energy, but also contributes a significant amount of vitamins A and D to the daily diet. Margarine is used as a spread in place of butter or for cooking.

Some margarines are high in polyunsaturated fats, which are recommended for those wishing to keep blood cholesterol levels down. Research indicates that saturated fats increases cholesterol in the blood stream, promoting fatty deposits in the arteries and leading to heart disease.

Margarine in cooking

Margarine is not suitable for frying at high temperatures but can be used for sautéing foods at moderate temperatures. Margarine can be used in pastry alone or combined with lard; it is particularly good for cakes, soft frostings, and sauces.

MARIGOLD

The heads and petals of this garden plant of Europe and North America are used fresh and dried as flavoring and coloring agents. The centers are often substituted for saffron, thus its appellation "the poor man's saffron."

MARINADE

A mixture of oil, wine, vinegar, or lemon juice and herbs in which meat or fish is soaked before cooking to give it flavor and make it more tender. Marinating is especially useful for cuts of meat which are suitable for quick methods of cooking, but are not of the best quality; the meat should be pounded and then left to soak for at least 2 hours in the marinade. Marinades are also used for kebabs and meat to be stewed or baked; also used in making salads.

A SIMPLE MARINADE

2 tablespoons salad oil
1 tablespoon lemon juice or vinegar
onion juice, chopped onion, shallot, or chives
salt
pepper

Mix all ingredients and use as required.

WINE MARINADE

1 sliced onion
$\frac{2}{3}$ cup dry white wine, red wine, or cider
1 bay leaf
6 cracked peppercorns
4 parsley stalks
2 tablespoons olive oil

Mix all the ingredients. Strain the liquid after use and add it to the gravy.

MARJORAM

A herb of the mint family with two varieties of culinary importance. Sweet marjoram has a delicate flavor and is an annual plant. It is particularly good served with lamb, but is also used in soups, salads, and meat dishes and is sometimes substituted for sage in stuffings for chicken and turkey.

Pot marjoram is a perennial also called wild marjoram but most commonly known as oregano. It grows throughout Europe and North America.

MARMALADE

A thick preserve traditionally made from unpeeled bitter oranges. The name derives from the Portuguese word *marmalada*, from the Latin word for quince, since the preserve was originally made from that fruit. In England, where marmalade is a great favorite for breakfast with toast and butter, the word now applies exclusively to a preserve made from Seville oranges (and sometimes other citrus fruits such as lemons, limes, and grapefruit). In France, however, the term "marmalade" means thick puree, made by stewing fruit until considerably reduced; many different fruits can be cooked in this way.

In addition to its use as a spread on toast or bread, marmalade is sometimes used in making puddings, tarts, and sauces.

Marmalade making

The process is similar to jammaking except that the peel of the fruit requires longer to cook and during the cooking, which takes about 2 hours, a considerable amount of moisture is evaporated, so a larger quantity of water must be used in the beginning. If the peel is not softened before the sugar is added, it will remain hard – prolonged boiling after the sugar is added does not soften the peel but it darkens the color of the marmalade and breaks down the pectin, causing it to lose its "jelling" properties.

When large quantities of marmalade are made, a marmalade cutter is well worth buying. Failing this, the peel can be put through a coarse grinder, but the appearance and the texture of the finished marmalade are not as good. When slicing the fruit by hand it is essential to have a sharp knife to cut the rind thinly; if desired, the cutting can be made much easier by partially cooking the fruit first; cut the rind in quarters and cook it with the required amount of water until it is soft, then slice it and complete the cooking.

BITTER ORANGE MARMALADE

3 lb Seville or other bitter oranges
juice of 2 lemons
3¾ quarts water
6 lb sugar

Wash the fruit, cut it in half and squeeze out the juice and the pits. Slice the peel thinly and put it in a pan with the fruit juices, water and pits (tied in cheesecloth).

Simmer gently for about 2 hours until the peel is really soft and the liquid is reduced by about half. Remove the cheesecloth bag, squeezing it well, add the sugar and stir until it has dissolved. Boil rapidly until setting point is reached – about 15 minutes. Let stand for about 15 minutes and then jar and cover in the usual way. *Makes about 10 lb.*

MARMALADE SAUCE

1 tablespoon marmalade
1 tablespoon superfine sugar
⅔ cup water
2 teaspoons cornstarch
a little lemon juice
coloring (optional)

Place the marmalade, sugar, and water in a saucepan and bring to a boil. Add the cornstarch, mixed with a little cold water, and boil until sauce is clear and cornstarch cooked – about 2 to 3 minutes. Add the lemon juice and a little coloring to improve the color of the sauce if necessary.

CALEDONIAN CREAM

A dark pungent marmalade enhances the flavor of the liqueur to make a rich, smooth dessert, a good dinner party choice, based on two of Scotland's best-known exports – Drambuie and marmalade. It freezes well in freezerproof glasses or tiny soufflé dishes, and thaws in 2 to 3 hours at room temperature.

6 teaspoons thin shred marmalade
2 tablespoons superfine sugar
4 tablespoons Drambuie
juice of 1 lemon
1 cup whipping cream

Mix together the marmalade, sugar, Drambuie, and lemon juice. Beat the cream until it is just beginning to hold its shape. Gently beat in the marmalade mixture until the cream stands in soft peaks – take care not to over-whip the cream. Serve in small glasses.

MARMITE

French term for a covered cooking pot, and hence for a broth cooked in such a pot. The name is also given to a brand of yeast extract (see Yeast Extract entry).

MARRON GLACÉ

A popular delicacy, made from chestnuts treated with syrup, which is served as a dessert or used as decoration on desserts; marrons glacés may also be rubbed through a sieve and beaten into a meringue mixture or blended with cream as a dessert.

CHESTNUTS IN SYRUP

1 cup granulated sugar
¾ cup glucose or dextrose
⅔ cup plus 2 tablespoons water
12 oz chestnuts, peeled and skinned (weight after
    preparation) or 12 oz canned chestnuts, drained
vanilla

Put the granulated sugar, glucose or dextrose, and water in a saucepan large enough to hold the chestnuts and heat gently together until the sugars are dissolved; bring to a boil. Remove from the heat, add the chestnuts (drained if canned ones are used) and bring to a boil again. Remove from the heat, cover and leave overnight, preferably in a warm place. On the second day reboil the chestnuts and syrup in the saucepan without the lid, remove from the heat, cover and again let stand overnight. On the third day add 6 to 8 drops of vanilla and repeat the boiling process as above. Warm some 2-cup canning jars in the oven, fill with the chestnuts and cover with the syrup. Seal in the usual way to make airtight.

Note: This recipe gives a delicious result, but the chestnuts are not exactly like the commercially prepared marrons glacés, which cannot be reproduced under home conditions.

MARROW

(See Vegetable Marrow entry.)

MARROW, BONE

(See Bone entry.)

MARSALA

An excellent sweet white wine made from grapes grown around the town of that name in Sicily. In Sicily it is traditionally served chilled with antipasto before the meal on special occasions. It is also frequently served with dessert. Marsala is also an excellent flavoring for sauces.

MARSHMALLOW

A white candy of an elastic, spongy texture, which derives its name from the marsh mallow plant, the root of which provided a gum originally used for making it. Today it is made from sugar, corn syrup, starch, and egg whites or gelatin. Marshmallows are traditionally roasted over an open fire on a long stick until lightly browned on the outside and runny inside. They are also used in frostings and desserts.

MARSHMALLOW SAUCE

½ cup sugar
3 tablespoons water
8 marshmallows
1 egg white
a few drops of vanilla

Dissolve the sugar in the water, then boil together for about 5 minutes. Add the marshmallows, cut into small pieces with scissors. Beat the egg white stiffly, then gradually fold in the marshmallow mixture. Add the vanilla. Serve poured over ice cream or fruit.

MARTINI COCKTAIL

(See Cocktail entry.)

MARZIPAN

Today, this term is generally used as equivalent to almond paste. The name is applied particularly to candies made of this paste. (See Candy entry.)

MASA

The dough from which tortillas are made. It used to be prepared by cooking dried, shelled corn in a solution of lime and water until the corn was partially cooked. The corn was then washed in several changes of water to remove the husks and any trace of lime. Following that it was ground by hand to a paste and patted into tortillas. Today dried masa (masa harina) is available and needs only the addition of water to be used.

MASKING

To cover or coat a cooked meat or similar dish with aspic, glaze, or sauce; also to coat the inside of a mold with jelly.

MATÉ

(See Yerba Maté entry.)

MATSUTAKE

An enormous mushroom, as large as 8 inches in diameter, that grows in the early fall in the pine forests around Osaka and Kyoto. It is so prized by the Japanese that during its brief season thousands throng the woods armed with pots, rice, and sake to pick and immediately savor the beefsteak-tasting mushroom.

MATZO

An unleavened bread eaten by Jews during the 7-day festival of Passover, commemorating their flight from Egyptian bondage. So great was their haste that the Jews were unable to leaven their bread. Matzo meal, ground matzo bread, is substituted for flour in many ceremonial Passover recipes.

MAYONNAISE

(See Salad Dressing entry.)

MAY WINE

A punch made of claret, champagne, and Rhine wine, flavored with woodruff. The term also applies to a still white wine flavored with woodruff.

MEAD

A drink made by fermenting honey and water with hops or yeast; cowslips or other wild flowers or spices are added for flavoring. It dates back to biblical times and was once a favorite in England. It is still made in California, England, and Poland.

MEAT

The flesh of animals such as pig (pork), calf (veal), steer (beef), sheep (mutton), lamb, deer (venison), and rabbit. The flesh of many other animals is eaten in different parts of the world.

Meat is the muscle tissue of the animal and consists of bundles of fibers held together by connective tissue, in the meshes of which are a number of fat cells. The fibers vary in length according to the type of animal and the cut of meat but broadly speaking the longer fibers are tough and require slow, moist cooking for best results.

Meat is an important source of protein; it also supplies valuable amounts of vitamins of the B group and a moderate amount of iron. The fat, which adds to the flavor, is of high energy giving value. The cheaper cuts of meat are just as nutritious as more expensive ones, provided that

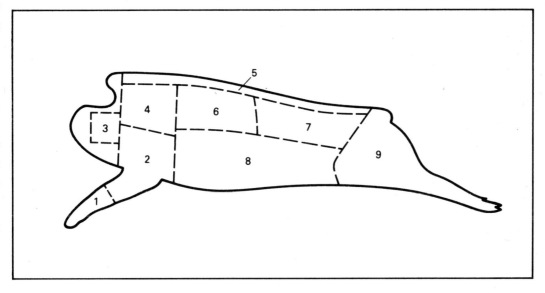

PORK

1. Foot. 2. Shank (Hock). Smoked and fresh hocks, arm roasts and steaks, fresh picnic, rolled fresh picnic, smoked picnic and canned picnic; canned luncheon meats. 3. Head. Jowl bacon, also used to make head cheese. 4. Boston Butt. Rolled Boston butt, smoked shoulder butt, blade steak, sausage meat, cubed steaks. 5. Fatback. Lard. 6. Rib Half of Loin. Blade loin roast, blade chop, country style backbone, back ribs, rib chop. 7. Center Cut Loin, Sirloin. Center loin roast, butterfly chop, rolled loin roast, loin chop, top loin chop, Canadian bacon, tenderloin, sirloin roast, sirloin chop. 8. Spareribs, slab bacon, sliced bacon, salt pork. 9. Ham (Leg). Smoked ham (shank and butt portions), smoked ham center slice, rolled fresh ham (leg), smoked ham boneless roll, canned ham, sliced cooked "boiled" ham.

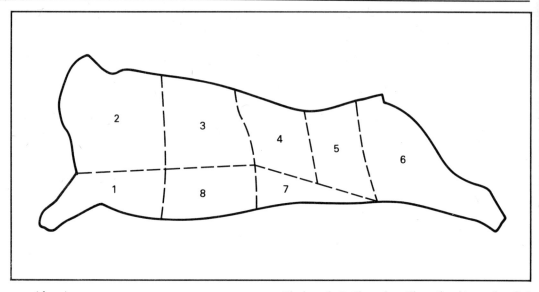

BEEF (above)
1. Shank (Shin). Shank cross cuts, fresh and corned brisket, stewing beef. 2. Chuck. Inside chuck roll, blade pot roast or steak, boneless shoulder pot roast or steak, chuck short ribs, arm pot roast, English (Boston) cut. 3. Rib. Standing rib roast, rib steak, Delmonico (rib eye) roast or steak. 4. Loin (Short Loin). Club steak, T-bone steak, Porterhouse steak, tenderloin steak (filet mignon). 5. Sirloin (Hip). Pin bone sirloin steak, flat bone sirloin steak, boneless sirloin steak, tenderloin steak (filet mignon). 6. Round. Round steak, top round steak, bottom round steak or pot roast, eye of round, standing rump, rolled rump, sirloin tip, sirloin steak. 7. Flank.

Flank steak. 8. Short plate. Short ribs, skirt steak, rolled plate, plate beef.

LAMB (below)
1. Shoulder. Square shoulder, rolled shoulder, cushion shoulder, arm chop, blade chop, Saratoga chop; neck slices. 2. Hotel Rack. Rib roast, crown roast, rib chops. 3. Trimmed Loin. Loin roast, rolled double loin, English chop, loin chops. 4. Leg. Sirloin roast, rolled double sirloin, sirloin chop, sirloin half of leg, shank half of leg, leg (sirloin on), leg (sirloin off), rolled leg, American leg, center leg, combination leg. 5. Breast. Fore Shank. Rolled breast, riblets, stuffed chops, brisket pieces.

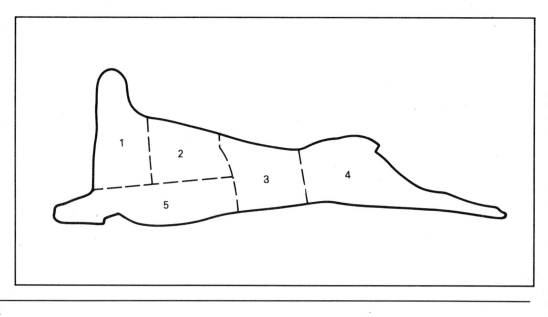

they do not contain a large proportion of bone or gristle.

Meat should not be eaten too fresh, for freshly killed meat lacks flavor and is likely to be tough. If it is kept for a while (the exact time varying with the kind of meat and the temperature at which it is kept) enzyme and bacterial action take place, breaking down the fibers, thus making the meat more tender and at the same time developing the flavor. This maturing process must not be allowed to continue beyond a certain point, otherwise the meat putrefies and becomes unwholesome.

A good butcher will usually advise about the selection of meat, but general rules are to choose meat which does not have an undue amount of fat; what fat there is should be firm and free from dark marks or discoloration. Lean meat should be finely grained with a marbling of fat, firm and slightly elastic.

Storing Meat

Fresh meat should be kept covered in a refrigerator or cool place. It should not be stored for too long before cooking as deterioration may occur. Frozen meat can be kept in the freezer compartment of a refrigerator.

Cooking Meat

Best quality meat and cuts may be cooked by the quicker methods, such as roasting, broiling, and sautéing. The coarser cuts are tougher and need a slow, moist method of cooking, such as braising, steaming, or stewing; grinding or shredding breaks down the long fibers mechanically and so helps to shorten the cooking time. Cured meat also requires long, slow cooking. For more detailed information see Beef and Lamb entries, also Roasting and Broiling entries.

MEATBALL

Ground meat formed into a ball and baked, fried, or stewed. A meatball usually contains egg and starch as binders, onion or garlic, and seasonings.

SPAGHETTI AND MEATBALLS

$\frac{1}{3}$ lb ground beef
$\frac{1}{3}$ lb ground veal
$\frac{1}{3}$ lb ground pork
4 slices bread, soaked in milk and squeezed dry
3 eggs
$\frac{1}{2}$ cup grated Parmesan cheese
2 tablespoons chopped parsley

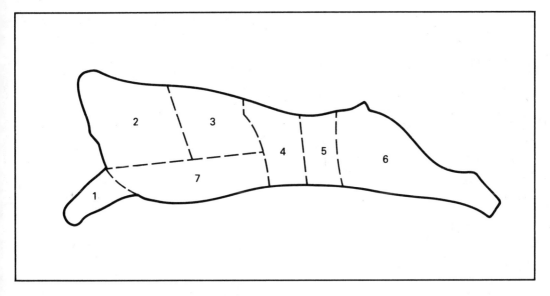

VEAL

1. Shank (Shin). Fore shank. 2. Shoulder. Neck, stewing veal, arm roast, arm steak, rolled shoulder, blade roast, blade steak. 3. Hotel Rack. Rib roast, crown roast, rib chop, Frenched rib chop. 4. Trimmed loin. Loin roast, rolled stuffed loin, loin chop, kidney chop. 5. Sirloin (Hip). Sirloin roast, sirloin steak, rolled double sirloin, cube steak. 6. Leg. Shank half of leg, standing rump, rolled leg, center leg, round steak, heel of round, boneless cutlets, rolled cutlets. 7. Breast. Rolled breast, brisket rolls, brisket pieces, stuffed chops. Veal for stew, grinding or cubing may come from any wholesale cut.

2 cloves garlic, chopped
salt
pepper
2 cups tomato sauce
½ lb spaghetti, cooked

Put the meats in a mixing bowl and shred the bread into them. Add the remaining ingredients and mix well. Form the mixture into 16 balls and place in a shallow baking pan. Bake in a 375° oven for 25 to 30 minutes, or until browned. Add the meatballs to the tomato sauce and simmer for 5 minutes. Serve over spaghetti.

MEAT EXTRACT

Meat extracts are made by cutting up meat, removing the tendons, grinding and boiling it; the mixture is then skimmed, filtered, and evaporated. Meat extracts contain small amounts of protein, minerals and some of the vitamins, and also have a strong flavor. They are of value for their stimulating action on the gastric juice and their vitamin content. A teaspoon of extract contains approximately as much riboflavin and niacin as 2 oz of roast beef. They make a pleasant drink, can also be added to soups, stews, and gravies and are available in cubes or paste form.

MEAT LOAF

Ground meat formed into a loaf and baked. The meat may be beef, pork, or veal, or any combination of these. In addition to meat, the loaf usually contains eggs and a filler and flavoring agents such as chopped vegetables and herbs, sauces or whatever strikes the cook's fancy. The secret of a good meat loaf is a light hand in mixing the ingredients. Meat loaves are sturdy family fare, go well at picnics and make delicious sandwiches from leftovers. Making individual loaves shortens the cooking time.

INDIVIDUAL MEAT LOAVES

1½ lb ground beef
2 eggs
1 cup prepared bread stuffing
1 can (8 oz) tomato sauce
½ cup chopped onion
salt
¼ teaspoon thyme
chili sauce

Combine all ingredients except the chili sauce and mix lightly. Spoon into six 6-oz custard cups. Brush with the chili sauce and bake in a 350° oven for 40 minutes, brushing occasionally with chili sauce, until browned. If desired, the meat may be shaped into a loaf and baked in a shallow pan for 1½ hours.

MEDLAR

There are several varieties of this fruit, which is of Central European origin and grows in the Southern United States and the south of Europe. Medlars are related to the pear; they are not unlike a rose hip in shape, but about the size of a plum, and of a russet-brown color. They are gathered in November and should not be eaten until the fruit is soft and mealy; they usually need to be kept for 2 to 3 weeks after gathering until mellow and "bletted" or softened. They may be eaten raw and also make good preserves. Medlars were introduced in the United States by the Jesuits.

MÉDOC

Red Bordeaux wines made in the Médoc district of France. The wines' properties vary from region to region: St Estèphe, Pauillac, St Julien, Central Médoc, Margaux, and Southern Médoc, the latter producing some of the finest wine.

The Gironde river stretches along the area, its gravel banks giving the area and its wines a character and quality. Although some of the Médoc wines are of excellent quality and predictably costly, there are many lesser classed ones which are affordable and suitable for serving at family meals.

(See Bordeaux wines entry.)

MELBA SAUCE

A sweet sauce which is made from fresh raspberries and served over ice cream with poached fresh peaches. It was created by Auguste Escoffier of London's Savoy Hotel around the turn of the century for Australian opera singer Dame Nellie Melba.

MELBA SAUCE

4 tablespoons currant jelly
⅓ cup sugar
⅔ cup raspberry puree from 8 oz raspberries, sieved
2 teaspoons arrowroot or cornstarch
1 tablespoon cold water

Mix the jelly, sugar, and raspberry puree and bring to a boil. Blend the arrowroot with the cold water to a smooth cream, stir in a little of the raspberry mixture, return the sauce to the pan, bring to a boil stirring with a wooden spoon until it thickens and clears. Strain and cool.

MELBA TOAST

(See Toast entry.)

MELON

The fruit of a creeping plant grown outdoors in sunny moist climates or indoors in greenhouses. There are numerous varieties. Except for the cantaloup, which is an excellent source of vitamins A and C, melons have little nutritional value, but they make a refreshing dessert.

CANTALOUPE OR MUSK MELON

This is one of the best-known and best-flavored melons. It has a segmented exterior and flesh of salmon-color, with a delicious flavor. When ripe it should have the characteristic melon fragrance, should yield slightly to pressure at the blossom end, and have no trace of a stem.

CASABA

A large round melon with a furrowed rind, golden yellow when ripe, and with a white flesh.

CHARENTAIS

These are small (French) melons (suitable for 2 people) with yellowish-green skin, deep yellow flesh, a sweeter and somewhat more pronounced taste than some melons and a rather perfumed aroma.

CRENSHAW

A large melon, round at the base and tapering to a point at the stem end. This generally smooth green-and-gold melon has a salmon-colored flesh.

HONEYDEW

When ripe, honeydews have a creamy yellow smooth skin and the blossom end yields to slight pressure. They are usually oval in shape and the flesh is greenish in color, sweet and fragrant. Large honeydews are usually better than small ones.

OGEN

Oval melons from Israel with greenish yellow segmented skin. The flesh is greenish yellow, juicy but not too sweet. As they are small, one is served to each person.

WATERMELON

These round or oval melons have a light or dark green skin and the flesh of various colors, frequently red, in which the seeds are imbedded. They are watery and somewhat insipid, but cool and refreshing.

To serve melon: Chill thoroughly, cut into wedges, remove seeds and serve with sugar and ground ginger or a garnish of fresh fruit.

A hollowed-out melon may be filled with fruit salad or ice cream to make a decorative dessert.

PICKLED MELON

2 lb prepared melon, cubed
2 tablespoons salt dissolved in 8 cups water, for brine solution
2 cups water
⅔ cup distilled vinegar
1 small stick cinnamon
1 teaspoon ground cloves
2¼ cups sugar
2 cups cherries (see note)

Soak the prepared melon overnight in the brine solution. Drain. Combine the 2 cups water, vinegar, cinnamon, cloves, and sugar and bring to a boil. When the sugar has dissolved, add the melon and cherries. Simmer, covered, for 30 to 40 minutes, until the melon is clear and tender. Jar and cover.

Note: Use either canned cherries or canned maraschino cherries, well drained.

MELTING

To convert a solid into liquid by gently heating. Some food, such as chocolate, needs very careful handling and is best melted over hot water.

MENU

The list of dishes to be served at one meal. For a formal meal it can be written on cards, placed on the table, the dishes being given in order of serving. (See Party entry.) Restaurants should provide a menu giving the choice of dishes available.

In recent years dinner menus have been simplified, as it is unusual for people to spend as long over their meals as in the past. Even for a formal dinner not more than 5 courses are usually served, while lunch may consist of 2 or at the most 3 courses.

MERINGUE

A confection made from white of egg and sugar and baked in a very slow oven. Meringues are usually plain but a flavoring such as coffee, chocolate, or chopped nuts may be included. When filled with whipped cream, ice cream, marshmallow, or fruit, meringues make a delicious dessert; small meringues or a piped or piled meringue mixture may be used as a topping for various desserts. Meringue can be made into shells and filled with fruit and cream.

Mixing: To each egg white allow $\frac{1}{4}$ cup sugar. The best texture is obtained by using superfine or powdered sugar. Separate the egg whites carefully, place in a clean dry mixer bowl and beat until stiff. Beat in half the sugar, then fold in the remainder lightly, using a metal spoon.

Shaping: There are two satisfactory methods.
1. With two spoons; dip one into a jug of cold water, shake off excess drops and fill with the meringue mixture. Using a knife smooth the mixture along the sides of the spoon until it resembles the shape of a finished meringue case, with a ridge along the top. With the second wet spoon, half lift the mixture out of the first spoon, then, preserving its shape and keeping the ridge on the top, allow it to slide out onto the prepared pan or board, using the first spoon to free it from the second spoon.
2. With a pastry bag fitted with a plain $\frac{1}{2}$-inch tip, squeeze out the mixture into pyramids, rounds, fingers, or ovals etc. Alternatively, place meringue into a pastry bag fitted with a fancy tip.

Baking: Ideally meringues should be baked on hardwood boards, but failing these, pans can be used quite successfully; they should be smooth and quite free from grease or crumbs; line with waxed paper and oil very lightly with olive oil, rubbing it with the fingertips.

Dredge the meringues lightly with superfine sugar, put in a 225° oven until they are firm and crisp both on top and underneath, but not colored. This may take 3 to 4 hours. As the meringues should not color and to maintain the necessary low temperature the oven door can be left ajar.

MERINGUE À LA CHANTILLY

For 12 meringue shells (6 whole meringues) allow $\frac{2}{3}$ cup heavy cream. Sweeten and flavor it with 2 tablespoons of sugar and a drop of vanilla and whip stiffly. Sandwich the meringue cases together in pairs with the cream (which may be either spread with a knife or piped) and place the meringues in paper cases. If the cream is piped, use a pastry bag fitted with a star tip and finish with a row of stars where the meringues join. Sprinkle the cream with chopped nuts, crushed candied violets, or flaked chocolate.

When the meringues are to be served as the dessert for lunch or dinner they may, if desired, be accompanied by a chocolate sauce.

MERINGUE TOPPING FOR TARTS, ETC.

Allow up to $\frac{1}{4}$ cup superfine sugar to each egg white. Beat the egg white until very stiff, then fold the sugar in lightly. Pipe on top of the (cooked) tart or pudding and put into a 300° oven for 30 minutes or a 425° oven for about 10 minutes till crisp to the touch and very lightly colored.

MESCAL

An alcoholic beverage made in Mexico and South America from the maguey, a species of agave. The fleshy leaves are chewed by Indians as a drug.

METABOLISM

The chemical reaction that takes place in the body enabling it to make use of food for energy, building, and repair.

The carbohydrates are absorbed into the blood as sugars; these are then either used in the tissues to provide energy or else stored as glycogen in the liver or muscles. Any excess of sugar is converted into fat and leads to obesity. When energy is required, the carbohydrate is oxidized and broken down into carbon dioxide and water.

Fat is also used to produce energy and is a more concentrated source than carbohydrates. It is stored in the body and supports certain organs such as the kidneys, acting as a kind of protection and energy store.

The amino acids from proteins are built again into proteins and used for new tissue to repair the old – indeed proteins form part of every cell in the body. Some of the protein eaten is used to provide energy, if carbohydrate is not eaten at the same time. Eventually protein in the body breaks down and is excreted to be replaced by fresh protein.

People differ in their rates of metabolism. Some people can burn up energy and food much quicker than others and can therefore consume larger quantities of food without putting on weight. People with a slow metabolism can eat small quantities of food, yet still suffer from weight increase. Certain drugs can change body metabolism, but these should never be taken without medical advice.

METRICATION

Today the metric system is used in all the world's industrialized nations except the United States. The Metric Conversion Act of 1975 made the conversion voluntary and polls show that Americans oppose the switchover 2 to 1. Nonetheless, many cookbooks and magazines now give metric measurements as well as traditional American measures. The exact conversions are too complicated to use in recipes, hence the approximate equivalent is used. Care is always taken to insure that the recipes work, but if traditional and metric quantities are given, only one should be followed. See metric conversion charts on page 444.

MICROWAVE COOKING

Microwave cooking utilizes electronic energy which passes through the mass of food, cooking it simultaneously throughout. It is important to note that the heat is produced within the food itself and not conducted from an outside source. Waves are then reflected by revolving blades and then by contact with the sides of the oven. Glass, porcelain, china, paper, and plastic transmit microwaves and thus remain cool; avoid foil containers which shield the food.

This method of cooking is now widely used in the home as well as in restaurants and eating establishments. It is particularly valuable for cooking foods from frozen in a very short time. Also, they are cheaper to run than conventional ovens. One disadvantage is that food does not brown, so colorful decoration and garnishing are important. However, a browning dish is now available within the microwave; this helps to overcome the problem of browning with some dishes. Microwave cooking does not tenderize meat so good cuts are preferable. Other cuts can be tenderized by pounding or marinating.

Microwave Ovens
These are units which can sit on top of a work surface without taking up too much room. The oven cavity is entirely metal and contains the microwaves which are deflected off the walls and base to be absorbed by the food. The door and surrounding frame is provided with special seals constructed to insure that the microwaves are confined within. As the door is opened the power is automatically shut off.

Reputable manufacturers insure that the microwave oven is electrically safe and that the radiation leakage is insignificant.

MILK

Milk is one of the most complete of all foods. In a mixed diet it is particularly significant as a source of protein, calcium, and riboflavin. It is especially important for growing children, pregnant women, nursing mothers, and the elderly. The latter find it particularly valuable as it does not require preparation.

Milk is a very versatile food as it can be taken as it is or made into many interesting and nutritious dishes.

Care of Milk
As milk is a perishable food the following points should be remembered:
1. Do not leave milk in the sunlight as it destroys the B vitamins.
2. Keep milk in a cool place, preferably a refrigerator.
3. Milk should always be used in rotation, the supply not exceeding that of 2 or 3 days.

Grading of Milk
All milk sold in the United States for interstate consumption is pasteurized, except for a small quantity of raw milk sold from farms with certified herds and governed by state laws, some of which permit sale and others not. Dairy cooperatives, which serve regions, combine all the milk of that region, standardizing the taste of milk from various herds.

Pasteurization is a process of heat treatment applied immediately before bottling destroys any pathogenic (disease-carrying) organisms. Milk is heated to 161° for 15 seconds and then quickly cooled to below 50° and bottled. The pathogenic organisms are destroyed and the milk souring organisms reduced in number.

WHOLE MILK
Fresh milk containing 4 percent butterfat. It has not been homogenized and upon standing will form a cream line, the butterfat rising to the top of the container.

HOMOGENIZED MILK
Also fresh milk containing 4 percent butterfat. In the course of processing, the butterfat is broken

down into fine globules distributed throughout the milk. As a result, the cream never rises. Although this milk is easier to digest, it allows the processor to add older milk to fresh milk without fear of detection by curdling.

SKIM MILK

Milk from which the butterfat has been removed. It has about half the caloric value of whole milk and the same protein and mineral values. It is usually enriched with vitamins A and D.

BUTTERMILK

Pasteurized skim milk that is treated with a specific bacteria culture to give it a sour, refreshing taste. It contains more lactic acid than skim milk and is more easily digested. Originally, buttermilk was the residue of buttermaking.

SOUR MILK

Pasteurized milk left to sour simply spoils and becomes unfit for consumption. If a recipe calls for sour milk, add 1 tablespoon lemon juice or distilled white vinegar to the measuring cup and fill to the 1-cup mark with fresh or evaporated milk. Allow to stand until curdled. Curdled raw milk can be used in cooking.

CONDENSED MILK

Whole or skimmed milk reduced by evaporation and usually sweetened with sugar. The water content is reduced by 60 percent. It has a shelf life of about 6 months. After opening, the milk will keep for a considerable time as the low proportion of water and high proportion of sugar do not promote bacterial growth.

EVAPORATED MILK

Whole milk freed from 50 percent of its water content. It can be used in place of fresh milk by substituting $\frac{1}{2}$ cup water for every cup milk required. It has a shelf life of 6 months and should be treated like fresh milk after opening.

DRY MILK SOLIDS

Air-dried particles of whole or skim milk from which all but 5 percent of the moisture has been removed. Unopened dry milk should be stored in a cool, dry place and after opening be refrigerated. To reconstitute dry milk, place 3 to 4 tablespoons in a cup measure. Add water to fill. In baking dry milk should be mixed with the flour.

See Cream and Yogurt entries.

Milk Shake

A creamy cold beverage made of milk, ice cream, flavoring or syrup blended together. To make, mix $\frac{3}{4}$ cup of milk with 2 scoops of ice cream and 2 teaspoons vanilla or 2 tablespoons coffee, chocolate, maple, strawberry or other flavoring syrup. Blend in an electric blender until frothy.

MILLE-FEUILLES

Layers of puff pastry filled with jam and/or cream or pastry cream; the top is often sprinkled with powdered sugar, or it can also be made with cheese for an appetizer.

MILLE-FEUILLES PASTRY

$7\frac{1}{2}$ oz package frozen puff pastry, thawed
2–3 tablespoons raspberry jam
$\frac{1}{2}$ cup heavy cream, whipped
glaze
1–2 tablespoons chopped nuts

Roll the pastry into a strip $\frac{1}{4}$ inch thick, 4 inches wide, and 12 inches long. Brush the baking sheet with water, lay the pastry on it and cut it from side to side in strips 2 inches wide, but don't separate the slices. Bake in a 450° oven for about 10 minutes. Separate the strips and cool them; split each into two and sandwich them together in threes or fours with jam and cream spread between layers. Cover the tops with glaze and sprinkle chopped nuts at each end.

Note: Ready-made pastry should be rolled thinner than homemade.

MILLE-FEUILLES GÂTEAU

$\frac{1}{2}$ package (17$\frac{1}{4}$ oz size) frozen puff pastry, thawed
1 quart fresh raspberries
superfine sugar
1$\frac{1}{4}$ cups heavy cream, whipped
glaze
3 tablespoons roughly chopped walnuts

Roll out the pastry very thinly (this is easier to do if it is rolled between sheets of waxed paper) and cut into three 6-inch rounds. Place on dampened baking sheets, prick and bake in a 450° oven for 8 to 10 minutes, until crisp and golden brown. Cool on a cooling rack.

Reserve a few raspberries for decoration and then crush and sweeten the remainder. Sandwich the pastry rounds together with layers of cream and raspberries spread between, cover the top with glaze and decorate with raspberries and nuts.

MILLET

A cereal which is easily grown in dry regions and is the staple food of many people in Africa and in some parts of Asia. With the introduction of new methods of cultivation, including irrigation, millet tends to be replaced by wheat and is thought to be inferior. It is true that millet is not as pleasant to eat, but it has quite a high protein value.

There are many varieties and names including sorghum, kaffir corn, finger millet, and pearl millet.

Like most cereals, millet is husked and then ground into meal. It can also be fermented to produce an alcoholic drink.

MILT

The soft roe of fish, also the spleen of animals.

MINCE

The British name given to ground meat. (See Hamburger entry.)

MINCEMEAT

The minced fruit mixture used as a filling for mince pies, which are part of the traditional Christmas fare in Britain. The original mincemeat included cooked lean beef, though today this is omitted.

A rich mincemeat is best when allowed to mature for a month after it is made, but if a larger amount of apple and no brandy are included it should not be kept more than a week or it may ferment.

Mincemeat is usually made into mince pies or mince tarts. It is always tasty in less traditional desserts; it blends well with apples and pears.

MINCEMEAT

3 cups currants, cleaned
3 cups golden raisins
3 cups black raisins
3 cups chopped mixed citrus peel
1 lb cooking apples, peeled and cored
1 cup almonds, blanched
2¼ cups firmly packed dark brown sugar
8 oz shredded suet (optional)
1 teaspoon ground nutmeg
1 teaspoon ground cinnamon
grated rind and juice of 2 lemons

Finely chop the prepared fruit, mixed peel, apples, and almonds. Add the sugar, suet (if used), spices, lemon rind and juice and mix all the ingredients thoroughly together. Cover the mincemeat and let stand for 2 days. Stir well and put into jars. Cover as for jam and allow to mature for at least 2 weeks before using.

Note: For mincemeat that will keep well, use a firm, hard apple; a juicy apple may make the mixture too moist.

MINCE PIES

To make individual mince pies, line muffin pans with 3-inch rounds of pastry dough. Fill each with mincemeat and moisten the edges with cold water or white of egg. Cover with rounds of pastry and press the edges together. Make a small hole in the top of each pie, brush with white of egg and sprinkle with sugar. Bake in a 450° oven for 20 minutes, or until the pies are well risen and nicely browned.

If desired, serve dusted with powdered sugar.

MINCING

To chop or cut into small pieces with a knife or in a food processor.

MINERALS

Various chemical substances which are necessary for the efficient working of the body are referred to as "minerals." Those which are most likely to be deficient in the diet are calcium and iron and it is important to include food rich in these substances. Traces of other minerals – copper, iodine, cobalt, fluorine – are also important but these are not likely to be in short supply. Other chemicals, such as sulfur, potassium, sodium, phosphorus, and magnesium are present in a normal diet in an adequate amount for health.

MINERAL WATER

Natural mineral waters containing various minerals, and sometimes charged with carbonated gas, spring from the earth in many places. A great many of these are claimed to have medicinal properties and at some places the waters are bottled and sold (e.g., Vichy and Seltzer water).

Commercially the name "mineral water" is given to various carbonated liquids, such as soda water, lemonade, etc., intended for table use. (See individual entries for details.)

MINESTRA

An Italian term for thick soup.

MINESTRA DI CAVOLFIORE

1 large cauliflower
½ onion, peeled and chopped
3 tablespoons oil
4 tablespoons butter
4 cups chicken broth
¾ cup rice
½ cup Parmesan cheese, grated

Remove green leaves from cauliflower, separate into flowerets and wash. Sauté onion in a large saucepan with all the oil and half the butter until browned. Add chicken broth, cauliflower and rice. Cover and simmer for 20 minutes. To serve, pour into a soup tureen, stir in the remaining butter, and sprinkle with Parmesan cheese.

MINESTRONE

The most celebrated Italian soup, made from a variety of vegetables and pasta and served with grated Parmesan cheese. A number of different recipes exist.

MINESTRONE

½ leek, shredded and washed
1 onion, finely chopped
1 clove garlic, crushed
2 tablespoons butter
4 cups chicken broth
1 carrot, cut into thin strips
1 turnip, cut into thin strips
1 stalk celery, trimmed and thinly sliced
3 tablespoons elbow macaroni
¼ cabbage, washed and finely shredded
½ cup diagonally sliced green beans
3 tablespoons fresh or frozen peas
1 teaspoon tomato paste or 4 tomatoes peeled and
   sliced
1–2 strips of bacon, chopped and fried
salt
pepper
grated Parmesan cheese

Lightly sauté the leek, onion, and garlic in the melted butter for 5 to 10 minutes, until soft. Add the broth, bring to a boil, add the carrot, turnip, celery, and macaroni and simmer, covered, for 20 to 30 minutes. Add the cabbage, beans, and peas, cover and simmer for a further 20 minutes. Stir in the tomato paste or tomatoes, bacon, and season-ing to taste. Bring back to a boil. Serve the grated Parmesan cheese in a separate dish.

MINT

An aromatic perennial plant used to flavor a number of dishes. A sprig of mint is cooked with new potatoes and peas, mint sauce is served with lamb or mutton, and chopped mint may be added to salads. A sprig of mint can be added to lemonade, other drinks or sorbets to give a refreshing flavor, while a mint-flavored syrup can be used to sweeten tea.

There are several kinds of mint which have varying uses.

SPEARMINT

The everyday garden mint used for flavoring vegetables and in mint sauce.

BOWLES MINT

Has a green furry leaf, a more delicate flavor, and does not grow wild.

APPLEMINT

Has a rounded variegated leaf, a delicate flavor; used in fruit cups and chutneys.

PEPPERMINT

This is used for flavoring chewing gum, tooth-paste and for medicinal purposes. The flavoring, peppermint oil, is extracted from this herb.

FRESH MINT SAUCE

small bunch mint, washed
2 teaspoons sugar
1 tablespoon boiling water
1–2 tablespoons vinegar

Put the mint leaves and the sugar on a board and chop finely. Put into the sauceboat, add the boiling water, and stir until the sugar has dissolved. Stir in the vinegar to taste. The sauce should sit for 1 hour before being served.

MINT SAUCE FOR WINTER

2 cups wine vinegar
⅔ cup young mint
2 tablespoons sugar

This is prepared in the same general way but no water is added and the mint leaves must be completely dried before they are chopped. The sauce will then keep through the winter.

MINT JELLY

5½ lb cooking apples
4½ cups water
bunch fresh mint
4½ cups vinegar
sugar
6–8 tablespoons chopped mint
green coloring, optional

Wash and coarsely chop the apples, put in a large saucepan with the water and bunch of mint and simmer until really soft. Add the vinegar and boil for 5 minutes. Strain through cheesecloth. Measure the liquid and return it to the pan with 1 lb sugar to every 2 cups liquid. Stir until the sugar has dissolved and boil rapidly until a "jelly" is obtained on testing. Stir in the chopped mint and a few drops of coloring if you wish. Skim, jar, and cover in the usual way.

MINT JULEP

(See Julep entry.)

MIRABELLE (MYROBALAN)

A small, round plum, golden yellow or red in color, which is grown in various parts of Europe and Great Britain, and ripens in July and August. In France, particularly in Alsace, a liqueur of the same name is made from the fruit. Called Cherry plums in Great Britain, they are rather mealy and uninteresting when eaten raw, but are excellent stewed or made into tarts and are also good for preserving. The skins are tough, but they can be slipped off the cooked plum quite easily.

MIREPOIX

A mixture of carrots, celery, and onion, often including some ham or bacon, which are diced, sautéed in fat and used as a "bed" on which to braise meat.

MIRLITON

(See Chayote entry.)

MIXED GRILL

(See Broiling entry.)

MIXED SPICE

A blend of ground or powdered cinnamon, nutmeg, and cloves. It sometimes includes any or all of the following: coriander, caraway, cassia, ginger, cardamom, and allspice. Mixed spice is used in Great Britain to flavor puddings, cookies, and cakes.

MOCHA

A strongly flavored coffee imported from Arabia. It is used mainly in blended coffee since most people find it too rich unless mixed with other coffee beans.

The word "mocha" is often used to describe cakes and pies flavored with coffee and is sometimes applied to a mixture of coffee and chocolate flavorings.

MOCK TURTLE SOUP

A brown soup made from calf's head which is supposed to resemble real turtle soup. After cooking, the pieces of meat from the head are removed and then cut into tiny pieces which when cool are added to the soup at the last minute.

MOLASSES

The general term used for the thick, brown syrupy drainings from raw sugar or the syrup obtained from the sugar during the process of refinement. It varies in color from deep amber to dark brown; the lighter the color the better the grade.

The best grades are made from the first boiling and crystalization of cane sugar juice. Successive boilings produce the darker mixture, low in sugar content, called blackstrap that is used mainly to feed cattle. Molasses drained from beet sugar is very bitter and unpleasant tasting.

Today molasses is used in cooking mainly as flavoring, though it was once a common sweetener in the United States.

Shoofly Pie, a traditional Pennsylvania Dutch favorite, is a rich molasses sponge cake baked in a crust and so named because it was so sweet that flies had to be continually shooed away as it cooled on the window sill.

SHOOFLY PIE

1 8- or 9-inch pie shell
1 teaspoon baking soda
1 cup boiling water
1 cup molasses
¼ teaspoon salt
1 cup flour
⅓ cup firmly packed brown sugar
¼ cup solid shortening
ice cream

Prick the bottom and sides of the pie shell with a fork, fill with pie weights and bake in a preheated 350° oven for about 5 minutes. In a mixing bowl combine the soda with the boiling water and mix until soda is dissolved. Stir in the molasses and salt and blend well.

In another bowl, combine flour and brown sugar. Add shortening and cut into dry ingredients with a fork or a pastry blender until mixture resembles fine crumbs.

Pour molasses mixture into prebaked pie shell and sprinkle the brown sugar crumb mixture over the top. Bake in a preheated 375° oven for about 10 minutes. Reduce heat to 350° and continue baking for 30 minutes, or until center of the pie is set. Serve hot or cold with ice cream, if desired.

BOSTON BROWN BREAD

This rich molasses bread is traditionally served with Boston Baked Beans.

1 cup rye flour
1 cup cornmeal
1 cup whole wheat flour
2 teaspoons baking soda
1 teaspoon salt
¾ cup molasses
2 cups buttermilk

In a large bowl, combine rye flour, cornmeal, wheat flour, baking soda, and salt. Blend the molasses and buttermilk together and stir into the dry ingredients. Blend well and pour into 2 well-greased pudding molds (or fill a 1 lb coffee can two-thirds full) and cover securely with a well-greased lid or piece of heavy-duty foil. Tie lid or foil down securely and place on a rack in a heavy deep Dutch oven filled with about 1 inch of boiling water, cover pot and steam over low heat for about 3 hours.

MOLD

A hollow dish which can be of varying shapes, used for making certain desserts and other dishes. Molds can be made of plastic, metal, glass, or china and usually have indentations which are printed on the food when it is turned out. The food is placed in the mold while in a liquid form then chilled or cooked to become a solid mass. (See recipe below.)

The term also applies to a furry, green growth which consists of minute fungi. It will grow on meat, cheese, bread, and sweet food if the correct conditions of warmth and moisture are present. The growth usually indicates that the food is not fresh. Although not harmful, the mold gives food an unpleasant taste and appearance.

Certain mold growths are responsible for the flavor and color in cheeses such as Roquefort, Stilton, and Camembert (outside skin). However, these are controlled and deliberately introduced.

VEAL, HAM AND TONGUE MOLDED SALAD

2 cups aspic
3 hard-cooked eggs, sliced
½ lb cooked veal, diced
½ lb cooked tongue, diced
½ lb cooked ham, diced

Line an oblong cake or bread pan with almost-setting aspic and decorate it with slices of hard-cooked egg. Chop up any remaining egg and mix it with the diced meat. Put the mixture into the pan and cover with aspic. When set, turn out and serve, cut into slices.

A colorful accompaniment is a salad of cooked asparagus and tiny red tomatoes stuffed with cubed cucumber and peas in mayonnaise.

MOLE SAUCE

A Mexican sauce with nearly as many variations as there are of curry in India, some mole sauces dating from Aztec times. The essential ingredient of them all is chili pepper; the word mole deriving from *molli* which means a "sauce flavored with chili." Though many mole sauces are hot, there are also milder variations. Among the most popular versions is green mole, made with chilis, tomatoes, garlic, onion, coriander, ground pumpkin seeds, almonds and walnuts. But surely the most famous is Mole Poblano (mole Puebla style), the rich sauce that owes its dark brown color to the bitter chocolate it contains. Although the taste of chocolate is hard to detect in this sauce, that unusual ingredient is responsible for its unique character. Mole poblano is used with pork and chicken, and most notably with turkey in Mole Poblano de Guajolote, one of Mexico's favorite holiday meals.

MOLE POBLANO

10–12 dried hot green chilis, stems and seeds removed
⅔ cup almonds
1 medium onion, coarsely chopped

3 medium tomatoes, peeled, seeded, and coarsely
    chopped
½ teaspoon each ground cinnamon, ground cloves,
    ground coriander seeds, and anise seeds
1 clove garlic, minced
½ cup raisins
2 tablespoons sesame seeds
1 flour tortilla, cut in thin strips
salt
pepper
2 tablespoons lard or butter
2 oz bitter chocolate
2 cups chicken stock

Place chilis in a small bowl, pour about 2 cups of
boiling water over them and let soak for about 1
hour.

Place almonds in a food processor and process
until finely ground. Add onion, tomatoes, spices,
garlic, raisins, sesame seeds, tortilla strips, chilis
and their soaking liquid, and season with salt and
pepper. Process until the mixture is pureed and
very smooth.

In a large skillet, melt the lard or butter. Add
the mole puree and simmer, stirring, for about 6
minutes. Stir in chocolate and cook, stirring, over
low heat until chocolate is melted. Stir in the
stock and cook, stirring, for a few minutes
longer.

Pour sauce over turkey, chicken or pork pieces
that have been precooked, and let the meat
simmer in the mole sauce for 30 minutes or so
over low heat.

MOLLUSK

A large, general category of invertebrates found
both on land and in water and usually protected
by a hard shell of one or two parts. The soft,
unsegmented bodies inside the shells of many
mollusks are eaten widely; some of them considered delicacies. The most sought-after land
mollusk is the snail. Sea mollusks sought after for
their delicate flesh include oysters, clams, scallops, mussels, abalones. Other edible mollusks
include cuttlefish, squid, octopus, periwinkles,
limpets, and conch.

MONKFISH

An exceedingly ugly fish, with an enormous
head and a broad gaping mouth, that is found in
the Atlantic from Newfoundland to the Caribbean, as well as off the coasts of many European
countries. It is known by a number of other
names: lote, goosefish, bellyfish, sea devil, and,
perhaps most familiar, anglerfish. The last name
derives from the fish's manner of catching

its prey by "angling" with a rod-like appendage
on its head that lures small fish into its large
mouth. Despite its grotesque appearance, the
monkfish has firm white flesh with a very sweet
flavor which has been compared to that of
lobster. Until recently the monkfish was considered a "trash" fish in the United States, but it has
now begun to appear more regularly in fish
markets and has started to command the respect
of fish lovers. It is suitable for almost any cooking
method, and is particularly good for skewering
and grilling. The Mediterranean monkfish is an
important ingredient in bouillabaisse.

MONOSODIUM GLUTAMATE (SODIUM GLUTAMATE)

This is the sodium salt of the amino acid called
glutamic acid – an almost tasteless substance
which constitutes part of the casein of milk. It
brings out the flavor of other foods, and is often
added to manufactured meat, fish, soups, and
other products; fruit and sweet dishes are less
suitable for this treatment. The amount required
is very small – about 1 in 3,000 parts. MSG, as it is
called, is often used with a rather heavy hand in
Chinese cooking and has been blamed in recent
years for causing an allergic reaction dubbed
"Chinese restaurant syndrome;" among the
symptoms are dizziness and headaches.

Consequently, the use of MSG has been
greatly curtailed in home and restaurant cooking, as well as in manufactured products such as
baby food.

MONTEREY JACK

An American cheese produced in Monterey
County in California from pasteurized cow's
milk and which resembles a fine mild Cheddar. It
can be made from whole or skim milk. When
young the cheese is soft and mild. Aged varieties
are sharper. Aging usually takes from 3 to 6
weeks. Dry Jack is aged for at least 6 months and
is a hard, sharp cheese intended for grating.

MOREL

A succulent edible fungus which is grayish-
yellow to black and has a spongelike
honeycombed cap. It grows in woods during the
spring. Morel is used in cooking to garnish soups
and sauces or as a side dish sautéed in butter. It is
available in a dried form to use as a flavoring for
sauces or meat, poultry or fish. It is one of the
most delicious and expensive of all mushrooms.

MORNAY SAUCE

A classic French sauce consisting of a basic
Béchamel or white sauce to which grated cheese
has been added. It was named for De Mornay, a
friend of France's King Henri IV, who was said to
have been responsible for its invention. Some
recipes also call for the addition of heavy cream
and an egg yolk. Others use chicken stock or fish
stock. In most cases grated Gruyère or Parmesan,
or a combination of the two are used. The sauce is
particularly good over eggs, fish, chicken, and
vegetables. It can also be used on veal or pasta.

MORNAY SAUCE

2 cups Béchamel (see entry)
2 tablespoons heavy cream
¼ cup grated Gruyère cheese
¼ cup grated Parmesan cheese
salt
pepper
pinch of nutmeg

Bring the Béchamel to a boil in a medium
saucepan. Stir in the cream. Remove from the
heat, add Gruyère and Parmesan and beat with a
wire whisk until cheeses are melted and the sauce
is smooth. Season to taste with salt, pepper, and
nutmeg.

MORTADELLA

A large sausage made in Bologna, Italy; it consists
of finely ground pork, beef and pork fat, flavored
with coriander and white wine, and, sometimes,
pistachio nuts. The mixture is stuffed into casings, then smoked. The American version is
generally not smoked and often lacks the flavor
and texture of the original.

MOSEL

The name given to wines made in the vineyards
in the Mosel area of Germany. They resemble
Rhine wine, but have a very fine flavor, and are
dry and clear. They can be served as a drink
without food or with light meals.

MOULARD DUCK

A domestic breed of duck which has just started
to be produced in the United States. It is a cross
between the Muscovy and the white Peking
duck, and is being raised both for its flavorful
flesh and the highly prized fattened liver or foie
gras – recently available fresh in this country.

MOULES MARINIÈRE

(See Mussel entry.)

MOUNTAIN ASH

(See Rowan Berry entry.)

MOUSSAKA

A dish eaten in Balkan and Near Eastern countries. It is one of the most popular and well-
known dishes in Greek cookery. There are many
variations, but it generally contains meat (usually
lamb) and eggplant.

EGGPLANT MOUSSAKA

2 eggplants, sliced
3–4 tablespoons olive oil
4–5 medium-sized onions, peeled and sliced
1 lb raw beef or lamb, ground
4 tomatoes, peeled and sliced
⅔ cup beef broth
3 tablespoons tomato paste
2 eggs
3 tablespoons milk
3 tablespoons cream
salt and pepper

Sauté eggplants in half of the oil for about 2 to 4
minutes, then arrange them in the bottom of an
ovenproof dish. Sauté the onions and meat until
lightly browned – about 3 minutes. Place layers
of onion and ground meat on top of the eggplants
and add the slices of tomato. Mix the broth and
tomato paste and pour into the dish. Bake in a
350° oven for about 20 minutes. Beat together the
eggs, milk, and cream, season well and pour this
mixture over the meat. Put it back into the oven
for 15 to 20 minutes, until the sauce is set and the
mixture is golden and firm to touch.

MOUSSE

A mousse is a light creamy dish which may be hot
or cold, sweet or not. It has as its base a white or
custard sauce, or a fruit puree to which eggs and
whipped cream are often added. A cold mousse
can be frozen but when a gelatin mixture is used it
only needs to be chilled.

RASPBERRY MOUSSE

3 packages (10 oz each) frozen raspberries, thawed
*   and drained or 1 lb fresh raspberries, sieved, to*
*   make ½ pint puree*

sugar to taste
⅔ cup heavy cream, whipped
4 teaspoons gelatin
3 tablespoons water or raspberry juice
2 egg whites, beaten
whipped cream for decoration

Mix the raspberry puree, sugar, and cream. Put the gelatin and water or fruit juice in a bowl, stand the bowl in a pan of hot water and heat gently until the gelatin is dissolved. Allow to cool slightly. Pour into the raspberry mixture in a steady stream, constantly stirring, and fold in the beaten egg whites. Pour into a dish and leave in a cool place to set. Decorate with whipped cream.

SALMON MOUSSE

2 (7½ oz) cans salmon
1 cup milk
2 tablespoons butter
3 tablespoons flour
2 eggs, separated
⅔ cup heavy cream, lightly whipped
2 tablespoons tomato catsup
1 teaspoon anchovy paste
1 teaspoon lemon juice
salt
pepper
4 teaspoons gelatin
4 tablespoons warm water
slices of cucumber to garnish

Drain the juice from the salmon and add enough milk to make 1 cup. Remove the skin and bones from the fish and mash the flesh until smooth. Melt the butter, stir in the flour and cook for 2 to 3 minutes. Remove the pan from the heat and add the egg yolks. Allow the sauce to cook slightly and stir in the cream, catsup, anchovy, lemon juice, and seasoning to taste and add it to the salmon. Dissolve the gelatin in the water by putting it in a small bowl over a pan of hot water; stir into the salmon mixture. Beat the egg whites stiffly and fold these into the mixture. Pour it into a 7-inch soufflé dish and chill until firm. Garnish with slices of cucumber before serving.

MOUSSELINE SAUCE

Hollandaise sauce to which beaten egg white or whipped cream has been added just before serving, giving a frothy effect. Serve as soon as possible; it is a good accompaniment for fish (e.g. sole) or green vegetables such as asparagus.

A sweet mousseline sauce can be made from eggs, sugar, and sherry beaten together over hot water; it is served with sponge cakes and fruit.

MOZZARELLA

A white Italian cheese traditionally made from buffalo milk. It is very soft and moist and should be eaten when freshly made and unripened. Mozzarella is often used in making pizzas. Smoked mozzarella has a golden skin. Now most mozzarella is made with cow's milk and it is produced widely outside of Italy, especially in the United States.

MUESLI

A cereal which was first made in Switzerland for health reasons by Dr Bircher-Benner toward the end of the nineteenth century. It consists of a mixture of raw cereals which includes some or all of the following: oats, wheat, rye, millet, and barley flakes; to these are added dried fruit, nuts, sugar, bran, wheatgerm, and apple flakes. Muesli has now become a popular breakfast cereal served with milk and sometimes yogurt or cream.

There are many commercial varieties on the market, most of which have a high sugar content.

MUFFIN

A small, round sweet bread or cake served hot with butter and usually eaten for breakfast. The origin of the word is uncertain, but it may have come from the word *Muffe* which means "cake" in low German. Muffins are made from batters of white, whole-grain, and rice flours, cornmeal, bran, etc., and often contain nuts, fruit, or berries. Today most muffins use baking powder as the leavening agent.

BLUEBERRY MUFFINS

¼ cup butter, melted
2 eggs, lightly beaten
¾ cup half-and-half
⅓ cup sugar
¾ teaspoon salt
2 teaspoons baking powder
1¾ cups all-purpose flour
1¼ cups blueberries

In a large mixing bowl, combine butter, eggs, half-and-half, and sugar and beat until well blended. In a separate bowl, combine salt, baking powder, and flour. Add dry ingredients to the liquid and blend just long enough to moisten dry ingredients. Fold blueberries into the batter and pour batter into greased muffin pans, filling each about three-quarters full. Bake in a 400° oven for about 25 minutes.

Cranberry-nut muffins: Substitute ¾ cup of split cranberries and add ½ cup of chopped walnuts.

Raspberry muffins: Substitute 1 cup raspberries and, if desired, add 1 teaspoon grated orange or lemon rind.

MULBERRY

A fruit similar to the blackberry but larger. The black mulberry of Asian origin is the tastiest variety. The red mulberry, an American variety, has red berries, ripening to a deep purple color when ready for picking. Mulberries are eaten raw with sugar for dessert and they may also be stewed in syrup, made into pies or flans, canned, or made into wine. As mulberries have a low pectin content they do not make satisfactory jams or jellies when used alone, but can be combined with apple.

MULBERRY AND APPLE JAM

3 pints mulberries
2 cups water
1 lb apples (prepared weight)
6¾ cups sugar

Wash the mulberries and simmer them in half the water until they are soft. Peel, core, and slice the apples, weigh them and simmer gently in the remaining water until they are very soft. Combine the mulberries and the apples and add the sugar. Stir until this is dissolved and then boil the jam until setting point is reached. Jar and cover in the usual way. *Makes about 5 lb.*

MULLED WINE OR ALE

These are made by heating, spicing, and sweetening the wine or ale. The hot liquor is sometimes poured over beaten eggs.

MULLED RED WINE

5 cups red wine
½ lemon, sliced
piece of cinnamon stick
4 cloves or pinch of grated nutmeg
¼ cup sugar

Heat all the ingredients together but do not boil. Pour into a hot jug and serve at once.

MULLED ALE

5 cups ale
1 tablespoon sugar
pinch of ground cloves
pinch of ground nutmeg
pinch of ground ginger
1 glass rum or brandy

Heat all the ingredients except the rum or brandy to nearly boiling point. Add the rum or brandy with more sugar or flavorings if required and serve at once.

MULLET

A saltwater fish, which may be of two different unrelated families.

RED MULLET
This is a striking looking fish, bright pink in color; one variety also has 2 to 5 bright yellow bands from head to tail. Red mullet are only 2 lb to 3 lb in weight when fully grown and are at their best from April to October. The flesh is firm and white and has a delicious but very delicate flavor, so it should be grilled, broiled or baked. The best red mullet are found in the Mediterranean. But a similar fish is found on the Atlantic coast of the United States.

Clean the fish thoroughly, retaining and replacing the liver, which is regarded as a delicacy. Score the fish twice on each side, season well, and sprinkle with lemon juice. Wrap in wax paper, adding a few pats of butter, lay in a greased, ovenproof dish and bake in a 400° oven for 15 to 20 minutes. To serve, arrange in a hot dish, still in the paper, which should be opened up to show the fish.

GRAY MULLET
This has a greenish back, with a silvery underside. Gray mullets reach 10 lb to 12 lb in weight when fully grown. They are very plentiful in both the Atlantic and Pacific Oceans. The most important species found in United States waters are the striped mullet and the smaller white mullet. When large they are treated as cod; small ones may be cooked in the same way as red mullet, although the flavor is not so good. The flesh is white and firm and easy to digest.

MULLIGATAWNY SOUP

A curry-flavored soup of Anglo-Indian origin, made with meat or chicken broth.

MULLIGATAWNY SOUP

1 thick slice bacon, diced
2 tablespoons butter
2 onions, chopped
1 carrot, chopped
½ turnip, chopped
1 sour apple, peeled and chopped
1 tablespoon curry powder
1 teaspoon curry paste
½ cup all-purpose flour
4 cups chicken broth
salt
pepper
bouquet garni
squeeze of lemon juice
1–2 tablespoons half-and-half

Sauté the bacon lightly, add the butter and when this has melted, sauté the vegetables, apple, curry powder and paste. Stir in the flour, then gradually add the broth. Bring to a boil, stirring, add salt, pepper, bouquet garni, then cover and simmer gently for about 1 hour, skimming occasionally. Sieve the soup or puree in a blender, return it to the saucepan and boil. Add more seasonings if necessary and stir in the lemon juice and half-and-half. Serve accompanied with boiled rice.

MUNG BEAN

This tiny light green bean, also known as the green gram, is the source of the most common type of bean sprout. It is grown widely in India, China, and other parts of Asia, and is incorporated in many Indian and Oriental dishes. Mung beans are high in protein and vitamins, have a fresh flavor and a crunchy texture. The Chinese call it the "tooth vegetable" because of its texture which is particularly good in salads. Mung beans sprout quickly and without soil if kept in a warm, damp spot. In their dried form, mung beans can be used in soups and stews or ground into bean flour.

MÜNSTER

A semi-hard cheese from the Münster Valley on the border between France and Germany. Often square in shape, it is yellow in color and has a red rind. Münster is made from whole milk, flavored with caraway or aniseed, and is good for both table and kitchen use. Münster made in the United States is made with pasteurized milk, is milder, and also yellow in color.

MUSCADET

A fresh, dry white wine made from Muscadet grapes grown in the Loire vineyards of France. Also produced in Italy and Chile. It is often drunk as an apéritif and is also suitable to serve with light meals.

MUSCATEL

The name is applied to strong sweet wines made from Muscat grapes in France, Spain, and Italy. In the United States an inexpensive sweet amber-colored wines goes by that name. The name is also used to describe raisins made from Muscat grapes.

MUSCOVY DUCK

This domestic duck, also known as the Barbary duck, is descended from a wild species found in Mexico and South America, and is characterized by a very large breast. It was imported to Europe in the 1700s and is now raised in most countries of the world. Muscovy has a stronger flavor than the Long Island variety which is descended from the Peking duck, and takes longer to cook than the latter. It can be prepared by the same method as wild duck (see Wild Duck entry).

MUSH

Cornmeal boiled in water or milk until it forms a soft mass.

MUSHROOMS

Several varieties of edible fungi are included under this name.

Mushrooms and other fungi should never be eaten if there is the slightest doubt about their identity and the only safe way of recognizing the edible types is to learn their botanical characteristics from a really reliable illustrated book or chart. There are various more or less superstitious beliefs – for instance, that cooked poisonous fungi will blacken a silver spoon, while edible ones will not, or that edible fungi all have a skin that peels easily; however, none of these methods of telling edible from poisonous mushrooms is reliable.

CULTIVATED MUSHROOMS

These are grown on a very large scale and are available year round. They belong to the genus *Agaricus* related to the field mushroom that is known to the French as the Champignon.

Mushrooms in Cooking

The food value of mushrooms is negligible but their rich woodsy flavor makes them a good addition to stews, sauces, soups, omelets, or burgers and they provide a quickly made snack when served on toast or combined with sautéed and broiled foods. They can also add interest served raw in a salad or marinated "à la Grecque" style. Wild mushrooms need to be washed well, drained and, if necessary, peeled. Trim stems or remove completely; the stems are useful in soups or stuffings.

Cultivated mushrooms need to be wiped with a damp cloth or washed and drained.

BAKED MUSHROOMS

Wash and drain the mushrooms, or wipe them, and place them, stems up, in a greased baking dish. Put a small pat of butter on each mushroom, season with salt and pepper and cover with greased foil. Bake in a 375° oven for 15 to 30 minutes, or until cooked.

BROILED MUSHROOMS

Wipe the mushrooms and trim the stems level with the caps. Melt $\frac{1}{4}$ cup butter for every lb mushrooms. Dip the caps in butter and then put them in the broiler pan, cap up. Broil for 2 minutes, turn them, sprinkle the gills with salt and pepper and broil for 2 to 3 minutes longer.

SAUTÉED MUSHROOMS

Melt $\frac{1}{4}$ cup butter per 1 lb mushrooms in a skillet. Add the mushrooms, stems up, season with salt and pepper and if you wish add a squeeze of lemon juice. Cover the pan and cook over a moderate heat for 4 to 5 minutes. Do not turn the mushrooms over, and the juice will remain in the caps.

MUSKELLUNGE

Also known as the "muskie," this freshwater North American game fish is the largest member of the pike family, and is considered to be very good eating. It is found in the Great Lakes, as well as in northern rivers and lakes and can weigh from 15 to 60 lb or more. (The largest recorded catch was 8 feet long and 110 lb.) It can be broiled, baked, or prepared by any method suitable for cooking pike.

MUSKMELON

(See Melon entry.)

MUSSEL

A greenish-black bivalve mollusk. Take care to gather mussels from a suitable source, as they are sometimes unfit to eat. Mussels should be alive when bought – discard any with gaping shells as the fish inside will be dead.

Mussels can be purchased in jars. Before use, they must be drained and the mussels soaked.

Preparation and cooking: Wash the mussels in several changes of water, scraping and scrubbing each shell separately until it is perfectly clean. Finally, lift them out of the water, leaving any sediment behind.

Put $\frac{1}{2}$ inch water in a saucepan and add the mussels. To improve the flavor, add a slice of onion, a bay leaf, some parsley stalks, thyme, and pepper. Cover the pan tightly and cook, shaking the pan frequently, over a gentle heat for about 2 to 4 minutes, or until the shells open. Drain well, reserving the liquor and removing the beard. Serve plain with lemon juice, salt and pepper, and brown bread and butter, or accompanied by a white sauce made from the liquor. Mussels can also be added to fish soups and stews and are an important ingredient in dishes such as Paella.

MOULES MARINIÈRE

3 lb mussels
butter
4 shallots or 1 medium onion, finely chopped
$\frac{1}{2}$ bottle dry white wine
chopped parsley
2 sprigs thyme, if available
1 bay leaf
freshly ground black pepper
flour

Put the mussels in the sink under cold running water, and scrape off the mud, barnacles, seaweed, and beards with a small sharp knife. Discard any that are open or loose (unless a tap on the shell makes them close) or any that are cracked. Rinse again and soak until there is no trace of sand. Melt a large piece of butter and sauté the shallots until soft but not colored. Add the wine, a small handful of chopped parsley, the thyme, bay leaf, and a generous shake of pepper. Simmer and cover for 10 minutes. Add the drained mussels a handful at a time. Cover and steam, shaking until the shells open; this will take about 3 to 5 minutes. Holding the mussels over the saucepan to catch the juices, remove the top shells and place the mussels in warm, wide soup plates. Keep them warm. Strain the liquor and boil to reduce it by half. Thicken it a little by adding a small piece of soft butter creamed with 2 teaspoons flour. Pour over the mussels, sprinkle with more parsley and serve at once.

MUSTARD

There are two major species of mustard seed which may be ground to make mustard – yellow or white and brown or black. The black seeds contain myronic oil, which gives the true piquant flavor but makes them of poor keeping quality; the white seeds, although inferior in flavor, keep better. Manufactured mustard powder is usually a mixture of both varieties of mustard seed, with a cereal – wheat flour or some other type – added to absorb the oil and retard fermentation. Powdered black mustard is seldom on sale.

To make mustard: Place a little powdered mustard in an egg cup and mix to a smooth, soft paste with the top of the milk or water. Transfer to the mustard jar.

It is also available prepared, in jars, in a wide variety of styles.

AMERICAN MUSTARD
Made from white seeds only and made as a very mild mustard.

FRENCH MUSTARD
This is made from powdered dark mustard seeds, mixed with vinegar or wine that has been flavored with garlic, tarragon, thyme, parsley, mace, and other spices; salt is also added.

DIJON MUSTARD
Mixed with the juice of unripe grapes.

BORDEAUX MUSTARD
Mixed with unfermented wine.

CREMONA MUSTARD
An Italian mustard mixed with wine vinegar with crystalized fruit added.

Mustard can be used in cooking to bring out the flavor of an ingredient such as cheese or to counteract an oily taste as in salad dressing. It is also widely used as a seasoning with meats such as beef, pork, bacon, and liver.

MUSTARD SAUCE

1 cup white sauce
1 tablespoon dry mustard
2 teaspoons sugar
1 tablespoon vinegar

Make the sauce using all milk or half milk and half broth from fish or a chicken bouillon cube. Blend the mustard, sugar, and vinegar to a smooth cream and stir into the sauce. Serve with fish.

To vary the flavor, use some of the many different mustard mixes now available, adapting the amount added to taste.

MUSTARD AND CRESS

The hardy mustard plant is frequently grown in Britain, in conjunction with cress, a peppery-tasting green with round leaves cut when still quite young and small. Wash well, to remove seed cases and any grit, then drain. Use in salads, as a garnish, or as the British do as a sandwich filling.

MUSTARD GREENS

The leaves of the brown, leaf, or Indian mustard plant, indigenous to Europe and Asia and transplanted to the United States where it grows wild as a weed. The seeds of this plant are ground to make the condiment mustard, and the dark, strong-tasting leaves are used in the cooking of the deep South, particularly in the Soul Food of American blacks. Mustard greens can be prepared in the same manner as collard greens, which are usually flavored with fat back and cooked for long periods of time.

MUTTON

The flesh of a full-grown sheep, as opposed to lamb, which comes from an animal under a year in age. The best mutton comes from well-fed sheep of good breed, about 2 to 3 years old and the meat should be hung in a cool, airy place for about 2 weeks after slaughtering, to improve the flavor and tenderness.

ROAST MUTTON
Cook as for Lamb. (See Lamb entry.)

NAPOLEON

A classic French pastry rectangular in shape, made of several sheets of puff pastry, spread with pastry cream and stacked 2 or 3 inches high. It is usually topped with a dusting of powdered sugar or a thin icing.

NASTURTIUM

The yellow, orange, or red flower petals of this New World plant were once very popular in salads and are still occasionally used as garnish. The leaves and stems may also be added to salads. The green, berrylike seeds are also edible and when pickled make a reasonable substitute for capers. Nasturtiums are also called Indian cress.

NAVARIN

French mutton stew usually also including tomatoes, onions, and potatoes. Navarin Printanier, a spring version of the ragout, also includes peas, turnips, carrots, and other vegetables.

NAVY BEAN (PEA BEAN)

A variety of kidney bean so named because it has been a staple for the United States Navy since the 1800s. Navy beans are the seeds of a leguminous plant indigenous to North America, which was taken back to Europe by the early explorers. Because they are highly nutritious, containing about 24 percent protein, and inexpensive, they have been called the poor man's meat.

Navy beans are used in Boston Baked Beans, a New England favorite that dates back to the time when Puritan women of Boston would prepare these beans with molasses and salt pork for the Sabbath.

BOSTON BAKED BEANS

4 oz salt pork, cut into several strips
2 cups navy beans, soaked overnight and drained, liquid reserved
1 teaspoon salt
$\frac{1}{3}$ cup firmly packed dark brown sugar
$\frac{1}{4}$ cup dark molasses
1 tablespoon dry mustard

Place a few strips of the salt pork in the bottom of a large earthenware bean pot or Dutch oven. Add beans and sprinkle with the salt. In a mixing bowl, combine sugar, molasses, and mustard and blend well. Pour in reserved soaking liquid from beans and stir until well mixed. Pour liquid over the beans and top with remaining strips of salt pork. Cover and bake in a 300° oven for about 5 hours, adding more water if necessary. Remove cover and continue baking for 1 hour longer. Serve with Boston Brown Bread (see page 264).

NEAPOLITAN

A name frequently given to desserts, cakes, ices, etc., made with layers of two or more colors, e.g. white (or cream), pink, pale green and coffee or chocolate, each layer being appropriately flavored. The layers are assembled before baking, setting, or freezing or they can be sandwiched together afterward, as is most convenient. Neapolitan dishes should be presented or cut so that the different colors show to the best advantage.

NECTARINE

The fruit of a type of peach tree, which is found in both free- and cling-stone varieties. The smooth, shiny skin is like that of a plum, but the flesh resembles that of a peach in appearance and flavor, indeed some people consider the ripe nectarine superior to the peach. They can replace peaches in any recipe, but are best eaten fresh as a dessert fruit.

NEGUS

A type of mulled wine, generally a mixture of port, red wine, or sherry, spice (such as nutmeg), lemon, sugar, and hot water.

NESSELRODE PUDDING

A rich and elaborate dessert made from chestnuts, egg yolks, cream, and sometimes candied fruits, which is molded and frozen.

NETTLE

Young stinging nettles, which have a pleasant, slightly bitter taste, may be cooked as a vegetable. Like spinach, nettles shrink during cooking so allow a cup per person. Wear gloves, to protect the hands, sort out weeds, and remove the nettle roots. Wash, drain, and plunge in boiling water for 2 minutes, then pour off the water and cook very gently without water until they are tender, as for spinach. Drain and chop well, add seasoning, a pat of butter and 1 tablespoon cream for every 2 lb nettles.

NEUFCHÂTEL CHEESE

A soft whole-milk cheese prepared in Normandy and other parts of France. It is usually made in rectangular shape, the pieces weighing about 3 oz.

NEW ENGLAND BOILED DINNER

A hearty meal-in-one-dish usually made of corned beef, cabbage, potatoes, and other vegetables boiled together. Originally salted beef was used. It can also be made with poultry or other meats and is served with horseradish and mustard. It is still traditional fare in New England.

NEW ENGLAND BOILED DINNER

4–5 lb corned beef
2 cloves garlic
4 medium onions
½ teaspoon black peppercorns
10 small red new potatoes
6 carrots
1 rutabaga, chopped
1 medium head green cabbage, cored and quartered

Place corned beef in a large Dutch oven, cover with cold water and bring to a boil. Skim during the first 15 minutes of cooking. Cover and cook for about 2 hours. Add the garlic, onions, peppercorns, and potatoes and simmer for 15 minutes. Add carrots and rutabaga and simmer for 30 minutes more. Remove meat and vegetables, add the cabbage to the broth, and boil for 3 or 4 minutes, until just tender. Meanwhile slice the corned beef and arrange on a platter, surrounded by the vegetables. Drain cabbage and arrange on the platter with the beef and vegetables. Serve with horseradish and corn muffins.

NIACIN

B₂ vitamin. (See Vitamins entry.)

NIÇOISE

When used to describe a dish this French term means "in the manner of Nice" the principal city of the Mediterranean coast of France. Items prepared Niçoise style can include many ingredients, but nearly always have tomatoes, olives, and anchovies, all of which are abundantly available in Southern France. Perhaps the best-known Niçoise dish is Niçoise salad, of which there are many versions, including the one that follows.

SALADE NIÇOISE

½ lb boiled new potatoes, diced
2 tomatoes, quartered
2 hard-cooked eggs, quartered
1½ cups steamed baby green beans
⅓ cup pitted ripe olives
    (Niçoise olives, if possible)
1 can (7 oz) tuna fish, drained and flaked
4 anchovy fillets
3 tablespoons French dressing
chopped parsley to garnish

Arrange the potatoes around the edge of a serving platter. In a mixing bowl, toss together the tomatoes, eggs, beans, olives, and tuna fish. Pile in the center of the serving platter. Cut anchovies in half lengthwise and arrange them in a lattice pattern over the salad. Pour the dressing over the top and garnish with parsley.

NOBLE ROT

A beneficial mold, *Botrytis cinerea*, that attacks grapes, shriveling them, increasing the sugar content and intensifying the flavor. It gives the Sauternes of France and the Beerenauslese and Trockenbeerenauslese Rhine wines of Germany their special character. California wines affected by the noble rot are usually labeled Late Harvest or Selected Late Harvest. They are largely made from Johannisberg Riesling but a few have been made from the sémillon, chauvignon blanc, and chenin blanc. Noble rot is known in France as *la pourriture noble* and in Germany as *Edelfäule*.

NOCKERLN

A light Austrian dumpling made of flour, butter, eggs, and milk and frequently served in stews and soups. Another version is made with sugar, egg yolks, butter, and stiffly beaten egg whites, and is served as a dessert with fruit or in fruit soups.

NOODLES

The word noodle comes from the German *Nudel* and is the general form for a wide variety of usually thin flat strips of dough that show up in many different cultures and cuisines. The dough is usually made of flour, eggs, and water, although in some Italian noodles or pasta, the eggs are omitted. Noodles are sold fresh and dried and can be boiled, fried, or baked.

Italian pastas are among the best known and loved noodles of the world and come in a wide variety of lengths, widths, and shapes. (See separate Pasta entry.)

Noodles can be served broken up in soups or as an accompaniment or garnish with the main dish instead of potatoes; they may also form a main dish when served with a meat sauce.

Somewhat different noodles are a staple food in Asia, where they are often made from wheat and rice flour, mixed with egg and water. In China the paste is shaped or "thrown" by hand into the long thin strings, which vary in diameter from that of the Italian spaghetti to that of the finest vermicelli. Chinese noodles can be served in a sauce of meat and vegetables; in soup or fried. There is, however, some difference in the preparation of fried noodles.

NORMANDE SAUCE

A classic French white sauce served with fish; it is made with fish broth and enriched with butter and egg yolk.

NORMANDE SAUCE

1 cup white sauce, made with clam broth
1 egg yolk
1 tablespoon butter
lemon juice

Make the white sauce in the usual way, cook and beat well. Cool slightly, then beat in the egg yolk and reheat carefully without boiling. Stir in the butter a little at a time and finally add lemon juice to taste.

NOUGAT

A chewy candy, usually white or pink, containing chopped candied or dried fruits, nuts etc. (See Candy entry.) Montélimar nougat is a famous white nougat made with boiled sugar, egg white, chopped nuts, and cherries.

NOYAY

A liqueur originally made in France, but now produced in other countries. It is rather sweet and is flavored with cherry pits, which give a taste resembling bitter almonds; it may be white or pink in color.

NUTBREAD

A sweet teabread made with chopped nuts, as well as, frequently, dates, and leavened with baking powder. It is often served with breakfast or with tea. Cranberries, dried apricots, and other fruits are often added to nutbread recipes.

NUTMEG

The seed of a tall, evergreen tree, grown in various tropical countries. The fruit splits when ripe, to reveal a single seed, surrounded by a husk (which when dried is known as mace). When the seeds are dry they are opened and the light-brown kernels or nutmeg are removed. Small ones are used for the extraction of their oil (nutmeg butter or oil of mace), while the larger ones are usually left as they are for export as whole nutmeg. Ground nutmeg is more widely sold but some people prefer to buy whole nutmeg and grate them as required, since the flavor is better.

Nutmeg is used as a flavoring for various types of food – cakes and desserts – as well as cream sauces.

NUTRIENT

A chemical component of food (sometimes called a food factor). In the body the nutrients perform the following functions.
(a) Production of energy.
(b) Growth and repair of tissues.
(c) Regulation of body processes.
The nutrients are proteins, carbohydrates, fats, vitamins, minerals, and water. Some of them carry out more than one of the above functions – for example, proteins can be used both for growth and repair and also to produce energy, while some of them are concerned with controlling body processes.

All food contains at least one and usually several nutrients. At one extreme, glucose contains only one – carbohydrate – but milk contains all six categories of nutrients. (See individual entries.)

NUTRITION

The science of food in all its aspects, from the growing of the foodstuffs to their use in the body by animals and humans. Usually the word is taken to mean human nutrition. Our knowledge of the subject has increased rapidly over the last century and during that time most of the essential food factors have been discovered and identified. The main factors, as mentioned in the preceding entry are: proteins, carbohydrates, fats, vitamins, minerals, and water. Roughage is also supplied by food.

It is not possible to estimate exactly how much of these food factors is necessary or to state how much is contained in different foodstuffs, so average figures only can be quoted for any one individual's requirements or for the composition of any food. (See Diet, Metabolism, Protein, and Vitamins entries.)

NUTS

There are many varieties of edible nuts, among them: Almond, Brazil, cashew, chestnut, coconut, filbert, hazel, hickory, peanut, pecan, pistachio, and walnut. (See individual entries.)

Although nuts are not usually eaten in large enough quantities to play an important part in the diet, they are a valuable food and vegetarians are able to use them to a considerable extent as a substitute for meat. This is due to the fact that nuts contain a large proportion of vegetable protein. The fat content of the nuts is considerable. The fat is often extracted and used as oil.

(See Almond oil entry, under Almond.) Carbohydrates (starch and sugar) are also present, the chestnut being the richest source of these factors.

Apart from their use as a dessert, nuts add flavor to many dishes. Salted nuts are served with cocktails and drinks, chopped nuts are used in desserts, candies, main dishes, salads, cakes and cookies, while peanuts make excellent "butter" for pastries and add richness to cakes, cookies, etc. Some nuts, particularly the attractively shaped almond and walnut and the delicate green pistachio, make good garnishes.

To shell nuts: Use a well-designed pair of crackers or strike the nut with a heavy hammer or weight, taking care not to crush the meat.

To blanch nuts: Hazelnuts may be oven-blanched by heating in the oven for a short time, until the inner skins become brittle enough to rub off with the fingers. Chestnuts should have the skin slit at both ends with a sharp knife and can then either be boiled for about 10 minutes, or put in the oven for a few minutes; then it should be quite easy to strip off both the outer shell and the inner skin. For almonds, pour boiling water over and leave for about 2 minutes; the skins may then be slipped off easily.

SALTED NUTS

Almond, walnuts, peanuts, cashew nuts, etc. can be salted and a mixture of these nuts makes a very attractive appetizer for cocktail parties. To each $\frac{1}{2}$ cup blanched nuts heat about 1 tablespoon butter or oil in a skillet. Distribute the nuts in a thin even layer over the surface of the skillet and sauté slowly, stirring continuously, until the nuts are a uniform, delicate brown. Remove them from the skillet and drain, then sprinkle the nuts generously with salt, and spread them out to cool and become crisp before serving. A little paprika may also be sprinkled over the nuts.

SPICED NUTS

Follow the same procedure as for salted nuts, including the browning stage; then to each $\frac{1}{2}$ cup of nuts mix $\frac{1}{2}$ teaspoon salt and $\frac{1}{2}$ teaspoon mixed spices of your choice such as ground caraway, cardamom, curry, mace, nutmeg, coriander, cloves, etc., and sprinkle freely over the nuts. Allow them to cool and become crisp before serving.

OATS

A cereal grain, *Avena*, which is widely cultivated throughout the world; it will grow in colder and wetter climates and poorer soils than any other cereal and also in hotter climates than wheat or rye. It was one of the earliest grains to be cultivated in Europe. In the United States it is used mainly as fodder, but also for breakfast food and baking.

The seeds are husked and the grain ground or rolled in different ways to give the various grades of oatmeal and rolled oats. The latter are produced by treating the grains with heat while passing them between rollers; quick-cooking rolled oats are produced by the application of greater heat, which partially cooks the grain.

All types of oatmeal have much the same food value and contain carbohydrates, protein, fat, iron, calcium, and vitamin B. Oats have very little gluten and therefore they cannot be used for breadmaking. Since oatmeal contains fat, it does not keep as well as some other cereals, so it should be bought in small quantities and stored in a closed container in a dry place.

Oatmeal and rolled oats are used for making breakfast cereal, pancakes, cookies, scones, biscuits, and granola.

There are many brands of "quick oats" which are specially treated to speed up the making of oatmeal; cooking directions will be found on the packet. The pinhead and coarse types of oatmeal need longer cooking, though some people contend that the time can be shortened if they are soaked overnight.

Oatcakes

An unleavened form of bread found in the north of Britain. The ingredients include oatmeal, water, salt, and fat.

OAT BARS

6 tablespoons butter, softened
½ cup firmly packed brown sugar
½ cup rolled oats

Grease a shallow 8-inch square pan. Cream the butter and sugar together in a mixing bowl. Add the oats and work them into the butter until thoroughly blended. Spread mixture evenly into the pan, pressing down evenly with a spatula. Bake in a 425° oven for about 15 minutes, until golden brown. Cool in the pan briefly. Break or cut into bars. Oat bars may be stored in an airtight container for up to one week.

OATMEAL COOKIE

(See Cookie entry.)

OCEAN PERCH

The commercial name for the Atlantic rockfish. It is also called sea perch, not to be confused with the Pacific perch, which is also called sea perch but is another type of rockfish. Ocean perch is more commonly seen packaged in fillets and frozen than fresh in the markets.

OCTOPUS

This saltwater cephalopod mollusk gets its common name from the Greek words *octo*, meaning eight, and *pod* meaning foot, because of its eight suction-cup-covered tentacles. Octopi can vary in size from less than a foot long to gigantic, monster proportions, but the most common species are seldom longer than three feet. Like cuttlefish and squid, octopus is eaten widely in Japan and the Mediterranean. The Japanese enjoy octopus raw. In Greece, Italy and France it is often sautéed or deep-fried quickly. Young tender octopus needs only very brief cooking. It can be prepared in almost any method suitable for squid. Ancient Romans ate octopus and considered it to have an aphrodisiac effect.

OEUFS À LA NEIGE

A feather-light, classic French dessert consisting of large scoops of stiffly beaten egg whites and sugar which are poached gently in sweetened, vanilla-flavored milk. The poaching milk is then strained and used to make a Crème Anglaise, a custardlike sauce that is the traditional accompaniment to the poached "eggs." Oeufs à la Neige and Crème Anglaise are usually served cold.

OEUFS À LA NEIGE

8 egg whites
1¼ cups superfine sugar
5 cups milk
¼ cup sugar

In a large bowl, beat the egg whites until very stiff. Sprinkle the sugar over them and fold in lightly so the whites do not lose their volume.

Pour the milk into a shallow, straight-sided skillet, add the sugar and stir to blend well. Bring to a simmer. Using 2 large spoons, mold egg whites into egg shapes and drop them, a few at a time, into the simmering milk. Poach, turning them so that they poach evenly, until they are firm. Remove and let drain. When all oeufs are poached, strain the poaching milk and use it to make a Crème Anglaise. Serve oeufs cold, floating on a pool of the cold Crème Anglaise.

OFFAL

The term used in Britain for variety meats, derived from "off fell" referring to the edible parts of the animal that are cut out or "fall out" during preparation of the carcass. (See Variety Meat entry.)

OIL

A fat of vegetable, animal, or mineral origin, which is liquid at normal temperatures.

Oils are a chemical combination of three molecules of fatty acids and one molecule of glycerol. The fatty acids may be of different types and this leads to the difference in characteristics between, say, a firm fat such as beef fat and a liquid one such as olive oil. Oils have a preponderance of unsaturated fatty acids which make them liquid instead of solid. Oils are used for frying, baking, roasting, and in cake, bread, and pastry making.

Vegetable oils

These are often used in place of other fats. The main varieties are:

COCONUT OIL
The nut from the coco palm yields a variety of oils with a strong flavor; these require a lot of refining before they can be used for culinary purposes. They contain a high proportion of saturated fatty acids.

CORN OIL
This is extracted from the germ of the seed of the corn plant. It has a high percentage of unsaturated fats, and can be used for all culinary purposes.

COTTONSEED OIL
Extracted from the seeds of the cotton plant. This oil is much used in the United States, particularly in the food industry.

GRAPESEED OIL
An oil of delicate flavor, which is good for cooking foods at very high temperatures.

HAZELNUT OIL
An extremely expensive, but very delicately nutty-flavored oil extracted from hazelnuts. It is an excellent ingredient for salad dressings.

OLIVE OIL
Extracted from the ripe olive. It has a strong but excellent flavor particularly good for salad dressings. (See Olive entry.)

PALM KERNEL OIL
Oil extracted from the nuts of palms. It is a white or pale yellow color and used in the manufacture of margarine.

PEANUT OIL
Oil which is extracted from the kernel of the peanut plant.

SAFFLOWER OIL

One of the most polyunsaturated of vegetable oils and a very good choice for those concerned with keeping cholesterol levels down. It is tasteless with a very high smoking point, and is used in cooking and in salad dressings. It is, however, not recommended to use this oil exclusively as it lacks vitamin E.

SOYBEAN OIL

Taken from the soybean which is a member of the Leguminosae family. The oil is much used in commercial food processing. Its strong flavor makes it less suitable for salads.

SUNFLOWER OIL

This is taken from the seeds of the *Helianthus annuus*. It has a pleasant rather neutral taste and can be used for all culinary purposes. It also has a high ratio of unsaturated fatty acids.

WALNUT OIL

Extracted from the nut of the walnut (*Juglans regia*). It has a delicate but distinctive flavor, but does not keep well.

Fish Oils

The oils extracted from cod and halibut liver are valuable sources of vitamins A and D.

Mineral Oils

These are not normally eaten. Although liquid paraffin has certain medicinal uses, it is inadvisable to use it in cooking, as it tends to prevent the absorption of nutrients.

PASTRY MADE WITH OIL

2½ tablespoons oil
1 tablespoon cold water
1 cup all-purpose flour
pinch salt

Put the oil and water into a bowl and beat well with a fork to form an emulsion. Mix the flour and salt together and add to the mixture to make a dough. Roll this out on a floured board or between waxed paper.

This is a slightly more greasy pastry than one made with solid fat so it is more suitable for meat or vegetable pies or other main dishes prepared in a crust than for sweet pies. Bake in a 400° oven.

Note: This pastry is best used as soon as it is prepared when it is a soft dough. If it has to be stored, wrap in a plastic bag and store in the refrigerator for no longer than 24 hours. Before using, remove from plastic bag and leave at room temperature for one hour.

OKRA (GUMBO)

A vegetable grown in America, the East and West Indies, Africa, India, and the Mediterranean countries. The young pods, which resemble immature cucumbers, are used as a vegetable and in soups. Okra appears frequently in the cooking of the Southeastern United States, particularly in Creole dishes. One of that cuisine's best-loved dishes, Gumbo, takes its name from the vegetable's African appellation. See Gumbo entry for recipe.

OLIVE

The fruit of the olive tree, which grows in sunny, warm climates, particularly in the Mediterranean region. There are many different varieties. Each fruit contains a large, single pit to which the flesh clings. The size of the olive varies considerably, according to the variety. Olives may be picked when green or when fully ripe and black.

The flesh of the olive contains an oil which has many uses in cookery. The olive itself has a sharp flavor and is therefore popular as an appetizer. Olives can also be added to dishes and when stuffed with pimientos are used for appetizers and as a garnish.

Both plain and stuffed olives are bought pickled in brine. To prevent turning the green olives black take them out with either stainless steel or wooden tools. Serve the olives on cocktail picks or piled in a dish. Any surplus may be put back into the brine.

Olive Oil

The oil obtained from ripe olives. There are three grades: the best or "virgin" oil is straw yellow, the "first quality" is yellowish and the "second quality" faintly greenish. Subsequent pressings produce an inferior oil that is whitish in color. Most olive oil available in the shops is second grade. Olive oil is used in cooking extensively in Europe. It makes excellent salad dressings and mayonnaise and can be used for frying, in marinades and batters and for greasing pans.

To obtain the best results with many dishes it is considered essential to use pure olive oil because of its distinctive flavor, e.g., in mayonnaise. Olive oil has only a moderate amount of unsaturated fatty acids, so cannot be classed as cholesterol-lowering.

OLLA PODRIDA

A Spanish dish, consisting of a type of stew which usually contains meat or poultry, chickpeas and chorizo sausages.

OMELET

A dish made of beaten eggs topped with a wide range of foods from jelly to lobster, then folded over envelope style.

With care anyone can master the art of omelet making. Delicate handling is needed but a little practice perfects the knack – do not be discouraged if your first two or three omelets are not successful. Two points about omelets that make them particularly convenient are the short time they take to make and the way they use up odds and ends – such as cooked meat, fish, or vegetables – either in the omelet itself, as a filling, or as an accompaniment.

Have everything ready before beginning to make an omelet, including the hot plate on which to serve it.

Omelet Pans

Special little omelet pans are obtainable and should be kept for omelets only. If you do not own such a pan, however, a heavy-bottomed skillet can equally well be used. Whether of cast iron, copper, enameled iron, or aluminum, the pan should be thick, so that it will hold sufficient heat to cook the egg mixture as soon as this is put in. Thus the omelet can be in and out of the pan in about 2 minutes – one of the essentials of success, slow cooking and over-cooking both make an omelet tough. A 6-inch to 7-inch pan takes a 2- to 3-egg omelet.

To season an omelet pan put 1 tablespoon salt in the pan, heat it slowly, then rub well with a piece of paper. Tip away the salt and wipe the pan with paper toweling. To clean the omelet pan after use, do not wash it but wipe it clean with paper toweling, then with a clean cloth. Nonstick pans are ideal for omelets and do not need seasoning.

A few minutes before you want to cook an omelet place the pan on a very gentle heat to insure that it is heated evenly right to the edges – a fierce heat would cause the pan to heat unevenly. When the pan is ready for the mixture it will feel comfortably hot if you hold the back of your hand about 1 inch away from the surface.

Note: Manufacturers of nonstick pans advise that heating the empty pan will damage the surface, so add the fat before heating the pan.

FAT FOR GREASING OMELET PANS

Undoubtedly butter gives the best flavor, but unsalted margarine can be used as a substitute. Bacon fat can also be used.

Types of Omelet

Basically, there are only two different kinds, the plain and the soufflé omelet, in which the egg whites are beaten separately and folded into the yolk mixture, giving it a fluffy texture. Plain omelets are almost invariably savory and soufflé omelets are most commonly sweet and served as a dessert. There are many different omelet variations, achieved by the different ingredients added to the eggs or used in the filling.

PLAIN OMELET

Allow 2 eggs per person. Beat them just enough to break down the egg; don't make them frothy as overbeating spoils the texture of the finished omelet. Season with salt and pepper and add 1 tablespoon water. Place the omelet pan or skillet over a gentle heat and when it is hot add a pat of butter to grease it lightly. Pour the beaten eggs into the hot fat. Stir gently with the back of the prongs of a fork or wooden spatula, drawing the mixture from the sides to the center as it sets and letting the liquid egg from the center run to the sides. When the egg has set, stop stirring and cook for another minute until it is golden underneath and still creamy on top. Tilt the pan away from you slightly, and use a spatula to fold over a third of the omelet to the center, then fold over the opposite third. Turn the omelet out onto the warmed plate, with the folded sides underneath, and serve at once. Do not overcook or the omelet will be tough.

OMELET FILLINGS

Fines herbes: Add 1 teaspoon mixed dried herbs or 2 tablespoons finely chopped fresh herbs to the beaten egg mixture before cooking. Parsley, chives, chervil, and tarragon are all suitable.

Cheese: Grate $\frac{1}{3}$ cup cheese and mix 3 tablespoons of it with the eggs before cooking; sprinkle the rest over the omelet after it is folded.

Tomato: Peel and chop 1 to 2 tomatoes and sauté in a little butter in a saucepan for 5 minutes, until soft. Put in the center of the omelet before folding.

Mushroom: Wash and slice $\frac{1}{2}$ cup mushrooms and cook in butter in a saucepan until soft. Put in the center of the omelet before folding.

Bacon: Chop four strips bacon and sauté in a skillet until crisp. Put in the center of the omelet before folding.

Ham: Add ¼ cup chopped ham and 1 teaspoon chopped parsley to the beaten egg before cooking.

Fish: Flake flesh of cooked fish and heat gently in a little cheese sauce. Put in the center of the omelet before folding.

Shrimp: Thaw ⅓ cup frozen shrimp (or use the equivalent from a can) and sauté in melted butter in a skillet with a squeeze of lemon juice. Put into the center of the omelet before folding.

WESTERN OMELET

4 slices bread
3 tablespoons butter, softened
3 eggs
salt
cayenne pepper
2 slices ham, minced
½ medium green pepper, minced
½ small onion, minced
prepared mustard

Spread bread with butter (about 1 tablespoon in all). Melt remaining 2 tablespoons of butter in a medium skillet. Meanwhile beat eggs lightly and season with salt and cayenne. Add ham, pepper and onion to the skillet and sauté until softened.

Pour in the beaten eggs and cook over low heat until lightly browned on the bottom. Turn the omelet and brown briefly on the other side. Cut omelet in half and place each half on a slice of buttered bread. Spread with mustard and top with a second piece of bread. Serve warm.

SPANISH OMELET

3 tablespoons olive oil
2 large potatoes, peeled and cut into ½-inch cubes
2 large onions, coarsely chopped
salt
freshly ground black pepper
6 eggs, lightly beaten

In a medium-sized skillet, gently heat the olive oil. Add the potatoes and onions and season with salt and pepper. Sauté, stirring occasionally, for 10 to 15 minutes until golden brown. Drain off excess oil and quickly stir in the eggs. Cook for 5 minutes, shaking the pan occasionally to prevent sticking. If you wish, place under a hot broiler to brown the top. Turn out onto a serving plate.

Note: This is the basic Spanish omelet, but other vegetables may be added, such as chopped fresh red pepper, tomatoes, peas, mushrooms, spinach. Either add them raw at the beginning or stir cooked vegetables into the eggs (peas and spinach should be added already cooked).

SAUSAGE AND PEPPER OMELET

6 pork link sausages
1 large green pepper, cored, seeded and cut in julienne strips
1 small bunch of scallions (white and tender green part only), cut in 2-inch lengths
½ cup canned white beans, drained
3 tablespoons butter
6 eggs, lightly beaten
salt and pepper

In a large skillet, sauté sausages over medium heat until well browned and cooked through. Remove from the pan and drain all but about 2 tablespoons of fat from the pan. Add the green pepper and scallions and sauté until softened. Add white beans and sauté briefly. Melt butter in a large saucepan. Season the beaten eggs with salt and pepper and turn into the skillet. Turn the sautéed peppers, scallions, beans and sausages into the pan and let cook slowly until eggs set and brown slightly. Turn out onto a serving plate and cut into wedges. Serve hot.

SOUFFLÉ OMELET

2 eggs
1 teaspoon sugar (or salt and pepper to taste for an entrée omelet)
2 tablespoons water
butter

Separate the yolks from the whites of the eggs, putting them in different bowls. Beat the yolks until creamy. Add the sugar (or seasoning) and the water and beat again. Beat the egg whites until stiff but not dry. At this point place the skillet containing a piece of butter over a low heat and let the butter melt without browning. Turn the egg whites into the yolk mixture and fold in carefully, using a spoon. Grease the sides of the skillet with the butter by tilting it in all directions and then pour in the egg mixture. Cook over a moderate heat until the omelet is a golden brown on the underside. Put under the broiler until the omelet is brown on the top. Remove at once as overcooking tends to make it tough. Run a spatula gently around the edge and underneath the omelet to loosen it, make a mark across the middle, add any required filling and fold the omelet over. Turn it gently onto a warm plate and serve at once.

SOUFFLÉ OMELET FILLINGS

Jam: Spread the cooked omelet with warm jam, fold it over and sprinkle with powdered sugar.

Rum: Substitute 1 tablespoon rum for half the water added to the egg yolks before cooking. Put the cooked omelet on a hot dish, pour 3 to 4 tablespoons warmed rum over it, ignite and serve immediately.

Apricot: Add the grated rind of an orange or tangerine to the egg yolks. Spread some thick apricot puree or jam over the omelet before folding it and serve sprinkled with sugar.

Entrée: Any of the fillings already given for plain omelets can be used for soufflé omelets.

BAKED SOUFFLÉ OMELET

4 eggs
2 tablespoons sugar
6 almonds, blanched and finely chopped
2 tablespoons water
pinch salt
butter
sugar for sprinkling
jam or stewed fruit, optional

Separate the yolks from the whites of the eggs and beat the yolks thoroughly with the sugar. Add the almonds and the water. Beat the egg whites and the salt stiffly and fold into the yolk mixture. Grease a shallow ovenproof dish with butter and put the omelet mixture into it. Bake in a 350° oven for 15 to 20 minutes, sprinkle with sugar and serve at once.

A little jam or some stewed fruit may be put at the bottom of the dish before the egg mixture is added.

ONION

A type of bulb, widely grown throughout the world, which is eaten as a vegetable and is also used to flavor soups, stews, and sauces. The onion is often regarded as the most important vegetable in the kitchen, for its flavor improves almost every dish except desserts. It has, however, little food value – a small amount of vitamin C and some minerals.

Since there are innumerable varieties of on-ions, with new hybrids cropping up annually, their classification is confusing. Appellations often overlap and contradict one another. However, some of the main varieties found in United States markets are as follows:

ALL-PURPOSE ONION
As the name implies, these onions are suitable both for cooking and for eating raw. Their flavor is strong, but less pungent that that of silverskins and the skin is usually yellow. These are also called new onions.

BERMUDA ONION
A mild variety, often classed as a sweet onion, which is typically 2 to 4 inches in diameter, flattened on one or both ends and with yellow, white or red outer skin. Because their flavor is not too strong, these are good in salads and sandwiches.

MINIATURE OR PEARL ONION
This tiny white variety, also called button onion, is often pickled and used as a garnish. The unpickled type is sometimes served creamed.

SILVERSKIN ONION
One of a number of varieties most suitable for cooking because of their strong, pungent flavor, and firm texture that holds up well under heat. They have silvery white skins and are also called, simply, white onions.

SPANISH ONION
Similar to the Bermuda, with the same mild, sweet flavor, but larger and more spherical, with yellow or white skin.

(See Scallion, Leek, and Shallot entries.)

Preparation
Cut the top from each onion but retain the root end for if this is cut the pungent vapor which attacks the eyes is released. Remove the peel.

To chop: Cut the onion in half from stem to root and place the cut side down on the board. Slice down through the onion lengthwise (not cutting quite to the root) then slice across at right angles, first horizontally and finally vertically. The onion will fall into rough cubes which can be chopped finely if the dish requires it.

FRENCH ONION SOUP

3 tablespoons butter
3 cups sliced onion
3¾ cups beef stock

1 tablespoon dry sherry
salt and pepper
4 slices French bread
½ cup grated Gruyère cheese

Melt the butter in a large saucepan, add the onions and sauté over medium heat for about 5 minutes. Pour in the stock and bring to a boil. Add the sherry and season with salt and pepper to taste. Cover and simmer for 45 minutes.

Ladle the soup into 4 ovenproof bowls and float a slice of bread on top of each. Sprinkle each with the grated cheese and place under a preheated broiler to brown. Serve immediately.

BOILED ONIONS

Cook in boiling salted water until tender, 30 to 45 minutes, according to size. Drain carefully and cover the onions in a white or brown sauce before serving.

BAKED STUFFED ONIONS

4 medium-sized onions
2 tablespoons fresh bread crumbs
salt
pepper
½ cup grated cheese
little milk
butter

Cook the onions in boiling salted water for about 25 minutes, removing them before they are quite soft; drain and cool. Scoop out the centers, using a pointed knife to cut the onion top and a small spoon to remove the centers. Chop the centers finely, mix with the crumbs, seasoning, and half the cheese and moisten with milk if necessary. Fill the onions and place them in a greased ovenproof dish. Put small pats of butter on top and sprinkle with the remaining cheese. Bake in a 400° oven for about 35 minutes, until the onions are cooked and browned.

Serve with a white sauce, season well, and flavor with grated cheese. A tomato sauce makes a good alternative.

FRIED ONION RINGS

These are often used as a garnish. Preferably, make them with the large Spanish onions. Slice the onions and separate them into rings, dip in lightly beaten egg white, toss in seasoned flour and fry in hot fat, for about 5 minutes, until tender. Drain and serve hot. (Rings can also be coated with a batter.)

ONION AND RED PEPPER QUICHE

3 tablespoons butter
1 onion, thinly sliced
1 red pepper, cored and thinly sliced
1 9-inch partially baked unsweetened pastry shell
4 eggs, lightly beaten
2 cups light cream
salt
cayenne pepper
1¼ cups crumbled blue cheese

Melt the butter in a heavy skillet, add onion and pepper slices and sauté until softened. Sprinkle onion and pepper evenly over the partially baked pastry shell. In a large mixing bowl, combine eggs, cream, salt and cayenne to taste, and blue cheese and beat until well mixed. Pour the egg–cheese mixture into the pastry shell over onion and pepper. Bake for 15 minutes in a 425° oven. Reduce temperature to 350° and bake for 30 minutes longer, or until custard is set. Cut in wedges and serve hot or cold.

BEEF-STUFFED ONIONS

4 large onions
1 small red pepper, cored and cut in julienne strips
½ cup lightly sautéed, lean ground beef
⅓ cup fresh bread crumbs
1½ teaspoons finely chopped parsley
salt
pepper
grated nutmeg
6 tablespoons melted butter
2 tablespoons dry sherry

Parboil onions for 10 minutes. Drain and run under cold water. Scoop out the centers, leaving enough flesh to make a sturdy shell; coarsely chop the scooped-out onion flesh and place in a large mixing bowl. Add red pepper, ground beef, bread crumbs and parsley to mixing bowl with chopped onion. Season with salt, pepper, and nutmeg to taste, and toss until well mixed. Brush the inside of the hollowed-out onions with butter and season with salt and pepper. Divide the pepper and beef filling in four and stuff into the onions, piling it up generously. Place stuffed onions in a well-greased shallow baking dish. Add sherry to the remaining butter and pour over each of the onions. Cover with foil and bake in a 300° oven for about 1 hour, until tender.

ORANGE

The fruit of an evergreen tree, native to China, which grows in hot climates in many parts of the world. There are two main varieties, sweet and bitter (or Seville); the latter type, which comes chiefly from Spain, is used mainly for making marmalade. Sweet oranges grown in the United States include principally the Valencia (Florida, California, and Arizona) and the Navel (California, Arizona). The tangerine, or mandarin, is considered distinct from the orange, but the Temple orange, a hybrid tangerine, represents a considerable share of the orange crop. Oranges are available year-round and are grown in California, Florida, Arizona, Sicily, Spain, Portugal, Malta, Israel, and South Africa.

Oranges have a high vitamin C content – 1 orange providing well over the daily requirement.

Preparation: For fruit salads, prepare the orange as follows: working over a plate to catch the juice and using a sharp knife, remove all the skin, peeling the orange like an apple and cutting deep enough to disclose the pulp. Hold the orange in the left hand and remove each segment, cutting away any remaining pith or membrane.

ORANGE FLAVORINGS FOR CAKES, DESSERTS, ETC. Grate the rind, taking only the colored part, not the underlying white pith. The juice can also be added to cakes and other desserts in small amounts.

ORANGE RINDS
These may be dried and stored for future use and they may also be candied. Fresh orange rinds may be made into baskets in which to serve orange jelly, sorbets, or mousse mixtures, etc.

SWEET ORANGE SALAD

Peel some oranges and separate the flesh in segments. Arrange these in a serving bowl, sprinkle with sugar and Kirsch and chill for about 1 hour. Toasted almonds may be sprinkled over the salad just before serving or simply sprinkle with sifted powdered sugar and granulated sugar.

TANGY ORANGE SALAD

2 sweet oranges
chopped tarragon and chervil, if available
1 tablespoon salad oil
2 teaspoons vinegar
1 teaspoon lemon juice
watercress, to garnish

Peel the oranges and remove all the white pith, then cut the fruit in thin slices, removing the pits.

Put the pieces in a salad bowl and sprinkle with the tarragon and chervil, if used. Add the oil, vinegar, and lemon juice and let stand for a short time. Garnish with watercress.

ORANGEADE

A drink made from fresh oranges and served cold. There are various brands on the market, but it can also be made at home.

ORANGEADE

2 oranges
1 lemon
$\frac{1}{4}$ cup sugar
2 cups boiling water

Wash the fruit and thinly pare off the colored part of the rinds, free of all the white pith. Put the rinds and sugar into a bowl and pour the boiling water over. Let cool, stirring occasionally; add the strained juice of the oranges and the lemon.

ORANGE-BLOSSOM WATER

A flavoring distilled from orange blossoms, used in making desserts and pastries.

OREGANO (ORIGAN)

This a wild marjoram, which is a bushy herb of the mint family. It is much used in Italian cooking on pizza, pasta dishes, as well as in salad dressings, and as an ingredient in South American dishes such as Chili con Carne.

ORGEAT

A beverage, originally made from barley, later from almonds and sugar.

ORTOLAN

A delicately flavored wild bird, about 6 inches long. In Europe, ortolans are caught in nets and fattened in captivity before being killed for the table.

OSSO BUCO

A popular dish in Italy, made from knuckle of veal which is cut into pieces, sautéed and then stewed with garlic, onion, and tomato. The meat is served on the bone with spaghetti or rice. See Veal entry for recipe.

OUZO

A Greek liqueur, flavored with aniseed.

OXTAIL

When skinned, this makes an excellent stew or soup, but as there is a large percentage of bone, one oxtail serves only about four people.

OXTAIL CASSEROLE

1 oxtail, cut apart at the joints
2 tablespoons fat or oil
2 onions, sliced
3 tablespoons flour
2 cups beef broth
pinch of dried, mixed herbs
bay leaf
2 carrots, sliced
2 teaspoons lemon juice
salt
pepper

Sauté the oxtail in the fat or oil until golden brown, then place it in a casserole. Sauté the onions and add to the meat. Sprinkle the flour into the fat in the skillet and brown it, add the broth and gradually bring to a boil, then pour over the meat. Add the herbs, bay leaf, carrots, and lemon juice, season, cover and cook in a 375° oven for 30 minutes, then reduce heat to 300° and simmer very gently for $2\frac{1}{2}$ to 3 hours more.

OYSTER

A bivalve mollusk with a flat rough gray shell. They are in season from September to April. Oysters usually live in the mouth of a river or in a bay near the shore, the cultivated ones being reared in special beds. There are many varieties of oysters. Four types are now cultivated in the United States The Eastern, or American, oyster which flourishes along the Atlantic sea coast and goes by various names including Blue Point, Wellfleet, Chincoteague, and Malpeque, depending on which region they come from. Two varieties, the tiny Olympia oyster and the larger Pacific, or Japanese, oyster, are cultivated on the West coast. And recently the French bélon oyster has been cultivated in Maine.

When oysters are bought the shells should be firmly closed and they should come from a reliable source.

OLD-FASHONED OYSTER STEW

$1\frac{1}{2}$ pints shucked oysters, with their liquor
2 cups milk
2 cups half-and-half
salt
cayenne pepper
1 tablespoon Worcestershire sauce
3 tablespoons butter

In a large Dutch oven, combine oysters, their liquor, milk, half-and-half, and season with salt and cayenne pepper. Stir in Worcestershire and simmer for about 5 minutes. Add butter and heat until it melts. Serve immediately, very hot.

BROCCOLI IN OYSTER SAUCE

$1\frac{1}{2}$ tablespoons soy sauce
$2\frac{1}{2}$ tablespoons sweet sherry
2 tablespoons oil
2 cloves garlic, minced
2 teaspoons minced fresh gingerroot
1 large head broccoli, broken into flowerets, thick stems quartered and cut into 2-inch lengths
$\frac{1}{4}$ teaspoon salt
3 tablespoons oyster sauce

In a small bowl combine soy and sherry. In a large wok heat the oil until just before smoking, distributing it well around side of wok. Add garlic and ginger and toss briefly in oil. Add the broccoli and salt and stir-fry for 1 minute over high heat. Add soy mixture, stir-fry for a few seconds, then cover and cook 30 seconds. Remove cover and continue to stir-fry until most of the liquid is evaporated and broccoli is tender. Add oyster sauce, toss broccoli in it and stir-fry until sauce simmers. Serve.

Oyster sauce

A dark brown, viscous Cantonese seasoning made from a fermentation of oysters and soy sauce. It is sold in bottles in most well-stocked supermarkets and used for flavoring and coloring of a large number of Chinese dishes.

ANGELS ON HORSEBACK

Simmer oysters in their own liquor until the edges curl. Wrap each in a thin slice of bacon, thread on a skewer and broil until the bacon is cooked. Prepare small rounds of toast and place two bacon rolls on each round; garnish with parsley and serve very hot.

PAELLA

Considered by many to be Spain's national dish, Paella is made from rice and a variety of ingredients depending on what is available, although chicken and shellfish (especially crayfish and mussels) are regarded as traditional. Paella is cooked and served in a special large, shallow pan.

PAELLA

6–8 mussels
2–4 oz Dublin Bay prawns or frozen scampi
1 small cooked lobster
1 small chicken
4 tablespoons olive oil
1 clove garlic, crushed
1 onion, chopped
1 green pepper, chopped
4 tomatoes, peeled and chopped
$\frac{1}{2}$–$\frac{3}{4}$ lb long-grain rice
$1\frac{1}{2}$–$2\frac{1}{2}$ pints chicken broth
salt
pepper
little powdered saffron
$\frac{1}{4}$ lb frozen peas

The quantities given in this recipe should serve at least eight people.

Shell the mussels and peel the prawns, if fresh. Remove the lobster meat from the shell and dice it, retaining the claws for garnishing. Cut the meat from the chicken into small pieces. Put the oil into a large paella pan or skillet and sauté the garlic, onion, and green pepper for 5 minutes, until soft but not browned. Add the tomatoes and chicken pieces and sauté until the chicken is lightly browned. Stir in the rice, most of the broth, the seasoning and saffron (blended with a little of the broth). Bring to a boil, then reduce the heat and simmer for about 20 to 25 minutes, until the chicken is tender and the rice just cooked.

Stir in the mussels, prawns, lobster, and peas and simmer for a final 5 to 10 minutes, until heated through. Serve garnished with a few extra pimiento or green pepper strips and the lobster claws. Mussels in their shells can also be used as a garnish.

PAIN PERDU (MOCK FRITTERS)

There are various forms of this simple French dish, the original French Toast, which makes a good way of using up leftover bread.

PAIN PERDU

1 French roll or some stale bread or cake
milk
ground cinnamon
butter for frying
1 beaten egg
sugar

Cut slices of bread 1 inch thick and trim to a neat shape, then soak them in milk, adding flavoring such as ground cinnamon to taste. Melt the butter in an omelet pan, dip the bread in the egg, put it carefully in the pan and sauté to a light brown on both sides. Sprinkle with sugar and cinnamon or serve with jam as desired.

PALM HEARTS

Also called swamp cabbage, this smooth ivory-colored shoot from the cabbage palm or palmetto indigenous to swampy areas in Florida and South America has the look of a white asparagus, the flavor of an artichoke and a silky texture. It is used in salads and is available canned.

PALMIER

A French classic consisting of puff or flaky pastry, sprinkled with sugar, rolled, and thinly sliced.

PALMIERS

8 oz ready-made puff pastry
granulated sugar
jam
powdered sugar

Roll the pastry out evenly until it is $\frac{1}{16}$ inch thick and about 20 inches long, then sprinkle generously with granulated sugar. Fold the ends over to the center until they meet and press down firmly. Sprinkle generously with more sugar and fold the sides to the center again, press and sprinkle with sugar. Place the two folded portions together and press, then with a sharp knife cut into $\frac{1}{4}$-inch slices. Place cut edge down on a baking sheet, allowing room to spread and bake in a 425° oven for 6 to 7 minutes, until golden brown. Turn them and bake for a further 6 to 7 minutes. Cool on a rack and just before serving spread jam on half the slices, sandwich with the remaining slices and dredge with powdered sugar. (If preferred, whipped cream may be used instead of jam.)

PALM OIL

The oil extracted from the pulp of the palm fruit (not to be confused with palm kernel oil; see Oil entry). It is reddish in color and fairly soft in consistency. It is also used in the manufacture of margarine.

PALM WINE

In many tropical countries a wine is made by fermenting the sap of various palms, particularly date and coconut palms.

PANADA

A very thick sauce, made from a roux, 4 tablespoons butter and $\frac{1}{2}$ cup flour to 1 cup liquid. It is used to bind meatballs, fish cakes, etc., and as a basis for such dishes as soufflés. Its flavor depends partly on the liquid used and on whether or not the roux from which it is made is allowed to brown slightly. Seasoning and extra flavoring are added as required.

A panada based on bread crumbs is often used for meatballs, quenelles, etc. To make this soak 8 oz bread (without crust) in 2 to 3 tablespoons milk or broth, then squeeze it dry in a cloth. Melt 2 tablespoons fat, add the bread and beat to a smooth paste. Season and flavor as required.

PANCAKE

An American breakfast favorite, this soft, flat cake cooked on both sides on a griddle or in a hot greased skillet, is traditionally served slathered with butter and maple syrup and accompanied by bacon or sausages. American pancakes trace their history back to the Indians who made soft balls of cornmeal into a kind of pancake they called *nokehick*. These cornmeal cakes as well as similar flat cakes New World settlers had made back home, such as the Dutch *pannekoeken*, evolved into the modern pancake of which there are several versions including buckwheat, buttermilk, johnnycakes, flapjacks, blueberry, etc. All are made from batters of various types of flour usually mixed with milk, eggs and frequently butter.

BLUEBERRY PANCAKES

1½ cups flour
2 tablespoons sugar
1 teaspoon salt
2 lightly beaten eggs
1¼ cups milk
3 tablespoons butter, melted
½ cup fresh blueberries, dusted lightly with flour

In a large mixing bowl blend the flour, sugar, and salt. Beat the eggs, milk, and butter together and pour into the dry ingredients, mixing just enough to moisten dry ingredients; batter may be slightly lumpy. Stir in the blueberries and spoon batter onto a very hot, well-greased griddle or skillet. When bubbles appear on top of pancakes, turn them over and cook until second side is lightly browned. Serve immediately with lots of butter and maple or other syrup.

PANDOWDY

An American dessert consisting of sliced apples, sweetened with maple syrup, cinnamon, cloves and brown sugar, dotted with butter, topped with a crumbly crust and baked. The origin of the name is unknown, perhaps deriving from the pan it is cooked in and its homey, unglamorous or "dowdy" nature.

PANETTONE

A festive Italian sweet yeast bread studded with raisins and candied citrus peel and served traditionally at Christmas time. It is a specialty of Milan.

PANETTONE

1 package active dry yeast
⅔ cup lukewarm water
¼ cup sugar
1 teaspoon salt
3 egg yolks, lightly beaten
3½ cups all-purpose flour
10 tablespoons butter, softened
½ cup raisins
½ cup chopped candied citrus peel

In a small bowl, combine the yeast with the water and 1 teaspoon of the sugar. Let stand for 10 minutes, until frothy.

In a large mixing bowl combine the salt, egg yolks, remaining sugar, and the yeast mixture. Stir in about 2 cups of the flour, then gradually beat in 8 tablespoons of the softened butter. Knead in the remaining flour.

Turn the dough onto a lightly floured work surface and knead until firm and elastic. Place in a lightly oiled bowl, cover with a damp towel and let rise in a warm place until dough is doubled in bulk. Turn dough out onto a floured surface, punch down and knead raisins and citrus peel into dough until evenly distributed. Place dough in a well-greased 7-inch round cake pan, cover with oiled plastic wrap and let stand in a warm place until dough rises to the top of the pan. Melt the remaining 2 tablespoons butter. Remove plastic wrap from dough and brush with some of the melted butter. Bake in a 400° oven for 20 minutes. Reduce heat to 350° and bake for 35 to 45 minutes longer. Remove cake from the pan and brush the top and sides with remaining melted butter. Cut in thin wedges and serve.

PANTOTHENIC ACID

One of the B vitamins. (See Vitamins entry.)

PAPAW

One of the varieties of custard fruit, grown in the Southern parts of the United States and in the tropics. It is green, with greenish-white flesh, and is generally not pleasant to eat. There is, however, one edible variety which when ripe turns brown, with yellow flesh.

It is unrelated to the papaya which is also called "pawpaw."

PAPAYA

A tropical fruit, originally found in the Caribbean and Central and South America, but now grown in most countries with a suitable climate; it forms an important food in some regions. There are a number of varieties, differing in color and size. Ripe papayas can be eaten like a melon, with sugar; when not quite ripe, they can be boiled like a vegetable and served with an oil and vinegar dressing.

The fruit produces an enzyme, papain, which breaks down meat fibers and is therefore the basis of meat-tenderizing powders.

In the United States, it grows in Florida and Hawaii. It is also called pawpaw.

PAPPADAM (POPPADUM)

Thin, round Indian breads resembling tortillas, made from lentil flour and often seasoned with garlic, red chilis, and black pepper. Available in packages in Indian markets, these breads puff up dramatically and become crisp when quickly fried. They can be served with hors d'oeuvres.

PAPRIKA

The red powder obtained from the fruit of a capsicum or chili pepper originally made in Hungary, but now made in many other countries including the United States. The strength of paprika varies greatly, some types being quite mild; the best kind is that known as Szegediner from Hungary. The characteristic sweet, aromatic taste of paprika makes it a very good addition to many dishes and it is indispensable in Hungarian goulash. It goes well with tomato; add up to 1 teaspoon mild paprika to 1 cup tomato sauce. When paprika is used in appreciable quantities it gives a pink coloring to a dish or sauce. To obtain maximum benefit from the flavor it should be "sweated" with any vegetables or meat. It may also be used as a garnish sprinkled on appetizers or other foods for color. As paprika does not keep well it should be bought when needed.

PARBOILING

To part-boil: the food is boiled in the normal way, but for only half the time until somewhat softened, and is then finished by some other method.

PARCHING

To brown in dry heat.

PARFAIT

A type of frozen sweet, similar to a mousse, but somewhat richer; beaten eggs are usually included to give lightness. The term also applies to layers of ice cream or ices garnished with sauces. Both desserts are served in tall glasses.

FRUIT PARFAIT

½ cup sugar
2 tablespoons water
1 egg white
few drops of lemon or other extract
1¼ cups heavy cream, whipped
fruit salad and whipped cream to serve

Boil the sugar and water to 225°. Pour a thin stream onto the stiffly beaten egg white, beating continuously. Beat until thick. Cool, add the extract and the whipped cream. Pour into ice trays, cover with foil and freeze.

Meanwhile, prepare some fruit salad, then chill it. Divide over each serving of parfait and top with whipped cream.

PARING

To peel or trim.

PARMENTIER

The name of the man who introduced the potato into France in the eighteenth century. The name is now applied to a number of potato dishes.

POMMES PARMENTIER

Peel 2 lb potatoes and cut into ½-inch dice. Fry in hot fat – shallow or deep – until crisp, golden brown and soft throughout. Season and serve at once.

PARMENTIER SOUP

1 lb potatoes
3–4 leeks

2 tablespoons butter
2 cups chicken or veal broth
seasoning

Sauté the potatoes and leeks in the butter, stir in the broth and simmer until the potatoes are soft. Sieve the soup and return to a boil, then season to taste.

PARMESAN CHEESE

A hard Italian cheese made from partially skimmed milk. In Italy it is referred to as Grana owing to its granular texture. Parmesan has an excellent flavor and is used grated for cooking. It is expensive but only a little is required, owing to its strong flavor. It can be purchased already grated in jars or it may be bought in a piece and grated as needed. If carefully stored, Parmesan will keep for years.

PARSLEY

This herb, with its curled, bright green leaves, is invaluable as both flavoring and garnish. The three main varieties are domestic, extra curly dwarf, and Italian. The domestic and curly are most commonly used as garnish. The Italian has flat leaves and a slightly stronger flavor and is often added to soups. There is a turnip-rooted type, grown for its large roots; the green foliage of this type can also, of course, be chopped and used for flavoring but it is inferior in flavor to other varieties. What is often referred to as Chinese parsley is actually cilantro or coriander leaves.

Parsley is a good source of vitamin C, but so little is eaten that it is not really significant.

To chop parsley: Wash the parsley to remove the grit, squeeze it dry in a cloth and chop it finely.

PARSNIP

This root vegetable, which is available from fall to spring, has a characteristic strong flavor which appeals to many people. Parsnips may be boiled and then served either in pieces or mashed, with seasoning, a little cream or milk and butter, or they may be put in the pan with the roast. A less common way of cooking is to dip strips of boiled parsnip in batter and fry them in hot fat. A homemade wine may also be prepared from parsnips.

Parsnips, like all root vegetables, contain carbohydrates and therefore have a higher energy value than green vegetables.

Preparation and cooking: Wash, peel off the tough skin, and remove the hard center core. Cut in slices, strips, or dice and leave in water until ready for cooking. Boil in a covered pan in 1 inch of salted water for 30 to 40 minutes, until tender. Drain and toss in butter, seasoning, and grated nutmeg.

To roast parsnips, parboil for 5 minutes in salted water, drain, place in fat around a roast and roast for 1 hour.

PARSNIP CROQUETTES

1 lb parsnips, cut into chunks
2 medium potatoes, peeled and cut into chunks
salt
pepper
2 tablespoons butter, softened
½ cup plus 2 tablespoons all-purpose flour
1 large egg, beaten
1 cup bread crumbs
¼ cup blanched almonds, finely chopped
vegetable oil for frying

Place parsnips and potatoes in a large saucepan of boiling salted water and boil for about 20 minutes, or until tender. Drain vegetables and return to the pan over low heat to evaporate any excess moisture, stirring to avoid sticking.

Transfer vegetables to a mixing bowl, let cool slightly, then mash until smooth. Season with salt and pepper, beat in butter and ½ cup of the flour and blend until well mixed. With well-floured hands, form the puree into about 8 croquettes. Roll each croquette in remaining flour, dip each in beaten egg then roll in the bread crumbs mixed with the chopped almonds until thoroughly and evenly coated. Chill for 1 hour.

Heat the oil in a deep-fryer or a large, straight-sided skillet to 375°. Fry croquettes, a few at time, turning until golden brown on all sides, about 5 minutes. Drain on paper towels and keep hot while frying remaining croquettes.

PARTRIDGE

A game bird of Europe and the British Isles. The most common and widespread European partridge (*Perdix perdix*) has been introduced into the United States and Canada, most successfully in the Midwest and Prairie Provinces. It is known as the gray, or Hungarian, partridge. The chukar, a red-legged European variety, does well in the West from southern Canada to northern Mexico, extending as far east as Colorado. Partridge is also raised on game farms. Allow one bird per serving.

Preparation, roasting and serving: As soon as possible after shooting, hang the bird head downwards for 3 to 4 days in a cool, airy place. Pluck, singe, and clean it, season the inside with pepper and salt and replace the liver. Stuffing may be added if desired (either a simple stuffing made of bread crumbs, parsley, etc., or a more elaborate one containing chopped mushrooms). Truss the partridge in the same way as poultry, pressing up the breast to give it a plump, rounded appearance.

During the cooking the bird must be well basted to prevent the breast from drying while the legs, which the heat takes longer to penetrate, are cooking. As an additional precaution the breast may be covered with grape leaves and bacon – trim a fine grape leaf to rectangular shape, spread it lightly with butter and lay it on the breast with a thin slice of bacon of the same size on top; fix it with a piece of string and remove it before the bird is served. Cook in a 425° oven; the average time is 25 minutes.

Remove the trussing strings and serve the bird at once with a good thin brown gravy made in the roasting pan.

The choice of garnish and accompaniments is very much a matter of taste. Quarters of lemon and watercress, seasoned and sprinkled with a few drops of vinegar, are often served. Bread sauce and browned crumbs are liked by some, while potato chips and a salad are indispensable additions. A crisp lettuce salad, sprinkled with a little chopped tarragon, is a favorite. A partridge can also be made into tasty dishes by broiling, poaching, or stewing with other ingredients.

PARTRIDGE CASSEROLE

2 medium-sized onions, skinned and sliced
2 stalks celery, trimmed and sliced
¼ lb mushrooms, sliced
¼ lb bacon, chopped
1 tablespoon oil
2 tablespoons butter
2 partridges, cleaned and cut up
3 tablespoons flour
1¾ cups broth
1 (16 oz) can tomatoes
salt
pepper
⅔ cup red wine

Sauté the onions, celery, mushrooms, and bacon in the oil and butter for about 5 minutes, until golden brown. Remove from the skillet and line the base of a casserole with them. Sauté the partridge for about 5 minutes then add to the casserole with the vegetables. Stir the flour into the skillet and cook for 2 to 3 minutes. Gradually stir in the broth, bring to a boil and stir until it thickens. Add the tomatoes, salt, pepper, and wine. Pour the sauce over the partridge, cover and cook in a 350° oven for 1 hour.

PARTRIDGE WITH GRAPES

2 young partridges
2 tablespoons vegetable oil
¾ cup light broth
6 tablespoons dry white wine
salt
freshly ground white pepper
1 tablespoon cornstarch
1 egg yolk
2 tablespoons heavy cream
4 oz white grapes, skinned, halved, pitted
chopped parsley to garnish

Halve the partridges and remove the back bones. Carefully pull off the skin. Heat the oil in a large skillet and lightly brown the birds on both sides. Add the broth and wine, season and bring to a boil. Cover tightly, simmer gently on top of the stove for about 25 minutes or until tender. Drain partridges, keep warm on a serving dish. Blend together cornstarch, egg yolk, and cream. Add to pan juices with grapes, cook gently without boiling, until sauce thickens. Adjust seasoning. Spoon sauce over partridges and garnish.

TO FREEZE
Prepare as above to the point of covering, then simmer for 20 minutes only, pack, and freeze. To use, thaw, reheat, covered, on top of stove and complete as above.

PARTY

Whether a party is to be large or small, formal or simple, it will have a greater chance of success if you plan it beforehand. See Planning a Party entry on page 448 for a guide to quantities for parties.

Buffet Parties

These provide an easy way of entertaining a large number of people; they have become very popular, as they need less space than a formal dinner or lunch and are less expensive.

If possible, arrange the buffet table in the middle of the room and have smaller tables set at convenient points to prevent congestion. Try to provide sufficient chairs for guests to be seated if they wish.

All the food should be easy to eat (preferably without the use of a knife) and set out so that the guests can easily help themselves. Plates, forks, spoons, and napkins should be placed near the dishes.

Soup may be served at one end of the buffet table; coffee or other hot drinks may be served there or at a separate table. Cold drinks and glasses should, if possible, be placed on a third table, to avoid congestion.

Cocktail Parties

If a large number of people are invited, the room should be arranged as for buffet parties. (See Cocktail entry for some popular drinks recipes.) Wine, also tomato juice or orange juice, should be offered as alternatives to cocktails. To accompany the drinks, serve small hot or cold canapés and snacks, such as olives, salted nuts, stuffed prunes, salty crackers and toast fingers spread with cream cheese, pâté, flaked sardines or other fish. Potato chips accompanied by a dip are also popular. Plain slightly sweet crackers are good with wine or sherry.

Wine and Cheese Party

The main requirements are an assortment of cheese (say 3 to 4 types for a small party and 6 to 8 for a larger one), with a variety of breads, crispbreads, and crackers. Choose well contrasted cheeses but have one mild kind for the less adventurous; allow about 2 oz to 3 oz per person. The cheeses will look attractive arranged on a wooden board or platter; Cheddar cheese may be cut into cubes and served on cocktail picks. Provide also tidbits such as potato chips, onions, olives, radishes, pickles, salami, and tiny sausages.

Other items that can be served at a wine and cheese party include:

Welsh rarebit, cut into neat squares
Smoked salmon and grape rolls on picks
Pitted grapes, stuffed with cream cheese and speared on sticks
Salted almonds
Cheese straws and assorted cocktail crackers
Cubes of cheese and pineapple
Smoked fish cut into small pieces.

If you are serving both bread and crackers allow 3 oz crackers per person (more for big eaters) and the equivalent of 2 slices of bread. Thus, for a party of 20 get 2 large rye loaves, 2 long French breads, and 3 lb to 4 lb crackers. 1 lb butter gives about 100 teaspoon-size pats.

Dips are popular; for these have bowls of one

or two kinds of dip, surrounded with breadsticks, chunks of crisp French bread, potato chips, or celery stalks.

Almost any drink can be served, from bottles of wine to iced or hot wine punch. It is wise to also have soft drinks and hot coffee.

There is no strict rule as to what wine is best with each cheese, so a choice of red or white can be offered. Allow about half a bottle per person. Some port or sherry – the classic accompaniment to cheese – can be served, while for any guests that do not care for wine, beer is a welcome alternative.

RED WINES
Bordeaux or California Cabernet Sauvignon Burgundy or California Gamay Beaujolais Red Chianti or California Zinfandel wine, e.g. Châteauneuf du Pape, or California Petit Syrah.

WHITE WINES
Bordeaux or California dry Sémillon Burgundy or California Pinot Blanc or Chardonnay.

ROSÉ WINES
From Provence, Portugal, or California.

Informal Dinner Parties
The menu for these informal meals usually consists of three courses, followed by coffee, though very informal gatherings can be even more simple. Anyone who has to be both cook and hostess should choose at least some dishes which can be prepared beforehand or plan for first courses that take little preparation, such as raw oysters or slices of purchased pâté; here are two sample menus:

Spring or Early Summer

> Crème Vichyssoise
> Veal Cutlets
> Green Beans
> Duchesse Potatoes
> Cherries in Wine

Fall or Winter

> Moules Marinière
> Tournedos with Béarnaise Sauce
> Braised Belgian Endive
> Potato Parmentier
> Rum and Chocolate Gâteau

Formal Dinner Parties
The number of courses at a formal meal may vary from three to five or more. Often menu cards are provided for each person or one to each small table if this is the seating arrangement.

At a large celebration dinner, place cards can be used on the table. At an informal dinner the hostess indicates where the guests are to sit. This begins with the senior lady guest who sits on the right of the host; the ladies are seated first and then the men are shown their places.

The full menu for a dinner or banquet in former times comprised these courses:

Appetizer
Soup (choice of clear or thick)
Fish
Entrée
A roast (with vegetables)
Sorbet (only served at very formal meals)
Poultry or game, with salad
Entremets: dressed vegetables, and other side dishes.
Glace (ice: only served at very formal meals)
Dessert (fresh fruit, bonbons, petits fours, cakes, etc.)
Coffee

Simplified menus are now made up in one of the following ways:
1. Appetizer or soup; fish, meat, game, or poultry, with vegetables; dessert; coffee.
2. Soup; fish; game; dessert.
3. Soup, game, and dessert.
4. Appetizer, main course, dessert, cheese.

Note: A first course of iced melon, melon cocktail, oysters, or any simple appetizer may be followed by soup, or the soup may be omitted altogether.

SERVING THE MEAL
1. The first course (appetizer, fruit cocktail, etc.) is usually placed ready on the table, either in individual dishes or (in the case of hors d'oeuvre) grouped in the center of the table.
2. Soup, fish, and entrées are usually served at the table by the hostess. For a more formal occasion, they can be served at a side table, and handed to the guests by a waitress. Food and plates are served and removed from the left, with the left hand, while drinks, with the glasses or cups, are served and removed from the right.
3. It is usually more convenient to carve roasts and fowl at a side table.
4. Sauces are served in a sauceboat and other accompaniments in serving dishes.
5. Desserts are served at table, or, if in individual dishes, they are handed around.
6. Cheese and crackers are served on dishes so that the guests can help themselves.

Luncheon Parties

These are usually less elaborate than dinner parties, though a formal luncheon is served exactly like a formal dinner, the chief differences being a simpler menu and table setting; there is no formality when entering the dining room and place cards are not used, except for very large functions.

For informal luncheons it is common practice to serve two courses only, followed by coffee.

Children's Parties

These can be given for various occasions, although birthday parties are the most popular. As different age groups require different amusements and food it is advisable not to have too wide an age range. For older children a theme adds interest; this can be introduced with decorations and dress, then carried through to the food and games.

The food should be novel in presentation, but the actual tastes and textures should not be too unfamiliar. Include pizzas, hot dogs, hamburgers, toasted sandwiches or spaghetti and meatballs. For cakes, you can have cup cakes, éclairs, cookies, brownies, or iced cake. Ice cream is usually popular, but avoid having too many rich things, for some children are easily upset. As a centerpiece, make an attractively iced birthday or party cake. This can sometimes be based on a favorite object or character, such as a train, boat, or a popular cartoon character. Plan the table to look pretty, but keep it simple for young children.

Popular drinks for small children are orange and lemon drinks, milk or milk shakes. School children may like these and also enjoy fresh lemonade, apple cider, and other fruit juices.

Tea Parties

For light afternoon tea, serve a good Indian or China tea (or both) and offer such things as thinly cut bread and butter topped with smoked salmon or prosciutto, open biscuits, thin layer sandwiches or rolled sandwiches, assorted fancy pastries and éclairs or petits fours and assorted cookies. In winter, hot cheese toast or hot butter biscuits or teacakes can be included.

Bridge Parties

These are planned to suit the time of day – for an afternoon party serve a light tea; if the guests arrive after dinner, serve coffee or tea, small sandwiches, pastries, petits fours, or cookies during an interval.

Wedding Receptions

It is a matter of choice as to whether this is a very formal occasion, informal, large or small gathering. For a summer wedding a garden setting is delightful, but it is wise to have a tent or to make some alternative arrangements for bad weather.

Buffet refreshments are easy to arrange, especially for a large number of guests, and are suitable for any time of day. A sitdown meal, however, is especially appropriate after an early wedding and makes a more dignified setting for the ceremonies of cutting the cake and proposing the toasts.

Buffet Wedding Breakfast

(For general arrangements see Buffet Parties entry.) Suggested menus are given below, the first one being for a midday reception and the second for an afternoon function. (For quantities required, see the list at end of entry.)

Tomato Juice Cocktail (or Jellied Consommé)
Chaudfroid of Chicken
Salmon Fingers
Cocktail sausages
Bouchées
Shrimp Puffs
Fruit Salad in Melons
Chocolate Soufflé
Meringues
Chocolate Éclairs
Wedding Cake
Champagne
Punch
Tea
Coffee

Lobster Salad
Chicken and Ham Bouchées
Asparagus Rolls
Salmon Éclairs
Shaped Sandwiches
Macaroons
Iced Petits Fours
Meringues
Fruit Tartlets
Wedding Cake
Champagne
Punch
Tea
Coffee

Sit-down Wedding Breakfast (Midday)

Either a hot or cold luncheon may be served; following are two suggested menus:

Consommé
Baked Salmon Steaks
Hollandaise Sauce
Asparagus Tips
New Potatoes
Strawberry Flan
Wedding Cake
Sherry
Champagne
Coffee

Iced Consommé
Smoked Trout
Horseradish Sauce
Cold Roast Duck
Orange and Lettuce Salad
Potato Salad
Raspberry Soufflé
Wedding Cake
Burgundy
Champagne
Coffee

Choose wines and beverages to suit the food served; champagne or sparkling white wine is best for the toasts – allow at least one glass per guest, more if possible. Cocktails and sherry may be served while the guests are being received. Wine should be available at either a buffet or a sit down meal. Coffee (hot or iced) is served at morning receptions and tea and coffee in the afternoons.

PASHKA

A sweet dish originally made in Russia: it is made from cottage cheese, cream, almonds, and dried fruit and is set in a wooden mold. It can also be molded in an earthenware flowerpot. It is a rich dish traditionally served at Easter with cake.

PASSION FRUIT

(See Granadilla entry.)

PASSOVER (PESACH)

The Jewish festival commemorating the deliverance of the Jews from Egypt as recorded in the Old Testament. The festival begins on the evening of the 14th day of the first month of the religious calendar (usually March or April) with a ceremonial meal, called a Seder which is followed by a second Seder the next evening. Ceremonial foods are served and only the unleavened bread, called matzo, can be eaten during the seven days of the festival to commemorate the fact that the fleeing Jews had no time to let their bread rise before taking flight.

PASTA

Pasta, which originated in Italy, is now produced in many countries. It is made from the flour of a very hard wheat, durum wheat, which grows particularly well in parts of Italy. Pasta constitutes the staple food in these parts, supplying energy, protein, and some vitamins and minerals. It performs the role that bread serves in other regions.

Basically, the paste or dough is made from flour, salt, oil, and water. Eggs are an added ingredient as is spinach or other food that colors the dough. The dough is next forced through perforations of various shapes, or rolled out and cut, then allowed to dry.

There is an immense number of different pasta shapes, each with its own name. Some of these are familiar and often the name itself gives some indication of the size or shape. Here are a few.

Vermicelli (little worms)	Macaroni
Spaghetti	Farfalle (butterflies)
Stelle (stars)	Ravioli (envelopes containing a meat or cheese mixture)
Alfabeto (Alphabet)	
Conchiglie (shells)	Cannelloni
Tagliatelle (noodles)	Lasagne

Most pasta is sold in dried form and keeps quite well, but is really best used when fairly fresh. After cooking and draining it can be served in many different ways. In Italy pasta is popular served quite simply tossed in butter and grated cheese: it is also served with a variety of tomato, meat and other sauces, and as accompaniment to casseroles, broiled and sautéed meat in place of potatoes, and in soups.

Outside of Italy, pasta dishes are served as a single course, as a main dish for lunch or supper or occasionally to replace potatoes with a meat dish. Since pasta consists almost exclusively of starch, it is not usual to serve another starchy food with it; macaroni and cheese, for example, is better served with tomatoes than with potatoes.

(See Macaroni, Spaghetti entries etc.)

Freezing pasta: Most pasta dishes can be frozen successfully but it is only really worthwhile for those that need further preparation. They can be cooked straight from frozen.

Cooking and serving pasta: The Italians serve 2 oz to 4 oz of pasta per person but elsewhere 1½ to 2 oz is more usual. It should be cooked in a large quantity of rapidly boiling salted water until just resistant to the teeth (*al dente*); it should not be allowed to become mushy and slimy. When the pasta is cooked it should be drained immediately and served on a heated dish. A lump of butter or a little olive oil can be stirred in; grated Parmesan cheese can be mixed into the pasta or served separately.

Pasta that has been stored for some time will require longer cooking time than a fresher product.

Vermicelli	5 minutes
Spaghetti	12 to 15 minutes
Macaroni	15 to 20 minutes
Fancy shaped	10 minutes
Ridged	20 minutes
Tagliatelle	10 minutes
Lasagne	10 to 15 minutes
Stuffed pasta	15 to 20 minutes

These cooking times give a softer pasta than that preferred in Italy.

When used as an ingredient in soups and stews, pasta is often added raw up to 30 minutes before the dish is ready to serve.

SPAGHETTI ALLA BOLOGNESE

(Using a traditional Italian meat sauce)

FOR THE SAUCE
2 oz bacon, chopped
butter
1 small onion, chopped
1 carrot, chopped
1 stalk celery, chopped
½ lb ground beef
¼ lb chicken livers, chopped
1 tablespoon tomato paste
⅔ cup dry white wine
1 cup beef broth
salt
pepper
8 oz spaghetti
grated Parmesan cheese to serve

To make the sauce, sauté the bacon lightly in a little butter for 2 to 3 minutes, add the onion, carrot, celery and sauté for a further 5 minutes until lightly browned. Add the beef and brown lightly. Stir in the chopped chicken livers. After cooking them for about 3 minutes, add the tomato paste and wine, allow to simmer for a few minutes and add the broth and seasoning.

Simmer for 30 to 40 minutes, until the meat is tender and the liquid in the sauce is well reduced. Adjust the seasoning if necessary.

Meanwhile cook the spaghetti in the usual way in fast-boiling water for about 10 to 15 minutes. Drain and serve in a heated dish with the sauce poured over. Serve the cheese sprinkled over the sauce or in a separate dish.

CANNELLONI WITH CHEESE SAUCE

8 large cannelloni or 32 rigatoni
salt
¼ lb mushrooms, chopped
4 tablespoons butter
1 can (6½ oz) pimientos, drained
1 can (8 oz) garden peas, drained
2 cloves garlic, crushed
1 can (7½ oz) salmon or tuna, drained and flaked
⅔ cup fresh white bread crumbs

FOR THE SAUCE
4 tablespoons butter
4 tablespoons flour
2½ cups milk
1½ cups grated Cheddar cheese
salt
pepper

Cook the pasta in salted water for the time directed on the package; drain well. Meanwhile sauté the mushrooms in the butter; add three-quarters of the pimiento, diced, the peas, garlic, fish, and bread crumbs. Cook over a low heat for 5 minutes, stirring.

Make up the sauce as for Spaghetti alla Bolognese, using 1¼ cups of the cheese. Stuff the pasta with the fish filling so that it protrudes slightly at each end. Arrange side by side in an ovenproof dish. Pour the sauce over. Garnish with the remainder of the pimiento, cut in strips, and sprinkle the rest of the cheese over. Bake in a 400° oven for 30 minutes, until bubbly and golden brown.

CANNELLONI AU GRATIN

10 oz cannelloni
1½ cups ricotta cheese
1 hard-cooked egg, finely chopped
1 tablespoon chopped parsley

½ cup chopped mushrooms
salt
pepper
1 egg, beaten
1¼ cups cheese or tomato sauce
bread crumbs
grated Parmesan cheese

Cook the cannelloni and drain. Make the stuffing by combining the ricotta with the hard-cooked egg, parsley, mushrooms, salt, pepper, and beaten egg.

Stuff the cannelloni carefully and lay in a buttered ovenproof dish. Coat with sauce and sprinkle with bread crumbs and cheese. Bake in a 400° oven for 15 minutes.

HOMEMADE NOODLES

2 cups semolina or all-purpose flour
½ teaspoon salt
2 eggs, beaten
1 teaspoon oil
1 teaspoon warm water

Sift the flour and salt into a bowl. Make a well in the center and add the remaining ingredients. Gradually incorporate the flour into the liquid ingredients, until the dough can be gathered into a ball. Knead for about 10 minutes, until smooth. Cover with a bowl and let rest for 10 minutes.

Divide the dough into two portions and roll out very thinly. To cut manicotti, lasagne, or cannelloni, leave the dough flat. Cut into 3-inch squares for manicotti, 4- to 4½-inch squares for cannelloni, and into 2-inch strips for lasagne. Dry, covered with a cloth, for 1 hour before cooking. To cut other noodles, roll up, or fold, the dough into a roll. Cut crosswise, at ¾-inch intervals for tagliatelle ¼-inch for fettuccine, or however desired. Unfold, cover, and dry for 1 hour before using. Fresh pasta will cook much more quickly than dried. For freshly made pasta, bring salted water to a boil, add pasta, stir and cook for 15 seconds to 1 minute after the water returns to boiling.

Any noodles which are not required immediately should be hung in a warm, dry place (near the stove, or before the fire) until crisp and dry; they can then be stored for a short period. Pasta that has been dried from 1 to 4 days will need to cook from 1 to 3 minutes after water returns to boiling.

TAGLIATELLE CON PROSCIUTTO

8 oz tagliatelle
8 oz prosciutto ham, chopped

butter
grated Parmesan cheese

Cook the tagliatelle in rapidly boiling water in the usual way for about 10 minutes. Meanwhile lightly sauté the ham in a little butter for 2 to 3 minutes. Drain the pasta, mix with the butter and ham and serve on a hot dish, sprinkled with the cheese.

Note: If using fresh pasta, start sautéing ham first as pasta only needs to cook about a minute.

CREAMY CHEESE LASAGNE

2 quarts milk
2 slices onion
2 slices carrot
bay leaf
6 peppercorns
8 tablespoons butter or margarine
1 cup flour
⅔ cup sour cream
½ lb cooked ham, finely diced
1 lb cheese, grated (mixture of Cheddar, Edam, blue cheese)
salt
pepper
12 oz lasagne

Place the milk, onion, carrot, bay leaf, and peppercorns in a saucepan, bring to a boil, then remove from the heat. Cover the pan and leave to infuse for 20 minutes, then strain.

Melt the butter in a saucepan and stir in the flour. Cook gently for 1 minute, stirring constantly. Gradually stir in the strained milk, stirring briskly until the sauce is smooth. Bring to a boil, then reduce the heat and simmer for 3 minutes. Remove from the heat; stir in the sour cream, finely diced ham, three-quarters of the cheese and salt and pepper to taste.

Arrange the uncooked pasta and sauce in layers (starting with pasta and ending with a good covering of sauce) in a lightly greased 5-pint shallow ovenproof dish. Sprinkle with the remaining cheese.

Bake in a 400° oven for about 1¼ hours or until golden brown and the pasta just tender; cover if necessary.

Note: Any combination of cheese can be used but add salt sparingly if using much blue cheese.

PASTEURIZATION

A method of partially sterilizing a liquid by heat treatment, first discovered by Louis Pasteur when experimenting with wine. (See Milk entry.)

PASTILLE

A small lozenge or hard candy usually flavored with fruit juice.

PASTRAMI

A Jewish-American delicatessen specialty which takes its name from the Romanian word "pastra," which means to preserve. It is made from beef, usually a boneless plate or brisket cut, that has been liberally rubbed with spices such as garlic, peppercorns, cayenne, coriander, etc., then dry-cured for a week or more. It is then rinsed, re-seasoned with a seasoning paste heavy on crushed peppercorns and smoke-cured for several hours. Before serving, it is usually steamed, then sliced against the grain and served hot on rye bread with mustard as the famous hot pastrami sandwich.

PASTRIES

A name loosely applied to fancy cakes, usually frosted or decorated. They include a vast assortment of different types, such as meringues, éclairs, mille-feuilles, rum babas, cream puffs, various types of small iced cakes, tarts, etc. (See individual entries.)

PASTRY

A combination of flour, water, and shortening that is baked. It may be sweetened or not, depending upon whether it is to be used for a sweet or savory pie or tart. Pastry differs by the type of shortening used (butter, vegetable shortening, lard, suet, oil), the amount of shortening used (the more shortening the "shorter" the crust) and how the shortening is introduced to the flour (cut in, rubbed in, rolled in, or melted and stirred in).

Ingredients for Pastrymaking

FLOUR
All-purpose flour should be used for most pastries, but bread flour is better for puff pastry.

LEAVENING AGENT
Baking powder is generally used in suet pastry. Steam acts as the leavening agent in puff and flaky pastries, in combination with the air enclosed between the layers of the paste. In choux pastry the leavening agents are eggs plus steam.

FAT
Butter and lard used to be the fats most commonly used, but today margarine, vegetable shortenings, and pure vegetable oils are also used. Butter gives the best flavor and should always be used for puff pastry. Lard is suitable for pie crusts, used with butter or margarine in the proportion of half butter or margarine to half lard.

General Hints on Pastrymaking

1. Coolness is important for good results. Handle the pastry as little as possible and always use the fingertips for rubbing in the fat. Rich pastries are improved by being made on a cold slab and placed in a refrigerator between rollings so that the pastry remains firm.
2. Always sift the flour and salt together into the mixing bowl, as this helps to lighten the mixture. Additional air is incorporated by lifting the flour from the bowl with the fingertips when rubbing in. Always rub in with a light, rather than a heavy hand.
3. The liquid should be very cold and must be added carefully; an excess causes a sticky, unmanageable dough and any extra flour then added will alter the proportions of the ingredients and cause the pastry to be tough. Chill the liquid in the refrigerator before use.
4. Rolling out must be done lightly and firmly; do not roll more than necessary. Always use firm, light strikes, rolling in one direction only.
5. Pastry requires a hot oven. Too slow an oven causes pale, hard pastry; see the pastry recipes given here and the individual recipes throughout the book.

Pre-baked Shells

Pastry shells are baked unfilled if the filling would otherwise make the crust soggy or if the filling itself should not be baked. If a filling is to be added and baked, then the shell is only partially baked.

Line the container with pastry and decorate the edge. Prick the pastry all over with a fork and cover with waxed paper. Half fill with metal pie weights or rice and bake in a 450° oven for about 12 minutes. Remove the weights and paper. If the pie is to be baked after filling, continue with the recipe. Otherwise, return the shell to the oven for about 10 minutes or until completely baked.

SHORT–CRUST PASTRY
1. Crumble the fat into the flour between the thumb and fingertips.

2. Add the water and stir until mixture begins to stick together in large lumps.

3. Gently knead the mixture together, to give a firm smooth dough.

SHORT-CRUST PASTRY

1⅔ cups all-purpose flour
pinch of salt
9 tablespoons butter or margarine
4 tablespoons water

Mix the flour and salt together. Cut the fat into small lumps and add it. Using both hands, rub the fat into the flour between finger and thumb tips. After 2 to 3 minutes there will be no lumps of fat left and the mixture will look like fresh bread crumbs. So far as possible, sprinkle the water evenly over the surface (uneven addition may cause blistering when the pastry is cooked). Stir it in until the mixture begins to stick together in large lumps. With both hands, collect it together and knead lightly for a few seconds, to give a firm, smooth dough. The pastry can be used immediately, but it is better when allowed to rest for 15 minutes before use. It can also be covered in plastic wrap and kept in the refrigerator for a day or two.

When the pastry is required, sprinkle a very little flour on a working surface and the rolling pin, not on the pastry, roll out the dough evenly in one direction only, turning it occasionally. The usual thickness is about ⅛ inch; do not pull or stretch it. Use as required. The usual oven temperature is 400° to 425°.

This amount is sufficient to cover a 5-cup pie dish, a 9-inch flan dish, or to make a top and bottom crust for a 7-inch pie plate.

Note: For a slightly richer pastry increase the fat to 6 tablespoons.

SHORTENING PASTRY

2½ cups all-purpose flour
1 teaspoon salt
¾ cup vegetable shortening
⅓–½ cup ice water

In a large mixing bowl, combine the flour and salt and blend well. Add the shortening and cut it into the dry ingredients with a fork or a pastry blender until mixture is the texture of coarse meal. Sprinkle just enough ice water into the mixture to make it stick together. Shape pastry into a ball. Cover with plastic wrap and chill until ready to roll out. Makes a double 9- to 10-inch crust.

OIL PASTRY

2½ tablespoons oil
1 tablespoon cold water
1 cup all-purpose flour
pinch of salt

Place the oil and water in a mixing bowl and beat well with a fork to form an emulsion. Mix the flour and salt together and add to the liquid to make a dough.

Roll this out on a floured board or between waxed paper. Fit into a 9-inch pie pan and bake in a 400° oven until lightly browned.

This is a slightly more greasy pastry than those made with solid fat so it is more suitable for nonsweet pies, such as meat pies, than for dessert pies.

GRAHAM CRACKER OR COOKIE CRUMB CRUST

1½ cups finely ground graham cracker or other
  sweet cookie crumbs
½ cup granulated, powdered sugar, or light brown
  sugar
1 teaspoon ground cinnamon (optional)
6 tablespoons butter, melted

Place crumbs in a large mixing bowl. Add sugar and cinnamon and blend well. Pour in the melted butter and mix until crumbs are well moistened. Turn mixture into a 9-inch pie pan and press evenly over the bottom and sides of the pan. Place another pie pan of equal diameter in the pan and press down firmly. Remove second pan, trim any excess crumbs and chill crumb crust thoroughly before filling.

SUGAR CRUST (FLAN) PASTRY

2 cups all-purpose flour
pinch of salt
9 tablespoons butter
3 tablespoons sugar
1 egg, beaten

Mix the flour and salt together and rub in the butter with the fingertips, as for short-crust pastry, until the mixture resembles fine crumbs. Mix in the sugar. Add the egg, stirring until the ingredients begin to stick together, then with one hand collect the mixture together and knead very lightly to give a firm, smooth dough. Roll out as for short-crust pastry and use as required. This pastry should be cooked in a 400° oven. This recipe is enough for an 8-inch ring.

SUET-CRUST PASTRY

This is the famous pastry of Great Britain, used to make a soft crust for dumplings and puddings.

2 cups self-rising flour
$\frac{1}{2}$ teaspoon salt
$3\frac{1}{2}$ oz shredded suet
7 tablespoons cold water

Mix together the flour, salt, and suet. Add enough cold water to give a light, elastic dough and knead very lightly until smooth. Roll out $\frac{1}{4}$ inch thick.

This pastry may be used for both sweet and savory dishes and can be steamed, boiled, or baked; the first two are the most satisfactory methods, as the pastry is inclined to be hard.

This quantity is sufficient for a 4- to 5-cup pudding bowl.

Flaky Pastries

FLAKY PASTRY

Probably the commonest of the flaked types, it can be used in many sweet and savory dishes; sausage rolls and pies are particularly popular. Good flaky pastry is judged by the evenness of the flakes when it is cooked, and the rolling and the even distribution of the fat are two important factors in achieving this result.

ROUGH PUFF PASTRY

Similar in appearance and texture to flaky although not quite so even. It is quicker and easier to make and can be used instead of flaky in most recipes.

PUFF PASTRY

The richest of all the pastries. It gives the most even rising, most flaky effect, and crispest texture. It should be handled very carefully. It is used for bouchées, vol-au-vents, and pastries.

The following general hints apply to all flaky pastries:
1. The fat should be the consistency of soft butter. Lard alone is too soft and margarine too hard, but a mixture of half lard and half margarine gives good results.
2. Make the flour dough of the same consistency as the fat, so that they mix easily together. Use a little lemon juice to make the pastry more pliable.
3. See that the air is evenly distributed during the rolling process and avoid bursting the air bubbles. Keep the edges of the pastry straight and the corners square.
4. Keep the pastry cool and allow it to rest between rollings and before baking, to avoid shrinkage.
5. Bake in a hot oven.

ROUGH PUFF PASTRY

2 cups all-purpose flour
pinch of salt
10 tablespoons butter
7 tablespoons cold water to mix
squeeze of lemon juice
beaten egg to glaze

Mix the flour and salt; cut the butter (which should be quite firm) into cubes about $\frac{3}{4}$ inch across. Stir the butter into the flour without breaking up the pieces and mix to a fairly stiff dough with the water and lemon juice. Turn onto a floured board and roll into a strip 3 times as long as it is wide. Fold the bottom third up and the top third down, then turn the pastry through 90° so that the folds are at the sides. Seal the edges of the pastry by pressing lightly with a rolling pin. Continue to roll and fold in this way 4 times altogether. Leave to rest wrapped in waxed paper for about 30 minutes before using. Roll out and use as for flaky pastry brushing with beaten egg before baking.

Rough puff gives a similar result to flaky pastry, but the flakes are not usually as even, so where even rising and appearance are particularly important, e.g. with patties and vol-au-vents, it is better to use flaky pastry. On the other hand, rough puff has the advantage of being quicker to make.

The usual oven setting for rough puff is 425°.

FLAKY PASTRY

2 cups all-purpose flour
pinch of salt
10 tablespoons butter
7 tablespoons cold water to mix
squeeze of lemon juice
beaten egg to glaze

Mix together the flour and salt. Soften the butter by working it with a knife on a plate; divide it into 4 equal portions. Rub one quarter of the softened butter into the flour and mix to a soft, elastic dough with the water and lemon juice. On a floured board, roll the pastry into an oblong 3 times as long as it is wide. Put another quarter of the butter over the top two-thirds of the pastry in flakes, so that it looks like buttons on a card. Fold the bottom third up and the top third of the pastry down and turn it through 90° so that the folds are now at the side. Seal the edges of the pastry by pressing with the rolling pin. Reroll as before and continue until all the butter is used up.

Wrap the pastry loosely in waxed paper and leave it to rest in a refrigerator or cool place for at least 30 minutes before using.

Sprinkle a board or table with a little flour. Roll out the pastry $\frac{1}{8}$ inch thick and use as required. Brush with beaten egg before baking, to give the characteristic glaze.

The usual oven setting for flaky pastry is 425°.

PUFF PASTRY

2 cups all-purpose flour
pinch of salt
14 tablespoons butter, preferably sweet
7 tablespoons cold water
squeeze of lemon juice
beaten egg to glaze

Mix the flour and salt. Work the butter with a knife on a plate until it is soft, then rub a good-sized lump of it into the flour. Mix to a fairly soft, elastic dough with the water and lemon juice and knead lightly on a floured board until smooth. Form the rest of the butter into an oblong and roll the pastry out into a square. Place the block of butter on one half of the pastry and enclose it by folding the remaining pastry over and sealing the edges with a rolling pin. Turn the pastry so that the fold is to the side, then roll out into a strip 3 times as long as it is wide. Fold the bottom third up and the top third down and seal the edges by pressing lightly with the rolling pin. Cover the pastry with waxed paper and leave to rest in the refrigerator for about 20 minutes. Turn the pastry so that the folds are to the sides and continue rolling, folding, and resting until the sequence has been completed 6 times altogether. After the final resting, shape the pastry as required. Always brush the top surfaces with beaten egg before cooking, to give the characteristic glaze of puff pastry.

The usual oven setting for puff pastry is 450°.

Note: Even without a freezer, uncooked home-made puff pastry keeps 2 to 3 days, wrapped in a cloth or foil in the refrigerator.

To freeze uncooked flaky and puff pastry: prepare as above up to the last rolling before freezing. Roll into an oblong shape, wrap in foil, then overwrap

FLAKY PASTRY
1. Dab on one quarter of the fat over the top two-thirds of the pastry.

2. Fold the bottom third of pastry up over center third, then fold top third over.

3. Turn the pastry so that the folds are now at the side. Seal pastry edges.

HOT-WATER CRUST PASTRY
1. Beat in melted lard mixture quickly to form a soft dough.

2. Working quickly, lightly pinch the dough together and knead in the bowl until the dough is smooth.

3. Cover the dough in the bowl with a plate and leave to rest for 20–30 minutes.

in a freezer bag. Seal the bag and label it giving the date and quantity of pastry. To thaw, leave the pastry in the wrappings overnight in the refrigerator for best results, but if you are in a hurry it can be thawed at room temperature for 3 to 4 hours. This kind of pastry is time-consuming to make, and it is therefore well worth storing some in the freezer.

HOT-WATER CRUST PASTRY

This dough is used for the raised meat pies of Great Britain.

1 lb all-purpose flour
2 teaspoons salt
$\frac{1}{2}$ cup lard
4 tablespoons milk or milk and water

Mix the flour and salt. Melt the lard in the liquid, then bring to a boil and pour into a well made in the dry ingredients. Working quickly, beat with a wooden spoon to form a fairly soft dough. Use hands to lightly pinch the dough together and knead until smooth and silky. Cover the dough in a bowl with a plate. Leave to rest for 20 to 30 minutes for the dough to become elastic and easy to work. Use as required.

CHOUX PASTRY

$\frac{1}{4}$ cup butter
$\frac{1}{2}$ cup water
$\frac{1}{2}$ cup all-purpose flour, sifted
2 eggs, lightly beaten

Melt the butter in the water and bring to a boil; remove from the heat and quickly tip in the flour all at once. Beat with a wooden spoon until the paste is smooth and forms a ball in the center of the pan. (Take care not to overbeat or the

CHOUX PASTRY
1. Melt the butter and water over a moderate heat. Bring slowly up to a boil and remove from the heat.

2. Tip in the flour all at once. Beat with a wooden spoon until the paste is smooth and forms a ball in the center of the pan.

3. Beat in the eggs, a little at a time, beating well after each addition to trap as much air into the mixture as possible. Continue beating until a sheen is obvious.

mixture becomes fatty.) Allow to cool for a minute or two. Beat in the eggs a little at a time, beating vigorously – this is important – to trap in as much air as possible. Carry on beating until a sheen is obvious. Use as required. Some people prefer to chill a handmade paste in the bag for about 30 minutes before piping. The usual oven setting is 400° to 425°.

Note: When beating by hand with a wooden spoon, the arm tends to tire, the beating speed to reduce and as a result the final consistency is often too slack to retain its shape. In this case a little of the egg may have to be omitted – and remember to use large eggs for the hand method.

PASTRY CREAM (CRÈME PÂTISSIÈRE)

A thick, sweet white sauce with egg yolks added. It is used as a filling for cakes and sweet pastries, e.g. éclairs.

VANILLA PASTRY CREAM

1 whole egg, separated
1 egg yolk
¼ cup sugar
2 tablespoons flour
2 tablespoons cornstarch
⅔ cup milk
vanilla

Cream the egg yolks and sugar together until really thick and pale in color. Beat in the flour and cornstarch and a little cold milk to make a smooth paste. Heat the rest of the milk in a saucepan until almost boiling and pour onto the egg mixture, stirring well. Return the mixture to the saucepan and stir over a low heat until the mixture boils. Beat the egg white until stiff. Remove the custard mixture from the heat and fold in the egg white. Again return the pan to the heat, add the vanilla to taste and cook for a further 2 to 3 minutes. Cool before using.

PASTY

(See Cornish Pasty entry.)

PÂTE

This French word literally means paste and is usually used to denote pastry, dough or batter, it is also used for Italian pasta.

PÂTÉ

Strictly speaking, this French term means a meat pie (sweet ones being more usually called tourtes). By extension it is sometimes applied to a meat paste, made from minced or pounded game, poultry, meat, liver (foie gras), fish etc., and shaped like a pie. A pâté of this type is usually served as an appetizer, accompanied by lettuce leaves, sliced lemon, and toast and butter.
 (See Foie Gras entry.)

CHICKEN LIVER PÂTÉ

1½ lb chicken livers
4 tablespoons butter
1 medium-sized onion, skinned and finely chopped
1 large clove garlic, skinned and crushed
1 tablespoon heavy cream
2 tablespoons tomato paste
3 tablespoons sherry or brandy
melted butter, optional

Rinse the chicken livers and dry thoroughly on paper toweling. Sauté them in the butter until they change color. Reduce the heat, add the onion and garlic, cover and cook for 5 minutes. Remove from the heat and cool. Add the cream, tomato paste, and sherry or brandy. Puree in a blender or press through a sieve. Turn into individual dishes. Cover tops with melted butter if you wish. Chill.

FARMHOUSE PÂTÉ

8 slices lean bacon
1 lb pork liver
1 lb chicken livers
½ lb pork belly or fat back
2 cups fresh white bread crumbs
2 eggs, beaten
2 cloves garlic, crushed
½ teaspoon salt
⅓ cup red wine
2 tablespoons brandy
2 teaspoons finely chopped thyme or 1 teaspoon dried thyme
½ cup pistachio nuts, coarsely chopped
pepper

Stretch the bacon slices with the blade of a knife and use them to line the bottom and sides of a greased 2-lb loaf pan or 2-pint terrine. Let the bacon hang over the sides. Set aside.
 In a food processor or with a sharp knife, mince the pork liver, chicken livers, pork belly and combine in a large mixing bowl. Add the

bread crumbs, eggs, garlic, salt, wine, brandy, thyme, and pistachios and season with pepper. Spoon the mixture into the loaf pan and level the surface. Fold the bacon over. Cover with foil, then stand the pan in a roasting pan half filled with hot water. Bake in a 325° oven for 2½ hours or until the pâté and the juices are just faintly pink.

Remove from the oven, pour off excess fat and let cool slightly. Then place heavy weights on top of the foil to compress the pâté into a firm block for slicing. When cooled completely, chill overnight. When ready to serve, turn pâté out onto a serving platter and slice thickly.

SMOKED TROUT PÂTÉ

8 oz smoked trout
4 tablespoons butter
1 cup fresh white bread crumbs
finely grated rind and juice of 1 lemon
salt
freshly ground black pepper
pinch grated nutmeg
⅔ cup half-and-half
⅔–1¼ cups aspic

Remove the skin and bones from the trout and finely chop the flesh. Melt butter in a small pan and pour it onto the bread crumbs with the lemon rind and juice. Season well with salt, pepper, and nutmeg. Add the fish to the bread crumbs and fold in the half-and-half. Spoon the mixture into 6 ramekins. Prepare aspic and when it is on the point of setting, spoon it over the fish mixture. Chill.

PÂTISSERIE

When correctly used, this term applies to highly decorated pastries, as produced by a French pâtissier or pastry cook, e.g. mille-feuilles, palmiers, cream puffs, and napoleons. It is often used more widely to denote any small fancy cakes and pastries.

PATTY PAN SQUASH

(See Squash entry.)

PATTY SHELLS

A shell of flaky or puff pastry in the form of a miniature pie or vol-au-vent. Small vol-au-vents are called bouchées in French. When the patties are closed the filling is put in before baking; it can consist of raw or cooked meat, poultry or game,

sometimes with additional ingredients such as mushrooms. For open patties, the filling is added after the pastry shells are baked and consists of cooked meat, poultry, game, shellfish, mushrooms, or similar ingredients, moistened with a sauce; see the recipes below.

To fill 24 patty shells.

MUSHROOM

Melt 2 tablespoons butter in a small pan and sauté 3 oz button mushrooms, coarsely chopped. Put on one side, wipe the pan and melt a further 2 tablespoons butter. Stir in 3 tablespoons flour and cook for 1 minute. Slowly beat in ⅔ cup milk and bring to a boil, stirring; cook for about 2 minutes. Fold in the mushrooms and enough cream to give a thick pouring consistency – about 3 tablespoons. Season to taste with salt, pepper, and a dash of Worcestershire sauce.

SHRIMP SAUTÉ

Use 4 oz shelled shrimp to replace the mushrooms and add 1 teaspoon chopped parsley and a little lemon juice instead of the Worcestershire sauce.

CHICKEN SAUTÉ

Use 1 small onion, finely chopped to replace the mushrooms; replace the Worcestershire sauce with Tabasco, and add ¾ cup diced cooked chicken before reheating.

PAUPIETTES

Paupiettes is the French word for thin slices of meat or fish wrapped securely around a filling and braised in wine or stock. They are most frequently made with thinly sliced veal or beef, but fish paupiettes are popular and even thinly sliced turkey or other fowl can be used. The fillings vary widely, including vegetables, bread crumbs, rice and meat.

PAUPIETTES DE VEAU

1 lb veal fillet, cut in 8 thin slices
8 thin slices cooked ham or bacon
⅓ cup bread crumbs, soaked in milk and squeezed dry
3 tablespoon raisins
¼ cup pine nuts or blanched slivered almonds
4 tablespoons grated Parmesan cheese
2 tablespoons chopped parsley
salt
pepper
1 tablespoon oil

2 tablespoons butter
⅔ cup dry white wine
parsley sprigs for garnish

Lay veal slices flat between waxed paper and pound lightly with a wooden mallet to flatten. Place a piece of ham or bacon on top of each slice of veal.

In a mixing bowl, combine bread crumbs, raisins, nuts, cheese, and parsley and season with salt and pepper. Divide stuffing between the veal slices, roll up tightly and secure with a wooden pick.

Heat the oil in a skillet and add the butter. Add the paupiettes and sauté until lightly browned all over. Add the wine, cover and cook very gently, turning once, for 20 to 25 minutes, until tender.

Transfer the paupiettes to a warmed serving platter and keep warm. Bring pan juices to a boil, stirring and cook until they have reduced. Spoon over the meat, garnish with parsley and serve immediately.

PAWPAW

(See Papaya entry.)

PEA

Green peas are the seeds of a climbing plant, of which there are numerous varieties, ranging in height from 1½ feet to 5 feet. The seeds are contained in a green pod which is not usually eaten, except in the case of the sugar variety. The peas themselves vary in size from the small "petits pois," with a diameter of about ⅛ inch to large ones nearly ½ inch in diameter.

The most familiar variety is the English or garden pea (*Pisum sativum*); when young, this is the "petit pois" of France.

There are also the Chinese snow pea (or super pea) and the sugar snap pea, a relatively recent hybrid between the English and the snow pea that is very sweet.

The season for fresh peas lasts for only about 2 months, but they are sold preserved in various ways: frozen, canned, dried, and dehydrated.

Frozen peas are very popular as they taste similar to fresh peas and there is no preparation required. Dried peas add considerably to the protein in the diet. Today, however, they have largely been replaced by frozen and canned peas.

Split peas are dried peas that have had the outer skin removed.

Dehydrated peas, which are dried by modern methods, retain many of the characteristics of fresh peas.

In addition to the protein already mentioned, peas supply a useful amount of vitamin C and A. Dried peas do not contain any vitamin C, but canned garden peas, dehydrated and frozen peas retain most of theirs, so their food value is very much the same as that of fresh peas.

Preparation and Cooking

FRESH PEAS
Shell and wash, place in boiling salted water with about 1 teaspoon sugar and a sprig of mint and cook until tender – about 10 minutes.

PETITS POIS
These are tiny, young garden peas popular in France. They are generally cooked with the addition of a little chopped onion and butter.

CHINESE SNOW PEA (SUGAR PEA)
Wash the pods in salted water, then "top and tail" them.

DRIED PEAS
Soak overnight in hot water containing ½ teaspoon bicarbonate of soda for every 8 oz peas. Put into fresh cold water, add salt, a sprig of mint, and an onion and boil gently until tender – about 2½ hours. Serve tossed in butter or a white, cheese or tomato sauce.

SPLIT PEAS
Prepare and cook in the same way as dried peas. They are used chiefly in soups and can also be substituted for lentils in various recipes.

PEA SOUP (USING DRIED PEAS)

6 oz dried peas
2 pints water
1 large onion, chopped
1 small carrot, chopped
1 small piece of turnip, chopped
2 tablespoons bacon drippings
seasoning
bouquet garni
⅔ cup milk

Wash the peas and soak overnight in the water. Sauté vegetables lightly in the melted drippings. Add the peas, the water in which they were soaked, seasoning, and bouquet garni, then simmer gently for 1½ to 2 hours, until the vegetables are reduced to a pulp. Remove the bouquet garni, add the milk, reheat, and serve. If desired, the soup may be sieved before the milk is added.

PEA BEAN

(See Navy Bean entry.)

PEACH

The single-pitted fleshy fruit of the peach tree, which is grown chiefly in warm areas such as California, Italy, and the South of France. It is native to China.

There are two main varieties of peach, the freestone and the cling-stone. In the former the skin and pit separate easily from the golden flesh, but in the cling-stone type the flesh is firmer and is freed from the pit with difficulty. Peaches bruise readily and the bloom is easily rubbed off, so they should be handled gently and as little as possible.

Peaches contain some vitamin C and some carotene. As the fruit contains little acid, extra must be added when it is used for jammaking.

Peaches can be frozen in syrup or as a puree. (See Freezing entry for methods.)

(See Canning, Drying entries, etc. for methods of preserving; for dried peaches, see Dried Fruit entry.)

Serving peaches: The fruits are usually served whole as a dessert fruit. They may, however, be cut up and used for fruit salads, tarts, cold desserts, ices, etc. They look attractive when cut in halves and pitted; a glaze helps to keep them moist and prevents any discoloring. Peaches are sometimes stewed or pureed and used to make a delicious soufflé. Canned or bottled peaches may be made into party desserts such as peach condé or melba and pies. Pureed peaches, sweetened and mixed with whipped cream, make a good cake filling.

PEACH MELBA

ice cream
halved peach
Melba sauce
whipped cream
chopped almonds

Place the ice cream in sundae glasses, then add a halved peach to each, hollow side down. Cover with the Melba sauce (see separate entry) and decorate with whipped cream and chopped almonds.

PEACHES IN LIQUEUR

Choose peaches which are not too ripe, plunge them into boiling water and leave for 3 minutes, then peel. Place the peaches in a serving bowl and cover with a light sugar syrup (see below), pouring it over while still hot; flavor with peach brandy and let cool. Serve very cold, with fresh cream.

To make the light syrup, boil 2 cups water and 1 cup sugar for 5 minutes, then skim. If desired, the syrup may be flavored by adding a piece of lemon rind while it is being boiled.

PEANUT (GROUNDNUT)

The seed of a leguminous plant grown in hot climates. The flowers bury themselves in the earth when they wither and the pod containing the nuts is therefore formed underground (hence the name groundnut). The pod is pale yellow and crinkled and it cracks easily to reveal 2 to 3 brown nuts. The nuts are usually roasted for a few minutes and the brown skins may then be easily removed by rubbing them.

Peanuts are valuable for the oil they contain, which is used in the manufacture of margarine and other fats. They have a high percentage of vegetable protein and fat and also contain iron, niacin, and thiamin, so they are a protective food and good provider of energy. Both the nuts and peanut butter are a useful addition to the diet and in some countries they are very important.

More than a billion pounds of peanuts are produced in the United States annually, the majority used for their oil and for cattle feed.

Salted Peanuts
(See Nuts entry.)

Peanut Brittle

A thin, crunchy candy made with caramelized sugar and corn syrup and peanuts.

PEANUT BRITTLE

3 cups sugar
1¼ cups light corn syrup
1 cup water
4 cups shelled peanuts
1 teaspoon baking powder
1 teaspoon vanilla
½ teaspoon salt

In a large, heavy saucepan, bring the sugar, corn

syrup and water to a boil and boil until sugar has completely dissolved and mixture registers 300° on a candy thermometer. Meanwhile, spread the peanuts evenly over a large marble slab or over two well-greased baking sheets. In a small bowl, blend the baking powder, vanilla and salt. Continue to heat the sugar mixture until it reaches 315°. Add the baking powder mixture quickly, then pour mixture over the peanuts. Working quickly, smooth out the surface with your hands in oiled plastic gloves and stretch and turn the sheets until they are thin and smooth. Let harden and cool, then break into irregular pieces.

Peanut Butter

A brownish-yellow, oily paste, with either a "smooth" or "crunchy" texture, made from peanuts. It may replace butter for use with bread, crackers etc., and it is most palatable when spread thickly with jelly in a sandwich. It is used in making some cakes and cookies.

PEANUT BUTTER COOKIES

¼ cup peanut butter
grated rind of ½ orange
¼ cup superfine sugar
3 tablespoons light brown sugar
¼ cup butter
1 egg
2 tablespoons raisins, chopped
1 cup flour
1 teaspoon baking powder
¼ teaspoon salt

Cream together the peanut butter, orange rind, sugars, and butter until light and fluffy. Beat in the egg, add the raisins and stir in the flour, baking powder, and salt to make a fairly firm dough. Roll the dough into small balls about the size of a walnut and place well apart on an ungreased baking sheet; dip a fork in a little flour and press criss-cross lines on each ball. Bake in a 350° oven for 25 minutes, until risen and golden brown. Cool on a rack.

PEAR

The fleshy fruit of a tree widely grown in most temperate zones, which is rounded at the base, and tapered at the stem. Many different varieties of dessert and cooking pear are grown. Some are very juicy and sweet and when absolutely ripe these make an excellent dessert fruit, though if allowed to become overripe they are mushy and insipid. They make good cold desserts when combined with other fruit, cream, ice cream, etc. A dessert pear which is ready for eating should yield to slight pressure at the stalk end.

Pears ripen from the end of summer to the beginning of winter and some types will keep until Christmas; they should be stored well apart, on wooden shelves, in a temperature from 40° to 60°.

The Bartlett, an English pear known there as the Williams Bon Chrétien, is the most common pear in the United States, accounting for about ¾ of our total pear production. It is yellow-skinned, with white smooth flesh and is highly aromatic. Its growing season is from July to November and it is grown in Washington and Oregon.

Other varieties produced there include the Anjou; the Bosc; the Seckel, a small hybrid of the Oriental type; the Comice, a juicy French variety; and the Kieffer.

The Conference pear, an English variety, is a good all-round fruit suitable for eating, cooking, and canning.

To cook pears: Peel, halve, or quarter and remove the cores, then cook as described in Compote of Pears, under Compote. Pears usually require a little additional flavoring, such as clove, lemon, ginger, or cinnamon and combine particularly well with a chocolate sauce. They are delicious poached in cider and brown sugar. Pears are also good with cheese; a simple appetizer can be made by halving a pear, removing the core and filling with a cheese mixture. (See Canning entry.)

POIRE HÉLÈNE

Put some lemon or vanilla ice cream into sundae glasses, place one canned pear half in each, top with chocolate sauce (see recipe under Sundae entry) and decorate with shredded or chopped almonds or candied violets.

POACHED PEARS

4 firm pears
⅓ cup granulated sugar
water
2 oranges
¼ cup superfine sugar

Peel the pears, cut into quarters and core. Dissolve the sugar in ¾ cup water in a small saucepan, bring to a boil and boil for 5 minutes. Add the pear quarters and simmer, covered, until the fruit is tender. Using a potato peeler, pare the rind from ½ orange and cut into very fine strips. Cook in a little water until tender – about 5 minutes. Rinse the rind in cold water. Peel the oranges free of pith and cut into segments.

Dissolve the superfine sugar in a pan shaking occasionally – do not stir. Bubble until golden, then pour it onto a greased pan. When brittle, crack with a rolling pin. Turn the drained pears into a serving dish and top with orange segments. Add the orange strips to the pear juice and pour over the fruit. Scatter caramel over and chill.

PECAN

A nut native to America, closely related to the hickory nut. The meat is somewhat similar to the walnut in appearance, but with a brittle, reddish-brown shell, and thinner and longer in shape. Pecan trees are cultivated in Texas, Georgia, Oklahoma, and Florida. Pecans are used in cakes and ice creams and in the popular classic southern pecan pie. (See Pie entry for recipe.)

Praline

A confection made in the United States originating in New Orleans. It was, perhaps, some Créole cook's failed attempt to make the French praline (see Praline entry). Louisiana pralines are softer and chewier than the French ones, with American pecans instead of almonds. The sugar and nut mixture is dropped onto a flat surface to make a sweet, flat round candy.

PRALINES

1 tablespoon butter
4 tablespoons water
3 cups light brown sugar
1¼ cups whole or chopped pecans

Combine butter and water in an enameled saucepan and heat until butter is melted. Stir in the brown sugar and continue to stir and heat until sugar is completely dissolved and the mixture registers 238° on a candy thermometer. Stir in the pecans. Remove saucepan from the heat and continue to stir the mixture until it loses its glossiness. Drop in tablespoonfuls onto a well-greased baking sheet and let cool.

PECTIN

A jelling carbohydrate substance, occurring naturally in the cell walls of many plants, which in combination with sugar causes jam to set. (See Jam entry.)

PEMMICAN

Well-dried buffalo or deer meat, pounded to shreds and mixed with melted fat; a concentrated food used originally by North American Indians and then by trappers and other travelers.

PEPPER

There are several varieties of pepper, obtained by grinding the fruits of certain plants which have a hot, pungent taste. For the vegetable, see separate Green Pepper entry.

WHITE PEPPER

This comes from the fully ripened berries of a climbing tree or tropical shrub. The outer skin is removed and the berries cleaned. It can be bought whole or ground and is less pungent and aromatic than black pepper. It is good to use in light sauces as it does not discolor them.

BLACK PEPPER

This comes from the berries picked while still green and left to dry in the sun until they shrivel and darken. It is available whole or ground but is at its best when freshly milled.

GREEN PEPPERCORNS

These are the unripe berries picked and canned without drying out. Their fresh pungent flavor is totally different from the dried varieties. Green peppercorns add an unusual tang to broiled meat or poultry. They can also be mashed and added to sauces.

CAYENNE PEPPER

A very hot and well-flavored pepper made from certain powdered capsicums. It is useful for many cooking purposes (especially highly flavored sauces), but is usually too hot to serve as a table condiment.

PAPRIKA

This comes from the fruit of a Hungarian tree. It is red and has a fine aromatic taste and since it is not as hot as other peppers, can be used more liberally.

PEPPERMINT

A European plant, similar to garden spearmint, but with a more pronounced odor and taste. An oil and a flavoring extract are made from the plant, the oil being obtained by distilling the plant with water and the extract consisting of the essential oil mixed with spirit. The oil has the stronger flavor, while the strength of the extract varies according to the degree of dilution.

Peppermint forms a popular flavoring for confectionery, drinks, and occasionally for desserts and it is also used medicinally. Desserts, candy, ice cream, etc., that have been flavored with peppermint are often colored green.

PEPPERONI (PEPERONI)

A spicy, air-dried Italian sausage popular in the United States, particularly as a pizza topping and sliced as an appetizer. It is smaller, firmer, and more highly seasoned than its relative salami. It is usually made from a pork and beef mixture.

PERCH

A freshwater fish of delicate flavor, many species of which are found throughout the world. The most common are the yellow perch found in the United States and the river perch of Europe. Both varieties are very similar, averaging about 1 lb in weight and 10 to 12 inches long. Perch has a characteristic sharp front dorsal fin and is of a greenish-brown color on the back and a light color below. Perch should be cooked as soon as possible after catching.

Preparation and cooking: The scales are more easily removed if the fish is plunged into boiling water for 2 minutes. Trim, clean, and wipe the fish, score it on both sides and broil or fry in butter.

Alternatively, place it in a well-buttered ovenproof dish, cover with pats of butter and then pour white wine and fish stock over it in equal parts; cover with foil or buttered parchment and bake for about 20 minutes in a 400° oven. Drain off the liquid and reduce by boiling. Add 4 tablespoons butter little by little, stirring constantly, and finally add 2 teaspoons finely chopped parsley. Serve the fish with the sauce poured over it and garnish with fried croûtons, lemon quarters, and parsley.

PERIWINKLE

A small black shellfish. To prepare winkles, wash them well in several waters to remove the sand and boil for 20 minutes in salted water.

PERNOD

An apéritif that takes its name from a French firm which used to distil absinthe. The modern Pernod is based on aniseed and contains no absinthe, which is now prohibited in France. Pernod is usually served with one part of Pernod and three parts water and topped up with chunks of ice.

PERRIER

A natural gaseous mineral water from the south of France, colorless and tasteless.

PERRY

The fermented juice of a hard, astringent type of pear (unsuitable for eating). Perry is made in a similar way to cider and is popular in England and the Normandy region of France.

PERSIMMON (DATE PLUM)

A fall fruit that appears in two main species, the American and the Japanese or kaki, both of which are grown in the United States. The Japanese is larger and generally considered to be of a better quality than the American. Persimmons are about the size of a small plum, with a leathery orange skin covering a yellow or orange-colored pulp; some have seeds, but the best varieties are seedless. The unripe green fruit is very astringent and even the ripe fruit is somewhat acid and bitter, though at the same time sweet. Persimmons are eaten raw and used for flavoring ices and jellies and for making preserves. Early Americans used them for breads and puddings.

PESACH

(See Passover entry.)

PESTO

A fresh, uncooked Italian sauce made with fresh basil leaves, garlic, grated Parmesan cheese, pine nuts and olive oil, all crushed with a mortar and pestle or ground in a food processor and blended to a creamy consistency. It is a specialty of Genoa and is excellent served on pasta, in soups, over potatoes, or in any number of other creative ways.

PESTO

2 cups fresh basil leaves
2 cloves garlic
3 tablespoons pine nuts or chopped walnuts
salt
¼ cup grated Parmesan cheese
½ cup olive oil
2–3 tablespoons softened butter

Place the basil, garlic, and nuts in a marble mortar or the bowl of a food processor and season with salt. Grind ingredients to a paste with the pestle or process in the food processor until reduced to a paste. Add the cheese and grind or process until evenly blended. Add olive oil a few drops at a time, blending with a wooden spoon or the processor constantly. When all the oil is incorporated, quickly blend in the softened butter.

PETITE SIRAH

A red varietal wine produced in California from the Petite Sirah (or Petite Syrah) grape. It has a rich, somewhat spicy bouquet and a character that has been compared to that of a Rhône wine from southern France.

PETIT FOUR

Petits fours are very small, rich, sweet cakes, served as a dessert at the end of a dinner, also with coffee or afternoon tea. Two typical recipes are given here. (See Macaroon, Meringue, Éclair entries etc.)

ALMOND PETITS FOURS

2 egg whites
1½ cups ground almonds
½ cup superfine sugar
few drops almond extract
maraschino cherries and angelica to decorate

Line 2 baking sheets with parchment paper or rice paper. Beat the egg whites until stiff and fold in the ground almonds, sugar, and almond extract. Place the mixture in a pastry bag fitted with a ½-inch star tip. Pipe small stars, circles, pinwheels, and fingers onto the baking sheets. Decorate each with a small piece of cherry or angelica and bake in a 300° oven for 15 to 20 minutes, until just beginning to color. Cool on a wire rack.

FROSTED PETITS FOURS

Make some genoise sponge cake (see Genoise entry), pour it into a shallow rectangular pan and bake in a 350° oven for 30 to 35 minutes, until firm and golden-brown. When it is cool, cut it into small fancy shapes – oblongs, squares, rounds, triangles, diamonds, crescents, etc. – and coat with warmed apricot jam.

Make some cake frosting in different colors and coat some of the cakes with it. Others may have a pat of almond paste, or a complete layer, placed on top before the frosting is added. Decorate the petits fours with candied flowers, nuts, pieces of maraschino cherry, piped butter frosting and so on; when the icing and decorations are quite dry and set, place the cakes in small fancy paper cups.

PETIT POIS

(See Pea entry.)

PETIT SUISSE

A French cream cheese.

PFANNKUCHEN

A kind of German pancake usually made of a yeast, milk, flour and egg batter which, instead of being cooked on a griddle, is generally deep fried. Pfannkuchen puff dramatically and are served hot sprinkled with sugar and lemon juice or jam. The Berliner Pfannkuchen is traditionally served just after the stroke of midnight on New Year's Eve in Germany with hot spiced wine or cold eggnog.

PHEASANT

One of the choicest and most beautiful game birds, the pheasant, believed to be a native of China, is found in many parts of the world.

Not native to North America, the ring-necked pheasant was introduced from Europe into Canada and the United States where it established itself. Wild pheasant is found in almost every State; it is also raised commercially here and one of the few game birds that does not totally lose its gamy flavor when domesticated. Although the colorfully plumed cock is more beautiful, the hen is generally more tender.

Traditionally pheasants were hung for from 4 to 12 days before serving, especially in Europe, but increasingly they are served fresh without being hung. A pheasant will serve 2 to 3 people depending on size. Pheasants are available frozen.

Preparation and roasting: Pluck, singe, and clean as for any game bird. Cut off the head and neck close to the body, leaving sufficient of the neck skin to fold over the back and cover the opening. Then remove the inside through a slit cut in the vent and wipe the bird inside and out with a damp cloth – do not wash it. Scald and skin the feet.

Put a piece of butter seasoned with pepper, salt, and lemon juice inside the bird. (Alternately, put inside ¼ lb of fatty beef, cut in small pieces, seasoned with pepper and salt, which will enhance the flavor and help to make the flesh more juicy.) To truss the bird, push the thighs back close under the wings and the body, then tie the second joints of the legs firmly together, making the feet stand up. Cut off the tips of the claws and either skewer or sew down the neck skin at the back. Tie 2 to 3 slices of fat bacon over the breast of the pheasant and roast in a 425° oven for about 30 minutes to 1 hour, according to size, basting frequently with butter or bacon fat. Unlike most game, pheasant should be well cooked rather than slightly underdone.

The usual accompaniments are bread sauce and thin gravy. Cranberry sauce, currant jelly, green salad, orange salad or stuffed oranges, or sautéed hominy can also be served.

Pheasants may also be mixed with veal, ham and mushrooms in a stew, or cooked in a casserole with onion, tomato, bacon, and sherry or other ingredients such as apple, celery, grapes, cream, and wine.

BURGUNDY PHEASANT

1 tender pheasant
3 shallots, finely chopped
1 tablespoon oil
4 tablespoons butter
6 small onions
2 tablespoons sugar
1 cup red Burgundy
2 oz button mushrooms
1 tablespoon flour
salt and pepper

Prepare the bird as for roasting. Put the shallots inside the pheasant with its liver. Heat the oil and 2 tablespoons of the butter in a skillet and sauté the pheasant gently until brown all over. Meanwhile, leave onions whole and boil them in salted water until tender. Drain. Melt 1 tablespoon butter in a separate skillet, add 2 tablespoons sugar, stir, add the onions and cook slowly until coloring. Put the pheasant in a casserole with the onions. Add the wine and mushroom stems to the juices in the pheasant pan and reduce by about half. Melt an additional tablespoon of butter in the onion pan, sauté the mushroom caps and add them to the casserole. Stir the flour into the juices and when bubbling gradually stir in the liquor from the other pan. Add seasoning, simmer to thicken, and strain over the pheasant. Cover and cook in a 350° oven for about 30 minutes or until tender.

PHEASANT CASSEROLE

1 pheasant
flour
butter for sautéing
4–6 oz mushrooms
2 slices bacon
salt and pepper
broth
little port wine (optional)

Cut up the bird and dip the pieces in the flour. Heat the butter in a skillet and sauté the pieces of pheasant until they are golden brown. Put them in a casserole with the sliced mushrooms, chopped bacon, salt, pepper, and sufficient broth to half cover the pheasant; a little port wine may be added with the broth if desired. Cook gently in a 350° oven for about 1 hour.

PHOSPHORUS

One of the essential minerals, used by the body for a number of vital purposes. It is one of the constituents of bones and teeth and is concerned in the life and structure of all the cells of the body. An ordinary balanced diet is unlikely to be deficient in this mineral, which is found in many foods.

PHYLLO PASTRY

Onion skin-thin, Middle Eastern pastry leaves made from a flour-and-water dough that closely resembles strudel dough. It is the basis of such popular Greek specialties as baklava, a golden confection made from honey and nuts sandwiched between layer upon layer of phyllo leaves, and spanakopita, spinach-and-feta cheese-filled phyllo. A factorymade phyllo is now available in most well-stocked groceries and supermarkets and is a good substitute for fresh homemade phyllo which is tricky to make.

PICADILLO

This Cuban dish has become highly popular in the United States. Serve it as the Cubans do with rice and black beans.

PICADILLO

$\frac{1}{2}$ lb ground beef
$\frac{1}{2}$ lb ground pork
1 minced onion
1 cup canned tomatoes
2 minced cloves garlic
1 tablespoon vinegar
salt
pepper
1 teaspoon ground cinnamon
$\frac{1}{4}$ teaspoon ground cumin
1 bay leaf
$\frac{1}{2}$ cup seedless raisins
$\frac{1}{2}$ cup almonds

In a large Dutch oven combine the beef, pork, and onion and sauté until lightly browned. Add the tomatoes, garlic, vinegar, salt and pepper to taste, cinnamon, cumin, bay leaf, raisins, and almonds. Cover and simmer for about 1 hour, adding water during cooking if necessary.

PICCALILLI

A relish usually made of cauliflower, green tomatoes, cucumbers, cabbage, onions, pickles, and other ingredients marinated in a mustard–vinegar dressing and seasoned with turmeric. It is of Anglo-Indian origin and is eaten with cold meats. (See Pickle entry for recipe.)

PICKEREL

A separate species of the pike family found in the United States from the Great Lakes to Texas, including the redfin pickerel of the Southeastern states and the grass pickerel found from Canada to Alabama. Like pike, pickerel have lean, mild-flavored flesh that can be prepared by any method suitable for pike. Pike perch and Walleye are also frequently loosely referred to as pickerel. (See Pike entry.)

PICKLE

The term generally refers to any vegetable or fruit that has been steeped in a flavored brine solution for varying lengths of time for the purpose of preserving them.

The best-known type of pickles are those made from cucumbers steeped in brine flavored with, for instance, vinegar, peppercorns, dill seeds, coriander, cloves, garlic, ginger, cardamom, and other spices.

There are many varieties of pickled cucumber; dill pickles, kosher pickles, sour pickles, sweet pickles, gherkins, cornichons.

Many other types of foods lend themselves to the process including watermelon rind, cauliflower, hot and sweet peppers, beets, cabbage, onions, tomatoes, apples, lemons, plums, and even walnuts.

The art of pickling grew out of the need to preserve food for consumption during the cold winter months. Salt meat and fish are sometimes referred to as "pickled."

Preparation for Pickling

Use a reasonably large aluminum, stainless steel or enamel pan – not copper or brass, as the acid in the vinegar will react with the metal to give traces of the very poisonous salt, copper acetate.

VEGETABLES

Choose sound, fresh vegetables and prepare as for cooking, cutting or breaking them into small pieces (except for such ingredients as small pickling onions and nasturtium seeds, which are left whole).

FRUIT

Treat according to kind – remove pits and cores, wipe lemons and slit the peel through in several places, as though the fruit were going to be quartered.

Brining

This is intended to remove some of the water present in vegetables, which otherwise would dilute the vinegar, so that it would look cloudy and the pickle would not keep well.

Fruit is not brined.

DRY BRINING

This is suitable for very watery vegetables, such as cucumber, zucchini, tomatoes, etc. Place the prepared vegetables in a deep bowl, sprinkling salt between the layers, cover and let stand overnight. Only a small amount of salt is needed – 2 teaspoons to 1 lb of vegetables.

WET BRINING

This is suitable for vegetables such as cauliflower, onions and shallots. Allow 4 tablespoons salt to 1 pint water (sufficient for about 1 lb vegetables). Place the prepared vegetables in a deep bowl, cover with the brine and let stand overnight.

Root vegetables such as artichokes and beets must be cooked in half-strength brine until they are tender.

After brining, rinse the vegetables thoroughly and drain them. If it is not possible to pickle them immediately, they may be placed in a fresh brine, made like the first one, and left until required.

SPICED VINEGAR

The vinegar used for pickling is usually flavored with spices (often including ginger and chilis). The flavor may be varied according to the fruit or vegetable to be pickled, but the following is a typical mixture:

1 quart vinegar
2 tablespoons blade mace
1 tablespoon whole allspice
1 tablespoon cloves
7-inch stick cinnamon
6 peppercorns

Put the vinegar and spices in a pan, bring to a boil and pour into a bowl. Cover with a plate to preserve the flavor and leave for 2 hours, then strain the vinegar and use as required.

An even better result is obtained if the spices are left to stand in unheated vinegar for 1 to 2 months.

NOTES
If the individual spices are not available, use 1 oz to 2 oz pickling spice. Different brands of pickling spice will vary considerably, e.g. some contain whole chilis, and give a hotter result.

For such things as cocktail onions, white (distilled) vinegar is usually used; it is occasionally replaced by dilute acetic acid.

Packing and Storing
Pack the fruit or vegetables into dry, wide-necked jars to within 1 inch of the top and pour on the vinegar, leaving a ½-inch space at the top to prevent it touching the lid of the jar. Cover fruit with hot vinegar and vegetables with cold.

Proprietary brands of synthetic skin are suitable for covering pickles. If metal covers are used, they must be lined with waxed paper or coated inside with melted paraffin wax so that the vinegar does not come into direct contact with the metal. Alternate coverings are corks wrapped in waxed paper; parchment paper covers; glass tops used with preserving jars; and calico dipped in melted paraffin wax or coated with melted candle grease.

The jars do not need sterilizing after filling and covering, as the growth of bacteria is prevented by the acid in the vinegar and by the salt and spices.

Pickles should be stored in a cool, dry, dark but airy place, as exposure to sunlight often spoils their color, and they should always be left for 2 to 3 months before being eaten, otherwise the flavor is not fully developed. Cabbage is an exception, for it usually tastes better if it is eaten while it is still crisp.

PICKLED RED CABBAGE
Remove the outer leaves and shred the rest of the cabbage finely. Dry-brine for 24 hours, drain, pack loosely into jars, cover with cold spiced vinegar and cover as usual. Do not store for longer than 2 to 3 months or the cabbage will lose its crispness.

PICKLED CUCUMBER
Cut the cucumbers into quarters lengthwise, then into ½-inch slices, and dry-brine them for 24 hours. Drain and pack into jars, cover with cold spiced vinegar and cover the jars.

PICKLED ONIONS
Use small pickling onions. Remove the skins carefully, without cutting the onions, wash and wet-brine for 24 hours. Drain, wash and dry, put into jars, fill up with cold spiced vinegar and cover the jars.

PICKLED WALNUTS
Walnuts should be pickled while still green and before the hard shell has formed. Wipe the nuts, prick them well, rejecting any that feel hard, and put them in a bowl. Cover with brine and allow to soak for 8 days, then throw away the brine, cover with fresh brine and resoak for 14 days.

  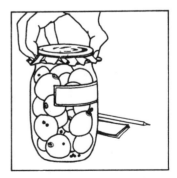

PICKLING: PACKING AND STORING
1. Pack fruit or vegetables into dry wide-necked jars to within 1 inch of the top.

2. Pour on the vinegar, leaving a ½-inch space at the top to prevent it touching the lid of the jar.

3. Cover and label giving date and contents of the jar. Metal covers must be lined with waxed paper or coated with melted paraffin wax.

311

Wash and dry the walnuts and spread them out, exposing them to the air until they turn black. Have some hot spiced vinegar ready, put the walnuts into pickle jars, cover with the hot vinegar and cover when cold. Allow pickled walnuts to mature for 5 to 6 weeks before using them.

PICKLED CAULIFLOWER (ITALIAN STYLE)

2 heads cauliflower
vinegar
1 tablespoon dried marjoram
seasoning
$\frac{1}{4}$ red pepper
olive oil

Divide the cauliflower into flowerets, boil them in salted water for 5 minutes, drain well, put in a bowl and cover with boiling vinegar, then leave for 24 hours. Lift out the flowerets, drain well, and put them in layers in a jar, sprinkling the marjoram, seasoning, and chopped red pepper between the layers. Pour a mixture of two-thirds olive oil and one-third vinegar over the pickle until there is at least 1 inch of liquid over the last layer. Cover and store in a cool place.

To serve, lift out the flowerets, pour over them some of the liquid from the jar and garnish with strips of red pepper and capers.

MIXED SWEET PICKLE RELISH

$\frac{3}{4}$ cucumber, washed
1 lb tomatoes, halved and seeded
$1\frac{1}{2}$ lb zucchini, peeled and seeded
1 quart malt vinegar
$1\frac{1}{4}$ cups white vinegar
$1\frac{3}{4}$ cups sugar
4 teaspoons salt
2 tablespoons turmeric
$\frac{1}{2}$ teaspoon ground mace
$\frac{1}{2}$ teaspoon ground mixed spice
2 large pieces gingerroot, crushed
$\frac{1}{2}$ teaspoon celery seed

Mince the vegetables coarsely. Add the vinegars, sugar, salt, and spices. Tie the ginger and celery seed in a cheesecloth and add to the mixture. Stir, bring to a boil and simmer for 3 hours, until dark in color and of a fairly thick consistency. Remove the cheesecloth bag, pour into warm jars, seal and store in a cool place.

PICCALILLI

6 lb prepared vegetables (zucchini, cucumber, beans, small onions, cauliflower)
1 lb salt
10 cups water
$1\frac{1}{3}$ cups sugar
1 tablespoon dry mustard
$1\frac{1}{2}$ teaspoons ground ginger
3 pints white vinegar
4 tablespoons flour
2 tablespoons turmeric

Dice the zucchini and cucumber, slice the beans, halve the onions and break the cauliflower into small flowerets. Dissolve the salt in the water and add the vegetables. Cover and let stand for 24 hours.

Remove the vegetables, rinse and drain. Blend the sugar, mustard, and ginger with $2\frac{1}{2}$ pints vinegar in a large saucepan, add the vegetables, bring to a boil and simmer for 20 minutes. Blend the flour and turmeric with the remaining $\frac{1}{2}$ pint vinegar and stir into the cooked vegetables. Bring to a boil and cook for 1 to 2 minutes. Pour into jars and cover.

PICNIC MEALS

This is a particularly popular way to eat a meal in the summer months. For some reason the food always tastes better eaten out of doors.

A picnic can be a highly organized affair to include plates, knives, forks, and a three-course meal, or an impromptu event with a few finger foods and paper napkins. Often the informal picnic is more enjoyable, especially for children.

There is a great deal of equipment available to make transporting food more pleasant and simple. Insulated coolers which keep food hot or cold are popular and can be used to carry most of the meal. Reusable chemical ice packs can be packed in the cooler to keep foods chilled. Plastic cups with fitted lids are also useful. Old yogurt and cottage cheese containers can be used for transporting relishes, sauces, cheese spreads, mousses, etc. Wide-neck vacuum flasks are useful for carrying ice cream, fruit salad, or yogurt. An ordinary vacuum flask can be used for hot soup and hot or cold drinks. Other useful items to include are salt, pepper, can opener, bottle opener, sugar, paper napkins, damp cloths (keep in polyethylene bag), and a large plastic bag for garbage.

The food eaten will depend on taste and the occasion. Many of the recipes in this book and others will provide suitable fare. It's wise to avoid packing highly perishable foods such as mayonnaise in hot weather.

PIE

The name given to various large and small combinations of pastry usually with a sweet filling, although they may also be filled with meat, fish, or vegetables. In single-crust pies the filling is placed in a deep dish or pan and covered with pastry; in open-faced pies (also called tarts or flans) an undercrust is filled with the mixture. Some pies have both a top and a bottom layer of pastry; many of those having only a bottom pastry shell are given a topping of meringue or something similar. There are also lattice-top pies with open-top crusts.

Many different types of pastry can be used for the crust including sweet or unsweetened short crust, puff pastry, or graham cracker crumb crust. (See Pastry entry.)

DEEP-DISH RHUBARB PIE

1½–2 lb pink rhubarb
2 oz preserved gingerroot
6–8 tablespoons sugar
1 tablespoon cornstarch
powdered sugar

PASTRY
2 cups all-purpose flour
pinch of salt
½ teaspoon ground ginger
8 tablespoons butter or margarine
water to mix
milk to glaze

Trim and thickly slice rhubarb. Chop ginger and add. Combine sugar and cornstarch and toss with fruit. Turn into a 3-cup pie pan. Sift together the flour, salt, and spice into a mixing bowl. Cut in the butter. Add just enough water, about 7 teaspoons, to give a manageable dough. Roll out and use to cover the pie pan, crimp and decorate edges. Brush pastry with milk. Place on a baking sheet and bake in a 425° oven for 15 minutes; reduce heat to 350° and bake for 20 to 30 minutes more until the crust is pale golden and the rhubarb tender. Sprinkle with powdered sugar to serve.

Note: For plum variation, replace rhubarb with halved pitted plums, gingerroots with a piece of cinnamon stick and the ground ginger with cinnamon.

DOUBLE-CRUST PIE

Prepare the filling. Make the vegetable shortening. Divide the dough into halves, then roll out one half and line the bottom of the pie pan, taking care to press the pastry well into the curves of the pan; wet the rim of the pastry and place the filling in the center. Roll out the other piece of pastry for the top, put it in position, easing it onto the rim, and press it down firmly. Cut off any surplus pastry as above, then press the edges of the pastry together, trim them with a knife and decorate with scallops, or other decorative edge. Brush top with beaten egg or with milk. Bake for 15 minutes in a 425° oven, then reduce the temperature to 350° and bake 15 to 20 minutes longer, depending on the filling. When cooked, sprinkle with powdered or granulated sugar if desired.

LINING A PIE
1. Cut a strip of pastry to fit the rim of the pie dish. Gently press onto the rim.

2. Roll out the remaining pastry to fit the top of the dish, and press pastry edges together firmly.

3. Cut off any surplus pastry. Flake the pastry edges with a knife and scallop the edge.

OPEN-FACED PIES
(See Flan and Tart entries.)

APPLE PIE

1½ lb cooking apples, peeled, cored, and quartered
¼ cup water
½ cup soft brown sugar
1 tablespoon cornstarch or arrowroot
½ teaspoon salt
1 teaspoon ground cinnamon
2 tablespoons lemon juice
2 tablespoons butter
½ teaspoon vanilla extract
1 recipe shortening pastry (see pastry entry)
milk to glaze

Simmer the apples with the water until soft. Mix together the sugar, cornstarch or arrowroot, salt, and cinnamon, and add to the cooked apples. Stir in the lemon juice and cook, stirring, until fairly thick. Remove from the heat, stir in the butter and vanilla and cool. Roll out half the pastry and line an 8½-inch greased pie pan; put the cooked apples in the pastry shell. Roll out the remaining pastry to make a top layer. Dampen the edges of the pastry on the pan and cover with the top, pressing the edges well together; trim and scallop the edges. Make short slashes with a knife on the top. Brush the top with milk, put the pan on a baking sheet and bake in a 400° oven for about 1 hour. Cover loosely with foil after 30 minutes to prevent it over-browning. Serve hot or cold, with whipped cream or ice cream.

PECAN PIE

8 tablespoons solid shortening
2 tablespoons butter
1½ cups flour
salt
3 tablespoons water

FOR THE FILLING
3 eggs
1 tablespoon milk
¾ cup sugar
⅓ cup maple or corn syrup
4 tablespoons butter, softened
½ teaspoon vanilla extract
1½ cups pecans or walnuts, halved

Cream together the shortening and butter. Gradually stir in the sifted flour and salt; cream well after each addition. Add the water and mix thoroughly with the hands. Knead lightly with extra flour, as this pastry is sticky to handle. Chill.

Roll out the pastry and line a 9-inch pie pan; flute the edge. Chill this shell while preparing the filling.

Beat the eggs and milk together. Boil the sugar and syrup together in a saucepan for 3 minutes. Slowly pour over the beaten eggs and stir in the butter and extract. Use half the nuts to cover the base of the pastry shell, spoon the syrup mixture over and cover with the remaining nuts. Bake in a 425° oven for 10 minutes. Reduce the heat to 325° and cook for 45 minutes longer, until the filling is set. Serve warm or cold with unsweetened whipped cream.

PIG

(See Pork entry.)

PIGEON

There are many species of this bird of the Columbidae genus, which is found world wide, both wild and domesticated.

Some of the best varieties for eating are the wood pigeon, the stock dove, and the rock dove. (Little distinction is made between pigeons and doves.)

A squab is a young pigeon under 4 weeks old and weighing less than 14 oz. They are tender and flavorful but without much meat. Squab can be split and sautéed or roasted.

Mature domestically raised pigeons can also be roasted.

Pigeons are particularly prized by the Chinese who prepare them in many delicious ways.

ROAST PIGEON OR DOVE

Prepare and truss the birds, allowing one for 1 to 2 people. Cover the breast with a slice of fat bacon, place a small shallot inside the bird and roast for 20 to 30 minutes in a 400° oven. Serve each bird on rounds of fried bread, garnish with watercress, etc.; serve with gravy.

If desired, the pigeons may be stuffed before roasting with a stuffing made as follows: Mix 2 chopped fried pigeon livers, 2 teaspoons chopped onion, 1 tablespoon chopped parsley, 3 tablespoons bread crumbs, 1 cooked, chopped slice of bacon, salt, cayenne pepper, and a pinch of nutmeg; bind with a beaten egg.

PIGNOLI

(See Pine Nut entry.)

PIG'S FEET OR TROTTERS

A variety of delicious and nourishing dishes may be made from pig's feet or trotters. After being boiled in water flavored with herbs, they may be served hot, with an onion sauce, or cold; alternatively they may be broiled (either plain or after being egg-and-bread crumbed), stuffed, fricasseed, or made into soup.

PIKE

There are several species of this thin, flat-headed freshwater fish in North America, including the giant muskellunge and the smaller pickerel (see separate entries). Its lean flesh is firm and white. Because of its voraciousness, pike is frequently referred to as river wolf or freshwater shark and is much admired by sport fishermen for its fighting nature.

Though a respected food fish in Europe, the pike has not been greatly sought after in North America, mainly because the taste is somewhat bland and the flesh is laced with small bones. Nonetheless, it is very suitable for many preparations, most notably fish mousses such as that used for quenelles, classic French poached fish mousse in a rich sauce. It can also be baked, broiled, and grilled on skewers, as well as prepared with a wide variety of sauces.

BAKED STUFFED PIKE

4 mushrooms
¼ lb fat bacon
3 anchovies, chopped
1⅓ cups fresh white bread crumbs
seasoning
1 teaspoon thyme, chopped
1 teaspoon parsley, chopped
1 teaspoon chives or onion, chopped
1 egg yolk
1 lb pike fillets
fish broth
⅔ cup white wine
hollandaise or anchovy sauce

Make a stuffing as follows: Fry mushrooms with fat bacon, then chop them both; add chopped anchovies, bread crumbs, some seasoning and chopped thyme, parsley, and chives or onion; bind with egg yolk.

Spread the stuffing over half the fillets, cover with the other fillets, place in a shallow ovenproof dish and pour over a little broth mixed with the white wine. Bake for 1 hour in a 350° oven. When the pike is cooked, place it on a dish and pour hollandaise or anchovy sauce over it; garnish with baked tomatoes.

PILAF (PILAU, PILAW)

An Oriental and Middle Eastern dish, consisting of rice flavored with spices and cooked in stock, to which meat, poultry, or fish may be added. There are many versions and the method of serving varies considerably, but a very common way of serving a pilaf is to pile the rice on a dish and imbed the meat or poultry in it. Fried onion rings, broiled tomatoes, seeded raisins, and blanched almonds, etc., form a suitable garnish.

LAMB PILAU

1–1½ lb loin of lamb
3 cups chicken broth
1 cup long-grain rice
pinch ground cinnamon
pinch ground cloves
salt
pepper
½ cup currants or raisins
4 tablespoons butter

Trim the meat and cut it into even-sized pieces. Cover with the broth and simmer until tender, then lift out, drain, and set aside. Wash the rice well and sprinkle into the liquid in which the meat was cooked; add the spices, seasoning, and currants. Bring to a boil, then cover and simmer very gently for about 15 minutes, until all the liquid is absorbed and the rice is just soft. Remove from the heat and leave covered for about 15 minutes to dry out. Sauté the meat in half the butter until lightly browned and stir the remaining butter into the rice mixture. Serve the rice piled on a dish with the meat in the center. If desired, this dish can be garnished with wedges of tomato or fried onion rings.

PILCHARD

Better known as the sardine, this small fish is abundant from the southern coast of Portugal to the British Isles and Scandinavia, where it can be enjoyed fresh from July to December. It is, however, usually found canned, both in oil and in tomato sauce.

Pilchards are also fished off the coasts of Spain, France, and Italy, particularly Sardinia, the island from which the fish probably derived its more common name. In North American waters there is a species of herring that is sometimes called a "false pilchard," more commonly known as a sprat.

Pilchards, like herrings, are economical and nutritious. They supply protein, fat, calcium and vitamin D.

Serving: Canned pilchards may be eaten without further preparation, accompanied by a green salad, or they can also be used as a sandwich filling or a topping for appetizers; the fish may be heated in their oil and served with mashed potato, or mashed and mixed with other ingredients and baked.

PIMENTO

(See Allspice entry.)

PIMIENTO

A red Spanish pepper with a sweet, pungent flavor, used in salads and as a vegetable. Also available canned. It is sometimes incorrectly called "pimento."

PIMMS

A British proprietary cocktail marketed as 'Pimms No. 1 Cup." It is gin based, and is served with ice and diluted with sparkling lemonade, garnished, if desired, with sliced fruit, cucumber, or mint.

PINEAPPLE

A tropical fruit, almost cylindrical in shape, which grows on a short stem from the middle of a tuft of gray-green pointed leaves. It has a hard, ridged skin of deep orange and firm but juicy flesh. There are many varieties which differ in size and color, the three main ones being the Queen, Cayenne, and Spanish. Generally the best quality ones are darker yellow, softer and sweeter than the other varieties. Fresh pineapples, which have a delicious flavor, are grown in tropical areas around the world – including Hawaii (which produces over 70 percent of the world crop), Brazil, Cuba, the Azores, Mexico, Sri Lanka, and the Canary Islands. Canned pineapple is more widely bought and is available in slices, cubes, chunks and whole, crushed and in other cuts such as "fingers" and tidbits. Pineapple juice is canned both sweetened and unsweetened. The quality is graded in various ways.

Preparation of fresh pineapple: Peel the pineapple fairly thickly, removing the "eyes." When served as dessert, pineapple is usually cut in wedge-shaped slices from top to the base, but if preferred, it may be further cut into chunks.

Pineapple in Cookery

In both the fresh and the canned form, this fruit can be used in a variety of sweet and non-sweet dishes – including pineapple snow, hot or cold soufflé, fritters, to accompany pork, on grilled meats and so on. When crushed and mixed with cream it forms a good cake filling; when combined with cream cheese, tomato or cucumber and mayonnaise it makes an excellent salad.

Fresh pineapple should not be used in gelatin mixtures unless previously boiled, as it contains an enzyme which prevents the jelly from setting, but the canned fruit may be used without boiling.

The pineapple case can be cut in half lengthwise and used to serve fruit mixtures or dips.

COLD PINEAPPLE SOUFFLÉ

1 can (15 oz) crushed pineapple
1½ tablespoons gelatin
4 large eggs, separated
½ cup sugar
2 tablespoons whisky
⅔ cup half-and-half
⅔ cup heavy cream
chopped pistachio nuts and whipped cream for
    decoration

Prepare a 6-inch (1½-pint) soufflé dish. Drain the pineapple. Reserve 4 tablespoons juice and pour it into a small bowl. Sprinkle over the gelatin. Place the bowl over a pan of hot water and dissolve the gelatin. Beat the egg yolks, sugar, and whisky in a large deep bowl over a pan of hot water until they are thick and pale. Remove the bowl from the heat and add the crushed pineapple. Add a little pineapple mixture to the gelatin and pour back into the soufflé mixture. Leave to cool, beating occasionally.

When the mixture is not quite cold, beat the creams together until thick. Fold into the cool, but not set, pineapple base. Beat the egg whites until stiff but not dry, pour the pineapple cream base over the whites and fold in lightly. Turn the mixture into the prepared soufflé dish and chill. To serve, remove the paper collar, decorate the edges with pistachio nuts and pipe with whipped cream.

PINEAPPLE SURPRISE

1 pineapple
strawberries, grapes, etc.
sugar
ice cream

Remove the top of the pineapple with the leaves and keep for decoration. Scoop out the central part of the pineapple and cut the flesh up into small pieces, mixing it with some fresh strawberries, raspberries, pitted grapes, or other fresh fruits as available. Add a little sugar and chill the mixture in a refrigerator. Put the fruit in layers in the pineapple shell alternating with some well-frozen ice cream, replace the pineapple leaves on top and serve at once.

BAKED PORK CHOPS WITH PINEAPPLE

Trim off the excess fat from 4 pork chops and lay them in a shallow baking dish. Cover with waxed paper and bake the chops in a 350° oven for $\frac{3}{4}$ to 1 hour. About 10 minutes before the cooking time is up, open a small can of pineapple slices, remove the waxed paper and place a slice of drained pineapple on top of each chop; pour $\frac{2}{3}$ cup of pineapple juice over and season. Return the chops to the oven to brown. Serve with the cooking liquid, which can be thickened slightly with cornstarch.

PINE NUT

A small, oblong, delicately flavored nut obtained from pine cones, notably that of the piñon. They are eaten raw or roasted and are an important ingredient in Italian (as pignoli), Turkish, Balkan, and Middle Eastern cooking.

PINOT CHARDONNAY

(See Chardonnay entry.)

PINOT NOIR

A varietal red wine produced in California. Although experimentation has improved the quality of this wine, it has yet to achieve the complexity of Burgundy wines grown from the same grape in France.

PINTO BEAN

A mottled bean, usually bought dried, raised chiefly in the South West of the United States.

PIPÉRADE

A Basque egg dish, containing sweet peppers, onions and tomatoes. It sometimes also includes ham. (See Egg entry.)

PIPING

The process of forcing a smooth, soft mixture (such as frosting, creamed potatoes, etc.) into fancy shapes. The mixture is placed in a paper or fabric pastry bag and forced through a special metal tip. There are many shapes and sizes to give different patterns. Piping forms an attractive way of decorating cakes, candies, petits fours and appetizers – even the simplest piping helps to give a professional touch to an ordinary dish.

Mixtures for Piping

These must be free of all lumps, which might block the tip. The sugar for royal icing, for instance, must be passed through a fine sieve before being used. During the final mixing, stir rather than beat the mixture to break down any large air bubbles. The mixture should be of such a consistency that it can be forced easily through the tip, but will retain its shape. If it is at all runny in the bowl, it will be too soft for piping. Cream should be whipped until it holds its shape and loses the glossy look. Potato and meringue mixture should be mixed to a soft not stiff consistency.

Filling the Pastry Bag

CLOTH BAG
Turn the bag so that the seam is on the outside and insert the tip. Hold the bag in the left hand, folding the top hem back in the left hand, and fill with a spoon, pushing the mixture off the spoon with the covered thumb of the left hand. To leave both hands free to fill the bag, place it over a cylindrical grater or tall wide glass. When the bag is about two thirds full, turn up the top hem. Place the bag on a flat surface and press the contents toward the tip. Twist round with the right hand until the mixture shows through the tip. At intervals stop piping and repeat this twisting process, to keep the mixture in one mass.

PAPER BAG
1. Fold a 10-inch square of parchment paper into a triangle.
2. Holding the right angle of the triangle toward you, roll over one of the other corners to meet it. Roll the second corner over in the opposite direction to meet the first at the back of the bag.

Adjust the two corners over one another until a point is formed at the tip.

3. Fold over the corners several times to secure them in position.

4. Cut a small piece from the tip of the bag and drop in the required metal tip.

5. Place enough mixture in the bag to fill it about one third. (Any more than this will leak out of the top.) Fold over the top edges of the bag several times and press down.

Method of Piping

The usual rule is to press with the left hand and guide with the right, but some people manage better the other way around. For sugar frosting stars and rounds, piped duchesse potatoes, etc., the bag must be held perpendicular to the surface, but for shapes like leaves the angle at which the bag is held, the movement of the hand, and the speed of pressure may all be varied to alter the shape of the leaf.

Éclairs: Use a plain ½-inch tip and pipe in finger lengths 2 inches to 3 inches onto a greased and damped baking sheet.

Meringues: Use a plain ½-inch tip and pipe in mounds onto lightly oiled parchment paper laid on a baking sheet.

CAKE FROSTING

The beginner is advised to draw the design for cake frosting, etc., on parchment paper and then prick it out by pushing a pin through the paper (the piping later covers these lines). Freehand piping can only be done successfully when one has a good deal of experience.

Trellis piping: Either butter frosting or royal icing may be used for trellis patterns that lie flat on the surface of the cake, but only royal icing is suitable for a raised trellis pattern.

To work trellis straight onto the cake, first prick out the pattern, then pipe the icing through a writing tip, holding this about 1 inch above the cake, so that the icing falls in straight lines. Allow the first set of lines to dry a little, then pipe perpendicular lines across them to give the trellis effect. To make the pattern stand out well, a third set of lines can be piped over the first set, giving a raised effect.

Icing flowers: For these royal icing must be used; if desired it may be tinted but the colors should be kept very delicate. The pastry bag should be fitted with a petal tip and an icing nail or flat-topped cork is needed, also some small squares of parchment paper. For each separate flower, stick a square of paper onto the nail or cork, using a tiny dab of icing.

To make a rose, pipe a cone of icing in the middle of the paper to form the flower center, and allow this to dry for a minute or two. Pipe the first and second petals, holding the tip as upright as possible, with the thick side of the tip at the base. Turn the nail around very slowly to pipe the successive petals; do not make too many, as this gives a shapeless, crowded effect. For the final ring of petals, work the top edge outward in a pleasing natural curve. When the flower is finished, remove it from the nail, on its paper, and leave it on a flat surface to dry for 24 hours. Attach the rose to the cake with a little freshly made icing.

To make pansies, narcissi, and other flowers, use the same petal tip, holding it with the thick

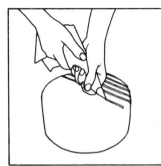

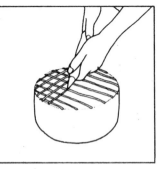

PIPING A RAISED TRELLIS
1. Pipe icing in straight lines, so that the icing falls onto the cake approximately ½ inch apart.

2. Pipe lines of icing approximately ½ inch apart across the first set of lines.

3. Pipe a third set of lines in the same direction as the first. Allow to dry out.

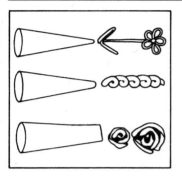

SPECIAL PIPING EFFECTS
1. *Plain, small writing tube*
2. *Plain, medium-sized writing tube*
3. *Petal nozzle for icing flowers*

4. *Flat star nozzle*
5. *Star (or rosette) nozzle*

6. *Small star nozzle*
7. *Petal nozzle*

edge to the center of the icing nail and the thin edge outward. Pipe the petals to suit the particular flower. When the flower is hard and dry, pipe a spot of dark yellow icing into the little hole left in the center between the petals.

Leaves are made in a similar way, with a leaf tip.

PIQUANT SAUCE

A well-flavored French sauce consisting of an espagnole sauce base flavored with shallots, white wine, chopped gherkins, and herbs. It is served with fish and boiled or roasted meat.

PIQUANT SAUCE

2 shallots or a small piece of onion, skinned and
   finely chopped
butter
$\frac{2}{3}$ cup wine vinegar
1 cup espagnole or demi-glace sauce
2–3 gherkins, finely chopped
1 tablespoon chopped parsley

Sauté the shallots or onion in butter for about 10 minutes, until really soft but not browned. Add the vinegar and boil rapidly until reduced by about half. Stir in the sauce and simmer for 15 minutes. Add the gherkins and parsley and serve without further cooking.

PIROSHKI (OR PIROZHKI)

A small Russian turnover, filled with meat or seafood and baked. Piroshki make excellent canapés.

PISSALADIÈRE

A tart filled with tomatoes, onions, black olives, and anchovy fillets. It is said to have originated in Greece but is mainly found in the South of France.

PISSALADIÈRE

PASTRY
1 cup flour
pinch of salt
5 tablespoons butter
1 egg

FILLING
1 tablespoon olive oil
2 tablespoons butter
1½ lb onions, finely sliced
½ teaspoon salt
pinch of pepper
pinch of nutmeg
3 egg yolks
3 tablespoons milk
4 oz package cream cheese

GARNISH
16 anchovy fillets
16 black olives

Make pastry adding sufficient egg to bind the mixture together. Wrap pastry in foil and chill for 2 hours. Heat the oil in a skillet, add butter and onions. Sauté, covered, for 30 minutes until soft and pale golden. Add seasoning and nutmeg. Use the pastry to line a 9-inch fluted flan or tart pan placed on a baking tray. Line with parchment paper and baking beans. Bake in a 400° oven for

20 minutes. Remove beans and parchment paper.

Blend together egg yolks, milk, and cheese, then mix in the onion. Pour filling into pastry shell and return to oven for 20 minutes more or until set. Arrange anchovy fillets in a lattice over flan with black olives. Bake for 10 minutes.

PISTACHIO NUT

The fruit of a tree which is grown in Southern Europe, Western Asia, and Mexico. The small, bright-green kernel, which is sweet and delicate in flavor, is covered with a yellowish-red skin and a bluish husk. The nuts are sold shelled and blanched. They can be chopped or sliced and used to decorate various types of desserts, cakes, and ices or salted like almonds. They also make a flavoring for ice cream.

PISTOU

A famous fresh vegetable soup from the area of Nice in the South of France. It is flavored with basil, ground to a paste with garlic and olive oil (pistou) added just before serving.

PITA

A small individual Mideastern bread. Although made from yeast, the pita is flat and round. It contains a "pocket" used to fill with food.

PIZZA

An Italian dish made from yeast dough, rolled into a flat round and covered with tomato, grated cheese, anchovies, or other additions such as ham, egg, mushrooms, olives, and onion.

It is brushed with oil and baked. They are best eaten straight from the oven with a mixed green salad. Pizzas freeze very well and can be reheated from frozen in about 30 minutes.

Pizzas are a popular fast-food item in this country and elsewhere as they provide an economical, quick meal. Pizzas are usually available to take away or eat on the premises. At home pizzas are ideal for informal entertaining: a large one can be made and cut into slices or serve small individual ones.

PIZZA NAPOLETANA

$\frac{2}{3}$ cup water
$\frac{1}{2}$ teaspoon sugar
1$\frac{1}{2}$ teaspoon dry yeast or $\frac{1}{2}$ oz fresh yeast

2 cups flour
1 teaspoon salt
4 tablespoons lard or butter
cooking oil

FOR THE TOPPING
1 lb onions, chopped
2 (16 oz) cans tomatoes, drained
2 teaspoons dried marjoram
salt
pepper
4 oz Bel Paese or Mozzarella cheese, cut into small dice
2 (2 oz) cans anchovy fillets, drained
black olives

Warm the water to about 100° and dissolve the sugar in it. Sprinkle the dry yeast over and let stand in a warm place until frothy. If you are using fresh yeast, blend it with the water and use at once; omit the sugar. Mix the flour and salt, cut in the lard and pour in the yeast mixture. Hand mix and beat until the dough leaves the sides of the bowl. Knead on a floured board until smooth and elastic. Put the dough in an oiled plastic bag, let rise in a warm place until doubled in size. Turn the dough onto a floured surface and roll to a long strip. Brush with oil and roll it up like a jelly roll.

Repeat 3 times. Grease a 12-inch round baking sheet or pizza pan and roll out the dough to fit this. Brush with oil. Sauté the onions in a little oil until soft but not colored. Spread to within $\frac{3}{4}$ inch of the edge of the dough. Arrange the tomatoes on top, sprinkle with marjoram and seasoning and bake in a 450° oven for 20 minutes. Scatter the cheese over the top, lattice with anchovy fillets, and arrange olives in the spaces between lattice. Cover loosely with foil and cook for 20 minutes more. Serve hot in wedges, with a green salad.

QUICK PIZZA

1 cup flour
1 teaspoon baking powder
$\frac{1}{2}$ teaspoon salt
5 tablespoons oil
4 tablespoons water
1 small onion, chopped
1 can (16 oz) tomatoes, drained and chopped
2 teaspoons mixed herbs
2 tablespoons butter
$\frac{1}{4}$ lb cheese, cut into small cubes
few olives and anchovy fillets

Mix the flour, baking powder, and salt and stir in 1 tablespoon oil and enough water to mix to a fairly soft dough. Roll out into a 7-inch round and cook on one side in the remaining oil in a large skillet. Meanwhile, make the topping by sautéing the onion, tomatoes, and herbs in the butter. Turn the dough over and spread with the tomato mixture, the cheese, and a few sliced olives and/or anchovy fillets. Cook until the underside is golden and place under a hot broiler until the cheese is golden and bubbling. Serve hot, cut in wedges – it goes well with a green salad.

PIZZA SPECIAL

2 oz onion, thinly sliced
2 tablespoons vegetable oil
1 lb ripe tomatoes, skinned
4 tablespoons mango chutney
¼ lb sliced cooked ham
salt
pepper
10 oz package brown bread mix
6 oz St Paulin cheese, chilled

Soften the onion in the heated oil in a skillet. Add the coarsely chopped tomatoes and mango chutney and sauté until mixture resembles a puree. Shred the ham coarsely and mix into the tomato mixture with seasoning to taste. Cool.

Mix and knead the dough according to package instructions. Roll out to fit a foil-lined and lightly greased 13 × 9 inch jelly-roll pan. Spread the tomato mixture over the dough. Grate the cheese over it evenly. Leave to rise in a warm place for about 1 hour. Bake in a 425° oven for about 25 minutes or until golden brown and crisp.

PLAICE

A European flatfish with characteristic red spots on the dark side and with eyes of uneven size on the same side of its head. Often referred to as the "poor man's sole," plaice vary in size from the small dab to a fish weighing approximately 10 lb. The medium ones have the best flavor; the very small ones are not worth buying, as they are mostly bone. When fresh, plaice has firm flesh and the spots are bright, which dull upon keeping. Plaice are in season year round, but are at their best toward the end of May. Plaice are not found in American waters, though the name is often used for flounder and fluke here.

Preparation and cooking: Plaice may be cooked whole or in fillets. (See Fish entry for method of filleting, etc.) Small plaice (and also dabs) are fried whole.

Frying is one of the most common methods of cooking plaice. Fillet, skin, and dry the fish, dip it in seasoned flour or coat with egg and bread crumbs and fry in hot deep fat. Garnish with slices of lemon and fried parsley and serve separately a well-flavored sauce such as anchovy, shrimp, etc., or maître d'hôtel butter.

Plaice fillets may, if preferred, be breaded and then placed in a greased baking pan dotted with butter and covered with waxed paper and baked for 20 minutes in a 400° oven. Alternatively, the breading may be omitted, in which case the fish should be coated with a sauce after baking – cheese, parsley, shrimp, vinaigrette, hollandaise and tartare are all suitable; use the bones (if available) to make fish broth for the sauce.

PLANKING

To cook (usually to serve) meat or fish on a special wooden board. The plank should be of well-seasoned hardwood, oblong or oval in shape. It is heated in the oven, then oiled with olive oil or melted butter and the meat or fish is placed on it, dabbed with pieces of butter or bacon and cooked in a hot oven or under a broiler (provided it can be placed at a safe distance from the heat).

PLANTAIN

A tropical fruit resembling a banana – in fact some of the many varieties are almost indistinguishable from bananas, though rather bigger and coarser. The ripe fruit of the better types has sweet, soft flesh. The coarser varieties, and also the unripe fruit, can be cooked by baking or frying.

Plantain is also the name of a weed found in Britain, which used to be dried and made into a drink before tea was introduced.

PLOVER

A small wild bird, several varieties of which are hunted and eaten in Europe, but are illegal to hunt in the United States.

PLUM

A fruit of the genus *Prunus*, supposed to have developed originally from the sloe. Many hundreds of varieties of plum are grown throughout the world, ranging in color from gold to very dark purple, and varying considerably in size. Some are suitable for dessert, some for cooking purposes and a few may be used in either way.

Most of the plums grown commercially in the United States are hybrids of the Sino-Japanese plum, crossed either with the European or the wild American species. Among the most common American varieties are the sweet juicy Burbank; the slightly tart Santa Rosa; and the large purple Stanley which is good for drying.

The skins of plums are inclined to be tough, and it is better to remove them when the raw fruit is used in fruit salads, etc.

Plums are used for all the usual fruit desserts, such as pies, sweet flans, mousses, fruit salad, etc.; they may also be frozen, pickled, dried, canned, or made into jam.

PLUM JAM

6 lb plums
1½ pints water
6 lb sugar

Wash the fruit, cut in halves and remove the pits. Crack some of the pits and remove the kernels. Put the plums, kernels and water in a pan and simmer gently for about 1 hour, or until really soft. Add the sugar, stir until dissolved and boil rapidly until setting point is reached. Jar and cover in the usual way. *Makes about 10 lb.*

Note: Alternatively, cook the fruit without pitting, removing the pits with a slotted spoon as the jam is boiling.

CANNED AND DRIED PLUMS
(See Canning and Drying entries.)

UPSIDE-DOWN PLUM CAKE

2 tablespoons butter
2 tablespoons light brown sugar
¾ lb red plums
¼ cup whole unblanched almonds
½ cup sugar
2 eggs
1 cup flour
1 teaspoon baking powder
½ cup ground almonds
½ teaspoon almond extract

Butter a 7-inch ring mold, using all of the butter. Sprinkle the base with the brown sugar. Halve and pit the plums. Place each plum half face down in the base of the pan with a whole almond inside the cavity. Place all the remaining ingredients in a mixing bowl and beat well with an electric mixer or wooden spoon until light and smooth — 2 to 4 minutes. Turn the creamed mixture into the pan and smooth the surface. Bake in a 375° oven for about 1 hour, until risen and golden brown.

PLUM PUDDING

A famous rich English steamed pudding, served at Christmas and known by the British as Christmas Pudding. It is made with suet, spices, dried fruits, and nuts. After steaming, it is flavored with brandy and wrapped to mature until Christmas, when it is resteamed and served hot. Plum pudding, decorated with a sprig of holly and brought to the table flaming with brandy, is usually served with a custard sauce or hard sauce and is an important feature of the English Christmas dinner.

PLUM PUDDING

4 cups fresh white breadcrumbs
3 cups all-purpose flour
1 teaspoon salt
½ teaspoon ground mace
½ teaspoon ground ginger
½ teaspoon ground nutmeg
½ teaspoon ground cinnamon
¾ lb suet, shredded
2 cups granulated sugar
1½ cups soft brown sugar
½ lb mixed candied peel, chopped very finely
12 oz currants
8 oz golden raisins
1¼ lbs seedless raisins
6 oz blanched almonds, chopped
2 apples, peeled and chopped
grated rind and juice of 1 lemon
grated rind and juice of 1 orange
⅓ cup brandy
3 eggs, beaten
about ⅔ cup milk

Mix together in a large mixing bowl all the dry ingredients, the almonds, apples and orange and lemon rind. Mix the lemon and orange juice and the brandy with the beaten eggs and add to the dry ingredients, with enough milk to give a soft dropping consistency.

Cover the mixture lightly and leave overnight. Half-fill 3 saucepans with water and put them on to boil. Grease 3 pudding bowls – 2-cup, 4-cup and 5-cup capacities. Stir the mixture before turning it into the prepared bowls, cover with greased waxed paper and with a clean dry cloth or foil.

Steam over rapidly boiling water as follows:
2-cup pudding 5 hours
4-cup pudding 7 hours
5-cup pudding 9 hours

When the puddings are cooked, remove them from the pans and allow to cool. Remove foil or cloth but leave the paper in position. Recover with a fresh cloth or foil and store in a cool place.

On the day of serving steam the pudding as follows:
2-cup pudding 2 hours
4-cup pudding 3 hours
5-cup pudding 3 hours

Turn out onto a hot dish and serve with hard sauce or a sweet white sauce flavored with rum.

Note: Do not put the aluminum foil directly onto the pudding, as the fruit eats into it after some weeks; this does not harm the pudding, but the foil ceases to be watertight.

POACHING

To simmer a food such as fish very gently in milk, water, or other liquids. (See Fish and Egg entries.)

POLENTA

A substantial type of cornmeal porridge eaten in Italy; in some parts of the country it is a staple food. It is used to make gnocchi and some bread and cakes; it is often used as a substitute for semolina. Polenta is left to cool and is then cut up into pieces, fried and served with bacon, etc., as a breakfast or supper dish.

POLENTA

3 cups water
2 teaspoons salt
2 cups finely ground cornmeal
freshly ground black pepper

Bring the water and salt to a steady boil in a saucepan. Slowly pour in the cornmeal, stirring all the time with a wooden spoon until a smooth mixture is formed. Lower the heat and simmer, stirring frequently, for 20 to 25 minutes or until it resembles thick porridge. Add pepper to taste. If a thicker polenta is required, continue cooking over a very low heat until almost too thick to stir.

Serve with a meat, tomato, or mushroom sauce poured over it, and pass grated Parmesan cheese separately. Thick polenta can be shaped on a wooden board to a flat cake when cold, cut into slices and fried, broiled, or baked to serve with small roast birds or with a hot sauce.

POLISH SAUSAGE

(See Kielbasy entry.)

POLLACK (COALFISH)

The name given to two very similar species of fish caught off the North Atlantic coasts of North America and Europe: the *Pollachius pollachinus*, found off European coasts, and the *Pollachius virens*, inhabiting North American waters.

Both resemble cod and may be prepared in the same ways.

POMEGRANATE

The fruit of a tree grown in Southern Europe, the Eastern countries, and South America. Pomegranates are about the size of an orange, of a yellowish-red color and contain a mass of pulpy red grains. The fruit can be squeezed to obtain the juice, which when strained free of pits is used in drinks and for flavoring ices. In Persia the fruit is made into wine; a Mexican liqueur called Aguardiente is also made from pomegranates.

POMPANO

A fish with a beautiful silvery skin and a deeply forked tail, caught off the coast of Florida and in the Gulf of Mexico. Thought to be one of the tastiest fish served in the United States, it is mostly consumed locally. It is considered at its height as served at Antonine's, a New Orleans restaurant, in parchment (en papillote) with a sauce of shrimp and crabmeat. It is equally good cooked in a simple fashion.

SAUTÉED POMPANO WITH PARSLEY BUTTER

4 pompano fillets
6 tablespoons butter
salt
pepper
½ cup dry white wine
3 tablespoons chopped parsley

Pat the fillets dry with paper towels. Melt 4 tablespoons of the butter in a large skillet and saúté the fillets flesh side down for about 2 minutes, just to set the flesh. Turn and saúté skin side down until done. Remove the fillets to a warm platter, discard the butter in the pan and season to taste. Add the wine and cook down over high heat, scraping the pan, until the liquid is syrupy. Swirl in the remaining butter, add the parsley and serve over the fillets.

PONT L'ÉVÊQUE CHEESE

Originally made in Normandy, France. It is a semi-hard fermented cheese, yellow in color with a very delicate flavor. It is a summer and autumn cheese made from whole or skim milk. The cheese is usually sold in flat woodchip boxes.

POOR BOY

A turn-of-the-century New Orleans sandwich made on a split loaf of French bread. Poor boys were usually filled with meat and cheese, but their contents could be as varied as the Hero.

POPCORN

Grains of a variety of corn which explodes when roasted. The best corn for the purpose is the small cob variety known as Non-pareil. The heat converts the water in the grain into steam and causes the grain to burst open with a "pop." The grain so treated often develops odd shapes and usually turns inside out.

POPE'S NOSE

The tail of a fowl, also known as the parson's nose.

POPOVER

A hollow light muffin made from the same batter as Yorkshire pudding.

POPOVERS

2 eggs
⅔ cup all-purpose flour
1 cup milk
½ teaspoon salt

Beat the eggs in a mixing bowl. Add the remaining ingredients and beat to combine. Fill greased medium muffin pans ¾ full and bake in a 450° oven for 20 minutes. Reduce heat to 350° and bake 15 minutes longer. Serve immediately with plenty of butter.

POPPADUM

(See Pappadam entry.)

POPPY SEED

The small deep-blue seeds of one type of poppy flower are sprinkled on top of rolls, bread, and certain cakes as a decoration; they are also used as a filling for yeast cakes and strudels; they have a mild but distinctive flavor.

PORGY

A small but important commercial fish of coastal North America, ranging from ½ to 2 lb. It is usually served whole, broiled or dipped in flour and pan-fried.

PORK

The meat of the pig eaten fresh, as distinct from bacon and ham, which are cured. The best pork comes from young animals and is recognized by its smooth, thin skin, firm flesh, and white fat.

Pork must be well cooked, to prevent the danger of infection by trichinosis, caused by worms which are present in the meat. When thoroughly cooked, pork should look white – pink-colored pork should never be eaten. It requires long, slow cooking, but because of the large amount of fat it contains, roast pork seldom requires basting during cooking. To counteract its richness, roast, broiled, or saúténed pork is usually accompanied by something sweet and tart, such as applesauce.

Like other meats, pork is a good source of animal protein and also of vitamin B_1 or thiamin.

Cuts of Pork and how to cook them

Leg	Roast
Shoulder (blade-bone)	Roast
Rib and Loin –	
one piece	Roast
cut into pieces	Saúté, broil, or bake
Spare rib	Roast

BROILED OR SAUTÉED PORK

Pork steaks and rib or loin chops are suitable for broiling or sautéing. For broiling, the meat should be at least ¾ inch thick. Set the temperature for 350° and broil 2 to 3 inches from the heat. Broil until the top side is brown, season with salt and pepper and turn. Broil on the second side until brown. Pork ¾ to 1 inch thick should take a total of 20 to 25 minutes' cooking time.

Use a small amount of fat when sautéing and turn frequently. The time should be about the same as for broiling.

ROAST PORK

Pork should be roasted to an interior temperature of 170°. An oven temperature of 325° to 350° insures even cooking and minimal loss of weight. Roast a center loin cut 30 to 35 minutes per lb and a rolled roast 35 to 40 minutes per lb. Roast a whole leg 22 to 26 minutes per lb, a half leg, 35 to 40 minutes per lb. A whole rolled leg is roasted 24 to 28 minutes per lb.

SWEET AND SOUR PORK

This is a Chinese method of cooking small pieces of pork in batter and serving it with a "sweet and sour" sauce containing both vinegar and sugar, as well as soy sauce and other ingredients. There are various recipes, but here is a typical one:

FOR THE SAUCE
2 oz pickles, chopped
1 carrot, grated
2 onions, chopped
½ (8 oz) can pineapple slices, chopped
2 tablespoons oil
3 tablespoons soy sauce
⅔ cup broth, water, or pineapple juice
2 tablespoons sugar
2 tablespoons vinegar
1 tablespoon cornstarch
1 teaspoon salt

1 lb pork shoulder
oil or fat for frying
2 eggs
2 teaspoons flour
2 teaspoons cornstarch

First make the sauce. Fry the pickles with the vegetables and pineapple in the oil for 10 minutes. Add the soy sauce, liquid, sugar, and vinegar, then simmer for 15 minutes. Mix the cornstarch with 3 tablespoons cold water, stir into the sauce and simmer for 5 minutes longer, until the mixture is translucent. Season to taste and keep hot. Cut the pork into 1½-inch cubes and fry until brown. Beat the eggs with the mixed flour and cornstarch. Dip the pieces of pork into the egg mixture and fry in deep fat until golden-brown, then drain well. Pour the sauce over the pork.

LOIN OF PORK CHASSEUR

2¼ lb pork loin
2 tablespoons oil
6 tablespoons butter
2 onions, sliced
½ lb button mushrooms
3 tablespoons flour
⅔ cup broth
⅔ cup white wine
salt and black pepper
chopped parsley
croutons

Cut the pork into 1¼- to 1½-inch slices. Heat the oil in a skillet, add the pork, and cook quickly to brown and seal the surface. Remove from pan, transfer to an ovenproof casserole. Heat 4 tablespoons of the butter in the skillet, add the onions and cook slowly until soft. Add the mushrooms and quickly sauté. Remove while still crisp and place over the meat. Blend the flour into the remaining pan juices, adding remaining butter and gradually add the broth and wine. Blend to a smooth consistency. Bring to a boil and simmer for 2 to 3 minutes. Adjust seasoning and pour into the casserole.

Cover and cook in a 350° oven for about 45 minutes, or until pork is fork tender. Serve sprinkled liberally with chopped parsley. Garnish with croutons or toasted French bread.

PORRIDGE

A hot breakfast cereal which originated in Scotland and is usually made of oatmeal, boiled in salted water. The name is also sometimes given to a type of thick soup made from corn, buckwheat, etc.

OATMEAL PORRIDGE

2 tablespoons medium oatmeal
2 cups water
salt

Measure out the oatmeal, bring the water to a boil, then sprinkle in the oatmeal, stirring well. Continue to stir until boiling point is again reached and boil for a few minutes, then allow to simmer (in a double boiler if possible) for 30 minutes to 2 hours, according to the size of the grains, until the oatmeal is well swollen and tender. More boiling water may be added to make the porridge of a pouring consistency.

Commercially prepared oats or rolled oats can be cooked in minutes, following package directions.

PORT

A fortified wine made from grapes in Upper Douro, Portugal. Not all of the wine made in this district is made into port, production being carefully restricted by the government. To make port, partially fermented red wine is run into the barrel a quarter full of brandy; this stops the fermentation. As the wine still contains at least half of its grape sugar a strong sweet mixture results. The grape skins are retained during the short fermentation by treading, so that they can be used to color and preserve the port.

The port is left to rest in vats before being taken to Vila Nova de Gaia, where it is kept in warehouses before being shipped from the nearby port of Oporto.

PORTER

A dark-brown English beer, the color and flavor being due to roasted malt and sometimes to added burned sugar. Stout can be made by adding molasses to porter.

PORTERHOUSE STEAK

(See Steak entry.)

PORT-SALUT (PORT DU SALUT) CHEESE

A semi-hard cheese, made originally by Trappist monks in the west of France. It is made from renneted cows' milk in a flattened round shape, weighing 3 lb to 4 lb. Port-Salut is very good when eaten plain, but its flavor is scarcely strong enough for it to be used in cooked cheese dishes. Serve with black grapes, crusty French bread, or crisp crackers.

POSSET

A drink of medieval times made of sweetened milk curdled with treacle, ale, or wine, etc. which used to be given to anyone who had a cold.

POTAGE

Today the general French name for soups of all kinds; originally it was a kind of thick hearty soup with meat and vegetables.

POTATO

This everyday vegetable, so widely used, is one of the best and cheapest of the starchy foods. In the United States about 120 lb of potatoes are consumed per capita each year. The edible part of the plant is the tuber or thickened stem.

The potato plant was originally a native of South America and was introduced into Europe during the sixteenth century. At first the potato was a curiosity, eaten only by the rich, but, by the nineteenth century it had become a staple article in the diet of the poorer classes; in the case of the Irish, it became their most important food, so much so that a failure in the potato harvest in the mid 1800s, led to famine and disaster.

Potatoes contain more starch than other vegetables; their vitamin content is low, but as they are eaten in such large quantities, they are an important source of vitamin C. (This applies particularly to new potatoes and to potatoes cooked in their skins.) The protein content is not high, but may be important if large quantities of potato are eaten. Potatoes also contain small amounts of minerals. Potatoes can be divided into three types: waxy and new potatoes, mature or starchy potatoes and all-purpose, a form of mature potatoes.

Waxy or new potatoes have a high moisture and sugar content, are small and round in shape and have thin skins that may be white or red. They hold their shape well and are good boiled whole and in salads and soups and pan-fried. They are not good for deep-frying.

Mature or starchy potatoes have low moisture and sugar content and high starch content. They include the Russets, or Idahos. They are long potatoes, regular in shape with a slightly rough skin and are excellent for baking and French fries. If expense is no object, they are also good for mashing.

All-purpose potatoes are not always as starchy as russets and not as regularly shaped, but they can be successfully cooked in any manner.

Potatoes should be kept in a cool, dark place (not the refrigerator). Exposure to light, natural or artificial, causes them to turn green and taste bitter. Any green portion should be cut away before cooking.

Preparation and Cooking

Potatoes should be peeled as thinly as possible, with either a special potato peeler or a sharp, short-bladed knife. New potatoes are scraped or brushed. The potatoes should be cooked as soon as possible after peeling or scraping, but if it is necessary to let them stand for a while, they should be kept under water, to prevent discoloration. There are literally hundreds of recipes for cooking potatoes.

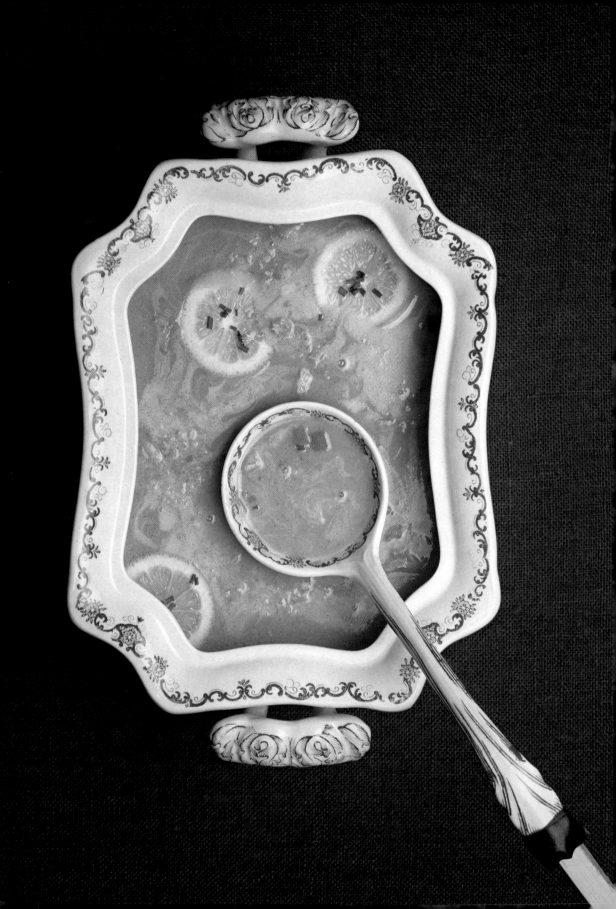

BOILED POTATOES

Scrape, brush, or peel the required number of even-sized potatoes and place in enough boiling salted water to cover them, adding a sprig of mint to new potatoes. Boil them gently till cooked: the time varies according to age, type, and size, from 15 to 30 minutes. Test with a knife and drain when they are tender. If they have been cooked in their skins, hold each on a fork and remove the skin or if using new potatoes leave the tender red skins on; shake them gently over a low heat to dry off. Potatoes may, if desired, be boiled in the oven; choose a pan with a well-fitting lid, place in the coolest part of the oven and allow about twice the usual time.

Very floury potatoes break up easily, so are best boiled slowly till nearly cooked. Drain them and leave with the lid on in a warm place, to finish cooking in their own steam. Old waxy potatoes should be put on to boil in cold water and sprinkled with chopped parsley when served. Toss new potatoes in melted butter and sprinkle with chopped parsley.

STEAMED POTATOES

Scrub the potatoes and remove a $\frac{1}{2}$-inch strip of skin round the center of each or peel completely. Steam for about 1 hour, or until tender.

MASHED POTATOES

Boil or steam the potatoes in the usual way, drain and dry off over a low heat then mash with a fork or a potato masher and beat in a piece of butter, seasoning to taste and adding a little hot milk. Beat them well over a gentle heat till really hot and fluffy and serve in a heated dish, sprinkled with chopped parsley.

BAKED POTATOES

Choose even-sized potatoes, scrub and dry, prick and bake in a 400° oven until they feel soft when pinched – about 45 minutes to 1 hour for small potatoes and 1 to $1\frac{1}{2}$ hours for large. To serve, cut open and insert a generous pat of butter.

ROAST POTATOES

There are two methods of roasting, the first giving a harder skin than the second. It is usual, though not essential, to peel potatoes before roasting.

First method: Cut the potatoes into suitable-sized pieces and dust with salt. Melt some bacon dripping in a shallow roasting pan, add the potatoes, turn them over in the hot fat and bake in a 425° oven for 45 minutes, until brown and tender, turning them over once.

Second method: Peel and cut the potatoes into suitable-sized pieces and boil them for 10 minutes in salted water, then drain off the water thoroughly. Put the potatoes into a roasting pan containing hot fat and turn them over in the fat. Cook in a 425° oven for 45 minutes, until brown and tender, turning them over once.

SAUTÉ POTATOES

After boiling the potatoes until they are just cooked, cut into slices $\frac{1}{3}$ inch thick. Sauté slowly in a little butter or other fat and turn when the first side is browned. Serve very hot, sprinkled with a little chopped parsley and chives.

FRIED POTATOES

Sticks: Peel the potatoes, cut them into even $\frac{1}{4}$-inch slices and then cut the slices into strips. Place them in cold water and leave for at least 30 minutes, then drain them and dry well in a cloth. Heat some fat to a temperature of 385°, place the potatoes in a frying basket (not too many at a time), and lower them into the hot fat. Cook for a few minutes, stirring them to insure even cooking, then remove the basket from the fat. When the fat has reached a slightly higher temperature, about 395°, place the basket of potatoes in it again and fry them until they are golden-brown. Drain on paper towels, season and serve very hot.

Chips: Scrub and peel the potatoes, then slice them very thinly into rounds. Fry them in deep fat at 395° until they are golden brown, shaking them frequently.

Curls: These are the same as chips, but are cut in long strips round and round the potato and are fried in the curled form.

Soufflé potatoes: Choose waxy potatoes for these. Peel and cut them into $\frac{1}{8}$-inch slices, then soak in cold water for 1 hour or longer. Drain and dry the slices and fry them slowly in deep fat until a few of them begin to come to the top. Remove the potatoes and raise the temperature of the fat to 395°. Plunge the precooked potatoes into the hot fat, adding a few at a time until they puff up.

DUCHESSE POTATOES

1 lb cooked potatoes
2 tablespoons butter
1 tablespoon cream or milk
1 egg
salt and pepper

Press the potatoes through a sieve or a ricer. Melt the butter in a saucepan and add the potatoes. When warm, add the cream and beaten egg (reserving a little for glazing), season well and mix together thoroughly. Turn out onto a floured board and divide into small squares, place these on a greased baking pan, brush over with the beaten egg and mark into lines with the back of a knife. Brown in a 450° oven and pile neatly in a hot vegetable dish.

If preferred, this mixture may be piped onto the pan in rosettes through a large star tip, or a fluted tip may be used to make rings or "baskets." The potato may also be piped round a dish as a border. Glaze and bake as above.

POTATO SALAD

Choose waxy potatoes, cook them and cut into ½-inch dice. Mix together some mayonnaise and chopped chives, green onions or parsley. Pour this over the potatoes and toss gently until well combined. Season with salt and pepper.

POTATO LATKES (PANCAKES)

1½ cups drained grated potatoes
1 egg, beaten
2 tablespoons grated onion
1 tablespoon matzo meal
salt
pepper
½ cup chicken fat or butter

Combine the ingredients, except the chicken fat, mixing well. Heat a large skillet and add the fat. Drop the potato mixture by the tablespoonful into the skillet and cook until browned on both sides. Serve with applesauce or as an accompaniment to pot roast or other meats.

POT-AU-FEU

A traditional French dish of meat and vegetables.

POT-AU-FEU

2¼ lb lean beef (brisket, flank, or shoulder)
5¼ pints water
salt

1 carrot, quartered
1 turnip, quartered
1 onion, quartered
1 parsnip, quartered
2 small leeks, quartered
2 stalks celery, quartered
bouquet garni
1 small cabbage, halved
2 tablespoons seed pearl tapioca
pepper

Tie the meat securely to keep it in one piece, put into a large saucepan, add the water and 2 teaspoons salt, cover and simmer for 2 hours. Add the vegetables (except the cabbage) and the bouquet garni and cook for another 2 hours. Put the cabbage into the pan and continue cooking for a final 30 minutes, or until it is soft. Strain off most of the liquid, put into a pan, bring to a boil, sprinkle in the tapioca and simmer for about 15 minutes. The meat can be served separately, with the vegetables and any remaining cooking liquid. Adjust seasoning before serving.

POT-ROASTING

A method of cooking meat in a saucepan or casserole with fat and a very small amount of liquid; it is particularly good for less tender cuts of meat.

POT ROAST

3 lb beef shoulder or chuck roast
seasoned flour
3 tablespoons fat
water
carrot
turnip
potato

Rub the meat all over with seasoned flour, then brown it in hot fat. Slip a low wire rack under the meat, add a cupful of water, cover tightly and cook gently until tender – 1½ to 2 hours – turning the roast occasionally. Add some cut-up carrot, turnip, and potato and continue cooking for 1 hour. Place the meat on a hot dish, with the vegetables, and serve separately a gravy made with the juices in the pan.

POTTAGE

A thick, well-seasoned meat or vegetable soup, usually containing barley or a similar cereal, or a pulse such as lentils. When cooked, the soup should be of the consistency of thin porridge.

POTTED FOOD

A method of packing food into pots with butter for temporary preservation. It is employed by the British to keep shrimp and pastes of meats and cheese for use at teatime and for snacks. The process with meats is very similar to the French one for making rillettes.

POTTED BEEF

1 lb lean stewing beef
1 beef bouillon cube
⅔ cup hot water
1 clove
blade of mace
salt
pepper
4 tablespoons butter
bay leaves

Cut off gristle and fat from meat and put in casserole with bouillon cube, crumbled and dissolved in hot water, the clove, mace, and seasoning. Cover casserole well and cook in a 325° oven for 2½ to 3 hours or pressure cook for 20 minutes. Discard clove and mace. Drain off broth and reserve.

Grind cooked meat twice, add meat juices and 2 tablespoons melted butter. Adjust seasoning. Press into ramekins or individual soufflé dishes. Cover with remainder of butter, melted. Garnish with bay leaf. Chill. (As potted meat contains no preservative it will keep only for a few days in refrigerator.)

POTEEN (POTHEEN)

An Irish whiskey illicitly made from barley. It is very crude and is injurious to health.

POULTRY

This term includes all the farmyard birds (as distinct from the edible wild birds, which are classed as game). General instructions regarding preparation, etc., are given here, but detailed information about the under-mentioned types of poultry, together with roasting instructions and recipes, will be found under individual headings:

Chicken	Guinea Fowl
Duck	Pigeon
Goose	Turkey

CHICKENS
The present-day classification is as follows:

Rock Cornish game hen: special breed of young chicken, 4 to 6 weeks old; ¾ to 2 lb

Broiler: 9 to 12 weeks old; 1½ to 2½ lb

Fryer: 9 to 12 weeks old; 2½ to 3½ lb

Roaster: 3 to 5 months old; 3½ to 5 lb

Capon: castrated male, under 8 months; 5 to 8 lb

Stewing chicken, male or female, over 10 months; 3½ to 6 lb

TURKEYS

Fryer-roaster: under 16 weeks old; 4 to 9 lb

Young turkey: 5 to 7 months old; 8 to 22 lb

Yearling turkey: under 15 months old; 10 to 30 lb

DUCK

Broiler or fryer: under 8 weeks old; 2 to 4 lb

Roaster duckling: under 16 weeks; 4 to 6 lb

GOOSE

Young goose: under 6 months old; 6 to 10 lb

GUINEA HEN

Young: domestic relative of the pheasant, about 6 months old; ¾ to 1½ lb

PIGEON

Squab: 3 to 4 weeks old; under 1 lb

Pigeon: over 4 weeks old; 1 to 2 lb

Choosing Poultry
When selecting fresh poultry choose a bird which is fresh and plump, with a well-rounded breast and thin, moist, tender skin. To tell whether it is young, test the breastbone, when held between the thumb and first finger, this should feel soft and flexible; in an older bird, the gristle turns to bone, which feels hard and rigid.

Frozen poultry is widely available from butchers and supermarkets. This is of good quality and prepared for immediate use once thawed. It may not have quite as much flavor as fresh poultry so extra seasoning should be added in cooking. It is essential to thaw frozen birds thoroughly before cooking.

GIBLETS
Remove and wash the liver, gizzard, and heart (cut away any blood vessels round the heart) and put them with the neck (scrape this well) into a pan, cover with water and simmer gently for 45 minutes to 1 hour. The broth obtained is used for making gravy.

Stuffing and Trussing

Turkey and fowls are stuffed at the breast end (though it is not usual to stuff very young chickens). Loosen the skin, pack the stuffing firmly and evenly into the breast and tuck the flap of skin under. Any stuffing that remains can be put into the tail end, baked separately in 2 casseroles or rolled into balls and cooked in the dripping in the roasting pan.

Ducks and geese are stuffed at the tail end.

The object of trussing is to keep the bird a good shape so that it will be easy to carve. A trussing needle (a long needle with an eye large enough to take fine string) is useful for the job, but if one is not available, a skewer and a length of fine string may be used.

Place the tips of the wings toward the backbone so that they hold the neck skin in position. Then set the bird on its back and press the legs well into the side, thus raising the breast. Slit the skin of the tail end and put the tail through this.

Insert the threaded trussing needle close to the second wing joint on the right side, passing it through so as to catch the corresponding joint on the left side. Insert the needle again in the first joint of the same wing (i.e. the left side), pass it through the flesh at the back, catch the tips of the wing and the neck skin and pass it out near the first joint of the wing on the right side. Tie the two ends of the string in a bow. To truss legs, re-thread the needle and insert it through the gristle at the right side of the tail. Pass the string over the

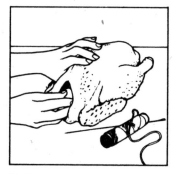
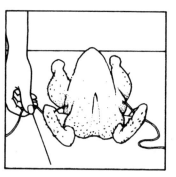
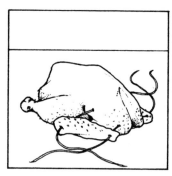

STUFFING AND TRUSSING FOWL
1. Loosen the skin and pack the prepared stuffing firmly yet evenly into the breast cavity until no more stuffing will fit.

2. Insert the trussing needle close to the second wing joint (on the right side), passing it out through the corresponding joint on the other side.

3. Insert the needle again into the first joint of the same wing, pass needle through flesh at the back catching tips of pinions, neck skin and right wing.

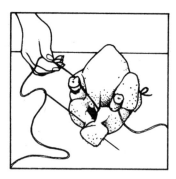
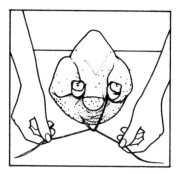
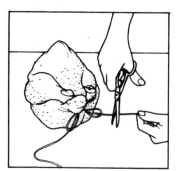

4. To truss legs, insert needle through gristle at right side of 'pope's nose', over right leg, through base of breast bone.

5. Carry thread over the left leg, through gristle at left side of 'pope's nose' then behind legs.

6. Tie together firmly to keep it in position

right leg, through the skin at the base of the breast bone, over the left leg, through the gristle at the left side of the tail, then carry it behind the legs and tie firmly to keep it in position.

Lacking a trussing needle, insert the skewer right through the bird just below the thigh bone. Turn the bird on its breast. First, catching in the wing tips, pass the string under the ends of the skewer and cross it over the back. Turn the bird over and tie the ends of the string together round the tail, at the same time securing the drumsticks.

Boning

For certain dishes, such as galantine, it is necessary to bone poultry before cooking it. Cut off the tip of the wings and bone the bird carefully as follows. Using a small, sharp knife, slit down the center back and separate the flesh from the bones, gradually turning the flesh inside out. Remove the bones, then continue working around the bird to the breast bone. Work the flesh from the breast bone and remove the carcass. Finally, turn the bird the right side out.

Cooking Poultry

The most traditional method is to roast poultry, but interesting stews and casseroles can be made with the addition of vegetables, fruit, broth, and wine. The birds may be left whole, cut up, or first cooked and the flesh removed. The latter is popular for serving in a rich creamy sauce. Poultry is frequently used in Chinese and Indian dishes as it blends well with spices.

POUND CAKE

An unfrosted cake baked in a loaf pan, so called because the ingredients of the cake call for 1 lb each of butter, sugar, eggs, and flour. This half recipe may be doubled to make two cakes. Pound cake is also the base for some fruitcakes.

POUND CAKE

1 cup butter, softened
1 cup sugar
5 eggs, separated
1 tablespoon brandy
½ teaspoon vanilla
2 cups all-purpose flour
½ teaspoon salt
½ teaspoon mace

Cream the butter with the sugar until fluffy. Beat in the eggs yolks one at a time, and then the brandy and vanilla. Combine the flour, salt, and

mace in a sifter, sift over the batter and stir in. Beat the egg whites until stiff but not dry and fold into the batter. Bake in a greased 8 × 4 or 9 × 5 inch loaf pan in a 325° oven for about 1 hour, or until the cake springs back when lightly touched in the center. This cake will keep for several weeks if stored in the refrigerator and freezes well.

WHITE FRUITCAKE

1 recipe pound cake (above)
8 oz seedless raisins
8 oz currants
4 oz candied cherries

Prepare the batter as above, folding the fruit in with the flour. Pour the batter into a greased and lined 8 × 3 inch round pan. Bake in a 275° oven for about 2½ hours, or until the cake tests done.

PRAIRIE OYSTER (PRAIRIE COCKTAIL)

A drink sometimes given to invalids and also to those suffering from a hangover; it is made from an unbroken raw egg, and so slightly resembles an oyster in appearance and consistency. It is also considered to be a good cure for the hiccups.

PRAIRIE OYSTER

½ teaspoon Worcestershire sauce
squeeze of lemon juice
pinch of salt
1 egg

Put the sauce, lemon juice, and salt into a wine glass and break in the egg.

PRALINE

A confection of almonds or pecans and caramelized sugar, often used as a center for chocolates and to flavor and decorate desserts; also the name of a French candy, an almond encased in sugar. In the United States' South pecans are substituted for almonds and made into flat round drop candies. (See Pecan entry.)

To make praline: Rinse ¼ lb unblanched almonds in cold water. Place ½ cup sugar and ½ cup water in a heavy-bottomed saucepan and heat gently until the sugar has melted. Bring to a boil, add the almonds and continue boiling, brushing the sides of the pan with a damp pastry brush to prevent sugar crystals forming. When the mixture is a rich brown caramel color (i.e. at a temperature of about 380° to 400°), pour it onto an oiled baking sheet or marble slab. Allow to cool and set, then break it up coarsely with a rolling pin and store in an airtight tin, to use as required.

PRAWN

Prawns resemble large shrimp with a more slender body and longer legs. When caught they are of a grayish-brown color, but after boiling they turn bright pink, which makes them a decorative addition to a salad, main dish, or appetizer. They have an excellent flavor and make a good stuffing for white fish, omelets, pastry shells, etc. Prawns are used in sauces, scalloped and curried dishes, also in appetizer cocktails. The majority of prawns sold are frozen. In restaurants and in the market the term prawn is often used to describe large shrimp that are not prawns at all. The only American varieties are found in Southern United States waters from North Carolina to Texas. They are also raised in Hawaii.

Preparation and Serving

For most purposes, prawns are taken out of the shells and the black "vein" down the back is removed. The heads are usually kept for decoration.

To serve prawns simply, shell them, garnish with lemon and parsley and serve brown bread and butter as an accompaniment.

To boil freshly caught prawns: Wash the prawns thoroughly. Heat some water, adding salt in the proportion of 1 tablespoon salt to 2 cups of water; when it boils put in the prawns and cook for about 8 minutes. Skim off the scum during the boiling and drain the fish thoroughly.

PRESERVATIVE

This term legally denotes any substance which is capable of inhibiting, retarding, or arresting the process of fermentation, acidification, or other decomposition of food or of masking any of the evidences of putrefaction. It does not include the traditional preservatives, salt, saltpeter, sugars, vinegars, acetic or lactic acid, alcohol or potable spirits, spices, herbs, hop extract, essential oils for flavoring, glycerine, or any substance added by the process of curing known as smoking.

Preserving

One of the greatest advances in human nutrition has been the discovery of various methods of keeping food in good condition from the season when it is abundant to the winter and spring seasons, when few cereal and vegetables crops are available and when it is correspondingly difficult to feed animals.

The main causes of deterioration of food are the micro-organisms, the molds, bacteria, and yeasts. Food is also spoiled by staling or drying and by being contaminated with dirt or pests, but preserving is generally directed against the above-mentioned micro-organisms.

Molds grow on many foods, but particularly on cheese, meat, and sweet foods. They are not harmful and can be scraped off, but they do indicate that the food is old or has not been stored properly. Moldy bread is harmful to birds, however.

Bacteria attack many foods and some types are harmful. Acid foods are less likely to be infected by harmful bacteria than other foods. Bacteria can be destroyed by heat, some more quickly than others.

Yeasts grow in sugary foods, fermenting the food in the growing process and therefore producing alcohol.

To sum up, the micro-organisms are not always harmful (and are in actual fact important in many processes, such as the making of cheese and wine). However, to keep food for some time it must be protected from these organisms.

The methods are, broadly speaking:
1. Heat treatment
2. Refrigeration
3. Drying (dehydration)
4. Treatment with chemicals.

Some methods have been in use for centuries. Drying, for example, was certainly applied to fish and meat 4,000 years ago. The addition of chemicals, particularly salt, sugar, and vinegar, is also traditional. Canning and, more recently, freezing and new methods of drying, are now widening the scope of preserving, so that it is possible to obtain an enormous variety of foods from all parts of the world and at all times of the year.

Some foods (e.g. grains, and such root vegetables as potatoes) require comparatively little special treatment, suitable storage conditions being sufficient, but the perishable foodstuffs such as meat and eggs require very careful preservation.

In the home, the chief methods used are freezing, canning and the making of jam, jelly, marmalade and pickles, candied fruit, and wines. Drying, salting, and smoking are today rarely carried out at home. (See Canning and Freezing entries.)

PRESSURE COOKING

A pressure cooker cuts down lengthy cooking times and saves fuel and money. It is a great help for specific jobs like cooking legumes, making stock, steamed puddings, etc., which will otherwise be very time-consuming.

There are a wide range of pressure cookers on the market today of varying sizes and finishes. Large families and freezer owners will find a big one most useful; otherwise, as a rough guide you'll need an 8 pint model for a household of 2 to 3 people; 10 pint to 13 pint model for 4 to 6 people. For preserving and steaming puddings you need a cooker with a 3 pressure control (usually low, medium, and high, or 5 lb, 10 lb, and 15 lb), while for processing large canning jars you will require one of the models with a domed lid or a canning pressure cooker. If the pan is to be used on a solid hotplate, check that it has a thick heavy base.

Directions for use vary from make to make so you should read and follow the manufacturer's instructions carefully.

With most cookers the prepared food is put into the pan with the required quantity of liquid, the lid closed and fixed into position, and the pressure cooker placed over high heat (unless otherwise stated). When steam flows from the valve on top, the weights are put into place and the contents brought to pressure – recognizable by the muttering noise produced. At this point the heat is reduced and the timing of the cooking period calculated from then.

To get the best from your pressure cooker there are a few points to note. Quantities and times here are for use with 8 pint to 12 pint models.

1. Do not overfill the cooker – it should never be more than two thirds full for solid foods and half full for liquids, cereals, and preserves. Models with a domed lid may be filled with solids to within 1 inch to 2 inches of the pan rim.

2. Cooking times will vary according to the quality of the food and the thickness of the pieces. When in doubt (e.g. with root vegetables that seem particularly young and tender) cook for a slightly shorter time than stated in the table. If necessary you can always bring the cooker to pressure again for a minute or so but nothing can be done about overcooked food.

3. Before opening the pan, let the pressure drop to normal. This is done either quickly or slowly, according to what is being cooked. For example, cereals and legumes, which tend to froth up and clog the vent, should be allowed to reduce slowly.

To reduce pressure quickly, take the pan to the sink and run cold water over it for a few seconds without wetting the valve or the vent. Follow the manufacturer's directions for lifting the weight, making sure there is no hissing before removing the weight and the lid. If hissing persists, run more cold water until it stops. To reduce pressure slowly, leave the pan at room temperature until the weight can be lifted without hissing.

4. All pressure cookers should have a safety valve designed to operate and release steam if the pressure rises above 20 lb. This may occur if the pan boils dry or the vent becomes blocked by dirt, grease, or food. If the valve does blow, inspect the vent, clean it if necessary and see that

COOKING VEGETABLES

VEGETABLE	PREPARATION	TIME
Artichokes, Jerusalem	Peel and place in water containing lemon juice until required	7 to 9 mins., depending on size
Beets	Wash and trim off the leaves.	20 to 35 mins., depending on size
Carrots – old	Peel and dice or cut in rings.	3 to 4 mins.
Carrots – young	Scrape and leave whole if small.	4 to 6 mins., depending on size
Legumes	Soak for 30 minutes; add 5 cups cold water and 1 teaspoon salt.	20 mins. for white beans, butter beans, and dried peas 15 mins. for split peas and lentils
Onions	1. Trim off root; skin and leave whole. 2. Chop or slice.	5 to 10 mins., depending on size 3 to 4 mins.
Parsnips	Peel, core, and cut in halves (quarters if large).	6 to 7 mins., depending on size and age.
Potatoes – old	Peel. If medium-sized, leave whole. If large, cut in quarters.	8 to 10 mins., depending on size 6 mins.
Potatoes – new	Scrape and leave whole, unless large.	7 to 9 mins., depending on size
Rutabaga, Turnips	Peel and dice.	4 to 5 mins., depending on size

there is sufficient liquid in the pan before replacing the safety valve, resetting the pressure and cooking again.

5. Pressure cookers should be kept completely clean. The vent should be inspected and washed after each use and the gasket or rubber ring round the lid kept free of grease and food particles. Store the pan with the lid upturned in it.

If steam escapes round the rim, remove the rubber gasket, rub it with oil, stretch it slightly and replace. Renew the gasket if steam continues to escape.

Stocks and Soups

Any recipe may be used though it may be necessary to reduce the liquid to conform with the maximum amount the pan can take. Put all ingredients into the cooker (the rack should not be used), bring to a boil without putting the lid on, skim the surface and put the lid in place. Lower the heat and bring slowly to high (15 lb) pressure then reduce the heat and cook for 45 minutes. Except when making soup from legumes reduce the pressure quickly using cold water.

Meat and Poultry

You have a choice of three methods.

Boiling: This is suitable for salt meat such as corned beef or tongue. Soak the meat overnight in cold water. Drain, put the meat in the pan without the rack and add 1 small onion, 1 carrot, and a stalk of celery and cover with water. Allow 15 to 20 minutes per lb, depending on the thickness and size of the meat.

Pot roasting: This is the nearest to pot roasting that can be achieved in a pressure cooker. It is suitable for lean cuts such as topside which become a little dry if roasted in the ordinary way in the oven, and fresh brisket.

Rub some seasoning into the meat and brown it all over in hot fat. Put the meat on the rack and add water as follows: 1 cup for a roast of 3 lb or less; $\frac{2}{3}$ cup extra for every further 2 lb meat. Allow 15 to 18 minutes per lb, depending on the size and thickness of the meat.

Braising: Prepare the meat and a bed of vegetables for ordinary braising, add the normal amount of liquid and allow 15 to 18 minutes per lb, depending on the size and thickness of the meat.

Chops and liver can be prepared as for a large piece of meat, but are cooked for 7 to 8 minutes only.

BOILING FOWL

Pressure cooking is ideal for softening older and tougher birds. Rub seasoning over the outside, put the bird on the rack, add $1\frac{1}{4}$ cups to 2 cups water, depending on the length of cooking, and cook for 10 to 12 minutes per lb, according to size and age. If you wish you can finish the bird by browning it in a 425° oven for about 15 minutes.

Alternatively, brown the bird in hot fat, put it on a bed of browned vegetables, add just enough water to cover these and cook for 10 minutes per lb.

STEWS AND CASSEROLE DISHES

Most recipes for a stew or casserole can be adapted for use in a pressure cooker; reduce the cooking liquid if necessary so that it does not exceed $2\frac{1}{2}$ cups and add any thickening (usually in the form of blended flour or cornstarch) at the end of the processing in the pressure cooker.

Beef stew: The best flavor and color are obtained if the meat is tossed in seasoned flour and browned lightly before cooking. Cook for about 20 minutes (depending on the quality of the meat).

Irish stew: Prepare in the usual way and cook for 15 minutes.

Veal stew: Prepare in the usual way and cook for 12 to 15 minutes.

Oxtail stew: Prepare in the usual way and pressure-cook for 40 to 45 minutes. Leave overnight, skim off the fatty layer and pressure-cook for a further 5 to 7 minutes before serving.

Tripe and onions: Cook the blanched and prepared tripe and onions for 15 minutes. Use the liquid to make a white sauce in the usual way.

ROOT VEGETABLES

1. Choose vegetables of the same size or cut them into even-sized pieces.
2. Cook at high (15 lb) pressure and time them accurately.
3. Use $1\frac{1}{4}$ cups water for all vegetables except beet, which requires $2\frac{1}{2}$ cups. Sprinkle the vegetables with seasoning.
4. Bring quickly to pressure and reduce the pressure quickly.
5. Put in first the vegetables that require the longest cooking time. After the necessary period, reduce the pressure, open the cooker, add the other vegetables and continue cooking until ready.

PUDDINGS

The best method for making traditional steamed puddings is with a pressure cooker.

For best results:
1. Never fill a bowl more than two-thirds full.
2. Cover the bowl with double parchment paper.
3. Stand the bowl on the rack in the pan and add $\frac{2}{3}$ cup boiling water for every 15 minutes of the total cooking time, plus $1\frac{1}{4}$ cups.
4. Cover the pan, heat until the steam flows and allow it to flow freely for the specified time.
5. Put on the weights, bring to pressure and cook for the required time.
6. Reduce the pressure slowly.

Pudding	Steam without pressure for:	Pressure	Time at pressure
Sponge: $2\frac{1}{2}$ cups	15 mins.	Low (5 lb)	25 mins.
Sponge: individual	5 mins.	Low (5 lb)	15 mins.
Plum Puddings: 1 lb	15 mins.	High (15 lb)	$1\frac{3}{4}$ hours
$1\frac{1}{2}$ lb	30 mins.	High (15 lb)	$2\frac{1}{2}$ hours
$2\frac{1}{4}$ lb	30 mins.	High (15 lb)	3 hours

Before serving plum pudding, pressure cook at 15 lb pressure, without any preliminary steaming, for a further period: 1 lb 20 minutes; $1\frac{1}{2}$ lb 30 minutes; $2\frac{1}{4}$ lb 45 minutes.

PRETZEL

A brittle, hard, salted bread, originally made in Germany; it is formed into a looped shape resembling a letter B, sometimes said to be the initial of the alternative form, Bretzel. It is sprinkled with salt and sometimes cumin seeds. Pretzels are made with a dough of flour, water, and yeast and traditionally eaten with beer.

PRICKLY PEAR

The watery, refreshing fruit of various types of cactus plants. It may be eaten raw or stewed. Often called "Indian fig."

PRIMEURS

Early forced vegetables and fruit.

PROCESSED CHEESE

A medium-soft cheese manufactured by special processes from ordinary cheese of various kinds, e.g., Cheddar, Dutch, Gruyère. The rind is removed and the cheese is then ground, melted, and mixed with emulsifiers and colorings, after which it is molded into various shapes and wrapped in foil. The heat to which it is subjected during the processing arrests the further growth of bacteria, therefore it keeps well.

Processed cheese has less food value than ordinary cheese as the percentage of water is higher and that of the other in-nutrients slightly lower. It creams well with butter for sandwich spreads and can be used in some cheese dishes; it has a mild uniform flavor which limits its use a little.

PROFITEROLE

Small balls baked from choux pastry. Forced out the size of a walnut, the balls are brushed over with beaten egg and milk and baked in a 425° oven for 15 to 20 minutes. When the profiteroles are cooked, a hole is made in the side, or the puffs are split, and a filling of ice cream, pastry cream, or whipped cream is inserted. Serve the profiteroles with a dark chocolate sauce poured over them.

A cheese, poultry, or meat filling can be used for puffs. Very small profiteroles are used to garnish consommé.

PROOF

(See Spirit entry.)

PROOFING

(See Bread entry.)

PROSCIUTTO

The famous Italian ham of Parma, made from pigs raised on a diet of chestnuts and whey from the equally famous Parmesan cheese of the area, and salt-cured. Although prosciutto is frequently an ingredient in cooking, it is generally eaten raw, sliced wafer thin, as part of an antipasto or accompanied by melon or figs.

PROTEIN

A substance which is an essential constituent of animal and plant cells. In animals, all the muscular tissue of the body is composed of proteins, therefore protein is vitally necessary for the growth and repair of the human body, both for growing children and for adults; it also provides energy and heat.

Proteins are made up of a number of amino-acid units and there may be more than 20 different kinds of amino acids in a single protein. The different kinds and different arrrangements of the amino acids differentiate one protein from another. In general, it can be said that animal proteins usually contain the essential amino acids in proportions suitable for human needs, while vegetable proteins may be lacking in one or other of these acids and may therefore need to be supplemented by other protein foods, either animal or vegetable.

There is a continual turnover of protein in the body – it moves in and out of the tissues and is lost in various ways from the skin, hair, nails, and other tissues. Protein is also used in producing hormones and enzymes. The amounts required vary enormously from individual to individual, so it is impossible to say exactly how much is required. Slightly more is needed by children and by pregnant and nursing mothers than by other adults. A man doing heavy work does not, however, require any more than a man in a sedentary occupation.

ANIMAL PROTEIN
The following are good animal protein foods. Meat of all kinds; game, poultry; fish; milk and milk products; cheese; eggs.

VEGETABLE PROTEIN
Plants can form their own protein from organic materials, and animals, which are unable to do this, can assimilate the protein made by plants. The foods providing vegetable protein are: soy beans (used in the form of flour); peanuts and other nuts; cereals, especially wholegrain; peas, beans, and lentils.

PRUNE

The purplish-black dried fruit of several special types of plum tree, the best known of which is the d'Agen plum, a native of France, but now also grown in California. The finest prune is the French Imperial, which has a thin skin, small pit, and good flavor. Of the prunes grown in California, the Santa Clara is the best grade and

the Californian the next. Prunes are also grown in South Africa and Australia.

The fruit is dried in various ways, some being sun-dried and some by a mixture of both methods. Some are dipped in a caustic solution to help the drying.

Prunes supply energy and small amounts of carotene (vitamin A) and iron; they have a slightly laxative effect.

Stewed prunes (see Dried Fruit entry) may be served with yogurt, custard, cream, or ice cream, or with a cereal for breakfast. They can also be used in a variety of hot puddings; they can be pureed for use in desserts.

Prunes are sometimes included in meat dishes, as in the two recipes given here.

STUFFED PRUNES

Fill pitted prunes with anchovy butter, cream cheese with chopped nuts or other stuffings, using a pastry bag or a spoon. Serve on cocktail sticks, biscuits or toast, or in salads.

PORK AND PRUNE CASSEROLE

$\frac{1}{4}$ lb prunes
1 lemon
1 lb pork
$\frac{1}{4}$ cup all-purpose flour
salt
pepper
1 tablespoon bacon drippings

Cover the prunes with cold water, soak for a few hours, then stew them with the rind of a lemon until tender. Strain off the juice and reserve. Pit the prunes. Wipe the pork, cut it into neat pieces and coat in the seasoned flour. Melt the drippings in a skillet and sauté the pork until brown, then place the pork and prunes in alternate layers in a casserole. Make some brown gravy with the remaining fat, flour, and about 1 cup of the prune juice and pour this over the pork. Add the juice of the lemon, cover with the casserole lid or waxed paper and cook in a 350° oven for about 1 hour. Serve in the casserole and accompany with new boiled potatoes and a green vegetable.

PRUNE AND APPLE ROLL

Make in the same way as a jelly-roll cake, substituting a mixture of soaked chopped prunes, chopped apple, sugar, and marmalade for the jelly. Serve with a custard sauce flavored with vanilla.

PRUNELLE

A pale-green, plum-flavored French liqueur.

PTARMIGAN

A small wild bird of the grouse family, which is found in Alaska, Northern Canada, and Europe, including Scotland. It turns white during the winter months. The willow ptarmigan of North America is the prized red grouse of Great Britain, while the rock ptarmigan of Alaska and Canada is called the ptarmigan in Great Britain, and mountain grouse. It is rarely seen in markets.

The flavor of the willow ptarmigan is so good that it is considered the best game bird of Great Britain. Cook as for grouse.

PUDDING

In the United States, the word generally refers to a sweet custard-like dessert, cooked or uncooked and served hot or cold. Common pudding bases include fruit, rice, tapioca, cornmeal and lemon, chocolate or vanilla custard creams.

There are also steamed puddings, such as plum pudding, particularly popular desserts in Great Britain. Yorkshire pudding is a popover-type batter, cooked in hot beef drippings and served traditionally with roast beef. Blood puddings are a kind of sausage.

PUFF BALL, GIANT

The largest member of a family of fungi of rounded shape; it may grow to 12 inches or more in diameter and while it is at the young stage, the flesh is white and cheesy, and can be eaten. To cook it, peel, slice ½ inch thick, dip in bread crumbs and egg and sauté.

PUFF PASTRY

(See Pastry entry.)

PULLET

A young hen or female fowl.

PULQUE

An alcoholic beverage, made in Mexico from maguey, the American century or agave plant. Fermented by the Aztecs before the arrival of Cortès, pulque has about the same alcoholic strength as beer. It is now surpassed in popularity in Mexico by tequila.

PULSES

The dried seeds of such plants as beans and peas. The most commonly used pulses are butter, white and soy beans, dried and split peas and lentils.

Generally speaking, pulses are useful because of their protein content (when cooked, they have about a quarter of the protein content of cheese) and their calorific value, which in the cooked pulses is similar to that of boiled potatoes and one-third that of bread. They are particularly valuable in Eastern diets which might otherwise be short of protein. They also supply a certain amount of the B vitamins. Sprouting pulses (like the bean sprouts eaten in China) also supply some vitamin C.

To cook pulse foods: Soak the pulses for 12 to 24 hours in warm water, to which a good pinch of bicarbonate of soda may be added. (This soaking is not essential for red lentils, though they soften more quickly if soaked.) Place the pulses in a pan, cover with fresh water, add seasoning and a bouquet garni and simmer gently for 2 to 3 hours, until tender. (Lentils take only 30 minutes to 1 hour.)

See the individual entries for further details and recipes.

PUMPERNICKEL

A German black bread made of coarse rye flour.

PUMPKIN

A member of the gourd or squash family, which can grow to a very great size. The sweet, orange-colored flesh of the pumpkin is used in soups, meat, and other non-sweet dishes as well as in pumpkin pie. Pumpkins have a pleasant flavor and make an interesting change in the menu. They should be allowed to mature before being eaten, the flavor is not at its best in the young vegetable.

Preparation and cooking: The best method of preparing pumpkin is to peel it, cut it up, and remove the seeds. It may then be baked with a roast. The seeds may be dried and roasted. They make a good snack and are popular in Mexican cooking.

Alternatively, cube and boil in water for 15 minutes, or until tender. (Add salt, unless making a sweet dish.) Another method is to blanch the pumpkin in boiling water and finish the cooking in the oven, adding a large piece of butter.

PUMPKIN PIE

The traditional Thanksgiving dessert in the United States.

1 lb pumpkin
½ recipe shortening pastry (see Pastry entry)
2 eggs, beaten
½ cup sugar
4 tablespoons milk
pinch ground nutmeg
pinch ground ginger
2 teaspoons ground cinnamon

Cut the pumpkin into pieces, remove any seeds and stringy inside part and cut off the outside skin. Steam the pieces of pumpkin between 2 plates over a pan of boiling water until tender, 15 to 20 minutes, and drain thoroughly. Mash well with a fork or puree in an electric blender.

Roll out the pastry and use it to line an 8-inch flan ring or deep pie pan; trim and decorate the edges. Beat the eggs with the sugar. Add the pumpkin, milk, and spices. Blend well and pour into the pastry shell. Bake in a 425° oven for 15 minutes, then reduce the temperature to 350° and bake for 30 minutes more or until the filling is set. Serve warm, with cream.

PUNCH

A drink made from a mixture of ingredients, one of which should be a spirit. It is said to derive its name from the Hindu word *panch*, meaning five, because it was originally made from five ingredients – the spirit arrack, sugar, spice, lemon juice, and water. Punches became popular in Europe in the seventeenth century. Nowadays a punch may have a base of white or red wine, cider, beer, cold tea, or champagne and sherry, whisky, rum, brandy, or a fruit liqueur may be added.

There are many types of punch, some served hot and some cold; they make good drinks for parties, as they are generally less expensive than spirits or fine wines. A glass of hot rum punch makes an excellent welcome to guests arriving on a cold winter's night and milk punch is a warming "night-cap," while a refreshing cold fruit punch is a popular addition to a buffet party. Fruit punches can be made without any alcoholic ingredient, the sparkle being provided by ginger ale or soda water. Fresh fruits, cut in a decorative fashion, are often served in a fruit-based punch.

RUM PUNCH

7½ cups cold water
2 cups sugar
1 lemon
4 oranges
1¼ cups strong tea
1–2½ cups rum

Put the water and sugar in a pan with the thinly pared rinds of the lemon and 1 orange. Stir until the sugar is dissolved, bring to a boil and boil for 5 minutes. Remove the pan from the heat and add the juice of the lemon and all the oranges, the tea, and the rum. Strain and serve hot or cold.

PUREE

Fruit, vegetable, meat, or fish which has been pounded, sieved, or blended (usually after cooking) to give a smooth, finely divided pulp. A soup made by sieving or blending vegetables with a liquor in which they were cooked is also called a puree.

The thickness of the puree depends on the amount of liquid present before sieving; a puree of cooked green peas or potatoes, for example, is very stiff and can be piped for decoration. Tomato puree, on the other hand, is soft and runny and usually requires thickening before it can be used. When making a fruit puree it is advisable to use very little water for stewing the fruit, otherwise the puree will be too thin.

The food is usually sieved or blended while still warm; in the case of meat and fish, the bones and gristle must first be removed and the flesh ground. The ground meat can then be pureed in a food processor or pounded in a mortar.

PURI

A wheat cake of Pakistan and northern India, made on special occasions; it is fried in deep fat.

PURL

An old-fashioned English winter drink, made by gently warming ½ pint of ale, adding a dash of bitters and a liqueur glass of whisky or brandy.

An alternative recipe was made by warming 1 pint of ale with ½ pint milk, sweetening to taste and adding a wine glass of gin, brandy, or whisky.

PURSLANE (PUSSLEY)

A weed that creeps along the ground. It has a red stem and fleshy green leaves. It is used as a salad vegetable or flavoring agent.

PYRIDOXINE

One of the B vitamins. (See Vitamins entry.)

QUAIL

A game bird of both the Old and New Worlds. The common quail of Europe is netted in the Mediterranean area on its migratory path from Africa. The bird has become so scarce in Great Britain that it is now a protected species. Although efforts to introduce the common quail into North America have failed, there are several related indigenous species. Most widespread is the bobwhite, which ranges from the Gulf of Mexico and the eastern seaboard of the United States north to Wisconsin and the edge of the Great Lakes. Quails of western and southwestern United States include the scaled, California, Gambel's, mountain and harlequin quails. Quails are also raised on game farms.

There are recipes for quails in aspic, stuffed quail, and braised quail. They can be broiled, grilled, pan-fried or roasted. The French stuff them with foie gras and truffles, the Americans with cracker crumbs, bacon, and celery. The results are equally delicious. The eggs are also used in various ways. (See Egg entry.)

ROAST QUAIL

Allow 2 birds per person. Pluck and singe and if necessary draw it from the neck end. Remove the head and neck, cut off the wings from the first joint, pick out the shot and wash the bird. Scald and scrape the feet. If desired, place a large oyster in the center of each bird. Turn the wings under to hold the neck skin in place, push the legs forward toward the wings and secure in position with fine string. Wrap the bird in a grape leaf and a piece of fat bacon and roast in 450° oven for 15 to 20 minutes. Remove the string, grape leaf and bacon and place each bird on a round of fried bread or toast that has been spread with the pounded quail liver cooked in butter. Garnish with watercress and brown gravy.

QUASSIA

A tree found in South America and the West Indies, from which is extracted a bitter oil, used for medicinal purposes and to flavor apéritifs.

QUEEN CAKE

A small, light, rich cupcake of Great Britain, containing fruit such as golden raisins, dates, candied cherries, or crystalized ginger.

QUEEN OF PUDDINGS

A pudding made in Great Britain of custard and bread crumbs, spread with jam and then topped with meringue. Usually it is flavored with lemon rind and vanilla. For variety, apricots or peaches instead of jam may be placed on top of the custard mixture after it is set and before it is covered with the meringue.

QUEEN OF PUDDINGS

2 cups milk
2 tablespoons butter
grated rind of ½ lemon
2 eggs, separated
¼ cup sugar
1½ cups fresh white bread crumbs
2 tablespoons raspberry or strawberry jam

Warm the milk, butter, and lemon rind. Beat the egg yolks and half of the sugar lightly and pour in the milk, stirring well. Strain over the bread crumbs, pour into a greased 4-cup ovenproof dish and let stand for 15 minutes. Bake in a 350° oven for 25 to 30 minutes, until lightly set; remove from the oven. Warm the jam and spread it over the pudding. Beat the egg whites stiffly and add half the remaining sugar, beat again and fold in the remaining sugar. Pile the meringue on top of the jam and bake for 15 to 20 minutes, until the meringue is lightly browned.

QUENELLE

Quenelles consist of fish or meat, cooked, pureed, sieved, or pounded to a forcemeat consistency and bound with beaten egg; this mixture is molded into egg shapes with a spoon or dropped from a pastry bag straight into simmering stock or water. Depending upon their size, quenelles may be served as a garnish, appetizer, or main course.

FISH QUENELLES

$\frac{1}{2}$ lb cod or any similar white fish – pike is the
 classic choice
2 tablespoons butter
3 tablespoons flour
4 tablespoons milk
1 egg, beaten
1 tablespoon heavy cream
salt
pepper

Cook the fish and puree it in an electric blender or food processor. Melt the butter, stir in the flour and cook for 2 to 3 minutes. Remove the pan from the heat and gradually stir in the milk. Return the pan to the heat and stir until the sauce thickens. Remove from the heat and stir in the fish, egg, cream, and a generous amount of salt and pepper. Mix together until thoroughly combined.

Grease a large skillet, fill it three-quarters of the way with water and heat to simmering point. Using 2 wet spoons, make the fish mixture into egg-shaped or oval pieces, put into the pan and simmer for about 10 minutes, basting well, until the quenelles are swollen and just set. Remove them from the pan with a slotted spoon and serve coated with a well-flavored sauce, such as mousseline or Normande.

QUETSCH

A pure white, potent liqueur distilled in France (chiefly in Alsace) from the type of plum of the same name and flavored with the plum-pit kernels.

QUICHE

A custard tart, a specialty of Lorraine and Alsace. It may be served as an appetizer, the main course for lunch or supper and, if made in bite-sized tarts, an accompaniment to cocktails. There are many variations to the filling, as mushrooms, fish, celery, corn, ham, peppers, or almost anything can be included.

QUICHE LORRAINE

short-crust pastry, made with $1\frac{1}{4}$ cups flour, etc.
 (see Pastry entry)
3–4 oz lean bacon, chopped
2–4 oz Gruyère cheese, thinly sliced
2 eggs, beaten
$\frac{2}{3}$ cup half-and-half
salt and pepper

Roll out the pastry and use it to line a 7-inch plain flan ring or layer cake pan, making a double edge. Cover the bacon with boiling water and leave for 2 to 3 minutes, then drain well. Place in the pastry shell with the cheese. Mix the eggs and the cream, season well, and pour into the shell. Bake in a 400° oven for about 30 minutes, until well risen and golden.

There are many variations on this traditional dish – it can be made with bacon or cheese or both. The cheese and bacon given above may be replaced by 3 oz blue cheese mixed with 6 oz cream cheese.

In some recipes lightly boiled rings of onions or leeks are used instead of, or as well as, the bacon.

QUICK BREAD

Any bread made with leavening that expands during cooking and does not require a period previous to baking.

QUICK FREEZING

The commercial process of freezing food. It is a very much quicker process than home freezing. The difference is that the temperature drops at great speed through the water-freezing zone (known as "the zone of maximum crystal formation"). Between 32° and 25°, water freezes into ice crystals. If this happens slowly the crystals are large and tend to damage the cells of the food; if it takes place rapidly, the crystals are small, the cells remain undamaged and less deterioration takes place in the appearance and texture of the food.

Quick freezing is carried out in three main ways:

1. Plate Freezing: the food is packed in rigid containers and placed between metal shelves in which a refrigerant, often liquid ammonia at −26° circulates, freezing the packed food in 2 to 3 hours.

2. Air Blast Freezing: the food is placed on metal trays and loaded onto trolleys, which then move slowly through a tunnel in which air at −22° is forced in the opposite direction. This takes 2 to 3 hours.

3. Flo Freezing: an ideal method for small foods, e.g. peas, corn. Cold air at −40° is forced upwards through perforated trays as the food moves along a tunnel and is frozen in 3 to 8 minutes. This method keeps individual items separate, they can then be packed in polyethylene bags.

After quick freezing the food is transferred to a cold storage at −20° until required for distribution. It leaves the factory in insulated trucks at −18° and is stored in stores at less than 0°. Freezing preserves the color and flavor of foods better than other methods of preserving and also retains the nutritional value. (See Freezing entry.)

QUINCE

The hard, dry-textured fruit of a tree belonging to the apple family, native to Asia, which grows in temperate climates. When ripe, in September or later, quinces become golden-yellow or slightly reddish in color and resemble apples or pears in appearance. They have an unusual and powerful smell and are therefore best stored apart from other fruit.

Quinces are not suitable for eating raw, but are good when baked like apples and they make excellent jams and jellies, alone or mixed with apples, cranberries, or pumpkin. In Portuguese the name for this fruit is *marmelo*; from this came the word marmalade, which originally meant quince jam.

To insure a good set when making quince jam or jelly, the juice of 2 lemons can be added to the water in which the fruit is cooked.

QUINCE JAM

2 oz quinces (prepared weight)
4½ cups water
3 lb sugar

Peel, core, and slice the quinces and then weigh them. Put them in a pan with the water and simmer very gently until the fruit is soft and mashed. Add the sugar, stir until dissolved and boil the mixture rapidly until setting point is reached. Jar and cover the jam in the usual way.

QUINCE JELLY

4 lb quinces
rind and juice of 3 lemons
15 cups water
sugar

Wash the quinces and chop. Simmer, covered, with 10 cups water, the lemon rind and juice until tender – about 1 hour; strain through a jelly bag. Return the pulp to the pan and add the remaining water. Bring to a boil, simmer for 30 minutes, then strain. Combine the two juices and measure. Bring to a boil and add 1 lb sugar to each 2¼ cups of juice extract. Return to boiling and boil vigorously until setting point is reached. Jar and cover in the usual way.

(See Quince Butter entry, under Fruit Butter entry.)

RABBIT

A small rodent belonging to the hare family. Although extremely popular in Europe, where both wild and domesticated rabbits are eaten, it has never been very popular in the United States, perhaps because of its association with the Easter bunny. For farmers and country people over the world, however, it forms a veritable feast.

Rabbits give a white meat which has a low fat content and a high percentage of animal protein, so they form an easily digested, nutritious food, especially suitable for those on a light diet. A really good rabbit has an excellent flavor, rivaling that of chicken.

Preparation and cooking: Wild rabbit should be gutted within a few hours of killing. The heart, liver, and kidneys should be saved. Before cooking, it should be washed and soaked in salted water for a time, to make the flavor less strong. If desired, it may then be cut up somewhat like a chicken. Separate the hind legs from the body to give two thighs. Cut the loin section into several pieces across the back and split the rib section into two pieces along the backbone.

Rabbits may be cooked in any way suitable for chicken, although only young, tender ones should be roasted or sautéed. They are frequently used in a fricassee (see Fricassee entry), braised, or jugged; they make a good pie filling and lend themselves well to such dishes as terrines. In casseroles the meat blends well with coriander, saffron, tomatoes, cider, prunes, and vegetables.

ROAST RABBIT

Fill rabbit with veal stuffing (see Forcemeat entry) and sew it up. Truss it by tying the legs in a bent position, so that the rabbit is in a sitting attitude. Cover with bacon or a little fat and for the first 45 minutes cover with greased foil also. Bake in a 350° oven for 1 to 1½ hours, until tender. Serve with gravy.

RACLETTE

A cheese dish, a specialty of the canton of Valais in Switzerland. The local cheese is placed in front of the fireplace and scraped off as the exposed surface is melted. The cheese is eaten with unpeeled boiled potatoes and accompanied with white wine.

RADISH

This small red or white-and-red vegetable has a characteristic, slightly hot flavor which makes it a useful addition to many kinds of salad. It is available year round.

Radishes should be eaten while young and tender and are best served raw. If they are to be eaten whole, cut off the tops, leaving ½ inch of stalk, and remove any large roots, then wash them well. Larger radishes may be blanched briefly in salted water. Serve with a well-seasoned white or parsley sauce. When used as a garnish, radishes may be sliced thinly, or cut into "roses" or "lilies." (See Garnish entry.)

Radish tops may be cleaned and cooked in salted water like other green vegetables.

RAGOUT

A stew of small pieces of meat or poultry and vegetables, browned in a little fat and then gently simmered. It can be flavored with mushrooms, port wine, tomatoes, etc. A lamb ragout is often known by the French name Navarin. A white ragout, such as Irish stew, is not browned and has no thickening other than the potatoes cooked with it.

RAGOUT OF POULTRY

1 duck or chicken
seasoning
all-purpose flour
butter or oil for sautéing
4 cups broth
1 tablespoon vinegar
4 cloves
8 allspice
8 peppercorns
1 clove garlic, chopped

Roast the bird for 25 minutes, if it is young; otherwise cut it in parts, dip in seasoned flour, and sauté until brown in butter or oil. Place in a casserole and brown $\frac{1}{4}$ cup flour in the fat remaining in the pan. Add the broth, vinegar, spices (tied in cheesecloth), and garlic, then pour into the casserole and cook in a 325° oven for 1 hour or longer, until tender (old birds will need $2\frac{1}{2}$ hours). Alternatively, the ragout may be simmered gently in a saucepan on top of the stove. If desired, include $\frac{1}{4}$ lb mushrooms or tomatoes or substitute a wine glass of red wine for the vinegar.

RAISED PIE

A pie made with hot-water crust pastry (see Pastry entry), which becomes firm during baking and retains its shape. Raised pies are usually served cold and after baking are filled up with stock which sets into a jelly. They are popular fare in Great Britain and a staple of pubs that serve a buffet of cold foods.

There are two ways of shaping a raised pie: (1) by using a special raised pie mold or a greased cake pan; (2) by molding the pie by hand, sometimes with a jelly jar or small can as a basis.

Making a Raised Pie
See step-by-step illustrations on the next page. Pastry made with 4 cups flour is required to fill a 6 × 3 inch round cake pan.

Cut off a quarter of the pastry, wrap it in waxed paper and leave it in a warm place. Mold the remaining pastry around the cake pan, jelly jar, or the hand; if a mold is used, press the pastry well into the mold. In both cases, take care to make the base and sides of the same thickness. Add the filling. Roll the smaller piece of pastry into a round and cover the pie, pinch the edges together and flute the border or cut with scissors and bend down alternate pieces. Pin a stiff paper band around the pie to keep the shape; make a hole in the center top and add a few leaves made from pastry trimmings. Brush with beaten egg and place on a greased baking sheet. Bake in a 425° oven for 20 minutes, then reduce heat to 300° and bake for $1\frac{1}{2}$ hours more or until the meat feels cooked when tested with a skewer run through the center hole. Allow the pie to cool for a few minutes, then remove it from the pan or mold. Fill the spaces in the pie with jelly stock made from the meat bones.

RAISED VEAL AND HAM PIE

hot-water crust pastry made with 4 cups flour (see
  Pastry entry)
12 oz stewing veal, diced
4 oz ham, chopped
1 tablespoon chopped parsley
grated rind and juice of 1 lemon
salt and pepper
little broth or water
1 hard-cooked egg
beaten egg to glaze
jelly stock

Make a pastry shell. Mix the veal, ham, parsley, lemon rind and juice, season with salt and pepper and moisten with a little broth or water. Half fill the pastry shell with this mixture. Put the hard-cooked egg in the center, add the remaining meat mixture, cover and decorate the pie. Make a small hole in the center with a sharp knife, to allow you to test whether the meat is cooked and to fill with jelly stock when cooked. Glaze the top with a little beaten egg and tie a band of wax paper around the pie. Bake in a 425° oven for 15 to 20 minutes, then reduce the heat to 350° and continue cooking $1\frac{1}{4}$ hours or longer until the meat feels tender when tested with a skewer. When cold, fill the pie up with jelly stock made by dissolving 2 teaspoons gelatin in $1\frac{1}{4}$ cups chicken broth. Leave to set.

RAISIN

Raisins are green or black grapes which have been dried either in the sun or by artificial means.

MAKING A RAISED PIE
1. Mold three-quarters of pastry around a jelly jar to cover sides.

2. Ease pastry 'mold' out of jelly jar and fill with pork mixture.

3. Cover top of pie and pinch edges together.

4. Secure with a stiff paper band around the pie. Make a hole in the center.

5. Allow the pie to cool for a few minutes after baking, then add stock.

6. When cold top up with any remaining jellied stock.

There are seedless varieties, but the best flavored type – the muscatel – has seeds. Raisins come from various countries, including southern Spain, Greece, California, Australia, South Africa, and Crete; the choice Malaga muscatels are usually sold at Christmas time. Raisins are mostly available dried, cleaned, and packed.

They are used in cakes, pies, puddings, chutneys, jam, and mincemeat and a wine can be made from them. Their food value lies in the iron they contain and also in their sugar content; the total amount usually consumed is, however, so small that raisins contribute little to the diet beyond their agreeable taste.

(See Sultana entry.)

RAITA

A mixture of yogurt and fresh vegetables or fruit, the Indian equivalent of a salad. Raitas are served as side dishes or an accompaniment to spicy foods.

EGGPLANT RAITA

1 small eggplant (about 12 oz)
oil for frying
1 cup plain yogurt
salt
2 teaspoons ground cumin
1–2 teaspoons chili powder

Cut the eggplant into $\frac{1}{8}$-inch slices. Add about $\frac{1}{4}$ inch of oil to a skillet and fry the slices until golden brown. Mash the cooked eggplant. Beat the yogurt with the salt and mix in the eggplant. Sprinkle with cumin and chili powder.

RAKI
(See Arrack entry.)

RAMEKIN

A small fireproof china or glass container. In France ramekin also indicates a tartlet with a kind of cream cheese filling.

RANCIDITY

(See Fats entry.)

RAPE

A Eurasian plant cultivated for animal fodder. The seeds yield an oil used for soapmaking and also for lubrication purposes.

RAREBIT

(See Welsh Rarebit entry.)

RASPBERRY

A wild or cultivated juicy fruit from a prickly shrub of the genus *Rubus*, native to North America and Europe; it may be red, purple, black, yellow, or white in color and cap- or thimble-shaped. Raspberries have quite a good vitamin C content.

The full flavor of raspberries is best appreciated when they are eaten immediately after picking, either alone or with cream and sugar. They also make excellent jam; for this purpose, use dry and slightly underripe fruit, as the pectin content is then at its highest. Raspberries have a good flavor when canned by either the oven or the water-bath method of sterilization, though the color is not as a rule very good. (See Canning entry.) Raspberries freeze well; the flavor is best preserved when they are frozen in sugar. The fruit may also be used for homemade wine, raspberry syrup, and raspberry vinegar.

Raspberries are excellent for use in flans, ice creams, gâteaux, shortcakes, meringue tartlets, cold soufflés or molds, fruit salads, and fools. Raspberry jam with a little added lemon juice gives a good flavor to puddings, cakes, etc. Raspberry sauce is good with ices and cold desserts.

To prepare the fruit, remove the hulls. If the fruit is dirty, wash it in a colander, but avoid this if possible, as washing spoils both shape and flavor.

RASPBERRY FOOL

Sprinkle 2 quarts raspberries with sugar to taste and leave for 4 hours, then puree and strain. Mix the puree with 3 cups whipped cream, custard, or a mixture of both, color if required, chill and serve.

RASPBERRY JAM

2 quarts raspberries
2 lb sugar

Wash and hull the fruit and simmer very gently in its own juice for about 15 to 20 minutes, or until really soft. Add the sugar, stir until dissolved and boil rapidly until setting point is reached. Jar and cover in the usual way. *Makes about 3½lb.*

RATAFIA

A liqueur or cordial flavored with the kernels of cherries, almonds, peaches, or other kinds of fruit, also a flavoring extract used in cooking.

The name is also applied to a type of cookie formerly eaten with the liqueur and now usually flavored with ratafia extract. These cookies somewhat resemble macaroons, but are smaller and browner; they may be served with wine, used whole to decorate trifles and other cold desserts, or crushed and mixed with cold custards or creams.

RATATOUILLE

A casserole or stew of vegetables, originating in Provence. It can be served hot as a vegetable or cold as an appetizer.

RATATOUILLE

4 tomatoes
2 eggplants
1 small green pepper
2 onions
3 zucchini
½ cucumber
3 tablespoons olive oil
2 tablespoons butter
seasoning
1 clove garlic, crushed
chopped parsley

Peel and slice the tomatoes; wipe and slice the eggplants; seed the pepper and slice; slice the onions, zucchini and cucumber. Heat the oil and butter in a flameproof casserole (preferably enameled iron) and add the prepared vegetables, seasoning, and crushed garlic. Stir well, cover tightly and place in a 350° oven for 1 to 1½ hours. Serve garnished with chopped parsley.

RAVIGOTE BUTTER

A green-colored butter, made by adding fresh aromatic herbs to creamed butter, served with broiled meat, etc. To make it, take 1 tablespoonful each of tarragon, parsley, chives, chervil and, if available, burnet, wash them and squeeze them dry in a clean towel; chop the herbs finely, pound with a finely minced or chopped shallot and if desired a little garlic. Season, mix with 3 to 4 tablespoons creamed butter and let it harden before serving.

Ravigote Sauce

A French salad dressing containing pounded hard-cooked egg yolks and highly flavored with chopped herbs and garlic.

A hot sauce of the same name is made by adding a generous amount of ravigote butter and some wine and vinegar (reduced by boiling) to a velouté sauce base. It is served with boiled poultry.

RAVIOLI

Square envelopes of pasta, usually containing a well-seasoned mixture of ricotta cheese or ground meat. They are boiled like macaroni and served with tomato sauce and grated cheese, or used as a garnish for soups. The filling may consist of cooked chicken or meat moistened with a sauce, or creamed or pureed vegetables.

RÉCHAUFFÉ

A dish of reheated food. A variety of réchauffés can be made from leftovers of cooked food, so that they become appetizing dishes in their own right. In general, the aim should be to reheat rather than recook the food and it is usually necessary to combine it with a well-flavored sauce or other accompaniment. As cooked food does not absorb flavors this must come from other ingredients.

Take great care in storing leftover food that is going to be used in réchauffés. Meat, fish, milk products, and vegetables in particular are easily contaminated with the germs that cause food poisoning. They should therefore not be left by the side of the range in a warm kitchen. Instead they should be cooled as rapidly as possible and placed in the refrigerator. When the food is to be reheated, it should then be allowed to cook for 15 minutes – this will destroy any microbes that may have contaminated it.

Using Leftover Meat

Trim the meat from the bones, removing fat, gristle, and any inedible parts. Cut or grind the meat finely and use for such dishes as beef croquettes, rissoles, hash, cottage or shepherd's pie. Additional moisture in the form of a sauce or gravy is usually necessary – for example, a panada or thick binding sauce for croquettes and rissoles.

To season white meats (veal, poultry, rabbit), use lemon rind and juice, parsley, herbs, nutmeg, and tomato; for other meats, use onion, tomato, mushroom, curry paste, or piquant table sauces.

Meat may also be sliced and reheated in a sauce. Use a white or light-coloured one for white meats and a brown one for red meat or game.

Using Leftover Fish

Free the fish from skin and bone and flake it – this is best done while the fish is still warm. (The bones and trimmings may be used for stock or sauce.)

Any sauce left over from the original dish should be used and may prove sufficient for binding and moistening the fish mixture, which can be served as fish cakes, croquettes, cutlets, scallops, fish pies and kedgeree. A mixture of white and smoked fish will sometimes make a better-flavored dish than white fish alone.

Cooked fish, which tends to be rather insipid, needs to be very well seasoned and attractively flavored; lemon; parsley, and anchovy are the most popular additions. Lemon and parsley are also used for garnishing.

Using Leftover Vegetables

These can be mixed with cooked pasta or rice to serve as a salad or added to soups, sauces, and quiches.

(See Croquette, Hash, Rissole, Russian salad (under Salad), and Soup entries.)

RECIPE

The list of ingredients and the instructions for making a dish. With some types of dish it is possible to vary the nature and amount of the ingredients and the method of mixing and cooking, so that there are often many different recipes for one dish. With certain classic or specialized recipes, however, particularly those devised by the great chefs of the last century or so, there is only one really "correct" or authentic version.

Beginners should follow recipes carefully and learn the basic methods for cakes, pastry, sauces, etc., before attempting too much in the way of variation. Basic recipes will be found under the appropriate headings throughout this book. The recipes are for four unless otherwise stated.

The quantities given in a recipe can usually be doubled or halved without further alteration, but when quantities are varied beyond this, the proportions of the ingredients often require modification; this applies particularly to such ingredients as leavening agents, flavoring and mixing liquids, which may need to be used in slightly smaller proportions when the quantities are increased. When you want to cook a large quantity of some particular mixture it is often better to make two moderate-sized batches rather than one very big one. This insures better quality results.

RED CABBAGE

(See Cabbage and Pickle entries.)

RED CURRANT

(See Currant entry.)

RED MULLET

(See Mullet entry.)

RED PEPPER

(See Green Pepper entry.)

RED SNAPPER

Any of various marine fish of tropical and subtropical waters with a pink body. The red snapper caught in the area of the Gulf of Mexico is a particularly delicate and tasty fish. Smaller red snappers, weighing around 5 lb, are often sold whole, while larger ones, ranging up to 2 or 3 feet in length and weighing as much as 30 lb, are cut into steaks and fillets. Red snapper may be prepared in any way that sea bass is.

REDUCE, TO

The process of boiling a mixture (especially when making a sauce, soup, or syrup) in an uncovered pan to evaporate surplus liquid and give a more concentrated result.

REFRIGERATION

This is a means of artificially cooling food in an appliance called a refrigerator.

A domestic refrigerator, the interior of which is normally maintained at a temperature between 35° and 45°, chills but does not freeze food. This temperature enables perishable food to be stored under ideal conditions for the short period necessary between purchase and consumption – usually a matter of a few days at the most. It is a mistake to leave highly perishable food longer than this, for although deterioration is much slower than at ordinary room temperature, the bacteria are not destroyed and slow changes occur if the food is kept too long in the refrigerator.

How to Use a Refrigerator

1. Since variations of storage temperature encourage the growth of microbes, the refrigerator should be opened as little as possible and hot food should never be placed in it.
2. Never pack food in too tightly, as this prevents the free circulation of the air.
3. As the air in the refrigerator is dry and will absorb moisture from any exposed food, see that everything (particularly moist food and uncooked cake and yeast mixtures, biscuit doughs, and pastry) is covered before being refrigerated. Special storage containers are available, made from plastic, but china and glass bowls covered with a plate, with a lid of foil or with a piece of plastic wrap are equally satisfactory. Foil and plastic can also be used to wrap items like cheese, and polyethylene bags are also very useful.
4. Strong-smelling foods such as fish should be stored for as short a time as possible. Remember to cover them closely, or else you may find the flavor is transferred to other foods.
5. Vegetables should be prepared before being stored in the special crisper or in a polyethylene bag or plastic box.
6. Pack the food in accordance with the temperature in the different parts of the refrigerator. The coldest part is below the frozen food storage compartment, and as the air at the base gets warmer, it rises toward this compartment and is then rechilled. Foods requiring the lowest temperature (e.g. meat, fish) should be placed directly under the frozen food storage compartment. Anything that is not wanted too cold, such as cooking fat, is best kept in the warmest position, so fats and eggs are generally stored in racks or compartments in the door.
7. Frozen foods should be stored only for the recommended length of time. This depends on the refrigerator. Recommended times are as follows:

Max. Temperature of Frozen Food Compartment	Max Storage Time for:	
	Frozen Foods	Ice Cream
0°	2 to 3 months	2 to 3 months
+10°	4 weeks	1 to 2 weeks
+21°	1 week	1 day

8. Sliced cooked meats, eggs, and cheese should be removed from the refrigerator about 1 hour before being served. Fruit juices, salads, chilled desserts, etc., are usually best if served straight from the refrigerator.

Storage times in a Refrigerator

Dairy Produce

Butter, Fats, etc.	2 to 4 weeks
Milk, Cream	3 to 4 days
Custards, Milk Puddings	2 days
Hard Cheeses	1 to 2 weeks
Soft Cheeses	1 week
Eggs	10 to 14 days
Bacon	7 to 10 days

Meat and Poultry

Raw Meat:	
Roasts	3 to 5 days
Chops, Steaks	2 to 4 days
Stewing Meat	2 to 4 days
Ground Meat, Liver, Kidneys etc.	1 to 2 days
Fresh Poultry	2 to 3 days
Frozen Poultry	2 to 3 days in refrigerator section
Cold Roast Meat	3 to 5 days
Meat Pies, Casseroles	2 to 3 days
Cooked Poultry	2 to 3 days

Fish

Raw Fresh Fish	1 to 2 days
Cooked Fish	2 days
Lightly Smoked Fish	1 to 2 days
Heavily Smoked Fish	2 to 3 months

Fruit

Soft Fruit	1 to 3 days
Citrus Fruit	10 to 14 days
Other Fruit	3 to 7 days

Vegetables

Salad Ingredients	3 to 6 days
Greens	5 to 7 days

REHEATED FOOD

(See Réchauffé entry.)

REINDEER

The meat of young reindeer, both cows and steers, resembles mild venison; the tongues are excellent when smoked. For method of cooking see Venison entry.

RELISH

A condiment, sauce, or pickle taken with food to give added flavor. The name used to be applied to dishes of the appetizer type, served after the soup and fish, to stimulate the appetite.

RÉMOULADE SAUCE

Into $\frac{2}{3}$ cup mayonnaise, fold $\frac{1}{2}$ teaspoon each of French and English mustards, 1 teaspoon each of chopped capers, gherkin, parsley, and chervil, and 1 anchovy fillet, finely chopped.

RENDERING

To extract fat from meat trimmings. (See Fats entry.)

RENNET

A preparation made from the stomach of a calf and containing the rennin, which possesses the property of coagulating casein in milk to form a fairly solid, easily digested clot. When served as a dessert, this clotted milk is known as junket. Rennet is also used to form the curd in cheese-making.

REUBEN SANDWICH

A creation of New York City's Jewish delicatessens, the Reuben spread over the United States and is now not only a classic hearty sandwich but in miniature is served as a cocktail appetizer. While there is some disagreement as to whether the bread should be pumpernickel or rye, there is no controversy about the contents – corned beef and Swiss cheese embracing a moist interior of sauerkraut mixed with Russian dressing. The sandwich is then broiled and controversy re-enters on the question of whether the cheese should be melted in the process or the inside of the sandwich remain cold.

RÉVEILLON

The supper eaten in France on Christmas Eve after midnight mass. It consists of a very elaborate supper and is often provided by the wealthy members of the town or village. The chief dish is usually "boudin noir" – black pudding. The name also applies to a feast held on New Year's Eve.

RHUBARB

Rhubarb is, botanically speaking, a vegetable, being the stalks of the plant, but since it is cooked and eaten like fruit, it is commonly included under that heading. The stalks, which vary in color from green to red, are best picked when young; they are ready for eating in the spring and early summer, before the majority of home-grown fruits are available. Rhubarb has a pleasant, refreshing flavor, particularly when the better varieties are grown. It has little food value, but may add a small amount of vitamin C to the diet. The leaves should be discarded and no attempt should be made to use them as greens as they can be poisonous.

Preparation and cooking: Remove the leaves from the rhubarb, wash the stalks and "string" them if they are old, then cut into 3-inch lengths.

Rhubarb easily breaks down into an unattractive, stringy mass, so it needs to be cooked slowly and gently (preferably in the oven). Use a very small quantity of water and cook in a 300° oven or simmer on top of the stove for a few minutes until tender, sweeten to taste with sugar or syrup. The addition of orange juice and rind gives a pleasant flavor.

In season at the same time as strawberries, the two combine to make delicious pies and conserves. Because of its sharp flavor, rhubarb makes a good fruit fool and it can be made into jam, preferably mixed with other fruits; when used alone, it is often flavored with ginger. Rhubarb may also be canned. It can be frozen in a syrup, dry pack, or as a puree. (See Freezing entry.)

RHUBARB MOUSSE

This mousse has a hint of surprise – marmalade.

1 lb rhubarb, prepared weight
½ cup sugar
⅔ cup water
6 tablespoons ginger marmalade
1 envelope unflavored gelatin
¼ cup water

1 egg white
⅔ cup heavy cream

Cut the rhubarb into 1-inch lengths. Put the rhubarb, sugar, water, and 5 tablespoons of the marmalade in a saucepan and cook until the rhubarb is tender. Puree it in a blender or put it through a sieve. Dissolve the gelatin in the water in a small bowl over a pan of hot water. Stir this into the rhubarb. When it is on the point of setting, fold in the stiffly beaten egg white. Divide between 6 stemmed glasses and chill. Whip the cream until it just holds its shape, fold in the remaining tablespoon of marmalade and use to top the mousse.

RIB (HOTEL RACK)

One of the basic retail cuts of meat. In beef and veal this cut extends from the shoulder through the twelfth rib, and contains a total of five ribs. The rib section of the lamb contains from seven to ten ribs, depending upon how many ribs have been left with the shoulder section. The rib cut of pork includes part of the shoulder blade and contains 10½ to 12 ribs, depending upon what has been left with the shoulder. The term "hotel rack" is used for the rib sections of the lamb and veal.

Beef cuts from the rib include the Standing rib roast, Rib steak, Boneless rib steak, and the Delmonico (rib eye) roast or steak.

Veal hotel rack cuts include the Rib roast, Crown roast, Rib chop and Frenched rib chop.

Pork cuts extend into the loin with the Center loin roast and Canadian bacon (rib eye of the rib and loin eye of the loin). Other cuts include the Blade loin roast, Rib chop, Butterfly chop (boneless hinged rib or loin chops), Blade chop, Back ribs and Country-style backbone.

Lamb cuts from the hotel rack include the Rib roast, Crown roast, rib chops, and Frenched rib chops.

RIBOFLAVIN

One of the B vitamins. (See Vitamins entry.)

RICE

This cereal is extensively cultivated in hot, moist climates such as that of India, Java, China, Japan, and parts of the United States and it is the staple food of half the human race. In some parts of the world two harvests a year can be obtained.

After threshing, the rice grain is left in its

tough husk; in the milling process, first this husk and then the inner skin are removed. Since most of the B vitamins are found in the inner skin, white "polished" rice has less food value than "unpolished" brown rice, though the latter has the slight disadvantage of taking longer to cook. Attempts are now being made to preserve more of the nutritive value of rice by steaming it before milling, so that the thiamin and nicotinic acid are absorbed by the white grain; this "parboiled" or "converted" rice is then polished and is greatly superior in nutritive value to ordinary white rice.

Shapes of Grain

There are three main kinds of rice grain – long, medium, and short,

The long slender grains are fluffy and separate when cooked so they are ideal in combination with other foods and for rice used as an accompaniment to dishes such as curries and stews. Medium- and short-grain rice are more moist and sticky. The medium grains are very suitable for dishes where the rice needs to be molded or bound together (e.g. rice rings, stuffings, and croquettes). Short-grain rice is used for rice puddings and other sweet rice dishes.

Types of Rice

REGULAR MILLED, LONG-GRAIN WHITE RICE

The hulls, germ, and most of the bran layers are removed. The rice is white in color, with only a bland, very slight flavor when cooked.

BROWN RICE

Whole unpolished grains of rice with only the inedible husk and a small amount of bran removed. It takes longer to cook than white rice (about 40 minutes), and more liquid. It is fawn color when cooked, and has a chewy texture and a pleasant, nutty flavour.

PARBOILED OR CONVERTED RICE

Cooked before milling by a special steam pressure process, which helps to retain the natural food value. It takes longer to cook than regular milled white rice (20 to 25 minutes), absorbs more liquid ($2\frac{1}{4}$ parts water to 1 part rice), but more easily produces a perfect result, with grains that are fluffy, separate, and plump when cooked.

PRECOOKED OR INSTANT RICE

This is completely cooked and then dehydrated. It is useful when in a hurry as it only needs heating in boiling water for about 5 minutes or as directed on the package.

RISOTTO RICE

Known as Arborio, a plump Italian rice which gives risotto its essentially creamy texture, with each grain firm in the center and slightly chewy.

WILD RICE

This is not actually rice, but seeds from a wild grass. Grown in the United States, it is expensive and not widely available, but delicious for special occasions, particularly with game.

Preparing and Cooking Rice

Rice sold in unbranded packages or loose should be washed before it is cooked. Put in a strainer and rinse it under cold water until all the loose starch (white powder) is washed off – it is this loose starch which prevents rice drying out into separate grains when cooked.

Storing and Reheating Rice

The rice can be cooked in quite large quantities and any not required can be stored in a covered container in a refrigerator for up to a week without any deterioration. To reheat, place about $\frac{1}{2}$ inch water in a pan, add some salt, bring to a boil and add the rice. Cover tightly, reduce the heat and simmer very gently for about 5 minutes. Place the rice in a strainer and rinse under hot water. Shake strainer to dry off rice; place over a saucepan of rapidly boiling water for 5 minutes to reheat rice and separate the grains.

BOILED RICE

Place 1 cup long-grain rice in a saucepan with 2 cups water and 1 teaspoon salt. Bring quickly to a boil, stir well and cover with a tightly fitting lid. Reduce heat and simmer gently for 14 to 15 minutes. Remove from the heat and before serving separate out the grains gently, using a fork. (The rice will not need draining.) If a drier effect is required, leave the rice covered for 5 to 10 minutes after it has been cooked. The grains should then be tender, but dry and quite separate. 1 cup rice gives 3 to 4 servings. Here are some points to remember when using this method:
1. Do not increase the amount of water or the finished rice will be soggy.
2. Do not uncover the rice while it is cooking or the steam will escape and the cooking time will be increased.
3. Do not stir the rice while it is simmering – it breaks up the grains and makes them soggy.
4. When the rice is cooked, do not leave it longer than 10 minutes before serving or the grains will stick together.

CURRIED RICE

1 onion, finely chopped
2 tablespoons butter
1 cup long-grain rice
⅓ cup currants or seedless raisins
½ teaspoon curry powder
2 cups chicken or beef broth
salt
pepper
2 tablespoons blanched almonds, slivered and
*   browned (optional)*

Sauté the onion in the butter for about 5 minutes, until soft. Add the rice and cook for 2 to 3 minutes, stirring continuously. Add the fruit, curry powder, broth, and seasoning and bring to a boil. Stir and cover with a lid, reduce the heat and simmer gently for 14 to 15 minutes. Stir in the almonds (if used) and serve.

Good with meat or chicken.

FLAVORED RICE

Although rice is most usually cooked in water, it can also be cooked in other liquids to give extra flavor and variety. The water may be replaced by any of the following:

Chicken or beef broth (fresh, canned, or made from a cube); canned tomato juice, undiluted, or use half and half with water; orange juice – use half and half with water.

Alternatively, rice can be flavored as in the following recipes:

SAVORY RICE
Sauté some chopped onion, pepper, celery, or bacon in a little butter in the pan before adding the rice.

HERBY RICE
Add a pinch of dried herbs with the cooking liquid (e.g. sage, marjoram, thyme, mixed herbs).

RAISIN RICE
Add seedless raisins (or currants) with the cooking liquid; a pinch of curry powder can also be added.

VARIETY RICE
When the rice is cooked stir in any of the following: diced pineapple, chopped canned pimiento, slivered brown almonds, grated cheese, chopped fresh herbs.

FRIED RICE

1 cup cooked long-grain rice
2 eggs, beaten
4 tablespoons peanut oil
½ teaspoon salt
½ onion, finely chopped
½ cup mushrooms, thinly sliced
2 tablespoons frozen peas
2 slices cooked ham, diced
2 teaspoons soy sauce.

The rice used in this dish should be cooked the day before using. Make a plain omelet from the eggs, cut it into thin strips and set aside. Sauté the rice, preferably in a nonstick pan, for about 5 minutes in 2 tablespoons very hot oil with the salt until light golden brown, stirring gently all the time; remove from the pan and set aside. Sauté the onion in the remaining oil for about 3 minutes, until lightly browned; add the remaining vegetables, rice, and the ham and cook for 3 minutes, stirring gently. Stir in the soy sauce and shredded omelet and cook to heat through.

RICE PUDDING

¼ cup short-grain rice
2 tablespoons sugar
2¼ cups milk
butter
whole nutmeg

Wash the rice and put it into a buttered 4-cup ovenproof dish with the sugar. Add the milk, dot with butter, and grate some nutmeg on top. Bake in a 300° oven for about 2 hours; stir it after about 30 minutes.

VARIATIONS
1. Add ⅓ cup dried fruit to the pudding.
2. Add 1 teaspoon ground cinnamon to the pudding before baking it; omit the nutmeg.

(See Kedgeree, Pilaf, and Risotto entries.)

RICE PAPER

A thin, semi-transparent, edible paper made from the pith of a plant grown in China. Macaroons and similar delicate cookies are often baked on the rice paper, which need not be pulled away before the cookies are eaten.

RICE WINE

A potent wine made in China and Japan. It resembles sherry in appearance and flavor.

RICKEY

An unsweetened long drink made originally from gin and seltzer, flavored with fresh lime. Today any unsweetened combination of liquor, fruit juice, and a carbonated beverage served in a short highball glass over ice is known as a rickey.

RICOTTA

An Italian unsalted cottage cheese. It is used for filling ravioli, and in cannelloni or lasagne dishes; also used in cheesecakes and cassata, a rich Sicilian cake, and other pastries.

RIESLING

A type of green grape used to make wines which are usually given this name. It is the classical German grape producing the best wines in that country. Most of the grapes are grown in the Mosel and Rheingau areas. The wines are comparatively expensive as the Riesling only gives about half as much wine per plant as other varieties of grapes. Good Riesling wines are also produced in Austria and Alsace. The grapes are also grown in Australia, South Africa, Chile, and California but the climates are too hot for producing the excellent wine made in Germany.

RIGATONI

A large Italian pasta, tubular with a ribbed surface, about 3 inches in length. It is considered a good pasta with hearty sauces.

RIGATONI WITH SAUSAGE

8 oz sweet or hot Italian sausages, sliced
1 tablespoon oil
1 onion, chopped
1 clove garlic, chopped
8 oz mushrooms, sliced
2 cups tomato puree
bay leaf
salt and pepper
8 oz rigatoni, cooked
grated Parmesan cheese

Cook the sausage in a skillet with the oil for about 10 minutes. Pour off most of the fat and add the onion and garlic. Cook until the onion is wilted and add the mushrooms. When they in turn are limp, add the tomato puree and bay leaf. Simmer for 30 minutes and season with salt and pepper. Place the rigatoni in a baking dish and cover with the sauce. Sprinkle liberally with cheese and bake in a 350° oven until bubbling and browned.

RILLETTES

A French preparation of pork. The meat is cooked very gently and slowly in pork fat, seasoned with salt and pepper and spices and pounded or shredded. The meat is packed into ramekins and sealed with fat. Rillettes keep well in the refrigerator for as long as 2 weeks if the seal remains unbroken.

PORK RILLETTES

2 lb fatty pork, cut into $\frac{1}{4}$-inch dice
8 oz pork back fat, cut into $\frac{1}{4}$-inch dice
$\frac{1}{2}$ cup water
bouquet garni
2 cloves garlic, crushed
bay leaf
allspice
salt and pepper

Combine the pork, back fat, water, bouquet garni, garlic, and bay leaf in a heavy casserole and place in a 300° oven for $2\frac{1}{2}$ hours. Reduce heat to 275° and cook $2\frac{1}{2}$ hours longer, stirring from time to time to prevent sticking.

Drain the meat in a strainer, discarding the bouquet garni and bay leaf, and shred it. Season with allspice, salt, and pepper and pack into 4 individual ramekins. When the reserved fat has cooled, pour the clear part of it over the rillettes to seal. Refrigerate until solidified. Serve as a first course or as an appetizer with drinks.

RISOTTO

A famous Italian dish made by boiling rice in stock and flavoring it with onion, cheese, mushrooms, kidneys, white wine, etc., according to the type of risotto. Here are two typical recipes.

CHICKEN RISOTTO

$\frac{1}{2}$ fowl or 2–3 good-sized chicken parts, uncooked
6 tablespoons butter
2 small onions, finely chopped
1 stalk celery, finely chopped
1 green pepper, seeded and finely chopped
$\frac{1}{2}$ sliced mushrooms
1 clove garlic, crushed
3 strips bacon or slices of ham, chopped
$\frac{2}{3}$ cup dry white wine
chicken stock
salt and pepper
chopped fresh herbs as available
1 cup long-grain rice
grated Parmesan cheese

Skin the chicken, bone it and cut the flesh in strips. Melt 2 tablespoons of the butter and sauté half the chopped onion and the garlic for 5 minutes, until soft. Add the chicken, the remaining vegetables, and the bacon or ham and sauté for a few minutes longer, stirring continuously. Add the wine and let it bubble until well reduced; just cover with chicken stock and add the seasoning and herbs. Cover and simmer for about 1 hour, until the chicken is tender. Drain off the juices; make up to 2 cups with more stock if required.

Sauté the remaining onion in 2 tablespoons remaining butter for about 5 minutes, until soft. Add the rice and stir until transparent. Add the chicken stock and bring to a boil. Cover and simmer for 10 minutes. Fold in the chicken mixture, stir well, and continue cooking until the two mixtures are well blended and the liquid absorbed. Stir in the remaining butter and some Parmesan cheese and serve.

SHELLFISH RISOTTO

1 onion, chopped
6 tablespoons butter
1 cup long-grain rice
$\frac{2}{3}$ cup dry white wine
4 cups chicken stock
salt and pepper
1 clove garlic, crushed, optional
8 oz shrimp
grated Parmesan cheese

Prepare the risotto as above, using 4 tablespoons of the butter. Just before the rice becomes tender, gently sauté the garlic (if used) and the shellfish in the remaining 2 tablespoons butter for 5 minutes. Stir into the risotto and serve with cheese.

A few sliced button mushrooms can be sautéed with the shellfish or a few frozen peas or strips of canned pimiento can be added to the risotto just before the rice is cooked. Other shellfish, such as crab or lobster meat (fresh or canned) may also be used; or a mixture of shellfish, with possibly a few mussels (canned or fresh).

RISSOLE

A rissole is a small croquette enclosed in a thin envelope of pastry before being fried or baked and served as an hors d'oeuvre.

In Great Britain the term has come to mean a small roll or round cake, made of cooked ground meat bound with mashed potatoes, which is coated in egg and bread crumbs and fried in hot fat. They are served as a supper or light luncheon dish, with a brown or tomato sauce.

RISSOLES BRITISH STYLE

$1-1\frac{1}{4}$ cups cooked ground beef
$\frac{1}{2}$ small onion, grated
1 lb potatoes, boiled and mashed
1 tablespoon sweet pickle
salt
pepper
beaten egg
dry bread crumbs for coating
shallow fat for frying

Mix the meat, onion, and potatoes and add the pickle and a generous amount of seasoning. Stir until well blended. Turn onto a floured board, form into a roll, and cut into slices about 1-inch thick. Shape these into round cakes, coat with the beaten egg and then with crumbs. Fry on both sides in the fat until golden. Drain well on absorbent paper before serving.

VARIATIONS
1. Replace the ground meat by a can of corned beef, finely chopped.
2. Omit the pickle and season with 1 tablespoon chopped parsley, 1 teaspoon mixed dried herbs or 1–2 teaspoons curry powder.

ROACH

A small freshwater fish of the carp family found in the waters of northern Europe. It has white flesh, which turns red when cooked. It must be well cleaned with salt to counteract its muddy flavor. It is usually sautéed or broiled.

ROASTING AND BAKING

A method of cooking by radiant heat. True roasting is done on a spit in front of an open fire or on a rotisserie. The meat turns continuously to cook it evenly throughout; to keep it succulent it should be basted frequently. (See Rotisserie entry.)

The term roasting is usually applied to cooking meat in an oven although in a strict sense this is baking. Many cuts of meat are suitable for roasting (see individual meat entries). Poultry and game can also be roasted; younger birds only should be used, the older ones being more suitable for stewing and braising.

To cook roasts from frozen, see individual Beef, Lamb, and Pork entries.

Roasting Meat in the Oven
Meat is roasted in the oven either at the traditional high temperature of 425° when it is seared

quickly on the outside, giving a good, meaty flavor, or in a 375° oven when the roast is more moist, there is less shrinking and (since the fibers are broken down) the meat is more tender, though some people consider that the flavor is not quite so good.

Arrange the shelves in the oven so that the meat is in the center. Put the meat in a roasting pan so that the largest cut surfaces are exposed and the thickest layer of fat is on top; this automatically bastes the roast. If the fat is thin, top the meat with $\frac{1}{4}$ cup butter or lard. Do not prick the meat with a fork or anything sharp while it is cooking or you will lose some of the juices. If you turn or lift the joint, use two spoons.

BASTING

If the hot fat and juices from the pan are spooned over the roast several times during the cooking period, the flavor is improved and the meat is moist and juicy.

ROASTING ON A RACK

If the meat is cooked on a rack standing inside a roasting pan, the finished result will be less fatty.

ROASTING IN A COVERED PAN

Using a covered pan produces a moist roast (and incidentally keeps the inside of the oven clean). However, because the meat is in reality being steamed, it is pale in color and doesn't have as good a flavor as when it is roasted in an open pan. You can remove the lid during the last 30 minutes of the cooking time and brown the roast.

ROASTING IN FOIL

If the meat is wrapped in aluminum foil before it is put in the roasting pan it will be moist and tender and will not shrink so much. However, foil wrapping has the same effect as roasting in a closed pan and the meat will not develop as much flavor and color. The foil should therefore be opened during the last 30 minutes of the cooking time, so that the roast can become crisp and brown.

ROASTING WRAPS AND BAGS

The main purpose of these is to keep the oven clean while the meat roasts. The bag or wrap also collects the meat juices together, and if a little flour is sprinkled inside the bag before inserting the meat, you have ready-made gravy at the end of the cooking time. The packages usually recommend cooking times and temperatures – usually up to 400°. Instructions suggest piercing or slitting the bag or wrap before cooking, to allow for expansion of air. To obtain crisp, browned meat, the wrap or bag should be opened during the last 30 minutes of the cooking time.

ROASTING ON A SPIT

The latest roasting method is in effect a return to the older ways. Cookers are available with an attached spit roaster, or you can buy one separately. Meat roasted on an open spit has a much better flavor than oven-roasted meat; spit-roasting in the oven, however, shows little difference from ordinary oven roasting. (See Rotisserie entry.)

MEAT THERMOMETERS

Some people find a meat thermometer a great help when roasting meat. Insert it into the thickest part of the roast before it is put into the oven. When the thermometer registers the required internal temperature (see chart), the meat will be correctly cooked. The thermometer is particularly useful with beef, insuring that you can have it rare, medium, or well done, to your particular taste. (It is, of course, still necessary to work out the approximate length of cooking time, in order to know at what time cooking should be started). Make sure the thermometer does not touch the bone.

A thermometer is essential if you are cooking meat from frozen.

USING A MEAT THERMOMETER

BEEF:

Rare	140°
Medium	160°
Well done	170°

VEAL	170°

LAMB:

Medium	160°
Well done	170°

PORK:

Cured cooked	140°
Cured uncooked	160°
Fresh	170°

POULTRY	185°

Pot Roasting

This method of cooking meat in a covered pan is particularly suitable for small, compact pieces and for cuts which are inclined to be tough, such as breast (boned, stuffed, and rolled); brisket; round; chuck.

ROBERT SAUCE

A piquant sauce containing onion, dry white wine, vinegar, espagnole or demi-glace sauce and mustard. A quick version may be made by substituting stock for the espagnole, but the sauce will not have the same full flavor.

ROBERT SAUCE

1 small onion, finely chopped
2 tablespoons butter
⅔ cup dry white wine
1 tablespoon wine vinegar
1¼ cups espagnole or demi-glace sauce
1–2 teaspoons mild prepared mustard
pinch of sugar
salt and pepper

Sauté the onion gently in the butter for about 10 minutes without browning. Add the wine and vinegar and boil rapidly until reduced by half. Stir in the sauce and simmer for 10 minutes. Add the mustard, a little sugar, and extra seasoning if necessary.

Serve with hot or cold meats, especially chops, steaks, pork, and goose when the tangy sauce will liven up the bland flavor of the meat.

ROCAMBOLE

A European plant, related to the onion, which bears "fruits" at the top of the stem; these resemble garlic, but are not so pungent.

ROCK CAKE

British cookies containing fruit and spice, which are baked in small heaps on a pan or baking sheet. The mixture must not be too wet or the cookies will spread and lose their "rocky" shape.

ROCKET

(See Cress Entry.)

ROCKFISH

(See Striped Bass entry.)

ROE

The spawn or milt of a fish. In many cases it is only suitable for cooking as part of the fish, but the roes of shad, herring, and cod are often used to make separate dishes. Sturgeon's roe, commonly called caviar, is an expensive delicacy used as an appetizer or for cocktail savories.

COD ROE

To cook raw roe, tie in cheesecloth and poach gently in salted water with a few peppercorns, until it is tender (30 minutes to 1 hour, according to thickness). Lift it out and allow to cool. Cut the roe in slices, dip in seasoned flour, eggs and crumbs and sauté in hot butter until golden brown. Serve on toast or with sautéed potatoes, accompanied by sliced lemon or tartar sauce.

SMOKED COD'S ROE

It may be served as an appetizer, accompanied by slices of lemon and toast or brown bread and butter. Smoked cod's roe also forms the basis for the famous Greek appetizer, Taramasalata.

ROEBUCK

The male roe deer, a small Eurasian deer, the meat of which is known as venison. (See Venison entry.)

ROLL, BREAD

Rolls may be made in numerous shapes and from many kinds of dough; certain textures are traditionally associated with certain shapes, thus finger-shaped sandwich or bridge rolls are soft; Vienna rolls, made with water, are crisp and very light; soft rolls (which may be made in various shapes) are made with milk, croissants are made from a dough with extra butter rolled into it.

Rolls become tough when stale, but this can be remedied by sprinkling with water and reheating in a 350° oven to freshen them. This process cannot be repeated because the rolls will remain hard.

SOFT ROLLS

1½ teaspoons active yeast
1 teaspoon sugar
about ⅔ cup tepid milk
2 cups bread flour
1 teaspoon salt
2 tablespoons margarine or lard

Dissolve the yeast and sugar in the milk and leave until frothy. Mix the flour and salt and rub in the fat. Add the yeast liquid and mix to a fairly soft dough, adding a little more milk if necessary. Beat well and knead on a floured board until smooth. Allow to rise in a warm place (about 75°) until doubled in size, knead lightly on a floured board, divide into 8 pieces and shape in any of the following ways:

BRAID

Divide a small piece of dough into three, shape each into a long roll and braid together, joining the ends securely.

TWIST

Divide a piece of dough into two, shape into long rolls, twist together and secure the ends.

PARKER HOUSE

Roll the dough out and cut into 3-inch circles. Brush with melted butter, make a crease across the center and fold so that the dough does not quite overlap; press to seal.

FAN TAN

Roll the dough into a rectangle and cut into 6 strips, each about $1\frac{1}{2}$ inches wide. Brush with melted butter and pile the strips evenly on top of each other. Cut into 1-inch lengths and set to rise and bake in greased muffin pans.

CLOVERLEAF

Shape the dough into 1-inch balls. Bake in greased muffin pans, 3 balls in each cup.

CRESCENT

Roll the dough into a circle and cut into 16 pieces. Roll each piece into a crescent, starting at the large end. Curve slightly on the baking sheet.

KNOT

Shape each piece into a long roll and tie a knot.

Unless directed to place the roll in a muffin pan, put it on a greased baking sheet. Let all rolls rise.

QUICK WHOLE-WHEAT ROLLS

Substitute 1 cup whole-wheat flour for 1 cup bread flour in the Soft Rolls recipe. Divide into 12 pieces, place on a floured baking sheet, cover with greased plastic wrap and leave to rise until doubled in size. Bake at the top of a 425° oven for about 20 minutes.

ROLLMOP

A marinated herring fillet, usually rolled round a small gherkin or onion and secured with a pick. They are served as appetizers.

ROLY-POLY

A traditional suet pudding of Great Britain. Pastry made with suet is rolled into a rectangle, spread with a filling such as jam or mincemeat and rolled up like a jelly roll. It is loosely wrapped in greased aluminum foil (but tightly sealed) and steamed for $1\frac{1}{2}$ to 2 hours over boiling water. Roly-poly is usually served with a custard sauce. To make, use the pastry in Steamed Suet Pudding, roll it into a 9 × 11 inch rectangle and spread with about 6 tablespoons mincemeat. Brush the edges of the pastry with milk before rolling from the short side.

ROMAINE

(See Lettuce entry.)

ROMANO

An off-white Italian grating cheese with a sharp tangy flavor. It is made with a combination of cow's and goat's milk.

ROOT VEGETABLES

This term includes such vegetables as carrots, beets, turnips, rutabagas, parsnips, radishes, and salsify; it is often used also for potatoes and Jerusalem artichokes, though these are actually tubers, also for kohlrabi and celeriac (which are swollen stems) and onions, which are bulbs. Most of these vegetables are cooked and eaten hot, though some, especially carrots, may be used raw in salads. Cold cooked beets, carrots, turnips, parsnips and, of course, potatoes, may be included in salads. Radishes are seldom cooked, but are usually used raw as an appetizer or in salads.

Cooking: For the general preparation and cooking see the individual vegetable entries. The most usual ways of cooking root vegetables are boiling, steaming, and baking.

Frozen and dehydrated root vegetables should be treated according to the instructions on the package.

Serving: Boiled root vegetables are usually drained and tossed with seasoning and a little melted butter. Parsnips, turnips, and rutabagas may be mashed with a little milk, seasoning, and butter or cream. Carrots when old may be served with a sauce. Potatoes may be treated in a multitude of ways.

ROQUEFORT

A cheese of a pale cream color, with a blue mold; it originated in the South of France and is made with ewes' milk. The characteristic pungent flavor is acquired by storing the cheeses in the natural caves in the Roquefort district for about 40 days while they mature. The atmospheric conditions in this part of France make the French type superior to other types produced elsewhere.

ROSE HIP

Hips, the fully ripe dark red fruits of the wild rose, are valuable for their high vitamin C content. They are not suitable for eating raw, as they are sour and have many hard seeds and irritating silky hairs. When cooked they may be made into an agreeable preserve or a pleasant-flavored syrup, which may be taken by itself or used to add extra sweetness and food value to sauces and cold desserts.

ROSEMARY

A fragrant evergreen shrub of the mint family, native to the Mediterranean region and now widely cultivated as a flavoring herb. It has grayish leaves and blue flowers and the fragrance and taste are refreshing and somewhat piny.

In its fresh state, rosemary is generally used in chopped form, while the dry leaves may be used whole or finely ground. It is a good addition to stuffings, stews, roast meat, herb dumplings, and many similar dishes, but must be used sparingly. It is particularly good with lamb, chicken, or rabbit.

ROSE WATER

This is either distilled from rose petals or prepared from rose oil and is usually employed to give a pleasant flavor and aroma to a cooked dish. It is widely used in Middle Eastern cooking.

ROSOLIO

A bright red liqueur made in Italy and France; it is flavoured with either oil of roses or tangerine rind, orange juice, and orange blossom.

ROTISSERIE

A method of cooking which has developed from the old-fashioned spit over an open fire. The main advantages are that the meat bastes itself, there is little splashing, and the flavor, which some consider to be better than oven-roasted meat. Rotisserie units are fitted on many ranges and separate electric and battery-operated units are also available.

A rotisserie attachment consists of:

A *Shaft* on which the food is impaled.

Holding Forks which slide on the shaft and can be secured by thumbscrews to hold the food firmly in place.

The *Motor* into which the loaded shaft is fitted.

The *Tray* placed under the revolving shaft to catch the drippings from the food as it cooks.

GENERAL HINTS FOR USING A ROTISSERIE UNIT
1. Prepare the food in the usual way.
2. Push one end of the holding forks onto the shaft and secure it. Place the food on the shaft, pushing this through the center of the food. Push on the second holding fork and secure.
3. Turn on the heat and allow the broiler or oven to get very hot.
4. Place the loaded shaft in position (follow instruction booklet with cooker).
5. Turn on the rotisserie motor and allow the shaft to revolve several times before leaving it, to make sure there is no obstruction and that it is turning evenly.
6. Reduce the heat and cook the food as instructed by the manufacturers.

The food may be basted from time to time with the fat and juices in the tray or with any suitable flavoring. A slice of onion or garlic can be added to the drippings to give extra flavor.

Kebab cookery (see Shish Kebab entry) has become more popular. Special Kebab attachments are now supplied with some rotisserie units. These consist of a number of skewers which are revolved by the rotisserie motor.

ROUGHAGE

The name given to carbohydrate which is not available to the body as food, passing through without being assimilated. Most roughage consists of cellulose, the fibrous material which composes much of the stiffer structures of vegetables and cereal foods. Roughage is digested to a very small degree by bacterial fermentation in the intestines and makes a quite insignificant contribution to the diet. Its great value is in stimulating the contraction and evacuation of the bowels. There is some medical evidence to show that diseases of the bowel have increased in recent years due to food becoming more refined. Hence, there is considerable publicity to encourage more roughage to be included in the diet.

ROULADE

A thin slice of meat covered with a stuffing and rolled up. It is also a rolled cake made from a soufflé-type batter. It can be filled with a savory mixture and served as an hors d'oeuvre or with something sweet, in which case it becomes a dessert.

ROUND (LEG AND HAM)

A retail cut of meat. The round of beef corresponds to the leg (round) of veal, the leg (ham) of pork and the leg of lamb. The only bone contained in center cut steaks from the round, leg, or ham is a cross-section of the leg bone.

Beef round is divided into the Sirloin tip and the Round, which includes top, bottom and eye of round. A beef round steak does not contain any part of the sirloin tip, which is a separate cut, but the tip is contained in veal, lamb, and pork steaks.

Beef cuts from the round include the Round steak (with portions of the top, bottom and eye of round all included), Top round steak, Bottom round steak or pot roast, Eye of round roast, Standing rump roast, Rolled rump roast, and Heel of round roast.

Veal cuts include the Round steak, Boneless cutlets, Standing rump roast, Shank half of leg, Center leg, and Rolled leg.

Pork cuts from the ham (leg) include Smoked or fresh ham shank portion, Smoked or fresh ham butt portion, Smoked ham center slice, Rolled fresh leg, Smoked ham boneless roll and Canned ham.

Lamb leg cuts include the Sirloin half of leg, Shank half of leg, Leg (sirloin on or off), the Rolled leg, Leg chop (steak), and the Hind shank.

ROUX

This mixture, which forms the foundation of many sauces, is made by cooking together equal amounts of fat and flour. For white roux the mixture is cooked until it resembles a cream colored paste, for blond roux it is cooked to a pale fawn color; and for brown roux to a rich golden brown.

SIMPLE WHITE SAUCE – ROUX METHOD

FOR CREAMED FOODS AND AS A BASE FOR OTHER SAUCES
2 tablespoons butter or margarine
2 tablespoons flour
1 cup milk or milk and stock
salt and pepper

Melt the butter and the flour and stir with a wooden spoon until smooth. Cook over a gentle heat for 2 to 3 minutes, stirring until the mixture (called a roux) begins to bubble. Remove from the heat and add the liquid gradually, stirring after each addition to prevent lumps forming. Bring the sauce to a boil, stirring continuously, and when it has thickened, cook for 1 to 2 minutes longer. Add salt and pepper to taste.

FOR SOUFFLÉS
3 tablespoons butter or margarine
3 tablespoons flour
1 cup milk or milk and stock
salt and pepper

Make the sauce as above.

BINDING CONSISTENCY (PANADA)
3 tablespoons butter or margarine
⅓ cup flour
1 cup milk or milk and stock
salt and pepper

Melt the butter, add the flour, and stir well. Cook gently for 2 to 3 minutes, stirring, until the roux begins to bubble and leave the sides of the pan. Off the heat, add the liquid gradually, bring to a boil, stirring continuously, and cook for 1 to 2 minutes after it has thickened; add salt and pepper to taste. This very thick sauce is used for binding mixtures such as croquettes.

ROWAN BERRY

The bright red fruit of the mountain ash. Rowan berries are occasionally used in making a jelly to serve with game and may also be pureed and added to applesauce to vary the flavor.

ROYAL ICING

The hard, white icing, made from egg whites and sugar, which is used for coating Christmas and other cakes that are to be decorated and kept for some time. It is usually applied over a coating of almond paste.

ROYAL ICING

Allow 4 egg whites to every 2 lb powdered sugar; 1 tablespoon glycerine may be added to give a softer texture. Sift the sugar twice. Separate the eggs, place the whites in a bowl, and

FLAT ICING A CAKE
1. Work icing with a spatula in a to-and-fro motion across cake until covered.

2. Draw a metal ruler across the top of the cake, then again at right angles to the first stroke.

3. Work the remaining icing onto the side of the cake then draw a dough scraper around the side.

stir slightly – just sufficiently to break up the albumin, but without including too many air bubbles. Add half the sugar and stir until well mixed, using a wooden spoon; beat for about 5 to 10 minutes, or until the icing is smooth, glossy, and white. Cover the bowl with a damp cloth and let stand for at least 30 minutes, to allow any air bubbles to rise to the surface.

Gradually add the remaining sugar until the required consistency is obtained. When the icing is intended for flat work, stand a wooden spoon upright in it – if the consistency is correct it will fall slowly to one side. For rough icing, the mixture should be stiff enough for peaks to be easily formed on the surface when you pull it up with the spoon. Add any desired coloring. If possible, leave the icing overnight in an airtight container in a cool place before use. To obtain an extremely smooth result, just before using the icing, remove 1 tablespoon of it and mix to a coating consistency with water, return it to the rest and mix until smooth.

NOTES
1. Royal icing can be made quite satisfactorily in an electric mixer; set the control on medium speed and whisk the egg whites slightly. Add the sifted sugar gradually until the mixture is of the required consistency. It is important to avoid overbeating and to allow the icing to stand for 24 hours before using it.
2. When using royal icing, it is advisable to keep the bowl and/or pastry bags covered with a damp cloth or a polyethylene bag to prevent a crust forming on the icing.

To rough-ice a cake: Place 1 teaspoon of the icing on the cake board and put on the cake firmly, centering it accurately. Spoon the icing on top of

the cake. Working with a spatula in a to-and-fro motion until the air bubbles are broken, cover the top and side of the cake evenly. Now draw a clean ruler or spatula across the top of the cake evenly and steadily, until the surface is smooth. Using a round-bladed knife, draw the icing up into peaks around the side and in a 1½-inch border around the top of the cake or as liked. Before the icing is set, you can put on one or two simple decorations.

If you want a very simply decorated cake, put almond paste on the top of the cake only and then royal icing on the top and down the side for about 1 inch, so that the almond paste is hidden. Rough-ice the side and make a border around the cake as above. Decorate as desired and tie a ribbon around the cake below the icing. For this sort of decoration use half the suggested amounts of almond paste and royal icing.

To flat-ice a cake: Place the cake on a cake board. Spoon about half the icing on top of it and with a spatula work with a to-and-fro motion across the icing until the air bubbles are broken and the top of the cake is well and evenly covered. Some of the icing will work down the side of the cake so return this to the bowl. Now draw an icing ruler or the spatula across the top of the cake evenly and steadily. Draw it across again at right angles to the first stroke until the surface is smooth. If possible, leave the cake for 24 hours. (In this case, put the icing from the bowl into a polyethylene bag and store in the refrigerator.)

Put the cake and board on an upturned plate or a turntable and work the remaining icing onto the side of the cake. Draw a ruler, knife, or dough scraper around the side until it is smooth. Smooth out the seam between the top and side, then leave to set for at least 24 hours. Finally, remove any unevenness with a sharp knife.

If liked, apply a second layer of icing to give a smoother finish. Save a little of the royal icing and mix it with a little water to give a coating consistency; pour onto the center of the cake then, using a knife, spread it over the top and down the side. Knock the board gently up and down on the table to bring any air bubbles to the surface, so that they can be burst with a pin before the icing sets. Leave to harden for 2 to 3 days.

ROYAL JELLY

The food given to certain bee larvae, which causes them to become queen bees.

It is claimed – without any scientific proof – to have certain magical effects on human health.

ROYAN

A delicately-flavored fish similar to a sardine, caught off the coast of France.

RUBBING IN

A method of incorporating fat into flour, used in Great Britain for making short pastries and plain cakes. The fat and flour are rubbed between the fingertips until the mixture resembles fine bread crumbs. It is similar to cutting in (see separate entry).

RUM

An alcoholic beverage distilled from molasses and made chiefly in the Caribbean region, especially where sugar cane is a major crop – Jamaica, Barbados, Trinidad, Guyana, Martinique, Cuba, Virgin Islands and Puerto Rico. Two types are generally available: Puerto Rican, or light; and Jamaican, or dark. The former is used for cocktails such as the Daiquiri (labeled "white") or highballs (labeled "golden"). The stronger tasting Jamaican rums are used for hot toddies and punches (see Punch entry). Familiar to travelers in the Caribbean is planter's punch, made with a variety of rums and fruit juices.

RUNNER BEAN

(See Beans, Green entry.)

RUSK

This may mean a type of sweetened tea biscuit, a piece of bread or cake dried in the oven, or a commercially-made product intended especially for young children and invalids. Both the last two types of rusk are frequently given to babies when they are teething and also to older children to keep their teeth in good condition. Plain rusks are sometimes served with cheese as an alternative to crackers or bread.

RUTABAGA

A plant of the cabbage family, also known as the Swedish turnip (or Swede). The stem swells underground to form a large fleshy root, orange-yellow in color. It contains more vitamins A and C than does the white turnip. Considered a cool climate crop, most of the rutabagas eaten in the United States are imported from Canada. It can be served as a separate vegetable and used in soups or in other dishes combined with bacon or cheese.

Preparation and cooking: Rutabagas should be peeled thickly, so that all the tough outer skin is removed. They may be sliced, diced, or cut into fancy shapes. Keep them covered with water and cook as soon after peeling as possible. Boil till tender in a little salted water with the lid on, about 30 to 60 minutes (according to size and age). Drain and mash with a little salt, pepper, grated nutmeg and a piece of butter. Or, roast them as follows: Cut in chunks or fingers and cook around a roast, or in a separate pan with drippings, allowing 1 to $1\frac{1}{4}$ hours, according to the size of the pieces. Serve round the roast.

RYE

A hardy cereal which will grow in cold climates and in poor soil. The grain, which is brown and hard, with a slightly sour taste, is often mixed with other flours in breadmaking, and is used for making pumpernickel bread. It is also used for making special thin, dry, crisp crackers.

The composition of rye flour varies with its source and the milling, the protein content being double and the calcium treble in the whole-grain flour, as compared with a low-extraction rye one; the calorific values of high-extraction rye flour are about the same as those of white flour (see Flour entry), but the calcium content is slightly higher in rye flour. The gluten content of rye flour is very poor and unless some other flour is mixed with it it makes a damp, heavy bread.

A whisky distilled from rye is popular in the United States and the Russian drink Kvass is also made from it.

SABAYON

This French version of the Italian zabaglione denotes a sweet sauce served hot with warm desserts. It can also be cooled and served as a dessert accompanied by delicate cookies or as a sauce for fresh fruits. It is a light frothy mixture made from eggs, sugar, and wine or sherry; it is not quite as thick as zabaglione.

SABAYON SAUCE (COLD)

$\frac{1}{4}$ cup sugar
$\frac{1}{3}$ cup water
2 egg yolks, beaten
grated rind of $\frac{1}{2}$ lemon
juice of 1 lemon
$2\frac{1}{2}$ tablespoons rum or sherry
$2\frac{1}{2}$ tablespoons half-and-half

Dissolve the sugar in the water and boil for 2 to 3 minutes, until syrupy. Pour slowly onto the yolks, beating until pale and thick. Add the lemon rind, lemon juice, and rum or sherry and beat a few minutes longer. Fold in the cream and chill well.

Serve with fresh fruit, particularly berries.

SABLEFISH

A marine food fish of the Pacific coast of North America. It is sold whole, filleted or as steaks and is kippered and smoked. Broil or bake whole fish, steaks, or fillets and sauté steaks or fillets.

SACCHARIN

A white crystaline powder, manufactured from coal tar, which has remarkable sweetening properties. It has no food value and passes through the body unchanged: it is therefore used to sweeten food for people suffering from diabetes or other illnesses in which sugar is forbidden, or for those who wish to lose weight. In times of sugar-shortage saccharin has been widely used in drinks, cakes, puddings, etc. There is some controversy over the addition of artificial sweeteners to food, as large doses have shown ill-effects in animals. However, saccharin is permitted in certain foods, but it should be shown as an ingredient on the label.

The sweetening power of saccharin is about 550 times more than that of sugar. It is sold in the form of small white tablets, containing 0.2 grains of saccharin: $\frac{1}{2}$ to 1 tablet is generally enough to sweeten a cup of tea or coffee. Saccharin tablets dissolve much more readily in hot liquids than in cold. The taste is improved if a little sugar is added with the saccharin.

Saccharin in Cooking

For sweetening fruit juice, jellies, and molds use 1 to 2 tablets to 1 cup juice.

For junket and milk puddings use $\frac{1}{2}$ to 1 tablet to 1 cup milk.

For puddings and cakes use 3 tablets saccharin and 6 tablespoons sugar to 2 cups flour.

NOTES
1. When saccharin is used for sweetening stewed fruit, milk puddings, etc., the tablets should be added after cooking or a bitter taste results.

2. Saccharin is not satisfactory for canning owing to a bitter flavor which develops. It is preferable to can the fruit in water and to add saccharin at the time of serving.

3. It is important to use some sugar with the saccharin in cakes and puddings, as this helps to give the desired texture.

JAM MADE WITH SACCHARIN

As saccharin has neither setting nor preserving qualities, it is necessary to add gelatin to obtain a good set. The jars containing the cooked jam must be sterilized and hermetically sealed, otherwise it will not keep satisfactorily. It is advisable to put the jam in small jars, since it does not keep well once the jar is opened.

SACHERTORTE

A world-famous chocolate cake made originally at the Sacher Hotel in Vienna, Austria. It was invented by Eduard Sacher in 1832 while in the employ of the legendary Austrian statesman Prince Metternich. When Sacher opened his hotel, the cake became associated with it. The Sachertorte depends for leaven upon air beaten into the batter.

SACHERTORTE

$\frac{2}{3}$ cup sweet butter, softened
$\frac{3}{4}$ cup sugar
8 egg yolks
6 oz semisweet chocolate, melted and cooled
10 egg whites
$\frac{2}{3}$ cup flour
apricot jam

Cream the butter and half of the sugar in a mixer bowl until very light and fluffy. Beat in the egg yolks, one at a time, then gradually add the chocolate, beating in as much air as possible.

Beat the egg whites until soft peaks form, then gradually beat in the remaining sugar. Fold in the egg whites lightly into the chocolate mixture alternately with the flour (sift the flour over the surface). Pour the batter into a greased and floured 8-inch springform pan. Bake in a 350° oven for 1$\frac{1}{4}$ hours, or until the cake shrinks from the side of the pan.

When the cake is cool, remove from the pan and invert. Slice in half horizontally and cover with apricot jam. Sandwich the cake together and cover the top with jam. Place the cake on a wire rack and pour chocolate glaze over it. Refrigerate until the glaze is firm.

CHOCOLATE GLAZE

3 oz unsweetened chocolate
$\frac{3}{4}$ cup heavy cream
1$\frac{1}{4}$ cups sugar
1 teaspoon corn syrup
1 egg, beaten
1 teaspoon vanilla

Combine the chocolate, cream, sugar, and syrup in a saucepan and cook over low heat, stirring constantly, until the chocolate is melted. Increase heat and bring to a boil; cook without stirring for 5 minutes. Pour a little of the mixture into the egg and stir. Pour back into the chocolate mixture and stir over low heat until the glaze makes a thick coating on the back of a spoon. Remove from heat and add the vanilla. When the glaze reaches room temperature, place the cake on a wire rack and pour the glaze over it. Refrigerate before serving.

SACK

An old name for various white wines, particularly those from Spain and the Canaries; sherry is the only modern representative of the family.

SADDLE OF LAMB

This comprises the undivided loin section from both sides of the animal, from the end of the ribs to the leg. When trimmed and ready for roasting it weighs 3$\frac{1}{2}$ to 4 lb and feeds 4 to 6 people. It is an expensive but elegant roast.

SAFFLOWER OIL

An oil extracted from the seeds of a flowering plant. It is classed with other vegetable oils (such as corn oil and sunflower oil), as it contains a high proportion of polyunsaturated fatty acids.

The dried and powdered flowers are also used as a coloring in foods and cosmetics.

SAFFRON

The yellow powder obtainable by drying the flower stigmas of the *Crocus sativus*. It has an aromatic and slightly bitter taste and is used as a flavoring for certain cakes and buns and for bouillabaisse and for various rice dishes, such as risotto Milanese and paella. It is also used to color certain foodstuffs (e.g. alcoholic beverages). Saffron must not be kept more than about a year, as after that time the color and flavor deteriorate. Always store in small air-tight containers.

SAGE

A strongly flavored herb with a slightly bitter taste. There are several varieties, red and green sage being used for culinary purposes. The leaves, in both fresh and dried form, are used to flavor meat dishes, stuffings, cheese and lentil dishes, soups and salads; the flowers may be used in salads. Sage tea was drunk to a considerable extent in England before the introduction of tea; it was thought to be a mild tonic and to soothe a sore throat. It was made by infusing $\frac{3}{4}$ oz fresh sage or $\frac{1}{4}$ oz dried sage in $2\frac{1}{4}$ cups boiling water. It was served with sugar and lemon to taste.

SAGE AND ONION STUFFING

2 large onions, chopped
2 tablespoons butter
2 cups fresh white bread crumbs
2 teaspoons dried sage
salt
pepper

Put the onions in a pan of cold water, bring to a boil and cook until tender, about 10 minutes. Drain well, add the remaining ingredients and mix well. Serve with pork or poultry.

SAGO

This pearly grain, obtained from the powdered pith of a type of palm, is similar in its uses to tapioca, appearing in puddings and as a thickener. Sago contains little beyond starch.

ST PIERRE

(See John Dory entry.)

SAKE

A Japanese alcoholic drink made by fermenting rice. It is colorless and quite still and is usually served warm in tiny porcelain bowls.

SALAD

The term "salad," which is used in some form in most European languages, is derived from the Latin, *sal*, salt, since a salad originally meant something "dipped in salt." The most widely used kind is probably that made of uncooked green plants, but an infinite variety of vegetables and fruits can be used, either cooked or uncooked, to make delicious dishes, many of which form a meal in themselves combined with a portion of protein, such as fish, cheese, egg, cold meat, etc. Salads can also include cooked rice or pasta, nuts, dried fruit and herbs.

The nutritive value of salads obviously varies according to the foods used. Their vitamin C content is increased if the ingredients include a good percentage of raw fruits or vegetables, but the vitamin C in salad plants is quickly lost, so it is important to use them as soon as possible after they are gathered and to prepare them carefully.

Salads should be attractively presented, either in large dishes or salad bowls or individual plates or hors d'oeuvre dishes. They are usually served with French dressing, mayonnaise, or something similar.

Salad plants and vegetables should be left uncut until required for use; then, using a sharp stainless knife, shred them coarsely rather than finely, to conserve the vitamins.

GREEN VEGETABLES
Wash quickly but thoroughly in running cold water, shake well over the sink and dry them by shaking in a salad basket or cloth. Shred lettuce with a stainless knife or break up the leaves with the fingers. Shred raw cabbage, Brussels sprouts, etc.

RAW CARROT
Peel or scrape and, if not used at once, keep covered in cold water. Grate just before serving.

LEFTOVER COOKED ROOT VEGETABLES
Dice neatly.

POTATOES
Boil the potatoes and when cold mix with French dressing; mayonnaise may be added to hot or cold potatoes.

BEETS
Cook, then dice, cut into strips or slice. If desired, beets may be allowed to stand for a time in vinegar. Raw beets may be grated and added to salads in small quantities to add flavor and a crunchy texture.

PEAS AND BEANS
Cook and allow to cool before adding to the salad.

CAULIFLOWER
This may be added cooked or uncooked: in either case, break it into flowerets – very small ones, if raw.

CELERY AND BELGIAN ENDIVE
Pull apart and wash or scrub each piece, then divide into suitable lengths.

CUCUMBER
Wipe and peel either completely or in strips; slice thinly. If the skin is unwaxed, it can be scored with a fork to give a decorative edge.

FRUITS
Prepare according to kind. The peel may if desired be removed – in the case of tomatoes, this is done more easily if the fruit is first dipped into boiling water for a moment.

CANNED VEGETABLES OR FRUIT
Any of these can be added to a salad. They should be well drained before use.

Garnishes for Salads
The following is a brief list; choose the garnish to contrast pleasantly with the salad.

Crimped slices of cucumber or lemon; celery curls; root vegetables cut into balls or fancy shapes; radish roses or lilies; diamond-shaped pieces of green beans, etc.; sliced hard-cooked egg; sieved egg yolk; egg whites chopped or sliced and cut into fancy shapes; whole flowers or petals of nasturtium, wild rose, or violet; balls of cream cheese, anchovy butter, etc.

It is important not to overgarnish a salad as it will not look appetizing.

Green Salads
These consist of one or more plants such as lettuce, endive, or watercress, tossed in a French or similar dressing. Prepare the salad plants, shake and dry them carefully and, if they are not required at once, leave covered in the refrigerator. Just before serving rub a clove of garlic or an onion around the inside of the salad bowl, add the dressing and toss the salad in it. If a still more delicate garlic flavor is desired, rub a clove of garlic on a cut piece of bread, toss this with the salad and then discard it.

Salads containing just one dressed vegetable or fruit are quite common, e.g. tomato and orange salads.

Good salad combinations include: Tomato and onion salad; celery and walnut salad; watercress and orange salad; cucumber and onion salad; pepper and onion salad.

RUSSIAN SALAD
(in aspic)

1 small cauliflower, cooked
1 envelope unflavored gelatin
1¾ cup chicken broth
4 tablespoons cooked peas
2 tablespoons cooked diced carrot
2 tablespoons cooked diced turnip
3 potatoes, cooked and diced
1 small beet, cooked and diced
2 tomatoes, peeled and diced
2 oz ham or tongue, diced
2 oz cooked shrimp
2 oz smoked salmon, cut in strips, optional
3 gherkins, chopped
1 tablespoon capers
few lettuce leaves, shredded
2–3 tablespoons salad dressing
4 olives
4 anchovy fillets

Divide the cauliflower into small sprigs. Make up the aspic with the chicken broth, following the manufacturer's instructions. When it is cold, pour a little into a ring mold and turn this round until the sides are coated with jelly. Decorate with a little of the peas and diced vegetables and allow to set. Set layers of vegetables, meat, fish, gherkins, and capers alternately with layers of aspic in the mold, reserving some of the vegetables. When the mold is set, turn it out. Toss the lettuce and remaining vegetables in the salad dressing and pile into the center of the mold. Decorate with olives and anchovy fillets.

Note: Failing a ring mold, use an ordinary mold; the remaining vegetables can be served in a border round the salad.

TOMATO SALAD

4 tomatoes
small piece of onion and ½ an apple (optional)
salt
pepper
3 tablespoons olive oil
1 tablespoon vinegar
chopped fresh basil or dried oregano to garnish
    (optional)

Peel the tomatoes, if desired, by first immersing in boiling water. Slice them and arrange neatly in a shallow dish; sprinkle with the chopped onion and apple, if using, and salt and pepper. Mix the oil and vinegar and pour over the salad. Garnish with herbs.

TOSSED FRESH SPINACH SALAD

⅓ cup salad oil
2½ tablespoons white wine vinegar
½ teaspoon dried basil or 1 teaspoon fresh
   chopped basil
salt and pepper
2 teaspoons finely grated lemon rind
4 oz fresh spinach
1 lettuce heart
6 radishes, trimmed and sliced
6 green onions, trimmed and sliced

Put the oil and vinegar in a screw-top jar with the basil, salt, pepper, and lemon rind. Shake well and leave to stand. Wash the spinach thoroughly, discarding any tough stems, then dry thoroughly. Wash and dry the lettuce. Using your fingertips, shred the spinach and lettuce into bite-size pieces. Mix with the sliced radishes and green onions, toss with the dressing and pile into a serving dish. Serve as a side salad with broiled or cold meats.

WALDORF SALAD

3 crisp eating apples
chantilly dressing
¾ cup finely diced celery
¼ cup chopped walnuts

Peel and slice the apples and immediately toss with the dressing. Gently fold in the remaining ingredients. Serve in lettuce cups if desired.

SALAD DRESSING

While there are many recipes for salad dressings, there are only two standard ones – French dressing and mayonnaise.

The success of a salad dressing depends very much on the quality of the ingredients. Pure olive oil is considered the best to use for dressings as it gives the most delicate and pure flavor. However, it is more expensive than salad oils which usually consist of a blend of oils. These will make a satisfactory dressing.

Use the finest mild-flavored cider vinegar, or better still, a good French wine vinegar. Avoid crude or strongly flavored brands, which are likely to make the dressing less palatable. Lemon juice can be used in place of some or all the vinegar if desired and is preferred by some people. Herb-flavored vinegars, such as tarragon, may be included, but in small quantities, or the flavor of the herb may predominate.

Seasonings, such as salt and pepper, should be measured carefully; their presence should not be accentuated in the finished dressing.

Using salad dressings: French dressing should be put on the salad shortly before serving, as greens become limp after the dressing has been on any length of time.

Mayonnaise gives a better flavor if mixed with potatoes and other vegetables while they are hot. When mayonnaise is intended to coat vegetables, etc., it is best put on just before serving, unless it is set with gelatin.

Salad dressings will tarnish silver, so wooden, glass, china, or plastic utensils should be used.

FRENCH DRESSING (SAUCE VINAIGRETTE)

French dressing, consisting of oil and vinegar with seasonings, is the simplest of all dressings and is usually preferred by the connoisseur. It may be varied by adding various flavoring ingredients such as chopped chives or herbs or piquant ingredients such as a relish or chopped pickles, olives, and so on: a few of these variations are given below.

pinch salt
pinch pepper
pinch dry mustard
pinch sugar
1 tablespoon vinegar
2 tablespoons salad oil

Put the salt, pepper, mustard, and sugar in a bowl, add the vinegar and stir until well blended. Beat in the oil gradually with a fork. The oil separates out on standing, so if necessary beat the dressing immediately before use. If you wish, store it in a screw-top bottle, shaking it vigorously just before serving.

The proportion of oil to vinegar varies with individual taste, but use vinegar sparingly. Cider, wine, tarragon or any other vinegar may be used.

VARIATIONS
To the above dressing add any of the following:

clove of garlic, crushed
1–2 teaspoons chopped chives
½–1 teaspoon curry powder
2 teaspoons chopped fresh parsley
½ teaspoon dried marjoram and a pinch of
   dried thyme
1 teaspoon chopped gherkins or capers
1 teaspoon chopped olives
1–2 teaspoons sweet pickle
1 tablespoon finely sliced or chopped stuffed
   olives
1–2 teaspoons Worcestershire sauce
1–2 teaspoons chopped fresh mint

1 tablespoon finely chopped anchovies
pinch of curry powder, $\frac{1}{2}$ hard-cooked egg,
 finely chopped, 1 teaspoon chopped onion
 (this is called Bombay dressing)
2 tablespoons blue cheese, crumbled
1 tablespoon finely diced pepper

Vinaigrette

There are many different interpretations of vinaigrette dressing; generally, it means a French dressing to which have been added one or more of the following: finely chopped gherkins, chives, shallots, capers, parsley, or other herbs.

Some writers use the term to mean simply a plain French dressing.

Mayonnaise

This is essentially an emulsion of oil and raw egg yolks, with seasonings and vinegar or lemon juice to give piquancy. Occasionally whipped or sour cream is used to replace some or all of the oil.

The process of making mayonnaise is rather lengthy, unless a mixer is available. However, it may be made in fairly large quantities and stored for some weeks in the refrigerator.

In addition to its use with ordinary salads, mayonnaise is served with such dishes as cold lobster, with certain cold vegetables (e.g. asparagus, globe artichokes) and to blend fillings for cocktail snacks; it may also be stiffened with gelatin and used to make a chaudfroid dish.

CLASSIC MAYONNAISE

1 egg yolk
$\frac{1}{2}$ teaspoon dry mustard
$\frac{1}{2}$ teaspoon salt
dash of pepper
$\frac{1}{2}$ teaspoon sugar
about 1 cup salad oil
1 tablespoon white vinegar

Put the egg yolk in a bowl with the seasonings and sugar. Mix thoroughly, then add the oil drop by drop, stirring briskly with a wooden spoon or whisk, until the sauce is thick and smooth. If it becomes too thick add a little of the vinegar. When all the oil has been added, add the vinegar gradually and mix thoroughly. If liked, lemon juice may be used instead of the vinegar.

NOTES

To keep the bowl firmly in position, twist a damp cloth tightly around the base – this prevents it from slipping. In order that the oil may be added 1 drop at a time, put into the bottle neck a cork from which a small wedge has been cut.

Should the sauce curdle during the process of making, put another egg yolk into a bowl and add the curdled sauce very gradually, in the same way as the oil is added to the original egg yolks.

VARIATIONS

Using 1 cup mayonnaise as a basis, add a flavoring as follows:

Blue cheese: Add 2 tablespoons crumbled blue cheese.

Caper: Add 3 tablespoons chopped capers, $1\frac{1}{2}$ teaspoons chopped pimiento and 1 teaspoon tarragon vinegar. Goes well with fried or broiled fish.

Celery: Add $1\frac{1}{2}$ tablespoons chopped celery and $1\frac{1}{2}$ tablespoons chopped chives.

Chantilly: Add $\frac{1}{2}$ cup whipped cream. Goes well with salads containing fruit, chicken, or rice.

Cucumber: Add $\frac{1}{4}$ cup finely chopped cucumber and $\frac{1}{2}$ teaspoon salt. Goes well with fish salads, especially crab, lobster, and salmon.

Herbs: Add 3 tablespoons chopped chives and $1\frac{1}{2}$ tablespoons chopped parsley.

Horseradish: Add $1\frac{1}{2}$ tablespoons horseradish sauce.

Piquant: Add $1\frac{1}{2}$ teaspoons catsup, $1\frac{1}{2}$ teaspoons chopped olives, and a pinch of paprika.

Russian: Add $\frac{1}{4}$ cup chili sauce, 1 tablespoon prepared horseradish, and minced onion to taste. Goes well with eggs, seafood, and mixed greens.

Thousand Island: Add $\frac{1}{4}$ cup chili sauce, 1 tablespoon finely chopped green pepper, 1 tablespoon finely chopped pimiento, and $\frac{1}{2}$ tablespoon minced onion. Goes with mixed greens and seafood.

Tomato: Add $\frac{1}{2}$ tomato, peeled and diced, 1 green onion, chopped, a pinch of salt, and $1\frac{1}{2}$ teaspoons chopped parsley.

These variations can also be made with ready-made dressings.

In small quantities, mayonnaise can only be made in a blender if the blades are set low enough to beat the egg yolk. It sometimes helps to add 1 tablespoon warm water or to use a whole egg. It is easier to make mayonnaise in large quantities.

SOUR CREAM DRESSING

1 cup sour cream
3 tablespoons white vinegar
small piece of onion, finely chopped
½ teaspoon sugar
1 teaspoon salt
pinch of pepper

Mix all the ingredients thoroughly. Serve with baked potatoes.

YOGURT DRESSING

Yogurt can be used in salad dressings in the same way as sour cream. Use 1 to 2 teaspoons lemon juice or wine vinegar and flavor with chopped green onions, chives, parsley, or other fresh herbs, or a little curry powder.

SALAMI

A type of dry sausage produced in Italy, Hungary, and various other European countries. It is made from finely chopped lean pork, pork fat, highly seasoned, flavored with garlic, and moistened with red wine. The sausages are air-dried or smoked and if properly stored will keep for a very long time. Salami is eaten as an appetizer or with other cold meats and salad. It can be filled with a savory mixture and rolled up, used in sandwiches or as a garnish.

SALLY LUNN

A plain type of teacake baked in cake pans of various sizes. Sally Lunns are served hot, split and buttered. Alternatively, they may be served cold, topped with a glaze.

The name is said to have come from a pastry cook who sold the original bun-sized cakes on the streets of Bath in Great Britain. Colonists brought the recipe to North America with them.

SALLY LUNN

¼ cup butter
¼ cup tepid milk
1 teaspoon sugar
2 eggs
1 package active dry yeast
5 cups all-purpose flour
1 teaspoon salt

FOR THE GLAZE
⅓ cup water
2½ tablespoons sugar

Thoroughly grease two 9-inch bread pans or a Bundt pan. Melt the butter in a pan, remove from the heat and add the milk and sugar. Beat the eggs and add with the warm milk mixture to the yeast. Blend well. Add to the flour and salt, mix well and knead lightly. Put into the cake pans, cover with oiled polyethylene and let rise until the dough is doubled in bulk – about 45 minutes to 1 hour. Bake in a 400° oven for 15 minutes. Reduce heat to 350° and bake about 15 minutes longer. Turn the Sally Lunns out of the pans onto a wire rack. Make the glaze by heating the water and sugar to boiling point and boiling for 2 minutes. Use at once to glaze the hot buns.

SALMAGUNDI

An old English supper dish of the eighteenth century consisting of meat, salad, eggs, anchovy, pickles, and beets, diced and carefully arranged to form a pattern, and served on a bed of greens.

SALMI

A kind of ragout, usually made from game or poultry, which is cooked by a mixture of two processes, roasting and then stewing.

SALMI OF GOOSE

1 goose, lightly roasted
1 shallot, chopped
1 orange, peeled and segmented
⅔ cup stock
1¼ cups espagnole sauce
⅔ cup red wine
few green grapes, peeled
currant jelly

Remove the skin from the goose; cut off the legs and wings and set aside. Break the carcass into small pieces and put in a pan with the shallot, thinly pared orange rind and stock. Simmer for 30 minutes. Strain the stock from the pan, put it with the espagnole sauce, wine, and goose legs and wings into a saucepan and simmer until the meat is heated through – about 10 minutes. Arrange the goose parts on a serving dish and reduce the sauce to a syrupy consistency. Pour it over the goose and garnish with the grapes and sections of orange. Serve with currant jelly.

SALMON

A migratory round fish, weighing 6 to 60 lb, caught in rivers as it heads upstream to spawn. It is obtainable in fresh, canned, and smoked form. Most of the salmon eaten in the United States is caught on the West coast or is imported from Nova Scotia, Canada.

Salmon is at its best when the head and tail are small and the neck thick; it should be stiff, red in the gills and covered with bright silvery scales; the flesh should be of a bright red color.

Salmon is one of the oily fish and is thus digested more slowly than white fish, but it is a good source of vitamin D and has a higher energy value than white fish: it also provides animal protein and calcium.

Freezing: A whole salmon can be frozen with care. It must be very fresh (under 12 hours from catch). Wash, remove scales, and gut. Wash thoroughly under running water. Drain and dry. Place the fish unwrapped in the freezer until solid. Remove and dip in cold water. This forms thin ice over the fish. Return to the freezer. Repeat the process until the ice glaze is $\frac{1}{4}$ inch thick. Wrap in heavy-duty aluminum foil and support with a thin board.

To thaw, allow 24 hours in the refrigerator before cooking. Once thawed, use promptly. Salmon steaks and cuts freeze very well. They should be individually wrapped or interleaved.

Preparation and cooking: Scale the fish, holding it by the tail and using a knife. Gut it, then scrape and wash all the blood away, but do not wash the fish more than necessary. Salmon may be cooked whole or cut across into large pieces or steaks and it may be served hot or cold. Boiling, broiling, grilling, and baking are all good cooking methods for this fish.

CANNED SALMON

Canned salmon can be used in place of fresh fish, in scallops, molds, fish cakes, and with a well-flavored accompaniment like cheese sauce.

SMOKED SALMON

This delicacy, which is sold ready to serve, is eaten as an appetizer (sliced very thinly and served with lemon). It may also be used in salads and sandwiches. Smoked salmon offcuts can be bought at a reduced price and used for pâtés and pastes.

POACHED SALMON

This may be done on top of the stove or in a shallow covered casserole in a 375° oven. Whole fish and large pieces are usually cooked on the top of the stove completely covered in liquid. A special fish poacher is required for this.

Prepare the fish and wrap in cheesecloth or aluminum foil so that it is easy to remove, then place in the pan. Cover with salted water or court bouillon and simmer gently until the fish is tender. Allow about 10 minutes to the lb.

Smaller steaks or slices of salmon tend to break unless carefully cooked. Wrap in cheesecloth or foil and poach very gently, allowing 10 minutes to the lb. If to be eaten cold, allow the fish to cool in the cooking liquid before removing.

FOIL-BAKED SALMON

Line a baking sheet with a larger piece of foil, and butter the surface. Place the prepared salmon on the foil. Dot each steak with butter and season with salt, pepper, and lemon juice. Package loosely and cook in a 350° oven for 20 to 40 minutes, according to the thickness of the fish. Serve with maître d'hôtel butter or hollandaise sauce or garnish with poached diced cucumber, sliced lemon, and parsley sprigs. If it is to be eaten cold, leave it to cool still wrapped in the foil.

Foil-baked salmon can be prepared the day before it is required and stored in the refrigerator until just before serving. Cod steaks can also be cooked by this method.

SALMON MOUSSE

2 cans (7½ oz each) salmon
1¼ cups milk
2 tablespoons butter
¼ cup flour
2 eggs, separated
⅔ cup heavy cream, lightly whipped
2 tablespoons tomato catsup
1 teaspoon anchovy paste
1 teaspoon lemon juice
salt
pepper
1½ envelopes unflavored gelatin
¼ cup water
slices of cucumber to garnish

Drain the juice from the salmon and make it up to 1¼ cups with milk. Remove the skin and bones from the fish and mash the flesh until smooth. Melt the butter, stir in the flour and cook for 2 to 3 minutes. Remove the pan from the heat and gradually stir in the salmon liquid and milk.

Bring to a boil and continue to stir until the sauce thickens. Remove from the heat and add the egg yolks. Allow the sauce to cool slightly and stir in the cream, catsup, anchovy paste, lemon juice, and seasoning to taste and add it to the salmon.

Dissolve the gelatin in the water by putting it in a small bowl in a pan of hot water; stir it into the salmon mixture. Beat the egg whites stiffly and fold these into the mixture. Pour it into a 7-inch soufflé dish and leave to set in a cool place. Garnish with slices of cucumber before serving.

SALMON TROUT

A trout that resembles salmon, but when cooked has a slightly pinker flesh. While both salt- and freshwater species exist, the majority of these fish inhabit clear, cold freshwater. In North America they are found in the Great Lakes area and in Canadian Lakes to the north. It may be cooked in any way that salmon is. Salmon trout is also the name for the European sea trout. (See Salmon and Trout entries.)

SALPICON

The French name given to many different mixtures of chopped fish, meat, and vegetables in a sauce, used as stuffings or fillings. It usually means minced or diced poultry or game, mixed with ham or tongue and mushrooms (or truffles) bound with sauce and used for croquettes, appetizers, bouchée fillings, and canapés.

SALSIFY (OYSTER PLANT)

A white root vegetable similar to a parsnip in shape. It has a slightly sweet flavor, supposed to resemble that of oysters, which accounts for its common name. It will keep throughout the winter in the ground and stored in the sand. There is a black variety known as Scorzonera: both have a long tapering root.

Not seen much in North American markets, salsify is used in Europe as a vegetable and to flavor steak pies, etc.; the flower stalks may be cooked like asparagus. It contributes a small amount of vitamin C to the diet.

Preparation and cooking: Wash the salsify carefully, cutting a small piece off the end of each stalk. Scrape it lightly and place it in cold water, adding a few drops of vinegar to prevent discoloration. Boil it until tender in a small quantity of boiling salted water, with a few drops of vinegar added – 30 to 40 minutes. Serve with a white sauce.

SALT

Salt (sodium chloride) is a mineral deposit found in different parts of the earth. It has always been an important substance and much involved in trade. At one stage in history people were paid in salt and this has given us the word "salary," from the Latin word meaning money for the purchase of salt.

Salt is found in solid form, as rock salt, and in solution in both sea water and brine wells. Europeans are apt to use sea salt, while in North America rock salt prevails.

Salt is essential to life, but it is so widely used in cooking and as a condiment that there is normally no difficulty in insuring an adequate supply. When heavy manual work or high temperatures cause an unusual amount of perspiration, however, extra salt is often needed to prevent fatigue and cramp. On the other hand, low-salt diets are sometimes medically prescribed in certain conditions and illnesses, such as kidney and heart complaints.

TABLE SALT

Salt which is finely ground and usually mixed with a very small proportion of magnesium carbonate and calcium phosphate, to help keep it in a dry condition. Iodized table salt can also be obtained to insure a sufficient supply of iodine. Salt has a corrosive action on metals, so it should not be left in silver containers and any metal container should have a glass lining.

Commercially sold salt comes from two sources, salt mines and the sea. The most common varieties are:

Common table salt which comes from salt mines containing solid sodium chloride residue of extinct seas.

Sea salt which is extracted by evaporating sea water and is therefore more expensive than salt from mines. It is, however, superior in flavor to mined salt.

Kosher salt, coarse salt used by Orthodox Jews in preparing meat according to religious laws. It is also preferred by many non-Orthodox cooks for its coarse, jagged form that clings to food.

Rock salt, large pieces of salt used in ice cream freezers and as a bed for oysters. It contains more impurities than the more refined varieties of salt.

Seasoned salts are table salt that has been seasoned with ingredients such as onion powder, garlic powder, and other seasoning.

Using Salt

The use of the correct amount of salt improves the flavor of most savory dishes and many sweet ones. A pinch of salt should always be added to cakes and cookies, to help make the gluten in the flour more elastic, so that the mixture will rise better.

Fish being skinned and filleted can be held more firmly if the fingers are dipped in salt.

SALTED NUTS

(See Nuts entry.)

SALTING

This is one of the oldest methods of preservation and is still a useful way of keeping meat, fish, butter, and some vegetables such as beans. There are two methods, wet and dry, and in both cases sea or common salt, brown sugar, and saltpeter are used. Dry salting involves more work, but enables spices to be used, which give meat a better flavor.

WET SALTING (ALSO CALLED PICKLING)

Use a container of suitable size (not glazed earthenware, as the salt will injure the glaze) which can be stood on a shelf or on pieces of wood.

For a piece of pork or beef (usually brisket) weighing about 5 lb, add 1 to 1½ lb sea or common salt, ¾ cup brown sugar, and 2 tablespoons saltpeter to 1 gallon water; bring to a boil, strain into the container and allow to become cold. Put the meat in the liquid, cover and leave for 5 days, turning it daily.

DRY SALTING

This is specially suitable for thin flank or round of beef. Rub a mixture of salt, sugar, and saltpeter (in the above proportions) into the meat. The following day rub in a mixture of 1½ teaspoons black pepper, 3 teaspoons powdered allspice, 1 teaspoon ground ginger, ½ teaspoon ground cloves, and ½ teaspoon ground mace. Turn the meat daily for 1 to 2 weeks.

To cook salted food: Wash away surplus salt by rinsing the food in several changes of cold water, then cook in the usual way.

SALTPETER (POTASSIUM NITRATE)

This is used extensively in conjunction with common salt for the preservation of meat, e.g. in pickling and preparing corned beef.

It gives an agreeable reddish color to meat.

SAMBALS

Accompaniments to Indian and Pakistani dishes, particularly curries (see Curry entry).

SAMPHIRE (GLASSWORT)

A piquant-flavored succulent plant found along various rocky European coasts. The leaves can be pickled in vinegar or served fresh in salads or as a vegetable.

SAMSOE (SAMSØ)

A golden Danish cheese made on the island of Samsø. It is a cartwheel shape, about 16 inches in diameter and weighs 32 lb. It is often eaten fresh on the island but is stored for 5 months before being exported. (See Cheese entry.)

SAND CAKE

A Madeira-type cake containing cornstarch, ground rice, or potato flour.

SAND DAB

A small fish found in the Pacific off the coast of California in the United States. Its delicate flavor is best brought out by sautéing, but it may be baked in parchment or quickly broiled.

SANDWICH

Two slices of bread enclosing some kind of filling. Sandwiches are said to have been invented by Lord Sandwich, from whom they take their name. A wide range of shapes and sizes can be made, to suit different occasions, ranging from a snack or light lunch to afternoon tea, and the sandwiches can be served either hot or cold.

Preparing the filling: Meat should be sliced, minced, or cut small, and vegetables, apples, nuts, herbs, etc., should be chopped, shredded, or grated and bound with softened butter, mayonnaise, etc. On occasions when sandwiches have to be made in advance, avoid very moist fillings, which soak into the bread or biscuits.

Cutting: If possible, use bread which is about 24 hours old. When making wafer-thin sandwiches for afternoon tea, butter the slices before cutting, but for large numbers and for more substantial sandwiches, it is often quicker to slice the whole loaf before buttering. Providing the bread is not too new, the crusts may be removed before slicing, but they are usually left on when catering for children and teenagers or for informal occasions like picnics. When you are making large numbers of sandwiches, thinly cut sliced loaves are a great labor-saver. Fruit and nut breads, provided they are not over-sweetened, may be used for sweet sandwiches.

Spreading: Sandwiches inevitably use a fair amount of fat, but the butter or margarine will spread much more easily and economically if it is slightly warmed and softened beforehand.

Serving: To keep the sandwiches fresh, cover them with waxed paper, foil, or a dampened kitchen towel. If you have a freezer, sandwiches may be prepared a week or two in advance, wrapped and frozen. These should not contain hard-cooked egg or salad ingredients, as these are not suitable for freezing.

When several varieties of fillings are used, the type can be indicated by the garnish.

Types of Sandwich

FANCY-SHAPED
Cut the slices lengthwise and shape them with special cutters, e.g., into hearts, diamonds, etc.

CLUB SANDWICHES
These are appetizing for snack meals, especially when made with toast and served hot. Place different fillings between three or more layers of any type of bread or toast.

HOT SANDWICHES
Use hot rolls or bread toasted on one side.

OPEN-FACE SANDWICHES
Use a base of white or brown bread (cut into fancy shapes), small rolls, crispbread, or biscuits. (See Smørrebrød entry.)

PINWHEEL SANDWICHES
Make large rolled sandwiches with slices cut lengthwise off the loaf, and then cut them across to give a jelly roll effect.

NEAPOLITAN SANDWICHES
These are made of white and brown bread used alternately, with different-colored fillings between the layers. Cut $\frac{1}{8}$-inch slices lengthwise across the loaves, sandwich three or more together and cut across the layers. Arrange the sandwiches on a plate to show the striped effect.

ROLLED SANDWICHES
Use moist bread; butter it, cut it thinly, spread with filling or insert asparagus tips, etc., and roll.

BREAD BARS
Cut $\frac{1}{2}$-inch slices of bread into bars and spread the whole outside surface with the sandwich mixture. Roll the bars in chopped parsley, chopped nuts, or sieved egg yolks, etc.

SANDWICH LOAF
Cut a loaf horizontally into 4 slices, then remove all the crusts. Sandwich together, using a different filling for each layer — for example, flaked salmon, scrambled egg flavored with cheese, shredded lettuce and chopped ham bound with mayonnaise. Coat the outside with cream cheese and garnish. To serve, cut down into slices.

Fillings
In addition to a single filling such as meat, egg, cheese, etc., many unusual and interesting fillings may be achieved by combining two, three, or even more ingredients. Anything like pickles, celery, olives, etc., should be chopped small. Here are some popular mixures.
1. Beef with horseradish sauce, onion or pickles, and French mustard.
2. Chicken or other white meat with celery and mayonnaise or olives and tomato sauce.
3. Fish with tomato sauce and onion (or pickles), shredded cabbage, and mayonnaise.
4. Salmon or smoked salmon with lettuce and lemon juice or cucumber and tomato sauce.
5. Crab, lobster, and other shellfish with watercress and cucumber or tomato and mayonnaise.
6. Various kinds of cheese with celery and pickles, chives and parsley, or apple and chutney.
7. Egg (hard-cooked, scrambled or fried) with cream cheese and chives or capers and tomato sauce.
8. Vegetable mixtures such as fried mushrooms, tomato, and parsley; cooked peas, mint, and mayonnaise; olives, lettuce, and vinegar; pickled onion, cucumber, and piquant sauce.
9. Fruit mixtures such as apple, nutmeg, and brown sugar; mashed banana, chopped raisins, and orange juice; dried fruit, peanut butter, and sliced orange; dates, ginger, and chopped apple.

SANGRÍA

A Spanish hot-weather drink made of red wine and fruit juices. Sangría has many variations and is popular in Mexico and other parts of Latin America.

SANGRÍA

juice of 4 lemons, strained
juice of 1 orange, strained
½ cup sugar
1 bottle (¾ liter) red wine

Combine the fruit juices and sugar in a large pitcher and stir to dissolve the sugar. Add the wine. Serve in tall glasses over crushed ice.

SAPOTE

Fruit of the sapodilla or chicle tree, native to Mexico, Central America and parts of South America and now also grown in the United States in southern Florida. Because of its shape, the sapote is sometimes known as the Mexican custard apple. Among the several varieties are included the sapote, and the white, black, and yellow sapotes, of which the white is best known.

SAPSAGO

A hard cheese from skim milk curd, flavored with clover. Sapsago is usually served grated.

SARDINE

Originally this name was given to young pilchards caught off the shores of Sardinia; it is now applied to various somewhat similar fish in different parts of the world. In North American waters a "false pilchard" which is actually from the herring family goes under the name of sardine "sprat." French and Portuguese sardines are still chiefly young pilchards; in the Soviet Union they are usually young herrings; in Norway they may be either sprats (also known as brisling) or young herrings (sild).

Fresh sardines are delicious when broiled and are served in this way in many European seacoast towns. To most people, however, sardines are more familiar in their canned form, packed in tomato juice or more commonly in olive or other oil; the bones are usually left in. Canned sardines packed in good–quality oil improve in flavor if left to mature in the can for about two years. The bones eventually become soft enough to eat with the fish and they then form a good source of calcium. Sardines are also good sources of protein, fat, iodine, and vitamins A and D. They are more nutritious than white fish, but not so easily digested.

Sardines have many uses, from tiny cocktail tidbits and appetizers to such snacks as broiled sardines on toast; they are also popular in hors d'oeuvres and salads and as a sandwich filling.

SARSAPARILLA

A flavoring made from the dried roots of a Smilax plant; it was formerly used to make a refreshing still cold drink and is now used to flavor carbonated ones.

SASHIMI

A Japanese dish consisting of thin slices of raw fish, garnished with grated ginger and accompanied by a hot green horseradish paste called "wasabi" and by soy sauce. Because of parasites connected with freshwater fish, only marine fish of unquestioned freshness are suitable.

SASSAFRAS

A tree of North America with an aromatic bark. The Creoles of Louisiana learned from the Choctaw Indians how to make a tisane from the bark and how to use the powdered dried leaves, which they called "filé," as a seasoning and thickener for gumbo. Filé must be carefully treated and once added to a stew, the stew cannot be boiled without becoming inedible.

SATAY (SATE)

Grilled skewered foods of Indonesia and Singapore, sold on the streets by vendors with charcoal braziers. Satays are cooked on wooden skewers and may consist of meat, poultry, or seafood. They are usually accompanied with a spicy peanut sauce. Depending upon their size, satays are served as an appetizer or as a main course. They are best grilled but may also be broiled.

CHICKEN SATAY WITH PEANUT SAUCE

¼ cup lemon juice
2 tablespoons soy sauce
2 cloves garlic, crushed
1 teaspoon sugar
salt
12 oz boned chicken breast, cubed
6 green onions, shredded

PEANUT SAUCE
2 tablespoons crunchy peanut butter
2 tablespoons butter
1 tablespoon soy sauce
1 teaspoon lemon juice
½ teaspoon sugar
chili powder to taste
¼ cup half-and-half

Combine the lemon juice, soy sauce, garlic, sugar, and salt and add the cubed chicken. Marinate for several hours, then drain, reserving the marinade.

Thread the chicken pieces onto wooden skewers that have been soaked in water while the chicken was marinating, four to six pieces to a skewer. Grill or broil, basting with the reserved marinade and turning once, until browned and cooked through. Combine the sauce ingredients and bring to a boil, stirring until smooth. Add the remaining marinade and just heat through. Sprinkle the chicken with green onion and serve the sauce separately.

SATSUMA

(See Tangerine entry.)

SAUCE

A sauce is used to flavor, coat, or accompany a dish and may also be used in the actual cooking to bind the ingredients together.

A sauce can make or mar a dish and must be carefully prepared. Use a clean, thick pan to prevent burning. Since the flavor depends largely on the liquid used, employ water only as a last resort; always hold some liquid back for last-minute adjustments, as it is easier to add more liquid to a sauce which is too thick than to thicken a too-thin one. Taste the sauce before serving and adjust the seasoning if necessary.

Types of Sauce

THIN SAUCES
These are made with unthickened liquids, common examples being mint sauce and thin gravy. These sauces are quite simple to make.

THICKENED SAUCES WITH A ROUX BASIS
This class includes a large number of the most frequently used sauces, which are really variations of the two main "roux" sauces – white and brown. (See Roux entry.)

THICKENED BLENDED SAUCES
These are thickened by means of a starchy substance, which may be arrowroot or cornstarch. Arrowroot, when it is used with a clear liquid, gives a clear sauce, suitable for glazing tarts, etc. (See Glaze entry.) Whichever type of flour is used, it is blended with the liquid (milk, stock, water, or a mixture) and no fat is needed. For sweet sauces, fruit syrup or puree may be used and sugar is substituted for the seasoning.

SAUCES THICKENED WITH EGG
These can take the form of egg custard or hollandaise sauce (see entries), but in both cases the whole egg or egg yolks are cooked for a short time until they thicken. They must not, however, be overheated or the sauce curdles, i.e. the albumin hardens, shrinks, and separates out from the liquid. To prevent this, the cooking temperature of egg sauces must always be kept below boiling point.

MISCELLANEOUS SAUCES
Many well-known accompaniments are not made according to any of the methods listed above – for example, rum butter, melted butter and flavoring butters, horseradish sauce, mayonnaise and aspic mayonnaise, some chocolate sauces, jam, marmalade and syrup sauces (which may be thickened or thin).

(See individual entries for recipes.)

SAUERBRATEN

A famous German dish of pot-roasted marinated beef accompanied by a sweet-sour sauce made from the marinade and thickened with ginger-flavored cookies. While the principal ingredient of the marinade may be beer, wine, or buttermilk, it is wine vinegar that is traditional. With today's tender beef, the marinating agent and process is more a matter of flavoring than tenderizing.

SAUERBRATEN

2–2½ lb bottom round roast
1 cup wine vinegar
2 cups water
1 medium onion, sliced
4 peppercorns
1 bay leaf
¼ teaspoon thyme
1 clove
pinch of nutmeg
parsley sprigs
flour
butter
1 carrot, sliced
1 onion, quartered
1½ teaspoons catsup

SAUCE
¼–⅓ cup crushed gingersnaps
1 tablespoon sugar
¼ cup red wine
½ cup currants

Place the meat in a large ceramic bowl and add the vinegar, water, sliced onion, peppercorns, other seasonings and the parsley. Refrigerate for 3 days, turning occasionally. Drain, reserving the marinade.

Dredge the meat in flour and brown in butter. Place in a heavy casserole and add the remaining ingredients along with $\frac{1}{2}$ cup of the strained marinade. Cover and simmer for 2 to 3 hours, or until tender.

Remove the meat to a heated platter and skim any fat from the sauce. Puree in an electric blender and add enough of the reserved marinade to measure 1 cup. Place in a saucepan, add the remaining ingredients and boil until thickened. Serve the sauce over the meat. Sauerbraten is traditionally accompanied by red cabbage and potato dumplings.

SAUERKRAUT

This is cabbage which has been allowed to ferment in salt; it is a favorite dish in Germany and in the Alsace region of France where it is *choucroute* and is frequently served with sausages. Sauerkraut may often be bought ready prepared in delicatessen shops and it is also obtainable in canned form.

Preparation and cooking: Fresh sauerkraut need only be washed in several cold waters to remove the brine.

Boil the sauerkraut in a very little water for about 30 minutes. To give additional flavor, add a few bacon rinds, a ham-bone or 1 to 2 tart apples (peeled and sliced).

SAUSAGE

Meat mixed with fat, cereal, or bread and seasonings, with suitable coloring and preservative, and packed into a special skin or casing. The sausage skins used to be obtained from the entrails of pigs or oxen but may now be a synthetic product. Their size, of course, determines the diameter of the sausage. After being filled the sausages are "linked" by being twisted at the required intervals.

The primary ingredient of the majority of sausages is pork, but they can be made from many other types of meat, including beef or veal, lamb, mutton, venison, turkey, chicken, etc.

The meat used can be fresh, cured, pickled, salted, smoked, dried, or cooked. Flavorings are also widely varied – including herbs and spices such as pepper, dill, fennel, cumin, mace, parsley, and cayenne. Fillers such as fat, flour, and bread are often used.

Considering this range of possibilities for ingredients and treatment, it is not surprising that there is an almost endless variety of sausages and nearly every country has its own versions of many types of sausages. Some of the most well-known varieties include:

Chorizo of Spain and Mexico
Kielbasy of Poland
Bratwurst of Germany
Andouille of France
Mortadella of Italy
Lop Chong of China

All uncooked sausages should be cooked and eaten as soon as possible after purchase; if it is necessary to store them for a short time, they should be kept in a refrigerator.

Cooking: Sausages may be fried, broiled, grilled, baked or boiled. Extra fat is sometimes needed for frying and baking. Cook them slowly and turn them at frequent intervals to brown all sides.

They are also popular for barbecues and picnics.

Freezing: Sausages can be bought ready frozen or fresh ones can be stored in a freezer for up to 3 months. They can be thawed and cooked or cooked from frozen.

SAUSAGE MEAT

A mixture of ground pork similar to that used for sausages, but not filled into skins. It is cheaper and more convenient to buy the meat in this form for sausage rolls or stuffing.

SAUSAGE ROLLS

7 oz short-crust pastry, made with 7 oz flour, etc.
  (see Pastry entry)
$\frac{1}{2}$ lb sausage meat
flour
milk to glaze

Roll the pastry out thinly into an oblong, then cut it lengthwise into 2 strips. Divide the sausage meat into 2 pieces, dust with flour and form into 2 rolls the length of the pastry. Lay a roll of sausage meat down the center of each strip, brush down the edges of the pastry with a little milk, fold one side of the pastry over the sausage meat and press the two edges firmly together. Seal the long edges together. Brush the length of the two rolls with milk, then cut each into slices 1$\frac{1}{2}$ inches to 2 inches long. Place on a baking sheet and bake in a 400° oven for 15 minutes; to cook the meat thoroughly, reduce the temperature to 350° and cook for 15 minutes more.

Good sausage rolls can be made with bought puff pastry, fresh or frozen. Use one sheet (about 8 oz) of a 16 oz package and allow it to reach room temperature (which will take about 2 hours) before rolling it out, then it will be easier to handle. Make the rolls as above, but heat the oven to 350° and bake a further 15 minutes.

SAUSAGE STUFFING

1 large onion, chopped
1 lb ground pork
2 teaspoons chopped parsley
1 teaspoon dried mixed herbs
⅓ cup fresh white bread crumbs
salt
pepper

Mix all the ingredients together.

Use with chicken, or turkey, adapting the quantities as necessary. This stuffing is sufficient for a 9 to 10 lb oven-ready turkey.

SAUTÉ (SAUTER)

Food cooked rapidly in a small amount of fat in an open pan. The word is derived from the French *sauter*, to jump, and suggests the action of tossing the food in the hot fat.

The vegetables used in making soups, stews, and sauces are often sautéed to improve their flavor without spoiling the color of the finished dish. Sauté potatoes are boiled, cut into slices, and cooked in a little fat until lightly browned.

SAUTERNES

The sweet white wine from the vineyards in the Gironde, near the village of Sauternes. Château Yquem is the best of the Sauternes, which also include Bommes, Barsac, Preignacs, and Fargues. Sauternes is not a highly alcoholic wine, the average alcoholic content being 10 percent. It may accompany fish, poultry, and white meat, but is particularly suitable to serve with desserts.

SAVARIN

A rich yeast mixture baked in a ring mold; it is served soaked with a rum syrup and accompanied by cream or fruit salad. The dessert was named after Brillat-Savarin, a famous gastronomic writer of the eighteenth century.

SAVELOY

A short, thick sausage made from salted pork, lightly seasoned and colored red with saltpeter.

SAVORY

Two types of plant go by this name. Summer savory is an annual which grows to about 12 inches in height and has pointed leaves, with a flavor resembling thyme, but milder and more fragrant. The winter variety is perennial and grows like thyme. Both can be used either fresh or dried for flavoring salads, soups, stews, stuffing, etc.

SAVOURY

In Great Britain this term is applied to three different kinds of food: (1) the tidbits eaten with the fingers, which are often known as cocktail savouries; (2) the highly seasoned type of dish, frequently hot, which used to be served after the sweet course and before the dessert at a formal dinner; (3) a more substantial dish which can form the main course of a simple lunch, high tea, supper, or a snack meal.

SAVOY BISCUITS

Small sponge fingers better known in the United States as Ladyfingers, used particularly for making such sweets as Charlotte Russe.

SCALDING

The term applies to the process of heating milk almost to the boiling point, to retard souring.

It also means the process of pouring boiling water over food in order to clean it or to skin it (e.g. tomatoes, peaches). The food must not be left in the boiling water for any length of time, or it will begin to cook.

SCALLION

An onion which as developed no bulb – frequently used in Chinese and Oriental cookery. Also called Spring onions or Welsh onions, they have hollow green tops and 2 or 3 inches of white above the roots. The flavor is milder than that of an onion, and is particularly good for adding taste to salads and some sauces.

Shallots can be used as a substitute for scallions.

SCALLOP

A shellfish of delicate flavor which makes excellent eating. Scallops should be used only when they are very fresh and in full season, from October through March; they are at their best in January and February. The flesh should be very white. In United States markets scallops are sold out of the shell, cleaned and ready for cooking.

In Europe, where scallops are larger, they are sold live, in their shells with the orange coral or roe which is much prized for its flavor there.

Preparation and cooking: The simplest method of cooking scallops is to simmer them in salted water, court bouillon, or milk until tender, drain, dry and serve in their shells. They may also be sautéed or served in a Mornay sauce, garnished with chopped parsley.

For fried scallops, either boil them first, or soak them for 30 minutes in a mixture of salad oil and lemon juice, seasoned with pepper and salt; dip in egg and bread crumbs or batter and fry.

SCALLOP

A thin slice of meat, usually veal, either round or oval-shaped, cut from the top of the leg – or fillet, in the case of veal. The word also means a thin slice of fish. Scallops are often breaded, then fried and served with a rich sauce. (See Veal entry.)

SCALLOPED DISHES

Food (often previously cooked) baked, combined with a creamy sauce, topped with bread crumbs and surrounded by a border of piped potato. The term also applies to foods served in scallop shells or similar containers.

SCALLOP, TO

A way of decorating the double edge of the pastry covering of a pie. Make horizontal cuts with a knife close together around the edge of the pie, giving a fluted effect.

Now, using the back of the knife, pull the edge vertically at regular intervals to form scallops. These should be close together for a sweet pie and wider apart for a meat one.

SCAMPI

Very large prawns, native to the Adriatic. They are very similar to Dublin Bay prawns. Scampi are delicious when breaded and fried and served with hollandaise or tartar sauce and a crisp green salad. Also called a Norway Lobster.

SCHAV

(See Sorrel entry.)

SCHNITZEL

An Austrian name for a thin slice of meat, usually veal, which is breaded and fried. (See Veal entry for Wiener Schnitzel.)

SCONE

A light, plain quickbread containing very little fat which is popular in Great Britain. It is baked in a very hot oven or cooked on a griddle, and is usually eaten split open and spread with butter or filling. Scones can be eaten hot or cold, as a snack dish, with morning coffee, or as rolls for supper parties. They are best eaten fresh, but can be kept in a cake tin for a day, when they may be reheated in the oven or toasted. Scones also freeze very well for up to 3 months.

OVEN SCONES

2 cups all-purpose flour
½ teaspoon salt
3 teaspoons baking powder
2–4 tablespoons butter or margarine
⅔ cup milk
beaten egg or milk to glaze, optional

Preheat a baking sheet in the oven. Sift the flour, salt, and baking powder together then cut in the butter until the mixture resembles fine bread crumbs. Make a well in the center and stir in enough milk to give a fairly soft dough. Turn it onto a floured board, knead very lightly if necessary to remove any cracks, then roll out lightly to about ¾ inch thick, or pat it out with the hand. Cut into 10 to 12 rounds with a 2-inch cutter (dipped in flour) or cut into triangles with a sharp knife. Place on the baking sheet, brush if you wish with beaten egg or milk and bake toward the top of a 450° oven for 8 to 10 minutes, until brown and well risen. Cool the scones on a rack. Serve split and buttered.

EVERYDAY FRUIT SCONES

Add ½ cup currants, raisins, or chopped dates (or a mixture of fruit) to the dry ingredients in the basic recipe.

RICH AFTERNOON TEA SCONES

Follow the basic recipe, adding 1 to 2 tablespoons sugar to the dry ingredients and using 1 beaten egg with 5 tablespoons water or milk in place of ⅔ cup milk; ½ cup dried fruit may also be included.

Girdle (Griddle) and Drop Scones

Girdle scones have similar ingredients to the oven type, but are cooked on a hot griddle, electric hotplate, or heavy skillet. They are best served warm and spread thickly with butter.

Drop scones, which are thin, light, and spongy, are also known by the name of Scotch pancakes; they are made from a type of batter mixture. Drop scones are served hot or cold, with butter and syrup or jam.

SCORING

To make shallow cuts in the surface of food in order to improve its appearance or to help it cook more quickly. Fish has a better flavor if scored before being marinated; the crackling of pork is scored before roasting to prevent its pulling the roast out of shape and to facilitate carving.

SCOTCH BROTH

(See Broth entry.)

SCOTCH BUN

This traditional English spiced plum cake with a pastry crust, also known as Black Bun, is eaten at Hogmanay, New Year's Eve in Scotland. It is made several months (sometimes even a year) beforehand, so that it has time to mature.

SCOTCH EGG

(See Egg entry.)

SCOTCH WHISKY

The most popular spirit distilled from grain. It is made in Scotland from malted barley and blended with an unmalted grain spirit. The different brands depend on the part of Scotland from which the malt whisky comes. Both the malt whisky and the plain grain spirit must, by law, be matured for 3 years before being blended. The blending is very important and has to be carefully carried out to produce a whisky of the same flavor and color each year.

SCOTCH WOODCOCK

Toast spread with anchovy paste and topped with scrambled egg.

SCRAPPLE

A dish made by the Pennsylvania Dutch of the United States consisting of spiced pork and cornmeal sliced and fried until crisp. Originally this dish was a thrifty way of using all the scraps of pork left over at slaughter time.

SCRAPPLE

1½ lb pork shoulder or neck
1 cup yellow cornmeal
salt
1 onion, chopped
1 teaspoon dried sage leaves
1 teaspoon dried marjoram leaves
¼ teaspoon dried thyme leaves
dash of ground cloves
pepper

Simmer the pork in 1 quart water for 1 hour. Reserve the broth, bone the meat and chop. Place the cornmeal in a saucepan and stir in 1 cup water and 2 cups of the strained broth. Season with salt and simmer, stirring constantly, until thickened. Add the remaining ingredients, cover and cook for about 1 hour. Pour into a 9 × 5 inch loaf pan and refrigerate until chilled.

To serve, cut into slices and fry until crisp on both sides.

SCROD

A small cod, weighing 1½ to 2½ lb. Young haddock and pollack are sometimes also called scrod. See Cod entry.

SEA BASS

An important commercial and game fish, a member of a large family that includes the groupers. Sea bass is found off both coasts of North America, the Pacific variety being somewhat larger. The weight of a sea bass runs from ½ to 5 lb. Smaller fish are cooked whole, larger ones can be filleted, or even cut into steaks.

SZECHWAN DEEP-FRIED SEA BASS

1½ lb whole sea bass, drawn
1 teaspoon finely chopped gingerroot
3 green onions, chopped
2 teaspoons salt
2 tablespoons dry sherry
oil for deep frying
1 teaspoon freshly ground pepper
2 tablespoons sesame seed oil, heated

Make three diagonal slices on both sides of the fish. Combine the gingerroot, green onions, 1 teaspoon of the salt, and the sherry in a flat dish and marinate the fish for 30 minutes. Heat the oil in a wok or deep-fryer to 350°. Add the fish and fry until golden brown on both sides. Sprinkle with the pepper and remaining salt and pour the hot oil over the fish. Serve immediately.

SEA KALE

A European vegetable with a stalk somewhat like celery. A member of the mustard family, sea kale grows wild in Europe and is now cultivated in the United States, France, and England. Like celery, it is banked up with earth to keep it white, as it develops a strong and bitter taste when exposed to light.

SEARING

To brown meat quickly over high heat in a little fat before broiling or roasting it. Searing helps to seal the juices in meat. The term is sometimes used when vegetables are browned in fat before being used in soup- or saucemaking.

SEA SALT (BAY SALT)

Common salt obtained from sea water by evaporation. It is less pure than that obtained from the brine from salt wells.

SEASONING

This term usually refers to salt and pepper, but it may mean any herb or condiment, etc., added to improve the flavor of a dish. Seasoning can be varied to suit individual tastes, but it should be used in moderation, for the sake of those who dislike highly seasoned food.

SEA SQUAB

(See Blowfish entry.)

SEA TROUT

Any of several marine fish of the Atlantic and Pacific coasts of North America, but particularly the weakfish of the mid-Atlantic United States, where it is of importance as a game and commercial fish. Sea trout can be broiled, baked, or sautéed.

SEA URCHIN

Any of various echinoderms, marine animals with a soft body encased in a round limy shell protected by long spines. Several varieties, in particular the green and black sea urchins, are edible. They may be eaten raw from the shell or lightly boiled.

SEAWEED

Many types of seaweed are eaten in different parts of the world and in Iceland and other countries where fresh vegetables are scarce during the winter months, they form an important part of the diet, for seaweed has a good mineral content. Such types as dulse, laver, sloke, or rock weed are eaten by themselves or used in cooking. The seaweeds known as alginates (see below) may be used instead of gelatin to set jellies and creams. Sea oxeye and sea sandwort are often pickled or salted like sauerkraut. Other types, e.g., tangle stem, are burned for kelp, which is a source of iodine.

To cook: Wash the seaweed very well in several changes of water, then simmer it in milk or water for 2 to 3 hours, until tender; the flavor is better if milk is used. Drain, and serve tossed in butter and seasonings.

Alginates

Carbohydrates derived from seaweeds. They have the property of forming jellies, and are used by food manufacturers to improve the texture or consistency of such things as ready-prepared soups, jellies, ice cream, and meat and fish spreads. Thus agar-agar, derived from the stems of the *Gelidium algae*, is mainly used as a stabilizer for emulsions and in jellies and creams. Irish moss *Chondrus crispus*, is a thickening agent.

SEDER

A feast commemorating the exodus of the Jews from Egypt into the Promised Land, celebrated on the eve of the festival of Passover and, by Orthodox and Conservative Jews, on the second night of Passover as well. Unleavened bread and other ceremonial foods are served to recall the sojourn of the Jews in the desert.

SEED CAKE

A type of Madeira cake (see entry), flavored with caraway seeds and lemon rind or extract. Allow 2 teaspoons seeds for a cake made with 2 cups flour.

SELF-RISING FLOUR

(See Flour entry.)

SELTZER

An effervescing mineral water, originally exported from the German town of Nieder Selters, and now widely imitated in manufactured table waters.

SÉMILLON

A relatively rare varietal United States white wine made in California, sold dry or semi-sweet. It is made from the same grape that, when attacked by noble rot, gives Sauternes its very special character. California vintners have yet to experiment on a large scale with this grape and noble rot.

SEMOLINA

This is made from the endosperm of wheat, ground into small granules of various size. It supplies vegetable protein, carbohydrate, and thiamin; when combined with milk it makes a useful food, especially for children and invalids. Semolina is used for making gnocchi (see entry) and other pastas, for thickening soups (1 oz to about 2 cups liquid and blend with a little milk before adding), for making puddings, molds, and fruit mousses; and it is sometimes included in cookies to give a "nutty" texture. Finely ground semolina gives a smoother texture to molds and puddings, but the granular texture of the coarser variety is useful for gnocchi and for cakes and cookies.

SESAME

An herbaceous plant widely grown in the Orient. The seeds are used in cakes and confectionery and the oil extracted from them serves as a flavoring for both sweet and non-sweet dishes.

SEVICHE

A Latin American appetizer consisting of raw fish marinated in citrus juice, usually lime. Chopped tomatoes and green peppers are often included. The juice "cooks" the fish, giving it a solid texture. Only fresh saltwater fish may be used to make seviche; sole and red snapper are good choices.

SEVICHE

3 flounder fillets, cut into thin strips
1 cup lime juice
salt
1 onion, thinly sliced
ground dried chili peppers to taste

Combine all ingredients and marinate at least 8 hours. Serve on lettuce if desired.

SEVILLE ORANGE

A type of Spanish orange which is too bitter to be eaten as dessert, but is used for making marmalade, wines, and cordials; it can also be used for sauces and relishes, especially those to be served with duck. (See Marmalade entry.)

SHAD

The name given to several species of white fish belonging to the herring family, only a few of which, primarily the American shad, have gastronomic value in North America. Like the salmon, it migrates from the sea to the rivers for spawning, and is caught during the winter months only. There are several types, varying in length from about 1 foot to $3\frac{1}{4}$ feet.

Shad may be boiled, but is better broiled or baked, either plain or stuffed. When baked it is served with anchovy, hollandaise, or other piquant sauce. Shad may also be pickled, like herrings.

SHADDOCK

A large, rather coarse and bitter citrus fruit with a thick, bitter rind, related to the grapefruit. It is also called the pompelmous.

SHAD ROE

The eggs of the female shad, considered a delicacy in itself. The roe is contained in two sausage-shaped sacs, one of which comprises a serving.

Shad roe is difficult to cook well. It is delicate, breaks easily, and if overcooked is dry, mealy, and tasteless. While shad roe may be broiled, it must be watched carefully and basted frequently.

SHALLOT

A member of the onion family; each plant has a cluster of small bulbs. Some people consider that shallots have a better flavor than onions, and their smell does not cling so tenaciously. They may be used for flavoring in the same way as onions, the green tops being chopped and used for salads, sauces, and soups, and the bulb in stews and other dishes. Shallots are very suitable for pickling, on account of their flavor and small size. (See Onion and Pickle entries.)

SHALLOW FRYING

(See Frying entry.)

SHANDY (SHANDY GAFF)

A popular drink in Great Britain made of equal quantities of beer or lager and lemon soda. In the United States it is usually made with ginger ale and beer.

SHARK

(See Mako entry.)

SHARK'S FIN

The fins of a type of shark found in the Indian Ocean and used to make a soup which is regarded in the Orient as a great delicacy.

SHASHLIK

(See Shish Kebab entry.)

SHELLFISH

The name given to all edible crustacea (fish which have shells). The best-known types are clams, crabs, crayfish, limpets, lobsters, mussels, oysters, prawns, Dublin Bay prawns, scallops, shrimp, conch, and periwinkles. Shellfish should only be bought in season and when quite fresh; if they have to be kept before use, it is better to buy them alive and kill them shortly before eating. The food value of shellfish lies chiefly in their protein content; they contribute useful amounts of the B vitamins and mineral salts. (See individual entries.)

SHEPHERD'S PIE

A traditional dish in Great Britain consisting of well-flavored cooked meat, usually ground but sometimes sliced, with a "crust" of mashed potato, which is baked long enough to reheat and brown the potatoes. If leftover potatoes are used, they should be mashed while still hot. Purists maintain that only lamb or mutton should be used in a shepherd's pie.

SHEPHERD'S PIE

2 lb potatoes
4 tablespoons milk
2 tablespoons butter
pepper
salt
1–2 onions
bacon drippings
1 lb cooked ground cold meat
broth
2 teaspoons chopped parsley
½ teaspoon mixed herbs

Boil, strain and mash the potatoes and stir in the milk, butter, pepper, and salt. Chop or slice the onion and fry it in a small amount of bacon drippings. Mix the meat with a little broth, pepper, salt, parsley, and herbs. Place this prepared meat mixture in the base of a pie pan or shallow casserole and cover with the mashed potato, piling it up in the center and marking it with a fork. Bake in a 400° oven for 20 to 30 minutes. If necessary, put the pie under the broiler briefly to brown the top.

SHERBET

Originally an Oriental cooling drink made of fruit juice. The name now denotes a mixture of sweetened fruit juice and, in some cases, beaten egg whites, frozen to make a kind of ice.

In the frozen sherbets, milk is sometimes used instead of water, cream is sometimes included, and gelatin is added in some recipes. As the acidity of the fruit varies, it is important to taste the sherbet mixture before freezing it and to add more sugar if required. (See Sorbet entry.)

ORANGE SHERBET

1 cup sugar
⅔ cup water
2½ cups orange pulp and juice
2 tablespoons lemon juice
⅔ cup heavy cream
1 egg white

Boil the sugar and water for 10 minutes, skim and cool. Cut several oranges in halves crosswise and carefully remove the pulp and juice, discarding the seeds and hard centers. Measure the quantity required, add the lemon juice and combine with the cold syrup. Freeze the mixture until it is of a soft creamy consistency. Whip the cream and beat the egg white until stiff, then fold both into the sherbet. Freeze until stiff enough to serve.

SHERRY

Sherry is made in Jerez in Andalusia, Spain from white grapes (Palomino) which are machine pressed and run off into casks. Fermentation takes place in the cask with ample air space between wine and cork. The sherry yeasts form a crust (flor) on the wine which protects it from the air. This flor feeds upon the alcohol but does not weaken the wine, since water evaporates through the wood of the cask more rapidly than the spirit. After fermentation is complete any residual sugar is consumed by the flor, meaning that sherries with a yeast flor crust are always dry.

All sherries are blended wines, the system being unique. The wines, maturing in casks are stacked in tiers, each row representing the produce of a year. The bottom row contains wines that have been passed through a solera system of blending and the top casks hold the "new" wines. Wines from the bottom casks (6 to 7 years old) are run off and used to top up the casks above. A continuing blending process and standard quality is achieved by this process. The wine is then fined, using egg whites, and may be blended again to achieve standard quality for particular exports. Sherries are classified according to the way they develop.

(a) Palmas: dryest, used for amontillado and fino sherries.

(b) Cortados: full bodied, more alcoholic and used for oloroso sherries.

(c) Rayas: coarser wines which may be used for finos or olorosos depending on development.

The types are:
1. Fino – pale, dry wine
2. Oloroso – sweetish, dark wine
3. Amontillado – older, stronger fino
4. Amoroso – pale, sweet wine
5. Brown sherry – dark and sweet

Sherry is served as an apéritif and with soup; the dark brown sweet type is also served with dessert. Cooking sherry is used in sauces, soups, etc.

SHIITAKE

A Japanese mushroom, about $1\frac{1}{2}$ to 2 inches in width, available in dried form in the United States.

SHIRATAKI

The dried thread of starch extracted from a root plant. These gelatinous Japanese noodles require soaking before use. Canned, they can be used without soaking.

SHISH KEBAB

Strictly speaking, a kebab is a piece of meat, but what is often referred to as a kebab is a Shish Kebab, which is a dish that originated in the Orient, particularly in Turkey and other Arabic countries. Basically it consists of small pieces of meat (usually lamb or mutton) threaded onto skewers and broiled. Shashlik, the Russian version of the dish, is usually made with beef. The meat is well seasoned and sometimes marinated beforehand, and it may be combined with onions, mushrooms, tomatoes, peppers, and so on.

Kebabs can be cooked under a broiler or they are particularly popular for barbecuing. They are usually served on a bed of rice with sauces or relishes served separately.

GINGER-GLAZED LAMB KEBABS

1 lb boned leg or shoulder of lamb
MARINADE
3 tablespoons chopped stem ginger
1 tablespoon soy sauce
1 tablespoon tomato paste
2 green onions, chopped
salt and freshly ground black pepper
6 tablespoons chicken broth

Cut the meat into bite-sized pieces. Place in a small shallow dish. Combine all marinade ingredients in a small pan using the white part only from the onion. Heat gently for 5 minutes, cool and pour over the meat. Cover and refrigerate overnight. The next day, drain the meat, thread on 4 skewers and broil under a moderate heat for 30 minutes, brushing over with a little of the marinade. Turn several times to insure meat is cooked on all sides. Arrange skewers in a serving dish. Heat marinade, add any skimmed meat juices from the broiling pan, and pour over the meat. Serve garnished with the snipped green of the onions.

SHISH KEBAB

1 lb boned leg or shoulder of lamb
$\frac{2}{3}$ cup olive oil
1 clove garlic, crushed
1 small onion, finely chopped
$\frac{1}{2}$ teaspoon salt
$\frac{1}{4}$ teaspoon pepper
2 tablespoons lemon juice
4 small zucchini
bay leaves
8 small tomatoes
2 medium-sized onions, quartered

Cut the lamb into 1-inch pieces. Make the marinade by combining the olive oil, garlic, onion, salt, pepper, and lemon juice. Add the meat, cover, and marinate overnight in the refrigerator. Cut the zucchini at an angle into small wedge-shaped pieces, about 1½ inches long. Blanch in salted water for 2 to 3 minutes before using. Drain meat, reserving the marinade. Alternate the meat, bay leaves, and vegetables on 8 skewers. Brush well, particularly the vegetables, with the remaining marinade. Place skewers under a preheated broiler and broil for 15 to 20 minutes, turning frequently and basting to keep moist. Serve on a bed of boiled rice.

Note: If the tomato is added as the last item on the skewer then the cooking time can be adjusted; tomatoes, especially if ripe, take only 7 to 10 minutes.

SHORTBREAD

A thick, crisp cake of "short," biscuitlike texture, which is particularly associated with Scotland, but is widely popular. It has a high proportion of butter to flour, therefore no liquid is required to bind the mixture. Traditionally, the dough is pressed into wooden or earthenware molds to shape it, then turned onto a baking sheet. Shortbread keeps well if stored in an air-tight tin. It will also freeze.

SHORTBREAD

1¼ *cups all-purpose flour*
3 *tablespoons rice flour*
⅓ *cup sugar*
8 *tablespoons butter or margarine*

Grease a baking sheet. Sift the flours and add the sugar. Work in the butter with your fingertips – keep it in one piece and gradually work in the dry ingredients. Knead well and pack into a rice-floured shortbread mold or a 7-inch square shallow cake pan. If using a mold, turn out onto the baking sheet and prick well. Bake in a 325° oven until firm and golden – about 45 minutes. Turn out if necessary. When cool, sprinkle with sugar. Serve cut into wedges.

SHORTCAKE

A traditional American dessert consisting of a rich sweet biscuit, with a filling of fruit and cream. Small individual shortcakes can also be served.

STRAWBERRY SHORTCAKE

2½ *cups all-purpose flour*
3 *teaspoons baking powder*
½ *teaspoon salt*
4 *tablespoons butter or margarine*
½ *cup sugar*
1 *egg, beaten*
1–2 *tablespoons milk, optional*
1 *pint strawberries*
3–4 *tablespoons sugar for filling*
⅔ *cup heavy cream*

Grease a deep 8-inch square cake pan. Sift the flour, baking powder, and salt together and cut in the butter until the mixture resembles fine bread crumbs; stir in the sugar. Add the egg a little at a time to the flour mixture until this begins to bind together; use a little milk as well if necessary. Knead the mixture lightly into a smooth, light, manageable dough.

Turn the dough onto a floured board, form into a round and roll out until it is 8 inches across. Press it evenly into the pan and bake in a 375° oven for 20 minutes, or until golden and firm. Turn the cake out of the pan onto a cooling rack.

Hull and wash the strawberries and drain them well. Keep about a dozen berries whole for decorating and crush the rest with a fork in a bowl, sprinkling with 2 to 3 tablespoons of the sugar. Beat the cream and stir in the remaining sugar. When the cake is nearly or just cold, split, spread with half of the cream and all the crushed fruit and replace the top. Pile the remaining cream on the top of the cake and decorate with whole berries.

SHORT-CRUST PASTRY

(See Pastry entry.)

SHORTENING

The fat used in a dough, cake mixture, etc., is so named because it makes the mixture "short," or tender. Such fats and oils as butter, bacon drippings, lard, margarine, and nut oils all come under this heading.

Fats differ in their shortening powers; generally speaking, the more "workable" the fat, the greater its shortening power; thus lard is good for the purpose, but oils lack workability and must therefore be used somewhat differently to obtain good results.

(See Fats and Oil entries; also the individual entries for the different fats and oils. See also Cake and Pastry entries.)

SHORT LOIN

(See Loin entry.)

SHOULDER (CHUCK)

A retail cut of meat, called "chuck" on beef cuts. Shoulder cuts are divided into those from the arm and those from the blade.

Shoulder arm cuts may be identified by cross-sections of the arm bone and of the rib bones, while shoulder blade cuts may be identified by the blade bone.

Beef cuts from the shoulder include the Inside chuck roll, Chuck tender, Blade pot roast or steak, Boneless shoulder pot roast or steak, Chuck short ribs, Arm pot roast or steak, and English (Boston) cut.

Veal shoulder cuts include the Arm roast and steak, Blade roast and steak, Rolled shoulder, Neck and Stewing veal.

Pork shoulder cuts include the Boston butt, Rolled Boston butt, Smoked shoulder butt, Blade steak, Sausage, Fat back and Lard.

Lamb shoulder cuts include Square, Rolled and Cushion shoulder roasts, Arm and Blade chops, Saratoga chops, Neck slices and Kebab cubes.

SHREDDING

To slice a food such as cheese or raw vegetables into very fine pieces, which often curl as they are cut. To shred use a sharp knife or a coarse grater.

SHRIMP

A very small shellfish, of the same family as the crayfish, in season year round. There are several different varieties, the brown or gray common shrimp of Europe being quite similar to the *Crangor vulgaris* of the Pacific and Atlantic coasts of America. It is very plentiful, and is of a translucent gray color when caught, but becomes reddish-brown when boiled. The rose or pink shrimp, which is caught in deeper waters, has a more delicate flavor. Shrimp can be obtained frozen, potted, and canned. They can also be bought ready cooked.

Shrimp are served as appetizers, as a main dish or in sauces; they are also useful for garnishing, and for salads. Both dried and fresh shrimp are a very common ingredient in Oriental cookery. Shrimp paste is a common spread.

Cooking and serving: For those who catch their own shrimp, the process of boiling them is quite simple. Allow enough water to cover the shrimp well and add 6 teaspoons salt to every 4 cups of water. Bring the water to a boil, place the shrimp in a frying basket and plunge them in the water. Boil for about 6 minutes, or until the color changes. Drain the shrimp and spread out to cool. They may be served either in their shells or shelled.

SHRIMP BISQUE

8 oz cooked shrimp
2 tablespoons butter
1 tablespoon flour
4 cups fish stock or water
$\frac{1}{4}$ teaspoon paprika
$\frac{1}{2}$ cup cream
2 tablespoons dry sherry
salt and pepper
chopped parsley and chives to garnish

Shell and devein shrimp, reserving shells. Melt the butter in a saucepan and sauté shrimp shells for 5 minutes. Sprinkle with flour and pound well with a wooden spoon. Add fish stock or water, and paprika. Bring to a boil and simmer for 10 minutes, then strain. Reserve a few shrimp for garnish and place remaining shrimp and strained stock in blender or food processor. Blend or process until smooth. Heat gently, stirring continuously, then add cream, sherry, salt, and pepper. Do not let soup boil. Serve immediately, garnished with reserved shrimp, chopped, and parsley and chives.

SHRUB

A bottled cordial, made of different fruits, spirits and sugar, popular in the eighteenth century.

SIEVING

To rub or press food (e.g. cooked vegetables) through a sieve; a wooden spoon is used to force it through. (See Puree entry.)

SIMMERING

To keep a liquid just below the boiling point (i.e. at approximately 205°). First bring the liquid to a boil, then reduce the heat so that the surface of the liquid is kept just moving or "shivering" – bubbling indicates the temperature is too high.

Simmering is the method used for many dishes which require long, slow cooking, such as stews.

SIMNEL CAKE

A traditional British fruitcake with a layer of almond paste on top and sometimes another baked inside the cake. Originally this cake was baked for Mother's Day in England, in the days when many girls went to work away from home and Mothering Sunday as the British call it was one day in the year they were allowed home. It is now more usual to have Simnel cake at Easter.

SIMNEL CAKE

1¼ lb almond paste
2½ cups currants
1 cup raisins
¾ cup mixed candied citrus peel, chopped
2 cups all-purpose flour
pinch of salt
1 teaspoon ground cinnamon
1 teaspoon ground nutmeg
¾ cup butter or margarine
¾ cup sugar
3 eggs, beaten
milk to mix
apricot jam or beaten egg to use under almond paste
icing, optional

Line a 7-inch cake pan. Divide the almond paste into three; take one portion and roll it out into a round the size of the cake pan. Mix together the remaining ingredients, cutting the butter into the fruit and dry ingredients, then beating in the egg and milk. Put half of it into the prepared pan, smooth and cover with the round of almond paste. Put the remaining cake mixture on top. Bake in a 325° oven for about 1 hour, lower the heat to 300° and bake for 3 hours, until the cake is golden brown and firm to the touch. Allow to cool in the pan.

Take another third of the almond paste and roll out to a round the size of the pan; make small balls from the remaining third — 11 is the traditional number. Brush the top of the cake with apricot jam or beaten egg, cover with the round of the paste and place the small balls round the edge. Brush the paste with any remaining egg or jam and brown under the broiler. The top of the cake may then be coated with icing, made by mixing 3 tablespoons sifted powdered sugar with a little cold water until it will coat the back of the spoon. Decorate the cake with a tiny model chicken or a few colored sugar eggs.

SIRLOIN (HIP)

A retail cut of meat that includes the hip bone. The two bones in this cut are the hip bone and the back bone, the latter frequently removed. Sirloin steaks and chops all contain different looking bones depending upon the position of the cut on the hip bone. Moving from the front to the back of the hip, these are known as the pin bone, flat bone (widest part of hip), round bone and wedge bone (nearest the leg).

Beef sirloin cuts include the Pin bone, Flat bone, Wedge bone and Boneless sirloin steaks.

Veal sirloin cuts include the Sirloin roast and steak and the Rolled double sirloin roast.

Pork sirloin cuts include the Sirloin roast and chop.

Lamb sirloin cuts include the Sirloin roast and chop and the Rolled double sirloin roast.

SKATE

A coarse white fish with a large proportion of bone, in season from September through April. It is sold cut into pieces and slashed, the thickest pieces, taken from the middle cuts, being the best to buy; if large it is sometimes filleted. Skate is usually fried or baked and it can be poached in milk flavored with bay leaf and a little nutmeg and served with a piquant sauce.

Preparation: Wash the fish well in salted water, skin it and remove the bones at each side. Cut into pieces, or fillet if large enough.

SKATE TOLEDO

2 tablespoons butter
1 clove garlic, optional
1 large onion, cut into rings
1 large green pepper, thinly sliced
1 cup long-grain rice
2 cups chicken broth
4 large tomatoes, peeled and chopped
black pepper
2 wings of skate
seasoned flour
oil
chopped parsley

Melt the butter in a skillet and add the crushed clove of garlic if used. Add the onion and pepper and cook gently without browning for about 5 minutes. Stir in the rice and chicken broth. Simmer steadily, stirring occasionally, until the rice is cooked and all the liquid absorbed, 15 to 20 minutes. Just before the rice is cooked stir in the chopped tomatoes. Season with pepper.

While the rice is cooking wash and dry the fish and cut each wing into two or three pieces. Coat thoroughly in seasoned flour.

Heat $\frac{1}{2}$ inch of cooking oil in a skillet and fry the fish quickly on both sides until pale golden brown, about 5 minutes. Drain on paper toweling.

Pile the rice in the center of a serving dish surrounded by the fish and sprinkle with freshly chopped parsley.

SLING

A cocktail usually made with gin, rum, or whisky, and fruit.

SLIVOWITZ (SLIVOVICA)

A Hungarian brandy made from a particularly large, sweet type of plum.

SLOE

The wild plum or fruit of the blackthorn. Sloes are small, with a purple skin and very tart yellow flesh. They are used with other fruits to make jellies and are also made into liqueurs and cordials such as sloe gin.

SLOW COOKERS
(See Crock Pot entry.)

SMELT

A small, delicately flavored fish from 4 to 12 inches long, closely allied to the salmon family. Smelts are in season from September through April, after which time they go up the rivers to spawn, in the same way as salmon.

Preparation and cooking: Pull out the gills, when the entrails should also come out if the fish is lightly squeezed. Wipe and dry well, but avoid washing and cook immediately. Frying is the usual method – roll the fish in seasoned flour, beaten egg, and bread crumbs and fry in hot fat. Serve garnished with fried parsley and accompanied by hollandaise, tomato or shrimp sauce.

SMOKED HADDOCK, SMOKED SALMON

(See Haddock and Salmon entries.)

SMOKING

The process of preserving meat and fish by drying them in the smoke of a wood fire. It is essential to use a wood fire and sawdust is usually thrown over it to create dense smoke. The flavor given to the food depends on the variety of wood employed: juniper, oak, beech, hickory, etc., all give their own special flavor. Some old houses had chimneys specially constructed for smoking; in others a special outhouse was used.

Home-smokers are now available for use domestically. They are particularly suitable for fish, poultry, meat, and cheese. Food smoked in this way is for immediate consumption and not for preservation.

SMÖRGÅSBORD

In Sweden and to a lesser extent in the rest of Scandinavia this is the traditional way of serving food. It resembles a buffet meal or cold table and can be either an appetizer course or a full meal.

No matter how elaborate it may be, a Smörgåsbord starts with bread and butter and herring dishes, accompanied by boiled potatoes and followed by one or two small piquant dishes. The plates are then changed and egg dishes are served, with salads, cold meats, perhaps some dishes in aspic and finally (for a fairly elaborate meal) perhaps some hot dishes such as kidneys or meat balls; then come rye bread, cheese, and coffee.

SMØRREBRØD

Danish open-face sandwiches, consisting of an oblong slice of bread, generously buttered, topped with meat, fish, or cheese (often combined with egg or salad ingredients) and attractively garnished. They may be served for lunch, snacks, tea, or supper and are very suitable for informal entertaining. Provided you have a reasonable supply of bread and some cans of meat, fish, etc., in the cupboard, smørrebrød can also be produced at short notice for unexpected guests.

In Denmark, rye bread is traditionally used, but other firm-textured types can, of course, be substituted. Cut the slices into pieces about 4×2 inches and butter really well, right up to the edges – this not only adds to the flavor, but also holds the topping in place. Use a generous amount of topping – the smørrebrød are normally eaten with knife and fork, not with the fingers. To serve with cocktails or as a buffet party snack, make them half the size (the Danes call these tidbits *Snittere*).

When serving smørrebrød at a party, allow about 3 per person of the ordinary-sized ones and follow the Danish order, offering the fish first, then the meat, and finally cheese smørrebrød. They are best arranged on large, flat dishes, platters, or trays; if possible, have cake or fish servers. After preparing the trays of smørrebrød, cover with a slightly damp cloth or parchment paper and keep in a cool place until required. The Danes serve chilled Schnapps or lager with them, with perhaps a liqueur to accompany the cheese smørrebrød.

Smørrebrød Ingredients
The choice of ingredients is almost unlimited, but here are some of the most popular:

FISH
Herrings (spiced or pickled), mackerel fillets, slices of cold cooked white fish, smoked salmon, shrimp, etc., caviar.

MEAT
Ham (fresh or canned) roast beef, pork, etc., pork luncheon meat, chopped pork, spiced pork roll, salami, tongue (fresh or canned), bacon, liver sausage, and pâté. The slices of meat are often rolled.

CHEESE
Almost any type that lends itself to easy slicing or spreading can be used, including the veined kinds such as Danish Blue. If the slices are sufficiently pliable, they are often folded like meat slices, to look more appealing.

OTHER INGREDIENTS AND GARNISHES
Lettuce leaves, watercress, sliced hard-cooked egg, egg strips, sliced cucumber, tomato, radish, pickle, beet, green pepper, etc., potato and Russian salads, cooked peas, button mushrooms, sprigs of parsley or other mild herbs, onion rings, radish roses, twists of tomato, lemon, cucumber, orange, etc., horseradish sauce, mayonnaise, applesauce and fried apple slices (particularly with bacon), cooked prunes, pitted grapes, sliced stuffed olives, halved walnuts.

To make egg strips: Mix 4 eggs with 1 cup milk, beat well, strain and season. Cook slowly over hot water until set and when cold cut into strips. Or, scramble eggs in the usual way and press them lightly while cooking.

SIMPLE SMØRREBRØD TOPPINGS
Chopped pork, potato salad, watercress, sliced tomato
Crisp-broiled bacon with scrambled egg
Tongue with Russian salad and a tomato twist
Salami with onion rings
Pork luncheon meat, sweet pickle, sliced cucumber
Liver pâté with sliced pickle and a beet twist

Four Dish Smørrebrød

LUNCHEON MEAT WITH HORSERADISH
Arrange on each slice of bread 2 to 3 folded slices of pork luncheon meat. Add 2 teaspoons horseradish sauce mixed with a little heavy cream and top with a twist of fresh orange and a pitted cooked prune, one half each side of the orange.

TONGUE AND RUSSIAN SALAD
On each piece of bread arrange 3 small thinly cut slices of tongue, folding them to give height. Top with 2 teaspoons of Russian salad and add tomato and cucumber twists.

CHEESE AND BACON
First broil some bacon slices until crisp and leave them to cool. Arrange across each slice of bread alternate bacon slices and slices of Samsoe cheese. Garnish with cooked button mushrooms and watercress.

CAVIAR AND EGG
Put 4 to 6 slices of hard-cooked egg on each piece of bread. Pipe a little mayonnaise on the center of each ring and on this press 1 teaspoon caviar; garnish with a parsley sprig.

SNAIL, EDIBLE (ESCARGOT)

A cultivated variety of snail, highly esteemed in France; the best are said to be those fed upon grape leaves. Snails have a good flavor (thought by some people to resemble that of oysters), but little food value. After being cleaned and boiled for 5 minutes, the snails are taken from the shells, the intestine is removed and the flesh is stewed with herbs, etc., before being returned to the shells for serving. They may also be fried or prepared in various other ways. Snails may be bought in cans, ready prepared and often accompanied by cleaned shells ready for serving.

SNAILS À LA BOURGUIGNONNE

1 can snails (about 20)
1¼ cups white wine
1 onion stuck with cloves
2 cloves garlic, crushed
⅔ cup brandy
bouquet garni
salt
butter

FOR GARLIC BUTTER
8 tablespoons softened butter
½ shallot, finely chopped
1 clove garlic, crushed
1–2 teaspoons chopped parsley
salt
pepper

Remove the snails from the can and place in a pan with the rest of the ingredients. Simmer gently for 1 hour, remove from the heat and allow to cool in the liquor. Meanwhile, mix the ingredients for the garlic butter, blending well. Put a snail into each shell, fill up with butter and put the shells in an ovenproof dish. Bake them in a 450° oven for 10 minutes.

SNIPE

A small bird with a long bill and striped plumage, in season from August through March. Snipe should be eaten really fresh, so make sure when buying them that the bill is dry and feet supple. The American snipe, *Gallinago wilsoni*, or Wilson's snipe, is a favorite on the Mississippi Delta. It can be prepared in many ways, but roasting brings out its flavor most fully. (See Game entry for cooking.)

SNOEK

A fish related to the mackerel, the tuna, and the swordfish, is found in South African and Australian waters and off the coast of Chile. The fish grows to about 4 feet in length and may weigh up to some 18 lb.

SNOW PEA

This slender pea, eaten pod and all, is known by a variety of names, including the Chinese pea pod and, by the French, mange-tout. It is a popular ingredient of Chinese cooking but must have the string running the length of the pod removed before using.

STIR-FRIED SHRIMP WITH SNOW PEAS

1½ lb shrimp, shelled and deveined
1 tablespoon dry sherry
1 teaspoon cornstarch
2 teaspoons soy sauce
4 oz snow peas
½ teaspoon sugar
salt
4 tablespoons peanut oil

Put the shrimp into a bowl with the sherry, cornstarch and 1 teaspoon of the soy sauce. Mix well, then cover and chill for at least 30 minutes. String snow peas. Mix the sugar, salt, and remaining soy sauce for seasonings. Heat 2 tablespoons of the oil in a wok or skillet and cook shrimp, stirring over a high heat until color changes. Remove. Add remaining oil and stir-fry snow peas for 2 minutes. Return shrimp to wok and add seasonings. Toss until heated through, and serve immediately.

SODA BREAD

In this Irish type of bread the leavening agent is baking soda combined with buttermilk.

IRISH SODA BREAD

4 cups flour
2 teaspoons baking soda
2 teaspoons cream of tartar
1 teaspoon salt
4 tablespoons lard or solid shortening
1¼ cups buttermilk

Grease and flour a baking sheet. Sift together the dry ingredients twice. Cut in the lard. Mix to a soft but manageable dough with the liquid: the amount required will depend on the absorbency of the flour. Shape into a 7-inch round and mark into triangles. Place on the baking sheet and bake in a 425° oven for about 30 minutes. Eat while fresh.

SODA WATER

Water aerated with carbon dioxide and sold in bottles or syphons. Soda water also contains a little bicarbonate of soda, the proportion varying in different makes. It is alkaline and may help to neutralize the acidity of the gastric juice. The chief value of soda water, however, is to add sparkle and therefore to accentuate the flavor of certain drinks and punches.

Syphons and containers of the gas can be bought for producing soda water at home.

SOFT DRINKS

Non-alcoholic bottled or canned drinks, ready to drink or requiring dilution. They include carbonated beverages such as various tonic waters, colas, lemon-lime drinks, as well as still beverages which are ready to drink.

None of these drinks has much food value. The amount of fruit used in soft drinks is very small indeed and unless extra vitamin C is added, is of no particular value.

SOLE

Next to the turbot, the sole is considered the finest of all the flatfish. Its flesh is firm and delicate, with a delicious flavor. It is very easily digested and so is often given to invalids and convalescents. The real sole, called the Dover sole, is easily recognized by its dark brownish-gray back skin. Lemon sole is broader and its back is a reddish-brown color. The lemon, witch, and Torbay sole are not considered to have as fine a flavor as the true Dover sole. When fresh, soles are shiny and firm to the touch. Those without roes are superior in flavor. Sole is in season year round.

Soles are cooked by any of the usual methods, particularly frying and broiling. Fillets of sole are delicious steamed, baked, or poached and served with a rich, well-flavored sauce – cream, white wine, mushroom, or a similar type.

SOLE MEUNIÈRE

1 large sole, whole or filleted
salt
pepper
flour
butter
lemon
chopped parsley

Season the sole with salt and pepper, flour it lightly on both sides and sauté it in butter until the fish is cooked and golden-brown on both sides. Serve on a hot dish, sprinkled with lemon juice and parsley, then pour on some lightly browned melted butter.

SORBET

Originally an iced Turkish drink (the name being derived from the same origin as sherbet). The modern sorbet is a soft water ice, flavored with either fruit or liqueur and sometimes containing whisked egg white. A sorbet was previously served at a formal dinner before the roast, to clear the palate but nowadays it is more often served at informal meals as part of the dessert course, combined with diced fruit or fruit salad. Sorbets are too soft to mold and are served in goblets or glasses.

SORBITOL

A sugar substitute which is tolerated by diabetics and can be used in their diet in place of sugar. However, it does have a high energy value, so it is not suitable for slimming diets.

SORGHUM

(See Millet entry.)

SORREL

A wild plant with sharply pointed leaves and red flowers. It is often overlooked in English-speaking countries, but is very popular in France, where a cultivated variety is sometimes grown in gardens. In the United States sorrel is also known as sour grass and is called schav by the Jews. Sorrel has a strongly acid taste and can be used in small quantities to add flavor to lettuce and other salads, sauces, and other dishes. It may also be cooked like spinach and made into a puree for serving with poached eggs, sweetbreads, and some meat dishes, or it can be mixed with spinach to improve its flavor. Sorrel should be picked when young and fresh.

SCHAV

1 lb sorrel (sour grass)
2 medium onions, chopped
6 cups water
salt
1 tablespoon lemon juice
$\frac{1}{4}$ cup sugar
2 eggs, beaten

Cook the sorrel and onions in the water for 30 minutes. Add the salt, lemon juice, and sugar and cook briefly. Stir a little of the soup into the eggs, then return the mixture to the pot. Chill. Serve garnished with sour cream if desired.

SOUBISE SAUCE

A velvety onion sauce made by mixng $1\frac{1}{4}$ cups cooked pureed onions with $1\frac{1}{2}$ cups Béchamel sauce and 2 tablespoons cream. It can be served with any egg or vegetable dish and is a traditional accompaniment for cutlets.

SOUFFLÉ

A fluffy dish, either sweet or non-sweet, which is lightened by the addition of stiffly beaten egg whites. Success in making a soufflé depends largely on the adequate beating of the egg whites and their very light but thorough incorporation into the flour or other mixture. There are two types of soufflé, one served hot and the other cold.

Hot Soufflés

These are based on a panada and may be steamed or baked, but in either case they should be served very hot and eaten at once, as they rapidly sink. Use an ovenproof china or glass mold or a soufflé pan.

BAKED

Prepare the pan or mold by greasing it well with clarified butter or a tasteless cooking fat. Grease a round of parchment to fit the base and put in position. Tie a double band of greased parchment paper firmly round the pan so that it stands 3 inches above the top – this will protect the sides of the soufflé as it rises. Fill the prepared pan about two-thirds full and bake in a 350° oven for about 30 minutes, until well risen and golden-brown. Try to avoid opening the oven door until the soufflé is cooked. Remove paper band and serve immediately in the dish.

Baked soufflés can also be cooked in individual molds and are prepared in the same way; decrease the cooking time to 20 to 25 minutes.

STEAMED

Fill the pan only half-full, to allow for rising. Cover the top with a round of greased paper to prevent water dripping onto the surface. Steam gently in a steamer or in a saucepan of hot water. (If a saucepan is used, place the pan on a rack or inverted saucer to raise it slightly.) Cook until firm to the touch, $\frac{3}{4}$ to 1 hour. Remove the paper band, turn the soufflé out onto a hot dish, remove the round of paper from the top and serve at once.

Cold Soufflés

These are set with gelatin, the exact quantity varying according to circumstances – in very cold weather or when the soufflé can be set in a refrigerator, it may be necessary to use a smaller amount of gelatin. The usual method is to beat together the egg yolks, sugar, and flavoring (e.g. fruit juice, coffee, or chocolate) over hot water until the mixure is thick and creamy – the warmth melts the sugar and air can then be beaten in more easily. (Do not overheat the mixture, for if it gets too hot, the egg cooks and the inclusion of air then becomes impossible.) The dissolved gelatin is then added and the mixture allowed to cool to "setting point" (that is, when the mixture begins to set around the edges). Stir occasionally to insure that all the ingredients are evenly distributed. The cream (if used) is beaten to the same consistency as the mixture and then folded in. The egg whites must be beaten very stiffly and are folded in at the last moment.

Preparing and filling the dish: A cold soufflé should be prepared so that when served it appears to have risen like a hot one. A straight-sided china or glass soufflé dish is used; for these recipes it should be 2 to 3 inches deep; individual dishes are also available.

The dishes are prepared as follows: cut a strip of firm paper long enough to go around the pan, overlapping slightly and deep enough to reach from the bottom of the dish to about 2 inches above the top. Place it around the outside of the dish so that it fits exactly and pin it firmly in position or tie it with string. Take care to see that the paper forms a true circle, not an oval, otherwise the soufflé will not have a symmetrical appearance when finished.

Prepare the mixture according to the recipe and pour it at once into the soufflé dish or dishes, filling to 1 to 2 inches above the rim. Put in the refrigerator to set.

Serving a cold soufflé: Remove the strings or the pins very carefully and take off the paper collar. To do this, hold a knife which has been dipped in boiling water against the outside of the paper – this will melt the mixture slightly and enable the paper to be removed easily, leaving a smooth edge. Decorate the top with some suitable decoration, such as piped whipped cream, angelica, almonds, pistachios, etc.

The side of the soufflé mixture which stands above the dish may be decorated with chopped walnuts, fine cookie or graham cracker crumbs, and so on. Press the finely chopped nuts or crumbs onto the mixture with a broad-bladed knife, letting any loose crumbs fall away. Repeat the process until the side is covered evenly all over.

CHEESE AND RICE SOUFFLÉ

¼ cup long-grain rice
1 can (8 oz) tomatoes, drained
2 tablespoons butter
4 tablespoons all-purpose flour
1¼ cups milk
1½ cups cheese, grated
3 eggs, separated
salt
pepper

Cook the rice in the usual way until just soft. Put the tomatoes into a greased 2-pint soufflé dish or well-greased large ovenproof dish. Melt the butter in a pan, stir in the flour and cook for 2 to 3 minutes. Remove from the heat and gradually stir in the milk. Bring to a boil, stirring constantly, and when the sauce has thickened, remove from the heat, stir in the cooked rice, cheese, egg yolks, and seasoning to taste. Finally beat the egg whites stiffly and fold in lightly. Pour over the tomatoes and bake in a 350° oven for about 50 minutes until well risen.

VARIATION
1 small sliced onion and 3 to 4 chopped slices of bacon can be sautéed lightly and used with or instead of the tomatoes.

SOUFFLÉ AU CHOCOLAT

3–4 oz chocolate bits
2 tablespoons water
2 cups milk
¼ cup sugar
4 tablespoons all-purpose flour
butter
3 egg yolks
4 egg whites
powdered sugar

Butter a 7-inch, 3-pint soufflé dish. Put the chocolate bits in a bowl with the water and melt them over a pan of boiling water. Heat the milk, reserving a little, with the sugar and pour onto the melted chocolate. Blend the flour to a smooth paste with the remaining milk, and stir in the chocolate mixture. Return to the pan, stir over a moderate heat until boiling, then cook for 2 minutes, stirring occasionally. Add a large pat of butter, cut in small pieces, then leave until lukewarm. Beat in the yolks, then fold in the stiffly beaten whites. Turn the mixture into the soufflé dish. Bake in a 350° oven for about 45 minutes, until well risen and firm to the touch. Dust with powdered sugar before serving.

SOUL FOOD

The term used for a way of cooking evolved by Blacks in the deep South of the United States. The ingredients were simple as imposed first by the sociological conditions of slavery and after the Civil War by the economic conditions of poverty. Chitterlings; fat pork cooked with collards, and mustard greens; pig's ears, ribs and backbones; black-eyed peas; and sweet potatoes are some of the ingredients of soul food, prepared originally by slaves who tried to reproduce their African ways of seasoning and cooking.

SOUP

Soup, which is often served as the first course of a luncheon or dinner, or as the main course of a light lunch or supper, not only stimulates the appetite for the food that follows but also provides food value.

Soups are infinitely varied in flavor, texture, appearance, and nutritive value, but the majority of them may be divided into the thin soups (consommés and broths) and the thick soups (purees, thickened brown and white soups), the bisques (cream soups), and fruit soups. The choice of soup depends very much on the other dishes to be served. When the soup is intended merely as an appetizer to precede a substantial meal, choose a clear (consommé) type. If the main course is light, the soup may well be thick and nourishing. A main course soup should be a broth or thick type, with plenty of vegetables and perhaps a garnish such as cheese dumplings. The majority of soups are served hot, but in summer weather an iced soup is often appreciated. For luncheon or dinner parties, it is usual to allow ⅔ cup soup per person, but for family meals 1 cup or more per person is more usual.

Soups can have a basis of meat or vegetables, or a combination of these with cereals. Bisques and other fish soups are well known in some parts of the world and fruit soups are frequently served in Scandinavia. Broth made from meat, fish, or vegetables (see Stock entry) forms the best foundation for most soups, but milk, water, or a mixture may also be used.

Well-flavored soups can be quickly made by using the many varieties of canned, condensed, and cube-form broths or bouillon which are now available, particularly if they are mixed or diluted with milk or with chicken, meat or vegetable broth. Two soups of different flavors can be combined, while dehydrated or frozen vegetables or other ingredients can be added to give more variety, flavor, and texture.

Serving soup: Soup may be ladled out at the table into hot bowls or soup cups. An appropriate garnish adds greatly to the appearance, flavor, and often the nutritive value of a soup. In general, the more substantial garnishes are used with thickened soups and the lighter types with the thin consommés and the more delicate cream soups.

Soup Garnishes

BACON
Cut into small strips or dice and sauté or fry lightly.

SAUSAGES AND SAUGE MEAT
Leftover cooked sausages, cut into rounds or small strips, go well with vegetable soups such as pea, onion, or celery; they should be heated through in the soup just before it is served. Raw sausage meat may also be used; roll into balls about the size of a marble, coat with flour and either broil or sauté, or boil in the soup for 10 to 15 minutes.

CHEESE
Grate the cheese (preferably Parmesan or dry Gruyère) and if desired mix it with either chopped parsley or watercress; pass it separately or sprinkle it on the soup just before serving.

CHEESE OR HERB DUMPLINGS
(See Dumpling entry.)

FRIED OR TOASTED CROUTONS
(See Crouton entry.)

MACARONI, VERMICELLI, NOODLES, SHELLS
These are good in minestrone or any thin soup. Break into short lengths, if necessary, and add to the soup about 20 minutes before serving, and boil in the soup until tender.

RICE
Add dry boiled rice and freshly chopped parsley or chives just before serving the soup.

MUSHROOMS
Cut into thin slices and sauté. When using button mushrooms leave whole. Add to soup just before serving and heat through.

ONIONS AND LEEKS
Slice into rings or chop finely and sauté before adding to soup.

OTHER VEGETABLES
Cut raw carrot, turnip, etc., into "matchsticks" or small rounds, shred cabbage and slice celery and cook them separately for 10 minutes in some broth. Another method is to tie them in cheese-cloth and cook them in the soup. Then place the pieces in the individual soup plates or cups before serving. Frozen mixed vegetables may be added 5 to 10 minutes before serving.

Varieties of Soup

CONSOMMÉS
These are made from a good broth or stock and are clarified with egg shells and whites to give an appetizingly transparent liquid, which must be quite free of fat. Serve them either very hot or as iced jelly; garnish with julienne vegetable strips or asparagus tips, etc., and accompany with Melba toast, crisp rolls, or bread sticks.

BROTHS
A broth is an unclarified soup with meat cooked in it, though the meat is often removed and can be served separately. Strictly speaking, broths are thickened only by the vegetables cooked in them, but pearl barley, rice, etc., are often added to the more substantial types such as Scotch broth (see Broth entry).

PUREES
Meat or vegetable stock, milk, or water can all be used for these soups, which are thickened chiefly by the sieved or pureed vegetables, though it is usual to add a liaison of a starchy substance or eggs.

CREAM OF TOMATO SOUP

1 stalk celery, chopped
1 carrot, sliced
1 small onion, chopped
1 thick slice bacon, finely chopped
2 tablespoons butter
2 tablespoons flour
1½ lb tomatoes, quartered
2½ cups beef or chicken broth
bouquet garni
salt and pepper
pinch of sugar
2 tablespoons heavy cream
chopped chervil, basil, or parsley to garnish

Lightly sauté the celery, carrot, onion, and bacon in the butter for 5 minutes, until soft but not colored. Sprinkle in the flour and stir. Add the quartered tomatoes, broth, and bouquet garni, cover and cook gently for about 30 minutes, until soft. Remove the bouquet garni and sieve the soup or puree it in a blender or processor and sieve to remove the seeds. Return it to the pan with the seasonings, add the cream and reheat, but do not let it boil. Garnish with freshly chopped chervil or basil, when in season – otherwise use chopped parsley.

If the tomatoes lack flavor, add a little tomato puree. Canned tomatoes can be used to replace the fresh ones, adding their juice plus enough broth to total about $2\frac{1}{2}$ cups liquid.

THICKENED SOUPS

These are made of meat or vegetable stock, milk, or water and may contain meat, fish, vegetables, etc. The thickening can consist of a cereal of some sort or eggs. Thickened soups may be either brown or white.

BISQUE

These creamed fish soups are usually made from shellfish.

FRUIT SOUPS

The basis of these soups is diluted fruit juice or a puree of rhubarb, currants, raspberries, oranges, lemons, etc.; this is slightly thickened with arrowroot or cornstarch, and sweetened to taste. A little white wine may be added and sometimes a touch of spice.

Before serving, a spoonful of whipped cream may be put on the top of each bowlful. Fruit soups are often served with diced bread which has been baked until brown with a little butter and sugar, or with chopped nuts.

CREAM OF LEMON SOUP

2 tablespoons butter or margarine
$\frac{1}{4}$ lb onions, sliced
$\frac{1}{4}$ lb carrots, sliced
$4\frac{1}{2}$ cups turkey or chicken broth
1 large lemon
1 bouquet garni
1 tablespoon arrowroot
salt
freshly ground black pepper
$\frac{2}{3}$ cup half-and-half

Melt the butter in a large saucepan. Add the sliced vegetables and cook gently until tender, stirring frequently. Pour over the broth, bring to a boil, reduce the heat and simmer. Using a vegetable peeler, thinly pare the rind from the lemon. Pour

boiling water over the rind and leave for 1 minute; drain. Add the rind, juice of the lemon, and bouquet garni to the pan contents. Cover and cook for 1 hour or until the vegetables are really soft. Remove the bouquet garni. Puree the soup a little at a time in an electric blender or processor. In a clean pan, blend the arrowroot with a little of the soup then add the remainder, stirring. Bring to a boil, stirring. Adjust seasoning before adding the cream. Reheat but do not boil.

SOURDOUGH

A leaven made of of sour fermented dough. Although known since antiquity and not brought to the Western hemisphere until the time of Columbus, it is associated with the United States because of the prospectors who carried their sourdough starters with them to Alaska at the turn of the century, thus earning the nickname "sourdoughs." The starter, once made, is self-perpetuating when properly cared for and may be purchased or homemade. The bread of San Francisco has made sourdough a household word in the United States.

SOURDOUGH STARTER

1 cup milk
1 cup water
1 tablespoon sugar
1 cup all-purpose flour
1 package active dry yeast
$\frac{1}{2}$ cup warm water

Heat the milk and water and cool to lukewarm. Stir in the sugar and 1 cup of the flour and pour into a crock. Cover with a cloth and put in a warm place for 3 days. Add the remaining ingredients and let stand for 3 to 4 days, or until smelly, bubbly and well fermented. Refrigerate until needed.

When used, replenish sourdough with equal amounts of flour and water. When unused, sourdough needs to be "fed" every 7 to 10 days. Stir in 1 cup water and 1 cup flour.

SOURDOUGH BREAD

$1\frac{1}{2}$ cups lukewarm water
1 package active dry yeast
1 cup sourdough starter
3 tablespoons melted butter
6 cups all-purpose flour
2 teaspoons salt
2 teaspoons sugar
$\frac{1}{4}$ teaspoon baking soda

Measure the water into a large mixing bowl and dissolve the yeast in it. Stir in the starter, butter, 4 cups of the flour, and the salt and sugar. Stir until well combined, cover with a towel and let rise in a warm place until doubled in bulk, $1\frac{1}{2}$ to 2 hours. Stir in 1 cup of the remaining flour and soda. Turn the dough out onto a floured board and knead in the remaining 1 cup flour, adding more if the dough is still sticky. Knead until smooth and elastic. Shape into three leaves and place in greased 8×4-inch loaf pans. Let rise until double in size. Bake in a 375° oven for 40 minutes, or until the loaves sound hollow when tapped on the bottom. Turn out of pans; cool on racks.

SOUR GRASS

(See Sorrel entry.)

SOUVLAKIA

The Greek skewers of grilled lamb sold as a snack on the streets of large cities and tiny mountainside villages and served as a substantial course in homes and fine restaurants. Souvlakia are made with lamb marinated in equal amounts of oil and lemon juice flavored with salt, pepper, and oregano. The meat is then threaded onto wooden skewers and grilled over a brazier. The meat may be interspersed with pieces of onion, green pepper, and tomato.

SOYBEAN

The soybean, the most nutritious of all the bean family, is grown chiefly in the Far East, in the United States, and in Germany. Over 100 varieties are known, some early, some late; the color of the beans may be green, yellow, or brown. Unlike other beans, the soy contains very little starch. The protein is far superior in kind and quality to that of other vegetable foods and the fat content is about 20 percent; soy contains calcium, iron, thiamin, also some riboflavin and nicotinic acid. It is a very important item in countries where food is short.

To cook dried beans: Beans should be bought from a store where there is a regular turnover as stale beans never soften however long they are cooked. Pick over the beans and soak overnight in clear cold water. Do not leave too long in a warm atmosphere as they can start to ferment. As a short cut to soaking bring the beans to a boil, remove from the heat and steep for 1 to 2 hours. To cook pour off the water and cover with fresh

water. Bring to a boil, skim off any foam and boil gently for 1 to 3 hours. Dried beans are not easily digested unless well cooked.

Soybean curd is made from cooked and fermented beans and is used to supplement meat and fish in Eastern countries.

SOY SAUCE

A dark brown, pungent sauce made from soy beans, very widely used in Oriental cookery as a flavoring and seasoning.

SPAETZEL (SPÄTZEL)

A small egg noodle or dumpling, originally from the area around southwest Germany and Hungary. In its native surroundings spaetzel dough is made thick enough to roll out and cut into slivers or thin enough to push through a colander or a special spaetzel-maker that looks somewhat like a grater with an attachment.

SPAETZEL

$1\frac{1}{2}$ cups all-purpose flour
salt and pepper
2 eggs, lightly beaten
$\frac{1}{2}$ cup milk

Combine the dry ingredients and stir in the eggs. Add the milk and let stand 30 minutes. Force through a colander or spaetzel-maker into a large pot of boiling water. Cook until the spaetzel rise to the surface.

SPAGHETTI

One of the most popular and, in the United States, most familiar types of Italian pasta, shaped like long "strings." (The word literally means "little threads"). It is cooked as macaroni.

A common method of serving spaghetti is to eat it with tomato, meat, or cheese sauce. It is a staple food in Italy. It may also be broken up and added to soups. (See Pasta entry.)

SPAGHETTI WITH MUSHROOM AND TOMATO SAUCE

3 tablespoons butter
$\frac{1}{4}$ cup chopped green onions
8 oz fresh mushrooms, sliced
8 oz tomatoes, peeled and roughly chopped
$\frac{1}{2}$ cup chicken broth
salt and pepper
8 oz spaghetti, cooked
grated Parmesan cheese

Melt the butter in a skillet and add the green onions. Cook until soft and add the mushrooms and tomatoes. Sauté for 5 minutes, or until the mushrooms are soft. Add the chicken broth and simmer until the liquid is reduced. Season with salt and pepper and toss with the spaghetti. Serve with Parmesan cheese.

SPAGHETTI SQUASH

A yellow hard-shelled squash, about the size and shape of a football. Cook in boiling water for about 40 minutes or until tender. Cut in half lengthwise, and remove the seeds. Using a fork, shred out the flesh. Serve tossed with butter or your favorite spaghetti sauce.

SPARERIBS

A cut of pork usually consisting of ribs from the breast section. Country-style back ribs come from the loin section and have more meat than the regular spareribs, which, however are preferred by most rib fans. Barbecued spareribs are highly popular in the United States, particularly the Southwest, and are delicious barbecued Chinese fashion.

CHINESE BARBECUED SPARERIBS

1½ lb spareribs
¼ cup hoi sin sauce
2 tablespoons dry sherry

Chop the ribs into small pieces and marinate in the hoi sin sauce and sherry for 2 to 3 hours, turning occasionally. Cook over charcoal for 10 minutes, turning once or twice, or bake in a 425° oven for 15 to 20 minutes, or until browned.

SPEARMINT

(See Mint entry.)

SPICE

The general term covering a wide variety of aromatic seasonings which are used to flavor food. They are usually derived from woody shrubs found in the tropics. Spices were formerly used to disguise rancidity in the days before canning, dehydration, and freezing could be successfully used to preserve foods. The use of curry powder in India is one example. Spices are sold both individually or in combination (e.g. as mixed spice and curry powder). The best flavor is obtained from freshly ground spices, so they should be bought in small quantities.

Spices stimulate the appetite, but should be used with moderation, as too much produces an unpleasant flavor.

The following list gives some of the spices most commonly used in cooking (in many cases fuller details are given under the individual names): allspice, aniseed, cardamom, cayenne, chilis, cinnamon, cloves, coriander, cumin, curry powder, fenugreek, ginger, mustard, nutmeg, pepper, and saffron.

SPINACH

An annual or perennial plant with succulent green leaves. Spinach should be picked young and eaten as soon as possible after picking: it is then a good source of vitamin C and an excellent source of vitamin A. It also contains a good percentage of calcium and iron, but probably neither of these is available to the body, because they form insoluble salts with the oxalic acid also present.

Preparation and cooking: Allow ½ lb spinach per person. Wash well in several changes of water, to remove all grit, and strip off any coarse stalks. Pack it into a saucepan with only the water that clings to it, heat gently and cook until it is tender, 10 to 15 minutes. Drain it thoroughly, and reheat with a large piece of butter and a sprinkling of salt and pepper. Or, sieve the spinach and add 1 to 2 tablespoons of white sauce, cream, or sour cream. Reheat before serving.

Creamed spinach can form a bed for poached eggs, slices of hard-cooked egg, or scrambled egg and chopped bacon. Pieces of toasted bread make a suitable garnish. Spinach may also be added to soups, in which case it is best shredded and added 10 minutes before serving. Sorrel and spinach may be cooked together and served creamed, while young spinach leaves can be served in salads.

SPINY LOBSTER

(See Langouste entry.)

SPIRIT

Beverages made from an alcoholic-bearing liquid by distillation rather than fermentation, the result being of a high alcoholic content. The five main liquors of the world are Brandy, Whisky, Gin, Vodka, and Rum (see individual entries).

A great deal of skill is required to make a good distillation although in principle it is quite simple. Alcohol vaporizes at 78.3°C and water at 100°C, so to drive off the alcohol a temperature between these is applied to the alcoholic wash. The required flavorings are also driven off, leaving the water behind.

The strength of alcohol in the spirit is indicated by the proof. In the American proof system pure alcohol is represented by the figure 200, therefore the figure on the label only has to be halved to obtain the actual alcoholic strength. The British system is similar to the American, pure alcohol being represented by the figure 175.25/175. In other European countries alcoholic strength is coded by stating the percentage of pure alcohol in a spirit which is a more logical method.

Food can be both preserved and flavored with spirits; thus fruit is often preserved in brandy or gin, while rum, whisky, or brandy may be added to such things as rich cakes and mincemeat. Spirits can also be used in other cooking, including sauces.

SPIT ROASTING

Originally meat was always roasted by turning it on a spit in front of an open fire. Meat cooked in a modern oven, although referred to as a roast, is really baked. However, a rotary spit, worked by an electric motor or a clockwork mechanism, can now be fitted to many stoves. The spit can be situated inside the oven or combined with the ordinary broiler. Most backyard barbecue grills come with or can be fit with rotating spit attachments.

This method of cooking is very successful for good cuts of meat, poultry, and game. It insures very even cooking and an excellent flavor, as the meat is basted by its own juice. (See Rotisserie entry.)

SPLIT PEAS

(See Pea entry.)

SPONGE CAKE

A light cake, made of eggs, sugar, flour, and flavoring. (For Genoise sponge (which contains fat) and for Victoria sponge (which is made by the creaming method) see individual entries.)

SPOON BREAD

A cornmeal bread soft enough to be eaten with a spoon. (See Cornmeal entry.)

SPRAT

A small silvery fish of the herring family. Norwegian sprats are canned under the name of brisling.

SPRUCE BEER

A drink which is popular along the Western coast of Canada. It is made without barley, the branches, cones and bark of black spruce being boiled for several hours, then put into a cask with molasses, hops, and yeast and allowed to ferment.

SPUMONI

An Italian frozen dessert made in a mold. It usually consists of an outer coating of ice cream with an inner filling of contrasting ice creams or whipped cream mixed with nuts and candied fruits.

SQUAB

A young pigeon 4 weeks old or less. Squab generally weigh from 8 to 14 oz and have very delicately flavored, dark meat. They are available fresh or frozen and can be broiled, roasted, or stuffed and baked.

SQUASH

Any of various plants of the Cucurbita genus or the fruit of any of these plants. Squash are sometimes referred to as summer and winter squash, but a more accurate division would be soft- and hard-shelled squash.

Soft-shelled squash are immature squash that cannot be stored over long periods of time. They must be eaten fresh and have an easily pierced skin and edible seeds. They include the yellow crookneck, the dark green, cylindrical zucchini, and the pale green to white patty pans (scallops), disk-shaped with a fluted edge. Summer squash may be prepared by boiling, baking, sautéing, or frying.

Hard-shelled mature squash can be stored for long periods. They have an inedible rind and seeds. They include the dark green acorn squash, the large green and warty Hubbard squash, and the cylindrical brown to dark yellow butternut squash with its bulbous base. Mature squash may be cooked by boiling and served in chunks or mashed or, like the acorn, they may be halved, baked and eaten from the shell. (See separate entry for Spaghetti squash.)

SQUID

Any of various cephalopod mollusks with an elongated body, 10 arms, and a small internal shell. Squid also carry an ink sac, the juices of which are sometimes used to stew the squid. Squid are considered a delicacy by such Mediterranean countries as Greece, Italy, and Spain and by the Chinese and Japanese. To clean squid, turn inside out and cut off the mouth and discard the ink sac and transparent bone. Cut into thin slices or rings. Squid may be baked, deep-fried, or sautéed.

SQUID IN TOMATO SAUCE

1½ lb squid
4 tablespoons olive oil
2 cloves garlic
1 cup canned tomatoes
½ cup sherry
pinch of oregano
salt and pepper

Clean and slice the squid; set aside. Heat 2 tablespoons of the oil in a skillet and add the garlic; cook until brown and discard. Add the tomatoes and simmer for 10 minutes. Add the sherry, oregano, salt, and pepper and simmer for 20 minutes.

In a separate skillet heat the remaining 2 tablespoons oil and add the squid. Cover and sauté 2 to 3 minutes, until done. Add to the tomato sauce and serve over rice.

STARCH

Starch is a carbohydrate of a more complicated type than sugar. When it is digested, it is broken down into sugar before being absorbed by the body.

It is found in most vegetables and fruits – in very small quantities in green vegetables and most fruits and in quite large quantities in root vegetables, peas, beans, and cereals such as wheat and rice. It does not occur in animal tissues. In a raw state starch is insoluble in water so most foods containing starch are cooked to allow the grains to swell and gelatinize.

In general, starch is the biggest source of energy in the human diet throughout the world.

STEAK

A piece of meat cut from the shoulder (chuck), ribs, loin, sirloin, or leg of an animal. Thick sections of a fish such as cod or salmon are also called steaks. Unless otherwise qualified, however, the word is usually applied to cuts of beef. Steaks are usually broiled, grilled, pan broiled or pan fried. Steaks from the rib, loin, and sirloin are considered choicest.

ROUND AND TOP ROUND
This has a very good flavor but is not always very tender. The top round is sometimes sold as London Broil.

SIRLOIN
Not as tender as rib and loin cuts, but considered by many to be more flavorful. It is an excellent choice for broiling or grilling and one steak can feed as many as eight.

PORTERHOUSE STEAK
Cut from the loin and containing the finger bone (stem of the T-bone) and a good section of the tenderloin. Will serve 2 or 3.

T-BONE
Also cut from the loin, with a larger bone and smaller pieces of the tenderloin. Will serve 2 or 3.

TOP LOIN
An individual boneless steak cut from the Porterhouse or T-bone and excluding the tenderloin portion.

TENDERLOIN
A small, very tender individual steak from the tenderloin. When cut thick from the large part of the tenderloin, it is known as a Chateaubriand and serves 2.

CLUB
An individual steak cut from the loin and frequently containing part of the 13th rib.

RIB EYE (DELMONICO)
An individual steak cut from the eye of the rib.

RIB STEAK
An individual steak cut from the rib. Can also be boned.

FLANK STEAK
A thin steak from the flank. It is covered with a thin filament that should be scored before cooking to prevent curling and cut across the grain on the diagonal. Broil no more than a total of 6 minutes in a preheated broiler. This is the classic London Broil.

SKIRT

Thin small steaks cut from the plate. Slightly tough, they improve with marination.

BLADE AND SHOULDER

These steaks are cut from the shoulder and should be broiled only if they are of high quality.

Cooking and serving steaks: Steaks less than 1 inch in thickness are usually pan broiled on top of the stove. The pan may be covered with a slight sprinkling of salt or a small amount of fat to prevent the steak sticking. Thicker steaks are broiled or grilled. Steaks over 2 inches thick are finished in the oven after initial broiling or grilling. If desired, serve steaks with a Béarnaise sauce or maître d'hôtel butter.

Cooking times for steaks (in minutes)

Thickness	Rare	Medium Rare	Well-done
$\frac{3}{4}$ inch	5	9 to 10	12 to 15
1 inch	6 to 7	10	15
$1\frac{1}{2}$ inch	10	12 to 14	18 to 20

STEAMING

An economical method of cooking food in the steam from boiling water. It has the advantage of retaining mineral salts and the water-soluble vitamins B and C, which are apt to be dissolved out when food is boiled in water. Steamed food also keeps a better shape and often a better flavor. Disadvantages are that food may take longer to cook and the room can become filled with steam.

There are several ways of steaming, according to the equipment available. The chief points to remember are that the steamer must not be allowed to boil dry, which ruins the steamer and burns the food, and the water must not be allowed to stop boiling, which results in foods not being cooked properly.

Methods of Steaming

1. In a steamer with a perforated base placed over an ordinary saucepan. The steamer must fit the saucepan well, otherwise the latter quickly boils dry. Soups or a vegetable can be boiled in the bottom of the steamer, while fish is steaming in the steamer.
2. In a tiered steamer; this is an extremely useful utensil, but care must be taken to see that the steam enters all compartments and the regulator knobs should be checked each time it is used. Different dishes can be cooked in each tier without any fear of flavors becoming mixed.

3. In a large bowl or mold standing in a pan of boiling water. The water should reach halfway up the bowl or mold. For a delicate dish, such as a soufflé, the container should be placed on an upturned saucer, pastry cutter, or tin, to protect the base from the direct heat.
4. In a chafing dish.
5. By cooking with steam under pressure. The great advantage of this method is that food which normally takes hours can be cooked in a very short time. (See Pressure Cooking entry.)
6. Chinese style in bamboo steamer baskets over a wok of boiling water.

MEAT

Any roast can be steamed. Allow twice as long as for boiling. If using salted meat, soak for 3 hours beforehand.

POULTRY

The time depends very much on the size and age of the bird. A good way of cooking an old bird such as a stewing chicken is to steam it until tender, then to brown it in a 425° oven for 30 to 45 minutes.

ENGLISH-STYLE PUDDINGS

Though not common in the United States, steamed puddings are popular desserts in Great Britain. To keep out the moisture caused by condensation, cover the pudding with a double thickness of greased parchment paper or a cloth dipped in hot water and floured. A string should be tied around the pudding mold so that it may be easily lifted out of the steamer.

Suet puddings need 3 hours or longer. Sponge puddings in small dariole molds cook in 20 to 30 minutes; larger puddings take $1\frac{1}{2}$ to 2 hours, according to the size. Allow plenty of room in the mold for the pudding to rise.

CUSTARDS

The water should be only just boiling for these, as they curdle if the temperature becomes too high. Remove as soon as they are set.

(See individual entries for methods of steaming vegetables and fish.)

STEEPING

The process of pouring hot or cold water over food and leaving it to stand, either to soften it or to extract its flavor and color.

STERILIZATION

The process of freeing food (and utensils) from living organisms. It is often confused with boiling, but in true sterilization the temperature varies according to the food: some bacteria form heat-resisting spores which need to be brought to a temperature of 257° (i.e. above boiling point) or a longer time at a lower temperature, to kill them. The time required also varies, according to the food, the method of sterilization and the kind of bacteria likely to be present.

The simplest way of sterilizing utensils is to use one of the chemical liquids or tablets sold at chemists. These are dissolved in a specific amount of water. Instructions should be carefully followed to insure proper sterilization.

STERLET

A small sturgeon; the flesh is highly prized and the roe yields the finest-quality caviar. The swimming bladder is used to make isinglass.

STEWING

A method of cooking by moist heat in a small amount of liquid which is kept at simmering point. Long, slow cooking insures that flavors are well blended and that tough cuts of meat are made tender. Food can be cooked in a pan on top of the stove or in a casserole in the oven; both should have tight-fitting lids to reduce the loss of liquid from evaporation. The new slow cookers are particularly suitable for stewing as the food cooks at a very low temperature for several hours. (See Crock Pot entry.)

STEWED FRUIT
(See Fruit and Dried Fruit entries.)

Meat Stews

BEEF
For this type the meat, vegetables, and flour are fried before stewing. Stewing beef is commonly used for beef stew, but other meats such as oxtail, kidney, and liver may be used.

OTHER
Mutton, veal, or rabbit are also used for stews. The meat and vegetables are frequently not fried first. The English refer to these stews as "white" stews while beef stews are called "brown stews." Irish stew is an example of a thin stew, while a fricassee (see entry) is a thickened stew.

Suitable cuts for stewing

BEEF
Shoulder steak, chuck steak, shank, brisket, top round, oxtail.

VEAL
Knuckle, breast, shoulder, neck.

The cheaper and coarser the meat, the longer it takes to cook. Most types of stew require at least 2 hours and some varieties, such as oxtail and brisket, may take 3 or even 4 hours. Herbs, spices, and vegetables should be added in moderation to give flavor and interest to the dish.

BEEF STEW

1½ lb stewing beef
2 tablespoons fat or oil
2 onions, sliced
2 carrots, sliced
4 tablespoons flour
3¾ cups broth
salt
pepper
bouquet garni

Cut the meat into ½-inch cubes. Heat the fat or oil in a skillet, and sauté the onions and carrots until browned. Remove from the pan and sauté the meat until browned. Put the meat and vegetables in a casserole. Add the flour to the fat remaining in the pan, stir well and add the broth gradually; bring to a boil, season and add to the casserole, with the bouquet garni. Cover and cook in a 325° oven for about 2 hours. Remove the bouquet garni before serving.

IRISH STEW

1½–2 lb neck of lamb, cut into pieces
2 lb potatoes, peeled and sliced
2 large onions, sliced
salt
pepper
chopped parsley

Trim some of the fat from the lamb. Place alternate layers of vegetables and meat in a saucepan, seasoning with salt and pepper and finishing with a layer of potatoes. Add sufficient water to half cover. Cover with a lid and simmer very slowly for 3 hours. Serve sprinkled with chopped parsley.

Alternatively, cook the stew in a casserole in a 375° oven for 2½ to 3 hours.

STILTON CHEESE

Regarded as the "King of English cheeses." The blue-veined variety has a soft close texture when ripe: the blue veins are a penicillin mold which is allowed to grow in the cheese, as in Roquefort and Gorgonzola. These give the cheese a very strong flavor. Stilton gained its name not because it was made in the village of Stilton, but because this is where it was first sold. It is now only made in certain areas of England, including Melton Mowbray in Leicestershire, Dovedale in Derbyshire, and parts of Nottinghamshire.

It used to be considered fashionable to scoop Stilton out from the center of the cheese with a spoon or cheese scoop then pour port into the cheese to stop it hardening. Some experts consider this practice wasteful, suggesting that a more suitable way to serve the whole or half cheese is to cut down the cheese 1 to 2 inches and take wedges all round on this level.

There is also a white Stilton cheese which does not contain the blue veins. This is a mild crumbly cheese.

STIR-FRYING

A Chinese cooking technique used to cook small pieces of food quickly. Vegetables, meat, poultry, and shellfish, after being cut into slices, shreds, or chunks, are cooked in a small amount of oil over high heat in a metal pot with a rounded bottom. The food is added in the order of its cooking time and is stirred constantly while frying to prevent burning. The sloping, rounded wok in which it is cooked helps to keep the ingredients constantly in motion. This method of quick cooking was developed to offset the scarcity of fuel in China.

STOCK

The liquid produced when meat, bones, or vegetables are simmered with herbs and seasonings in water for several hours. Stock forms the basis of soups, sauces, stews, and many dishes, giving a far better flavor than when plain water is used. It has no food value apart from some minerals.

MEAT STOCK

Any meat (especially such cuts as shin of beef or shank and knuckle of veal) and any bones, whether fresh or already cooked, can be used to make stock. Place the bones (and the meat, if used) in a saucepan with a few flavoring vegetables (e.g. carrot, onion, celery) and add a few peppercorns, a clove, a bay leaf, a pinch of mixed herbs, bring to a boil, cover and simmer for 2 to 3 hours.

Green vegetables and starchy foods should not normally be included, as they cause the stock to sour rapidly. If they are added, the stock should be used at once.

If the bones or scraps of meat are fatty, the liquid should be strained after cooking and allowed to cool, so that the fat may be removed before the stock is used.

If the stock is not used at once, bring the pot to a boil each day, adding any extra bones or vegetables and more water as required; empty the pot after 3 to 4 days and start over. The bones are sometimes used for a second lot of stock.

VEGETABLE STOCK

This is made in the same way as meat stock using a selection of vegetables such as carrots, onion, rutabaga, turnip, celery, and peppers, but is simmered for a shorter time and it must be used quickly. A few bacon slices help to give flavor and richness.

FISH STOCK

Use the bones and skin from fresh or cooked fish, with flavoring, vegetables, herbs, and spices, and make as above, simmering for 20 minutes. Fish stock should be used within a day or two of making.

BOUILLON CUBES

These provide an easy way of making stock.

STOCKFISH

Cod which has been air-dried but not salted.

STOLLEN

A rich, sweet German Christmas bread, filled with raisins, candied fruits, and almonds. One side of the bread is folded over the other before baking to form a long oval. Stollen is dusted heavily with powdered sugar after baking and is served in thin slices. The city of Dresden in Germany is famed for this Christmas bread.

STOUT

A beer made with a dark malt. It is thus darker (and sweeter) than ale.

STRAWBERRY

A low-growing plant that is now cultivated all over the world. The wild strawberry fruit is delicious, but smaller than the cultivated varieties. Strawberries are a good source of vitamin C.

Large, perfect berries can be washed, left unhulled, served with sugar and eaten in the fingers. When cream is served as an accompaniment, the fruit is hulled beforehand. Strawberries may also be included in fruit salads and fruit cocktails; when pureed, they make delicious creams and ices and form the filling for the ever-popular strawberry shortcake (see Shortcake entry). Strawberries are not often used in cooked desserts, as they lose their shape, color, and flavor, nor do they can very successfully. Frozen strawberries are available for use when fresh ones are out of season, but they do not freeze well as they lose flavor and become watery when thawed. If strawberries are to be frozen at home they should be of a very good quality, or preferably made into a puree and then frozen.

Strawberries make a well-flavored jam, but as they are not rich in pectin it is often necessary to add lemon, pectin extract, or tartaric or citric acid, to help the jam set. These additions affect the flavor, and the truest strawberry taste is obtained when the jam is made with only a little added acid.

STRAWBERRY ICE

6 tablespoons sugar
1 cup water
1½ teaspoons lemon juice
1¼ cups strawberries, pureed
1 egg white
1½ tablespoons powdered sugar, sifted

Dissolve the sugar in the water over gentle heat. Bring to a boil and boil rapidly for 3 minutes. Cool. Stir in the lemon juice and strawberry puree. Pour into a freezer container and freeze until "slushy." Beat the egg white until stiff. Beat in the powdered sugar. Beat this into the strawberry mixture until evenly combined. Freeze until solid. To serve, use a melon baller to form small scoops.

STRAWBERRY JAM

3½ lb strawberries
3 tablespoons lemon juice
7 cups sugar

Hull and wash the strawberries, put in a pan with the lemon juice and simmer gently in their own juice for 20 to 30 minutes until really soft. Add the sugar, stir until dissolved and boil rapidly until setting point is reached. Allow to cool for 15 to 20 minutes then jar and cover in the usual way. *Makes about 5 lb.*

STREUSEL

A crumb topping for coffee cakes and fruit tarts made of flour, butter, sugar, and cinnamon. Cake crumbs may be substituted for the flour and chopped nuts added.

STRIPED BASS (ROCKFISH)

A game and food fish of the coastal waters of North America, of commercial importance on the East Coast of the United States, where its sale has been restricted because of chemical pollutants. Striped bass usually runs from 15 to 18 inches in length, although larger fish are sometimes seen on the market.

Striped bass is a versatile fish. It may be cooked whole or in fillets and may be broiled, baked, sautéed, or cooked en papillote. While it is wonderful poached and served hot with a hollandaise or shellfish sauce, it is equally delicious cooked in the same manner, chilled and served with a mayonnaise, gribiche or mustard sauce. Bake bass in a 425° oven or poach it for 10 minutes per inch at its thickest point. If stuffed, include the stuffing in the measurement.

STROGANOFF

A preparation of thinly sliced meat quickly cooked with onions and mushrooms and served in a thick sour cream sauce. This dish is celebrated as Boeuf Stroganoff (see Beef entry) and, although any steak cut may be used, is at its best when prepared with tenderloin.

STRUDEL

A form of pastry, very popular in Austria, Germany, and central Europe generally. It is made from a soft dough which is stretched out by hand until paper-thin, covered with one of a variety of fillings (e.g., apple, black cherries, nuts, poppy seeds, cheese, and vegetables) and rolled like a jelly roll.

STRAWBERRY

low-growing plant that is now cultivated
over the world. The wild strawberry fruit
delicious, but smaller than the cultivated
ieties. Strawberries are a good source of
amin C.

Large, perfect berries can be washed, left
hulled, served with sugar and eaten in the
gers. When cream is served as an accompani-
nt, the fruit is hulled beforehand. Strawberries
y also be included in fruit salads and fruit
ktails; when pureed, they make delicious
ams and ices and form the filling for the ever-
pular strawberry shortcake (see Shortcake
ry). Strawberries are not often used in cooked
serts, as they lose their shape, color, and flavor,
do they can very successfully. Frozen straw-
ries are available for use when fresh ones are
of season, but they do not freeze well as they
e flavor and become watery when thawed. If
wberries are to be frozen at home they should
of a very good quality, or preferably made
o a puree and then frozen.

Strawberries make a well-flavored jam, but as
y are not rich in pectin it is often necessary to
lemon, pectin extract, or tartaric or citric
d, to help the jam set. These additions affect
flavor, and the truest strawberry taste is
ained when the jam is made with only a little
ed acid.

STRAWBERRY ICE

blespoons sugar
p water
easpoons lemon juice
ups strawberries, pureed
g white
ablespoons powdered sugar, sifted

solve the sugar in the water over gentle heat.
ng to a boil and boil rapidly for 3 minutes.
ol. Stir in the lemon juice and strawberry
ee. Pour into a freezer container and freeze
l "slushy." Beat the egg white until stiff. Beat
he powdered sugar. Beat this into the straw-
ry mixture until evenly combined. Freeze
l solid. To serve, use a melon baller to form
ll scoops.

STRAWBERRY JAM

strawberries
blespoons lemon juice
ps sugar

Hull and wash the strawberries, put in a pan with
the lemon juice and simmer gently in their own
juice for 20 to 30 minutes until really soft. Add
the sugar, stir until dissolved and boil rapidly
until setting point is reached. Allow to cool for 15
to 20 minutes then jar and cover in the usual way.
Makes about 5 lb.

STREUSEL

A crumb topping for coffee cakes and fruit tarts
made of flour, butter, sugar, and cinnamon. Cake
crumbs may be substituted for the flour and
chopped nuts added.

STRIPED BASS (ROCKFISH)

A game and food fish of the coastal waters of
North America, of commercial importance on
the East Coast of the United States, where its sale
has been restricted because of chemical pollutants. Striped bass usually runs from 15 to 18
inches in length, although larger fish are sometimes seen on the market.

Striped bass is a versatile fish. It may be cooked
whole or in fillets and may be broiled, baked,
sautéed, or cooked en papillote. While it is
wonderful poached and served hot with a hollandaise or shellfish sauce, it is equally delicious
cooked in the same manner, chilled and served
with a mayonnaise, gribiche or mustard sauce.
Bake bass in a 425° oven or poach it for 10
minutes per inch at its thickest point. If stuffed,
include the stuffing in the measurement.

STROGANOFF

A preparation of thinly sliced meat quickly
cooked with onions and mushrooms and served
in a thick sour cream sauce. This dish is celebrated
as Boeuf Stroganoff (see Beef entry) and,
although any steak cut may be used, is at its best
when prepared with tenderloin.

STRUDEL

A form of pastry, very popular in Austria,
Germany, and central Europe generally. It is
made from a soft dough which is stretched out by
hand until paper-thin, covered with one of a
variety of fillings (e.g., apple, black cherries, nuts,
poppy seeds, cheese, and vegetables) and rolled
like a jelly roll.

STILTON CHEESE

Regarded as the "King of English cheeses." The blue-veined variety has a soft close texture when ripe: the blue veins are a penicillin mold which is allowed to grow in the cheese, as in Roquefort and Gorgonzola. These give the cheese a very strong flavor. Stilton gained its name not because it was made in the village of Stilton, but because this is where it was first sold. It is now only made in certain areas of England, including Melton Mowbray in Leicestershire, Dovedale in Derbyshire, and parts of Nottinghamshire.

It used to be considered fashionable to scoop Stilton out from the center of the cheese with a spoon or cheese scoop then pour port into the cheese to stop it hardening. Some experts consider this practice wasteful, suggesting that a more suitable way to serve the whole or half cheese is to cut down the cheese 1 to 2 inches and take wedges all round on this level.

There is also a white Stilton cheese which does not contain the blue veins. This is a mild crumbly cheese.

STIR-FRYING

A Chinese cooking technique used to cook small pieces of food quickly. Vegetables, meat, poultry, and shellfish, after being cut into slices, shreds, or chunks, are cooked in a small amount of oil over high heat in a metal pot with a rounded bottom. The food is added in the order of its cooking time and is stirred constantly while frying to prevent burning. The sloping, rounded wok in which it is cooked helps to keep the ingredients constantly in motion. This method of quick cooking was developed to offset the scarcity of fuel in China.

STOCK

The liquid produced when meat, bones, or vegetables are simmered with herbs and seasonings in water for several hours. Stock forms the basis of soups, sauces, stews, and many dishes, giving a far better flavor than when plain water is used. It has no food value apart from some minerals.

MEAT STOCK

Any meat (especially such cuts as shin of beef or shank and knuckle of veal) and any bones, whether fresh or already cooked, can be used to make stock. Place the bones (and the meat, if used) in a saucepan with a few flavoring vegetables (e.g. carrot, onion, celery) and add a few

peppercorns, a clove, a b[...]
herbs, bring to a boil, cov[...]
hours.

Green vegetables and [...]
normally be included, as [...]
sour rapidly. If they are [...]
be used at once.

If the bones or scraps [...]
liquid should be strain[...]
allowed to cool, so that [...]
before the stock is used.[...]

If the stock is not used [...]
a boil each day, addin[...]
vegetables and more w[...]
the pot after 3 to 4 days a[...]
are sometimes used for [...]

VEGETABLE STOCK

This is made in the same [...]
a selection of vegetables [...]
rutabaga, turnip, celery [...]
simmered for a shorter t[...]
quickly. A few bacon sl[...]
and richness.

FISH STOCK

Use the bones and skin fr[...]
with flavoring, vegetabl[...]
make as above, simmeri[...]
stock should be used w[...]
making.

BOUILLON CUBES

These provide an easy v[...]

STOCKFISH

Cod which has been air-[...]

STOLLEN

A rich, sweet German [...]
with raisins, candied fr[...]
side of the bread is folde[...]
baking to form a long [...]
heavily with powdered s[...]
served in thin slices. T[...]
Germany is famed for t[...]

STOUT

A beer made with a dar[...]
(and sweeter) than ale.

STUFFING

A mixture used to give flavor (and sometimes shape) to a dish. It may be placed in the body cavities (as with poultry), laid flat between two portions, spread on fillets before they are rolled, or mixed with ground meat, etc., as in galantines, to increase the bulk. It is also used to stuff vegetables to serve as an accompaniment or main dish. White bread crumbs, chopped vegetables, ground meat, pounded fish, rice, etc., are used as a base; vegetables, herbs, spices, and extracts, etc., are used for flavoring; and eggs, stock, gravy, sauce, milk, or mayonnaise bind the ingredients together; some fat is also necessary, usually in the form of melted butter, margarine, or cream.

(See separate entry for Forcemeat.)

NUT STUFFING

½ cup walnuts
¼ cup cashew nuts
6 Brazil nuts
¼ cup butter
2 small onions, finely chopped
4 oz mushrooms, finely chopped
pinch of dried mixed herbs
1 tablespoon chopped parsley
2 cups fresh white bread crumbs
1 large egg, beaten
giblet stock to moisten
seasoning

Finely chop the nuts. Melt the butter and sauté the onion for 5 minutes. Add the mushrooms and sauté for a further 5 minutes. Toss together the nuts, mixed herbs, parsley, and bread crumbs. Stir in the mushroom mixture with the beaten egg. If necessary, moisten with stock; season. *Makes enough for a 9 to 10 lb bird.*

CHESTNUT STUFFING

1 lb peeled chestnuts
½ cup broth
12 oz sausage meat
poultry liver
1 large onion
2 tablespoons butter
salt and pepper
¼ cup white wine

To peel the chestnuts, cook in boiling water for 5 minutes. Drain and peel. Cook in the broth for 30 minutes, then drain and chop roughly. Combine with the sausage. Chop the liver and onion and sauté in the butter for 2 to 3 minutes. Add to the chestnut mixture and toss with the remaining ingredients. *Makes enough for a 9 lb bird.*

STURGEON

A large shark-like fish, with an average weight of about 60 lb, which is caught in river estuaries and seas of the northern hemisphere and is in season from August through March.

Sturgeon is expensive, but its firm, white flesh is delicious if suitably prepared and cooked. When bought, it should have veins of a bluish color – not brown, which indicates that the fish is stale. It may be cooked in various ways and is particularly good when roasted and stuffed.

The precious roe of the sturgeon is known as caviar and is highly prized by gourmets and extremely expensive. (See Caviar entry.) The air bladder of the sturgeon is used to make isinglass (see Isinglass entry). The finest caviar comes from the beluga, largest of all sturgeon. The beluga live in the Black and Caspian seas and swim up the Danube and the Volga rivers to spawn.

SUCCOTASH

A traditional American dish made from corn and green or lima beans. The dish originated with the Narrangansett Indians.

SUCROSE

Common sugar (a chemical combination of glucose and fructose) as obtained from both sugar cane and sugar beet. When cooked with acid, sucrose is split into glucose and fructose; the former is less sweet and the latter sweeter than sucrose.

SUET

The fat around the kidneys and loins of sheep and cows that is a common ingredient in many traditional English recipes. In Great Britain it is bought either from the butcher, in the form of solid lumps of fat, or from the grocer, grated and packaged ready for use.

Suet is used in stuffings and mincemeat, in steamed suet puddings (including Christmas puddings) and in suetcrust pastry.

SUGAR

A crystaline, sweet-tasting substance obtained from various plants. The type normally used in the home is sucrose, derived both from sugar cane, grown in tropical and sub-tropical countries, and from sugar beet. Contrary to some people's impression, beet and cane sugar are of equal value. Other sources of sugar of various kinds are maple trees, sorghum (Chinese cane), millet, corn, certain varieties of palm trees and malted substances.

Types of Sugar

SUCROSE
This is contained in sweet fruits and in roots such as carrots, as well as in sugar cane and beet, which give a product that is chemically the same.

GLUCOSE
Contained in honey, grapes, and whole kernel corn.

FRUCTOSE
Contained in fruit juices and honey.

LACTOSE
Contained in milk.

MALTOSE
Formed during the germination of grain. (See individual sugar entries.)

Food Value of Sugar
Sugar is a good source of energy and is easily and speedily digested. However, it should not be taken in place of more valuable foods.

If eaten to excess it may lead to obesity.

Commercially Prepared Sugars
These are varieties of cane and beet sugar which are all the same in structure.

Granulated: A refined white sugar with coarse granules. It is used for most sweetening purposes and is the most economical sugar.

Superfine: A fine white sugar mostly used in cakes and puddings.

Cube: Refined white sugar which is compressed into cubes for convenient table use.

Powdered: White sugar which is ground to a fine powder. It is used for making frosting, sorbets, ice creams, and meringues.

Brown sugar: Light and dark, a soft sugar used in baking.

Maple sugar: Extracted from the sap of the maple tree, has a characteristic flavor. In sweetening power it is similar to cane and beet sugar.

Malt sugar: Found in the malting of cereals, etc.

Molasses: This by-product arising during the refining of sugar is a viscous liquid, consisting of an unrefined solution of sugar in water. Its sweetening power is about one-third less than that of sugar.

Uses of Sugar
Sugar sweetens food and is an essential ingredient in all cakes and desserts. Combined with either fat or eggs in rich cakes, it helps to hold air; in dough mixtures it makes the cake lighter in texture.

Sugar is also useful as a preservative (e.g. in jammaking), since bacteria and molds find it difficult to live in highly concentrated sugar solutions such as those found in jam, 60 to 70 per cent.

Sugar-boiling
This process is the basis of most candymaking and is also employed in some frosting and for making caramels. The sugar is first dissolved in water and brought to a boil. At this stage the thermometer will register 212° and the mixture will remain at this temperature until enough water has been evaporated to produce a syrup consistency. Then the temperature will start to rise, continuing as more water evaporates. The syrup first becomes very thick but pale, darkening gradually, until finally at 350° it becomes dark brown. At this stage it is no longer sweet and it can be used for darkening gravy.

A candy thermometer is desirable for this work but for simple candy it is possible to use instead the home tests described below.

The list gives the various stages between boiling point and caramel, with their special names and the method of testing. Although definite temperatures are quoted for the different stages, the sugar passes almost imperceptibly from one stage to the next.

SOFT BALL
(235° to 245°) When a drop of the syrup is put into very cold water it forms a soft ball; at 235° the soft ball flattens on removal from the water, but the higher the temperature, the firmer the ball, till it reaches the Firm Ball Stage. Used for making fondants and fudge.

HARD BALL
(245° to 265°) The syrup, when dropped into cold water, forms a ball which is hard enough to hold its shape, but is still pliable. Used for making caramels and marshmallows.

SOFT CRACK

(270° to 290°) The syrup, when dropped into cold water, separates into threads which are hard but not brittle. Used for toffees.

HARD CRACK

(300° to 310°) When a drop of the syrup is put into cold water, it separates into threads which are hard and brittle. Used for hard toffees.

CARAMEL

(310°) Shown by the syrup becoming golden brown. Used for making praline and caramels, also for flavoring caramel custard, etc. (See Candy entry.)

Crystalization

The technique of dissolving and boiling sugar needs great care, as the syrup has a tendency to recrystalize if not handled correctly.

The chief causes are: (1) agitation of the mixture by stirring or beating, and (2) the presence of any solid particles such as sugar crystals or grit in the syrup while boiling.

To obtain a clear syrup, therefore, the pan must be perfectly clean and the sugar must be completely dissolved before the mixture is allowed to boil. Should any crystals form on the sides of the pan after boiling has begun, they should be brushed down with a clean pastry brush dipped in cold water. Also, there must be no stirring or agitation of the mixture, but a wooden spatula can be used to tap the grains of sugar onto the bottom of the pan while dissolving, to hasten the process. Once the sugar is dissolved and the syrup has been brought to a boil, it can be heated rapidly to the exact temperature stated in the recipe and at once removed from the heat, so that the temperature does not rise any higher.

SUKIYAKI

A combination of meat and vegetables cooked in a saucepan and known in Japan, because of its appeal to foreign palates, as the "friendship dish." The ingredients of the sukiyaki are beautifully arranged on a platter and brought to the table where the food is cooked in a shallow heavy iron pan atop a charcoal brazier, gas flame or electric plate. An electric skillet would do as well. Beef is the traditional meat, while poultry, pork or other combinations are considered to be variations.

SULTANA

The raisin of a seedless species of grape vine, which is grown in many regions, principally California, Greece, Crete, Australia, and South Africa. Originally sultanas came only from Turkey, being shipped from the port of Smyrna.

The best sultanas are pale yellow, with such thin skins that they are almost transparent; the inferior grades have many dark fruits mixed with the light. Sultanas have a pleasant fruity flavor and are used extensively in cakes, cookies, mincemeat, pickles, curries, etc.

The chief nutritional value of sultanas is represented by the iron they contain and the energy provided by the sugar.

SUNDAE

An ice cream concoction usually served in a shallow dish or a tall glass, with a sweet sauce, syrup such as chocolate, caramel or marshmallow whip poured over it and topped with fresh or crystalized fruit, nuts, or grated chocolate and whipped cream.

Some suitable sauces are given below.

STRAWBERRY SAUCE

Boil $\frac{1}{4}$ cup sugar with $\frac{2}{3}$ cup water until they form a syrup and add 1 cup crushed strawberries. Remove the pan from the heat and chill very thoroughly before using.

RASPBERRY SAUCE

Make as for strawberry sauce. If canned fruit is used, replace the water with the liquid from the can and use sugar only if required. The mixture may be rubbed through a fine sieve to remove the seeds.

CHOCOLATE SAUCE

Melt 2 oz chocolate and 1 tablespoon butter in a bowl over hot water, then remove from the heat and stir in 1 tablespoon milk and 1 teaspoon vanilla extract. Use hot or cold.

CARAMEL SAUCE

Melt 1 tablespoon brown sugar, 1 tablespoon corn syrup, and 2 tablespoons butter in a heavy saucepan and boil for 1 minute. Add 1 tablespoon milk and serve hot. If desired, add $\frac{1}{4}$ cup chopped walnuts or the grated rind of $\frac{1}{2}$ a lemon.

SUNFISH (YELLOW PERCH)

A freshwater fish found largely in shallow lake waters of North America. It is an important commercial fish of the Great Lakes and is caught by sportsmen as well. Sunfish are small, rarely exceeding 1 lb and are sold filleted or whole. Small fish may be sautéed or pan fried whole. They may also be baked in a 425° oven on a bed of onions moistened with wine. Dot with butter and baste occasionally. Cook for 10 minutes per inch measured at the thickest part.

SUNFLOWER OIL

An oil extracted from sunflower seeds. It is an almost odorless, pale yellow oil with a mild flavor that makes it excellent for cooking and for use in salad dressings. It is also high in poly-unsaturates.

SUNFLOWER SEEDS

The seeds of the sunflower plant that was once considered a weed. The plants are now cultivated for the seeds which are an important commercial snack food and in favor among health-food fans and vegetarians for their high protein content.

SUPRÊME SAUCE

A white sauce made like a Velouté sauce, with a base of well-reduced chicken stock; cream, butter, or egg yolks may be added just before the sauce is served. (See Menu Glossary entry.)

SUSHI

A Japanese food of vinegared rice and raw fish served as a snack or as an appetizer. There are three types of sushi: Vinegared rice spread with small pieces of fish and rolled in edible seaweed; vinegared rice served in a bowl and decorated with bits of fish, shellfish, and vegetables; and the most popular form, small balls or rectangles of vinegared rice topped with bits of raw fish. In Japan sushi bars are found everywhere in large cities and sushi is a favorite ingredient of lunch and picnic boxes.

SWAN

In the Middle Ages this large white water fowl with a taste resembling that of a goose was considered a great delicacy and was often served at royal banquets and special occasions. It is seldom eaten now because its meat is generally very oily and tough unless taken from a very young swan or cygnet.

Swans are still considered royal birds in England where they are served at the annual Swan banquet put on by the Swan wardens of the Vintner's Company in the City of London.

SWEDE (SWEDISH TURNIP)

(See Rutabaga entry.)

SWEETBREAD

The culinary term for the glands in the throat and near the heart of the lamb and calf.

The most delicate sweetbreads are lambs', but these are rather more expensive than the other kinds. Both heart and throat sweetbreads can be bought, the heart sweetbread (pancreas) being the better, as it has fewer membranes and is a nicer shape.

In addition to their protein content, sweetbreads contribute a little fat and thiamin.

To prepare sweetbreads: Use very fresh; wash and soak in cold water for several hours, changing the water as it becomes discolored. Blanch by covering with cold water with a few drops of lemon juice added, bring slowly to the boiling point and boil for 5 minutes. Drain, put in cold water and pull off any fat and skin that will come away easily. Use as required; sweetbreads may be cooked in various ways and we give a couple of typical recipes.

SAUTÉED SWEETBREADS

Allow 1 lb lambs' or calves' sweetbreads for 4 people. Soak them for 3 to 4 hours in cold water, drain and put into a pan. Cover them with water and the juice of $\frac{1}{2}$ lemon, bring slowly to a boil, then simmer for 5 minutes. Drain and leave in cold water until they are firm and cold, then strip off any stringy tissue.

Press the sweetbreads well between paper towels, slice and dip into beaten egg and fresh bread crumbs. Cut a few slices of bacon into strips and sauté lightly until just crisp; drain and keep hot, then sauté the sweetbreads in the same fat until golden. Toss the bacon and sweetbreads together and serve at once with tartar or tomato sauce.

CREAMED SWEETBREADS

1 lb sweetbreads, prepared as for sautéed
  sweetbreads, above
½ onion, chopped
1 carrot, chopped
few parsley stalks
½ bay leaf
salt
pepper
3 tablespoons butter
4 tablespoons flour
1¼ cups milk
squeeze of lemon juice
chopped parsley to garnish

Put the sweetbreads, vegetables, herbs, and seasoning in a pan with water to cover and simmer gently until tender – 45 minutes to 1 hour. Drain and keep hot, retaining 1¼ cups of the cooking liquid. Melt the butter, stir in the flour and cook for 2 to 3 minutes. Remove the pan from the heat and gradually stir in the sweetbread liquid and the milk. Bring to a boil and continue to stir until it thickens, season well and add a few drops of lemon juice. Reheat the sweetbreads in the sauce and serve sprinkled with parsley.

SWEET CICELY

The name given in Europe to an aromatic herb with a sweet flavor resembling aniseed. The herb looks a little like parsley and grows wild in Europe.

SWEET POTATO

This plant (which is no relation to the ordinary potato) is a native of South America, but is now cultivated in other parts of the world with a similar climate. The tubers have a tender, sweet, and slightly perfumed flesh and are usually served as an accompaniment to meat, but may also be eaten as a dessert such as a sweet potato pie. They are fresh or in canned form; the canned sweet potatoes may be mashed with butter and milk, sweetened, and flavored with spice, etc., then used as a filling for a pie or tart, or they may be heated and served with roast meat.

The chief food value of sweet potatoes lies in their starch content and sugar; they also contain vitamin C and some B vitamins.

Sweet potatoes may be baked in their jackets and served with a pat of butter or any of the following: soured cream; grated cheese and chopped onion; hot meat sauce; spicy tomato sauce; honey.

SWISS CHARD

A leafy green vegetable. The green part of the leaves should be prepared and cooked as spinach and the midribs as celery.

SWORDFISH

A large marine game and food fish weighing up to 600 lb, found in coastal waters over the world. It is a particularly popular fish in the United States. The swordfish gets its name from the long swordlike extension of its upper jaw.

Swordfish has a flesh firm enough to skewer and cook as kebabs. It is sold in steaks and may also be sautéed, grilled, broiled, or baked but must be watched carefully as it becomes tasteless if overcooked.

SYLLABUB

An old English dessert, traditionally made by gently pouring fresh milk, in a thin stream, over wine, cider, or ale, resulting in a frothy mixture which was sweetened to taste and flavored with spices and spirit. Alternatively, cream was whisked with wine, sugar, and grated lemon rind until frothy; as the froth formed, it was skimmed off, to be served piled on small almond-flavored cookies.

SYLLABUB MADE WITH WINE

2 egg whites
½ cup sugar
juice of ½ lemon
⅔ cup sweet white wine
1¼ cups heavy cream, whipped
crystalized lemon slices

Whisk the egg whites stiffly and fold in the sugar, lemon juice, wine, and cream. Pour the mixture into individual glasses and chill for several hours before serving. Decorate with the lemon slices. The mixture will separate out as it stands.

SYRUP

A solution of sugar dissolved in water and concentrated by being heated; the syrup is often flavored with fruit juice or extract. The chief uses of syrup in cookery are for sweetening such things as cold beverages, stewed fruit, and fruit salad, for preserving, glazing, candying, and crystalizing fruit, and for making candies.

The term syrup also denotes the uncrystalizable fluid separated from sugar-cane juice in the process of refining molasses.

TABASCO

A very hot, red sauce made from a kind of capsicum (pepper), originally grown in Mexico.

TABOULEH

A refreshing Middle Eastern salad made from bulgar (cracked wheat) and flavored with mint.

TABOULEH

1 cup bulgar
2 tomatoes, peeled and chopped
¼ cup chopped green onions
1 cup chopped parsley
½ cup chopped mint
¼ cup olive oil
¼ cup lemon juice

Soak bulgar for 1 hour, or according to package directions. Drain. Toss with ingredients.

TACO

The Mexican version of a sandwich, a taco is a rolled tortilla with a filling. Tacos may be eaten as is or broiled, fried, or baked. (See Tortilla entry.)

TAHINI

A baste made of toasted sesame seeds, popular in the Middle East where it is used to flavor cakes, cookies, and sauces.

TAMALE

A Mexican dish of Aztec origin made of corn husks spread with masa and wrapped around a filling of meat, poultry or vegetables. The little package is tied and steamed before eating.

TAMARILLO (TREE TOMATO)

An oval to egg-shaped fruit, native to South America and grown commercially in New Zealand. The mature fruit can be plum red, purplish, or yellow. It can be eaten raw or cooked, but is usually first submerged in boiling water for 1 minute and then stripped of its bitter skin.

TAMARIND

The fruit of a tropical tree grown in the East and West Indies and similar regions. The leaves and flowers are eaten as a vegetable, while the acid, juicy pulp found in the pods is used to make preserves, sauces, and chutneys and figures largely in Oriental curries and other dishes. The seeds are ground into a meal and baked as cakes.

TAMMY

To squeeze a sauce through a fine woolen cloth to strain it and make it glossy.

TANDOORI

Food of northern India that is first marinated in a spicy yogurt dressing and then threaded onto spits and baked in a tandoor over hot coals. It is the tandoor, a clay oven, that gives these dishes their name. (See Curry entry for Tandoori Chicken recipe.)

TANGELO

(See Ugli entry.)

TANGERINE

A small, very sweet type of orange, with a skin which is easily removed.

Tangerines are usually served as dessert, but may also be used in making fruit salads, cakes, etc., and the small, brightly colored sections are useful for decorating desserts and gâteaux. To remove the pith, dip the sections quickly into boiling water and scrape them with a knife.

Tangerines can be made into very good marmalade, provided extra pectin or lemon juice is added to insure a good set. The peel may be preserved like that of oranges (see Candied Fruit entry.)

There are several other citrus fruits somewhat resembling tangerines such as the ones described below. The South African *naartje* is also a form of tangerine.

CLEMENTINE

A form of tangerine grown in North Africa. It has closer rind, more like that of an orange, is practically seedless, and not quite so sweet as the ordinary tangerine.

MANDARIN

Also known as the clove or noble orange. Mandarins were originally grown in China, but are now cultivated in Spain, Italy, Malta, and Algeria. They are small and flat in shape, with a thin, tender rind which is easily separated from the flesh. They are slightly larger, sweeter, and darker in color than the ordinary tangerine.

SATSUMA

A prized form of mandarin grown in Spain.

KUMQUAT, AND UGLI

These are related to tangerines. (See entries.)

TANSY

An herb with bitter, aromatic leaves. It was widely used in earlier centuries, traditionally at Easter time. A "tansy" was a baked egg custard flavored with tansy leaves.

TAPAS

Spanish appetizers, ranging from olives and toasted almonds to small skewers of anchovy, cheese, foie gras, ham, and smoked fish and sophisticated miniature sandwiches. Although a specialty of the bars of Madrid, tapas are available throughout Spain.

TAPIOCA

This cereal is obtained from the roots of the cassava plant (see Cassava entry), which grows in hot countries like Central and South America, Malaya, and the East and West Indies. Tapioca is sold in different forms, the most common being flakes (large, irregularly shaped pieces) and pearls, which cook more quickly.

Tapioca contains very little protein and consists almost entirely of starch. Its chief uses are for making puddings and as a thickener.

TARAMASALATA

A Greek dip made from tarama, the dried roe of the gray mullet. The roe is available in cans.

TARAMASALATA

4 slices white bread, crusts removed
milk
4 oz tarama
1 small onion, chopped
1 clove garlic, chopped
¼ cup lemon juice
¾ cup olive oil

Soak the bread in the milk and squeeze dry. Shred into the blender and add the tarama, onion, garlic, and lemon juice. Process until smooth, then add the oil gradually, making sure each addition is absorbed before adding more.

TARO

Taro tubers (also known as coco yams) are a staple diet in the Pacific islands; they can be boiled or baked or made into a kind of bread. Taro must be well cooked or fermented to break down the poisons it contains.

TARRAGON

An aromatic herb which is similar to wormwood. This herb has long, narrow leaves which have a mild licorice flavor. There are two varieties, Russian and French; the latter is more delicate in flavor and is the one grown for culinary purposes. It is used in tarragon vinegar which the French use for mixing mustard. It combines well with chicken and fish and is the correct flavoring for tartar sauce.

TARRAGON CHICKEN

2 tablespoons butter
2 slices bacon, chopped
2 onions, sliced
2 carrots, sliced
4 chicken parts
2 oz chicken livers
3 tarragon sprigs
1¼ cups chicken broth
1 tablespoon sweet sherry
salt and pepper
1 teaspoon cornstarch
tarragon sprigs

Melt the butter in a skillet and add the bacon, onions, and carrots. Cook until wilted, then transfer to a casserole. Brown the chicken on both sides and transfer to the casserole. Brown the chicken livers and place around the chicken. Add tarragon, broth, sherry, seasoning. Cover and cook in a 325° oven for 1 hour. Thicken the gravy with cornstarch and pour back over chicken; season. Garnish with fresh tarragon.

TART, TARTLET

A large or small open pastry shell with a filling such as fruit, jam, lemon curd, cake mixture, custard, etc. The term is often used interchangeably with "pie" or "flan."

Tarts are usually made of short-crust or flan pastry. The filling is usually cooked in the pastry shell but in the case of a custard tart, the pastry may be filled with pie weights and prebaked before the filling is added.

Metal, enamel, or ovenproof glass or china pans, square baking pans, and flan rings may all be used for tarts and individual tartlet pans of various sizes.

TART BAKED AFTER FILLING

Make the pastry and roll it out into a round a little larger than the pie pan or dish to be used. Fit the pastry evenly and neatly on the pan, taking care not to pull or stretch it and making sure that there are no air bubbles underneath. Trim around the pan with a sharp knife and decorate the edge as desired. Place on a baking sheet. Add the filling and bake in a 425° oven for about 10 minutes, to set the pastry; then lower the heat according to the recipe and bake until the filling is cooked.

LATTICED TART

This is an attractive way of finishing tarts. For an 8-inch pie pan about 5 to 6 oz pastry will be required. Line the pan with the pastry, reserving about one-third of it for the decoration. Spread the jam or other filling over the pastry. Cut strips of pastry ¼ inch wide and arrange them lattice fashion over the filling. Moisten the edge of the tart with water, then lay a strip of pastry the width of the rim all the way around, covering the ends of the criss-cross strips, press down and decorate as desired. Glaze the pastry and bake in a 425° oven for 15 to 20 minutes.

TARTARIC ACID

A colorless, crystaline compound, occurring in various plants, especially in unripe grapes. For domestic purposes its acid salt — potassium tartrate, or cream of tartar — is more commonly used. This can be combined with soda to form an emergency baking powder. It is also used in candymaking.

TARTAR SAUCE

A mayonnaise sauce flavored with herbs, chopped capers and pickles, which is served with fish, salads, and such vegetables as Jerusalem artichokes.

TARTAR SAUCE

⅔ cup mayonnaise
1 teaspoon chopped fresh tarragon or chives
2 teaspoons chopped capers
2 teaspoons chopped pickles
2 teaspoons chopped parsley
1 tablespoon lemon juice or tarragon vinegar

Combine the ingredients and allow to stand for at least 1 hour before serving. Serve with fish.

TEA

A tropical evergreen shrub: the dried leaves are used to make a drink which is an infusion with boiling water. Various types and quality of tea depend on differences in soil, climate, and firing produce. It is grown in China, Pakistan, India, Sri Lanka, and Japan and was first introduced in Europe in the seventeenth century.

There are many varieties or grades of tea, but these are not classified on quality but on the size of the leaf. Those made from broken leaves are strong quick-brewing teas. "Dust" is a trade term for small particle leaves. These are not used alone but are blended with other leaves. Most teas now consist of blends.

Tea as such has little food value, though when served with milk and sugar it acquires the food values of these substances. A good infusion of tea, properly made, contains little tannin, but tea that has been standing for a long time will have an excessive amount of tannin extracted and this may be harmful if drunk in large amounts.

Types of Tea
There are several types of tea available:

GREEN TEA
Mainly produced in China. The leaf is steamed and dried quickly without being allowed to ferment and this preserves the green color. Green tea has a much more astringent taste than black tea and a liking for it is an acquired taste.

BROWN TEA
After being picked, the leaves are partially fermented before drying. Tea made from these leaves is pale brown in color, with a characteristic flavor. Oolong teas are examples of this type.

BLACK TEA
For this, the most popular type of tea, the leaves are fermented before drying; the brew made from black tea is darkish-brown and has a slightly astringent flavor.

Much of the world's black tea is imported from India and Sri Lanka. A large quantity of it is blended in England, where tea is extremely popular, and sold in branded packages. It is also possible to buy "pure" teas from Sri Lanka, Assam, and Darjeeling. The teas are usually blended to suit the average taste and water supply, but some firms specialize in making up teas to suit the water of a particular district.

Choosing and Storing Tea
Most teas now sold are ready-packed, so one cannot see the actual leaves when buying. Points to remember when trying a new brand are that a good tea is made up of small, well-rolled leaves and has a pleasing aroma, while a poor one has a large percentage of dust and stalk.

Since tea readily absorbs moisture, it must be kept tightly covered in a cool, dry place.

Making Tea
1. Boil water. (Soft water makes a darker tea, but many people do not think the flavor is as good as that of tea made with hard water.)
2. Warm the pot and add the tea. The quantity varies according to the type and blend. The average amount is 1 teaspoon tea to 1 cup of water.
3. Make the tea as soon as the kettle boils or the water will go "flat" and spoil the taste of the brew. Take the teapot to the kettle and pour the boiling water onto the leaves, then cover the pot to keep it warm.
4. Allow the infusion to stand for 3 minutes in the case of ordinary teas, 5 or 6 minutes for high-grade tea.

Serving Tea
Tea should be served really hot. Milk is usually served with black tea, but lemon can be offered as an alternative. Sugar should also be offered for those who prefer a sweet tea. High-grade teas are usually served with lemon.

ICED TEA

Prepare the tea, strain it, and pour into a tumbler part-filled with crushed ice. Add sugar and a slice of lemon and re-chill before serving – the quicker the chilling, the better the flavor and the clearer the tea.

TEAL

One of the smaller wild ducks, averaging about 14 inches in length. Teal, which is highly prized, is in season September through February and is at its best at Christmas. It is found in the Americas, Europe, and Asia. One bird per person is served. It is usually roasted in a 350° oven for 25 to 30 minutes and served garnished with watercress and slices of lemon.

TEFF

A plant with very small grains about the size of a pin head which grows in Abyssinia, where a bread made of meal ground from these grains is the staple article of diet.

TEMPERATURES FOR COOKING

Accurate temperatures are essential to insure good results in cooking – the most perfectly mixed cake will not survive being baked at the wrong temperature.

OVEN TEMPERATURES
The ovens of most modern electric and gas stoves are thermostatically controlled; once the thermostat has been set, the oven heat will not rise above the selected temperature.

WATER–BASED LIQUIDS

Boiling	212°
Simmering (approximately)	205°
Tepid and lukewarm (approximately)	98°
Freezing point	32°

TEMPERATURES FOR SUGAR-BOILING, PRESERVING, FRYING

To judge these, it is best to use a candy or jelly thermometer. (See individual entries and recipes for the exact temperatures required.)

TEMPURA

Japanese batter-dipped deep-fried seafood and vegetables, including seaweed and herbs. The foods are dipped in a flavored soy sauce before eating. Using an electric skillet or deep-fryer, tempura can be cooked at the table for an unusual dinner party. Arrange the foods on platters and let each guest cook his own. The foods should be thoroughly dry or the batter will not stick. Tempura may be served as an appetizer or main dish.

SHRIMP TEMPURA

24 large shrimp
1 egg
1 cup water
1 cup all-purpose flour
oil for frying

Shell the shrimp, leaving the tail intact, and devein. Beat the egg with the water and add the flour gradually. The batter should be slightly lumpy. Heat the oil to 360° and dip the shrimp in the batter. Cook for 2 to 3 minutes, or until golden brown.

DIPPING SAUCE

1 cup Japanese soy sauce
2 tablespoons freshly grated horseradish
2 teaspoons grated gingerroot

Stir the ingredients together to combine.

TENDERLOIN

The long tapering muscle that extends the entire length of the loin (short loin and sirloin) of an animal. In beef, the entire piece of meat may be roasted at once or it may be cut into steaks, filet mignons coming from the thin end in the short loin and the larger Chateaubriands coming from the thicker end in the sirloin.

TEQUILA

A Mexican spirit distilled from the heart of the maguey plant.

TERIYAKI

Japanese foods, usually fish, marinated in sake-flavored soy sauce to which sugar has been added, and then broiled. The sugar imparts a glaze to the cooked foods. Marinate seafoods for about 30 minutes, meats or poultry for several hours before broiling.

TERIYAKI MARINADE

1 cup soy sauce
1 cup sake or dry sherry
⅓ cup sugar

Combine ingredients.

TERRAPIN

A small turtle of North America, the flesh of which is considered a great delicacy.

TERRINE

An earthenware cooking dish and hence the meat, rabbit, game, fowl, or fish cooked (and often served) in the dish. (See Pâté entry.)

THIAMIN

One of the B vitamins (see Vitamins entry).

THICKENING

Any substance added to sauces, soups, etc., to give them a thicker consistency and to bind them. (In most sauces, of course, the thickening or liaison is an integral part of the mixture, e.g, the flour used in many sauces and the butter used in hollandaise and Béarnaise sauce.) A thickening also insures a smooth texture and holds heavy ingredients (whether sieved or not) in suspension – without a liaison such ingredients as lentils would separate out from a soup and settle at the bottom.

THICKENING FOR SAUCES
(See Sauce entry.)

THICKENING FOR SOUPS
Flour, rice flour, cornstarch, potato flour, sago, tapioca, semolina, egg, and cream are all used.

THICKENING FOR STEWS, ETC.

Flour, potato flour, and cornstarch can be used in the proportion of 2½ tablespoons thickening agent to 2½ cups of stock. Blood is also used in meat dishes such as jugged hare.

How to Add Thickenings and Liaisons

FLOURS AND OTHER POWDERED CEREALS

For soups or stews, mix smoothly with a little cold liquid, then add just before serving and boil for at least 5 minutes, stirring all the time.

(For Sauces see Sauce entry.)

SMALL GRAIN, E.G. SAGO, TAPIOCA

These must be added 15 to 20 minutes before serving and cooked until quite transparent.

EGG

The richer white soups and sauces may be thickened by eggs or egg yolks beaten up with a little cream, milk, or light stock or broth. Just before serving, add 2 to 3 tablespoons of the hot but not boiling sauce or soup to the beaten egg mixture, then stir this into the contents of the pan (which should not be quite boiling). Cook and stir for a few minutes on a very low heat or over boiling water in order to coagulate the egg albumin and form the liaison, but do not boil or the egg will curdle.

BEURRE MANIÉ (BUTTER AND FLOUR)

This provides a quick method of thickening the liquid in which meat, fish, vegetables, etc., have been cooked. Knead together ⅔ cup flour and ½ oz butter; add this a small piece at a time to the hot liquid, beating all the time, then bring to the boiling point; repeat until the sauce, gravy, or soup reaches the desired consistency.

THYME

A garden herb with a characteristic flavor, which is used in soups, sauces, stews, etc.; the variety known as lemon thyme is excellent for veal stuffing.

Thyme has a strong pungent flavor and should be used sparingly as it easily overpowers other flavorings.

TIFFIN

Anglo-Indian term for a light mid-day meal not used very much today.

TILEFISH

Any of various Atlantic marine food fishes. Their varied color markings give them their name. Tilefish are usually sold as fillets and are best broiled or sautéed.

TIMBALE

A round mold with straight or sloping sides made from ovenproof china or tinned copper used for molding meat or fish mixtures. Molds for hot timbale can be lined with macaroni, potato, or pastry, and cold molds are usually lined with aspic and decorated. Dishes cooked in the mold usually take on the name "timbale." They are a good way of using leftover meat, fish, vegetables, etc.

TISANE

French name for a medicinal tea or infusion, made with such herbs and flavorings as camomile, lime blossoms, lemon balm, fennel seeds, etc.

TOAD-IN-THE-HOLE

A dish made by cooking sausages or chopped cooked meat in a batter.

TOAD-IN-THE-HOLE

1 cup flour
½ teaspoon salt
1 egg
1¼ cups milk and water
1 lb skinless sausages

Sift the flour and salt into a bowl. Add the egg and half the liquid. Gradually stir in the flour and beat until smooth; stir in the remaining liquid. Grease a shallow ovenproof dish, put in the sausages and pour in the batter. Bake in a 425° oven for 40 to 45 minutes, or until the batter is well-risen and golden brown.

TOAST

Bread browned on each side under a broiler or in an electric toaster.

Toast may be buttered immediately on removal from the heat and placed in a covered dish to keep warm, but this uses more butter and it is less digestible than dry toast served with separate butter.

Fingers of hot buttered toast can be spread with a variety of toppings such as anchovy, peanut butter, flavored cream cheese, smooth pâtés, etc. Cinnamon toast is made by spreading it with a mixture of equal quantities of cinnamon and sugar and then returning it to the broiler to melt the sugar.

Fingers, rounds, diamonds, and other shapes of toast are often used as bases for cocktails.

TOAST MELBA

This light, crisp toast can be served instead of rolls.

Cut slices of bread $\frac{1}{8}$ inch thick and toast them slowly on both sides, so that they become very crisp; or they can be dried slowly in the oven until crisp and golden. Alternatively, cut $\frac{1}{4}$-inch slices, toast them on each side, split them through the middle and toast the uncooked surfaces. Melba toast can also be purchased ready-made.

TODDY

A drink made with rum or whisky, hot water, sugar, and lemon. In tropical countries the word is used for the sap of various palm trees and for the fermented drinks made from them.

TOFFEE

A toffee is made from a simple sugar mixture boiled to 310°. The majority of toffees contain butter, but some are made merely from sugar and water, with flavoring and sometimes coloring. (See Candy entry.)

TOMATILLO

A husk-covered Mexican vegetable that grows on ground vines and resembles a small green tomato. It is used for sauces and is now cultivated in the United States where it is sometimes called a "green tomato."

TOMATO

The soft, pulpy fruit of a trailing plant of South American origin, which is now widely grown in many parts of the world. There are many varieties of tomatoes, ranging from the size of small cherries to that of a large orange and in color from red to orange and yellow.

Tomatoes are a source of vitamin A and C, the vitamin C content being about half that of citrus fruit. Those grown outdoors and allowed to ripen on the plant contain a higher proportion of vitamins and flavor than those picked green.

The characteristic flavor of tomatoes is best enjoyed when they are picked ripe and eaten raw as a salad vegetable, but they are used in cooking for soups and many other dishes (e.g. stuffed tomatoes) and for forming a good flavoring for such things as stews and cheese dishes; the juice makes a refreshing drink. Broiled, baked, or fried tomatoes make a colorful garnish for hot dishes and raw tomatoes can be used in various ways for decoration.

(See Garnish, Salad and Soup entries.)

Ripening and storing tomatoes: If necessary tomatoes can be ripened indoors in one of the following ways:
1. Wrap them in paper and place in a drawer or a covered box or seal tightly in a brown paper bag.
2. Place them in a shady window.
3. In the case of large quantities, pack them in a box, with sawdust to separate each tomato from its neighbors. (Only tomatoes that have begun to turn color should be stored in this way.)

TOMATO SAUCE

2 tablespoons olive oil
1 onion, thinly sliced
2 cloves garlic, minced
1 can (33 oz) plum tomatoes
1 teaspoon dried basil
salt and pepper

Heat the oil in a skillet and sauté the onion and garlic until soft but not browned. Add the tomatoes and seasonings and simmer 30 minutes. If the sauce is acid tasting, add 1 teaspoon sugar.

TOM COLLINS

A drink made of gin, lemon or lime juice, sugar, and cracked ice shaken together and served with soda water.

TONGUE

The tongues of sheep, beef, calves, and pigs may be cooked in various ways and served either hot or cold. Pickled smoked or brined tongues take only half the normal time to cook, and are usually bought from a specialty butcher, but we give below directions for pickling them at home. Hot tongue is generally served with a sauce such as Cumberland, mushroom, or tomato. Cold tongue can be glazed with aspic and served with salad.

Like all meats, tongue is principally a protein food, with some minerals and B vitamins.

PICKLED TONGUE

Choose a tongue with as smooth a skin as possible; wash it very thoroughly, scraping it well and cutting off any gristle at the root end. Rinse in cold water and dry, then rub it over with coarse salt and leave it overnight.

Prepare a pickling liquid as follows:

2 cups salt
2 tablespoons saltpeter
1 cup brown sugar
1¼ gallons water

Boil for 5 minutes, keeping the surface well skimmed, then strain and let cool. Pour the pickling liquid over the tongue, completely covering it, cool and leave for 7 to 10 days.

TORTE

The name given to an open tart or rich cake-type mixture baked in a pastry shell. An Austrian 'torte' called 'Linzertorte' is a flan case of rich spiced pastry filled with raspberry jam then topped with latticed strips of pastry. A 'torte' can include other ingredients such as nuts, fruit, chocolate, and cream. In France savory mixtures are sometimes used as the filling for a rich base. The richness is offset by serving with a green salad.

LINZERTORTE

1 cup flour
½ teaspoon ground cinnamon
6 tablespoons butter
¼ cup superfine sugar
½ cup almonds
grated rind of 1 lemon
2 egg yolks
1 tablespoon lemon juice
1–1½ cups raspberry jam
whipped cream for serving

Sift the flour and cinnamon into a bowl and cut in the butter. Add the sugar, ground almonds, and the lemon rind. Beat the egg yolks and add with the lemon juice to the flour, to make a stiff dough. Knead lightly and let stand in a cool place for 30 minutes. Roll out two-thirds of the pastry and use to line an 8-inch fluted flan ring on a baking sheet. Fill with raspberry jam. Roll out the remaining pastry and cut into ½-inch strips. Use to make a lattice design over the jam.

Bake in a 375° oven for 25 to 35 minutes. Allow to cool, remove from the flan ring, and serve with whipped cream.

Note: Fresh or frozen raspberries can be used in place of the jam: reduce 1 pint raspberries with 1 tablespoon water, a lump of butter, and a little sugar to taste to a thick puree. Cool before serving.

TORTILLA

A kind of thin pancake eaten throughout Mexico, which is made from a dough of *masa* flour (corn kernels cooked with slaked lime, dried, and ground). The pancakes are shaped and flattened by hand and cooked on both sides on a hot griddle until dry. Mexican tortillas are served sprinkled with salt and rolled into a cylinder; if they are filled with beans, meat and a spicy sauce before rolling they are called Tacos.

In Spain, a tortilla is quite a different dish, consisting of beaten eggs and thinly sliced potatoes and onions cooked together in a kind of omelet, the recipe for which follows.

TOSTADA

A tortilla that has been fried until crisp and served covered with many combinations of meats and vegetables, sauces, and garnishes. Depending upon the amount of the filling and its size, the tostada can be served as an appetizer, snack, or main dish.

TREACLE

The British name for the sticky fluid similar to molasses remaining after sugar cane has been processed. Black treacle, which contains more of the harmless impurities than light treacle (called golden syrup), has a somewhat bitter taste.

TREE TOMATO

(See Tamarillo entry.)

TRIFLE

A traditional English dessert made with a sponge cake soaked in a liquid such as sherry or fruit juice, then covered with custard sauce and whipped cream and decorated. Trifles for a party can be quite elaborately decorated with such things as candied fruit, angelica, almonds, almond cookies, grated chocolate, and whipped cream. They may be made either in a large glass dish or in individual glasses or dishes.

Variations on the traditional trifle can be made with the use of convenience foods such as instant custards and canned fruit.

TRIPE

Part of the stomach lining of a cow, sold cleaned and usually parboiled. Tripe is pale cream in color and in texture may be like a honeycomb, depending on whether it is from the first or second stomach. It is, like all meats, a protein food and contains a little fat, some minerals and some B vitamins.

Preparation and cooking: If the tripe has not already been cleaned and blanched, treat it as follows: Wash it in several changes of warm water, scraping it thoroughly and removing any discolored parts and fat, cover with cold water, bring to a boil, then rinse. Repeat one or more times, until the tripe has a pleasant smell. Now put it in cold water, bring to a boil and simmer for 6 to 7 hours, then let stand overnight in the water in which it was cooked. It is at this stage that tripe is usually sold in shops.

After blanching, tripe needs to be simmered in milk and water until tender, usually a further 1 to 1½ hours. It can be served plain with boiled onions, or the liquid can be made into a white sauce, which can be flavored with tomato sauce, mushrooms, capers, etc.

Honeycomb tripe is excellent if it is cooked, cut into small pieces, dipped in batter and fried; serve it with chips, fried onions, or mushrooms and French mustard or tartar sauce.

TROUT

This fish of the salmon family is native to both the United States and Europe where there are varieties including salmon trout, lake trout, river trout, rainbow trout, and brook trout.

Trout require clean, well-oxygenated water to survive. In recent years techniques have been developed for rearing trout on fish farms. They can then be released into natural lakes, etc. or reared to sell for table use.

Salmon trout, also known as sea trout, frequent all the countries bordering the Atlantic, from Spain northwards, and are in season from March through August; they are cooked in the same way as salmon. Lake trout are also treated like salmon.

River trout, although smaller than salmon or lake trout, are much prized for their delicate flavor; they are found in rivers and mountain streams and are in season from March through early September, but are best April through August. Their color varies from silvery-white to dark gray and they may have red, brown, or black spots.

River trout have such a fine flavor that they are best cooked very simply, either broiled or breaded and fried. They may also be smoked or boiled.

TROUT AND ALMONDS

4 trout, about ¼ lb each
seasoned flour
¾ cup butter
½ cup blanched almonds, cut in slivers
juice of ½ lemon

Clean the fish, but leave the heads on. Wash and wipe them and coat with seasoned flour. Melt 8 tablespoons butter in a skillet and sauté the fish in it two at a time, turning them once, until they are tender and golden on both sides, 12 to 15 minutes. Drain and keep them warm on a serving dish. Clean out the pan and melt the remaining butter; add the almonds and heat until lightly browned, add a squeeze of lemon juice and pour over the fish. Serve at once, with lemon.

TRUFFLE

An edible fungus which is much esteemed for flavor and garnish. It grows underground usually under oak or nut trees. As the fungi have a characteristic smell they are located with the help of pigs and dogs.

French black truffles are one of the finest and most famous and are found in Périgord; they also take on this name. Another famous truffle is a white one found in Piedmont, Italy. Truffles are available fresh, at certain times of the year, and canned year round. Lately the black variety have begun to be sold frozen.

TRUFFLE, CHOCOLATE

(See Candy entry.)

TUNA FISH (TUNNY)

A fish found in warm seas, such as the Mediterranean. It is blue-gray above and silver below and grows to 10 feet in length.

Fresh tuna, when obtainable, may be broiled or boiled and served with a suitable sauce.

Canned tuna, usually prepared in oil, is imported from various parts of the world and may be used as an appetizer or in salads and cooked dishes.

TURBOT

A large European flatfish not found in American waters. The best ones are said to be those from the Dogger Bank, but they are also found off the coasts of Holland, Norway, and the British Isles. What is often referred to as the "American turbot" is actually a large flounder or a chicken halibut. Turbots are in season year round, but are at their best between March and August. They have a firm, creamy-white flesh with a characteristic and delicious flavor and are reckoned to be the finest of the flatfish. Because they are so big – they may weigh up to 50 lb – they are usually sold cut into slices or cutlets; when possible, choose thick cuts, which are easier to handle and cook and tend to have a better flavor. Turbot has a useful protein content.

To cook: Small fish may be baked whole after the head and tail have been removed, and the steaks or fillets from larger fish are equally good cooked in this way. Put the turbot in a greased ovenproof dish, sprinkle with seasoning and grated nutmeg and cover it with milk, milk and water, or white wine. Bake in a 350° oven; steaks need about 20 to 30 minutes; whole fish take longer, according to size. Serve with a sauce made from the cooking liquid flavored with anchovy paste or shrimp.

Fillets of turbot may be sautéed by dipping them in seasoned flour and cooking them gently in butter. Serve with lobster, shrimp or anchovy sauce and fried parsley. Turbot can also be steamed, broiled, or poached.

TURKEY

A large farmyard bird of American origin popular for its excellent flavor and its size. The birds are killed at 6 to 9 months. The majority are sold plucked and trussed, sealed in polyethylene and frozen. Small turkeys of about 5 lb can be bought but they are available in various weights up to 20 lb or more. Turkey parts and boned and rolled cooked turkey are also available.

Fresh turkey is available from many butcher shops and a good one can be recognized by the whiteness of its skin and broad, plump breast. The hen tends to be more tender than the tom and has less bone.

Turkey is the centerpiece of the traditional American Thanksgiving feast, and is also served for special occasions and at Easter.

Leftover turkey meat can be made into many interesting dishes. Fricassee, creamed turkey, galantines and pot pies are some examples.

Preparation: If frozen, the bird must be allowed to thaw out before cooking. Leave it for 2 to 3 days in a refrigerator, removing it a little while before cooking, for the flesh to reach room temperature; allow 20 to 30 hours in the refrigerator or about 18 hours in a warm kitchen. It is better to over- rather than underestimate thawing times as it is important that the bird is completely thawed before cooking. When the bird has thawed, remove the bag of giblets which is always packed in the body cavity. The giblets can be boiled with vegetables and flavorings to make gravy stock.

ROAST TURKEY

The stuffing for roast turkey may be bread, chestnut, veal, wild rice, or sausage, and should be placed in the body cavity at the breast end.

Sew and truss the turkey, after making it as plump and even in shape as possible. Before cooking, spread the bird with softened bacon drippings or butter; the breast may also be covered with strips of fat bacon. If you are going to cook it by the quick method (see below), you will obtain the best results by wrapping the bird in aluminum foil to prevent the flesh drying and the skin hardening. Foil is not recommended for the slow method, as it tends to result in a steamed rather than a roast bird.

Roast either by the slow method in a 325° oven or by the quick method in a 450° oven for times listed below.

Unless the bird is cooked in foil, baste it regularly, turning it over once to insure even browning. Foil, if used, should be removed for the last 30 minutes, so that the bird may be well basted and then left to become crisp and golden.

Roasting Times for Turkey

Weight	Hours – slow method	Hours – quick method
6 lb to 8 lb	3 to $3\frac{1}{2}$	$2\frac{1}{4}$ to $2\frac{1}{2}$
8 lb to 10 lb	$3\frac{1}{2}$ to $3\frac{3}{4}$	$2\frac{1}{2}$ to $2\frac{3}{4}$
10 lb to 12 lb	$3\frac{3}{4}$ to 4	$2\frac{3}{4}$
12 lb to 14 lb	4 to $4\frac{1}{4}$	3
14 lb to 16 lb	$4\frac{1}{4}$ to $4\frac{1}{2}$	3 to $3\frac{1}{4}$
16 lb to 18 lb	$4\frac{1}{2}$ to $4\frac{3}{4}$	$3\frac{1}{4}$ to $3\frac{1}{2}$
20 lb to 22 lb	$4\frac{3}{4}$ to 5	$3\frac{1}{2}$ to $3\frac{3}{4}$

GARNISH
Small sausages, meat balls, rolls of bacon, and watercress or other vegetables may be used to garnish the turkey. Serve it with brown gravy, cranberry or some other sharp sauce.

To carve a turkey: (See Carving entry.)

TURKISH DELIGHT

A popular chewy candy. The genuine Turkish delight sold in the Orient is made with dextrin or dextrinized flour and is flavored and perfumed with flower extracts but a fair substitute can be made by using either gelatin or cornstarch. (For recipe see Candy entry.)

TURMERIC

An East Indian plant of the ginger family. The roots, when dried and ground, have an aromatic, slightly bitter flavor. The powder is orange-yellow in color and is used as a food coloring. Turmeric adds the yellow color to curry powder and mustard pickles and to prepared mustard.

TURNIP

A root vegetable with a thick skin and white or yellow flesh. Turnips are obtainable year round, as they may be stored for long periods. They have a strong, sweet flavor and only a little is required for flavoring stews, soups, etc. Turnips contain a small amount of vitamin C.

Preparation and cooking: Peel thickly to remove the outer layer of skin and put under water to prevent discoloration. Young turnips are left whole, but the older ones should be sliced or diced, or they may be cut into matchstick pieces or balls for use as a garnish.

Cook as for other roots (see Vegetable entry). If turnips are used whole, drain them and toss in butter or cream, with added seasonings, or serve in white sauce.

TURNIP TOPS

This pleasant-flavored green vegetable is prepared and cooked like cabbage. Turnip tops are a good source of vitamins C and A.

TURNOVER

A large or small piece of pastry, folded over on itself and containing a filling of fruit, jam, ground meat, or other mixture.

JAM TURNOVERS

Cut some thinly rolled puff pastry into squares and spread one half of each with jam to within about $\frac{1}{2}$ inch of the edge of the pastry. Brush the edges with water, fold the other half of the pastry over and seal the edges tightly. Trim the edges with a knife and scallop them. Brush the top of each turnover with water and sprinkle with sugar. Bake in a 425° oven for 15 to 20 minutes.

Serve hot with a custard sauce or cold on their own with fresh cream.

APPLE TURNOVERS

1 package (16 oz) frozen puff pastry, thawed
$\frac{1}{4}$ cup superfine sugar
2 teaspoons arrowroot
1 lb cooking apples
egg white and granulated sugar to glaze

Roll out pastry sheets and cut out six 5-inch squares. Mix sugar and arrowroot together. Peel, core, and slice apples and cook with sugar mixture until just tender. Let cool. Divide apple between pastry squares. Dampen edges, fold over to make triangular shapes, and seal well. Chill for at least 2 hours. Bake in a 425° oven for 20 minutes. Remove from oven, brush with egg white, and sprinkle with sugar. Return to oven for 5 to 10 minutes. Serve warm.

TURTLE

Various types of turtles inhabit the rivers and lakes of the Americas and saltwater types are found in the warmer seas of the world.

Turtles vary in size and the so-called Green Turtle from the South Atlantic, which is used to make the famous turtle soup, may weigh several hundred pounds. The soup must be made from freshly killed turtles, so for this reason and because the method of making the soup is very complex, it is out of the question except for commercial firms or for the skilled staff catering for special functions.

Ready-made turtle soup may be bought in cans and a version may be made from canned or diced turtle. The soup should be served accompanied by meat balls.

TUTTI-FRUTTI

A confection, particularly ice cream, containing a mixture of candied fruits.

UDDER

Cow's udder, which is an easily digested and delicious meat, is prepared in some parts of the world like escalopes of veal.

UGLI (TANGELO)

A hybrid citrus fruit produced by crossing a grapefruit with a tangerine. It has loose, tough, rather thick skin of greenish yellow and is about the size of a grapefruit, but in shape is more elongated at the stem end. The taste is pleasantly sweet.

UNLEAVENED BREAD

Bread made with flour, but with no leavening agent. A good example of unleavened bread are Matzos.

UPSIDE-DOWN CAKE

This is made by lining a baking pan or dish with fruit and placing a sponge cake mixture over it, so that when the cake is cooked and turned out, the decoration will be on top. Fruits such as apricots, prunes, peaches, pineapple, etc., are especially suitable for this purpose, as they keep their shape well. Fresh, jarred, or canned fruit can be used. To give variety, the sponge mixture may be flavored with ginger, chocolate, lemon, etc. It may be accompanied by a sauce made from the fruit juice, thickened with arrowroot, or by cream.

PINEAPPLE UPSIDE-DOWN CAKE

4 tablespoons butter
¼ cup brown sugar
1 can (8 oz) pineapple rings, drained
8 tablespoons butter or margarine
½ cup superfine sugar
2 eggs, beaten
1½ cups flour
1½ teaspoons baking powder
½ teaspoon salt
2–3 tablespoons pineapple juice or milk

Grease a 7-inch round cake pan. Cream together the butter and brown sugar and spread it over the bottom of the pan. Arrange the rings of pineapple on this layer in the bottom of the pan. Cream together the remaining fat and sugar until pale and fluffy. Add the beaten egg a little at a time and beat well after each addition. Fold in the flour, baking powder, and salt, adding some pineapple juice or milk to give a dropping consistency, and spread on top of the pineapple rings. Bake in a 350° oven for about 45 minutes. Invert onto a dish and serve with a pineapple sauce made by thickening the remaining juice with a little cornstarch.

USQUEBAUGH

The Celtic form of the word whisky – literally meaning "Water of Life" (like the French *eau-de-vie*). It is also the name of an Irish liqueur made of whiskey or brandy, spices, etc., infused overnight.

VACHERIN

A fairly elaborate sweet, consisting of a "basket" made of meringue or macaroon mixture built up in rings on a pastry base, which is filled with cream or ice cream and fruit.

It is also the name of a cheese from the Jura region of France; a soft runny cheese with a firm rind, usually served with cream.

VANILLA

A flavoring made from the seed pods of a climbing plant of the orchid family, grown in Mexico and other tropical countries. When pods are fermented they turn brown and become covered with crystals of vanillin. When buying whole pods, see that these crystals are present and see also that the pods are not split for more than about one-third of their length.

A small piece of vanilla pod may be infused in the milk used for puddings, etc. Sugar may be flavored by mixing ground pods with it in the proportion of 4 pods to 1 lb or by placing a whole pod in the sugar jar. Store the flavored sugar in a jar with a tightly fitting lid and use as required for cakes, etc.

Vanilla Extract

This is made by soaking vanilla pods in alcohol or spirit of wine to extract the flavor; brown coloring is usually added. Vanilla extract is more variable in flavor than the pods, but is a more convenient form to use and quite satisfactory if a reliable brand is chosen. The synthetic vanilla flavoring is based on oil of cloves. (See Extract entry.)

VARIETY MEAT

The general term used for the edible internal parts of an animal. Ordinary meat is composed mainly of muscle, but the structure of offal varies considerably according to the particular part; thus the heart, tongue and tail, which are used for active work are very different from the liver, which is used for storage. (See individual entries.)

The following is a list of variety meats, also called organ meats:

Brains
Chitterlings
Feet (calf's, pig's, sheep's)
Heads (calf's, pig's, sheep's)
Hearts (beef, sheep's)
Kidneys (beef, calf's, pig's, sheep's)
Oxtail
Sweetbreads (calf's, sheep's)
Tongue (beef, calf's, pig's, sheep's)
Tripe
Liver (beef, calf's, pig's, sheep's)

VEAL

The term applied to the meat of a calf about $2\frac{1}{2}$ to 3 months old. (For Beef, see individual entry.) The flesh is pink and close-textured and contains less fat than beef or lamb, so the percentage of protein in veal is higher and its energy value lower than that of red meats. It contains some thiamin, iron, riboflavin, and calcium.

Fillet of veal, which comes from the leg, is the most suitable cut for sautéing. Chops usually come from the chump end of the fillet and cutlets from neck or loin. As veal comes from such a young animal, most parts are tender enough to be roasted, though breast is best braised or stewed. Since the meat is lean, sautéing in fat or roasting in added fat are very suitable methods of cooking and bacon or ham are often used as an accompaniment or garnish for veal.

Veal has not such a pronounced flavor as red meat and therefore needs a well-flavored sauce or gravy as an accompaniment. It combines well with bacon, tomatoes, mushrooms, etc., in casserole dishes.

Cuts of Veal and How to Treat Them

Shoulder (bladebone)	Roast or stew
Loin	Roast
Loin (when cut into chops)	Sauté or broil
Neck	Stew or roast
Neck (when cut into cutlets)	Sauté or broil
Fillet (i.e. top of leg) in the piece	Roast
Fillet (i.e. top of leg) if sliced	Sauté or fricassee
Knuckle	Stew or boil
Breast	Stew or braise
Breast (if boned, stuffed, and rolled)	Roast, stew, or braise

ROAST VEAL

Prepare the meat in the usual way. If the meat is to be stuffed, bone it, using a sharp knife, and wipe it well, insert some of the stuffing and tie securely. Season and place in a roasting pan with the fat side up and bacon drippings under the roast. If the meat is very lean, put some fat or bacon on top of it. Make any remaining stuffing into balls and place them around the meat.

Veal has a better flavor if roasted in a closed pan or in foil, although the appearance may not be quite as good. For the quick method allow 25 minutes per lb plus 25 minutes for roasts with bone; 30 minutes per lb plus 30 minutes for boned roasts. When cooking by the slow method allow 40 minutes per lb plus 40 minutes.

VEAL SCALLOPS

When cooking scallops by any of the methods described below it is not advisable to have more than 2 in the pan at once as they are difficult to turn over.

BREADED VEAL SCALLOPS

Allow 1 scallop per person and ask the butcher to pound it until really thin. Rub each piece with a cut lemon and sprinkle lightly with salt and black pepper. Coat with beaten egg and with fresh white breadcrumbs, patting them on well. Melt 4 tablespoons butter in a large skillet and sauté the veal gently (about 2 minutes on each side). Drain well on paper towels and serve with wedges of lemon and a green salad. Or if you wish, serve with vegetables and a tomato sauce.

VEAL SCALLOPS WITH PARMESAN CHEESE

Prepare and bread the scallops as above, then sauté gently in butter for about 1 minute on each side or until just tender. Cover each scallop with a thin slice of cooked ham and 1 tablespoon grated Parmesan cheese. Spoon a little of the butter over the cheese, cover the pan with a lid or large plate and cook for a further 2 minutes, until the cheese just melts. Serve immediately with sautéed or boiled potatoes, a crisp salad, or a green vegetable.

WIENER SCHNITZEL

Basically this famous Viennese dish is the same as veal scallop – that is, a large scallop, pounded, dipped in flour, in beaten egg and finally in white breadcrumbs, then fried in deep fat. Schnitzels are traditionally served quite simply with a wedge of lemon, although a more elaborate garnish of sliced hard-cooked egg, olives, and anchovies may be used.

OSSO BUCO

$2\frac{1}{4}$ *lb veal shanks*
salt
pepper
4 tablespoons butter
1 medium-sized onion, finely chopped
1 carrot, thinly sliced
1 stalk celery, thinly sliced
$\frac{2}{3}$ *cup dry white wine*
1 tablespoon flour
2 cups stock
$\frac{1}{2}$ *lb tomatoes, peeled and chopped*
pinch of dried rosemary
1 tablespoon chopped parsley to garnish
grated rind of $\frac{1}{2}$ lemon

Ask your butcher to saw the veal shanks into 2-inch pieces. Season with salt and pepper. Melt the butter, brown the veal all over and remove from the pan. Add a little more butter if necessary and sauté the onion, carrot, and celery until they are golden brown. Drain off any excess fat, return the meat to the pan and add the wine. Cover and simmer gently for 20 minutes. Blend the flour with a little stock to a smooth cream, add the remainder of the stock and add to the meat. Add the tomatoes and rosemary, cover tightly and continue to simmer for a further 1½ hours, or until the meat is tender. Arrange in a deep serving dish and sprinkle with a mixture of parsley and lemon rind. Serve with risotto and a dressed green salad.

VEGETABLE

Vegetables may roughly be classified as follows:
1. Roots and tubers, e.g. carrot, beet, salsify, radish, potato, Jerusalem artichoke, celeriac, parsnip.
2. Bulbs, stalks or stems, and buds, e.g. onion, sea kale, leek, celery, asparagus, chicory, eggplant, fennel, kohlrabi.
3. Leaves and flowers, e.g. cabbage, lettuce, sorrel, spinach, watercress, cauliflower, broccoli, globe artichoke, sprouts, endive.
4. Pods and seeds, e.g. green bean, broad bean, pea.
5. Fruit, e.g. tomato, cucumber, zucchini, avocado.
6. Dried legumes, e.g. peas, beans, lentils.
7. Seaweed, e.g. Irish moss.

Details of each vegetable will be found under the appropriate entry or under such collective entries as Legumes and Root Vegetables.

Food value

Vegetables are an essential part of a normal diet, since they provide vitamins and mineral salts, a good deal of roughage (cellulose) and, in the case of legumes, some protein and carbohydrates. They are also important as they help to make a meal look attractive and appetizing.

VITAMINS AND MINERALS

Vegetables provide vitamins A and C in important quantities. The amounts vary considerably, depending on the kind of vegetable, the season and the soil in which they grow. Carrots, for example, supply very large amounts of vitamin A, beet none at all; Brussels sprouts supply vitamin C, lettuce very little; the new season's potatoes contain far more vitamin C than old ones.

Minerals, principally calcium and iron, are also present in vegetables in variable amounts.

It is now considered more satisfactory to recommend one or two helpings of vegetables each day, including as wide a variety as possible, rather than to worry about the composition of individual vegetables.

Canned, frozen, and dehydrated vegetables retain their vitamin and mineral content, apart from a slight loss of vitamin C. Dried vegetables such as lentils and split peas contain no vitamin C.

PROTEIN, CARBOHYDRATE, FAT AND WATER CONTENT

Tubers, pods and seeds, and legumes provide the largest amount of protein; although this is not as good as animal protein, it is extremely useful. The energy value of vegetables, except for roots, which contain carbohydrates, is low. Generally speaking, vegetables (with few exceptions, e.g. avocado pears) contain no fat. However, when they are roasted, sautéed, or fried, they acquire extra energy value from the fat used.

Vegetables contain 76 to 90 percent water.

Choosing and Storing Vegetables

Green vegetables should be fresh, crisp and green – not yellow. Roots and tubers should feel firm. Most vegetables do not store well, so they should be bought frequently in small quantities. They are best kept in a cool dark place.

POTATOES

Store in a cool dark place, but they are best eaten soon after digging up.

ROOT VEGETABLES

Large quantities may be stored in sand; when brought into the house they should be wrapped in newspaper, to prevent evaporation.

GREEN VEGETABLES

Should be put in a rack. Lettuce and other salads keep best in a refrigerator, in the vegetable crisper or in a plastic bag. Parsley, mint, watercress, and cucumber, if not placed in a refrigerator, should be kept with the stalks in water.

Preparation and Cooking

All vegetables should be prepared as near to the time of cooking as possible, to retain their flavor and vitamin C content.

GREEN VEGETABLES

Separate the leaves (except for sprouts, cauliflower, and globe artichokes, which are left whole) and discard the tougher parts or discolored outer leaves. Wash quickly, soaking the leaves only if they are contaminated by flies or grubs – in this case, leave in salted water for about 15 minutes. Cut up if necessary, using a sharp knife to prevent bruising the leaves. Place at once in a pan containing about 1 to 2 inches of fast-boiling salted water. Cover with a tight-fitting lid, bring back to a boil as quickly as possible and boil just until crisp-tender. When cooked, the vegetables should be really green and just tender. Baking soda should not be added to greens during cooking, for although it gives a good green color, it destroys vitamin C.

ROOTS AND TUBERS

These should be washed if dirty and scraped or thinly peeled (except for turnips, which must be thickly peeled, and beet, which must not be peeled or cut at all before cooking). Cut into even-sized pieces, put in a pan and just cover with salted water. Bring to a boil and simmer until tender, allowing 20 to 30 minutes, depending on the vegetables.

PODS AND SEEDS

Green beans, if young, should be washed and left whole; if old, remove the strings on each side, then slice the pods. Peas and broad beans should be shelled. To cook, place in boiling salted water and simmer for about 15 to 25 minutes, until tender. A sprig of mint and a little sugar added to the cooking liquid improve the flavor of peas.

STEMS AND SHOOTS

They should be scrubbed and the leaves and base of the stems cut off. Asparagus is prepared by scraping off the lower leaves and trimming the base of the stems. During the preparation, celery and asparagus should be placed in water containing lemon juice to prevent discoloration. To cook asparagus, tie in bundles with cheesecloth and simmer in salted water containing some lemon juice for about 15 minutes until just crisp-tender.

DRIED PEAS, BEANS, AND LENTILS

Wash, then (except in the case of lentils) soak overnight with 1 teaspoon baking soda to 1 lb of legumes. Drain well, cover with fresh water and simmer for 1 to 1½ hours. (See Legumes and Pulses entries.)

Other Methods of Cooking

STEAMING

Potatoes, if steamed until just cooked, will retain more of their vitamin C content than do boiled ones. Greens, however, discolor badly and lose more of their vitamin C content than do boiled ones. To prepare vegetables, scrub them and peel (except potatoes); if very large, cut into even-sized pieces. Allow up to half as long again cooking time as is needed for boiling.

PRESSURE COOKING

A useful quick method of cooking all but green vegetables; the short cooking time reduces the loss of nutritive value to a minimum, but thiamin and vitamin C are partially lost. (See Pressure Cooking entry.)

ROASTING

Adds flavor and produces an attractive crisp finish, but there is a greater loss of vitamin C than with boiling.

Potatoes, also carrots, turnips, and parsnips, roast well when cut up and placed around a roast in the roasting pan, or may be cooked in fat in a separate pan. Peel or scrape the vegetables and boil them for 5 minutes in a little salted water (which can be saved to make gravy). Place them in hot fat and cook for 1 to 1½ hours, turning them over and basting once or twice during the cooking. If the meat is being cooked by the slow method, put the vegetables at the top of the oven to brown for the last 30 minutes.

FRYING AND SAUTÉING

These methods are particularly suitable for potatoes. Small cubes of zucchini and flowerets of cauliflower are delicious sautéed in butter or margarine, while small portions of such vegetables as cauliflower and cucumber may also be dipped in batter and fried. (See Fritter entry.)

BAKING

Potatoes can be baked in their skins (see Potato entry); this method avoids waste in preparation and conserves much of the mineral and vitamin content.

BRAISING

This is a good method for such vegetables as carrots, celery, onions, etc. (See Braising entry for cooking details.)

Serving Vegetables

The cooked vegetables should be drained well and served immediately, while the flavor and food value are at their best. (It is better to reheat them rather than to keep them hot for a long time.) The serving dishes should be hot and the vegetables arranged attractively, tossed in butter when appropriate and garnished with chopped parsley, paprika, or a suitable sauce which is added just before serving. Cold cooked vegetables can be served as part of a side salad.

Two or more vegetables should be served with each main meal. Salads go well with hot dishes as well as cold and can also be served as a separate course.

Preserving Vegetables
(See Freezer, Pickle, Canning, and Drying entries; see also Dehydrated Foods and Frozen Foods entries.)

VEGETABLES VINAIGRETTE

1 small head cauliflower, broken into flowerets
1 lb small onions
1 lb carrots, cut into small sticks
1 lb button mushrooms, dipped in lemon juice
1 lb snow peas, strings removed
1 lb green beans, trimmed
vinaigrette dressing

Select one of the vegetables above and cook in boiling water until just tender. Drain and place under cold running water to fix the color and stop the cooking. Place in a serving dish and cover with vinaigrette dressing. Marinate for at least 2 hours before serving, and serve chilled.

VINAIGRETTE DRESSING

3 tablespoons olive oil
1 tablespoon wine vinegar
1 clove garlic, crushed
salt
pepper
1 tablespoon finely chopped fresh herbs mixed
*   together (parsley, chives, tarragon, oregano)*

Combine the ingredients and spoon over the vegetables.

VEGETABLE MARROW

A member of the squash family, highly prized in Great Britain as the marrow but neglected in the United States in favor of other thin-skinned squash. Vegetable marrow should be eaten when young and only a quarter of its full-grown size.

VEGETABLE PEAR

(See Chayote entry.)

VEGETARIAN DIET

A true vegetarian diet, as the name suggests, should consist of vegetables and fruit only. Most followers of the regime interpret it as a non-flesh diet and permit themselves milk, cheese, and often eggs, and strictly speaking are lacto-vegetarians. The diet is bulky (especially the strict version), and it is therefore particularly suitable for those who are overweight. It is, however, likely to cause flatulence and is not suitable for people troubled with this condition. It may also be deficient in protein. Generally speaking, a lacto-vegetarian diet can be quite satisfactory if the person planning it has sufficient dietetic knowledge to keep it well balanced.

VELOUTÉ

A rich white sauce made with a foundation of light broth which is used as the basis of many more elaborate sauces such as Allemande, Mousseline, etc. The liquid used may be veal, chicken, or fish stock, according to the dish in question.

VELOUTÉ SAUCE

1 tablespoon butter
2 tablespoons flour
2 cups chicken or other light broth
2–3 tablespoons half-and-half
few drops of lemon juice
salt
pepper

Melt the butter, stir in the flour and cook gently, stirring well, until the mixture is pale fawn color. Stir in the broth gradually, bring to a boil, stirring all the time, and simmer until slightly reduced and syrupy. Remove from the heat and add the cream, lemon juice, and seasoning.
Serve with poultry, fish or veal.

Velouté Soup is a thick soup of creamy consistency.

VENISON

The flesh of a deer. Buck venison, which is considered superior to that of the doe, is in season October through December only.

Venison is usually cut into the haunch, fillet, loin, neck, and breast. Slow methods of cooking are better for neck and breast. But other cuts roast or sauté well, the haunch being the prime cut. When sautéing venison, treat it like a steak, but allow more fat.

VERBENA

A herb with a faint lemon flavor, which used to be used for making a herb tea.

VERJUICE

The juice of unripe grapes, apples, or crabapples. It was at one time used in sauces, etc., instead of lemon juice or vinegar.

VERMICELLI

An Italian pasta which is forced through very small holes and dried; the resulting fine "strings" (the Italian word literally means "little worms") are used in soups and for making puddings. (See Pasta entry.)

VERMOUTH

A drink with a white wine basis, fortified with spirit and flavored with herbs and other substances; the name is derived from the German word for wormwood, which gives vermouth its characteristic flavor. French vermouth is dry and lighter colored, the Italian type sweeter and darker. Vermouth is used in making various cocktails and is often served mixed with an equal quantity of gin. (See Cocktail entry.)

VICHY CARROTS

Young carrots, lightly scraped and cooked in water and butter until all the liquid has evaporated, and then glazed with the butter. Originally Vichy water was used as the cooking liquid – hence the name.

À la Vichy indicates that carrots have been used in a dish or form a large part of its garnish.

VICHYSSOISE

A cold leek and potato cream soup introduced by Diat, Chef des Cuisines of the Ritz-Carlton Hotel, New York.

CRÈME VICHYSSOISE

4 leeks, cleaned and sliced
1 onion, sliced
4 tablespoons butter
4½ cups light broth
2 potatoes, peeled and thinly sliced
salt and pepper
¾ cup cream
chopped chives to garnish

Lightly sauté the leeks and onion in the butter for about 10 minutes, until soft but not colored. Add the broth and potatoes. Season, cover, and cook until the vegetables are soft. Sieve the soup or puree it in an electric blender, stir in the cream, with more seasoning if necessary, and chill thoroughly for at least 2 hours. Sprinkle with chives before serving.

VICHY WATER

A mineral table water from one of the springs at Vichy in France. Types other than Celestin should be taken only on doctor's orders.

VINAIGRETTE SAUCE

(See Salad Dressing entry.)

VINEGAR

The liquid resulting from the alcoholic and later acetous fermentation of various grains and fruit. The process may be started by introducing "vinegar plant" or "mother of vinegar," a gelatinous mass of the bacteria which cause the fermentation. The by-products formed during fermentation give the characteristic flavor to vinegar and make it easily distinguishable from the colored and flavored acetic acid sometimes sold as vinegar (see Acetic Acid entry). Vinegar may be made from different substances, which give it varied flavors. In the United States cider apples are used; in the United Kingdom it is made from malted grains; while in France wine is employed. Other vinegars include balsamic, raspberry, and sherry.

By definition, wine vinegar is the only type that has a right to the name. Either red or green grapes can be used and occasionally raisins, though the last named give an inferior vinegar.

Vinegar is used as a condiment in piquant sauces and salad dressings, for sousing foods like herring and mackerel, for pickling and for marinating meat, etc. It is sometimes used with baking soda as leavening in cake and pudding mixtures. White wine vinegar, which is colorless, is used in white sauces. Vinegar flavored with herbs or spices is used for some sauces, especially spicy ones.

TARRAGON, CHILI OR CAYENNE VINEGAR

To 5 cups vinegar allow 1¼ cups tarragon leaves, 2 oz chilis or 1 oz cayenne pepper. Let the flavoring ingredient soak in the vinegar for 2 to 3 weeks, shaking the mixture occasionally, then strain and bottle the vinegar.

Wine vinegar is best for use with tarragon, but cider vinegar may equally well be used with chilis or cayenne.

VINTAGE

The word is translated from the French "vendage," which means grape harvest. Although there is a vintage each year, the term is usually used as "vintage year," meaning that the wines made in that year are of excellent quality.

They are made from one grape harvest which is exceptionally good. Individual wine growers may decide when a year can be termed a "vintage," or it may be a trade association decision.

VITAMINS

Chemical substances required in small amounts to keep a body healthy by regulating the metabolic processes. Since they are found in foodstuffs, a good mixed diet supplies an adequate amount of vitamins to the body.

Vitamins exist in more than one chemical form, but overall they are either fat soluble or water soluble. The former consists of vitamins A, D, E, and K, and the latter, the vitamin B complex of thiamin (B_1), ribloflavin (B_2), niacin, cholin, folic acid, vitamins B_6, B_{12}, paba, biotin, and pantotenic acid. Vitamin C is also water soluble but always occurs in different foods from the B vitamins.

If there is an absence or insufficient supply of vitamins in the diet, general and specific symptoms will result. General symptoms include a feeling of malaise and a restriction in the growth of children. If fat-soluble vitamins are taken in excess the accumulation in the body can be dangerous, but an excess of water soluble vitamins has little effect as most is eliminated in the urine.

Vitamin A

A deficiency causes the mucous membranes to dry up and a vulnerability to infection (particularly in the eyes, where it causes defective vision in dim light); children do not grow and their teeth do not develop satisfactorily. Vitamin A is stored in the liver, which, in normal individuals contains enough to last for one to two years.

Vitamin A is present in fish oils and variety meat (especially liver), and also in butter, eggs, cheese, sardines, salmon, herrings, and milk. Carotene, which is converted into vitamin A in the body, is present in carrots, green vegetables, apricots, and tomatoes and to a lesser extent in other fruits; carotene, however, is less well utilized by the body than vitamin A and the "activity" is usually assessed by dividing the carotene figures by three.

Vitamin A is fat soluble, and cooking has no effect on it. Taken in very large amounts it can cause poisoning as the effects are cumulative. Most cases of vitamin A poisoning recorded are children who have been given large amounts of fish liver oil.

The B Group of Vitamins

This consists of several vitamins which frequently occur together in food and were therefore originally mistaken for a single vitamin. Their functions are similar and are concerned with releasing energy from food in the body. The more important ones are:

Thiamin (Vitamin B_1)
Riboflavin (Vitamin B_2)
Niacin
Less important ones are:
Vitamin B6
Pantothenic acid
Biotin
Cyanocobalamin (Vitamin B_{12})

The vitamin B complex is contained particularly in yeast, liver, wheat germ and wholegrain breads and cereals.

Thiamin

A deficiency of thiamin leads to such symptoms as tiring easily, irritability, nervousness, headaches, sleeplessness, and loss of weight. Stiffness and cramp in the legs may be present, also palpitation and breathlessness, when the heart is affected; loss of appetite, indigestion, and constipation are other possible symptoms. An acute deficiency of thiamin leads to beriberi, prevalent in some parts of Asia.

Liver and edible food yeast, wheat germ and pork are rich sources. Bacon and other meat, potatoes, eggs, and milk also contain useful amounts; peas, beans, lentils, spinach, and cabbage contribute a little to the diet.

Prolonged cooking and the use of alkalis destroy the vitamin and since it is soluble in water, it is easily washed out. Meat loses about 5 percent when roasted or broiled, 20 percent when boiled, stewed, or fried. In breadmaking, about 15 percent of the vitamin in flour is destroyed and in cakemaking about 25 percent.

RIBOFLAVIN

When insufficient riboflavin is provided by the diet, cracks and sores appear on the skin at the corners of the mouth and the tongue becomes sore and red; the growth of children is checked.

Riboflavin cannot be stored in the body, so a regular intake is necessary. It is widely distributed in food, the richest sources being dried brewer's yeast, liver, meat extract, cheese, eggs, peanuts, beef, whole-grain bread, milk, and fish.

NIACIN

One of the B vitamins chiefly concerned with the utilization of starch and sugars in the body. It is found in meat, organs, fish, yeast, meat and yeast extracts, potatoes, flour and milk. It is soluble in water and heat-stable. Little loss is likely to occur with ordinary methods of cooking. A deficiency of niacin causes pellagra, the classical picture being dermatitis, diarrhea, and dementia. At one time this was a prevalent condition in the South of the United States, caused by a diet of pork and cornmeal.

Vitamin C (Ascorbic Acid)

Deficiency of this vitamin leads to proneness to catch infections, slow healing of wounds, poor teeth and bones, inflamed gums, poor circulation, and anemia, and in acute stages to scurvy.

Good fruit sources of vitamin C are oranges, grapefruit, lemon, rose hip syrup, and strawberries. The best vegetable sources are Brussels sprouts, broccoli, cauliflower, turnip greens, cabbage, tomatoes, spinach, asparagus, sweet potatoes, potatoes (unpeeled), and watercress. Other fruits and vegetables also contribute a little. (See entries.)

Vitamin C is lost during storage and cooking. Generally speaking, the degree of wilting in a vegetable is an indication of its vitamin loss. Grating, shredding, or mashing increases the vitamin C loss and a good deal is lost if vegetable cooking water is not used. Approximately 50 percent of the vitamin is lost in boiling potatoes, 60 to 75 percent in boiling green vegetables. The loss is greater with steaming, while pressure cooking compares favorably with ordinary methods. The loss is lessened if potatoes are boiled in their skins (about 15 percent loss) or baked in their skins (20 percent loss). Frying causes about 30 percent loss.

Vitamin D

Needed to help absorb calcium from the food to keep the bones and teeth strong and healthy; a deficiency will lead to tooth decay and rickets. It is obtained from sunlight and food (particularly fish liver oil, milk, liver, and egg yolks). In excess it can cause kidney stones and other deposits in the body, and care should be taken in giving fish liver oils and other fortified foods.

Vitamin K

A deficiency is extremely rare in a balanced diet and causes abnormal clotting of the blood. Vitamin K is found in vegetables, peas, and cereals. It can also be synthesized by intestinal bacteria.

VODKA

The Soviet Union's national drink, a strong, fiery, colorless liquor distilled mainly from wheat, though rye or potatoes can also be used. Vodka is not colored or matured. Apart from its use in the Soviet Union as an apéritif and elsewhere as a liqueur, it serves as the base of various cocktails.

Vodka is appearing more in the West and is frequently served in a similar way to gin. Served in tomato juice, it is a popular brunch drink in the United States known as a Bloody Mary.

VOL-AU-VENT

A shell made of very light, rich puff pastry filled with cut-up meat, poultry, game or fish in a richly flavored sauce. A vol-au-vent may be served as an entrée or main dish or at a buffet meal.

CHICKEN VOL-AU-VENT

$\frac{1}{2}$ package (17$\frac{1}{4}$ oz size) puff pastry
beaten egg
$\frac{3}{4}$ cup diced cooked chicken
1 cup well-flavored white sauce
mushrooms, watercress, and parsley to garnish

Roll out the pastry about 1 inch thick, place it on a greased baking sheet and cut it into a large round or oval. (Try not to cut nearer than $\frac{1}{2}$ inch to the edge of the slab of pastry.) With a smaller cutter or a knife mark a circle or oval within the larger one to form a lid, cutting about halfway through the pastry. Make scallops on the outside edge with the back of a knife and brush the top with beaten egg. Bake according to package directions. Remove the lid, scoop out any soft pastry inside and dry out the shell in the oven for a further 5 to 10 minutes.

Stir the chicken into the sauce and fill the vol-au-vent. Garnish and serve hot.

WAFER

A very thin, crisp, sweetened cookie, served with ice cream, etc. In addition to the conventional oblong, various fancy shapes are made.

WAFFLE

A crisp, golden-brown type of pancake, with deep indentations, made by baking a batter mixture in a special waffle iron, which cooks simultaneously on both sides. The irons may be made for use over a gas jet or electric ring or they may be electrically heated. Waffles, which are quickly prepared, are usually considered a breakfast food in the United States, although they can also serve as a base for creamed poultry or meats or with sauce or ice cream for dessert.

PLAIN WAFFLES

2 cups all-purpose flour
4 teaspoons baking powder
pinch of salt
1 tablespoon sugar
2 eggs, separated
½ cup butter, melted
1¾ cups milk

Mix the dry ingredients together in a bowl. Add the egg yolks, melted butter, and milk and beat to give a smooth batter. Beat the egg whites until stiff and fold into the batter. Heat the waffle iron. Pour enough batter into the iron to run over the surface. Close the iron over the mixture and leave for 5 minutes to cook, turning the iron if using a nonelectric type, until crisp and golden brown. Serve with butter and maple syrup.

WHEATGERM WAFFLES

Sprinkle 2 tablespoons wheatgerm over the batter immediately after pouring it onto the iron.

To preserve their crispness, waffles should be served immediately after the addition of any spread or filling.

SWEET ACCOMPANIMENTS
Butter and sugar; jam and cream; maple syrup; syrup and ginger; ice cream; fresh or stewed fruit.

SAVORY ACCOMPANIMENTS
Sausage, bacon, kidney, liver, tomatoes, mushrooms, ground meat, or melted cheese. If finely chopped or grated, such flavorings as bacon, kidney, mushrooms, or cheese may be added to the actual batter before the egg white is folded in.

WALLEYED PIKE

A game fish of northern North America, the walleyed pike is prized for its delicately flavored snow-white flesh and is considered by many to be among the tastiest of freshwater fish. Of good size, it is frequently filleted or baked.

WALNUT

The fruit of the walnut tree, many varieties of which are grown all over the world. The thin-shelled nuts are used for dessert, while the coarser types are crushed for the oil, which can be used in place of olive oil. Where the climate prevents the walnut from ripening well, they are often picked green toward the end of July, before the shell has formed, and are preserved as described under Pickle entry.

The walnut is a good source of vegetable protein and of fat and it contains small amounts of the B vitamins.

Walnuts can be used in the main dish of a meal, in salads, and in nut roasts for vegetarians. They are, however, more commonly used as dessert and in cakes, puddings, and candies, either as an ingredient or as a decoration.

WATER

Water is essential to life. It is the largest constituent of all animal and plant life. It makes up two-thirds by weight of the human body.

Pure water is a colorless, tasteless, and odorless liquid. At normal atmospheric pressure it boils at 212° and freezes at 32°. Most water contains dissolved gases, minerals, and minute particles of dust. "Hard" water is due to the presence of soluble calcium and magnesium salts, not present in "soft" water.

Clean water is taken for granted in most industrial countries. The basic supplies are treated by filtering and other methods to make them safe. Water is used in large quantities for drinking, cooking, other domestic uses, and for industrial purposes.

Part of its value to life is due to the fact that it will dissolve many substances; it is not chemically changed, but it acts as a vehicle in the body for oxygen and food and for removing waste products. It is also involved in many other processes. Without water the body cannot survive for more than a few days.

Water is continually being lost from the body and must be replaced by the intake of liquid and food. The principal source, of course, is drinking water and other drinks. Normally about 1 quart per day is required in a temperate climate. This is easily provided by, for example, 2 cups milk, one glass of water, and four cups of coffee, so it is clear that most of us drink more than this amount in a day.

The next most important amount comes from food, which also consists largely of water. This applies not only to such obvious things as gravy and custard – vegetables and fruit are largely water (up to 90 percent for some of them) and even cheese, meat, bread, and other apparently solid foods supply quite an appreciable amount of water. A small amount of water is formed in the body itself through the breakdown of protein, fat, and carbohydrates.

There is no evidence to show that it is harmful to drink with meals. In fact, it increases the secretion of digestive juices and softens the food.

WATER CHESTNUT

Small tubers, related to the myrtle, eaten in China and other parts of the Orient. They are similar in appearance to ordinary chestnuts before peeling. The flesh is crisp and white. Dried and ground, they are used as a thickener in Oriental cooking.

WATER CRACKER

A thin, crisp, plain cracker, usually served with butter and cheese.

WATERCRESS

A plant with small green leaves that grows in water. Commercially grown watercress is now available year round. The leaves have a pleasant, slightly hot, peppery taste and are excellent as an accompaniment to fish, game, or broiled food, in a salad or sandwiches, or made into a soup.

When eaten in large quantities, watercress is a useful source of vitamins A and C, also of iron and calcium.

Preparation and serving: Pick off the thick stalks and any tough or yellow leaves. Wash well in salted water, rinse and drain.

Watercress served as a salad may be left plain or tossed in French dressing; a sprinkling of chopped onion is sometimes added. For sandwiches it can be used either alone or mixed with cheese, tomato, etc. Sprigs or bunches of watercress may be used to garnish dishes and single leaves may be floated on the top of creamed soups.

WATER ICE

(See Ices entry.)

WATERLESS COOKING

A waterless cooker consists of a heavy aluminum pan with a tightly-fitting lid; this means that there is little evaporation and only the minimum amount of cooking liquid is needed – hence the name.

The food is placed in containers and the pan (on its base plate) is put on the stove. There is a steam vent in the lid to prevent a build-up of pressure in the pan, so although in the moist methods of cooking steam is produced and indeed helps to cook the food, it is not under pressure as in a pressure cooker. The pan can be used for pot-roasting, stewing, and braising, and for steaming and canning. Complete meals can also be cooked all at once, thus saving space, fuel, and washing-up. The fact that such a small amount of liquid is used helps to retain the soluble constituents of the foods.

WATERMELON

(See Melon entry.)

WATERZOETJE (DUTCH); WATERZOIE (BELGIAN)

In Brussels this is a dish of boiled chicken and white wine served in a creamy white sauce containing julienne strips of mixed vegetables. Elsewhere in Belgium and Holland it consists of a mixed fish stew containing julienne strips of vegetables. It is usually eaten like soup.

WEAKFISH

(See Sea Trout entry.)

WEDDING CAKE

The traditional rich fruitcake, with one, two, or more tiers, covered with almond paste and decorated with royal icing, which is served at the wedding reception. The bride makes the first cut and the rest of the cutting up is then usually done in the background. The top tier of a wedding cake is often saved for the first christening, for the cake is rich enough to keep if wrapped well.

WEDDING CAKE

(Quantities sufficient for a cake of three round tiers, baked in pans measuring 12 inches, 9 inches and 6 inches in diameter.)

$5\frac{1}{2}$ lb currants
2 lb sultanas
2 lb raisins
1 lb almonds
$1\frac{1}{2}$ lb candied cherries
1 lb mixed peel
1 lemon
$3\frac{1}{2}$ lb all-purpose flour
5 teaspoons ground cinnamon
3 teaspoons ground mace
pinch of salt
3 lb butter or margarine
3 lb sugar
24 eggs
1 cup brandy or rum

Grease the pans and line with a double thickness of greased waxed paper. Wash and sort through the dried fruit, blanch and chop the almonds, cut the cherries in half, chop the mixed peel, grate the lemon rind and strain the juice. Sift the flour, spices, and salt into a large mixing bowl. Stir in the prepared fruit, almonds, etc. Cream the butter and sugar until pale in color, then add the eggs, beating each one in separately; should the mixture curdle, stir in a little of the flour. Fold in the dry ingredients, stirring in the brandy or rum and lemon juice gradually. Pour the mixture into the prepared pans and bake in a 300° oven, reducing to 250° after 1 hour. Allow 3 to $3\frac{1}{2}$ hours for the 6-inch pan, $4\frac{1}{2}$ to 5 hours for the 9-inch pan and $7\frac{1}{2}$ to 8 hours for the 12-inch pan. When the cakes are cold, wrap them in foil and store for 2 to 3 weeks, thus allowing them to mature slightly before covering them with almond paste and royal icing. The table below shows the quantities of almond paste and royal icing required for cakes of various sizes. (See Royal Icing and Piping entries.)

Icing Quantities

These quantities are approximate. The amount of royal icing quoted should be enough to give two coats plus simple decoration.

Size of Cake	Almond Paste
5-inch round	$\frac{1}{2}$ lb
5-inch square	$\frac{1}{2}$ lb
6-inch round	$\frac{3}{4}$ lb
6-inch square	$\frac{3}{4}$ lb
7-inch round	1 lb
7-inch square	1 lb
8-inch round	$1\frac{1}{2}$ lb
8-inch square	$1\frac{3}{4}$ lb
9-inch round	$1\frac{3}{4}$ lb
9-inch square	2 lb
10-inch round	2 lb
10-inch square	$2\frac{1}{4}$ lb
11-inch round	$2\frac{1}{2}$ lb
11-inch square	$2\frac{3}{4}$ lb
12-inch round	$2\frac{3}{4}$ lb
12-inch square	3 lb
13-inch round	$3\frac{1}{4}$ lb
13-inch square	$3\frac{1}{2}$ lb

Size of Cake	Royal Icing
5-inch round	$\frac{3}{4}$ lb
5-inch square	$\frac{3}{4}$ lb
6-inch round	1 lb
6-inch square	1 lb
7-inch round	1 lb
7-inch square	$1\frac{1}{2}$ lb

8-inch round	1¾ lb
8-inch square	2 lb
9-inch round	2 lb
9-inch square	2¼ lb
10-inch round	2¼ lb
10-inch square	2½ lb
11-inch round	2¾ lb
11-inch square	3 lb
12-inch round	3¼ lb
12-inch square	3½ lb
13-inch round	3¾ lb
13-inch square	4 lb

WELSH RAREBIT

Melted cheese on toast. When eaten with tomatoes or similar vegetable, it makes a nourishing main course for lunch or supper. In Great Britain it is often served as a savory.

WELSH RAREBIT

2 cups grated Cheddar cheese
2 tablespoons butter
1 teaspoon dry mustard
salt
pepper
⅓ cup ale or beer
toast

Place all the ingredients except the toast, in a heavy-bottomed saucepan and heat very gently until a creamy mixture is obtained. Pour the cheese over the toast and put under a hot broiler until golden and bubbling.

Serve with broiled tomatoes and watercress garnish.

WHALE OIL

Oil extracted from the whale. At one time it was much used in the manufacture of oils and margarine, but it is now rarely used.

WHEAT

The grain that is grown in most parts of the world to provide flour for human consumption and also to some extent for use in cattle-feeding and in manufacturing processes.

There are two main groups of wheat, hard wheat which is rich in gluten and soft wheat which is richer in starch. The two varieties are blended according to availability and requirement.

The nutritional value of wheat is similar to that of barley, oats, and rye, though it varies somewhat with different varieties and in different climates. Although the protein of wheat is not so valuable as animal protein, it is nevertheless a body-building food and 1 lb of bread contains about a third of the daily protein requirements; wheat products also contain varying amounts of B vitamins, calcium, and iron.

(See Bread and Flour entries.)

Wheat Germ

The part of the grain that actually gives rise to the new plant; it is a rich source of the vitamin B complex. The germ is largely removed during the milling of white flour, but it can be obtained as a commercial preparation and eaten sprinkled on cereals, yogurt, etc.

WHELK

A marine snail with a conical twisted shell, eaten in Great Britain. Whelks are steamed, boiled, or batter-fried.

WHEY

The watery liquid which separates from the curd when milk is clotted, as during the making of cheese. It contains lactose, a trace of easily digested protein (lactalbumin) and calcium.

Whey is little used in human diet, but can be fed to hogs.

WHIPPING, WHISKING

The process of beating egg whites, cream, etc., until thick and stiff. A whisk or beater of some kind is usually employed, though some people prefer a fork. An electric mixer may also be used – follow the manufacturer's directions.

WHISKY, WHISKEY

The alcoholic beverage distilled from the fermented grain of cereals, chiefly barley, rye, and corn. The best-known type is distilled in Scotland, but whisky is also made in Ireland (where the spelling whiskey is preferred). The Canadian and United States types are made from rye or corn. Liqueur whiskies are good-quality matured liqueurs, while Drambuie is a liqueur made from Scotch whisky and heather honey.

The quality of whisky depends on the grain used, the process followed in its manufacture, the time allowed for maturing and the blending. Distillers usually aim at achieving by blending a more or less standard liquor, so that people will know what to expect when they ask for a certain brand.

Whisky is drunk neat or with water or soda water; rye whisky is often drunk with ginger ale. The quantity of water, soda, or ginger ale added depends, of course, on personal taste.

Whisky is also used as a basis of some mixed drinks such as Manhattan Cocktail, etc. (See Cocktail entry.) Whisky Sling is made by adding 1 cup boiling water to ⅔ cup whisky and sprinkling a little grated nutmeg on top.

WHITEBAIT

These tiny silvery fish, the young of the herring and the sprat, are served fried, accompanied by lemon. Being cooked in fat, they are a good source of energy and vitamin D is probably present in an appreciable amount; as the bones are eaten, whitebait also forms an excellent source of calcium. The fish must be eaten very fresh.

WHITE MOUNTAIN FROSTING (OR ICING)

The special feature of this frosting is that while it forms a crust on the outside, it never becomes really hard in texture like royal icing. It can be used on any type of cake. Any decorations (e.g. nuts, crystalized fruit) must be ready to put on immediately, before the frosting has time to set. *Note:* To make this frosting properly, it is necessary to use a candy thermometer.

WHITE MOUNTAIN FROSTING

1 cup sugar
¼ cup water
1 tablespoon white corn syrup
1 egg white
½ teaspoon vanilla

Gently heat the sugar in the water with the corn syrup, stirring until dissolved. Then, without stirring, boil to 240°. Meanwhile, beat the egg white stiffly. Remove the sugar syrup from the heat and when the bubbles subside, immediately pour it onto the egg white in a thin stream, beating continuously. Add the vanilla. Continue beating until the mixture thickens, shows signs of becoming dull round the edge, is almost cold, and stiff peaks form. Pour it quickly over the cake and swirl at once with a spatula. *Enough to frost one 8- or 9-inch layer.*

WHITE SAUSAGE

A farmhouse pork sausage made in Great Britain usually from cooked brain, tongue, lungs, heart, kidneys, etc., mixed with cooked pearl barley or oatmeal, seasoned and flavored to taste. The sausages are fried and eaten hot.

WHITE WINE

(See Wine entry.)

WHITE WINE CUP

crushed ice
3 bottles white wine
¾ bottle dry sherry
⅓ cup Curaçao
4 splits tonic water
3 slices of cucumber, a slice of apple, and a sprig of borage per jug

Mix all the ingredients together in one or more jugs and chill before serving. *Makes about 4 quarts.*

WHITE MOUNTAIN FROSTING
1. Place sugar, water and corn syrup in a saucepan. Stir over a gentle heat.

2. Without stirring, boil to 240°. Remove saucepan from heat.

3. Pour syrup onto stiffly beaten egg whites in a thin stream.

WHITING

A fish about 12 to 14 inches in length, with a gray back and silver underside. It is sometimes mistaken for a small haddock, but can be distinguished by the fact that it has no dark marks on the back. They are caught on the east coast of North America as far south as Virginia in the United States. As whiting does not possess a great deal of flavor, it needs to be accompanied by a good sauce, though when in prime condition it can be fried and simply served with lemon. Whiting is an easily digested fish and is therefore useful for those on diets. It has a good protein content and supplies some vitamin D.

BAKED WHITING

Prepare the fish, removing the heads and arrange in an ovenproof dish, head to tail. Add some milk, milk and fish stock or white wine, season and sprinkle with 1 teaspoon herbs. Bake in a 350° oven for 20 minutes. Make an egg, shrimp, tomato, anchovy, or hollandaise sauce with the liquid; this sauce may be poured over the fish, if they have been skinned; otherwise serve it separately.

WHOLE-GRAIN FLOUR

(See Flour and Bread entries.)

WIDGEON

A small bird of the wild duck family. The European widgeon is a regular visitor to the coasts of North America, although not usually in large numbers. The American widgeon, also known as the baldpate, extends from the United States north into almost all of Canada. Its diet of grass, grain, and plant roots makes it one of the tastiest of the wild ducks. It is plucked, drawn, and trussed like a duck, but is cooked for only about 18 to 20 minutes in a 450° oven. If well-done duck is desired, reduce the heat to 350° after the first 20 minutes and cook until done as wished.

WIENER SCHNITZEL

(See Veal entry.)

WILD BOAR

The flesh of the young animal, up to one year of age, is considered excellent. It is a traditional game in Europe, but in the United States can be found in the open only in Tennessee and North Carolina. The meat may be marinated first, and then cooked like pork.

WILD DUCK

There are many varieties of wild duck but those caught in the United States and Canada include the bufflehead, canvasback, block, ring-necked, ruddy, wood, eider, gadwall, scoter, scaup, shoveler, redhead, mallard, widgeon, pintail, and teal.

Wild duck has a fishy flavor which can be unpleasant. This can be reduced by marinating the bird in a strong liquid after being rubbed inside and out with a half lemon dipped in salt; or by placing a raw potato, an onion or apple inside the body during cooking.

The wild duck is lean, unlike the domesticated duck, therefore slices of fat should be used to bard it during cooking. The flavor is improved by the addition of red wine in basting and slight undercooking; this also makes the meat more tender. The flavor is again improved by flaming with gin, whisky, or brandy. It is important that wild duck is cooked within 24 hours of shooting, unless it has been bled, as it is likely to produce poisonous bacteria. Allow one duck for each person for larger birds such as the mallard and canvasback, and one and one-half birds for the teal and small ducks. For rare meat roast birds in a 400° oven, 12 minutes for small birds, 20 minutes for large ones.

WILD GOOSE

A highly prized game bird of North America that feeds largely on grain and grass sprouts and some marine vegetation. The best known and most prevalent goose of the United States is the Canada goose, which ranges north above the Arctic Circle. Dressed geese weighing $4\frac{1}{2}$ lb or under are probably young enough to roast. Cook in a 375° oven for $2\frac{1}{2}$ hours. Larger geese should be braised. A $4\frac{1}{2}$ lb goose feeds 3 to 4.

WILD RICE

The edible grain of a grass unique to North America that grows in water in the area of the Great Lakes. Most of the wild rice sold on the market grows on a Chippewa reservation, and only the Indians are permitted to harvest it, which they do from canoes. It is this rice, rather than the small cultivated crop, that is prized by the gourmet for its nutty flavor. It takes about 40 to 50 minutes to boil.

WILD TURKEY

A land bird native to the United States and parts of Canada. Wild turkeys are fairly common in open woodlands or forest clearings and feed on acorns, fruit and seeds. In the fall an adult tom turkey weighs with feathers about 15 lb, the hen about 7½ lb. Young male and female birds weigh about 10 and 5 lb respectively. Roast or braise adult birds. Young ones may be broiled or sautéed.

WINE

The produce of the alcoholic fermentation of fresh or dried grapes (raisins) or grape juice. There are also other types of wine made from fruits, vegetables, and flowers.

The yeasts which are present on the skins of grapes convert the glucose (grape sugar) into alcohol and carbon dioxide (the latter produces the bubbles during the fermentation). The length of the fermentation period varies – a short fermentation of 4 to 5 days gives a finer wine, more delicate in flavor; a longer period of 10 to 15 days gives a stronger, darker wine. After the first wine is drawn off, the residue can be pressed to produce slightly less alcoholic wines – called wines of the second (or third) pressing.

Dry wines are made by allowing complete fermentation leaving very little sugar. To make a sweet wine, fermentation is halted to retain more natural sugar. However, for some of the poorer sweet wines, sugar or a sweet wine concentrate is added. The best sweet wines are made from overripe grapes containing sweet juice which kills the yeast before fermentation is complete.

Wine is produced from both white and black grapes, but more usually from the black ones. The skins of black grapes, if left in during the fermentation, turn the wine red; if the skins are removed at an early stage the wine is a rose or pink. White wine is made from the juice only of white or black grapes.

Wine is produced in many countries. Italy is the world's largest producer but it is generally conceded that France produces the greatest quantity of fine quality wines. Spain is the third largest producer. Germany, Portugal, the Balkan countries, Algeria, Australia, South Africa, Chile, and Argentina are other wine-exporting countries.

The flavor of the wine depends on the species of grape, the weather, and the soil they are grown in and also on the degree and method of fermentation.

Since the early 1970s the United States has become an increasing competitor to French wines. There are now three times as many Chardonnay grapes in California as in France and twice as many Cabernet Sauvignon. It is important to remember that while French quality wines are marketed by the region in which they grow (e.g. Chablis, Médoc, etc.), quality wines in the United States are marketed by the variety of grape (e.g. Chardonnay, Cabernet Sauvignon, etc.).

Grapes

GAMAY
Makes first-class red wine when grown on granite; used in Beaujolais and also in California to make rosé.

SÉMILLON
This grape rots in warmth and humidity, producing luscious white wines; it is the grape used to produce the Sauternes of Bordeaux and is used extensively in Australia.

CHENIN BLANC
Used to make Vouvray and other white wines from Anjou and Touraine. It ages well because of a high acid content. Successful in California.

RIESLING
The classic German grape which is also planted in Australia, South Africa, Chile, and California. Wines produced from this grape in California are called Johannisberg Riesling or White Riesling.

CHARDONNAY
The grape of white Burgundy and Champagne. It gives a firm, full, strong wine; also used in northern California, where it is considered the most successful white wine variety in the United States.

MUSCAT
Either black or white grapes used to make a sweet white wine (except in Alsace and Bulgaria). Muscat wines are made all over the world.

PINOT NOIR
The grape of the Côte d'Or, used to make Champagne. The best red wine grape. Experimentation with this grape is being made in California.

GRENACHE
A sweet grape, usually blended with others. It is used for dessert wines.

CABERNET SAUVIGNON

A small tough grape which gives distinction to the wines of Bordeaux. It also produces the finest red wines of California.

SAUVIGNON BLANC

The chief white grape of Bordeaux. It makes a clean, light wine or it can be blended. California Sauvignon Blanc is marketed as Fumé Blanc or Blanc Fumé.

ZINFANDEL

A grape of European origin but now considered almost indigenous to California. It can produce excellent red wine.

Some of the best-known wines are as follows:

French Wines

BORDEAUX, RED

Claret is the greatest red wine in the world, comparable only to red Burgundy and available in much larger quantities. The five chief districts in France where these wines are produced are Médoc, St Émilion, Graves, Entre-deux-Mers, Pomerol, and Sauternes.

BORDEAUX, WHITE

The chief types are called after the regions, Graves (although the white Graves are not so good as the red); Sauternes (excellent sweet white wines) and Entre-deux-Mers (not so distinguished as the other two).
(See Bordeaux Wine entry.)

BURGUNDY, RED

This is made in a small strip of land called the Côte d'Or. The wine is slightly sweeter than claret.

BURGUNDY, WHITE

These districts produce wines named after them: Meursault and Montrachet, Chablis, and Pouilly-Fuissé. Meursault and Montrachet are among the best white Burgundies. Chablis is the driest in flavor.

BEAUJOLAIS

A red wine, produced on the fringe of the Burgundy district; it has not the highly esteemed reputation of Burgundy or Bordeaux and is therefore much cheaper.

RHÔNE, LOIRE, AND ALSACE

These regions also produce various wines, some of them very good but without the reputation of the foregoing.

CHAMPAGNE

Comes from the Champagne district between Rheims and Épernay. A secondary fermentation takes place in the bottle, forming carbon dioxide which dissolves in the wine. A sediment also forms, which is removed very carefully with the cork. A dose of sweetened wine is added, a new cork inserted and wired down. All this takes place about 5 years after the wine was started.

In all good wine countries other sparkling wines can be made by the *méthode champenoise*, but the makers are not allowed to use the name "Champagne."

Italian Wines

Chianti, in the wickered bottles, is the best known. Both red and white types are produced. There are also Barolo (which is perhaps the finest Italian wine), Valpolicella, Orvieto, Soave, and many others.

Spanish Wines

Spain is generally known for its sherry, but there are many other good Spanish wines, perhaps the best known being Rioja. Spanish wines are suitable for drinking and cooking and are available at a comparatively low price. Sherry is a nonvintage wine, fortified with brandy. It improves with age. The two basic types are Fino, pale and dry, and Oloroso, darker and mixed with a sweeter wine.
(See Sherry entry.)

German Wines

Hock is a general name covering the Rhine wines, including the districts Rheingau, Rheinhesse, Palatinate, and Nahe. They are generally good wines and the labeling regulations are strict. Liebfraumilch is a name that can be applied to almost any German wine. It usually indicates a medium dry Rhineland wine.

Mosel is produced along the Mosel valley. It has a pleasant, fresh taste and a low alcoholic strength which makes it an attractive drink for the summer and as part of a wine cup or punch.

United States Wines

Although New York state produces many fine wines and winemaking is a growing industry in Washington and Oregon, it is California that produces the greatest volume of wine in the United States. California wine is generally known by its method of marketing – generic and varietal. Generic wines are the jug wines, labeled with names of famous European wine regions, e.g. Burgundy, Chablis, etc. While of good value, the wines have little resemblance to those of the regions for which they were named. Varietal wines are the finer California wines, labeled with the variety of grape from which they are made. The chief growing regions of California are the San Joaquin, or Central, Valley, running from Lodi in the north to Bakersfield in the south. It is here that most generic wines are produced. Varietal wines are produced in the coastal countries that fan out from San Francisco – Napa, Sonoma, Mendocino, Alameda, and Santa Clara.

Fortified Wines

SHERRY
(See Sherry entry.)

VERMOUTH
A popular apéritif made in France, Italy and the United States; it is a nonvintage wine blended from three or four types, slightly fortified with brandy and finally flavored with herbs. The fortifying gives it a strength of about 30° which is not much less than that of sherry and port. (See also Vermouth entry.)

PORT
Made in Portugal, up the river from Oporto. It is a fortified wine, like sherry. (See Sherry entry.)

See also Madeira and Marsala entries.

Choice of Wine
This depends on personal tastes, but certain major rules will prove helpful.

Before a meal: Serve dry sherry, Dubonnet, chilled Champagne, or California sparkling wine.

With appetizers: Serve white Mosel, Alsace, Chablis, Graves, Chardonnay, or Riesling.

With soup: Serve dry sherry or Madeira.

With fish, veal, chicken, turkey (i.e. white meats): Serve a full white wine, chilled – e.g. white Burgundy, Chardonnay.

With beef, lamb, and mutton: Serve a fairly light red wine such as Beaujolais, red Graves, or Pinot Noir.

With duck, goose, pork, and game: Serve a fuller red wine such as Burgundy or Cabernet Sauvignon.

With desserts: Serve Sauternes, Champagne, Anjou, Palatinate Hock, sparkling wine.

With cheese and dessert: Serve a sweet or fuller sherry, port, or Madeira.

With (or after) coffee: Serve brandy, liqueurs.

In these days it is unusual to serve different wines for each course. Often an apéritif is followed by sherry with the soup, a wine with the main dish, and a liqueur with the coffee. A dry wine is best before rather than after a sweet wine and a light wine before a heavier one.

Buying Wine
Always study the label: vintage wine bears a date and is expected to mature well, because it is the product of a year when climatic conditions were good and the wine is therefore of the best quality. Unfortunately, there is some bad wine made in vintage years but there is also some good wine in nonvintage years, so the date serves only as a general guide to the buyer. Furthermore, even a superb wine can be ruined by bad storage, too much shaking in transit, bad bottling, etc. The only safe course, therefore is to deal with a trustworthy store.

Storage of Wine
Wine should be stored in a dry, dark cellar or cupboard at a constant temperature, with the bottles lying on their sides – this keeps the corks damp so that they do not shrink and let in air. The bottles should be rested on shelves or racks, so that they need not be disturbed as movement does not improve the wine.

Serving Wine
It is important to serve wine at the correct temperature or the individual characteristics will be lost. Red wine should be served at about 65° (Cambré). At this temperature it will become aromatic, but if allowed to become warmer the alcohol will start to vaporize. The bottle should be opened and left to stand in a warm room for several hours before serving rather than be subjected to heat.

It is easier to serve white or rosé wines perfectly as they usually only require refrigeration for one hour. A quicker method is to place the bottle in a bucket of cold water and ice. The ideal temperature for serving white wine is 45° to 50°; at this temperature it has a scent and piquancy. The wine should not be allowed to become icy or frozen as flavor will be lost.

Wine is often decanted before serving; this is important with old wines containing sediment, but younger wines can also benefit. Once in a decanter the oxygen helps to develop the scent and flavor of a young wine. Wines are sometimes decanted for esthetic reasons.

The wine glasses should be carefully chosen, for they can add greatly to the enjoyment of good wine by enabling one to appreciate its color and bouquet. Connoisseurs usually prefer colorless glasses although colored stems may enhance the color of the wine. Many different shapes in various sizes are made for serving different wines, but the more usual ones are shown in the list below; it is unusual nowadays to have a large number of wine glasses.

Sherry: A fairly small, long-sided glass

Burgundy, Claret and white wines: A large, bowl-shaped glass

Hock and Moselle: A long-stemmed glass with a fairly small cup-shaped bowl. Hock glasses usually have tinted stems.

Champagne and sparkling wines: A fairly large tulip-shaped glass or a tail thin "flute" is favored.

Port: a glass similar to that used for sherry but larger.

Brandy and liqueurs: A small glass although it has become fashionable to serve brandy in a bowl-shaped glass.

WINE VINEGAR

(See Vinegar entry.)

WINES, HOMEMADE

Home winemaking is becoming increasingly popular. Most people probably make wine because it is cheaper than buying it, but it is also a creative hobby. It can be linked with growing fruits and vegetables to use as a base for wines; or for those who live in the country, flowers and wild fruits can be picked while out walking.

There are many books and magazines giving information about home winemaking; also courses and practical instruction are held in many areas around the country. There are also wine clubs and circles where people can discuss and learn more about their hobby.

WINKLE (PERIWINKLE)

A small black marine snail. To prepare winkles, wash them well in several waters to remove the sand and boil for 20 minutes in salted water. Although found from Nova Scotia south to New Jersey, periwinkles do not enjoy the same popularity in North America as they do in Great Britain and Europe.

WINTER CORN SALAD

A hardy annual plant used in salads. It is also known as Lamb's Lettuce and is sometimes served cooked.

WINTER MELON

A large Chinese melon resembling in the color of its skin and flesh the honeydew, but tasting more like the zucchini squash. Weighing up to 30 lb, it is sold in Chinatown markets in the United States by the piece. It is usually served in soup and despite its name is available year round.

WON TON

A Chinese noodle dumpling enclosing a morsel of filling, somewhat similar in appearance to the Jewish kreplach. Won tons are usually served in soup (Won Ton Soup) but may also be deep-fried and passed as appetizers. Won ton skins are available in some supermarkets and can be made at home.

WOODCOCK

Either of two small game birds, one of the Old World. The American woodcock is an inland sandpiper, living in moist woodlands and swamps east of the Mississippi. It has a short neck and legs, a long bill, and mottled plumage.

Preparation and roasting: Allow one bird per person. Woodcock should be plucked very carefully, as the skins are very tender. They are not drawn. Arrange the birds on a trivet with bacon over the breasts, put a little butter on each bird and place in a pan, each bird on a square of toast. Roast in a 350° oven for 20 to 30 minutes. Serve on the toast, garnished with watercress and lemon. A rich brown gravy should be made in the roasting pan to serve with the birds.

WORCESTERSHIRE SAUCE

A commercial sauce, thin in consistency and spicy in flavor.

WORMWOOD

Name given to various wild plants that were used for medicinal tisanes, herb-flavored liqueurs, and absinthe. Its use is now forbidden as it has been proved to cause blindness.

YAKITORI

The Japanese version of broiled chicken, extremely seductive to Western tastes. Boned and cut-up chicken is threaded onto bamboo skewers alternately with green onions and grilled over charcoal, basting frequently with Teriyaki marinade. (See Teriyaki entry.)

YAM

The fleshy edible tuber of a tropical climbing plant; it somewhat resembles a sweet potato. A starch product, similar to arrowroot, is extracted from the yam.

YEAST

A microscopic single-celled plant that grows rapidly in favorable conditions. There are many different varieties, but all have similar characteristics and properties. As yeast grows it produces ferments which are capable of breaking down starch and sugars, converting them into carbon dioxide and alcohol. It is the production of carbon dioxide gas in breadmaking which causes the dough to rise, and the by-products that are formed during the working of the yeast ferments that give bread its special flavor. A different type of yeast is used in beer and winemaking. This has a higher alcoholic tolerance than other yeasts.

Carbohydrates, air, water, and warmth, in suitable proportions, are all necessary for the rapid growth of yeast. A certain amount of sugar enables it to grow quickly, though too much shrinks the cells and prevents budding. Too much salt and shortening also slow down the budding process. All liquids used for yeast mixtures should be lukewarm, as cold retards the growth, and excess heat kills the yeast plant. (This happens, of course, when the bread is put in the oven, but by that time the yeast has done its work.)

Yeast is a source of all the B vitamins, and is sometimes prescribed medically, either in its natural form or as one of the manufactured yeast extracts.

Types of Yeast

MOIST, COMPRESSED

This is the yeast usually supplied by bakers and is available in some supermarkets. When it is fresh, yeast in this form cuts cleanly, but it keeps fresh for only 2 to 3 days, after which it crumbles easily, becomes darker in color and has a stale smell. It is best to buy just enough yeast for immediate use, but if it has to be stored for a few days, keep it in a paper bag wrapped in a damp cloth or place it, well wrapped, in the refrigerator. It can, however, be stored in a freezer for up to 1 year.

ACTIVE DRY YEAST

This is a granular type sold in envelopes. There are different varieties and the manufacturer's instructions should be followed. When using dry yeast in a recipe specifying fresh yeast, allow half the quantity of the dry type. To add it to the other ingredients, dissolve 1 teaspoon sugar in a cup of liquid taken from the amount stated in the recipe: it should be warm (110°); sprinkle the dry yeast on top, leave in a warm place for 10 minutes, or until frothy, then mix with the dry ingredients and remaining liquid to make a dough.

BREWER'S YEAST

This semiliquid yeast is not now commonly used, but it can sometimes be bought from brewers. $\frac{2}{3}$ cup of good strong yeast or 1 cup of a weaker type will raise 7 lb of flour; $2\frac{1}{2}$ tablespoons brewer's yeast are equivalent to 1 oz of compressed yeast. The yeast can be made stronger by adding 1 teaspoon sugar to $1\frac{1}{4}$ cups of the liquid and leaving it for 3 to 4 hours. To remove its bitter flavor before use, cover the yeast with cold water and set aside for a day, then pour off the water and the thick yeast will remain. Brewer's yeast is also available in dry form.

Quantities for Making Bread and Rolls

The following table shows the amount of moist compressed yeast required to raise various quantities of flour:

$\frac{1}{2}$ oz yeast	1 lb flour
1 oz yeast	$3\frac{1}{2}$ lb flour
2 oz yeast	7 lb flour
20 oz yeast	280 lb flour

The above quantities apply to bread mixtures in which no shortening is used. For enriched mixtures, more yeast is required, since shortening retards the growth of the yeast. With a rich roll type of mixture any extra sugar, fruit, and shortening are best added after the first proofing, to give the yeast a better chance to grow, so producing a lighter dough. Sometimes a separate sponge is made using the yeast and some of the flour. This is left aside till it is full of bubbles, then added to the remaining ingredients.

RECIPES FOR USING YEAST
(See Bread, Bun, and Roll entries.)

YEAST EXTRACT

This product, made by treating yeast with acid, is rich in the B vitamins.

Yeast extracts resemble meat extracts, with which they are often confused, the main difference being that they contain the nitrogenous substance called adenine, while the meat extracts contain the nitrogenous substances creatine and creatinine. They can be used to flavor soups, stews, etc., and as a sandwich spread.

YELLOW PERCH

(See Sunfish entry.)

YERBA MATÉ

A South American shrub, the leaves of which are dried and used to make a drink called Paraguay tea. The natives prepare it by putting the leaves in a hollowed-out gourd and adding boiling water. A small tube, like a metal straw, is used to suck up the tea.

YOGURT

Yogurt is thought to have originated among the nomadic tribes of Eastern Europe. Traditionally it was a drink, made by allowing the natural milk flora to ferment the lactose (milk sugar) to lactic acid. A very sour yogurt results when there is no refrigeration to limit acid production.

Yogurt is manufactured on a large scale under very strict hygienic conditions in Western countries. Pasteurized milk is inoculated with a specific bacterial culture and incubated under controlled conditions to produce yogurt of the desired flavor and consistency.

Unless pasteurized after preparation, all yogurt contains live bacteria which remain dormant

MAKING YOGURT
1. Heat milk then blend yogurt and milk together. Place in a vacuum flask.

2. Turn into a bowl and cool quickly in a second bowl containing cold water.

3. Flavor yogurt with sugar, honey, fruit syrups or fruits as desired.

when kept at a low temperature. If it is stored at room temperature or above, the bacteria become active and produce more acid which impairs the flavor of the yogurt. It also causes the yogurt to separate and the bacteria are eventually killed. Yogurt should therefore be kept under refrigeration and should not be purchased if the sell-by date stamp on the lid has expired.

Manufacture of Yogurt

Yogurt is made from a skim milk base to which extra skim milk powder is added; this gives a total of 12 to 16 percent milk solids.

The milk is pasteurized and cooked to 100°, then inoculated with bacteria cultures, *Lactobacillus bulgaricus* and *Streptococcus thermophilus*. During incubation at 109° some of the lactose is fermented to lactic acid. When the acidity reaches the point of precipitating the casein (milk protein), the yogurt is rapidly cooled to 40°. If the yogurt is to be flavored before packaging, fruit in the form of a syrup is added.

Ready-frozen yogurts are available. A stabilizer may have been added to prevent separation on thawing, but usually there is sufficient sugar to prevent this happening.

Yogurt in the diet

As it contains skim milk, yogurt has a very good food value. It is a good source of protein, due to the addition of extra milk solids, calcium, and riboflavin. As most yogurt contains very little fat it does not supply much vitamin A and D; most brands of yogurt now have these vitamins added to make good the loss.

Yogurt is a good food to take in place of milk, which is important if children will not drink the latter. Yogurt can also be given to babies once weaning commences.

Use of Yogurt

Most yogurt is eaten straight from the carton and sometimes with fruit, but it can be used in many recipes to give a refreshing piquant flavor.

Natural yogurt can be added to many dishes such as chilled soups, cheese sauce, flans, cheese biscuits, goulash, stroganoff, salad dressing; or made into a topping for savory dishes by mixing $\frac{2}{3}$ cup yogurt with 1 egg (beaten).

Plain or fruit yogurts can be added to custards, rice puddings, other desserts, and cereals. Mix 1 carton of fruit yogurt with 1 cup cold milk to make a milk shake.

When adding yogurt to hot dishes, it is important to add it toward the end of cooking and just heat through gently. If the liquid boils the yogurt will cause curdling and separation.

Making Yogurt at home

There are several yogurt-making appliances on the market but it can quite easily be made in a large thermos bottle (a wide-necked one is best).
1. Sterilize equipment to be used by immersing in boiling water or by using a commercial sterilizing solution. (Saucepan, spoons, small bowl, thermos bottle, thermometer.)
2. Heat 1 quart milk to almost boiling. Cool to 110°.
3. Blend 3 heaping tablespoons of plain yogurt with a little of the milk in a bowl and mix into the remainder. Pour into the prewarmed thermos bottle, seal and leave for 7 hours.
4. Turn into a bowl and cool the yogurt quickly by standing it in a second bowl of cold water and beating the yogurt.
5. Cover the bowl and place in the refrigerator for 4 hours to allow the yogurt to thicken further.
6. The yogurt can be flavored with sugar, honey, jam, fruit syrup, or fruits as desired.

It will keep in a refrigerator for 4 to 5 days.

YORKSHIRE PUDDING

An English batter pudding traditionally eaten with roast beef, originating in Yorkshire where it is usually served separately, before the meat, accompanied by some of the hot beef gravy. Elsewhere the pudding is served with the meat. It may be cooked either in a separate pan, or around or under the roast. If preferred, the mixture can be made up as small individual puddings, or popovers. (See Popover entry.)

YORKSHIRE PUDDING

1 cup milk
2 eggs
$\frac{2}{3}$ cup flour
$\frac{1}{2}$ teaspoon salt

Combine the ingredients in the container of an electric blender and blend until smooth. Preheat a 9-inch-square baking pan and fill with about $\frac{1}{2}$ cup roast beef drippings or melted shortening. Add the batter and place in a 450° oven for 10 minutes. Reduce heat to 375° and bake 15 to 20 minutes longer.

YORKSHIRE RAREBIT

Welsh rarebit topped with ham and an egg.

YUCCA

(See Cassava entry.)

ZABAGLIONE

An Italian sweet, a frothy mixture of wine (usually Marsala), egg yolks and sugar, beaten over a gentle heat until thick; it is served hot in glasses. Sabayon sauce (see Sabayon entry) is a variation of zabaglione.

ZABAGLIONE

6 egg yolks
¼ cup sugar
6 tablespoons Marsala

Place beaten egg yolks, sugar, and Marsala in a deep bowl over a pan of hot, but not boiling, water. Beat continuously until thick and creamy. Pour at once into small glasses and serve immediately with macaroons or ladyfingers. If liked, a little fruit may be placed at the bottom of the glasses before adding the zabaglione mixture – pineapple goes particularly well.

ZAKUSKI

Russian appetizers, often a meal in themselves, served in Tsarist Russia in a separate room. They consist of many types of caviar, blinis, smoked sausages, cold meats, pickled fish, tvoroinki (cheese dumplings), and endless other hors d'oeuvres, all to be washed down with equal amounts of vodka.

ZEST

The thin, oily outer skin of citrus fruits. As a culinary term, it means a thin shaving of orange or lemon peel or the colored part of the peel, often rubbed off onto lumps of sugar.

ZINFANDEL

A varietal red wine produced from grapes grown largely in the San Joaquin Valley of California in the United States. Although European in origin, the grape is now considered indigenous to the United States. Zinfandels range from undistinguished through fruity wines meant to be consumed young and intense tannic wines that need time to develop. Late Harvest Zinfandels are also produced.

ZUCCHINI

These are a variety of long green summer squashes. They are normally cooked unpeeled, being either left whole or cut into rounds. They may be boiled in a minimum of water (allow 10 to 15 minutes), steamed, sautéed or fried and are served with melted butter and chopped parsley or tarragon. Or, cook them, dress with French dressing while still warm, then leave to become cold and serve as a salad. Zucchini are an essential ingredient in ratatouille, and can be added to casseroles, soups, and stews.

Allow ¼ lb per portion when served as an accompaniment.

In France and Great Britain they are known as courgettes.

ZWIEBACK

A sweetened bread cut into slices and toasted until dry. The name means "twice baked" in German.

COLOR PLATES

Between pages 14–15
Teddy Bear Cake
Trout with almonds
Sally Lunn; Hot milk spongecake; Swedish
  coffee cake

Between pages 38–39
A barbecue party
Cassoulet; Chili con carne; Lentil and bacon
  soup
Beef rolls
Spit-roasted beef

Between pages 70–71
Beef Wellington
Star cookies
Dundee cake
Christmas fruitcake

Between pages 102–103
Wedding cake
Carved roast chicken
Boned and rolled lamb chops
Roast Turkey, Buttered Brussels sprouts,
  Plum Pudding

Between pages 134–135
Cocktails: Daiquiri; Manhattan; Brandy
  cocktail; Harvey Wallbanger; Dry martini
Duck with Cherries; Tarragon Chicken;
  Chicken with Grapefruit; Chicken
  Normande
Charlotte russe; Syllabub with wine;
  Raspberry mousse; Cherry compote
Onion and red pepper quiche

Between pages 166–167
Oat Bars
Fondue
Berries
Strawberry ice; Lemon ice cream;
  French custard vanilla ice cream

Between pages 198–199
Herbs
Hors d'oeuvre
Molded fruit gelatin; Sundae; Chocolate ice
  cream
Oriental Salad

Between pages 230–231
Crown roast of lamb
Spiced lamb with eggplant; Cornish pasties
Lobster thermidor
A selection of dried fruit and nuts

Between pages 262–263
Sausage and pepper omelet
Beef-stuffed onions
A children's party
Pasta dishes

Between pages 294–295
A variety of pasta
Cream puff; Caramel sauce
Pâté
A picnic party

Between pages 326–327
Fruit pies
Ways of cooking potatoes
Two-crust apple pie; Potted beef; Country
  lamb potage; Farmhouse pâté
Shrimp bisque

Between pages 358–359
Strawberry jam
Party punch
Salads
Salads

Between pages 390–391
Appetizers
Strawberry shortcake
Vegetables Vinaigrette; Deviled eggs with
  caviar
Cold soufflé; Zabaglione

Between pages 414–415
Soufflé au chocolat
Spaghetti
A selection of spices
Steak and kidney pie

Between pages 430–431
Stock
Homemade candies
A selection of fresh vegetables
Wholewheat flowerpots; Poppyseed braid;
  Cheese pull-aparts; Crumpets

MENU GLOSSARY

Included in this alphabetical glossary are the French and other phrases most likely to be seen in restaurant and hotel menus. While it is easy enough to look up the name of foodstuffs such as *agneau* (lamb), it is not so easy to discover from a dictionary or phrase-book that *Sauté d'Agneau à l'hongroise*, for example, will have a cream and paprika sauce.

For ease of reference those terms usually describing a method of preparation or a garnish (which in formal menus are mostly preceded by the words *à la, au* or *en*) are given first, but listed according to the first letter of the main word. These are followed by the names of particular types of dish such as *brandade* and adjectives often applied to food, such as *brûlé*.

Part I

À l'Allemande: Applied to dishes finished or garnished with such German specialties as sauerkraut, smoked sausage, pickled pork, potato dumplings, or noodles tossed in butter. Also means dishes served with Allemande sauce.

À l'Alsacienne: With a fairly elaborate garnish, the best-known variation probably being smoked sausages, ham, and peas.

À l'Américaine: Denotes various methods of preparing meat, game, fish, vegetables, and eggs, the best known example being Homard à l'Américaine, where the sauce has a basis of tomato, onion, and herbs, cooked in wine or brandy.

À l'Ancienne: Literally, old-style. Usually means a dish with a mixed garnish, consisting of beans, cooked lettuce, and hard-cooked egg.

À l'Andalouse: Applied to a variety of recipes, but often involving the use of tomatoes and rice.

À l'Anglaise: Plainly cooked, usually boiled in stock or water.

À l'Archiduc: Applies to many dishes, usually seasoned with paprika and blended with cream.

À l'Aurore: Dishes served with tomato-flavored aurore sauce or items of a yellow color, often dome-shaped, suggesting the rising sun.

Au Beurre: Cooked or served with butter.

À la Bigarade: With orange or orange sauce.

Au Blanc: White or with white sauce.

Au Bleu: Fish such as trout, cooked immediately after they are caught by simmering in white wine with herbs, or in water containing salt and vinegar.

À la Bordelaise: Incorporating a wine sauce, mushrooms, or a garnish of artichokes and potatoes.

En Bordure: With a border of cooked vegetables.

À la Bourgeoise: "Family style," homey but appetizing cooking. Also means garnished with small carrots and onions and with diced lean bacon.

À la Bourgogne (Bourguignonne): With a garnish incorporating mushrooms, small onions, and bacon and cooked or served in red wine sauce.

À la Bretonne: Usually implies a garnish of haricot beans or bean puree. There is also a Bretonne sauce, used with eggs and fish, which includes onions or leeks and white wine.

En Broche (Brochette): Roasted or broiled on a spit or skewer.

À la Cardinal: With a scarlet effect, as when a fish dish is served with a coral or lobster sauce dusted with paprika or cayenne.

À la Carte: In a restaurant, food prepared or served to order and not part of a set (table d'hôte) meal. *

(À la) Catalane: With a garnish of eggplant and rice.

À la Chantilly: Including or accompanied by vanilla-flavored sweetened whipped cream.

À la Chasseur: Hunter's style. With a garnish of mushrooms cooked with shallots and white wine.

En Cocotte: Cooked and served in a small (or occasionally a large) casserole.

À la Colbert: Name given to two well-known dishes; Sole Colbert is a whole boned fish, coated with bread crumbs, fried and filled with herb butter. Consommé à la Colbert is garnished with small poached eggs.

(À la) Condé: Usually denotes the presence of rice. Also the name of a type of pâtisserie.

En Coquille: Served in the shell, or made to resemble a shell.

(À la) Crécy: Made or garnished with carrots.

À la Créole: Usually includes rice with – in the case of savory dishes – a garnish or sauce of red peppers and tomatoes. For sweet dishes, orange, banana, pineapple, or rum are often included.

En Croûte: Game, entrées, and appetizers, etc., served on a shaped slice of bread or pastry, which is toasted, fried, or baked.

En Daube: Braised or stewed.

À la Diable (Diablé): Deviled or highly spiced.

À la Diéppoise: Seawater fish garnished with crayfish tails and mussels and served with a white wine sauce.

À la Dubarry: A rich cauliflower soup or a cauliflower garnish.

À la Duchesse: Rich mashed potato, either made into fancy shapes, or used as a topping; also Béchamel sauce with tongue and mushrooms.

À la Financière: Meat or poultry in a rich brown Madeira sauce containing mushrooms and truffles, or with a garnish of truffles, olives, and mushrooms.

À la Flamande: Served with a garnish of braised vegetables and bacon or small pork sausages.

À la Florentine: Fish or eggs served with spinach.

À la Forestière: Meat or poultry with a garnish of mushrooms, ham or bacon and fried potatoes.

Au Four: Cooked in the oven.

Au Gras: Cooked and dressed with rich gravy or sauce.

Au Gratin: Sprinkled with bread crumbs and/or grated cheese and then browned.

À la Hollandaise: With hollandaise sauce (see recipe entry).

À l'Hongroise: Cooked in a cream sauce seasoned with paprika.

À l'Huile: With olive oil or olive oil dressing.

À l'Impératrice: Name given to various dishes and cakes, the best known being Riz (rice) à l'Impératrice.

À l'Impériale: Dishes with a rich garnish of foie gras, truffles, and kidneys.

À l'Indienne: Generally applied to dishes including curry or chutney, often served with rice.

À l'Italienne: Generally applied to dishes made partly or wholly of pasta and often with cheese and tomato flavoring.

À la Jardinière: Prepared or served with a variety of vegetables.

À la Julienne: See main entry, under Julienne.

Au Jus: Served with the natural juices or gravy.

Au Kari: Curried.

À la King: Served in a rich cream sauce (often flavored with sherry) and including mushrooms and green peppers.

À la Lyonnaise: With sautéed shredded onion as a principal ingredient.

À la Madrilène: Flavored with tomato.

Au Maigre: Without meat.

À la Maître d'Hôtel: With maître d'hôtel or parsley butter (see main entry).

À la Marinière: For Moules Marinière see Mussels entry. The term is also applied to fish dishes cooked in white wine and garnished with mussels.

À la Maryland: With a butter and cream sauce, often containing wine. Maryland Chicken has a garnish of corn fritters and sautéed bananas.

À la Meunière: Fish dredged with flour, fried in butter and served with the butter and chopped parsley.

À la Milanaise: Garnished with spaghetti, tomato sauce, and ham or tongue. Also food dipped in egg and a mixture of bread crumbs and cheese, then fried.

À la Minute: Quickly cooked, e.g. broiled foods, omelets.

À la Mode: Beef braised in the classic way; also dessert pie served with ice cream.

À la Montmorency: Name of various sweet dishes and cakes which include cherries.

À la Mornay: Coated with cheese (Mornay) sauce.

À la Nantua: Garnished (or in some cases made) with crayfish.

À la Napolitaine: With a garnish of spaghetti, cheese, and tomato sauce.

Au Naturel: Plain, uncooked (e.g. oysters) or very simply cooked.

À la Nesselrode: Implies the use of chestnuts.

À la Niçoise: As a garnish for meat, implies use of tomatoes, olives, and green beans; as a soup, garnished with tomato, flageolets, and diced potato; as a sauce, concentrated tomato purée blended with demi-glace.

À la Normande: Containing apples; or, in the case of fish, served with Normande sauce and garnished with shrimp, crayfish, or mussels.

À l'Orientale: Fish, eggs, vegetables, cooked with tomatoes and flavored with garlic and often with saffron.

En Papillote: Made or served in a paper case.

À la Parisienne: A garnish which varies considerably, but always includes small balls of sautéed potatoes called "pommes de terre à la Parisienne."

À la Parmesan: Including grated Parmesan cheese.

À la Paysanne: Peasant or simple country style. Meat or poultry, usually braised and accompanied by mixed vegetables, bacon, etc.

À la Périgueux (à la Périgord, à la Périgourdine): Made or served with truffles and sometimes foie gras.

À la Polonaise: Used for a variety of dishes; often implies presence of sour cream, beet, and red cabbage. With vegetables it means a sauce of crumbs browned in butter and mixed with chopped parsley and hard-cooked egg.

À la Portugaise: Most dishes with this title include tomato, onion, or garlic.

À la Poulette: Usually means a sort of fricassee of cooked meat or poultry in rich white sauce, garnished with onions or garlic.

À la Provençale: Containing olive oil, garlic, and often tomatoes.

À la Princesse: With a garnish of asparagus tips and truffles or noisette potatoes.

À la Printanière: Spring style, i.e. containing or garnished with small, young vegetables.

À la Reine: Implies that the dish is based on chicken.

À la Richelieu: Made with Richelieu sauce (a rich brown Madeira sauce) or garnished with mushrooms, artichoke bottoms, or stuffed tomatoes, etc. The name is also given to other dishes, such as a sweet pastry.

À la Royale: Applied to a variety of methods of cooking and serving. Consommé royale is garnished with tiny unsweetened custard cut-outs.

À la St Germain: Indicates the use of green peas.

À la Soubise: Flavored with onion or garnished with onion puree.

Table d'Hôte: A meal consisting of a certain number of courses at a fixed price; there is usually some choice of dishes within each course.

En Tasse: In a cup, especially of soups, etc.

Au Vert-pré: Garnished with watercress and straw potatoes and often served with maître d'hôtel butter; also, coated with green mayonnaise.

À la Vichy: Implies the use of carrots.

À la Vinaigrette: With a dressing of oil, vinegar, and herbs.

À la Walewska: Fish with a lobster sauce and garnish.

Part II

Aiguillette: A thin strip or slice of cooked poultry, meat, or fish.

Aillade: Name given to various sauces and accompaniments for salads, all strongly flavored with garlic.

Ballottine: A kind of galantine, made of meat, poultry, or fish, boned, stuffed, and rolled into a bundle. Also small balls of meat.

Barquette: Small boat-shaped pastry shells, used for both savory and sweet mixtures.

Brandade: A dish based on salt cod, flavored with garlic, which is popular in Southern France.

Brûlé: Literally, "burned" – in other words, the food is broiled or otherwise heated sufficiently to give it a good brown color.

Brunoise: A tiny dice of vegetables used as base for a soup or sauce or as a garnish.

Émincé: Cut in thin slices or shredded.

Estouffade (Estouffat, Étuve): Meat cooked very slowly in very little liquid, i.e. braised.

Frappé: Iced, frozen, or chilled.

Friandises: A variety of small sweets, preserved fruits, etc., served as petits fours or desserts.

Frit: Fried; *Friture*, fried food.

Glacé: This can mean either (1) iced or frozen; or (2) having a smooth, glossy surface or glaze.

Haché: Ground or chopped.

Hachis: Ground hash; food cut up finely.

Maison: In the style of the particular restaurant.

Matelote: A rich, well-seasoned fish stew made with red or white wine.

Mignardise: Small and dainty foods.

Mignon: Small, dainty, e.g. small portions of fillet of beef.

Navarin: A ragout of mutton and either potatoes and onions or mixed spring vegetables.

Noisette: A small, round, individual portion or slice of meat.

Pâte: Paste, dough, batter, pastry.

Pâté: A pie made with pastry or a terrine baked and served cold.

Paupiette: A small, thinly cut piece of meat wrapped around a filling of forcemeat, covered with a bacon slice and braised; similar fillets of fish are rolled around a piece of potato (which is later removed) and then fried; the hollow left when the potato is removed is filled with a rich white sauce.

Plat du Jour: The main dish of the day.

Poêlé: Braised, pot roasted.

Rafraîchi: Chilled.

Recherché: Choice, rare, dainty.

Renversé: Turned out, as of a molded dessert.

Rissolé: Baked or fried and well-browned.

Roulade: Meat roll or galantine.

Rubané: Built up of ribbonlike layers.

Soubise: Puree of rice and onions, or onions only.

Suprême: The best or most delicate part, e.g. breast of chicken. (See also Suprême Sauce entry.)

HANDY CHARTS

When using recipes in this book:

- As a general rule, the quantities given make 4 average servings.
- All spoonfuls are level measures, not rounded or heaping

CUP MEASURES

1 cup = 8 fl oz

Almonds		
(whole)	6 oz	1 cup
(ground)	4 oz	1 cup
Breadcrumbs		
(dry)	3 oz	1 cup
(fresh)	2 oz	1 cup
Cheese (grated)	4 oz	1 cup
Cracker crumbs	4 oz	1 cup
Cream	4 fl oz	1 cup whipped
Dried fruit	1 lb	3 cups
Flour	1 lb	4 cups
Rice	8 oz	1 cup
Sugar		
(brown)	6 oz	1 cup
(confectionary)	1 lb	3 cups
(granulated)	1 lb	2 cups

Liquid Measurements
1 American pint = 16 fluid oz
1 American cup = 8 fluid oz
1 imperial pint = 20 fluid oz
$\frac{1}{2}$ imperial pint = 10 fluid oz

SPOON MEASURES

All spoon measures are level.

10 tablespoons	$= \frac{1}{4}$ pt (150 ml)
1 tablespoon flour	$= \frac{1}{2}$ oz (15 g)
1 tablespoon cornstarch	$= \frac{1}{2}$ oz (15 g)
1 tablespoon breadcrumbs	$= \frac{1}{4}$ oz (10 g)
1 tablespoon ground almonds	$= \frac{1}{2}$ oz (15 g)
1 tablespoon whole blanched almonds	$= \frac{1}{2}$ oz (15 g)
2 tablespoons rice	$= 1\frac{1}{4}$ oz (35 g)
2 tablespoons sugar	$= 1\frac{1}{4}$ oz (35 g)
2 tablespoons shredded coconut	$= \frac{1}{2}$ oz (15 g)
2 teaspoons powdered gelatin	$= \frac{1}{4}$ oz (10 g)

AMERICAN MEASUREMENT	APPROX. METRIC EQUIVALENT
1 oz	25 g
2 oz	50 g
3 oz	75 g
4 oz	100–125 g
5 oz	150 g
6 oz	175 g
7 oz	200 g
8 oz	225 g
9 oz	250 g
10 oz	275 g
1 lb	0.45 kg
2 lb	0.9 kg
3 lb	1.36 kg
4 lb	1.81 kg
5 lb	2.26 kg
6 lb	2.72 kg
7 lb	3.17 kg
8 lb	3.62 kg
9 lb	4.08 kg
10 lb	4.53 kg
20 lb	9.07 kg
50 lb	22.67 kg

OVEN TEMPERATURES

Oven	°F	°C	Gas Mark
Very cool	250–275	130–140	$\frac{1}{2}$–1
Cool	300	150	2
Warm	325	170	3
Moderate	350	180	4
Fairly hot	375–400	190–200	5–6
Hot	425	220	7
Very hot	450–475	230–240	8–9

NOTE: To convert a Fahrenheit temperature into Centigrade/Celsius, subtract 32, multiply by 5 and divide by 9. Conversely, to convert Centigrade/Celsius temperatures to Fahrenheit, multiply by 9, divide by 5 and then add 32.

TIME-SAVING TIPS

Use any little time you have to spare to save extra-precious moments when you're busy.

A day or two in advance, chops herbs for garnishes, slice or chop mushrooms, onions, carrots (but never vegetables like parsnips, which discolor) and store them in covered containers in the refrigerator.

Segment or slice oranges and grapefruit, squeeze orange or lemon juice and grate the rind – citrus fruits can be prepared 2 or 3 days in advance.

Seed grapes (or use seedless ones!) and remove the pits from cherries up to 2 days in advance.

Use washed yogurt or cottage cheese containers and margarine tubs, all with lids, for storing these advance preparations. But remember to label them clearly. A frantic last-minute search for a spoonful of parsley saves neither time nor temper!

Chop, flake, grate or grind nuts. Toast nuts when you're using the oven or broiler. They all store for several weeks in a screw-top jar.

Practice batch cooking for the refrigerator or freezer to save time, fuel and washing up.

When spooning honey, flour the spoon first – it rolls off like a dream!

You know about dipping peaches, apples and tomatoes into boiling water for a few seconds before peeling them. Try the same trick for citrus fruits.

● Never waste anything, especially an opportunity to cook ahead. When you've removed the bones from any cuts of meat or poultry, or filleted fish, use the bones with chopped onion, carrots, celery and herbs to make a basic meat, poultry or fish stock. Freeze and store it for up to 3 months.

When you have some wine left over from one dish – or from a meal – use it to prepare another. Poach apples or pears in red wine spiced with cinnamon or cloves. Use wine instead of water to make a syrup for extra-special fruit salads, or freeze the wine in cubes.

MONEY-SAVING TIPS

BUTTER

1. To economize on butter, substitute oil for frying, margarine for creaming and sandwiches and reserve the luxury of butter for spreading on bread, crispbreads or toast.

2. If your family is heavy handed with butter, extend it. Beat 8 oz of butter until soft, then gradually beat in 4 tablespoons of hot water or you could use boiling milk. The bulk will be much increased and the butter can be spread more thinly even when cold.

CABBAGE

1. This leafy vegetable is available in many delicious forms. The base and core of a cabbage are heavy and must be discarded. Before buying a head of cabbage, be sure to check that the base is good to avoid wasting money, especially if some outer leaves have been stripped off because they have begun to decay.

2. Cooking cabbage in a closed casserole in the oven saves heat when the oven is in use, and conserves all the nutritional value which is often wasted when boiling cabbage in too much water.

3. Washed and finely shredded green cabbage has a nutty flavor, and combined with a dressing, makes an excellent alternative when salad greens are out of season.

CHEESE

1. To prevent the surface of cut cheese from becoming oily, cover tightly with plastic wrap and store near the bottom of the refrigerator. To prevent ripe, soft-crusted cheese from oozing once a wedge has been removed, wrap tightly in plastic wrap, pressing it closely to the cut surfaces.

2. To restore full flavor to cheese which has been stored in the refrigerator, remove the cheese at least two hours before serving. Allow it to stand until it returns to room temperature, then unwrap and serve.

3. To make sure a cheese sauce does not go either 'oily' or 'ropy', add grated cheese to the hot *cooked* sauce, remove from the heat, and stir until the cheese has melted. The sauce will soon become smooth again.

4. If cheese becomes hard and unfit for table use, grate it, mix with dry breadcrumbs and keep in a small container to use up quickly on vegetables, broiled and gratin dishes.

EGGS

1. To whisk egg whites for soufflés and desserts, whisk only until they stand in peaks, look shiny and cling to the whisk or beaters. If overwhisked until the whites look 'dry' they will not incorporate easily and may give a grainy texture to the finished dessert.

2. To prevent home-made meringue from "weeping," add a pinch of cream of tartar to the sugar.

3. Hard-cooked eggs sometimes show a line of discoloration around the yolks. To prevent this, cover the hot, drained eggs with cold water and allow to stand for 5 minutes before shelling them. Then tap the eggs gently all over against a hard surface until the shell is covered in cracks. Remove it together with the inner skin.

FRUIT

1. Never throw away orange or lemon halves which have been squeezed, without grating off the rind. This is useful to add flavor to many dishes and keeps well in small plastic containers. It is easier to grate the rind before cutting and squeezing the fruit.

2. If you are too busy to grate the rind, remove it in thin slivers, place on a baking tray and dry slowly in an oven as it cools down after use. The rind may need to be returned several times to the oven. When it is thoroughly dry, snip it up finely and store in an airtight container to use as flavoring.

3. To peel peaches and grapes easily for delicate desserts, plunge them first into very hot water for one minute, then into cold water. The skin will then slip off easily.

4. To remove the pits from cherries and grapes, use a new bobby pin, sterilized by standing it in boiling water until it becomes cool. Insert the rounded end of the bobby pin into the cherry or grape, hook it around the pit and pull out quickly. Do this over a bowl to catch any juice which may spurt out.

PASTA

1. Cook pasta in a large saucepan in plenty of salted boiling water. The saucepan must be large enough to allow the contents to boil really fast during cooking without boiling over. Do not cover the pan. According to size, the pasta will take anything from 4 to 15 minutes to cook. When ready it should be "al dente" or still reasonably firm when tested.

2. Drain the cooked pasta thoroughly. It is improved by rinsing immediately after draining with fresh hot water, both to prevent it from continuing to cook in its own heat, and to remove any excess starch.

3. If you are serving the pasta simply with a sauce, either return the drained pasta to the rinsed-out pan with a little melted butter in it to coat the strands, or turn it straight into the rinsed-out pan and stir in a little oil for the same purpose.

SALADS

1. Lettuce is delicate and once it goes limp cannot be revived. Break off leaves, do not cut them – cut stems turn brown within a few hours. Submerge gently in a colander in cold water, lift up and down several times to wash and leave to drain. Washing lettuce under a tap bruises it.

2. Outer leaves from lettuces, especially the hothouse variety, may not look crisp enough to use in a salad, but should not be discarded. Wash them carefully, shake dry and shred finely with kitchen scissors and use as a base for appetizers and cold meat dishes.

SAUCES

1. To make dressings or marinades which need to be emulsified (such as French dressing), put the dry ingredients in a screw-top jar, add the lemon juice, vinegar or wine, then the oil. Allow a small space for shaking, screw the top down firmly and shake vigorously until the mixture is blended.

2. To prevent a sauce from forming a skin while it is being kept hot, lay a damp circle of greaseproof paper over the entire surface of the sauce. Remove the paper and stir lightly just before using. Alternatively, for sweet sauces, sift a little powdered sugar over the surface; for white sauces, pour a thin layer of milk over the top. Stir these in just before serving.

STEWS

1. Cheaper cuts of meats, which are excellent for stewing, frequently contain a high percentage of fat. When the stew is cooked, allow it to become cold; the solidified fat can then easily be removed.

2. The quickest way of all to remove excess fat from a stew is to drop a few ice cubes into it. The fat will almost immediately solidify, clinging to the ice cubes, which can be quickly removed with a slotted spoon. Using layers of paper toweling to soak up surplus fat is wasteful.

3. Fat taken from a stew can be clarified for frying or roasting. Bring it to a boil in fresh water and allow to boil uncovered for 10 minutes, then cool. When the fat is cold, remove it with a slotted spoon, scrape all sediment off the underside, and place the fat on absorbent paper towelling to dry. This prevents it from spitting when used for frying or roasting.

SUGAR

1. If you are disappointed on opening canned fruit to find that the syrup is too light in strength, you can easily adjust it to your requirements. Drain the syrup and boil it until it reduces in quantity to make a heavier syrup, or heat it with added sugar and when this has dissolved boil it for a few minutes until sufficiently concentrated. Cool before pouring over the fruit.

2. If syrup from canned fruit is too heavy in strength, drain it and stir in sufficient water and a few drops of lemon juice.

3. Soft light brown and dark brown sugars tend to form a solid block in the pack when stored for more than a few weeks. Directions are usually given on the pack how to soften the sugar if this happens but, in general, the best way to soften the finer sugars is to empty the pack into a bowl and put a damp cloth across the top overnight.

4. If members of the family use a large quantity of sugar to sweeten drinks, it is cheaper to buy artificial sweeteners and insist that they are used to replace all or some of the sugar.

VEGETABLES

1. To clean new potatoes without losing the nutritional value just below the delicate skin, rub gently with a nylon scouring pad, and rinse before cooking.

2. To bake small potatoes which might otherwise fall between the bars of an oven grill, arrange them in the cups of a muffin tin.

3. To ripen green tomatoes, wrap each one separately in tissue paper or absorbent paper towelling. Place them together in the bottom of a drawer (with newspaper over the top) in a warm room. Examine the tomatoes at intervals and use those which have become ripe.

4. When your stock of root vegetables is reduced to a couple of carrots, one onion and part of a parsnip or turnip, make a mixture of diced vegetables, and cook them together with the colorful addition of some frozen peas.

SHOPPING AND CATERING GUIDE

Given below are the approximate quantities per head per meal to allow for family catering: they will serve as a guide to anyone who is catering for the first time.

MEAT
With bone 4–6 oz
Boneless 3–4 oz
For made-up dishes 2–3 oz

FISH
With much bone 6–8 oz
Little or no bone 3–4 oz
In combination dishes 2–3 oz

VEGETABLES (weight as purchased)
Artichokes (Jerusalem) 6 oz
Beans (broad) 8–12 oz
Beans (butter or haricot) 2 oz
Beans (runner) 6 oz
Beets (as a vegetable) 4–6 oz
Brussels sprouts 6 oz
Cabbage 8 oz
Carrots 4–6 oz
Celeriac 4–6 oz
Celery 1 large head for 4–5 persons
Greens (spring) 8 oz
Kale 6–8 oz
Onions (as a main vegetable) 6 oz
Parsnips 6 oz
Peas (green) 4 oz
Peas (dried) 2 oz
Potatoes 6–8 oz
Rutabagas 8 oz
Savoy cabbage 6–8 oz
Spinach 8–12 oz
Turnips 8 oz
Turnip tops 8 oz

CEREALS
Rice (for curry, etc.) 1–1½ oz
Macaroni 1–1½ oz
Oatmeal (for porridge) 1–1½ oz

BEVERAGES
Coffee (breakfast) 4 tablespoons per 4 people
Coffee (after dinner) 2 tablespoons per 4 people
Milk (in tea) 1¼ cups per 4 people
Tea 1 teaspoon per person

MISCELLANEOUS
Soup ⅔–1 cup
Sauces and gravies ¼ cup

PLANNING A PARTY

APPROXIMATE QUANTITIES FOR BUFFET PARTIES

	1 portion	24–26 portions	Notes
Soups: cream, clear or iced	⅓ pint	1 gallon	Serve garnished in mugs or cups
Fish cocktail: shrimp, tuna or crab	1 ounce	1½ pounds fish 2–3 heads of lettuce 1½ pints cocktail sauce	Serve in stemmed glasses, garnished with a shrimp
Meat: with bone boneless	5 ounces 3–4 ounces	7–8 pounds 5–6½ pounds	Cold roasts or barbecued chops Casseroles, meatballs, sausages, barbecued steaks
Poultry: turkey chicken	3–4 ounces (boneless) 1 piece 5–8 ounces	16 pounds (dressed) Six 2½–3 pound birds (dressed)	Serve hot or cold
Delicatessen: ham pâté for wine-and-pâté party	3–4 ounces 3–4 ounces	5–6½ pounds 5–6½ pounds	Halve the amount if pâté is starter course
Salad vegetables: lettuce cucumber tomatoes cabbage boiled potatoes	⅙ head 1 inch slice 1–2 1 ounce 2 ounces	3–4 heads 2 cucumbers 3 pounds 1½ pounds 3 pounds	Dress at last minute for winter salads for potato salads
Rice or pasta	1½ ounces (uncooked)	2 pounds	Can be cooked a day ahead, reheat in 5 minutes in boiling water
Cheese (for wine-and-cheese party)	3 ounces	4½–5 pounds at least 4 types	You'll need more if you serve a cheese dip too
Cheese (for crackers)	1–1½ ounces	1½–2 pounds cheese plus 1 pound butter 2 pounds crackers	Allow the larger amounts for an assorted cheese board

APPROXIMATE COFFEE AND TEA QUANTITIES

	1 Serving	24–26 Servings		Notes
Coffee				
ground, hot	⅓ pint	9–10 ounces coffee 6 pints water	3 pints milk 1 pound sugar	If you make the coffee in advance strain it after infusion. Reheat without boiling. Serve sugar separately.
ground, iced	⅓ pint	12 ounces coffee 6 pints water	3 pints milk sugar to taste	Make coffee (half sweetened, half not), strain and chill. Mix with chilled milk. Serve in glasses.
instant, hot	⅓ pint	2–3 ounces coffee 6 pints water	2 pints milk 1 pound sugar	Make coffee in jugs as required. Serve sugar separately.
instant, iced	⅓ pint	3 ounces coffee 2 pints	6 pints milk sugar to taste	Make black coffee (half sweetened, half not) and chill. Mix with chilled creamy mix. Serve in glasses.
Tea				
Indian, hot	⅓ pint	2 ounces tea 8 pints water	1½ pints milk 1 pound sugar	It is better to make tea in several pots rather than one oversized one.
Indian, iced	⅓ pint	3 ounces tea 7 pints water	2 pints milk sugar to taste	Strain tea immediately after it has infused. Sweeten half of it. Chill. Serve in glasses with chilled creamy milk.
China	⅓ pint	2 ounces tea 9 pints water	2–3 lemons 1 pound sugar	Infuse China tea for 2 or 3 minutes only. Put a thin lemon slice in each cup before pouring. Serve sugar separately.

QUANTITIES FOR PARTY DRINKS
Rough guide only, as drinking habits vary.

Type of Party	Drink Allowance
Buffet party	Allow each guest 2–3 cocktails plus coffee. Reckon a half-bottle of wine per person.
Dinner party	Two bottles of table wine are sufficient for 4 people.
Cocktail party	Reckon on 3–5 cocktails each and 4–6 different hors d'oeuvres in addition to the usual olives and nuts.
Drinks by the bottle	Sherry, port and straight vermouths give roughly 12–16 glasses per bottle. In single shots for cocktails, vermouths and liquors give just over 30 per bottle. Allow 16–20 drinks of liquor from a bottle when serving it with soda, tonic or fruit juices. Liqueurs served in liqueur glasses will give about 30 per bottle. A split bottle of soda or tonic makes 2–3 drinks. A 1-pint can of tomato juice makes 4–6 drinks.

STOCKING YOUR KITCHEN CUPBOARD

The following list gives guidance on the shelf life of different dry goods and suggestions as to basic perishables.

CODE
**** keeps well
*** keeps up to 6 months
** keeps for 2–3 months
* buy in small quantities
Basic essentials in heavy type

BEVERAGES
Cocoa★
Coffee★, instant and ground
Dried skimmed milk★★
Tea★

CANS★★★★
Fish – Anchovy fillets
   Salmon
   Sardines
   Tuna
Fruit – assorted

Juices – Orange
   Grapefruit
   Tomato
Meat – Chicken
   Corned beef
   Ham
   Liver pâté
   Stewed beef
Milk – Evaporated
   Condensed
Soups – Consommé
   Cream of chicken
   Cream of mushroom
Vegetables – **Beans**
   Carrots, baby
   Corn
   Mushrooms
   Peas
   Tomatoes, peeled
   Tomato paste

CEREALS
Barley, pearl★★★★
Breadcrumbs, dried★★
Cornflakes, etc.★
Cous cous★★★
Lentils and split peas★★★

Oatmeal, medium★★★
Oats, rolled★★
Pasta, macaroni,
noodles, etc.★★★
Rice, long and short grain★★★

COLORINGS★★★★
Coloring Set

CRACKERS
Cheese crackers★
Crispbreads★★

DRIED FRUIT★★
Apple rings
Apricots
Candied peel – mixed, citron
Dates
Peaches
Pears
Prunes
Raisins

DRIED VEGETABLES★★★
Beans, lentils, peas
Garlic, flaked
Onion, flaked
Potato, instant

EXTRACTS★★★★
Almond
Lemon
Orange
Peppermint
Vanilla

FLOURS★★★
Cake flour
Cornstarch
Plain flour
Wholewheat flour

HERBS (FRESH★ FROZEN★ DRIED★★★)
Basil
Bay leaf
Chives
Garlic
Marjoram

Mint
Mixed dried
Parsley
Rosemary
Sage
Tarragon
Thyme

LEAVENING AGENTS
Baking powder★★
Baking soda★★
Cream of tartar★★
Yeast, dry★★★

NUTS
Almonds, whole★★, sliced★, ground★
Cashew★
Coconut, shredded★★
Peanuts★★
Walnuts★

PICKLES★★★
Capers
Gherkins
Olives, green, black, stuffed
Onions, cocktail
Peppers

PRESERVES
Apricot★★★
Black cherry★★★
Cranberry jelly★★★
Corn syrup★★★
Honey★★★
Maple syrup★★★
Marmalade★★★
Raspberry★★★
Stem ginger★★★
Strawberry★★★

SAUCES
Chutney★★
Mayonnaise★
Tabasco★★★
Tomato catsup★★
Worcestershire sauce★★★

SPICES
Allspice★★★
Caraway seeds★★★

Cayenne★★★
Chilli powder★★★
Cinnamon★★★
Cloves, whole and ground★★★
Curry powder and paste★★★
Dill★★★
Ginger, ground★★★
Mace and **nutmeg**★★★
Mustard, ground and seeds★★★★
Paprika★★
Pepper, black and white★★
Poppy seeds★★★
Salt, fine and coarse★★
Sesame seeds★★★

SUGARS
Confectionary★★★★
Granulated★★★★
Lump★★★★
Soft dark brown★

MISCELLANEOUS
Bouillon cubes, beef, chicken, fish★★
Cherries, maraschino★★★
Chocolate, dark, dessert★
Gelatin, powdered★★★
Meat and yeast extracts★★★★
Mustard★★
Oil, olive and corn★★★
Parmesan cheese, grated★
Vinegar, cider, wine, tarragon, malt★★★★

BASIC PERISHABLES
(Best kept in refrigerator)
Bacon
Cheese, Cheddar etc.
Eggs
Fats – **Butter**
    Vegetable shortening
    Margarine
Milk and cream
Sour cream
Yogurt
Lemons
Parsley
Yeast, fresh

RECIPE INDEX

Almond(s), 3
  Petits fours, 308
  Pralines, 331–2
Almond paste, 3–4
  Marzipan candies, 62–3
Anchovy:
  Butter, 5
  Deviled eggs, 148
  Toasts, 61–2
Angel food cake, 5–6
Angels on horseback, 284
Apple(s), 6–10
  Apple ginger preserve, 10
  and Blackberry jam, 30
  and Celery stuffing, 79
  Chutney, 98
  Crab apple jelly, 110
  Dumplings, 8–9
  Jelly, 9–10
  and Mulberry jam, 268
  Pie, 8, 314
  and Prune roll, 336
  Sauce, 9
  Tarte tatin, 9
  Turnovers, 416
Apricot jam, 10
Apricot soufflé omelet, 281
Artichoke(s), 11–12
  Jerusalem, with tomatoes, 12
  Salad, 12
  Stuffed, 11
Asparagus and shrimp gratin, 13
Asparagus soup, Cream of, 13
Aspic:
  Ham and parsley in, 190
  Homemade, 13
  Jelly, 193
Aubergine see Eggplant
Avgolemono, 13–14
Avial (Aviyal), 126–7
Avocado:
  Appetizers, 14
  and Crab gratin, 14
  Dip, 15
  and Grapefruit salad, 15

Bacon:
  Angels on horseback, 284
  with Dandelion salad, 130
  and Lentil soup 239
  Omelet, 280
Baked Alaska, 220
Bamboo shoots, Stir-fried, 18–19
Banana(s):
  Boats, 19

  Flambé, in orange sauce, 19
  Ice cream, 218
Barbecue sauce, 20
Barley water, 21
Batter, 22
Bean(s):
  Black bean soup, 30
  Boston baked beans, 272
  Fava with garlic sausage, 156
  Frijoles refritos con queso, 229
Béchamel sauce, 24
Beef, 25–7, 254
  Beef-stuffed onions, 282
  Boeuf Stroganoff, 26
  Brisket, braised in red wine, 36–7
  Carbonnade of, 26–7
  Chili con carne, 94
  Flemish beef in beer, 76
  Goulash, 197
  Hamburger, 207
  Jerked, 225
  Pot-au-feu, 328
  Potted, 329
  Rissoles British style, 353
  Rolls, 27
  Steak and kidney pie, 27
  Stew, 26, 398
  Wellington, 26
Beurre manié, 28
Beurre noir (Black Butter), 28
Beurre noisette, 28
Bigarade sauce, 28, 140–1
Biryani, 127
Biscuit tortoni, 29
Biscuits:
  Buttermilk, 29
  Rolled baking powder, 29
  see also Cookies
Bishop, the, 29–30
Blackberry jelly, 30
Black-eyed pea balls, 31
Black forest torte, 89
Blintzes, Cheese, 32
Blueberry:
  Cobbler, 102
  Jam, 32
  Muffins, 267
  Pancakes, 286
Blue cheese dip, 136
Bouillabaisse, 35
Borsch, 34
Brains, 35–6
Brandy cocktail, 103
Brandy snaps, 37–8
Bread (and Rolls), 38–45

  Anadama, 5
  Boston brown, 264
  Brioches, 47
  Challah, 80–1
  Chapatti, 81
  Cheese pull-aparts, 44–5
  Corn, 113–14
  Croissants, 120
  Croûtons, 122
  French toast, 177
  Fried bread croustades, 122
  Garlic, 186
  Grissini (bread sticks), 202
  Irish soda bread, 387
  Johnnycake, 226
  Malt, 45, 248–9
  Pain perdu, 285
  Panettone, 287
  Poppy seed braid, 44
  Quick whole-wheat rolls, 356
  Scones, 376–7
  Soft rolls, 355–6
  Sourdough, 392–3
  Spoon, 114
  Toast melba, 412
  White, 43–4
  Whole-wheat flowerpots, 45
Bread and butter pudding, 45
Breadcrumbs, 45–6
Broccoli in oyster sauce, 284
Brose, 49
Broth:
  Chicken, 49–50
  Scotch, 49
Brownies, Rich, 110–11
Brussels sprouts, 50
Bubble and squeak, 50
Butter:
  Clarified, 51, 155
  Deviled, 133
  Frosting, 52, 179
  Fruit, 181
  Garlic, 387
  Herb, 211
  Lobster, 243
  Maître d'Hôtel, 248
  Melted (Drawn), 51
  Parsley, 323–4
  Quince, 181
Butterscotch sauce, 52

Cabbage, 53
  Pickled red, 311
Cabinet pudding, 53
Caledonian cream, 251

Calf's brain, 36
Calf's foot jelly, 60
Calf's head, 209–10
  Head cheese, 210
Calf's liver:
  Liver marsala, 242
  and Onions, 242
Canapés, 61–2
Candied citrus peel, 62
Candy, 62–5
Cannelloni, 66
  with Cheese sauce, 294
  au Gratin, 294–5
Caramel, 70
  Sundae, 403
Cardinal sauce, 71
Carrot cake, 72
Cassata alla siciliana, 75
Casserole(s), 76–7
  Chicken, 76
  Duck and orange, 141
  Flemish beef in beer, 76
  Oxtail, 284
  Partridge, 289–90
  Pheasant, 309
  Pork and prune, 336
  Rich rabbit, 76
Cassoulet, 77
Catsup (Ketchup), 77–8
Cauliflower, 78
  au Gratin, 78
  Minestra di cavolfiore, 262
  Pickled (Italian style), 312
Caviar, 78
  Deviled eggs, 148
Celery, 37, 78–9
  and Apple stuffing, 79
  Minted, and cucumber, 123
Celery root (Celeriac), 79
Champagne cocktail, 103
Champagne cup, 81
Charlotte russe, 82
Chasseur sauce, 82
Chateaubriand steak, 82
Chaud-froid sauce, 82–3
Chayotes, Ham-stuffed, 83
Cheese, 83–7
  Blintzes, 32
  Fondue, 165–6
  Hot cheese dip, 166
  Knaidlach, 230
  and Macaroni, 245
  Omelet, 279
  and Rice soufflé, 390
  Sauce and cannelloni, 294
  Soufflé, 87
  Straws, 87

  Toasted, 87
  Welsh rarebit, 429
  see also Cream cheese
Cheeseburgers, 207
Cheesecake, 88
  Cherry, 88–9
  Compôte, 89
  Jam, 89
Chestnut(s), 90
  and Brussels sprouts, 50
  Soup, 90
  Stuffing, 401
  in Syrup, 251–2
Chicken, 48, 90–2
  Arroz con pollo, 92
  Broth, 49–50
  Casserole, 76
  Coq au vin, 92
  Deviled, 133
  Fried, 91
  Fricassee, 177–8
  Galantine, 184–5
  with Grapefruit, 198
  Marengo, 91–2, 250
  Maryland, 92
  Normande, 9
  Poached, 91
  Risotto, 352–3
  Roast, 91
  Satay with peanut sauce, 372–3
  Tandoori, 127
  Tarragon, 408
  Vol-au-vent, 425
Chicken liver(s), 92–3
  Chopped, 242
  Paté, 301
  Pilaf, 93
  Rumaki, 17
  on Toast, 93
Chickpea(s) (Garbanzo), 93
  Salad with chorizos, 97
  with Sausages, 93
Chili con carne, 94
Chocolate, 95–6
  Cake, 95–6
  Chocolates, 96
  Easter eggs, 143
  Eclairs, 144
  Fudge, 63
  Fudge frosting, 96
  Ice cream, 218, 219
  Mousse, 95
  One-step shortening cake, 56–7
  Sauce, 96
  Sachertorte, 362
  Soufflé au chocolat, 390
  Sundae, 403

  Truffles, 65
Chop suey, 97
Chowder, 97
  Fish, 97–8
  Manhattan clam, 101
  New England clam, 100–1
Christmas fruitcake, 181–2
Christmas pudding, 322–3
Chutney, 98–9
Cider, 99
Cioppino, 100
Clam(s), 100–1
  Bake, 101
  Red clam sauce, 241
  White clam sauce, 100
Cobbler, 102
Cocktails (alcoholic), 102–3
Cocktails (non-alcoholic), 103–4
Coconut ice, 65
Coconut kisses, 104
Cod, 104–5
  Roe, 355
  Salt, 105
  Stuffed cod steaks, 105
Coeur à la Crème, 105
Coffee:
  Ice cream, 218
  Layer cake, 107
  Sauce, 106–7
  Swedish coffee cake, 107
  Walnut fudge, 63–4
Coleslaw, 108
Conserve, Strawberry and
  rhubarb, 109
  see also Jam; Jelly
Consommé, 109–10
Cookie crumb-crust, 162,
  297–8
Cookie(s), 110–12
  Brandy snaps, 37–8
  Chocolate chip, 110
  Florentines, 162–3
  Ladyfingers, 233
  Macaroons, 246
  Moravian ginger, 111
  Nürnberger lebkuchen, 236–7
  Nut refrigerator, 112
  Oatmeal, 111
  Orange glazed meltaways,
    111–12
  Peanut butter, 305
  Star, 112
Corn fritters, 113, 178
Corned beef hash, 113
Cornish pasties, 113
Cornstarch glaze, 194
Court-bouillon, 115

Crab, 115–16
  and Avocado gratin, 14
  Deviled crab canapés, 62
  Gumbo, 204
  Scrambled curried, 116
Crab apple jelly, 116
Cranberry sauce, 117
Cream cheese filling (Danish pastry), 131
Cream cheese frosting, 117
Cream horns, 118
Cream puffs, 118
Crème au beurre, 59
Crème chantilly, 118
Crêpes, 119
Croissants, 120
Croquettes:
  Egg, 147
  Parsnip, 289
  Savory, 121
Croutons, 122
Crumpets, 122
Cucumber, 123
  Buttered, 123
  and Mint fish salad, 104–5
  Minted celery and, 123
  Pickled, 311
Cumberland sauce, 123
Currant fool, 124
Currant jelly, 124
Curried fish, 160–1
Curry, 124–8
  Avial, 126–7
  Biryani, 127
  Rogan josh, 126
  Samosas, 126
  Sauce, 127–8
  Tandoori chicken, 127
  Vindaloo, 125–6
Custard, 128
  Baked, 128
  Caramel, 70
  Pie, 128
  Sauce, 128

Daikon, sweet-sour, 130
Daiquiri, 103
Dandelion salad with bacon, 130
Danish pastry, 131
Date(s), 131–2
  Bars, 132
  Pickled, 132
Demi-glâce sauce, 133
Deviled, 133–4
  Butter, 133
  Chicken, 133
  Crab Canapés, 62

Eggs, 147–8
  Ham, 133
  Turkey drumsticks, 134
Devil's food cake, 134
Dhal: Lentil puree, 134
Dips, 136
  Blue cheese, 136
  Fondue, 165–6
  Guacamole, 203
  Hot Cheese, 166
  Hot mustard, 136
  Hummus, 217
  Taramasalata, 407
Dobos torte, 137
Dolmades, 199
Double crust pie, 313
Doughnuts, 137–8
Dry martini, 103
Duck, 140–1
  with Bigarade sauce, 140–1
  with Cherries, 89
  and Orange casserole, 141
  Wild, 431
Dumplings, 141
  Apple, 8–9
  Cheese knaidlach, 230
  Matzo balls, 141
  Spaetzel, 393
Dundee cake, 141–2

Easter eggs, 143
Eccles cakes, 143
Eclairs, 144, 318
Eels, 144
Egg(s), 144–9
  Baked, 147
  Coddled, 146
  Croquettes, 147
  Deviled, 147–8
  Framed, 147
  Fried, 147
  Frittata, 178
  with Garlic soup, 186
  Hard-cooked, 146
  Hot stuffed, 148
  Huevos rancheros, 147
  Oeufs à la neige, 277
  Omelets, 279–81
  Pickled, 146
  Pipérade, 149
  Poached, 146
  Pork eggs foo yung, 169
  Scrambled, 147
  Scotch, 148
  Shirred, 147
  Soft-cooked, 146
Egg flip, 149

Eggplant (Aubergine), 149–50
  Baked stuffed, 149
  Fiesta, 149–50
  Moussaka, 266
  Raita, 344
  with Spiced lamb, 234–5
Egg rolls, 150
Elderberry jelly, 150
Empanadas, 151
Espagnole sauce, 152

Fettuccine alfredo, 156–7
Finnan haddie, Poached, 206
Fish, 49, 157–61
  Baked, 161
  Bouillabaisse, 35
  Chowder, 97–8
  Cioppino, 100
  Cocktail, 103
  Curried, 160–1
  Fish cakes, 161
  Gefilte, 188–9
  Kedgeree, 228
  Mint and cucumber fish salad, 104–5
  Provençale, 161
  Quenelles, 340
  Réchauffé, 346
  Seviche, 379
Flans, 162
Fondants and creams, 62, 165
Fondue, 165–6
Forcemeat, 169
French dressing (sauce vinaigrette), 104, 365–6
French toast, 177
Frittata, 178
Fritters, 178
  Corn, 113, 178
  see also Pancakes
Frosting, 179
  Chocolate fudge, 96
  Classic butter cream, 179
  Lemon cream cheese, 117
  Petits fours, 308
  Piping, 318
  Vanilla butter, 52
  White mountain, 430
Fruit, 179–81
  Butter, 181
  Canned fruit jam, 224
  Coupe Jacques, 115
  Crumble, 122
  Flan fillings, 162
  Flip, 149
  Fool, 181
  Freezing, 171–2

Fresh fruit cocktail, 182
Fruit pulp jam, 224
Molded fruit gelatin, 190
Parfait, 288
Salad, 180–1
Stewed, 180
Winter fruit salad, 181
Fruitcake, 181–2
Christmas, 181–2
Dundee cake, 141–2
Family, 182
Simnel cake, 384
White, 331
Fudge, 63–4, 183
Funnel cakes, 183

Game soup, 185–6
Garbure, 186
Garlic:
Bread, 186
Butter, 387
Sausage with fava beans, 156
Soup with eggs, 186
Gâteau St Honoré, 188
Gazpacho, 188
Gefilte fish, 188–9
Gelatin, 189–90
Basic dessert, 190
Clear lemon, 190
Jambon persillé, 190
Molded fruit, 190
Genoise, 190–1
Ginger, 191–2
Apple ginger preserve, 10
Ginger-glazed lamb kebabs, 381
Ice cream, 219
Moravian ginger cookies, 111
Ginger ale and beer, 192
Gingerbread, 192
Gingersnaps, 191
Glaze, 192–4
Chocolate, 362
Cornstarch, 193–4
Icing, 193
Meat, 193
Gnocchi, 195
Goose, 195–6
Salmi of, 367
Wild, 431
Gooseberry jam, 196
Gooseberry sauce, 196
Gougère, Ham, 196–7
Goulash, 197
Graham cracker pie crust, 197,
297–8
Grapefruit, 198–9
and Avocado salad, 15

Gravlax, Scandinavian, 199
Gravy, 199–200
Red-eye, 207
Gray mullet, 268
Greengage jam, 200
Grouse, Roast, 202
Guacamole, 203
with Bacon, 203
with Green chili peppers, 203
Guinea fowl, Roast, 203
Gumbo, 204

Haddock, 205–6
Baked stuffed fresh, 205
Julienne, 205–6
Poached finnan haddie, 206
Smoked, 205, 228
Halibut, Baked in wine, 206
Ham, 206–7
Broiled ham steak, 48, 207
Deviled, 133
Omelet, 280
and Parsley in aspic, 190
Raised veal and ham pie, 343
and Scalloped potatoes, 207
and Shrimp jambalaya, 224–5
Steak and red-eye gravy, 207
Tagliatelle con prosciutto, 295
Hamburgers, 208
Hard sauce, 208
Hare, Jugged, 209
Harvey wallbanger, 103
Head cheese, 210
Heart, 210–11
Baked stuffed, 210
Braised sliced, 210–11
Ragout of beef heart with
lemon, 76–7
Herring, 211–12
Hollandaise sauce, 213
Hopping John, 214
Horseradish sauce, 216
Hot cross buns, 216–17
Hot milk sponge cake, 57
Hummus dip, 217

Ice cream, 218–20
Baked Alaska, 220
Cassata alla siciliana, 75
French custard vanilla, 218–19
Lemon, 238
Peach melba, 304
Philadelphia, 219
Praline bombe, 219–20
Sundae, 403
Ices, 220–1
Granita di caffè, 198

Lemon, 220
Orange, 220
Pineapple, 220–1
Strawberry, 400
Icing:
Fondant, 165, 232
Piping flowers, 318–19
Royal, 358–60
see also Frosting
Icing glaze, 193
Indian pudding, 114
Irish stew, 398
Italian Bavarian cream, 23

Jam, 222–4
Apricot, 10
Blackberry and apple, 30
Blueberry, 32
Canned fruit, 224
Cherry, 89
Fruit pulp, 224
Gooseberry, 196
Greengage, 200
Mulberry and apple, 268
Plum, 322
Quince, 341
Raspberry, 345
Strawberry, 400
Jam soufflé omelet, 281
Jam turnovers, 416
Jambalaya, Ham and shrimp,
224–5
Jelly, 225
Apple, 9–10
Blackberry, 30
Calf's foot, 60
Crab apple, 116
Currant, 124
Elderberry, 150
Mint, 263
Jelly doughnuts, 137–8
Jelly roll, 57
Johnnycake, Rhode island, 226

Kasha varnitchkes, 228
Kebabs, 49
Ginger-glazed lamb, 381
Shish, 381–2
Kedgeree, 228
Key lime pie, 240
Kidneys, 48
with Sherry, 229
Steak and kidney pie, 27
Kippers, 230
Knaidlach, cheese, 230
Kohlrabi, 230
Kugel, 231

Kulich, 232

Ladyfingers, 233
Lamb (and Mutton), 233–5, 254
  Country lamb potage, 234
  and Potato pasties, 234
  Spiced, with eggplant, 234–5
Lasagne:
  Creamy cheese, 295
  al Forno, 236
Latkes, Potato, 328
Lebkuchen, Nürnberger, 236–7
Leek and potato bake, 237
Leek and potato soup, Cream of,
  237
Lemon:
  Cheesecake, 88
  Chiffon cake, 57–8
  Clear lemon gelatin, 190
  Cream of lemon soup, 392
  Curd, 238
  Meringue pie, 238
Lemonade, 239
Lentil, 239
  and Bacon soup, 239
  Puree (Dhal), 134
Linguine, 241
Linzertorte, 413
Liver, 48, 241–2
  Chicken liver pilaf, 93
  Chicken livers on toast, 93
  Chopped chicken livers, 242
Lobster, 242–3
  Butter, 243
  Newburg, 243
  Salad, 243
  Thermidor, 243

Macaroni and cheese, 245
Macaroons, 246
Mackerel, 246–7
Madeira cake, 247
Madeira sauce, 247
Madeleines, 247
Manhattan (cocktail), 103
Marinade(s), 250
  Teriyaki, 410
Marmalade, 250–1
Marrons glacés, 251–2
Marsala sauce, 247
Marshmallow sauce, 252
Marzipan candies, 62–3
Mayonnaise, Classic, 366
Meat loaves, Individual, 256
Melba sauce, 256–7
Melon, Pickled, 257
Meringue, 258

Lemon meringue pie, 238
Milk shakes, 260
Mille-feuilles, 260
Mincemeat, 261
Mince pies, 261
Mint, 262–3
  Julep, 227
Minted cucumber and celery, 123
Molasses, 263–4
Mole poblano, 264–5
Mornay sauce, 266
Moussaka, Eggplant, 266
Mousse:
  Chocolate, 95
  Raspberry, 266–7
  Rhubarb, 349
  Salmon, 267, 368–9
Mousseline sauce, 267
Muffins, 267–8
  Blueberry, 267
  Cranberry and nut, 268
  Date-bran, 131
  Raspberry, 268
Mulled ale, 268
Mulled red wine, 268
Mushroom(s), 269–70
  Baked, 270
  Broiled, 270
  Omelet, 279
  Patty shells, 302
  Sautéed, 270
  and Tomato sauce, 393–4
Mussels, 270
  Moules marinière, 270–1
Mustard sauce, 271

New England boiled dinner, 273
Noodles, 274
  Homemade, 295
  Kugel, 231
Normande sauce, 274
Nougat, 64
Nut stuffing, 401

Oat bars, 276
Oatmeal cookies, 111
Oatmeal porridge, 325
Oil pastry, 278, 297
Omelet, 279–81
  Fillings, 279–80
  Plain, 279
  Sausage and pepper, 280
  Soufflé, 280–1
  Spanish, 280
  Western, 280
One-step shortening chocolate
  cake, 56–7

Onion(s), 281–2
  Beef-stuffed, 282
  Boiled, 282
  French onion soup, 281–2
  Fried onion rings, 282
  and Liver, 241–2
  Pickled, 311
  and Red pepper quiche, 282
Orange(s), 282–3
  Bitter orange marmalade, 251
  Duck and orange casserole,
    141
  Orange snow, 190
  Sauce, with Flambé banana, 19
  Sherbet, 380
  Salad, 283
Orangeade, 283
Oriental salad, 24
Osso buco, 419–20
Oxtail casserole, 284
Oyster(s), 284

Paella, 285
Pain perdu, 285
Palmiers, 286
Panada, 286
Pancakes, 286
  Cheese blintzes, 32
  Crêpes, 119
  Potato latkes, 328
  see also Fritters
Panettone, 287
Parfait, Fruit, 288
Parmentier soup, 288
Parsnip croquettes, 289
Partridge, 289–90
Pasta, 293–5
Pasties:
  Cornish, 113
  Lamb and potato, 234
Pastry, 296–301
  Choux, 97, 300–1
  Flaky, 298–9
  Flan, 162, 298
  Hot water crust, 217, 300
  Oil, 278, 297
  Phyllo, 309
  Puff, 299
  Rough puff, 298
  Short-crust, 297
  Shortening, 297
  Suet-crust, 298
  Sugar-crust, 298
Pastry cream, 301
Pâté, 301–2
  Whirls, 61
Patty shells, 302

Pea(s), 303
  Black-eyed, 31, 214
  Snow peas with shrimp, 387
Peach(es), 304
  Dumplings, 141
  in Liqueur, 304
  Melba, 304
Peanut:
  Brittle, 304–5
  Butter cookies, 305
Pear(s), 305–6
  Compôte of, 109
  Chutney, 98–9
  Poached, 305–6
  Poire Hélène, 305
Pecan pie, 314
Pepper, 306
Peppers, Chili, 94
Peppers, Green (sweet), 201
  and Onion quiche, 282
  and Sausage omelet, 280
Perch, 307
Pesto, 307
Petits fours, 308
  Fondant fruits, 165
Pfannkuchen, 308
Pheasant, 308–9
  Burgundy, 309
  Casserole, 309
Philadelphia ice cream, 219
Picadillo, 309
Pickles, Pickled, 310–12
  Cauliflower (Italian style), 312
  Cucumber, 311
  Dates, 132
  Eggs, 146
  Melon, 257
  Mixed sweet pickle relish, 312
  Onions, 311
  Piccalilli, 312
  Red cabbage, 311
  Tongue, 413
  Walnuts, 311–12
Pigeon or dove, Roast, 314
Pig's feet or trotters, 315
Pike, Baked stuffed, 315
Pilaf (Pilau, Pilaw), 315
  Chicken liver, 93
  Lamb, 315
Pilchards, 315–16
Pineapple, 316–17
  with Baked pork chops, 317
  Cold pineapple soufflé, 316
  Ice, 220–1
  Surprise, 317
  Upside-down cake, 417
Pink gin, 103

Pipérade, 149
Piquant sauce, 319
Pissaladière, 319–20
Pizza, 320–1
  Napoletana, 320
  Quick, 320–1
  Special, 321
Plaice, 321
Plum cake, Upside-down, 322
Plum jam, 322
Plum pudding, 322–3
Poire Hélène, 305
Polenta, 327
Polish cheesecake, 88
Pommes parmentier, 288
Pompano, Sautéed with parsley
  Butter, 323–4
Popovers, 324
Poppy seed braid, 44
Pork, 324–5
  Baked chops with pineapple,
    317
  Broiled, 324–5
  Cassoulet, 77
  Chinese barbecued spareribs,
    394
  Eggs Foo Yung, 169
  Loin of Pork Chasseur, 325
  and Prune Casserole, 336
  Rillettes, 352
  Roast, 325
  Sautéed, 324–5
  Scrapple, 377
  with Stir-fried green beans,
    23–4
  Sweet and sour, 325
Porridge, Oatmeal, 325
Potato(es), 326–8
  Baked, 327
  Boiled, 327
  Cream of leek and potato soup,
    237
  Duchesse, 328
  Fried, 327
  Gnocchi, 195
  Ham and scalloped potatoes,
    207
  Kugel, 231
  and Lamb pasties, 234
  Latkes, 328
  and Leek bake, 237
  Mashed, 327
  Pommes parmentier, 288
  Roast, 327
  Salad, 328
  Sauté, 327
  Steamed, 327

  Stuffed cheese potatoes, 87
  Pot-au-feu, 328
Pot roast, 328
Potted beef, 329
Poultry, 48, 173–4, 329–31
  Ragout of, 343
Pound cake, 331
Prairie oyster, 331
Praline bombe, 219–20
Pralines, 306, 331–2
Prawns, 332
Profiteroles, 335
Prune(s), 336
  and Apple roll, 336
  Filling for danish pastry, 131
  and Pork casserole, 336
  Stuffed, 336
Pumpkin pie, 338
Punch, rum, 338

Quail, Roast, 339
Queen of puddings, 339–40
Quenelles, fish, 340
Quiche, 340
  Lorraine, 340
  Onion and red pepper, 282
Quince, 341
  Butter, 181
  Jam, 341
  Jelly, 341

Rabbit casserole, Rich, 76
Rabbit, Roast, 342
Ragout, 343
  of Beef heart with lemon, 76–7
  of Poultry, 343
Raised veal and ham pie, 343
Rainbow Coleslaw, 108
Raita, 123
  Eggplant, 344
Raspberry, 345
  Fool, 345
  Jam, 345
  Mousse, 266–7
  Muffins, 268
  Sundae, 403
Ratatouille, 345
Ravigote butter, 346
Ravigote sauce, 346
Red cabbage, Pickled, 311
Red-eye gravy, 207
Red mullet, 268
Rémoulade sauce, 348
Reuben sandwich, 348
Rhode island johnnycake, 226
Rhubarb:
  Betty, 82

Deep-dish rhubarb pie, 313
Mousse, 349
and Orange chutney, 99
Rice, 349–51
  Biryani, 127
  Boiled, 350
  and Cheese soufflé, 390
  with Chicken (Arroz con
    pollo), 92
  Chicken liver pilaf, 93
  Curried, 351
  Flavored, 351
  Fried, 351
  Kedgeree, 228
  Paella, 285
  Risotto, 352–3
  Wild, 431
Rice pudding, 351
Rigatoni with sausage, 352
Rillettes, Pork, 352
Risotto:
  Chicken, 352–3
  Shellfish, 353
Rissoles British style, 353
Robert sauce, 355
Rogan josh, 126
Roly-poly, 356
Rose hip syrup, 69
Roux, 358
Rum:
  Baba au rhum, 16
  Punch, 338
  Soufflé omelet, 281
Rumaki, 17
Russian salad, 364
Rutabaga, 360

Sabayon sauce (Cold), 361
Sachertorte, 362
Sage and onion stuffing, 363
Salad(s), 363–5
  Artichoke, 12
  Avocado and grapefruit, 15
  Caesar, 54
  Chickpea, 97
  Coleslaw, 108
  Dandelion salad with bacon,
    130
  Fruit, 180–1
  Grapefruit, 198–9
  Grapefruit and shrimp, 199
  Italin pepper, 201
  Lobster, 243
  Mint and cucumber fish, 104–5
  Orange, 283
  Oriental, 24
  Potato, 328

Russian, 364
Salade niçoise, 273
Tabouleh, 406
Tomato, 364
Tossed fresh spinach, 365
Veal, Ham and tongue molded,
  264
Waldorf, 365
Salad dressing, 365–7
  French (Sauce vinaigrette), 104,
    365–6
  Green goddess, 200–1
  Mayonnaise, 366
  Sour cream, 367
  Yogurt, 367
Sally Lunn, 367
Salmi of goose, 367
Salmon, 368–9
  Foil-baked, 368
  Mousse, 267, 368–9
  Poached, 368
  Scandinavian gravlax, 199
Samosas, 126
Sandwiches, 370–1
  Reuben, 348
  Smørrebrød, 385–6
Sangria, 372
Sardine pyramids, 61
Satay, Chicken, with peanut
  sauce, 372–3
Sauerbraten, 373–4
Sauerkraut, 374
Sausage(s), 48, 374–5
  with Chickpeas, 93
  Chorizos, 97
  Garlic, with fava beans, 156
  and Pepper omelet, 280
  with Rigatoni, 352
  Stuffing, 375
  Toad-in-the-hole, 411
Sausage rolls, 374–5
Scallop, 376
Scandinavian gravlax, 199
Schav, 388
Scones, 376–7
  Oven, 376
Scotch broth, 49
Scotch eggs, 148
Scrapple, 377
Sea bass, Szechwan deep-fried,
  377–8
Semolina gnocchi alla Romana,
  195
Seviche, 379
Shellfish risotto, 353
Shepherd's pie, 380
Sherbet, orange, 380

Sherry cobbler, 381–2
Shish kebab, 381–2
Shoofly pie, 263–4
Shortbread, 382
Shrimp, 383
  and Asparagus gratin, 13
  Bisque, 383
  Deviled eggs, 148
  and Grapefruit salad, 199
  and Ham jambalaya, 224–5
  Omelet, 280
  Oriental salad, 24
  Sauté patty shells, 302
  Stir-fried, with snow peas,
    387
  Tempura, 410
  Vindaloo, 125–6
Sidecar, 103
Simnel cake, 384
Skate toledo, 384–5
Smoked haddock see Haddock,
Smørrebrød, 385–6
Snails à la bourguignonne, 387
Snow peas, with Stir-fried
  shrimps, 387
Sole meunière, 388
Soubise sauce, 388
Soufflé, 389–90
  Cheese, 87
  Cheese and rice, 390
  au Chocolat, 390
  Cold pineapple, 316
Soufflé omelet, 280–1
  Baked, 281
Soup(s), 390–2
  Black bean, 30
  Borsch, 34
  Chestnut, 90
  Chicken broth, 49
  Classic consommé, 109–10
  Cock-a-leekie, 102
  Cream of asparagus, 13
  Cream of leek and potato, 237
  Cream of lemon, 392
  Cream of tomato, 391–2
  Crème vichyssoise, 423
  French onion, 281–2
  Game, 185–6
  Garbure, 186
  Garlic soup with eggs, 186
  Gazpacho, 188
  Lentil and bacon, 239
  Minestra di cavolfiore, 262
  Minestrone, 262
  Mock turtle, 263
  Mulligatawny soup, 268–9
  Parmentier, 288

Soup (*cont.*)
  Pea, 303
  Scotch broth, 49
Sour cream dressing, 367
Sourdough bread, 392–3
Sourdough starter, 392
Soybeans, 393
Spaetzel, 393
Spaghetti:
  alla Bolognese, 294
  alla Carbonara, 17
  and Meatballs, 255–6
  with Mushroom and tomato
    sauce, 393–4
Spanish omelet, 280
Spareribs, Chinese barbecued,
  394
Spiced vinegar, 310–11
Spinach, 394
  Tossed fresh salad, 365
Spoon bread, 114
Squid in tomato sauce, 396
Star cookies, 112
Steak and kidney pie, 27
Stock, 399
  Brown, 109
  Calf's foot, 60
  Court-bouillon, 115
Strawberry, 400
  Ice, 400
  Jam, 400
  Shortcake, 382
  Sundae, 403
Stuffed (dishes):
  Artichokes, 11
  Baked stuffed eggplant, 149
  Baked stuffed hearts, 210
  Baked stuffed onions, 282
  Baked stuffed pike, 315
  Beef-stuffed onions, 282
  Celery, 79
  Cheese potatoes, 87
  Cod steaks, 105
  Dolmades, 199
  Fresh haddock, 205
  Ham-stuffed chayotes, 83
  Hot stuffed eggs, 148
  Peppers, 201
  Prunes, 336
Stuffing, 401
  Apple and celery, 79
  for Baked haddock, 205
  Cheese and tomato, 105
  Chestnut, 401
  Nut, 401
  Sage and onion, 363
  Sausage, 375

Suet-crust pastry, 298
Swedish coffee cake, 107
Sweet and sour pork, 325
Sweetbreads, 404–5
  Creamed, 405
  Sautéed, 404
Sweet-sour daikon, 130
Syllabub made with wine, 405
Szechwan deep-fried sea bass,
  377–8

Tabouleh, 406
Tagliatelle con prosciutto, 295
Tandoori chicken, 127
Taramasalata, 407
Tarragon chicken, 408
Tartar sauce, 408
Tarte tatin, 9
Teddy bear cake, 57
Tempura, shrimp, 410
Teriyaki marinade, 410
Timbale shells, 22
Toad-in-the-hole, 411
Toast melba, 412
Toffee, molasses, 64
Tomato(es), 412
  Catsup, 77
  and Cheese stuffing, 105
  Cream of tomato soup, 391–2
  Green tomato chutney, 98
  and Jerusalem artichokes, 12
  and Mushroom sauce, 393–4
  Omelet, 279
  Puree, 68
  Salad, 364
  Sauce, 396, 412
  and Sweet peppers, 201
Tomato juice, 69
  Cocktail, 104
Tongue, 412
  Pickled, 413
  Veal and ham molded salad,
    264
Tripe, 414
Trout, 414
  and Almonds, 414
  Smoked trout pâté, 302
Truffles, Chocolate, 65
Turbot, 415
Turkey, 415
  Deviled drumsticks, 134
  Wild, 432
Turkish delight, 64–5, 416
Turnip, 416
Turnovers:
  Apple, 416
  Jam, 416

Upside-down pineapple cake,
  417
Upside-down plum cake, 322

Vanilla, 418
  Bavarian cream, 22
  Butter frosting, 51
  French custard ice cream, 218
  Fudge, 63
  Pastry cream, 301
Veal, 255, 418–20
  Breaded veal scallops, 419
  Cutlets in lemon sauce, 129
  Forcemeat, 169
  Ham and tongue molded salad,
    264
  Osso buco, 419–20
  Paupiettes de veau, 302–3
  Raised veal and ham pie, 343
  Roast, 419
  Scallops with parmesan cheese,
    419
  Wiener schnitzel, 419
Vegetable vinaigrette, 422
Velouté sauce, 422
Vichyssoise, Crème, 423
Vinaigrette dressing, 365–6, 422
Vindaloo, 125–6
Vinegar, 423–4
  Spiced, 310–11
Vol-au-vent, Chicken, 425

Waffles, 426
Waldorf salad, 365
Walnuts, pickled, 311–12
Wedding cake, 428–9
Welsh rarebit, 429
Western omelet, 280
Wheatgerm waffles, 426
White mountain frosting, 430
White sauce, 358
White wine cup, 430
Whiting, baked, 431
Whole-wheat bread, 44
  Flowerpots, 45
  Quick, 44
  Quick rolls, 356
Wiener schnitzel, 419
Woodcock, 435

Yogurt, 437–8
  Salad dressing, 367
Yorkshire pudding, 438

Zabaglione, 439
Zucchini, 439
  Chutney, 99